Understanding Modern Warfare

Understanding Modern Warfare has established itself as a leading text in professional military education and undergraduate teaching. This third edition has been revised throughout to reflect dramatic changes during the past decade. Introducing three brand new chapters, this updated volume provides in-depth analysis of the most pertinent issues of the 2020s and beyond, including cyber warfare, information activities, hybrid and grey zone warfare, multi-domain operations and recent conflicts in Ukraine, Gaza and Syria. It also includes a range of features to maximise its value as a learning tool: a structure designed to guide students through key strategic principles; key questions and annotated reading guides for deeper understanding; text boxes highlighting critical thinkers and operational concepts; and a glossary explaining key terms. Providing debate-driven analysis that encourages students to develop a balanced perspective, *Understanding Modern Warfare* remains essential reading both for officers and for students of international relations more broadly.

David Jordan is deputy head of the Defence Studies Department, King's College London, based at the Defence Academy of the UK, Shrivenham and a founding co-director of the Freeman Air & Space Institute. He also serves as a director of the RAF's Centre Air & Space Power Studies and has authored numerous articles and book chapters addressing air and space power issues.

James D. Kiras is dean and professor at the School of Advanced Air & Space Studies (SAASS), the US Air Force's premier school of strategy. He is the author of *Special Operations Success: Balancing Capabilities and Control* (2025) and *Special Operations Strategy: From World War II the War on Terrorism* (2006), and co-editor of *Into the Void: Special Operations Forces After the War on Terrorism* (2024), *Strategic Sabotage* (2021) and *Special Operations: Out of the Shadows* (2020).

David J. Lonsdale is senior lecturer in war studies at the University of Hull. He is the author of *Alexander the Great: Lessons in Strategy* (2008), *The Nature of War in the Information Age: Clausewitzian Future* (2003) and *Alexander, Killer of Men: Alexander the Great and the Macedonian Art of War* (2004), and co-author of *Understanding Contemporary Strategy* (2019).

Ian Speller is professor of military history, head of the Department of History and Strategic Studies at the National University of Ireland, Maynooth. He also lectures at the Irish Military College. He is the author of numerous works on maritime strategy and naval warfare, including *Understanding Naval Warfare* (2024) and *The Role of*

Amphibious Warfare in British Defence Policy, 1945–1956 (2001), and co-editor of *Small Navies: Strategy and Policy for Small Navies in War and Peace* (2014) and *Europe, Small Navies and Maritime Security* (2021).

Christopher Tuck is a reader in strategic studies in the Department of Defence Studies, King's College London, based at the Joint Services Command and Staff College, Shrivenham. He is the author of *Understanding Land Warfare* (2022) and *Confrontation, Strategy, and War Termination* (2013), co-author of *Amphibious Warfare: Strategy and Tactics from Gallipoli to Iraq* (2014) and co-editor of *British Propaganda and Wars of Empire: Influencing Friend and Foe* (2014).

C. Dale Walton is a retired professor of international relations at Lindenwood University and a senior fellow with Lindenwood's Hammond Institute. He is the author of *The Myth of Inevitable U.S. Defeat in Vietnam* (2002), *Geopolitics and the Great Powers in the Twenty-First Century: Multipolarity and the Revolution in Strategic Perspective* (2007) and *Grand Strategy and the Presidency: Foreign Policy, War and the American Role in the World* (2012).

Understanding Modern Warfare

Understanding Modern Warfare has established itself as a leading text in professional military education and undergraduate teaching. This third edition has been revised throughout to reflect dramatic changes during the past decade. Introducing three brand new chapters, this updated volume provides in-depth analysis of the most pertinent issues of the 2020s and beyond, including cyber warfare, information activities, hybrid and grey zone warfare, multi-domain operations and recent conflicts in Ukraine, Gaza and Syria. It also includes a range of features to maximise its value as a learning tool: a structure designed to guide students through key strategic principles; key questions and annotated reading guides for deeper understanding; text boxes highlighting critical thinkers and operational concepts; and a glossary explaining key terms. Providing debate-driven analysis that encourages students to develop a balanced perspective, *Understanding Modern Warfare* remains essential reading both for officers and for students of international relations more broadly.

David Jordan is deputy head of the Defence Studies Department, King's College London, based at the Defence Academy of the UK, Shrivenham and a founding co-director of the Freeman Air & Space Institute. He also serves as a director of the RAF's Centre Air & Space Power Studies and has authored numerous articles and book chapters addressing air and space power issues.

James D. Kiras is dean and professor at the School of Advanced Air & Space Studies (SAASS), the US Air Force's premier school of strategy. He is the author of *Special Operations Success: Balancing Capabilities and Control* (2025) and *Special Operations Strategy: From World War II the War on Terrorism* (2006), and co-editor of *Into the Void: Special Operations Forces After the War on Terrorism* (2024), *Strategic Sabotage* (2021) and *Special Operations: Out of the Shadows* (2020).

David J. Lonsdale is senior lecturer in war studies at the University of Hull. He is the author of *Alexander the Great: Lessons in Strategy* (2008), *The Nature of War in the Information Age: Clausewitzian Future* (2003) and *Alexander, Killer of Men: Alexander the Great and the Macedonian Art of War* (2004), and co-author of *Understanding Contemporary Strategy* (2019).

Ian Speller is professor of military history, head of the Department of History and Strategic Studies at the National University of Ireland, Maynooth. He also lectures at the Irish Military College. He is the author of numerous works on maritime strategy and naval warfare, including *Understanding Naval Warfare* (2024) and *The Role of*

Amphibious Warfare in British Defence Policy, 1945–1956 (2001), and co-editor of *Small Navies: Strategy and Policy for Small Navies in War and Peace* (2014) and *Europe, Small Navies and Maritime Security* (2021).

Christopher Tuck is a reader in strategic studies in the Department of Defence Studies, King's College London, based at the Joint Services Command and Staff College, Shrivenham. He is the author of *Understanding Land Warfare* (2022) and *Confrontation, Strategy, and War Termination* (2013), co-author of *Amphibious Warfare: Strategy and Tactics from Gallipoli to Iraq* (2014) and co-editor of *British Propaganda and Wars of Empire: Influencing Friend and Foe* (2014).

C. Dale Walton is a retired professor of international relations at Lindenwood University and a senior fellow with Lindenwood's Hammond Institute. He is the author of *The Myth of Inevitable U.S. Defeat in Vietnam* (2002), *Geopolitics and the Great Powers in the Twenty-First Century: Multipolarity and the Revolution in Strategic Perspective* (2007) and *Grand Strategy and the Presidency: Foreign Policy, War and the American Role in the World* (2012).

'This third revised and updated edition of *Understanding Modern Warfare* should be the basic textbook for all military academies and university courses on warfare!'

Beatrice Heuser, Head of Strategy Teaching at the German General Staff Academy, Hamburg

'An engaging and useful introduction to the challenges and complexities of modern warfare and strategy.'

William Stuart Nance, author of *Commanding Professionalism: Simpson, Moore, and the Ninth US Army*

Understanding Modern Warfare

David Jordan King's College London
James D. Kiras School of Advanced Air and Space Studies, Maxwell Air Force Base, USA
David J. Lonsdale University of Hull
Ian Speller National University of Ireland, Maynooth
Christopher Tuck King's College London
C. Dale Walton

CAMBRIDGE
UNIVERSITY PRESS

CAMBRIDGE
UNIVERSITY PRESS

Shaftesbury Road, Cambridge CB2 8EA, United Kingdom

One Liberty Plaza, 20th Floor, New York, NY 10006, USA

477 Williamstown Road, Port Melbourne, VIC 3207, Australia

314–321, 3rd Floor, Plot 3, Splendor Forum, Jasola District Centre,
New Delhi – 110025, India

103 Penang Road, #05–06/07, Visioncrest Commercial, Singapore 238467

Cambridge University Press is part of Cambridge University Press & Assessment, a department of the University of Cambridge.

We share the University's mission to contribute to society through the pursuit of education, learning and research at the highest international levels of excellence.

www.cambridge.org
Information on this title: www.cambridge.org/highereducation/isbn/9781009724494

DOI: 10.1017/9781009724524

When citing this work, please include a reference to the DOI 10.1017/9781009724524

First published 2008
Second edition 2016
Third edition 2026

A catalogue record for this publication is available from the British Library

A Cataloging-in-Publication data record for this book is available from the Library of Congress

ISBN 978-1-009-72449-4 Hardback
ISBN 978-1-009-72450-0 Paperback

Additional resources for this publication at www.cambridge.org/Jordan-3e.

Contents

Figures

Tables and Boxes

Tables

Boxes

Preface to the Third Edition

This book focuses on modern warfare, meaning that it addresses the conduct of war today, tomorrow and in the recent past. The topic was addressed in two previous editions and is tackled here in a revised and updated third edition that takes account of recent events, of new technology and of wider evolution in military thought and practice to address the topic in a comprehensive and sophisticated manner while retaining the earlier edition's emphasis on presenting ideas and arguments in a user-friendly manner. The authors were motivated to write the first edition of this book after an unsuccessful search to find a source that, in a single volume, could provide an authoritative yet accessible introduction to the theory and practice of modern warfare. As we noted at the time, there were numerous books that explored war and security in a general sense, and many others that addressed the history of war across the centuries, but none that gave the reader a thorough grounding in the critical issues, ideas, concepts and vocabulary needed to develop and articulate an understanding of the conduct of war in its various forms and in its different operating environments. Moreover, those works that did address aspects of this subject often did so in a manner that was difficult to understand, even for those already well grounded in the topic. This book was, and is still, designed to fill that gap.

The first edition was conceived almost twenty years ago, at a time when many chose to believe that 'modern warfare' was largely a thing of the past. Such analysis was often underpinned by some rather wishful thinking and reflected limited understanding of the realities of international relations and of relevant history; their conclusions have not aged well. Sadly, war and warfare remain topics as relevant today as they ever were, a point reinforced forcibly by the 2022 Russian invasion of Ukraine, or by Israeli military actions in Gaza in response to the Hamas-led terrorist outrages of 7 October 2023. This new edition provides an opportunity to reflect on the most recent developments in the field and to update our analysis to take account of advances in the theory and practice of modern warfare. In support of that, all chapters have been revised and re-written, engaging with the latest scholarship and events in order to bring the work fully up to date. In addition, we have added three entirely new chapters to address issues relating to hybrid warfare, joint warfare, and also on information and cyber operations, topics of growing relevance to any understanding of war today. The result, we hope, is a body of work that continues to reflect the latest developments and that presents these to the reader in a manner that equips them with the knowledge and information that they require to foster a sophisticated understanding of the subject matter. It seems unlikely that the need for such understanding will pass anytime soon.

As we noted in the preface to the previous editions, the contributors to this book have all benefited from experience teaching students at civilian universities and military establishments in many different countries. We owe these students, uniformed or otherwise, a debt of gratitude for the stimulus and challenge that they have provided over the years. Exposure to their different ideas and innumerable questions has forced each of us individually to explain and defend our views and opinions many times over. This book is therefore partly a result of such debates and, hopefully, will provoke and inform many more in the future. An additional debt is owed to our colleagues in the various departments and institutions in which we work. They are too numerous to mention individually but without their support works such as this one would not be possible. The authors would also like to thank their partners and families for their support and, often, their forbearance as the manuscript was completed on top of already rather full workloads. In light of this, and the challenges faced in meeting deadlines, we are all very grateful for the professional way in which Michael Watson and his team at Cambridge University Press guided us through the process. Finally, it is important to note that the ideas and opinions expressed in this book are those of the authors alone and do not represent the views of any group, organisation or institution.

Abbreviations

A2/AD	anti-access/area denial
AAA	anti-aircraft artillery
ABCS	Army Battle Command System
ACTS	Air Corps Tactical School
AFVs	armoured fighting vehicles
AI	artificial intelligence
AIP	air-independent propulsion
APT	advanced persistent threat
AQ	Al-Qaeda
ARIS	Assessing Revolutionary and Insurgent Strategies
ASAT	air-launched anti-satellite
ASCMs	anti-ship cruise missiles
ASCOPE	areas, structures, capabilities, organisation, people and events
ASEAN	Association of Southeast Asian Nations
ATB	Advanced Technology Bomber
BCTs	Brigade combat teams
BDA	battle damage assessment
BFT	Blue Force Tracking
BMD	ballistic missile defence
BRI	Belt and Road Initiative
BWC	Biological Weapons Convention
BWs	biological weapons
C2	command and control
C4I	command, control, communications, computers and intelligence
CAS	Chief of the Air Staff
CBI	China–Burma–India
CBWs	chemical and biological weapons
CEMA	Cyber Electro Magnetic Activities (Effects Group)
CEMO EMS	cyber electromagnetic activities
CENTCOM	US Central Command
CEO	cyber-enabled operations
CEP	circular error probability
CERTs	computer emergency response teams
CIA	Central Intelligence Agency
CNO	computer network operations
COIN	counterinsurgency operations
COP	common operating picture

COPD	Comprehensive Operations Planning Directive
CWC	Chemical Weapons Convention
CWs	chemical weapons
DCO	defensive cyber operations
DDoS	Distributed Denial of Service
DoS	Denial of Service
ELINT	early warning and electronic intelligence
EMF	Experimental Mechanized Force
EMS	electromagnetic spectrum
EU	European Union
FLN	*Front de Libération Nationale* (National Liberation Front)
FPV	first-person view (drones)
FSB	Russian federal Security Service
GBAD	ground-based air defence
GCMA	*Groupement de commandos mixtes aéroportés* (Mixed Airborne Commando Group)
GDP	gross domestic product
GLOC	*g*-induced loss of consciousness
GMLRS	Guided Multiple Launch Rocket System
GPS	Global Positioning System
GRU	Russian military intelligence
GWOT	Global War on Terrorism
HA/DR	humanitarian assistance and disaster relief
HAPSs	high-altitude pseudo-satellites
HIMARS	High Mobility Artillery Rocket System
HUMINT	human intelligence
HVAs	high-value assets
ICBM	intercontinental ballistic missile
IDF	Israeli Defence Force
IEDs	improvised explosive devices
IJO	integrated joint operations
INS	inertial navigation system
IP	Internet Protocol
ISAF	International Security Assistance Force
ISIS	Islamic State
ISR	intelligence, surveillance and reconnaissance
IUU	unreported and unregulated
JADC2	Joint All-Domain Command and Control
JADO	Joint All-Domain Operations
JDAM	Joint Direct Attack Munition
JFCC-NW	Joint Functional Component Command – Network Warfare
JSF	Joint Strike Fighter
JTF-CND	Joint Task Force – Computer Network Defense

JWC	Joint Warfighting Concept
LO	low observable
LUSVs	large uninhabited surface vessels
MACA	Military Assistance to Civil Authorities
MAD	mutually assured destruction
MDI	multi-domain integration
MDO	multi-domain operations
MDTF	Multi-Domain Task Force
MIGs	Marine Expeditionary Force Information Groups
ML	machine learning
MLEAs	maritime law enforcement agencies
MOU	Memorandum of Understanding
MSOs	maritime security operations
NATO	North Atlantic Treaty Organization
NCSC	National Cyber Security Centre
NCW	network-centric warfare
NPT	Nuclear Non-Proliferation Treaty
NSA	National Security Agency
OCO	offensive cyber operations
OIF	Operation Iraqi Freedom
OODA	observe, orientate, decide, act
OSINT	open-source intelligence
PGMs	precision-guided munitions
PLA	People's Liberation Army
PLAN	People's Liberation Army Navy
PMESII	political, military, economic, social, information and infrastructure
PNT	positioning, navigation and timing
RAF	Royal Air Force
RAM	radar-absorbing material
RCS	radar cross-section
RFC	Royal Flying Corps
RMA	revolution in military affairs
RPASs	remotely piloted air systems
RSCs	reconnaissance-strike complexes
RUSI	Royal United Services Institute
SACEUR	Supreme Allied Commander Europe
SAMs	surface-to-air missiles
SCADA	supervisory control and data acquisition
SCEPVA	Sovereign Cyber Effects Provided Voluntary by Allies
SDI	Strategic Defence Initiative
SEAD	suppression of enemy air defences
SLBMs	submarine-launched ballistic missiles
SOCMINT	social media intelligence

SOF	special operations forces
SORM	System for Operative Investigative Activities
SSBN	ship submersible ballistic nuclear
SSF	Strategic Support Force
SSKs	diesel-electric submarines
SSNs	nuclear-powered submarines
STOVL	short-take-off and vertical-landing (aircraft)
SVR	Foreign Intelligence Service
TNWs	tactical nuclear weapons
UAE	United Arab Emirates
UAVs	autonomous (unmanned) aerial vehicles
UK	United Kingdom
UN	United Nations
UNIFIL	UN Interim Force in Lebanon
UNSC	UN Security Council
US	United States
USAAC	US Army Air Corps
USAAF	US Army Air Force
USAF	US Air Force
USCYBERCOM	US Cyber Command
USMC	US Marine Corps
USN	US Navy
USSF	US Space Force
USVs	uninhabited surface vehicles
UUVs	uninhabited underwater vehicles
WEZ	weapons engagement zone
WMDs	weapons of mass destruction

Introduction to the Third Edition

IAN SPELLER

CHAPTER OUTLINE

This book focuses on modern **warfare**. It examines the conduct of **war** in its different environments and forms and provides an introduction to the issues, ideas, concepts, context and vocabulary necessary to develop an understanding of the subject. It is not a history book, although relevant historical examples are used throughout to illustrate the analysis. Rather, the book is designed to equip the reader with a sophisticated introduction to the concepts, issues and debates that will help them to understand current concerns and future possibilities and also to unpick past **campaigns**.

This subject is an important one. War and warfare have had a pervasive and often a pernicious influence on human affairs throughout history. Optimistic claims that we are evolving towards a less dangerous international **system**, or that humans are somehow becoming less violent, are not borne out by any reasonable analysis of relevant history and appear hard to sustain in the light of recent events.[1] Despite this, the conduct of war, as an academic field of enquiry, is not a subject that everyone is comfortable with. It requires one to study a phenomenon that many disapprove of and to think about things that some prefer to ignore. That such study is often encouraged or supported by armed forces eager to derive 'lessons' intended to improve future performance has done little to endear it to liberal academics. Insofar as they study war at all, most Western universities prefer to focus on 'war and society', examining the impact that war has had on wider society rather than focusing explicitly on warfare. The result has been a demilitarisation of the topic within much of academia, what Michael Howard called a 'flight to the suburbs'.[2] This is not a suburban book. It self-consciously focuses on the central activity of armed forces and on the urban centre of the subject, on warfare. It does so in recognition that this does not address the totality of war, which is about more than just warfare, but is based on the notion that one cannot understand modern war unless one also understands modern warfare.

The book is also based on the judgement that such understanding is important. To paraphrase Sun Tzu, the conduct of war is of such importance, quite literally the province of life and death, it is vital that it be studied carefully. It should never be forgotten that wars always result in death, destruction, waste and human suffering, all too frequently on a truly staggering scale (Figure 0.1). Unfortunately, ignoring the phenomenon is unlikely to make it go away and to do so fosters ignorance of something that has had, and continues to have, a major impact on human affairs. Whether one wishes to avoid warfare, to mitigate its impact or to prepare to conduct it more efficiently (and these are not mutually exclusive positions) it is important that it be studied. Indeed, one might suggest that in a democracy in the twenty-first century it is particularly important that as wide a range of people as possible should understand the nature of modern warfare in order that they are equipped to make intelligent judgements about the ways in which their own governments seek to employ military force. The requirement for military personnel to understand warfare should be too obvious to require further elaboration given the historical correlation between ignorance and military incompetence.

What Is War?

According to the *Oxford English Dictionary*, war is a 'hostile contention by means of armed forces, carried on between nations, states or rulers, or between parties in the same nation or state'.[3] Hedley Bull, the renowned scholar of international relations, described war more succinctly as 'organised violence carried on by political units against each other'.[4] Other definitions distinguish between armed conflict and war. These tend to focus on the scale and degree of violence employed, suggesting that 'wars' are characterised by large numbers of combatants, heavy casualties and/or high-intensity fighting. The Correlates of War project, for example, defines war as involving sustained combat by organised armed forces resulting in a minimum of 1,000 battle-related deaths between combatants in any given year. The Uppsala Conflict Database Project, on the other hand, focuses on 'armed conflict', defined as a 'contested incompatibility' involving at least twenty-five battle-related deaths within a year.[5] The collection and use of quantifiable data clearly poses some methodological challenges and the shortcomings of either definition are readily apparent. Is it really the case that a terrorist campaign that kills twenty-five people within twelve months is indicative of an armed conflict but one that kills twenty-four is not? Does a conflict really cease to be a war simply because the casualty figures slip below 1,000 in any given year? Such definitions tell us little about the nature or the character of war; they are best recognised for what they are, simply a means of gathering and handling data.

Other approaches focus on legal issues, identifying 'war' as a state of law that regulates armed conflict between groups, usually states. These reflect the conventional understanding of war, as articulated in international law and treaties, as organised rule-bounded violence conducted between the uniformed representatives of states. They tend to exclude the activities of substate groups whose use of

Figure 0.1 The heavy death toll and large-scale destruction associated with Israeli military operations in Gaza in from 2023 to 2025 demonstrate that modern warfare remains a phenomena capable of inflicting appalling suffering on both combatants and non-combatants. Source: https://tinyurl.com/3zp9d3d5

violence is not given the credibility or legitimacy associated with the term. Given that, thus far into the twenty-first century, most armed conflict has occurred either between substate groups or between such groups and conventional militaries, such definitions, while logically coherent, may be too restrictive. For the purposes of this book, Bull's more expansive approach seems more satisfactory(see Box 0.1).

BOX 0.1 DEFINING WAR

Carl von Clausewitz (1832): 'War is not merely an act of **policy** but a true political instrument, a continuation of political intercourse, carried on with other means.'[6]

L.F.L. Oppenheim (1906): 'War is a contention between two or more states through their armed forces, for the purpose of overpowering each other and imposing such conditions of peace as the victor pleases.'[7]

Mao Zedong (1938): 'Politics is war without bloodshed while war is politics with bloodshed.'[8]

Quincy Wright (1942): '[War is] a legal condition which equally permits two or more hostile groups to carry on a conflict by armed force.'[9]

Hedley Bull (1977): '[War is] organised violence carried on by political units against each other.'[10]

Colin Gray (2005): 'War is organised violence threatened or waged for political purposes.'[11]

UK Defence Doctrine (2022): 'In simple terms, war is defined as: a state of armed conflict between different countries or different groups within a country.'[12]

Contemporary Western approaches to war are profoundly influenced by the work of Carl von Clausewitz, whose posthumous magnum opus, *On War,* published in 1832, stated that war is 'an act of force to compel our enemy to do our will . . . a clash of major interests, which is resolved by bloodshed'. Famously, Clausewitz emphasised the political **nature of war**, stressing that '. . . war is not merely an act of policy but a true political instrument, a continuation of political intercourse, carried on with other means', a statement that is as widely known as it is frequently misused. Far from advocating war as an alternative to politics he intended to show that war was driven by politics and could only be understood in that context. The means of waging war can never be considered in isolation from the aim that they are designed to support. As Clausewitz put it, '[W]ar may have its own grammar, but not its own logic. The logic is determined by the political aim.'[13] Logic and grammar may collide, often with unfortunate consequences.

Not everyone views war in this way, a point that was emphasised by Anatol Rapoport in his introduction to an abridged edition of Clausewitz's work published by Penguin. Rapoport identified that not all people or groups viewed war as political or approached it in the rational and instrumental manner described in *On War.*[14] More recently, authors such as Mary Kaldor have argued that Clausewitz's approach is less useful within the context of so-called '**new wars**', where there may be no formal government, no clear political objectives and where many of the combatants may fight because they enjoy it or because it gives them access to the things that they value; they may have no interest in military victory in the traditional sense.[15] On the other hand, one might argue that even self-serving warlords have aims, even if these are associated with the continuation of the current conflict. For them, violence is indeed a tool of policy, even if that policy bears little relation to those traditionally adopted by states. It may well be the case that, as Kaldor and others have argued, some of those engaged in war are motivated by cultural imperatives or even perhaps by a non-rational urge to fight, but this does not mean that the conflict in which they participate is not directed towards some end. These ends may involve the achievement of wealth, security or prestige, they may be profoundly influenced by culture, identity, religion and/or ideology, and may be poorly defined or even barely understood, but they do exist. It seems fair to suggest that war remains political, in the sense that it is pursued in support of some or other policy, even if that policy involves the pursuit of goals that appear non-political in the narrowest sense of that word.

As will already be apparent, the study of war clearly requires an investigation that is not limited to the battlefield. Even works, such as this one, which focus explicitly on the conduct of military operations, must recognise that these occur within a broader context in which other factors intrude. That point is well understood by most western militaries, that commonly employ approaches such as the PMESII-ASCOPE analytical tool to integrate political, military, economic, social, informational and **intelligence** (PMESII) matters in their campaign planning, alongside an understanding of how these impact areas, structures, capabilities, organisation, people and events (ASCOPE); see Table 0.1. To understand war, and the conduct of war, requires one to understand more than just the battlefield.

War is a duel and this imposes a certain discipline (the enemy gets a say in how things are done); suboptimal approaches chosen for cultural reasons usually incur some cost. However, the purposes for which wars are fought and the manner in which they are conducted necessarily reflects the character of those who wage them. For this reason the character of each war is different and to understand this character one must engage with a number of disciplines. A sophisticated understanding of war requires one to engage with (at least) political, social, cultural, economic and technological matters. Any attempt to examine and explain war in its broadest sense is, therefore, a huge undertaking. As Azar Gat explained, '[W]ith war being connected to everything else and everything else being connected to war, explaining and tracing its development in relation to human development in general almost amounts to a theory and a history of everything.'[17] This book does not attempt to provide this. It is informed by an understanding of this complexity, and of the interdisciplinary nature of war studies, but the specific focus of this book is on the conduct of warfare.

What Is Modern Warfare?

US joint **doctrine** defines warfare as '"the how" – or the ways – of waging armed conflict against an enemy'. British defence doctrine defines it as 'the conduct of war primarily, but not exclusive, by military means'. It notes that war and warfare are not synonymous; there is more to war than warfare.[18] The study of warfare, therefore, is a

Table 0.1a An example of a typical PMESII-ASCOPE analysis, conducted in order to identify and address issues of relevance in campaign planning

	P Political	M Military	E Economic	S Social	I Information	I Infrastructure
A Areas	Areas – Political (district boundary, party affiliation areas)	Areas – Military (coalition /local national bases, historic ambush/IED sites)	Areas – Economic (bazaars, shops, markets)	Areas – Social (parks and other meeting areas)	Areas – Information (radio/TV/newspapers, where people gather for word-of- mouth)	Areas – Infrastructure (irrigation networks, water tables, medical coverage)
S Structures	Structures – Political (town halls, government offices)	Structures – Military/ Police (police HQ, military higher HQ locations)	Structures – Economic (banks, markets, storage facilities)	Structures – Social (churches, restaurants, bars, etc.)	Structures – Information (cell/radio/ TV towers, print shops)	Structures – Infrastructure (roads, bridges, power lines, walls, dams)
C Capabilities	Capabilities – Political (dispute resolution, Insurgent capabilities)	Capabilities – Military (security posture, strengths and weaknesses)	Capabilities – Economic (access to banks, ability to withstand natural disasters)	Capabilities – Social (strength of local and national ties)	Capabilities - Info (literacy rate, availability of media/ phone service)	Capabilities – Infrastructure (ability to build/maintain roads, walls, dams)

Table 0.1b An example of a typical PMESII-ASCOPE analysis, conducted in order to identify and address issues of relevance in campaign planning (cont.)

	P Political	M Military	E Economic	S Social	I Information	I Infrastructure
O Organisations	Organisations – Political (Political parties and other power brokers, United Nations)	Organisations – Military (Units of military, police, insurgent are present)	Organisations – Economic (banks, large land holders, big businesses)	Organisations – Social (tribes, clans, families, youth groups, non/inter government organisations)	Organisations – Info (NEWS groups, influential people who pass word)	Organisations – Infrastructure (Government ministries, construction companies)
P People	People – Political (Governors, councils, elders)	People – Military (Leaders from coalition, local national and insurgent forces)	People – Economic (bankers, landholders, merchants)	People – Social (religious leaders, influential families	People – Info (media owners, mullahs, heads of powerful families)	People – infrastructure builders, contractors, development councils)
E Events	Events – Political (elections, council meetings)	Events – Military (lethal/non-lethal events, loss of leadership, operations, anniversaries)	Events – Economic (drought, harvest, business open/ close)	Events – Social (holidays, weddings, religious days)	Events – Info (IO campaigns, project openings, CIVCAS events)	Events – Infrastructure (road/ bridge construction, well digging, scheduled maintenance)

Source: US Marines Training Command, 2017[16]

subset within the study of war. Warfare revolves around the use, and the threat to use, violence. Its study implies a particular focus on combat, the basic hard currency of war and the raison d'être for armed forces. This does not mean that political, social, cultural, economic and technological factors are not relevant. Nothing could be further from the truth. Such factors set the context within which warfare is conducted and all play a part in determining how different societies or organisations approach the conduct of war. For this reason it is important to remember that the character of war and of warfare continues to change, as does the character of those societies that wage war and, by extension, there will be more than one characteristic form of war (and of warfare) in existence at any given time.

This rather begs the question as to what we actually mean by 'modern' warfare. Michael Sheehan has defined it as 'the forms of warfare shaped by and reflecting the modern era of human history'.[19] Sadly, this shifts but does not solve the definitional problem. What is the 'modern era of human history'? Returning to the dictionary suggests that 'modern' means 'of or relating to the present and recent times' or 'being in existence at this time'.[20] This may not help us much as there is little consensus on either point. Different authors have interpreted 'present and recent times' in different ways. The starting point of Theodore Ropp's 1959 examination of war, *War in the Modern World*, for example, was 1415.[21] Some authors begin with the age of Marlborough or of Frederick the Great in the eighteenth century, the French Revolution of 1789 or the defeat of Napoleon in 1815. Others focus on the period from the outbreak of the American Civil War in 1861, from the start of the twentieth century, the end of the First World War, and so on.

There is no more agreement on what 'being in existence at this time' might mean. Some might suggest that this implies a focus on the latest technology, most recent doctrine and evolving 'best practice' amongst the most advanced militaries (Figure 0.2). Others might argue that some of the most effective practitioners of modern warfare have been substate groups able to exploit low-technology weapons and asymmetric **tactics** in support of their aims. Still more might claim that the idea of modern warfare is now rather passé and that we have entered a new era of 'post-modern warfare', 'fourth generation warfare', '**hybrid warfare**', 'war amongst the people' or some other apparently new form of war. In the first two decades of the twenty-first century, it become fashionable to conclude that future conflict would be predominantly asymmetric or 'hybrid', that it would occur between irregular combatants or between these and regular armed forces, and that interstate conventional warfare was a thing of the past. Such arguments were often built on weak foundations. The latter suggestion, in particular, seems particularly problematic in the context of recent interstate wars.

The use and the threat to use armed force is a recurrent feature of contemporary international relations. Statistics from the Heidelberg Institute for International Conflict Research suggest that there were twenty wars, twenty-five limited wars and 176 interstate conflicts conducted violently in 2013. Ten years later the figures were depressingly similar, with twenty-one wars, twenty-five limited wars and 174 violent crises. The major difference was less in the number of violent conflicts

Figure 0.2 British RAF and US Marine Corps F-35B aircraft over England in 2016. Expensive high-tech capabilities like these are important to an understanding of modern warfare but one must also engage with a range of lower technology and asymmetric capabilities to truly understand warfare today.

and more in their nature, with no interstate wars reported in 2013 compared with two in 2023 (Russia/Ukraine, Armenia/Azerbaijan).[22] While interstate wars may have declined recently in terms of size, intensity and import, this may not represent as radical a change as is sometime claimed, see Box 0.2. Further, it would seem premature to assume that there will never again be cause for one armed force to face another in a conventional conflict. As United States (US) hegemony is replaced by multipolarity, great powers may once again find cause to fight each other. New technology or new techniques may give lesser powers the ability to defend themselves without having to resort, in the first instance, to asymmetric tactics that see their institutions toppled and their cities occupied. It may be the case that the deterrent effect of nuclear weapons may wane with further proliferation or with the development of more reliable ways of shooting down incoming missiles. All of these issues (and more) are discussed in this book. The only thing that can be said with certainty is that the future is uncertain.

It is important also to recognise the impact created by the potential to prevail in conventional combat. Military force does not have to be used to be useful. When a Vietnamese coastguard vessel gives way to its Chinese counterpart (without firing a shot) in a dispute in the South China Seas, it may do so because it recognises that to open fire is to invite a conflict that it can only lose. The superior Chinese Navy may not be actively engaged but is clearly relevant to the outcome. Similarly, Russian

BOX 0.2 INTERSTATE WARS, INTRA-STATE WARS AND NON-STATE WARS

Across the centuries intra-state wars (i.e., wars within states) have occurred more frequently than interwar wars (those conducted between different states). The Correlates of War project identified that there were a total of ninety-five interstate wars between 1816 and 2007, of which thirty-eight occurred after the Second World War. Of the latter, nine came in the period after the end of the Cold War (i.e., since 1990). Over the same period (1816–2007) there were over 330 intra-state wars in addition to sixty-two non-state wars (where neither side was a state) and over 160 extra-state wars (where a state fought a non-state entity beyond its own borders). There were also many minor armed conflicts that did not meet the project's threshold for consideration. As a corrective to those who believe that interstate conflict now occurs much less frequently than before, it may be worth noting that in the first twenty-five years of the study (1816–1841) there were only two interstate wars, twenty-four non-state wars and over thirty intra-state ones. There were more interstate wars in the last twenty-five years of the study than in the first twenty-five. On the other hand it would be fair to say that recent interstate conflicts have lacked the scale and the impact of many of those before 1945. There has also been a reduction in the number of battle-related casualties (as wars have tended to be shorter and less intense). This has not necessarily led to a reduction in overall civilian casualties, and these almost always surpass those of combatants. For example, there were around 145,000 battle-related deaths during the war in the Democratic Republic of Congo from 1998 to 2001 but the war overall may have resulted in as many as 2.5 million deaths.[23]

tanks may not have fought battles against their Ukrainian counterparts in Spring 2014, but their perceived ability to do so helped to set the context within which Ukraine was inhibited from dealing with separatists in Crimea, leading to the secession of that region. Conventional military force was far from the only factor at play, but it is spurious to suggest that it was irrelevant. The 2008 Russo-Georgian War, in which Russian **joint forces** engaged with and defeated their Georgian counterparts (who were attempting to suppress pro-Russian separatists in South Ossetia and Abkhazia) provides an illustration of the costs of thinking otherwise. Ukraine appears to have learnt the lesson well. Resistance to the Russian invasion of 2022 did not rest solely on conventional forces but these were certainly central to the defeat of the initial onslaught and to continued Ukrainian survival in the face of ongoing Russian aggression. Similarly, the abject failure of Russian conventional forces in the early stages of this war set the context for the extension of the 'special military operation' into a long war that cost both sides dearly (Figure 0.3).

Figure 0.3 Burnt-out Russian tank in Kyiv Oblast, Ukraine, 2022. The 2022 Russian invasion of Ukraine provided an unwelcome reminder that conventional warfighting capabilities could still be important in determining victory or defeat in the twenty-first century. Source: https://tinyurl.com/3ws7bx8w

Similarly, the US and its allies may have spent a decade fighting insurgencies in Afghanistan and Iraq, typical of 'war amongst the people', but one should not forget why their enemies adopted asymmetric tactics; they had no other choice. Had the Taliban or Saddam Hussein been able to prevail in conventional warfare, the US and its allies would not have faced insurgencies in Iraq and Afghanistan; they could not have been there in the first place. Conventional superiority (across all domains) provided the context within which the enemies of the US were forced to try something else.

In the aftermath of the 2006 Israel–Hezbollah conflict, and in light of Western difficulties in Iraq and Afghanistan, it was often argued that modern warfare was becoming increasingly 'hybrid' in nature, with adversaries employing a variety of techniques and procedures, both conventional and unconventional, within the same battlespace and tailored to exploit enemy weaknesses. One might reasonably ask whether there has ever been a war that was not hybrid to some degree but, banal though it may be, the concept does at least focus attention on the complexity of current military operations and may help to foster an understanding that in order to achieve a satisfactory outcome in these, one requires an approach that brings together both military and civilian agencies in an integrated manner. It also supports the idea that, rather than concentrating on only one apparently dominant form of warfare, armed forces may be required to operate across a spectrum of operations that might include benign peacetime engagement, **peace operations**, limited military intervention, **irregular warfare** and/or major combat operations.

These issues are addressed throughout this book. The focus is on the kind of warfare that is 'in existence at this time' and our aim is to examine activities across the spectrum of warfare involving both conventional and unconventional forces. To examine these in a satisfactory fashion also requires an examination of military concepts, organisations and activities in 'recent times'. We have tried to avoid being overly prescriptive about what this might actually mean. The degree to which one needs to look back in order to understand the present varies depending on the subject. To understand current **strategy**, for example, one must deal with concepts and theories that were first articulated centuries ago. On the other hand, an understanding of air power theory implies a particular focus on the period since the Wright brothers' pioneering flight in 1903 (although, even here, apparently new theory is often grounded in concepts that are centuries old). We focus primarily on warfare in the twentieth and twenty-first centuries. This approach allows us to chart the evolution of thought and practice over an interesting, relevant and dynamic period. Where necessary it also draws on issues, events and concepts that pre-date this timescale. Sadly there is not the space in this one volume to provide a detailed examination of strategic history across the centuries and we have not tried to do so. The analysis is informed by the authors' historical understanding and examples are used throughout in order to illustrate and explain the conceptual analysis. The list of recommended reading at the end of this chapter provides guidance on a number of sources that do focus explicitly on relevant history, and familiarity with the concepts discussed in this book will help the reader to gain the best from such works.

How to Use This Book

The book is not intended to provide a history of modern warfare. Many such books exist already and there is not the space in this slim volume to provide a satisfactory historical narrative. Rather, the book examines the critical issues, ideas and concepts that one must engage with in order to develop and articulate an understanding of the conduct of war in its various forms and in its different operating environments. While it does not attempt to provide a history of modern warfare, the book does seek to introduce readers to both the *theory* and the *practice* of modern warfare. It is important to engage with both as one cannot properly be understood without reference to the other. The practice of warfare – what armed forces do and the way that they do it – is influenced by theoretical concepts and constructs or, where these are not expressed formally, by preconceived ideas that themselves represent an informal (sometimes an unconscious) equivalent to theory. Today such concepts are often expressed officially through military doctrine, adopting and adapting theoretical constructs in a manner designed to foster understanding amongst practitioners. Thus, one of the aims of this book is to examine and explain the concepts and ideas that underpin modern doctrine and that inform current practice.

BOX 0.3 PRINCIPLES OF WAR: AN ILLUSTRATION

Soviet Union	United States	United Kingdom
Offensive action	Objective	Selection & maintenance of the aim
Manoeuvre & initiative	Offence	Concentration of force
Concentration of force	Mass	Economy of effort
Economy of force	Economy of force	Maintenance of morale
Surprise & deception	Manoeuvre	Offensive action
Momentum	Unity of command	Flexibility
Annihilation	Security	Cooperation
Reserves	Surprise	Security
Cooperation	Simplicity	Surprise
	Restraint	Sustainability
	Perseverance	
	Legitimacy	

Academic commentators, professional think tanks and military doctrine writers have generated a plethora of templates, ideas and rules on the methods through which warfare can be conducted successfully. The manner in which these are often used is reflected in the way in which many militaries have articulated formal 'principles of war' to guide the effective application of military power; see Box 0.3. As this book makes clear, however, the conduct of war is an art and not a science. It cannot be made subject to immutable rules. Knowledge of 'principles' is less important than an understanding of the challenges faced when trying to apply them in any given context. A century ago Julian Corbett emphasised this point, writing that 'nothing is so dangerous in the study of war as to permit maxims to become the substitute for judgement'.[24] Knowledge of principles and concepts is not a substitute for judgement or understanding, merely a means of fertilising both. We hope, therefore, that in addition to informing the reader this book will act as a stimulus for thought and reflection on the subject.

For ease of use the book has been broken down into six main parts that examine strategy (Part I), land warfare (Part II), naval warfare (Part III), air warfare (Part IV), irregular warfare (Part V) and weapons of mass destruction (Part VI). Each of these parts consists of three chapters that each addresses a different aspect of the topic. The six parts have been written in such as way as to enable them to be read individually, and not necessarily sequentially. Part I, relating to strategy, does provide a useful foundation that is relevant to all other areas and thus it makes sense for readers to first acquaint themselves with the concepts and issues discussed there, particularly if they do not already have a sound grounding in strategic thought. The first chapter in each of the six parts introduces core concepts and these are then discussed and developed in the chapters that follow.

This new edition of the book includes an additional part that addresses the 'future operating environment'. Here we address issues that are critical to an understanding of warfare in the twentieth century. Chapter 18 examines **joint warfare** and operations in a multi-domain environment; Chapter 19 focuses on hybrid warfare and grey zone conflict; and Chapter 20 explores **cyber warfare** and information operations. The concepts and issues addressed in these chapters impact on the analysis elsewhere in the book and there is discussion of joint, hybrid and cyber challenges throughout most others chapters, but their salience to current defence debate warrants their inclusion here as discrete topics.

It should be remembered that the breakdown discussed previously is rather artificial. This is particularly true of the division of chapters into separate environments (land, sea and air). In truth these are all interconnected and operations in one usually depend on supporting activities in the others. This has been reflected in the particular emphasis placed by many armed forces on proficiency in **joint operations**, meaning those that involve cooperation between the different services. Such operations are notoriously difficult, requiring as they do competence across environmental (and thus institutional) boundaries. Nevertheless, it is now widely accepted that to prevail in warfare one must integrate activities across all relevant war-fighting domains. The US military currently lists five such domains: land, sea, air, space and cyber. The first three of these are discussed in Parts II–IV of this book, space is examined in Part IV under the general examination of air power and the importance of cyberspace is discussed throughout the book and in detail in Chapter 20.

The importance of joint operations represents a common theme across the various chapters in this book and is addressed in detail in Chapter 18. Another key theme is that modern warfare is more of an evolutionary phenomenon than it is revolutionary. Many of the important features of warfare in the twenty-first century have their origins in the gradual development of concepts and structures from earlier periods. A third theme is the importance of thinking about warfare in terms of different, but interrelated, levels of war (see Box 0.4 and Figure 0.4). These provide a framework

BOX 0.4 THE LEVELS OF WAR (ACCORDING TO US JOINT DOCTRINE)

Tactical: The level of war at which battles and engagements are planned and executed to achieve military objectives.

Operational: The level of war at which campaigns and major operations are planned, conducted and sustained to achieve major objectives within **theatres** of other operational areas.

Strategic: The level of war at which a nation, often as a member of a group or nations, determines national or multinational strategic security objectives and guidance, then develops and uses national resources to achieve those objectives.[26]

Figure 0.4 The levels of war (according to US doctrine).

within which one can categorise and rationalise military activity and are usually reflected in formal military **command** structures. One should note that the boundaries between the levels are often blurred and that each influences the other in both an upward and a downward direction. Thus, decisions at the strategic level will influence activity at the tactical and **operational levels**, while actions at the tactical level can have an impact on the levels above (indeed, there is not much point if they don't). Major General Charles Krulak's discussion of the 'strategic corporal' provides a good illustration of how, in complex environments, decision making can devolve lower and lower down the command chain, and also how decisions made at the tactical level (i.e. by corporals) can have a strategic impact.[25]

While Chapters 1–3 demonstrate that strategy is always of importance, the subsequent chapters illustrate that different environments and forms of warfare have seen continuity and change that manifest themselves in different ways at different levels of war. For example, as the chapters on naval warfare explain, changes at the tactical level of war do not necessarily invalidate established principles at the operational and strategic levels. Another recurrent theme is that it is evidently rarely easy to distinguish between continuity and change. Consequently, militaries have often found it difficult to predict accurately the future of warfare.

This last theme, in particular, is an important one. Adapting successfully to the future depends in part upon having a grasp of the past and the present. The future is not fixed, nor is it easily predicted. As the eighteenth century philosopher David Hume noted, 'Nothing that we imagine is absolutely impossible.' While *knowledge* of the past and present of warfare may provide part of the foundation for coping with the future, more important is developing an *understanding.* We hope that this book is a useful contribution to that process.

FURTHER READING

Baylis, J., J. Wirtz and J. Johnson (eds.), *Strategy in the Contemporary World*, 7th ed. (Oxford: Oxford University Press, 2022). This textbook provides a useful introduction to a range of topics of relevance to our understanding of conflict and strategy in the world today.

Black, Jeremy, *Rethinking Military History* (London: Routledge, 2004). A bold critique of much contemporary military history that includes a survey of key themes within the subject from 1500 to the present.

Black, Jeremy, *War. A Short History* (New Haven, CT: Yale University Press, 2022). Black provides a brief examination of the history of war since ancient times, offering valuable insight on a range of issues that remain relevant today. In particular he challenges the eurocentric bias evident in some other works.

Gat, Azar, *War in Human Civilization* (Oxford: Oxford University Press, 2006). In this thought-provoking book Gat combines many disciplines in an attempt to examine why people engage in war.

Gray, Colin S., *Another Bloody Century: Future Warfare* (London: Weidenfeld & Nicolson, 2005). A challenging look at war and at warfare from one of the world's leading experts on the subject.

Gruszczak, Artur and Sebastien Kaempf, *The Routledge Handbook of Future Warfare* (London: Routledge, 2023). An edited volume with contributions from a wide range of different perspectives, seeking to assess the likely nature of future warfare.

Lindley French, Julian and Yves Boyer (eds.), *The Oxford Handbook of War* (Oxford: Oxford University Press, 2012). This edited volume includes a series of short articles written by academics and practitioners that address a broad range of topics relating to the causes, conduct and consequences of war.

Parker, Geoffrey (ed.), *The Cambridge History of Warfare* (Cambridge, UK: Cambridge University Press, 2005). A collection of essays that examines the history of warfare since ancient times, with a particular emphasis on an apparent 'Western way of war'.

Roy, Kaushik and Michael Charney (eds.), *The Routledge Handbook of the Global History of Warfare* (London: Routledge, 2023). An edited volume containing a range of scholarly chapters that address different aspects of the history of warfare from ancient times to the present.

Townshend, Charles, *The Oxford History of Modern War*, 2nd ed. (Oxford: Oxford University Press, 2005). Written by some of the leading experts in the field, this book examines various aspects of war and warfare from the seventeenth to the twenty-first centuries.

ONLINE RESOURCES

There are numerous think-tanks and pressure groups that study the causes, conduct and consequences of war. The following all contain useful and interesting material.

Correlates of War project, www.correlatesofwar.org/. Initiated first by the University of Michigan, this is an academic project that seeks to collect and disseminate reliable statistics relating to international relations, and primarily to war.

The Stockholm international Peace Research Institute, www.sipri.org/. As the title suggests, this institute studies issues relating to war and peace and publishes useful annual reports relating to conflict, the arms trade, etc.

The RAND organisation, www.rand.org/. RAND is a major US think-tank that undertakes research in a number of areas, including international relations, diplomacy and security. The website includes links to numerous blogs, reports and articles.

The Uppsala Conflict Data Program, www.pcr.uu.se/research/ucdp/. Based at a Swedish university, this program seeks to provide data on active armed conflicts. The website includes numerous datasets and links to other publications.

The International Institute for Strategic Studies, www.iiss.org/. A London-based think-tank that supports research and publication in the field. Their website contains links to many useful articles and other valuable sources.

NOTES

1 See, for example, Philip Dwyer and Mark Micale (eds.), *The Darker Angels of Our Nature: Refuting the Pinker Theory of History and Violence* (London: Bloomsbury, 2021).

2 Michael Howard, 'Military History and the History of War', in Williamson Murray and Richard Hart Sinnreich (eds.), *The Past as Prologue: The Importance of History to the Military Profession* (Cambridge, UK: Cambridge University Press, 2006), p. 17.

3 See www.oed.com/.

4 Hedley Bull, *The Anarchical Society* (Columbia, NY: Colombia University Press, 1977), p. 178.

5 See Correlates of War Project, www.correlatesofwar.org/, and Uppsala Conflict Database Program, https://tinyurl.com/4rrrnbra.

6 Carl von Clausewitz, *On War*, ed. and trans. Michael Howard and Peter Paret (Princeton, NJ: Princeton University Press, 1976 [1832]), p. 99.

7 Quoted in Lawrence Freedman, 'Defining War', in Julian Lindley-French and Yves Boyer (eds.), *The Oxford Handbook of War* (Oxford: Oxford University Press, 2012), p. 19.

8 *Selected Military Writings of Mao Tse Tung* (Beijing: Foreign Languages Press, 1967), pp. 226–7.

9 Quincy Wright, *A Study of War*, Vol II (Chicago, IL: University of Chicago Press, 1942), p. 685.

10 Hedley Bull, *The Anarchical Society*, p.178.

11 Colin S. Gray, *Another Bloody Century: Future War* (London: Weidenfeld & Nicolson, 2005), p. 30

12 UK Ministry of Defence, *JDP 0-01. UK Defence Doctrine*, 6th ed. (2022), p. 3.

13 See Carl von Clausewitz, *On War*, ed. and trans. Michael Howard and Peter Paret (Princeton University Press, 1976), first publ. 1832.

14 Anatol Rapoport, 'Introduction', in Carl von Clausewitz, *On War* (London: Penguin, 1968). Unfortunately the Penguin edition of *On War* is poorly translated and badly edited, so is best avoided.

15 See Mary Kaldor, *New & Old Wars: Organized Violence in a Global Era*, 3rd ed. (Bristol: Polity, 2012). Also see Herfried Munkler, *New Wars* (Bristol: Polity, 2004).

16 US Marines Training Command, 'ASCOPE-PMESII', https://tinyurl.com/yv2cj6c7.

17 Azar Gat, *War in Human Civilisation* (Oxford: Oxford University Press, 2006), p. ix.

18 US Joint Chiefs of Staff, *Joint Publication 1. Vol. 1. Joint Warfighting* (2023), p. II-5. UK Ministry of Defence, *Joint Doctrine Publication 0-01, British Defence Doctrine*, 6th ed. (2022), p. 3.

19 Michael Sheehan, 'The Evolution of Modern Warfare' in John Baylis, James Wirtz and Colin Gray, *Strategy in the Contemporary World,* 4th ed. (Oxford: Oxford University Press, 2013), pp. 39–59.
20 See www.oed.com/.
21 Theodore Ropp, *War in the Modern World* (Durham, NC: Duke University Press, 1959).
22 Heidelberg institute for International Conflict Research, *Conflict Barometer 2013. No.22.* (2014) and *Conflict Barometer 2023 No.31,* https://hiik.de/ [24 July 2024]. /
23 Correlates of War Project, www.correlatesofwar.org/. Bethany Lacina and Nils Petter Gleditsch, 'Monitoring Trends in Global Combat: A New Dataset of Battle Deaths', *European Journal of Population,* 21 (2005), 145–66.
24 Sir Julian Corbett, *Some Principles of Maritime Strategy* (Annapolis, MD: Naval Institute Press, 1988 [1911]), p. 10.
25 Charles Krulak, 'The Strategic Corporal: Leadership in the Three Block War', *Marine Corps Gazette*, January 1999, https://tinyurl.com/3eyed6ae.
26 Joint Doctrine Publication 1-02, *Department of Defense. Dictionary of Military and Associated Terms* (August 2012).

PART I
Strategy

DAVID J. LONSDALE

1 The Study and Theory of Strategy

CHAPTER OUTLINE

KEY THEMES

- Strategy is neither war nor politics, and thus requires its own intellectual tradition.
- The nature of strategy must be respected.
- Strategy requires serious study removed from moral, political, operational and intellectual fads.
- **Strategic theory** can help the practitioner cope with complexity, but offers no guarantees.

Introduction

War is practised in many different environments and contexts. While this has always been the case, the modern period has witnessed a growing complexity to warfare. In the twentieth century the air, space and cyberspace environments took their place as theatres of war alongside the traditional environments of land and sea. With each new environment of warfare came distinct features, challenges and opportunities for the commander to deal with. In addition to these new arenas, the invention of nuclear weapons presented a severe challenge for those involved in using military force in the service of policy objectives. However, the twentieth and twenty-first centuries are not just notable for introducing new components to warfare. Older forms of warfare have also undergone substantial developments. Irregular warfare witnessed a degree of theoretical and practical maturation through the works and careers of men such as Mao and Robert Thompson. At the same time, regular forms of warfare have had to adapt to new technology and an increasingly joint approach. Finally, political and social developments have added to the challenges faced by commanders. In an age of ubiquitous social media, legal and moral restrictions on the use of force are more readily applied and upheld.

This book will explore the significance of the previously discussed changes to the character of war. Yet, despite the seeming novelty of warfare in the modern period, the very essence of war has remained the same. Across time and place, although the character of war has altered, the components that comprise its nature have remained constant. At the heart of that nature is politics. War is a violent political activity. Regardless of the specific context, each war has a guiding policy rationale. Ensuring that military means serve policy ends effectively is the realm of strategy. Each particular form of warfare, whether acting in isolation or operating in concert with others, must be guided by strategy: the process that ensures war has dynamic rational purpose.

In our quest to understand strategy, this opening chapter begins by identifying the need for an academic approach to the subject. Having explored the requirement for, and development of, the discipline of Strategic Studies, the work focuses upon the role of theory in strategy. To that end, the chapter provides a summary of the two great works of universal theory, Carl von Clausewitz's *On War* and Sun Tzu's *The Art of War*. Mention will also be made of Baron Antoine Henri de Jomini's *The Art of War*, and the most important works of modern theory.

The Study of Strategy

Since its inception during the Cold War, Strategic Studies has enjoyed mixed fortunes. During periods of perceived heightened threat (e.g., from terrorism or nuclear weapons), interest in strategy has flourished. However, changes in the international security environment, evident failures in strategy or moral repugnance towards war can undermine the perceived validity, desire and/or requirement for Strategic Studies.

It has also been difficult to maintain a unified, coherent approach to the study of strategy. Like many other academic disciplines, especially those tied so closely to the policy world, Strategic Studies suffers from fads and fashions. The subject tends to respond quite vigorously to the changing security environment. While this is understandable, and to some degree desirable – Strategic Studies should help inform the policy process – the tendency to 'trend' invariably dissects the discipline and leaves certain areas neglected. Thus, the 1990s were dominated by **peacekeeping** and revolutions in military affairs; whereas study of the post-9/11 world was primarily concerned with irregular warfare, before returning to great power conflict as tensions rose between the powerful nation-states. To some degree, nuclear weapons reflect the changing fortunes of the entire discipline. Strategic Studies was born as a response to the nuclear revolution, but nuclear strategy was then neglected during the initial post-Cold War era, only to be resurrected in the face of nuclear modernisation and nuclear threats between Russia and North Atlantic Treaty Organisation (NATO) over Ukraine. This tendency to fluctuate in response to the issue of the day is troublesome because nuclear weapons have been, and always will be, present in the arsenals of the great powers.

To clarify, in order to make sense of the complex strategic environment we need a vibrant, unified discipline of Strategic Studies, one that stays true to the nature of the subject. Richard Betts is convincing when he states that university 'faculties should decide what to cover on the basis of long-term evidence of what mattered in world politics rather than recent events, intellectual fads, or moral hopes'.[1] The study of strategy is essential to give military activity meaning beyond the battlespace.[2] Without an understanding of strategy, we cannot construct meaningful theories of victory. In this sense, victory cannot be defined merely in military terms. Rather, a strategic theory of victory is concerned with the achievement of policy objectives. Strategic Studies enables us to conceptually make this jump from the battlespace, and appreciate the true value of military actions. Thus, in the first instance this chapter seeks to outline the need for the continued development of Strategic Studies as an academic discipline, acting in the service of those who practise strategy in the real world.

The need for Strategic Studies is perhaps at its most intense in response to the complexity of strategy. This complexity, and the challenges it produces, is amply demonstrated in the recently concluded war in Afghanistan and the ongoing conflicts in Ukraine and Israel/Gaza. These conflicts represent quite different forms of war, irregular and regular (with a nuclear element), but still all entail the various complexities to be identified. Indeed, we can conclude that the complexity of strategy is such that achieving a satisfactory end state at reasonable cost, and within a reasonable time frame, is often more elusive than ill-informed comment would suggest. As a result, we must have realistic expectations of what is possible from both the theorist and the practitioner. As David Jablonsky notes, 'a true scientific product is not possible from the study of strategy'.[3] Strategy does not tolerate formulas for success; rather it calls for an approach more suited to art than science. Every strategic context is unique, and therefore requires its own unique mixture and application of strategic assets. To appreciate fully the challenges faced by those practising strategy, and to provide a common set of definitions and concepts, the first three chapters of this book seek to dissect the art of strategy. In undertaking this task, the work is by default asking the question: 'Why is strategy so difficult?', and seeking means to alleviate the challenges faced.

In many respects, the development of modern Strategic Studies can be attributed to one man and one invention. The man is Bernard Brodie; the invention is the nuclear weapon (see Figure 1.1). The unique characteristics of nuclear weapons, and the absence of a history of use – beyond the attacks on Hiroshima and Nagasaki at

Figure 1.1 The invention of nuclear weapons, used first at Hiroshima (depicted here) and Nagasaki in August 1945, played a key part in the development of the academic discipline of Strategic Studies.

the end of the Second World War – opened the door for civilian strategists to lead debates about strategy during the Cold War. The rise of the civilian strategic analyst is illustrated by Alain Enthoven, who made the following comment during a discussion on strategic plans: 'General, I have fought just as many nuclear wars as you have.'[4] Brodie's contribution was to call for a more systematic, academic approach to the subject. Ironically, Brodie's call somewhat backfired. In outlining the need for a more scientific approach to strategy, he inadvertently instigated an approach (systems analysis) that attempted to reduce the complexity of strategy to quantifiable mathematical phenomena. In response, Brodie called for the reintegration of politics and history into the subject.

Since strategy is a process that sits uncomfortably between two worlds occupied by politics and military power, it has historically suffered from the absence of an intellectual tradition of its own. Political theory has a long tradition stretching back to ancient Greece. Although strategic theory has been blessed with outstanding works such as Clausewitz's *On War* and Sun Tzu's *The Art of War*, much discourse relating to military matters has tended to be limited to a focus on tactical and operational issues. Indeed, Brodie bemoans the lack of any real successors to the two great theorists. Since 1949 a number of commendable theorists have emerged – Brodie amongst them – yet his comments regarding the anti-intellectual bias of the military still ring true: 'Soldiers usually are close students of tactics, but only rarely are they students of strategy and practically never of war!'[5] This seemingly odd statement can be explained by the following comment by Gray, citing historian Peter Browning: 'War is a relationship between belligerents; it is the whole context for warfare. Warfare is defined as "the act of making war".'[6] Understanding these two related, but distinct, concepts requires very different approaches. Worryingly, Brodie's lament that military staff colleges focus primarily, and intensively, on training, at the expense of true analytical reflection, could easily be an observation of the current situation. In modern military colleges, strategic theory often receives significantly less attention than subjects such as defence management and procurement. The result of such an approach is that the military tend towards an over-reliance on principles concerned with tactical and operational issues, such as the principles of war. Although the principles of war have value, they are ill-suited to understand the complex natures of war and strategy. Such an approach also misunderstands the role of theory. As Gray notes, 'strategic theory is about education, not training or doctrine'.[7] As Brodie again notes, within the cultural confines of the military, there simply is neither the inclination nor the time to engage in detailed analysis of strategic issues.[8] One might say that because there is no inclination, sufficient time is not created.

This should not necessarily be taken as an outright condemnation of the military profession's attitude to study. Nor should it be regarded as a call for an abstract, purely theoretical pedagogic approach. In many respects, it is understandable that a profession so rightly focused on practical considerations and results should neglect deep analytical ruminations. Also, since strategy is so bound up with intangible forces, such as morale and will, judgement, rather than endless analysis, is often the key to success. However, these two considerations, while somewhat understandable, do not excuse the neglect of academic analysis. Clausewitz, both a soldier and a scholar, was aware of the value of strategic theory: 'Theory exists so that one need not start afresh each time sorting out the material and ploughing through it, but will find it ready to hand and in good order. It is meant to educate the mind of the future commander, or, more accurately, to guide him in his self-education, not accompany him to the battlefield.'[9] In this sense, theory helps us to understand what matters in strategy, and gives us insight into how the many dimensions of strategy interact.

The relationship between theory and practical strategy is a complex one. An overly enthusiastic fixation on the practical can lead to analytical stagnation, and an obsession with today's problem. A theory constructed and developed beyond immediate policy concerns may therefore have more lasting value, and may be able to illustrate a range of tomorrow's policy issues. However, at the same time, theory devoid of policy relevance will not further the goal of better strategy, which must be an objective for Strategic Studies; bad strategy kills. It is therefore understandable that, as Raymond Aron observes, strategic theory often reflects the strategic issues of the day. Again, Betts summarises the relationship well: 'Neither theory nor policy can be optimised apart from each other. Central theoretical insights often flow from grappling with concrete questions rather than a priori constructs.'[10] Or, as Gray puts it: 'Most practitioners need to be educated to recognise the relevance of theory to their search for workable solutions to today's problems, whereas theorists must never forget that their labours ultimately only have meaning and value for the world of strategic behaviour.'[11] Ultimately, the strategist has to act, usually, if not always, without a complete understanding of the situation. At such times, judgement and moral courage come to the fore, albeit based on an intellect shaped by theoretical education. Additionally, the further development of strategic theory can help the strategic community improve its understanding of the complex relationships amongst the many dimensions in strategy.

In the absence of an intellectual strategic tradition within the military, Strategic Studies has had to develop its own identity within the civilian sector, within universities, think-tanks and research institutes. Initially centred in the latter, which resulted in a focus on current policy demands, the subject failed to establish a scholarly framework, as Lawrence Freedman notes. Again, akin to its relationship with the military, academic analysis finds little empathy in the world of policymakers, who want solutions, not further elucidation of the problems and complexities facing them. As Freedman notes, 'Policymakers became impatient with those qualities that academics believe to be the most valuable: long-term thinking, stretching the bounds of the possible, and taking complexity as a challenge rather than an excuse for not going into too much detail.'[12] Thus, alongside the need for a more academic approach in staff colleges, the maintenance of Strategic Studies in universities is equally critical for the development of a genuine analytical framework and tradition. Within such an environment, the strategic analyst is afforded the freedom and time to develop the interdisciplinary, analytical approach required to enhance understanding of strategy.

Again, these comments are not designed to denigrate the more practical aspects of military education and training, such as doctrine. However, while accepting the need for doctrine, all those concerned with the development of strategy should also embrace a theoretical approach in the Clausewitzian tradition, rather than a slightly more sophisticated version of Jomini's work (based as it is in principles and operational-level issues). Too often, the significance of Clausewitz's work is acknowledged, but only through the citation of an overused maxim. Clausewitz's real value exists in the intellectual development one experiences when dealing with the whole complexity of his theory. Despite the many instances when this chapter will extol the virtues of Clausewitz's work, it should not be taken as an advertising campaign for *On War*. We must heed Brodie's advice and go beyond Clausewitz. Strategic Studies, and thereby our understanding of strategy, cannot develop if all we do is reiterate Clausewitz's ideas. Clausewitz is a great starting point, but we must develop theory further. This can only be achieved by theorising in an intellectually permissive environment.

In light of the previous discussion, a fair question to pose is: Do we need academics involved in the strategic process? Could not the military and policymakers construct an effective understanding of strategy between themselves? Richard Betts thinks not: 'If civilian [academic] strategists are not to decide along with the professional military, either ignorant civilians will do it, disjoining political and military logic, or the military will do it alone.'[13] Strategy is a complex subject that requires multivariate analysis, based in deep conceptual and historical knowledge. It would be asking too much of political and military leaders to be able to acquire such knowledge and understanding while also excelling in their particular fields. Invariably, with their limited faculties and time, humans tend to become centred and encultured in their particular fields. Thus, since strategy straddles two worlds, we need a dedicated discipline and community focused on this very particular socio-political activity. The real challenge for Strategic Studies is how to remain useful in the service of policy and military realities, without forgoing the detailed analysis necessary to understand the complexities of the subject.

Strategic Theory

Efforts to understand the complexities of strategy have been aided by a number of key theorists. Although each particular form of warfare has its own dominant works of theory, there are universal theorists who grapple with the nature of war and the broader aspects of strategy. For the practitioner, these works help to identify and illuminate the various elements of strategy. In addition, they provide some advice, if limited, on how to cope with the challenges of strategy. However, the more prescriptive a work is, the less universal it tends to be. This is particularly the case with Jomini's work, which suffers in comparison with Clausewitz as a result.

Although these universal works provide enlightenment on strategy, the limits of theory must be kept in mind. As a general proposition, Wylie's assertion that no general theory can guarantee success should be treated as the first and most important thought on this issue.[14] In this vein, Clausewitz recognised that theory could only ever be second best to what military genius does: 'What genius does is the best rule, and theory can do no better than show how and why this should be the case.'[15] Unfortunately, military geniuses, perhaps in the vein of Alexander the Great, are rare indeed. Consequently, us mere mortals require aid from theory. Indeed, even some prospective geniuses would benefit from a greater theoretical understanding of strategy. Napoleon was undoubtedly in a class of his own at the tactical and operational levels, but his campaigns in Russia and Iberia reveal serious limitations at the strategic level. Theory has often performed a very practical function within strategy. One of the most striking examples of this is the relationship between the theory and practice of strategic bombing. The influence of theory was particularly evident during the interwar years, when the central theoretical tenets of both precision and area/morale bombing were formulated in the works of Douhet, Trenchard and Mitchell. Williamson Murray notes how pervasive the influence of theory can be, reaching into areas such as doctrine and force composition: 'The theories of Douhet and other early airpower advocates ... have exercised a great influence on the development of air forces since that time.'[16] In a similar manner, the theorists of nuclear strategy during the Cold War were said to have 'wielded enormous influence, not only over the way an entire generation's thoughts about military issues were shaped but also over the formulation of defence policy in the nuclear-weapon states'.[17]

To be useful to the practitioner, theory must coincide with reality. To this end, Murray and Grimsley's declaration that 'strategy is the art of the possible' is an important warning to those who would construct naively optimistic theories.[18] Again, Clausewitz is persuasive when he warns: '[Theory's] purpose is to demonstrate what war is in practice, not what its ideal nature ought to be.' In a similar vein, Brodie argues that: 'Above all, strategic theory is a theory for action.' Echoing Brodie's wise counsel, Daniel Moran stipulates that 'The goal of theory in any field is to improve our understanding of reality, and our ability to act effectively.'[19] Finally, Clausewitz summarises both the value and limits of theory: '[Theory] is meant to educate the mind of the future commander, or, more accurately, to guide him in his self-education, not to accompany him to the battlefield.'[20] Later on in the work he elaborates on these thoughts:

> Theory cannot equip the mind with formulas for solving problems, nor can it mark the narrow path on which the sole solution is supposed to lie by planting a hedge of principles on either side. But it can give the mind insight into the great mass of phenomena and of their relationships, then leave it free to rise into the higher realms of action.[21]

Clausewitz

Of the universal theorists, the first amongst equals is the aforementioned Carl von Clausewitz. Having served in the Prussian Army against Napoleon's forces,

Clausewitz's major work, *On War*, was posthumously published in 1832. *On War* is arguably the most influential work of strategic theory to date. Brodie is unequivocal about the value of Clausewitz's work, which he describes as 'not simply the greatest but the only truly great book on war'. Similarly, Gray, one of the most respected of modern strategic thinkers, describes Clausewitz as his constant companion.[22] The practitioners of strategy are no less impressed by the Prussian's credentials. The US Marine Corp (USMC)'s doctrinal publication *Warfighting* stipulates that Clausewitz's *On War* is 'the definitive treatment of the nature and theory of war'.[23]

Despite his prominence in modern strategic affairs, Clausewitz's work is often misunderstood and criticised. Much of this is due to the unfinished nature of the work, and the fact that Clausewitz chose a philosophical framework that, although popular in his day, is now rarely utilised. *On War* was published as a single volume after Clausewitz's wife gathered together elements of the unfinished manuscript. Indeed, in a book of 123 chapters, Clausewitz only considered the first to be fully complete. In addition, Clausewitz's use of the dialectical approach has led to some confusion. Rather than merely present one perspective, this philosophical method arrives at a synthesis after discussing the thesis and antithesis. Specifically, Clausewitz first presents a vision of war that is absolute, escalatory and unrestricted. He spends much of the rest of the book reining in this idea with the various means by which war is limited. So, for example, absolute war can never be achieved because it is limited by policy concerns and the play of friction, to name just two restraining effects. On this basis Clausewitz distinguishes between absolute war and real war. Unfortunately, some commentators have failed to grasp his approach, and have thus criticised Clausewitz for advocating unrestricted forms of war in the early sections of the book.

Clausewitz has come under fire from some of the most prominent writers in modern Strategic Studies. Martin van Creveld, perhaps in an attempt to bolster his view that war is becoming increasingly irregular in character, regards Clausewitz's work as being stuck in a state-centric view of the world, and therefore narrow in its utility. The military historian John Keegan likewise regards Clausewitz's view of war as being too narrow. Keegan argues that, rather than being merely an instrument of policy, war in fact is a cultural phenomenon.[24] These narrow interpretations of *On War* do a disservice to Clausewitz, whose work is far more universal. Clausewitz's focus on policy as the guiding force in war is anything but restrictive. It certainly is not limited to state-based war fought for purely rational and secular motives. The following statement from Clausewitz illustrates this point perfectly: 'Policy, of course, is nothing in itself; it is simply the trustee for all these interests against other states . . . we can only treat policy as representative of all interests of the community.'[25] The emphasis here is on the broad interpretation of the concept of policy, and the use of the term community. Thus, policy may refer to any objective for which war is waged. This can include religious issues, territorial disputes, resources or indeed as an expression of culture. Similarly, community can refer to any group that forms a strategic actor.

Clausewitz's vision of war is fairly complex and dense. Although it is not possible to fully express his ideas in just one chapter of a book, the main concepts can be summarised. However, it is worth noting that there is simply no substitute for spending time analysing *On War*. Amongst strategic thinkers Clausewitz comes closest to defining the nature of war. For Clausewitz war is a complex phenomenon, composed of rational and non-rational forces. This is expressed most clearly in the 'trinity', which describes how the nature of war is composed of three interactive forces: 'primordial violence, hatred, and enmity', 'the play of chance and probability' and 'its element of subordination, as an instrument of policy, which makes it subject to reason'.[26] The true nature of any particular war is to be found in the dynamic interplay of these three forces. Much emphasis is given to war's rational element as a tool of policy. However, this subjection to reason is tempered by non-rational forces that make war uncertain, chaotic and non-linear. For Clausewitz, war is infused by chance, emotions and significant levels of friction that prevent war from reaching the higher levels of operational efficiency.

Although Clausewitz spends much of his time in *On War* discussing the various complexities of strategy, he does offer a number of means through which to deal with the associated problems. In a work that places so much emphasis on the human element, it is not surprising that the primary factor that can mitigate the complexities of strategy is to be found in man. Indeed, Clausewitz's theory of war cannot be fully understood without reference to the role of the commander or, to use the correct terminology, the 'military genius'. Winston Churchill, a man who had to wrestle with strategy at the highest levels, is of the same mind: '[War's] highest solution must be evolved from the eye and brain and soul of a single man … Nothing but genius, the demon in man, can answer the riddles of war.'[27]

Although Clausewitz fought against Napoleon, it is clear that his notion of the 'military genius' was largely based upon the Corsican, albeit with the aforementioned limits still noted. Although the term genius tends to suggest that Clausewitz was referring to a few gifted individuals, we can utilise his concept to discuss the attributes of good command more generally. Thus, good command requires certain cognitive skills, certain moral qualities and an understanding of the human condition. More specifically, Clausewitz identifies a number of characteristics that a commander should possess. These include physical and moral courage, incisiveness, presence of mind, strength of will and character and an ambitious nature. Particular prominence is given to a general's intuitive ability, his *coup d'oeil*, and a determined character to pursue his decisions through to conclusion. Clausewitz was also conscious of the significance of leadership within the chaotic and stressful environment of war. Finally, and rather obviously, a Clausewitzian general must understand the process of strategy by which war is used for political effect.[28]

Important though the commander is, command as a whole cannot be reduced simply to the attributes of the individual. As Gray postulates, an astute commander may be unavailable when the next war occurs. Thus, a process of command must be designed to compensate for the potential lack of genius: 'War cabinets, general staffs, and chiefs of staff committees were invented to function as a surrogate for individual strategic genius.'[29] There are a number of examples of command systems that are able to produce consistently good results. One prominent example, often cited, is the Prussian General Staff. T. N. Dupuy goes as far as to suggest that the success of the Prussian/German General Staff can be attributed to the fact that 'it enabled men who individually lacked the qualities of a genius to perform institutionally in a manner that would provide results ordinarily achievable only by genius'.[30] Thus, we can conclude that the complexity of strategy can be somewhat unravelled by a judicious combination of the commander's qualities, the command structure and an appropriate command ethos.

In many respects, the main utility of Clausewitz's work for the practitioner may simply be the fact that he identifies the complexities of strategy. To be able to deal with a problem, one must first acknowledge and understand it. However, *On War* goes further. Aside from an important, if not always practical, focus on the military genius, Clausewitz provided a few conceptual aides. Most noteworthy in this respect is **'centre of gravity'**. This concept dominates much of modern military doctrine. Centres of gravity are defined by Clausewitz as follows: 'Particular factors can often be decisive . . . One must keep the dominant characteristics of both belligerents in mind. Out of these characteristics a certain centre of gravity develops, the hub of all power and movement, on which everything depends. That is the point against which all our energies should be directed.'[31] Wylie incorporates centre of gravity into his own theory regarding the search for strategic success:

> The basic problem facing the strategist throughout all these situations, through any war, any time, any place, is this: Where shall be the center of gravity of the war? . . . Control of the strategic weights or centers of gravity in any war, large or small, limited or unlimited, is a basic advantage that should be sought by any strategist. It is the fundamental key to the conduct of warfare.[32]

Wylie's statement identifies that there may be more than one centre of gravity for each belligerent, and therefore a number of routes to victory. Indeed, it is possible to identify centres of gravity at all of the levels of strategy. An airfield may act as the operational-level centre of gravity. At the same time, an individual leader or the public may be the centre of gravity at the grand strategic level. Although Clausewitz himself recognises that there may be various centres of gravity, he does conclude that it is preferable to 'trace them back to a single one'. Clausewitz's candidates for the centre of gravity are the army, capital city, public will, alliance cohesion or personalities of the leadership. Nonetheless, reflecting his emphasis on battle, Clausewitz concludes that 'the defeat and destruction of [the enemy's] fighting force remains the best way to begin, and in every case will be a very significant feature of the campaign'.[33]

In this respect, Clausewitz's work is noteworthy for the emphasis it places on battle. While this may seem rather obvious in a work about war, it is a refreshing counterpoint to the modern tendency to undervalue engagement with the enemy. Clausewitz was certainly aware of the limits of force, but he also stressed the dominance of the destructive principle and the value of defeating the enemy's forces. The latter is obviously not an end in itself but, as noted earlier, is usually an important step on the road to achieving policy objectives. Battlefield victory over the enemy destroys his ability to resist, thereby opening the door to **control.** Whether that control is enforceable may depend on effective utilisation of the non-violent tools of **grand strategy**. Nonetheless, success in battle will at least present a more permissive security environment.

Clausewitz's emphasis on battle is wise counsel in an age when we may be guilty of overthinking strategy in our search for overly complex and subtle answers to strategic dilemmas. Indeed, simplicity, one of the modern principles of war, is often overlooked; yet Clausewitz regarded it as an essential ingredient of his theory of war: 'It seems to us that this is proof enough of the superiority of the simple and direct over the complex ... rather than try to outbid the enemy with complicated schemes, one should, on the contrary, try to outdo him in simplicity.'[34] And for those who regard a direct, battle-orientated approach as intellectually immature, Clausewitz comments: 'The maximum use of force is in no way incompatible with the simultaneous use of the intellect.'[35]

Regardless of what constitutes the centre(s) of gravity in any particular war, the concept does act as a very useful analytical and planning tool. Nonetheless, as with all theory, it does not offer a guaranteed route to victory. Therefore, to fully appreciate the relative value of centres of gravity, we must ask a number of questions in each circumstance. Does the enemy actually have a centre of gravity? Can the enemy's centre of gravity be identified? The intelligence and analytical challenge posed by this last question should not be underestimated. For example, a debate still rages over what constituted the centre of gravity within the German war economy during the Second World War. This is not surprising when one considers the size of the task involved in trying to undertake an accurate macro-level analysis of the German economy at that time. Robert A. Pape acknowledges that the required information was simply not available.[36] Even with the benefits of historical research and hindsight, historians still disagree over which component of the German economy, at which period in the war, represented its key vulnerability. Understanding the functioning of the German economy at the time must have been even more of a challenge. These difficulties are compounded by the fact that often the intelligence acquired is based on a peacetime analysis of the enemy, rather than when they have mobilised their economy for war.

Even if a centre of gravity has been correctly identified, is it always possible to put it under sufficient pressure? As Beaufre argues: 'The enemy's vulnerable points must be set against our own capabilities.' For example, if the Wehrmacht represented one of Nazi Germany's centres of gravity, it was beyond the reach of certain countries at certain times. Until the D-Day landings, the Wehrmacht could not be sufficiently engaged by British and American military power. Furthermore, in 1939, although German forces were in contact with the Poles, the latter lacked the required capabilities to put the former under significant pressure. With such a mismatch in capabilities and opportunities it matters little that you have identified the enemy's key attribute; defeat will still occur. Finally, the Soviet Union, although able to

eventually defeat the Wehrmacht, could only do so at great cost. Most countries would not have been able to sustain such losses and deprivations.

There is much more that could be written about *On War*. For now, we must satisfy ourselves with this brief discussion of Clausewitz's significance to Strategic Studies. Nonetheless, Clausewitzian concepts will appear constantly throughout this book. Most obviously, the following chapter will discuss in detail the important concept of 'friction'.

Jomini

Before moving on to the work of Sun Tzu, the other great universal theorist, it is important to mention the work of Baron Antoine Henri de Jomini. Despite being a contemporary of Clausewitz, who also participated in the Napoleonic Wars, Jomini offers a distinctly different vision of war than the Prussian. In contrast to Clausewitz's emphasis on military genius overcoming the complexities of a chaotic world, Jomini provides readers with a number of principles, which if followed should lead to victory. Indeed, rather than describing war as a non-linear activity in which intangible forces dominate, Jomini's approach to war is rather geometric. In particular, Jomini stresses the advantages of interior lines of communication. Jomini's experience with the general staff may have been instrumental in shaping his planning-based approach to the subject of war. This may help to explain his greater emphasis on concepts such as lines of operation.

It is interesting to note that two strategic thinkers from the same period, and sharing some of the same experiences, can produce such radically different theories. In broad philosophical terms, both Jomini and Clausewitz display a tendency for the enlightenment's propensity towards rational analysis. Jomini, in particular, apes Newton in his quest to discover the fundamental principles underpinning the activity of war. However, whereas Jomini can be criticised for failing to escape the rationalism of the eighteenth century, Clausewitz managed to create a synthesis of the enlightenment's rationality and the non-rational approach of German Romanticism with its greater emphasis on the psychological, emotional, metaphysical and intuitive. Despite his apparent failings, Jomini proved particularly popular during the nineteenth century. However, over time the limitations of the prescriptive nature of Jomini's work have become evident. This emphasises the point that war cannot be reduced to a science, beholden simply to a series of maxims or principles.

Sun Tzu

The second great universal theorist pre-dates the Napoleonic period by over 2,000 years. The Chinese strategist Sun Tzu offers yet another different vision of war. Sun Tzu's work is influenced by the Taoist tradition with its emphasis on non-material force-multipliers. Thomas Cleary explains that Taoism can be understood as 'the ancient tradition of knowledge'.[37] In this sense, we may conclude that for Sun Tzu war in its ideal form becomes an intellectual and metaphysical exercise rather than a physical one. For Sun Tzu, war is a necessary evil that represents a departure from cosmic harmony.

In contrast to Clausewitz's emphasis on violent clashes of arms, Sun Tzu seeks attainment of policy objectives, preferably without the application of violence. For Sun Tzu, 'to win one hundred victories in one hundred battles is not the acme of skill. To subdue the enemy without fighting is the acme of skill.'[38] In order to achieve this, or indeed to gain victory at minimal cost should fighting occur, Sun Tzu puts great emphasis on the role of information and knowledge. Indeed, much of Sun Tzu's work is built around the need to acquire and use intelligence about factors such as the enemy, environment and oneself. With intelligence at the heart of his theory, Sun Tzu understandably highlights the significance of deception. His statement, 'All warfare is based upon deception', is revealing, since in order to deceive the enemy effectively one must exert control over information.

Whereas Clausewitz regards a more direct, battle-orientated approach as the most profitable, Sun Tzu is famed for the indirect approach. Rather than highlighting the gains to be made from destroying the enemy, Sun Tzu extols the virtues of absorbing the enemy's resources into one's own: 'Your aim must be to take All-under-Heaven intact. Thus your troops are not worn out and your gains will be complete.'[39] From the above it is understandable why the ancient Chinese strategist has become popular in the modern period. In many respects his approach is ideally suited to a Western, information-age, post-heroic approach to strategy that seeks minimal costs, and champions the manouevrist or effects-based approach to warfare.[40] Sun Tzu is also an obvious point of reference for irregular warriors, who lack resources and thereby gravitate towards the indirect approach.

Whereas Clausewitz's work may at times be criticised for being too dense and sometimes confusing, Sun Tzu suffers from the opposite problem. Although there is little to argue with in his ideas concerning the value of acquiring information, overall his work gives the impression that war is a controllable and predictable activity. Lawrence Freedman goes as far as to suggest, 'Sun Tzu believed that perfect knowledge could be obtained.'[41] In the chapter 'Energy', Sun Tzu provides a picture of combat that appears chaotic, but in fact 'there is no disorder'.[42] Organisation and good communications are the means by which order is produced from seeming disorder. Rather than Clausewitz's gritty 'real war', Sun Tzu provides something of an ideal vision of how strategy should be conducted. Taking Sun Tzu too seriously could leave the practitioner naively optimistic of what is possible in strategy.

While Sun Tzu and Clausewitz offer very different approaches to strategy, their ideas can be effectively combined. This has been most obviously and successfully done in Maoist strategic thinking. Mao's three-stage theory of revolutionary war utilises the indirect approach in the early stages, switches to Clausewitzian battle in the final stage, and throughout is infused by a clear adherence to the idea that war is very much a political instrument. Indeed, Mao was extremely conscious of the fact that his forces were political actors as well as being military units.[43]

Modern Theory

Taken together, the works of Clausewitz and Sun Tzu provide practitioners with a solid theoretical basis for their future undertakings (see Box 1.1). However, Gray is

BOX 1.1 STRATEGIC THEORY

Clausewitz

- War is a continuation of political intercourse.
- The nature of war is composed of rational and non-rational forces.
- Wars may differ in their character, but are all things of the same nature.
- Friction, which distinguishes war on paper from war in reality, impedes efficacy.
- War is violent, uncertain and competitive.
- There are many potential centres of gravity, but defeating the enemy's forces is usually the best place to start.

Sun Tzu

- The acquisition of knowledge is the key to success in strategy.
- Deception has a central role in war.
- More is gained through victory without battle/violence.
- Victory may be achieved through either a direct or an indirect approach.

right in his assertion that we need more than just the classics. At the level of general theory, three works suggest themselves. These are Luttwak's *Strategy: The Logic of War and Peace*, for its identification of the **paradoxical logic** of strategy and the need for harmony in the levels of strategy; Wylie's *Military Strategy: A General Theory of Power Control*, which is distinguished for its universally useful concept of control, and the related ideas concerning 'the-man-on-the-scene-with-a-gun'; and Gray's *The Strategy Bridge*, which is chosen for its conceptually comprehensive analysis of strategy, while maintaining the important idea that strategy represents a unified, practical undertaking.

Conclusion

As a consequence of the fact that strategy is neither politics nor war – rather it is the process that links one to the other – it is not endowed with a strong intellectual tradition of its own. That being the case, the discipline of Strategic Studies, based primarily in civilian institutions, plays an essential role in keeping the theoretical flame alive. Strategic theory, however, is not a self-justifying activity. In the strategic realm, theory plays an important role in educating the practitioner. To reiterate Brodie's important observation, 'strategic theory is theory for action'.

Although steadily growing, universal strategic theory is still thin on the ground. Thankfully, what exists is of high quality. Alongside important modern works (including Gray, Wylie and Luttwak), the theories of Clausewitz and Sun Tzu stand out. Together, these two works provide invaluable insights into the nature of war and the challenges of strategy. For those responsible for the practice of strategy, the great works of theory act as important tools in the difficult task of understanding this most complex and important of subjects. To paraphrase Sun Tzu, strategy is of such import that it should be thoroughly studied.

RESEARCH QUESTIONS

1. Why is the study of strategy important?
2. In what ways can theory aid the practitioner of strategy?
3. Does Clausewitz deserve his pre-eminence in modern strategy?
4. Is Sun Tzu's *The Art of War* especially well suited to the modern age?
5. How well does modern strategic theory build upon the classics?

FURTHER READING

Betts, Richard K., 'Should Strategic Studies Survive?', *World Politics*, 50 (October 1997), 7–33. Provides a compelling argument on why we need to keep the Strategic Studies flame alive.

Brodie, Bernard, 'Strategy as a Science', *World Politics*, 1/4 (July 1949), 467–88. A vastly important article that outlines the need for an intellectual development of Strategic Studies.

Clausewitz, Carl von, *On War*, trans. Michael Howard and Peter Paret (London: David Campbell Publishers Ltd, 1993). Quite simply the best work of strategic theory ever written. Clausewitz gets closer than anyone to defining the true nature of war.

Freedman, Lawrence, *Strategy: A History* (Oxford: Oxford University Press, 2015). A masterly and exhaustive exploration of the theory and practice of strategy.

Gray, Colin S., *The Strategy Bridge: Theory for Practice* (Oxford: Oxford University Press, 2010). Probably the greatest modern work of strategic theory. Gray's analysis is comprehensive and thought-provoking.

Handel, Michael I., *Masters of War: Classical Strategic Thought*, 2nd rev. ed. (London: Frank Cass, 1996). A great introduction to the classic works of strategic theory.

Jomini, Baron Antoine Henri de, *The Art of War* (London: Greenhill Books, 1996). A flawed classic; Jomini is still worth reading to see how a 'principles' approach to strategy can underestimate the challenge of complexity.

Luttwak, Edward N., *Strategy: The Logic of War and Peace* (Cambridge, MA: The Belknap Press of Harvard University Press, 1987). A modern classic that introduces the paradoxical logic and discusses harmonisation of the levels.

Mao Tse-Tung, *Selected Military Writings of Mao Tse-Tung* (Beijing: Foreign Languages Press, 1963). Mao is arguably one of the most important theorists and practitioners of irregular warfare. He also manages to combine the theories of Clausewitz and Sun Tzu.

Schelling, Thomas C., *Arms and Influence* (New Haven, CT: Yale University Press, 1966). An outstanding analysis of how military force can be used for strategic effect.

Sun Tzu, *The Art of War*, trans. Samuel B. Griffith (London: Oxford University Press, 1971). A rich work of strategic theory, which considers military strategy in its grand strategic context.

Watts, Barry D., *Clausewitzian Friction and Future War*, McNair Paper 52 (Washington, DC: Institute for National Strategic Studies, National Defense University, October 1996). The best analysis of Clausewitzian friction to date.

Wylie, J. C., *Military Strategy: A General Theory of Power Control* (Annapolis, MD: Naval Institute Press, 1967). Often overlooked, Wylie's little book provides an excellent discussion of strategic theory and introduces the central concept of 'control'.

ONLINE RESOURCES

https://clausewitz.com/: a site full of interesting papers on this most important of strategic thinkers.

https://ssi.armywarcollege.edu/: the website of the Strategic Studies Institute, which contains lots of in-depth analysis of important strategic issues.

www.militarystrategymagazine.com/: an online journal devoted to strategy.

https://thestrategybridge.org/: focused on developing thinking in strategy and military affairs.

https://warontherocks.com/: a site full of articles and podcasts on matters of strategic significance.

www.rand.org/: after many years, RAND continues to keep its finger on the pulse of important strategic matters.

https://nipp.org/: The National Institute for Public Policy offers a wide range of online publications dealing with important issues in contemporary strategy.

NOTES

1 Richard K. Betts, 'Should Strategic Studies Survive?', *World Politics*, 50 (October 1997), 41.

2 The term 'battlespace' refers to the environment in which warfare occurs. The term is used in place of the more traditional 'battlefield' to indicate the increasingly complex, and joint, operational environment. Hence, battlespace includes the traditional environments of land, sea and air. It also includes space, cyberspace and the electromagnetic spectrum more generally.

3 David Jablonsky, 'Why Is Strategy Difficult?', in Joseph R. Cerami and James F. Holcomb, Jr (eds.), *US Army War College Guide to Strategy* (February 2001), http://permanent.access.gpo.gov/lps11754/00354.pdf.

4 Quoted in Fred Kaplan, *The Wizards of Armageddon* (New York, NY: Simon and Schuster, 1983), p. 254.

5 Bernard Brodie, *War and Politics* (London: Cassell, 1973), p. 11.

6 Colin S. Gray, 'From Principles of Warfare to Principles of War: A Clausewitzian Solution', in Colin S. Gray, *Strategy and History: Essays on Theory and Practice* (London: Routledge, 2006), p. 82.

7 Colin S. Gray, 'Introduction', in Colin S. Gray, *Strategy and History: Essays on Theory and Practice* (London: Routledge, 2006), p. 2.

8 Bernard Brodie, 'Strategy as a Science', *World Politics*, 1(4) (July 1949), 486–7.

9 Carl von Clausewitz, *On War*, trans. Michael Howard and Peter Paret (London: David Campbell Publishers Ltd, 1993), p. 141.

10 Betts, 'Should Strategic Studies Survive?', p. 37.

11 Gray, 'Introduction', p. 5.

12 Lawrence Freedman, 'The Future of Strategic Studies', in John Baylis et al. (eds.), *Strategy in the Contemporary World*, 2nd ed. (Oxford: Oxford University Press, 2007), p. 360.

13 Betts, 'Should Strategic Studies Survive?', p. 3.
14 J. C. Wylie, *Military Strategy: A General Theory of Power Control* (Annapolis, MD: Naval Institute Press, 1967).
15 Clausewitz, *On War*, p. 136.
16 Williamson Murray, *The Luftwaffe 1933–1945: Strategy for Defeat* (Washington, DC: Brassey's, 1996), p. xxiv.
17 John Baylis and John Garnett, 'Introduction', in John Baylis and John Garnett (eds.), *Makers of Nuclear Strategy* (New York, NY: St Martin's Press, 1991), pp. 1–2.
18 Williamson Murray and Mark Grimsley, 'Introduction: On Strategy', in Williamson Murray, MacGregor Knox and Alvin Bernstein (eds.), *The Making of Strategy: Rulers, States, and War* (Cambridge, UK: Cambridge University Press, 1994), p. 22.
19 Daniel Moran, 'Strategic Theory and the History of War', in John Baylis et al. (eds.), *Strategy in the Contemporary World: An Introduction to Strategic Studies* (Oxford: Oxford University Press, 2002), p. 17.
20 Clausewitz, *On War*, p. 141.
21 Ibid., p. 578.
22 Colin S. Gray, *Modern Strategy* (Oxford: Oxford University Press, 1999).
23 H. T. Hayden (ed.), *Warfighting: Manoeuvre Warfare in the US Marine Corps* (London: Greenhill, 1995), p. 43.
24 John Keegan, *A History of Warfare* (London: Pimlico, 2004).
25 Clausewitz, *On War*, p. 606.
26 Ibid., p. 89.
27 Winston S. Churchill, quoted in M. Carver, 'Montgomery', in John Keegan (ed.), *Churchill's Generals* (London: Weidenfeld & Nicolson, 1991), p. 148.
28 Clausewitz, *On War*, pp. 100–12.
29 Gray, *Modern Strategy*, pp. 53, 108.
30 T. N. Dupuy, *A Genius for War: The German Army and General Staff, 1807–1945* (London: MacDonald and Jane's, 1977), p. 307.
31 Clausewitz, *On War*, pp. 595–6.
32 Wylie, pp. 76–7.
33 Ibid., p. 596.
34 Ibid., p. 272.
35 Ibid., p. 75.
36 Robert A. Pape, *Bombing to Win: Air Power and Coercion in War* (Ithaca, NY: Cornell University Press, 1996), p. 275.
37 Thomas Cleary, Translator's Introduction', in Sun Tzu, *The Art of War*, trans. Thomas Cleary (Boston, MA: Shambhala, 1988), p. 2.
38 ˙Sun Tzu, *The Art of War*, trans. Thomas Cleary (Boston, MA: Shambhala, 1988), pp. 77–9.
39 Ibid.
40 Edward N. Luttwak, 'Towards Post-Heroic Warfare', *Foreign Affairs*, 75/3 (1996), pp. 109–22.
41 Lawrence Freedman, *The Revolution in Strategic Affairs*, Adelphi Paper 318 (Oxford: Oxford University Press, 1998), p. 60.
42 Sun Tzu, *The Art of War*, pp. 92–3.
43 Mao Tse-Tung, *Selected Military Writings of Mao Tse-Tung* (Peking: Foreign Language Press, 1966).

2 Strategy Defined

CHAPTER OUTLINE

KEY THEMES

- Strategy is a process that connects military power with policy effect.
- Strategy has various levels that must be in harmony.
- Strategy is a complex, challenging activity.
- The difficulties of strategy can be mitigated, to some degree.

Introduction

Now that we have identified the need to develop an analytical approach to the subject, we must begin our exploration with some key definitions of strategy and its various levels. Having illuminated the essence of strategy, this chapter will analyse the various factors that make it difficult. In particular, the chapter will explore strategy's multidimensional nature; disharmony amongst the levels; the paradoxical logic; nature of war; friction; human participation; and war's polymorphous character. It is hoped that by the end of this chapter the reader will have a better understanding of the challenges involved in strategy, and how these can be dealt with so that the use of military force can best serve policy objectives.

Strategy Defined

Extant strategic literature contains various definitions of strategy. For Clausewitz, it can be understood as 'the use of engagements for the object of the war'.[1] Similarly, Gray defines strategy as 'the use that is made of force and the threat of force for the ends of policy',[2] whereas Andre Beaufre highlights the dynamic interaction between belligerents: 'The art of the dialectic of two opposing wills using force to resolve their dispute.'[3] This work defines strategy as *the process that converts military power into policy effect* (see Box 2.1). Importantly, this definition identifies the key relationship in strategy: that between policy and the military instrument. Furthermore, it acknowledges strategy as process. The latter is recognition of that fact that strategy is not tangible, but is dynamic and does have manifest effect.

As noted, the core relationship within strategy is that between military force and the policy objective. Gray describes this relationship as a bridge that links the military and political worlds.[4] Alternatively, Eliot Cohen described this relationship as an 'unequal dialogue' (see Figure 2.1).[5] In this sense, we can regard strategy as a process by which military force creates political effect. Although the supremacy of policy is established and well understood, and thereby military force must serve policy, it is not simply a case of the political leadership demanding what it requires from the military instrument. Indeed, Clausewitz notes that although policy must remain the supreme consideration in the conduct of war, '[T]hat, however, does not imply that the political aim is a tyrant. It must adapt itself to its chosen means.'[6] Thus, the military and political leaderships must engage in discussions concerning what policy requires and, just as importantly, what the military instrument can deliver. Hence, the significance of dialogue becomes clear in the quest for positive strategic effect. However, the dialogue lacks equity because the military instrument must ultimately serve policy goals.

A constructive dialogue may avert an obvious danger in such a relationship; namely, that policymakers may not understand the instrument at their disposal. As Gray notes, this danger can manifest itself in two ways: 'There is always a danger either that out of ignorance or incompetence policy will ask more of its military instrument than that instrument should be expected to deliver, or that policy will ask less of its "sword" than could, and perhaps should, be secured.'[7] To mitigate the potential for such failures, some modicum of education in strategic studies for policymakers would be welcome, but still would not guarantee success. Policymakers may

BOX 2.1 STRATEGY DEFINED

The process that converts military power into policy effect.

Figure 2.1 President Trump holds briefing with senior military leaders in the Cabinet Room of the White House in Washington, DC, on Wednesday 3 April 2019. Strategy serves political goals and acts as a bridge between the military and political world.

conduct poor strategy, even in the face of good strategic theory, for a host of different reasons. For example, domestic or party political considerations may influence policymakers. Note the reduced troop increases in Vietnam in 1967 for fear of the political repercussions of calling up reservists, or the rushed US withdrawal from Afghanistan during the Biden Administration. Alternatively, policymakers may simply lose focus on a strategic problem, turning their intention to other political matters instead. The latter is illustrated by British strategy, or lack thereof, during the later stages of the war in Afghanistan.[8] In such circumstances, if an enemy can remain strategically focused and committed, they can then take advantage of lapses in strategic sense by their opponents.[9]

This suggests that the relationship between policy and the military is seemingly at its most complex, or most challenging, in a modern democratic state. In such an environment the political and military leaderships often have little experience or understanding of their opposite number. In his excellent study of Field Marshal Sir Douglas Haig, John Terraine notes that within Haig's generation there was a substantial amount of mistrust and misunderstanding between the military and civil establishments. In addition, Terraine correctly concludes that Haig's 'absolute lack of interest in politics . . . cannot be considered as other than a serious defect'.[10]

That being said, the military-political divide in a democracy can offer some advantages. Left to their own devices, the military may wage war in a manner that is ultimately unsustainable from the perspective of the community they represent. In Algeria, the French military eventually largely contained the Front de Libération Nationale (FLN, National Liberation Front), but the methods used and the costs incurred ultimately proved too much for the French polity. During the US Civil War, Lincoln had to regularly push his overly cautious generals into action, partly because he was conscious of the growing popularity of the peace party in Washington as the war dragged on.

The complexities that emanate from the political–military relationship are not restricted to modern democratic states, however. Although on the surface this relationship seems much simpler for the likes of Alexander the Great or Napoleon, problems still existed. In these instances, the unification of the roles of political and military leadership creates its own problems. Without an external dialogue to assess the strategic rationale of decisions, there may be a corresponding absence of any effective check on the strategic efficacy of certain actions. In the case of Alexander this problem intensified over time as he became more confident, paranoid and increasingly sure of his divine destiny. By the time he had reached India, his campaigns had lost a degree of strategic focus and subtlety of method. The result of this deterioration in his **strategic performance** was a long, bloody campaign that eventually provoked a mutiny in the army. Thus, the complexities of the military–policy relationship seem to be less a problem of command organisation (although this can exacerbate the difficulties), as both modern democracies and imperial dictators alike struggle to bring together these two worlds effectively. The problem is more conceptual; it is about means and ends, which at times can be very different in their nature and may even sometimes appear contradictory. Nonetheless, as difficult as this relationship often is, it is the beating heart of war and the very driving force of strategy.

The Levels of Strategy

Successful strategic performance requires far more than merely overcoming the challenges involved in the process of matching means to ends. It also requires competent performance across all the levels of strategy. It will be instructive at this point to define the levels of strategy and comment on how they interact (see Box 2.2), for this is the very process of strategy. The highest level in the taxonomy of strategy is *policy*. Policy is simply the overall objective that is sought. The range of policy objectives is essentially infinite, as Clausewitz so ably described it: ‘Policy, of course, is nothing in itself; it is simply the trustee for all these interests against other states . . . we can only treat policy as representative of all interests of the community.’[11] Policy objectives should influence actions within the other levels of strategy; indeed, more specifically, they should strongly influence the methods used in the campaigns. However, this is easier said than done. Clausewitz’s comment that the policy objective should guide the military instrument often creates problems when the political and military objectives are discordant. Consider, for example,

BOX 2.2 THE LEVELS OF STRATEGY

- Policy: the objective(s) sought/the guiding rationale for war.
- Grand strategy: the coordination of the state's resources towards the attainment of the policy objective(s).
- Military strategy: the use of military force to achieve the policy objective.
- Operational: the conceptual and/or geographical linking of tactical actions to military strategy.
- Tactical: actions in the battlespace in the face of the enemy.

counterinsurgency campaigns, especially those with a strong nation-building element. The latter includes a range of activities and objectives, including those related to social wellbeing, infrastructure networks, economic development, trust in the political process, etc. How does one use a blunt military instrument to achieve what are often subtle socio-political objectives? As is often the case, Clausewitz provides us with the answer. He notes that when the policy and military aims are not the same, a military aim should be chosen that leads to the fulfilment of the policy objective indirectly.[12.] For example, you should endeavour to give yourself a strong military position from which to negotiate peace. Similarly, a stable security environment facilitates development projects in support of nation-building activities.

We should remember that politics, and therefore war, is about power. Perhaps at times we are guilty of over-thinking Clausewitz, and have tried to establish too direct a relationship between policy and war. War cannot always itself directly lead to a policy objective, but it can alter the power relationships by which policy can be pursued against the enemy. A more nuanced reading of Clausewitz would note that while strategy is about the use of military force to achieve policy objectives, this relationship is not always straightforward or direct. In the first instance strategy is about the acquisition and use of power. Once gained, an imbalance in power can be used to achieve policy objectives. Thus the attainment of power represents the hidden step in Clausewitz's concept of strategy. Although Clausewitz does not explicitly outline this step in terms of power acquisition, it is evident in his work when he notes that 'war is thus an act of force to compel our enemy to do our will'.[13] This statement represents a definition of power that is remarkably similar to that offered by Raymond Aron, the theorist of international relations: 'The capacity of a political unit to impose its will upon other units.'[14]

With sufficient power, one can engage in the many subtle activities that achievement of the policy objective calls for: nation-building, civic works, reconstruction and providing security, to name just four. If, however, the enemy still retains sufficient power themselves, they too can influence events, for example by coercing the population. In this sense, they may be able to challenge one's influence and authority. The relationship between military force and power is central to Wylie's aforementioned (Chapter 1) concept of control: 'The aim of war is some measure of control over the enemy.'[15] Control is not an absolute condition. Rather, Wylie notes that it can be 'direct, indirect, subtle, passive, partial or complete'.[16] Interestingly, for the purposes of understanding the role of military force in the acquisition of power, when describing the more indirect examples of control, Wylie is happy to use the term 'influence' instead. Thus, when thinking about strategy, we should remember that although the relationship between war and policy objectives is not always direct or obvious, the former relates to the latter through the medium of power.

Once a policy objective has been decided upon, a *grand strategy* must be devised through which to pursue it. Grand strategy encompasses all the instruments at the state's disposal: diplomatic, intelligence, military, economic and now cyber. Basil H. Liddell Hart succinctly outlines the function of grand strategy: 'To coordinate and direct all the resources of a nation, or band of nations, towards the attainment of the political object of the war – the goal defined by fundamental policy.'[17] One of the main challenges in grand strategy is choosing the right instrument, or the right balance of instruments, to fulfil the particular policy objectives sought. This decision should be arrived at after taking into account a number of factors, including the policy itself, available resources, nature of potential enemies, strategic culture and the geopolitical environment, to name just five. Indeed, one of the great challenges of grand strategy, as identified by John Lewis Gaddis, is 'the alignment of potentially unlimited aspirations with necessarily limited capabilities'.[18] Grand strategy also tends to be concerned with long-term objectives. Thus, short-term remedies must be handled in a manner that is not injurious to long-term interests.

The aspect of grand strategy of primary interest to us here is military strategy. Once it has been established how military force will be used to serve the ends of policy, the strategy must be put into practice. This is achieved through actions at the *tactical* and *operational* levels. The former is concerned with actions in the battlespace in the face of the enemy. Therefore, for example, tactics includes how forces are deployed, how they engage the enemy and how various units interact with one another. In essence, tactics is about the details of combat. Each contact with the enemy represents a tactical event that occurs in a distinct time and place. At first, one could be forgiven for thinking that success at the **military strategic level** stems from a victorious outcome in every tactical event. However, successful military strategy requires a more developed understanding of the significance of tactical events. Thus, it is possible that tactical 'failure' can make an effective contribution to the attainment of a military strategic end state. A striking example of the latter is the Tet offensive launched by the Viet Cong in 1968. After initial, but short-lived, success, Tet was characterised by a series of tactical failures. However, the fact that the Viet Cong was able to launch such a range of tactical actions across South Vietnam seriously undermined morale within the US. In this respect, it is the interactions amongst the different tactical actions (in the case of Tet, their cumulative effect on public and political perception in the US) and their relationship with the military strategic level that matter most. It is at this point that the *operational* level performs its role. The operational level links tactical engagements with the overall military strategy. Edward Luttwak aptly describes it thus: 'This operational level governs the consequences of what is done and not done tactically.'[19]

The operational level has both conceptual and material elements. Conceptually, the operational level provides a framework within which tactical actions can be understood and linked together so that they serve military strategy. So, for example, a series of tactical aerial bombing missions need to be considered as a whole so that they produce a decisive coercive effect on the enemy. Materially, we can think in terms of a geographic area of operations, within which the operational level commander moves their forces from objective to objective. From a geographical standpoint there are a number of factors that the operational commander must consider in their quest for success. These include **logistics** and lines of communication, movements of the enemy and decisive points in the theatre of operations such as cities and key terrain features.

It is worth noting that the validity of the operational level, although generally accepted, is not without its detractors. Gray, for example, expresses concern that the operational level may interfere with efficacious interactions between the tactical and strategic levels. Specifically, he warns that military commanders may substitute operational objectives (with which they are most comfortable) for strategic ones, and thereby disassociate military power from policy objectives.[20] Moreover, the traditional linear description of the levels of strategy, valid though it is, does not reflect the complexity and non-linear nature of strategy. This chapter will now analyse those features of strategy that make it so complex and such a difficult activity to get right.

Why Is Strategy Difficult?

The complexity of strategy is the product of a number of different factors, which taken together produce substantial challenges for practitioners. The aforementioned awkward relationship between policy and military force is but one such factor. There are many other considerations that must be dealt with by practitioners in their quest for strategic success (see Box 2.3).

Multidimensional Nature

The notion of 'dimensions' helps us to understand the many different factors that impinge upon or play a part in strategy. Depending upon which theorist you choose to read, the number of dimensions in strategy varies. Clausewitz identified five dimensions of strategy: moral, physical, mathematical, geographical and statistical. In the modern era, Michael Howard, in his 1979 article, 'The Forgotten Dimensions of Strategy', identified four dimensions. The four dimensions in Howard's taxonomy are technological, operational, social and logistical. The relative prominence of each dimension is dependent upon circumstance.[21] More recently, in *Modern Strategy*, Gray produced a considerably more developed

BOX 2.3 WHY IS STRATEGY DIFFICULT?

- The relationship between war and policy is difficult and awkward.
- Strategy is multidimensional, and success requires a level of competence in them all.
- Success requires harmony of actions amongst the levels.
- Strategy has a paradoxical logic. The enemy will attempt to offset one's advantages.
- The component's of war's nature are constant and must be respected.
- Friction prevents war from achieving its maximum operational efficiency.
- War is a human activity imbued with non-rational, emotional forces.
- War has a polymorphous character. It can take many forms, each of which requires a subtly different approach.

theory of the dimensions, and by doing so has dissected the art of strategy considerably further than either Clausewitz or Howard. In total, Gray identifies seventeen dimensions, which he organises into three categories: 'People and Politics', 'Preparation for War' and 'War Proper'. Within these categories the dimensions include society, culture, economics and logistics, strategic theory and doctrine, command and time, to name just six. Is seventeen the final and correct number of dimensions? As Gray himself notes: 'The precise number [of dimensions] does not matter so long as everything of importance is properly corralled.'[22]

For our purposes, the significance of identifying the dimensions of strategy, and Gray's analysis in particular, is that it highlights the substantial range of factors that must be considered and dealt with (see Box 2.4). The strategic waters are muddied further by the fact that complex interactions occur amongst the dimensions. And, as Gray notes, despite the range of dimensions and their complex interactions, success requires the practitioner to achieve a reasonable degree of competence in each of them. This challenge is further intensified by the fact that an enemy may have the advantage in one very significant dimension. For example, the English Channel gives Britain a substantial advantage in the geographical dimension over Continental foes. These significant dimensions, depending on the context, do not necessarily provide an automatic advantage, although they may provoke a degree of natural friction for the enemy. Rather, it is down to the practitioners themselves to exploit them to their advantage. Thus, the English Channel did not prove a substantial obstacle for the Roman or Norman invading forces. However, once the inhabitants of the British Isles had developed competent naval forces, the significance of the geographical dimension was substantially magnified. This implies that some of the dimensions can be controlled or manipulated to varying degrees. This is discussed in the section 'Dealing with the Difficulties of Strategy'.

BOX 2.4 GRAY'S DIMENSIONS OF STRATEGY

- People
- Society
- Culture
- Politics
- Ethics
- Economics and logistics
- Organisation
- Military administration
- Information and intelligence
- Strategic theory and doctrine
- Technology
- Military operations
- Command
- Geography
- Friction
- Adversary
- Time

Disharmony amongst the Levels

In order for the process of strategy to function effectively, the strategic practitioner has to achieve a degree of competence in each of the levels of strategy. However, they must also harmonise their actions amongst these levels. Actions at the tactical level must be in accord with those at the higher levels of strategy. Although this seems to be fairly straightforward advice, the realisation of it is far from easy. Clausewitz's following general point about strategy is especially relevant when considering harmony amongst the levels: 'Everything in strategy is very simple, but that does not mean that everything is very easy.'[23] Indeed, Edward Luttwak notes that the normal state of affairs is measured disharmony. In his work *Strategy: The Logic of War and Peace*, Luttwak paints a disturbing picture for strategists, one in which the challenges of achieving harmony are substantial. To illustrate, Luttwak cites the Japanese attack on Pearl Harbor. Although at the tactical and operational levels the attack was relatively successful, from the grand strategic perspective, this success proved problematic. The scale of the attack compelled the US to pursue a policy of unconditional surrender. From this position it can be argued that Japan was always destined to lose the resulting war. Thus, harmonisation of the levels of strategy is not necessarily concerned with achieving success within all the said levels. Rather, it is about ensuring that actions within each level support, rather than undermine, efforts in the other levels of strategy. More limited, less aggressive Japanese action at the tactical and operational levels, although almost certainly aggravating the US, may have provoked a more limited response, which may not have ended in total defeat for the empire.

Harmony also demands that both policy and grand strategy create a conducive and permissive environment for military strategy to play its part. The dangers inherent in getting this wrong are evident in the case of Germany in the Second World War. Germany's overly ambitious policy objectives and flawed grand strategy ensured that tactical and operational prowess could not be fully exploited. Germany simply acquired too many powerful enemies, who, because of the nature of the Third Reich and its objectives, were beyond negotiation. Much like in the case of Japan, the enemies of Germany were set on a course of unconditional surrender. Despite substantial battlefield success for Germany, their enemies were constantly able, and willing, to put fresh forces into the field.

To illustrate further we can also look to the Second Punic War, fought between Carthage and the Roman Republic. The Carthaginian commander, Hannibal, was astute at the tactical and operational levels. Thus, he was able to inflict a series of stunning battlefield defeats on Rome during his invasion of Italy. The most notable of these were the battles of Cannae and Lake Transimene. At the former Hannibal destroyed two Roman armies, killing 60,000 men in a single day. However, he failed to translate these successes into a favourable policy outcome. In a curious decision Hannibal chose not to attack Rome itself. Thus, the Republic survived and was able to continually exploit its vast manpower resources. Considering the nature of his enemy, Hannibal's outstanding successes on the battlefield were out of kilter with the situation at the strategic and grand strategic levels. The effects of this disharmony were magnified by Rome's strategy, masterminded by Fabius Maximus, of avoiding battle under anything but the most favourable circumstances. This Fabian strategy gave Rome the time it required to mobilise its resources. Thus, we can appreciate Luttwak's notion that the challenge of harmonising the levels of strategy is further complicated by the actions of the enemy, which ensures that a complex series of interactions is taking place within and amongst the levels of strategy of all belligerents.

Paradoxical Logic

Beyond the notion of harmony, Luttwak identified another central feature of strategy, which he terms the 'paradoxical logic'. This pervasive feature operates in many different ways, and can perhaps best be explained through a number of examples, which illustrate that the expected does not always occur, strength leads to weakness, and advantage does not always flow from a linear progression of events. Much of this is the result of interaction with a thinking enemy. For example, the paradoxical logic is at play when a **manoeuvre** that takes the more difficult, less logical route, catches the enemy off guard. Alternatively, the paradoxical logic suggests that a successful military operation may begin to produce diminishing returns over time. This may occur as advancing forces move further from their sources of supply at the same time that the enemy's lines of communication are shortened. Additionally, unless the enemy is knocked out of the fight, it is likely that they will adapt and learn to successfully counter your course of action. Russia has twice adopted such an approach against an invading force. In 1812 against Napoleon, and again in the 1942 campaign against Germany, Russian/Soviet forces traded space for time, refusing to give their enemies the chance to defeat their armies in the field.

More recently, the war in Iraq offers a prime example of the paradoxical logic in action. As in the 1991 Gulf War, US-led forces easily overcame their Iraqi counterparts. However, in 2003 the defeat of the Iraqi regular forces merely represented the first stage in the struggle. Those wishing to challenge the presence of US-led forces sought to offset the conventional superiority of their enemies, and opted for irregular warfare, blending elements of **insurgency** and terrorism. In this sense, the paradoxical logic began to operate at different levels for the US-led coalition. At the tactical and operational levels, roadside bombs inflicted casualties on US forces and their allies, while not allowing their conventional superiority to be brought to bear. In addition, the insurgents could avoid contact with the coalition forces entirely by targeting civilians with car and truck bombs. Such tactics, and the associated casualties and destruction, created pressure at the higher levels of strategy within the coalition. Understanding that they could not militarily defeat the coalition, the insurgents attempted to break the will of political communities in the coalition.

Although it is certainly possible to overplay the significance of the paradoxical logic – the enemy can sometimes be overwhelmed – interaction with the enemy is worthy of continued attention. This point is well made by Luttwak: 'Although each separate element in the conduct of warfare can be very simple … the totality of these simple things can become enormously difficult when there is a live enemy opposite, who reacts to undo everything being attempted, with his own moves and his own strength.'[24] The same point is more starkly made by General George Pickett who, when asked why the Confederates lost at Gettysburg, replied: 'I think the Union Army had something to do with it.'[25]

Nature of War

Those seeking to achieve policy objectives through the use of military force also have to contend with the nature of war. The nature of war is different from its character. The character of war is a constantly changing phenomenon. It changes depending upon a number of factors, including the geography of the battlespace, the belligerents and their level of technological development, to name just three. In contrast, the components that comprise the nature of war are unchanging across time and place. Like strategy, the nature of war is complex. It is composed of elements that are always present, but fluctuate in their relationships with each other. There are various conceptual means by which to describe the nature of war. As discussed in Chapter 1, Clausewitz's 'fascinating trinity' is one such conceptual device that encompasses rational and non-rational forces (policy, emotion and chance). The relative strength or influence of each of these forces varies with context. Thus, the nature of each particular war is unique, and can be found floating somewhere between these forces. From this position, Christopher Bassford concludes that the key to understanding the nature of war is appreciating the dynamics that occur within the trinity, and between the trinities of the various belligerents in a conflict.[26] For Alan Beyerchen, non-linearity is central to the nature of war. This non-linearity emanates from the many complex interactions that occur and the moral forces that infuse war. Within such a non-linear world, small fluctuations can have significant consequences.[27]

In addition to non-linearity and the interplay of rational and non-rational forces, the nature of war includes other, ever-present, aspects. Of particular significance are 'uncertainty' and 'violence'. In addition, war is of course characterised by human participation, and the many complexities this produces. These additional elements in the nature of war are reflected in another Clausewitzian concept, 'the climate of war', which the Prussian theorist describes as being composed of danger, exertion, uncertainty and chance.[28.]

Uncertainty in war comes from a number of sources. For Clausewitz, who declared that everything in war is uncertain, unreliable and/or incomplete information produces a metaphorical fog of war over the battlespace. In addition, uncertainty emanates from interactions between the opposing actors in war. These interactions produce non-linear results that are difficult to predict and challenging in terms of understanding their implications. Moreover, human participation infuses war with powerful moral forces of an unquantifiable nature. Uncertainty may be further enhanced by the geography of the battlespace, especially in dense environments such as forests and urban areas. Often, such environments are used by irregular forces, who themselves add to the uncertainty since they rarely assume regular formations or wear uniforms. Finally, as information has to be handled and interpreted by human users, uncertainty may be the product of human error or bias. Admittedly, the processing of information has been enhanced by the application of computers and artificial intelligence (AI), and thus certain causes of uncertainty may be less acute than before. Nonetheless, even in the face of these improvements, uncertainty still abounds. AI is not infallible, information technology tends to create more information and attendant information overload, and humans remain the ultimate consumers of information, with their foibles still in play.

Violence, or what Clausewitz describes as the 'dominance of the destructive principle', is inherent to the nature of war: 'War is a clash between major interests, which is resolved by bloodshed – that is the only way in which it differs from other conflicts.'[29] Although the levels of violence vary in war, it is always present or waiting in the wings. As Clausewitz notes: 'It is inherent in the very concept of war that everything that occurs *must originally derive from combat*'[30](emphasis in the original). Although there are those who promote less violent forms of war, its presence and influence can never be eradicated. In the early years of the post-Cold War world, when the threat of major clashes of arms seem to recede, and technology appeared to offer a more sparsely populated battlespace, much was made of so-called post-heroic and humane warfare.[31] These well-intentioned ideas soon disappeared in the violence of seemingly endless insurgencies and the bloody reality of war in Ukraine and Israel/Gaza. The retention of violence is primarily because war has a dialectic nature. As Clausewitz recognised, the competitive aspect of war creates an escalatory dynamic as each belligerent attempts to seek an advantage. Thus, even if one belligerent in a conflict extols a less-bloody method, the enemy may introduce higher levels of violence to gain the upper hand. The intensification of the destructive principle may seek to debilitate the enemy's capabilities, and/or break their will through the application of violence.

Strategy itself may require that enemy forces be physically destroyed, rather than just coerced or outmanoeuvred. In order to pursue the policy of unconditional surrender against Nazi Germany, as well as to leave post-war Germany militarily impotent, the Combined Chiefs of Staff issued the following directive to the commander Eisenhower: 'You will enter the continent of Europe and, in conjunction with the other Allied Nations, undertake operations aimed at the heart of Germany and the destruction of her armed forces.' Eisenhower goes on to note, 'This purpose of destroying enemy forces was always our guiding principle.'[32]

Violence complicates strategy because it provokes strong moral forces and has an attritional effect on the capabilities of the belligerents. Objectives must still be achieved despite the debilitating effect violence has on the commander, their forces, and possibly also on the will of the domestic population and political community. Thus, those involved in strategy must endeavour to maintain sufficient will and capabilities to pursue objectives in the face of destruction and human suffering.

The significance of this violent, uncertain and competitive nature must not be underestimated. Those who do submit to this error run the risk of being at a disadvantage. As Clausewitz warns us: 'Kind-hearted people might of course think there was some ingenious way to disarm or defeat an enemy without too much bloodshed'; he continues: 'If one side uses force without compunction, undeterred by the bloodshed it involves, while the other side refrains, the first will gain the upper hand.' In a similar vein, Clausewitz warned: 'The fact that slaughter is a horrifying spectacle must make us take war more seriously, but not provide an excuse for gradually blunting our swords in the name of humanity. Sooner or later someone will come along with a sharp sword and hack off our arms.'[33]

While this advice cannot be ignored without serious consequence, in the same instance war cannot be waged without reference to the social norms of the day. In a modern setting, certain actions in war are simply not possible from an ethical standpoint. As noted by Gray: '[War] should be waged militarily in such a manner as not to sabotage its political goals.'[34] A particularly brutal form of war may cause such a backlash that the policy objectives could be lost amongst the condemnation. As with so much in strategy, there is simply no straightforward solution to this dilemma. Instead, the strategists must rely upon their judgement to create the required balance. Again, Clausewitz is instructive:

> We can thus only say that the aims a belligerent adopts, and the resources he employs, must be governed by the particular characteristics of their own position; but they will also conform to the spirit of the age and to its general character. Finally, they must always be governed by the general conclusions to be drawn from the nature of war itself.[35]

Friction

The conduct of strategy is further complicated by the play of chance and the existence of friction. Again, this is an essential ingredient of Clausewitz's theory of war: 'No other human activity is so continuously or universally bound up with chance.' Friction can be understood as 'countless minor incidents – the kind you can never really foresee – [that] combine to lower the general level of performance, so that one always falls short of the intended goal'. For Clausewitz, friction is an essential ingredient in the reality of war: 'Friction is the only concept that more or less corresponds to the factors that distinguish real war from war on paper.'[36] The various factors that make up friction, and thereby complicate the practice of strategy, have found theoretical form in Clausewitz's 'unified concept of general friction', as identified by Barry D. Watts. In his excellent study on future war, Watts identifies the following taxonomy for the unified concept of general friction: danger; physical exertion; uncertainties and imperfections in information; friction in the narrow sense of resistance within one's own forces; chance events; physical and political limits on the use of military force; unpredictability stemming from interaction with the enemy; and disconnects between ends and means in war.[37.]

To complicate matters further, friction can occur as a result of, and be exacerbated by, the paradoxical logic. Paradoxical courses of action, for example to surprise an enemy, may forgo the normal, complete and logical procedures. As Luttwak states, these actions 'will further increase friction and therefore the risk of organisational failure'.[38] Naturally, certain elements of friction are also enhanced by the effects of interaction with the enemy. Losses of men and equipment in battle deplete the capabilities of a force, which in turn may hinder future operations. In addition, the enemy may actively seek to complicate one's actions. For example, the pace of an advance may be severely curtailed by the enemy blowing a bridge.

Human Complications

At its heart war is a human activity: 'In war and strategy people matter most.'[39] Thus, as Clausewitz reminds us, war is infused with human emotions and concerns: 'The art of war deals with living and moral forces.'[40] If we return to Clausewitz's climate of war, we see that much of it is concerned with the human dimension. Uncertainty is compounded by human perceptions, friction is partly due to human actions, and danger and exertion relate directly to human participation. Within the stress and exertion of war, human actors, whether generals or a foots soldier, may be negatively affected in relation to their ability to think and act effectively. This complicates the task of strategist by restricting their options and freedom of action. In addition, as Gray notes: 'War is usually so traumatic an experience that generally it follows a course and has consequences quite unintended by the belligerents. To go to war is to roll the iron dice.'[41] Thus, we can regard the effects of danger and physical effort as contributory factors to friction in war. The reality of human limitations, in both a physical and psychological sense, restricts the potential efficacy of armed forces.

Polymorphous Character of War

War does not take a single regular form, for which strategists can plan with certainty. Indeed, the reverse is true. In this sense, war can be said to have a polymorphous character. Historically, war has always taken several different forms. However, from an operational perspective the modern era has undoubtedly produced a more complex environment. Technological developments in the twentieth century facilitated the exploitation of the air, space and cyberspace environments. In addition, the century also witnessed further developments in the theory and practice of insurgency and terrorism. Finally, perhaps the greatest challenge for strategy has been the arrival of nuclear weapons. The extreme destructive nature of these weapons makes them difficult tools of policy. Each of these various areas of strategy will be discussed in detail in the following chapters. For now, we must recognise that many of them overlap, creating new opportunities and challenges in the different environments. For example, maritime strategy has had to incorporate both air power and nuclear weapons. Thus, commanders in each geographical environment, as well as those running an entire campaign, have to deal with a more complex battlespace.

The remainder of this book will discuss the range and complexity of forms war can take. In this sense, the character of any particular war can include weapons of mass destruction (WMDs), regular conflict between uniformed and similarly organised foes, and/or various forms of irregular warfare including terrorism and insurgency. The challenge posed by such a variety of forms concerns both the preparation and conduct of war. Each particular form of warfare requires a somewhat distinct set of capabilities, which in turn may require varied types of forces, equipment, doctrine and/or training. Charles Callwell, the Victorian theorist of irregular warfare, notes: 'The art of war, as generally understood [for regular forms of warfare] must be modified to suit the circumstances of each particular case. The conduct of small wars is in fact in certain respects an art in itself.'[42] Almost one hundred years after Callwell, Gray cautions against complacency in the face of the **polymorphous character of war**: 'Small wars can detract from the readiness of regular forces to take the field against other regular forces.'[43] For strategists, the challenge posed by this range of war forms is that they must endeavour to achieve a degree of competence across the spectrum of warfare. In this sense, one may require competence in a particular form of war without being too specialised so that one cannot easily adapt to another form.

The task of strategists is further complicated by the fact that particular wars often display a complex mix of different forms. Thus, the following counsel from Clausewitz is valid, but not always easy to achieve: 'The first, the supreme, the most far-reaching act of judgement that the statesman and commander have to make is to establish by that test the kind of war on which they are embarking.'[44] Wars such as the US war in Vietnam and the war of American Independence contain elements common to both regular and irregular warfare. However, even though each particular form of warfare presents its own unique challenges, they are all still forms of war. Thus, they take place within the same complex nature discussed previously. In particular, they are still violent, competitive conflicts acting in the service of policy. Thus, the battle of the wills is often paramount, albeit fought through physical means, and a theory of victory must exist. It is all too easy to give too much significance to the challenges of a particular form of warfare, while ignoring the common features of the nature of war. This is nowhere more evident than in counterinsurgency (COIN).

Modern COIN practice, at least partially based upon seminal works such as Thompson's *Defeating Communist Insurgency*, tends to be regarded less as a form of war and more as a security challenge, with popularity and legitimacy being the key to achieving the desirable end state. While there is certainly value in the hearts-and-minds aspects of COIN doctrine, we must never lose sight of the fact that COIN is still a form of war. In fact, an essential ingredient of COIN is inflicting serious military setback on the insurgents. This not only restricts their ability to undermine security in the contested territory but it also promotes a sense of authority for the local government and its allies. On this point Callwell is clear: 'Prestige is everything in such warfare.' Similarly, Julian Paget, in the classic work *Counter-insurgency Campaigning*, concludes that to win the support of the local population 'the government must demonstrate its determination and its ability to defeat the insurgents'.[45.] Finally, Steven Metz notes: 'It is less an assessment of a preferred future that drives insurgents or insurgent supporters than an assessment of who will prevail – the insurgents or the regime.'[46]

The successful British COIN campaign in Malaya provides a telling example. The campaign took twelve years, and included some fairly draconian methods. The latter included curfews, the mass forced relocation of 400,000 people, detention without trial and execution for possession of firearms or explosives. In addition, the insurgents were subjected to a protracted war of **attrition**, during which their numbers were slowly eroded, at the cost of 500 British deaths. In summary, rather than being a competition in popularity, COIN is rather a competition in authority and strategic pre-eminence. Once again, the contest over power is paramount. Undoubtedly, COIN has particular characteristics that must be respected. Yet, it is also a form of war that is beholden to the true nature of war and strategy.

Dealing with the Difficulties of Strategy

Despite the challenges of practising strategy, policy objectives are still attained through the use of force, albeit often at greater cost and over a longer time period than initially envisaged. Strategy gets done because there are a number of actions that can be taken to mitigate the effects of these difficulties. Not surprisingly, theory offers us a range of means of dealing with the difficulties of strategy. In *On War*, having explained the reality of friction, Clausewitz looks to the human dimension as part of the answer. Specifically, the traits of the military genius, such as determination and boldness, can go some way towards overcoming the effects of friction. Moreover, although it is true to say that Clausewitz's work is light on prescription, his discussion of centres of gravity offers important advice to the practitioner.

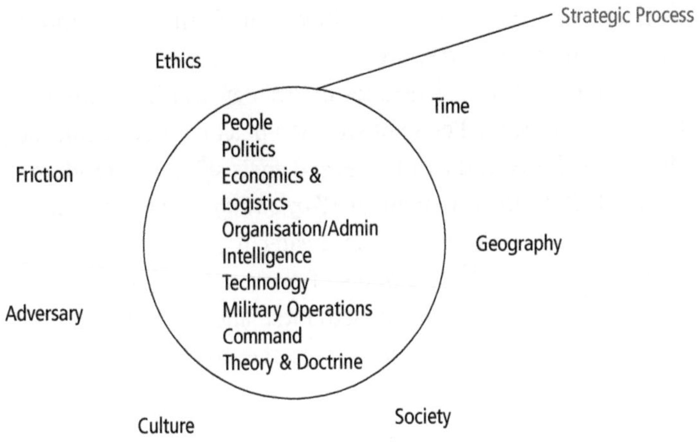

Figure 2.2 Internal/external dimensions.

Amongst the uncertainty and non-linearity of strategy, a planning methodology founded on centre of gravity analysis instils a degree of focus and structure. Centre of gravity is a contested term, but in essence refers to a feature of the enemy from which it draws its strength or that enables it to function effectively.

Looking to modern theory, Gray suggests a number of practical preparatory steps that can be taken to help improve strategic performance. These include good and ample equipment, high morale, rigorous training, imaginative planning, historical education, combat experience and sensitivity to potential problems.[47] The latter is served by both historical education and familiarity with theory. Indeed, as we develop strategic theory still further our understanding of the process also advances. This is evident, for example, in the dimensions of strategy taxonomy. As previously noted, on this subject Gray built upon the theories of Clausewitz and Howard. We can develop this work still further by seeking to exert some form of control over the dimensions, and thereby over the whole process of strategy.[48] The first step in this next stage of theory development is recognition that the dimensions exist as being either internal or external to the process of strategy, as seen from the perspective of a strategic actor (see Figure 2.2).

Those dimensions that are internal to the process can be controlled to some extent. For example, technological development can be manipulated to some degree through investment, experimentation, etc. Likewise, economics and logistics can be more adequately resourced and corralled in support of strategic endeavours. In contrast, the external dimensions appear to be beyond control of the strategic practitioner. Time marches on inexorably, and the enemy is a free agent, not a puppet dancing to our commands. However, although beyond direct control, these external dimensions can be influenced by actions in the internal category. Time cannot be stopped or slowed, but perceptions of it can be manipulated. One can prepare in a manner that is more tolerant of the passage of time. The strategic performance of Nazi Germany suffered because it failed to prepare for a long war. Regarding the enemy, President Lincoln and General Grant understood that aggressive simultaneous operations in all theatres helped limit Confederate options and gradually depleted their more limited resources.

This short discussion of dealing with the difficulties of strategy will hopefully offer succour to those overwhelmed with the challenge of strategic practice. That being said, despite the ability to mitigate the effects of the difficulties, there is still much wisdom in the following advice from the USMC doctrine manual *Warfighting*, where friction can be read as the difficulties of strategy in general: 'The greater requirement is to fight effectively within the medium of friction.'[49] Regardless of one's preparations, war and strategy are incredibly challenging socio-political activities, and thereby require a considerable commitment of resources and a strong will in order to prevail.

Conclusion

Strategy, *the process that converts military power into policy effect*, is a multilevel complex activity. This complexity emanates from its multidimensional nature; disharmony amongst the levels; the nature of war; the polymorphous character of war; the involvement of humans; the existence of an intelligent enemy; the play of friction; and the fact that it is the meeting point between the two different worlds of politics and military power. In the face of myriad difficulties, strategists must strive to control the process of strategy. As indicated in the previous chapter, in this daunting task they are aided by strategic theory, which orientates their mind towards strategic understanding. With such understanding in place, the practitioner can begin to use force in various ways to pursue the desired policy objectives. The proceeding chapter will explore these various uses of force conceptually, while also focusing on the modern strategic landscape

RESEARCH QUESTIONS

1. How does strategy function as a process?
2. Is success at the strategic level more important than success at the tactical and operational levels?
3. Why is strategy so complex?
4. Can the dimensions of strategy be controlled?
5. How do you maximise the chances for success in strategy?

FURTHER READING

Aron, Raymond, *Peace and War: A Theory of International Relations*, trans. Richard Howard and Annette Baker Fox (New York, NY: Anchor Press/Doubleday, 1973). One of the best discussions of war and power in international politics.

Baylis, John et al. (eds.), *Strategy in the Contemporary World: An Introduction to Strategic Studies* (Oxford: Oxford University Press, 2022). An excellent introduction to the theory and practice of strategy in the contemporary world.

Beaufre, Andre, *An Introduction to Strategy: With Particular Reference to the Problems of Defence, Politics, Economics, and Diplomacy in the Nuclear Age* (London: Faber and Faber, 1965). A classic work of strategic theory from the Cold War, which contains many insights into the complexities of the subject.

Callwell, Charles E., *Small Wars: A Tactical Textbook for Imperial Soldiers* (London: Greenhill Books, 1990). An insightful analysis of British imperial strategy with many pertinent observations for the contemporary environment.

Cohen, Eliot A., *Supreme Command: Soldiers, Statesmen, and Leadership in Wartime* (New York, NY: The Free Press, 2002). An interesting study of the relationship between policy and the military instrument. The work benefits from some good historical case studies.

Kane, Thomas M. and David J. Lonsdale, *Understanding Contemporary Strategy* (London: Routledge, 2019). A comprehensive introduction to strategy in all its forms.

Liddell Hart, Basil H., *Strategy: The Indirect Approach* (London: Faber and Faber, 1967). An interesting updating of Sun Tzu's main ideas.

Lonsdale, David J., *Alexander the Great: Lessons in Strategy* (London: Routledge, 2007). Alexander the Great is still the best example of how to overcome the complexities of strategy and achieve outstanding success.

Summers, Jr, Harry G., *On Strategy: A Critical Analysis of the Vietnam War* (Novato, CA: Presidio, 1982). An insightful and sobering analysis of what happens when strategy is not given its due respect.

ONLINE RESOURCES

https://clausewitz.com/: a site full of interesting papers on this most important of strategic thinkers.

https://ssi.armywarcollege.edu/: the website of the Strategic Studies Institute, which contains lots of in-depth analysis of important strategic issues.

www.militarystrategymagazine.com/: an online journal devoted to strategy.

https://thestrategybridge.org/: focused on developing thinking in strategy and military affairs.

https://warontherocks.com/: a site full of articles and podcasts on matters of strategic significance.

www.rand.org/: after many years, RAND continues to keep its finger on the pulse of important strategic matters.

https://nipp.org/: The National Institute for Public Policy offers a wide range of online publications dealing with important issues in contemporary strategy.

NOTES

1 Carl von Clausewitz, *On War*, trans. Michael Howard and Peter Paret (London: David Campbell Publishers Ltd, 1993), p. 177.

2 Colin S. Gray, *Modern Strategy* (Oxford: Oxford University Press, 1999), p. 17.

3 Andre Beaufre, *An Introduction to Strategy: With Particular Reference to the Problems of Defence, Politics, Economics, and Diplomacy in the Nuclear Age* (London: Faber and Faber, 1965), p. 22.

4 Colin S. Gray, *War, Peace, and Victory: Strategy and Statecraft for the Next Century* (New York, NY: Simon and Schuster, 1990).

5 Eliot A. Cohen, *Supreme Command: Soldiers, Statesmen, and Leadership in Wartime* (New York, NY: The Free Press, 2002), p. 208.
6 Clausewitz, *On War*, p. 87.
7 Colin S. Gray, 'New Directions for Strategic Studies? How Can Theory Help Practice?', in Colin S. Gray, *Strategy and History: Essays on Theory and Practice* (London: Routledge, 2006), p. 43.
8 Theo Farrell, *Unwinnable: Britain's War in Afghanistan* (London: Vintage, 2017).
9 The notion of strategic sense is discussed in Colin S. Gray, *Theory of Strategy* (Oxford: Oxford University Press, 2018).
10 John Terraine, *Douglas Haig: The Educated Soldier* (London: Cassell & Co., 2000), pp. 31, 53.
11 Clausewitz, *On War*, p. 606.
12 Ibid., p. 81.
13 Ibid., p. 75.
14 Raymond Aron, *Peace and War: A Theory of International Relations*, trans. Richard Howard and Annette Baker Fox (New York, NY: Anchor Press/Doubleday, 1973), p. 44.
15 J. C. Wylie, *Military Strategy: A General Theory of Power Control* (Annapolis, MD: Naval Institute Press, 1967), p. 66.
16 Ibid., p. 98.
17 Basil H. Liddell Hart, *Strategy: The Indirect Approach* (London: Faber and Faber, 1967), pp. 335–6.
18 John Lewis Gaddis, *On Grand Strategy* (London: Penguin, 2019).
19 Edward N. Luttwak, *Strategy: The Logic of War and Peace* (Cambridge, MA: The Belknap Press of Harvard University Press, 1987), p. 69.
20 Gray, *The Strategy Bridge*, pp. 20–1.
21 Michael Howard, 'The Forgotten Dimensions of Strategy', *Foreign Affairs*, 57 (1979), 976–86.
22 Gray, *Modern Strategy*, p. 24.
23 Clausewitz, *On War*, p. 178.
24 Luttwak, *Strategy: The Logic of War and Peace*, p. 7.
25 Quoted in R. L. DiNardo and Daniel J. Hughes, 'Some Cautionary Thoughts on Information Warfare', *Airpower Journal*, 9(4) (1995), 76.
26 Christopher Bassford, 'Primacy of Policy and the Trinity in Clausewitz's Mature Thought', in Hew Strachan and Andreas Herberg-Rothe (eds.), *Clausewitz in the Twenty-First Century* (Oxford: Oxford University Press, 2007), pp. 74–90.
27 Alan D. Beyerchen, 'Clausewitz and the Nonlinear Nature of War: Systems of Organised Complexity', in Hew Strachan and Andreas Herberg-Rothe (eds.), *Clausewitz in the Twenty-First Century* (Oxford: Oxford University Press, 2007), pp. 45–56.
28 Clausewitz, *On War*, p. 104.
29 Ibid., p. 149.
30 Ibid., p. 108.
31 Christopher Coker, *Humane Warfare* (London: Routledge, 2001), and Luttwak, 'Post-Heroic Warfare'.
32 Dwight D. Eisenhower, *Crusade in Europe* (London: William Heinemann Limited, 1948), p. 247.
33 Clausewitz, *On War*, pp. 83–4, 718.
34 Colin S. Gray, 'From Principles of Warfare to Principles of War: A Clausewitzian Solution', in Colin S. Gray, *Strategy and History: Essays on Theory and Practice* (London: Routledge, 2006), p. 86.

35 Clausewitz, *On War*, p. 718.
36 Ibid., pp. 119–21.
37 Barry D. Watts, 'Clausewitzian Friction and Future War', McNair Paper 52, Washington, DC: Institute for National Strategic Studies, National Defense University, October 1996, p. 32.
38 Luttwak, *Strategy: The Logic of War and Peace*, p. 14.
39 Gray, *Modern Strategy*, p. 97.
40 Clausewitz, *On War*, p. 86.
41 Gray, 'From Principles of Warfare', p. 87.
42 Charles. E. Callwell, *Small Wars: A Tactical Textbook for Imperial Soldiers* (London: Greenhill Books, 1990), p. 23.
43 Gray, *Modern Strategy*, p. 279.
44 Clausewitz, *On War*, p. 88.
45 Julian Paget, *Counter-insurgency Campaigning* (London: Faber and Faber, 1967), p. 176.
46 S. Metz and R. Millen, 'Insurgency and Counterinsurgency in the Twenty-First Century: Reconceptualising the Threat and Response', Strategic Studies Institute, US Army War College, PA, November 2004, p. 5, https://press.armywarcollege.edu/monographs/761.
47 Gray, *War, Peace, and Victory*, pp. 107–8.
48 David J. Lonsdale, 'Ordering and Controlling the Dimensions of Strategy', *Defence Studies*, 16/4 (2016), 390–407.
49 H. T. Hayden (ed.), *Warfighting: Manoeuvre Warfare in the U.S. Marine Corps* (London: Greenhill, 1995), p. 38.

3 The Practice of Strategy

CHAPTER OUTLINE

KEY THEMES

- Military force is a flexible instrument of policy.
- The contemporary strategic environment is complex and requires astute strategy.
- Certain trends, such as cyber power and military ethics, interact in complex and often unpredictable ways.
- After a hiatus, nuclear strategy is developing quickly.

Introduction

Strategy may be complex and difficult. And yet, as noted in Chapter 2, perhaps with the aid of theory, historical experience, adequate resources, a strong will and ideally military genius at the helm, strategists can, indeed must, utilise the military instrument in the service of policy. This can be done in a number of ways. Highlighting the fact that military power is a far more flexible instrument than many assume, this chapter explores the various uses of force in the modern world. These will be divided into five categories: defence, **deterrence**, **compellence**, offence and miscellaneous. It should of course be noted that the actual use of force will often simultaneously cover a number of these categories. It is important to remember that the categorisation of anything rarely reflects the complexities of reality in an absolute sense. Nonetheless, taxonomies enable us to make sense of an inherently complex reality.

Having discussed the use of force in general conceptual terms, the chapter will conclude by analysing the current and future state of strategy. It will utilize the Ukraine War as a vehicle to discuss some of the most important contemporary developments in strategy. In particular, the work will assess the continued influence of technological developments, via cyber campaigns and the use of unmanned systems; the return of nuclear weapons to centre stage; and the further development of military ethics.

The Use of Force

Defence

Generally speaking, defending the state/community is the primary function of military force. The defensive use of force has two functions: to repel an attack and to limit the damage caused. What actually constitutes an act of self-defence became something of a debate after the terrorist attacks of 9/11, and the Bush administration's response to it. Traditionally, it has been generally assumed that self-defence can only occur in the face of an armed attack, or if such an attack is imminent. However, the Bush administration's National Security Strategy declared, in response to more insidious threats, that both pre-emptive attacks and preventative war must be considered as forms of the defensive use of force. Of course, the problem with this position is that an overlap begins to develop between the defensive and offensive use of force. Such debates are of import for international lawyers and the character of the extant international system. However, from a strictly strategic position, if a preventative war achieves its motivating policy objectives, the process has functioned and perhaps it matters little how the action is categorised. In the unforgiving world of strategy, facts on the ground are more compelling than theoretical or legal arguments. This is not to say that perceptions or judgements of strategic actions are without value. Since, by its very nature, strategy has a political element, perceptions of legitimacy may be important. If observations of legitimacy matter, then how an act of force is perceived will have strategic bearing. Nonetheless, in matters of defence the perceptions/rights of the served community surely come first. Winning the legal argument will be cold comfort to a community reeling from a preventable attack.

Deterrence

The defensive use of force is a physical act. In contrast, deterrence and compellence are dependent upon the psychological effects of military power. Deterrence 'has the negative object of persuading an adversary not to take an action he might otherwise have done'.[1] This can be achieved through the threat of punishment and/or denial. Punishment seeks to deter an actor by threatening to respond in such a way as to make the costs of the enemy's actions outweigh the potential benefits. Deterrence by denial seeks to persuade an actor that his goals cannot be achieved.

Deterrence will be discussed in detail in C. Dale Walton's chapters on nuclear strategy. In the context of this chapter, it is worth noting that deterrence as strategy has its own challenges. By default, the efficacy of deterrence is difficult to prove, in that one cannot prove a negative. That does not mean, however, that deterrence is not a potent form of strategy. To have a chance of being successful, a strategy of deterrence must be credible. To achieve credibility, deterrence must fulfil four criteria: capability, commitment, communication and context. To deter, an actor must possess the capability and commitment to fulfil the threatened punishment or denial. Just as importantly, these must be communicated effectively; otherwise the basis for the deterrent effect remains hidden. Finally, all these features of deterrence must be contextually suitable for the situation at hand. Of particular significance to context, deterrence can be general or specific.[2] In the former, the deterring power must let it be known generally that they have the capability and will to respond in support of their interests. However, there may be times when a deterrence posture must be tailored to a specific threat or specific actor(s). In both cases, a display of military power may be required, or what is often described as 'posturing'.

Deterrence can apply to all forms of military power. Nonetheless, it is most closely associated with nuclear strategy. Depending upon the context, when nuclear weapons are involved the commitment criterion is problematic. For example, during the Cold War, when mutually assured destruction (MAD) had become a reality, the US had to persuade the Soviet Union that it was willing to commit suicide in order to defend Western Europe from Soviet attack. To do so credibly, the US had to jump through various strategic hoops, including the development of limited nuclear war and warfighting theory, alongside the requisite capabilities.

In the complex world of strategy, fulfilling the four previously mentioned criteria is not sufficient to guarantee success. As Lawrence Freedman notes: 'Deterrence works best when the targets are able to act rationally, and when the deterrer and the deterred are working within a sufficiently shared normative framework.'[3] Cultural differences regarding rational choices may cause a mismatch in the deterrence relationship. It is also plausible that some actors are beyond deterrence. This may be the case for some within radical terror groups. However, even radical terrorist organisations may be deterred from attacking certain targets if they are well protected enough. After all, failure to destroy the target can have negative strategic consequences for a terrorist campaign. To further illustrate, Gray notes that the recruitment of terrorist foot soldiers becomes more difficult if the cause appears to be losing momentum.[4] In both cases, deterrence by denial seems to have a role to play in deterring certain terrorist organisations, who initially seem beyond deterrence.

In the final analysis, despite the challenges of deterrence, it has always been, and will remain, an important instrument of strategy. Problems arise when too much is expected of it. Like all forms of strategy, deterrence has limitations. Thus, deterrence should be considered as merely one possible instrument of grand strategy: 'Deterrence does not offer a self-contained strategic relationship but is part of a wider set of relationships.'[5] In the final analysis, it must be recognised that the success or failure of deterrence will be decided by the actor to be deterred. Referring again to controlling the process of strategy, as an external dimension the enemy cannot be controlled, but their choices can be influenced by actions taken within the internal dimensions.

Compellence

Along the same lines as deterrence, compellence aims 'to be able either to stop an adversary from doing something that he has already undertaken or to get him to do something that he has not yet undertaken'.[6] Like deterrence, compellence relies upon the psychological effects of force. In this sense, the situation is not completely under one's control: 'The adversary must still have the capacity for organised violence but choose not to exercise it.'[7] Thomas Schelling, one of the most influential writers on the subject, describes this difference: 'There is a difference between taking what you want and making someone give it to you.'[8] Although compellence can be achieved without the application of violence, it is the threat of violence that still compels. Indeed, Schelling argues that the power to hurt is actually most effective when held in reserve. In this sense, it is the threat of more pain to come that compels. Compellence is particularly suited to pursuing limited objectives, or when the attacker wishes to engage in some form of post-conflict positive relationship with an enemy. Compellence may also prove useful for those with limited resources or without the will to sustain a long and costly attritional struggle. To this end, a carefully targeted application of force against valued assets of the enemy may bring success at reasonable cost.

Of course, the entire notion of compellence rests on one's ability to understand what the enemy values, and the amount of pain that will compel them to alter their behaviour. Sun Tzu's advice to know your enemy is especially useful in such circumstances. However, estimating the enemy's pain threshold is notoriously difficult. For example, during the 1999 Kosovo conflict, elements within the US leadership predicted that a mere three days of bombing would bring Serbia back to the negotiating table. In the end, the campaign lasted seventy-eight days. And, although the coercive air campaign did influence Serbia's decision-making process, other factors were also significant. Particularly worthy of mention were the withdrawal of Russian support from its traditional Serbian ally, and increasing discussion and preparations for a North Atlantic Treaty Organization (NATO) ground offensive.

Like deterrence, compellence clearly has its limitations. However, it is a vital form of strategy. In fact, few wars end with the absolute overthrow of the enemy. Thus, most conflicts cease when one side has been coerced. In this sense, the compellent use of force is central to strategic effect. However, curiously the ability to inflict pain for strategic effect is often overlooked. Schelling bemoans this lack of recognition: 'It is extraordinary how many treaties on war and strategy have declined to recognise that the power to hurt has been, throughout history, a fundamental character of military force and fundamental to the diplomacy based on it.' This problem, which Schelling noted in the 1960s, has only intensified in more recent times. It seems plausible that 'the power to hurt' has been increasingly undermined by social, ethical and legal concerns. Inflicting pain to achieve policy objectives does not sit well with prevailing liberal values. Nonetheless, unpalatable though it might be, much like the nature of war, the power to hurt remains an important ingredient in strategy.

Offence

Often missing from discussion on the use of force is the offensive use of military power. Again, as in the case of the power to hurt, Schelling recognises the many functions that an offensive use of force can perform: 'Penetrate and occupy, seize, exterminate, disarm and disable, confine, deny access.' Specifically, used in an offensive manner, military force can seize or destroy resources, force political change (which may include occupation) and degrade or eradicate an enemy. To this end, military force can be the instrument by which 'control' is exercised in a much more direct and physical sense than would be the case with deterrence or compellence. However, it must be remembered that the different uses of offensive force have varying strategic effect, dependent upon context.

Indeed, history offers very mixed results for the offensive use of force. Alexander the Great succeeded in Persia, but reaped diminishing returns in India. Similarly, Napoleon had many successes in Central and Western Europe, but ultimately failed in Iberia and Russia. Irregular war has a similarly mixed record. Alongside Fidel Castro, Che Guevara was victorious in Cuba, but failed miserably in Bolivia. Communist insurgents succeeded in Vietnam, but failed in Malaya. A similar tale of success and failure is evident in the contemporary strategic environment. At the time of writing, it appears that Russia will hold on to its 2014 gain of Crimea, but will have to accept the failure to capture the whole of Ukraine following the 2022 invasion. What does this all tell us? The offensive use of force has always been, and remains, an instrument of policy. However, like all forms of strategy, offensive military endeavours are challenging, and success and failure are dependent upon a complex set of interactions and judgements.

Miscellaneous

In addition to those previously mentioned, military force has many other, less headline-grabbing, uses (see Box 3.1). Falling within the miscellaneous category is a vast range of activities, including, but not limited to, policing, humanitarian aid, disaster relief, ceremonial, counter-smuggling operations and garrison duties. Some of these activities are often corralled under the heading of Military Assistance to

BOX 3.1 THE MANY USES OF FORCE

- Defence: to repel an attack or limit the damage should one occur.
- Deterrence: to dissuade an adversary from taking certain actions through the threat of punishment or denial.
- Compellence: to persuade an adversary to act in a certain way through the threat of, or actual, infliction of pain.
- Offence: many uses, including occupation, seizure, destruction, disarmament and confinement.
- Miscellaneous: includes policing, humanitarian aid, disaster relief, ceremonial, counter-smuggling operations and garrison duties.

Civil Authorities (MACA). The latter can include providing a stand-by fire-fighting force in the event of industrial action, or helping local civil authorities and water companies during floods. A larger MACA commitment can be witnessed in the use of the British Army in support of police operations in Northern Ireland. As the previous discussion indicates, military force is far from being a blunt and limited instrument. Rather, it represents a very flexible tool of policy, albeit one that is underpinned by the ability to deliver violence to exert influence and power. This of course is not the case in relation to some MACA activities, which instead are based upon the military's range of capabilities, skills and willingness to serve the broader community.

Strategy in the Contemporary Environment

Ukraine War

At the time of writing, one of the most pressing strategic issues is the war in Ukraine. Although it is still too early to provide a comprehensive analysis of this ongoing conflict, a few tentative observations can be made. Indeed, because of its significance the Ukraine War acts as a useful vehicle for discussing the contemporary strategic environment. Thus, this section will begin with an analysis of the war itself, to be followed by discussions of key debates in warfare that are prominent in the Ukraine conflict.

Some of the general coverage of the war tends to focus on the increasing use of unmanned systems (discussed later). At one level this is understandable since drones have made important contributions both at the frontline and in deep-strike missions. However, much of the fighting is being done with far more traditional means, especially infantry in trenches, armoured fighting vehicles (AFVs), and artillery. Another notable feature of the war is that neither side has been able to demonstrate **air dominance**. Indeed, the latter has been described as an air equivalent of no man's land. This is because Ukraine lacks the platforms to challenge for **air superiority**, while Russia has been unable to destroy the Ukrainian integrated air defence system.[9] As a result, both sides have increasingly relied on long-range drone and missile strikes. Moreover, without adequate air cover, ground offensives on both sides have struggled to achieve operationally decisive results.

The initial Russian offensive seemed to fail as a result of poor **combined arms**, specifically insufficient infantry and artillery support to armoured forces, command and control problems, inadequate logistics, insufficient forces for a country on the scale of Ukraine and underestimation of the Ukrainian resistance.[10] Anyone familiar with military history will be aware that wars often begin with poor tactical and operational performance until the various sides become more experienced. This was evident, for example, for British and American forces in the Second World War. Indeed, although German forces achieved remarkable results in 1939–1941, this was in part due to the poor quality of their enemies' performance in these early campaigns, which helped magnify the effect of German **operational art**. As the war in Ukraine has progressed, Russian forces have learned and adapted.[11] Consequently, the Ukrainian counter-offensives have struggled to make much progress.

In the absence of air superiority, armoured-led ground offensives in Ukraine have invariably proven costly and produced disappointing results. With the correct combined arms and joint approach, AFVs can be the spearhead of rapid operational advances. Against relatively poorly equipped, poorly led and poorly trained forces, such advances can at times achieve spectacular results, as evidenced by the 1991 Gulf War. However, as the Normandy and Eastern Front campaigns reveal, such offensives are often costly and logistically challenging. Without good air cover, the challenges are intensified, as illustrated perfectly by the German Ardennes offensive in late 1944. It thus comes as no surprise that the war in Ukraine currently has the characteristics of a stalemate, with defence having the upper hand. In early-to-mid 2023, there was some optimism in the West that Ukrainian forces could retake all their lost territory, including perhaps even Crimea. However, anyone familiar with Russian military history could speculate with reasonable confidence that Russia would show considerable resilience and construct effective defensive positions.

Development of Technology

With increasing regularity in the modern period, technological developments have intensified complications emanating from the polymorphous character of war. The war in Ukraine presents us with another chance to engage with the important subject of technology in war and strategy. In particular, certain technologies and technologically driven operations have attained a certain prominence in Ukraine. Many of these will be covered in detail in the forthcoming chapters. For now, it will prove useful to assess them within the broader context of the role of technology in war.

Cyber Power

The Ukraine War has acted as a contemporary test bed for cyber power, another potentially revolutionary technologically driven development in strategy. Indeed, one could make the case that the arrival of cyber power is as significant as air power, in that it introduces a new domain for strategic activity. Moreover, since it is largely a virtual form of strategic power, cyber seems to exemplify the non-violence of humane warfare. Consequently, much was expected of cyber operations in the Ukraine War. This is especially the case because in recent years Russia has been one of the more active cyber powers. Indeed, it is thought that Russia was behind the 2015 *BlackEnergy* and 2017 *NotPetya* cyber-attacks on Ukraine. The former knocked out sections of the Ukrainian energy grid, whereas the latter affected almost 10% of computers in the country.[12]

In terms of cyber activity, the early stages of the Ukraine War did not disappoint. According to Google's Threat Analysis Group, Russian cyber-attacks in Ukraine were 'an aggressive, multipronged effort to gain a decisive wartime advantage in cyberspace'.[13] Despite such efforts, once again cyber power failed to produce any significant operational or strategic effects in Ukraine. Indeed, when cyber and kinetic forces attacked the same targets, the latter were far more effective.[14] There appear to be three main reasons for these limited returns from the exercise of cyber power in the current conflict. Despite the oft-cited idea that cyber power is a cheap instrument of strategy, it seems Russia has not been able to sustain an effective campaign in Ukraine. The US$300 million *Stuxnet* operation against Iran in 2010 gives previous indication that cyber is not the cheap option it is often assumed to be. Additionally, and this comes as something of a surprise, it seems that Russia, despite its years of experience, did not execute a well-coordinated cyber campaign. Finally, Ukrainian cyber defences, strengthened by Western support, seem to have blunted much of the Russian offensive. As the United Kingdom (UK)'s National Cyber Security Centre (NCSC) notes, Ukraine has 'proved masterful in withstanding hostility through bolstered cyber defences, demonstrating the importance of resilient systems'.[15]

Although this is only one conflict, the experience of cyber power in Ukraine is a significant indicator. Once again, this much-hyped form of strategic power has fallen well short of its potential. Not only does this reveal something about cyber power but it also acts as a warning for those, like Fuller, who would elevate technology to be a decisive dimension in strategy: 'Tools or weapons, if only the right ones can be discovered, form ninety-nine per cent of victory.'[16] In contrast to Fuller's technological determinism, although technological developments can at times have a significant and lasting effect – see air power as an example – technology interacts in complex ways with the other dimensions of strategy. As a consequence of these complex interactions, the impact of technological developments is difficult to predict or ensure.

Unmanned Systems and AI

As already noted, the Ukraine War has also witnessed the further development of unmanned operations. In a hostile air environment, alongside long-range missile systems, drones provide a capability for reconnaissance and surveillance (including artillery spotting), battlefield support, **interdiction**, and targeted attacks against infrastructure and command and control facilities. In this sense, drones have been used in anti-armour, anti-personnel, and anti-ship missions. They have also been used in an anti-air role via attacks against airbases. One of the interesting features of the war has been the variation in unmanned systems used. Certainly, both sides have used dedicated military systems, but in other cases we have witnessed the use of adapted commercial drones. The latter has been described as the 'democratisation of drones', putting such systems in the hands of less wealthy strategic actors.

AI has not been as obviously prominent in Ukraine, but it is being used for information processing and analysis, encryption, etc. Indeed, the ongoing war has been described as a 'living lab' for AI-based warfare.[17] Furthermore, 2023 can fairly be described as the year when AI rose to public consciousness. Understandably, AI is often discussed alongside unmanned systems, as it seems to offer even greater levels of freedom from human limitations in warfare. Put simply, unmanned systems with some form of autonomy can operate with fewer restrictions in relation to physical characteristics, information processing and decision making. The result is a system that can operate at higher **tempo**, taking advantage of new operational concepts such as swarming. While this may seem like some sci-fi future, various levels of autonomy are already extant in military systems. In its most common use, an armed drone operates with a man-in-the-loop. In such an approach, human agency is required to authorise the release of munitions. Alternatively, a system may operate on the basis of man-on-the-loop, whereby the system is authorised to engage targets without human authorisation, but the process is monitored and can be overridden by human intervention. Finally, a fully autonomous system operates without any human intervention, including identification and destruction of targets. This last level of autonomy is evident in the anti-**radar** Harpy drone, and certain ship-based anti-missile defences, when speed of response is essential.

While we acknowledge the role unmanned systems and AI increasingly play in modern warfare, it is important that we take a measured approach to their development. Akin to any significant technological development, unmanned systems have led to changes in the character of war (see Figure 3.1). The key question is whether they will lead to a change in the nature of war. Specifically, are we witnessing the removal of human beings from the sharp end of warfare? The answer to both these questions is undoubtedly no. The reasons for this are many. Perhaps most importantly, we must remind ourselves that war is politics. In turn, politics is concerned with how human societies organise and govern themselves. Consequently, although the role of humans in war changes over time, humanity per se can never be removed from war. Humanity is intrinsic to the very nature of war. This leads us back to Wylie's concept of control. At some level, war is always concerned with controlling human affairs. Thus, and as evident again in Ukraine, the-man-on-the-scene-with-a-gun is central to control.

Secondly, because war is a human activity, moral considerations are also ever-present. The development of unmanned systems and AI pose complex ethical

Figure 3.1 An MQ-9 Reaper unmanned aerial attack vehicle descends into an airfield in Afghanistan. Such platforms illustrate the technological dimension of strategy and the rise of unmanned systems in modern warfare.

dilemmas. Certainly, the removal of humans from the sharp end of war presents some moral advantage, most obviously in the potential reduction in human casualties. However, the same technological innovations raise some troubling moral conundrums. Is it right for a machine to take a human life? Would this breach human dignity and be a violation of 'public conscience'? Does such a possibility undermine the moral basis of the warrior code? The latter is premised on the understanding that it is acceptable to take life in war only because those doing so are also subject to such a threat. What about the laws of war? Without intent, could the laws of war be applied to a machine? These and many other moral considerations may eventually lead to self-imposed restrictions on the use of unmanned systems.

Thirdly, the use of unmanned systems does not do away with friction or the paradoxical logic of strategy. In which case, the operational efficacy of unmanned systems will invariably fall short of expectations. Of course, unmanned systems remove certain causes of friction, those relating to human participation. However, as is amply evident in the fields of robotics and AI, unmanned systems fail and make errors.[18] Moreover, as identified by Luttwak, tactical and operational advantages will be offset via the paradoxical logic. Unmanned systems have already been subject to a range of counter-measures, including hacking, laser defences, nets, etc. In summary, unmanned systems and AI will undoubtedly play an increasing role in modern warfare. However, for the reasons identified previously, it is unlikely that they will come to rule the battlespace. Indeed, the most likely route to tactical and operational advantages is via human/machine hybrid systems, perhaps along the lines of the loyal wingman in air power.

Nuclear Weapons

The Ukraine War has brought into sharp relief another instrument of modern strategy, nuclear weapons. Having dominated much of the discourse during the

Cold War, nuclear strategy has been somewhat neglected since the collapse of the Soviet Union. Regarded by many as blunt instruments of a bygone era, some of the world's nuclear arsenals were neglected, and nuclear discourse became focused on arms control, disarmament and minimum deterrence. This trend reached its height during the Obama administrations, when the US naively sought to use its own nuclear weapons policy to kickstart multilateral nuclear disarmament. It soon became apparent, however, that the major potential adversaries of the US (Russia and China), far from disarming, were actually modernising and increasing the size of their nuclear arsenals. The Ukraine War has only intensified this reality. The West now finds itself involved in a tense standoff with a heavily nuclear armed Russia, with the latter regularly engaged in nuclear sabre rattling. This is perhaps best exemplified by the new RS-28 Sarmat super heavy intercontinental **ballistic missile (ICBM)**. In response to the deteriorating security environment, the Western powers have themselves invested in significant modernisation programmes. In the US, this includes new warheads and delivery systems, including the B-21 Raider, Columbia-class ship submersible ballistic nuclear (SSBN) submarine, and the LGM-35A Sentinel ICBM. Similarly, the UK is committed to replacing its Trident force, and has increased its nuclear warhead cap from a proposed 180 to 260.[19]

Also of concern in the field of nuclear strategy is the increasing development of so-called tactical or sub-strategic nuclear weapons. As evidenced by the Cold War, this is nothing new. Both superpowers had a range of nuclear capabilities, ranging from battlefield weapons designed to counter conventional forces, to intermediate and large long-range systems to strike the enemy's homelands. However, many seemed to have hoped that the days of tens of thousands of deployed warheads was over, and that nuclear weapons would be reduced to minimum deterrence postures centred on limited numbers of so-called strategic systems. Yet, at the time of writing, Russia has a clear numerical advantage in lower-yield weapons, as well as making significant developments in advanced delivery systems.[20] And with the arsenals of Russia, Britain and China increasing, it seems that more complex forms of nuclear strategy are back in business.

The upshot of these recent developments is that, after the hiatus of minimum deterrence and the abolitionist agenda, nuclear strategy may be returning to echoes of the so-called golden age. From the seeming simplicity of Massive Retaliation (1954), US nuclear strategy developed considerably during the Cold War. It eventually settled on the doctrine of Flexible Response and incorporated more mature thinking on countervailing and prevailing strategies. In the contemporary environment we see echoes of this in the operational thinking of the 2018 and 2022 Nuclear Posture Reviews, both of which discuss post-deterrence missions. Moreover, Russia has developed its operational thinking, returning to notions of escalation dominance and the pursuit of victory. Most concretely, Russia has adopted the doctrine of escalate-to-de-escalate, whereby lower yield nuclear weapons could be used to contain a failing conventional situation.

In addition to the modernisation of the arsenals of the established nuclear powers, new nuclear weapon states have emerged since the end of the Cold War. India,

Pakistan and North Korea have joined the nuclear club, with concerns that Iran is trying to join them. Thus, those tasked with navigating the field of modern strategy face a more complex, threatening, multipolar nuclear security environment. To deal with this emerging reality will take considerable intellectual engagement from the wider defence community and increased levels of investment in nuclear weapons.

Strategic Ethics

With fighting in populated areas and long-range missile attacks on cities, the Ukraine War has once more brought into focus the issue of military ethics. Built upon the foundation of the **Just War** tradition and corralled under the War Convention, modern military ethics present the strategist with both challenges and opportunities. This final section of the chapter outlines the challenge posed by the War Convention, before discussing how the strategist can respond to ensure that military ethics is given its proper due, without becoming a hindrance to strategic best practice.

Before we go any further in our discussion, it is important to note that moral concerns are an integral part of strategy, not some foreign interloper sent to impose an alien concept on the rational pursuit of strategy. Politics has a moral dimension (in a general sense, with differences evident over time and place). Thus, it follows that strategy likewise has a moral component. This is the case even if strategists are engaged in a struggle with the resultant ethical demands. The point to be made is that strategy cannot operate in a moral and ethical vacuum.[21] This is not to say that there exists a universally acknowledged and constantly applied set of ethics. At first glance, the acceptance of a moral dimension appears to sit uncomfortably with some traditional realist interpretations of the subject: 'States in anarchy cannot afford to be moral.'[22] Indeed, the master strategic theorist Clausewitz warns against the inclusion of moral concerns in the practice of strategy: 'If one side uses force without compunction, undeterred by the bloodshed it involves, while the other refrains, the first will gain the upper hand.'[23] However, although fairly blunt in their tone, these statements should not be seen as the abject dismissal of the existence of ethics in strategy. Rather, they represent a normative approach, one which will be modified in this chapter.

Strategy is practised within a moral framework best described as the 'War Convention'. This is described by Michael Walzer as 'the set of articulated norms, customs, professional codes, legal precepts, religious and philosophical principles, and reciprocal arrangements that shape our judgements of military conduct'.[24] Since this is a rather broad set of criteria which interact with strategy in complex and challenging ways, military ethics is often delineated within the Just War tradition. The latter is a philosophical device, albeit one with an eye on the practical, to bring together moral concerns with the necessity to wage war. In essence, Just War seeks to codify the conditions under which political violence is necessary and legitimate, and strives to limit the suffering and damage caused when war occurs.

The Just War tradition, which can be traced back to ancient Greece, Rome and early Christian theologians, is broken down into three components: *jus ad bellum*

BOX 3.2 JUST WAR

Jus ad bellum

- Just cause
- Right intention
- Last resort
- Legitimate authority
- Proportionality
- Reasonable prospect of success

Jus in bello

- Proportionality
- Discrimination

Jus post bellum

- Rights vindication
- Proportional political rehabilitation
- Economic reconstruction
- Proportional punishment of war criminals

(justification for going to war), *jus in bello* (the justice of how war is waged) and *jus post bellum* (justice after war) (see Box 3.2). The first is subdivided into six categories, all of which must be met for the recourse to war to be regarded as just: just cause, right intention (a better peace), last resort, legitimate authority, proportionality and reasonable prospect of success (to prevent unnecessary suffering). *Jus in bello* is divided into discrimination (between combatants and non-combatants) and proportionality. Finally, *jus post bellum* seeks to establish a lasting just environment, one that hopefully prevents a recurrence of the conflict, in addition to pursuing justice for those affected by the war. This includes rights vindication (addressing injustices that caused the war, as well as limiting the ambitions of the victor); proportional political rehabilitation and economic reconstruction (establishing stable socio-political structures); and proportional punishment of war criminals (for reconciliation and as a deterrent against future war crimes).[25]

It will be immediately apparent that many of the Just War categories are open to subjective interpretation. Even discrimination, which on the surface appears straightforward, is not always so. For example, how does one distinguish between combatants and non-combatants in complex irregular environments? Do civilians working in armament factories forgo their non-combatant immunity? These, and other issues, suggest that military ethics is prone to judgement, differences of opinion and misunderstandings. Nonetheless, the Just War tradition does provide a conceptual framework within which to understand the interplay between ethics and the demands of strategy.

Although Just War provides important insight and guidance into the tense relationship between military necessity and ethical obligations, for strategists it can be perceived as a somewhat prohibitive approach. There is a sense that ethical considerations 'limit' strategic options. This perspective is growing as ethical and legal demands play an increasingly prominent role in strategic affairs. However, a more positive approach to military ethics is possible: '**strategic ethics**'. This new approach, which remembers that war is politics (with its attendant moral dimension), incorporates ethics as a core component of strategy. This broader conception is not interested in 'military necessity', but rather concerns itself with 'strategic necessity'. The latter puts policy considerations first (as should all strategic activity), and in doing so ensures that ethical demands are considered fully and within proper context. With the emphasis on strategy (using force to achieve policy objectives), moral and political legitimacy have a heightened profile. At the same time, a focus on achieving victory (obtaining the policy objective) ensures that moral demands do not overwhelm the process of strategy. It is hoped that strategic necessity provides a more balanced and rational approach to the subject of military ethics.

Conclusion

As the following chapters in this book illustrate, war is a varied activity characterised by constant evolution. To be successful, practitioners must achieve tactical and operational proficiency in each of the environments in which war occurs. This represents a constant challenge because the technological and doctrinal landscape is ever-changing. However, proficiency at the lower levels is simply not enough. Every use of the military instrument must be guided by strategy: the first-order consideration. Strategy, that process by which military force serves policy objectives, must be the dominant thought in the mind of the commander. What an admiral does with his fleet, or what an insurgent does with his AK 47, must be guided by the policy objective.

Even with a good education in strategic theory as their aid, strategists must ultimately rely upon their own judgement to ensure that their use of force works towards the desired policy objectives. In this sense, strategists must translate theory into practice in a vast range of different, indeed unique, contexts. To this end, they can use force in a variety of ways and for a variety of purposes. Sometimes military force may be used in a direct manner in a defensive or offensive way. In addition, military force is often used in a more limited and indirect fashion, whereby the effects are felt more at the psychological level in the realms of deterrence and compellence. Finally, the flexibility of military force endows it with a host of other miscellaneous uses, from disaster relief to counter-narcotic operations.

With the above fully acknowledged, modern practitioners of strategy are better equipped to deal with the complex interplay of extant strategic challenges. These include the return of large-scale regular war, powered by new technological developments, an attendant growing threat from nuclear weapons, and an increasingly complex moral environment. Ultimately, regardless of how it is used, it must always be remembered that military force is premised on the ability to deliver violence in the pursuit of policy objectives. The Ukraine War and its consequences have brought this reality back into sharp focus. It is imperative that our understanding of war remains true to its true nature.

RESEARCH QUESTIONS

1. In what ways can military force serve policy in the contemporary environment?
2. Is the offensive use of force legitimate?
3. Does technology change the nature of war?
4. Should strategists account for moral concerns in the practice of strategy?
5. Do nuclear weapons require a different approach to strategy?

FURTHER READING

Art, Robert J., 'The Four Functions of Force', in Robert J. Art and Robert Jervis (eds.), *International Politics: Enduring Concepts and Contemporary Issues* (New York, NY: Longman, 2003). A concise and clear discussion of the various uses of force.

Bellamy, Alex, *Just Wars: From Cicero to Iraq* (Cambridge, UK: Polity Press, 2006). A comprehensive analysis of the Just War tradition.

Cohen, Eliot A., *The Big Stick: The Limits of Soft Power and the Necessity of Military Force* (New York, NY: Basic Books, 2016). An interesting discussion of the role of hard military power in various contexts.

Freedman, Lawrence, *Deterrence* (Cambridge, UK: Polity, 2004). A concise but thorough analysis of deterrence from one of the established experts in the field.

Lonsdale, David J., *The Nature of War in the Information Age: Clausewitzian Future* (London: Frank Cass, 2004). This book suggests that classical strategic theory is still our best guide to understanding modern warfare.

Scharre, Paul, *Army of None: Autonomous Weapons and the Future of War* (New York, NY: W.W. Norton & Company, 2018). A balanced analysis of unmanned systems and AI, and their potential impact on modern warfare.

Schelling, Thomas C., *Arms and Influence* (New Haven, CT: Yale University Press, 1966). A classic analysis of compellence and deterrence from the nuclear age.

Valeriano, Brandon and Ryan C. Maness, *Cyber War Versus Cyber Realities* (Oxford, UK: Oxford University Press, 2015). A balanced analysis of the potential and limits of cyber power.

Whetham, David (ed.), *Ethics, Law and Military Operations* (Basingstoke, UK: Palgrave MacMillan, 2011). A varied collection of essays, offering a range of perspectives, on the nature and role of military ethics and the Laws of War.

ONLINE RESOURCES

https://ssi.armywarcollege.edu/: the website of the Strategic Studies Institute, which contains lots of in-depth analysis of important strategic issues.

www.militarystrategymagazine.com/: an online journal devoted to strategy.

https://thestrategybridge.org/: focused on developing thinking in strategy and military affairs.

https://warontherocks.com/: a site full of articles and podcasts on matters of strategic significance.

www.rand.org/: after many years, RAND continues to keep its finger on the pulse of important strategic matters.

https://nipp.org/: The National Institute for Public Policy offers a wide range of online publications dealing with important issues in contemporary strategy.

NOTES

1 Colin S. Gray, *Maintaining Effective Deterrence* (Carlisle: Strategic Studies Institute, 2003), p. 25.

2 Lawrence Freedman, *Deterrence* (Cambridge, UK: Polity Press, 2004).

3 ibid., p. 5.

4 Gray, *Maintaining Effective Deterrence.*

5 Freedman, *Deterrence*, p. 4.

6 Robert J. Art, 'The Four Functions of Force', in Robert J. Art and Robert Jervis (eds.), *International Politics: Enduring Concepts and Contemporary Issues* (New York, NY: Longman, 2003), p. 155.

7 Daniel Byman and Matthew Waxman, *The Dynamics of Coercion: American Foreign Policy and the Limits of Military Might* (New York, NY: Cambridge University Press, 2002).

8 Thomas C. Schelling, *Arms and Influence* (New Haven, CT: Yale University Press, 1966), p. 2.

9 Michael Stefanovic, Robert Norris, Christophe Piubeni, Dave Blair, 'The Somme in the Sky: Lessons from the Russo-Ukrainian Air War', *War on the Rocks*, 9 February 2023, https://tinyurl.com/2edjtvb5.

10 Christopher Dougherty, 'Strange Debacle: Misadventures in Assessing Russian Military Power', *War on the Rocks*, 16 June 2022, https://tinyurl.com/2pjrwm6z, and Seth G. Jones, 'Russia's Ill-Fated Invasion of Ukraine: Lessons in Modern Warfare', *Center for Strategic & International Studies*, 1 June 2022, www.csis.org/analysis/russias-ill-fated-invasion-ukraine-lessons-modern-warfare.

11 Jack Watling and Nick Reynolds, 'Meatgrinder: Russian Tactics in the Second Year of Its Invasion of Ukraine', *RUSI Special Resources*, 19 May 2030, https://tinyurl.com/3es7jcwc.

12 Marcus Willett, 'The Cyber Dimension of the Russia–Ukraine War,' *Survival*, **46**(5) (October–November 2022), 7–26, 10.

13 Google Threat Analysis Group, 'Fog of War: How the Ukraine Conflict Transformed the Cyber Threat Landscape', https://tinyurl.com/mrx8ea42.

14 Jon Bateman, *Russia's Wartime Cyber Operations in Ukraine: Military Impacts, Influences, and Implications* (Washington, DC: Carnegie Endowment for International Peace, December 2022), p. 2.

15 National Cyber Security Centre, 'New Analysis Highlights Strength of Ukraine's Defence against 'Unprecedented' Russian Offensive', 20 April 2023, https://tinyurl.com/32e4hw4v.

16 J. F. C. Fuller, *Armament and History: A Study of the Influence of Armament on History from the Dawn of Classical Warfare to the Second World War* (London: Eyre and Spottiswoode, 1946), p. v.

17 Robin Fontes and Jorrit Kamminga, 'Ukraine: A Living Lab for AI Warfare', *National Defense*, 24 March 2023, https://tinyurl.com/4mpeb5wn, and Samuel Bendett, 'Roles and Implications of AI in the Russian-Ukrainian Conflict', *Center for a New American Security*, 20 July 2023, https://tinyurl.com/55788nnn.
18 See Paul Scharre, *Army of None: Autonomous Weapons and the Future of War* (New York, NY: W.W. Norton & Company, 2018).
19 Heather Williams, 'UK Nuclear Weapons: Beyond the Numbers', *War on the Rocks*, 6 April 2021, https://warontherocks.com/2021/04/u-k-nuclear-weapons-beyond-the-numbers/.
20 Mark B. Schneider, 'How Many Nuclear Weapons Does Russia Have? The Size and Characteristics of the Russian Nuclear Stockpile', *Occasional Paper*, 3/8, National Institute for Public Policy, August 2023, https://tinyurl.com/urjkj8u2.
21 Colin S. Gray, *Perspectives on Strategy* (Oxford: Oxford University Press, 2013).
22 Art and Waltz, quoted in Jack Donnelly, 'Realism', in Scott Burchill et al. (eds.), *Theories of International Relations* (Basingstoke: Palgrave Macmillan, 2005), p. 31.
23 Carl von Clausewitz, *On War*, ed. and trans. Michael Howard and Peter Paret (Princeton, NJ: Princeton University Press, 1976 [1832]), pp. 83–4.
24 Michael Walzer, *Just and Unjust Wars: A Moral Argument with Historical Illustrations* (Harmondsworth: Penguin Books, 1980), p. 44.
25 I would like to thank Philip Mayne for his advice on this section.

PART II
Land Warfare

CHRISTOPHER TUCK

4 Concepts of Land Warfare

CHAPTER OUTLINE

KEY THEMES

- Land, in the form of the ground that warfare is fought on, gives land warfare certain unique characteristics.
- These characteristics in turn shape the nature of the forces that fight upon land.
- Land warfare is complex: its prosecution requires navigating a wide array of competing trade-offs.

Introduction

Warfare on land has been pivotal to military outcomes throughout history. This is because human beings live on land; therefore, the capacity to seize and control territory often carries with it decisive political consequences. As the strategist Colin Gray has noted: 'The inherent strength of land warfare is that it carries the promise of achieving decision.'[1]

The next three chapters explore the key ideas, concepts, principles and debates associated with conventional, high-intensity land warfare in the twentieth and twenty-first centuries. At the heart of these chapters lies the idea of the so-called 'modern system' of land warfare. During the twentieth century, armies faced a range of problems resulting from the interaction between various forces for change, including the effects of increasing firepower and the problem of moving, feeding and supplying larger armies. Incrementally, armies found potential solutions for these problems by manipulating some of the core areas of continuity in land warfare, not least the nature of the land environment itself and the basic characteristics of armies. These solutions created a dominant set of themes in the conduct of land warfare: dispersal, combined arms, fire-and-manoeuvre depth and close cooperation with the other domains (joint and multi-domain operations). Collectively, these themes constitute modern-system land warfare.

As with the later parts of this book on maritime and air warfare, our discussion of land warfare begins with an exploration of some of the key concepts that lie at the heart of the subject. This provides an essential background to the development of the modern system of land warfare not only in terms of explaining the problems facing armies at the beginning of the twentieth century but also how important continuities, such as the effect of terrain and the flexibility of armies, have shaped potential solutions. Building on the concepts explored in this chapter, Chapter 5 then explores how and why the modern system evolved during the twentieth century. Whereas the modern system is essentially an evolutionary and adaptive development, more recent debates have often focused on the potential for revolutionary changes in the conduct of land warfare. Chapter 6 develops this idea and examines the debates on the future of land warfare.

Like all warfare, land warfare is shaped by the nature of the environment in which it is fought. Although this may seem like a statement of the obvious, it is important to understand that one of the key differences between warfare on land and the other environments is land itself. The modern system has been shaped decisively by the way that land (in terms of terrain) can be used to mitigate the effects of firepower. The air and sea environments are fundamentally different in this respect. This means that there is no equivalent of a modern system in air and maritime warfare. It also means that, whereas the key developments in land warfare during the period have been (to use the 'levels of strategy' outlined in Chapter 2, p. XX) at the tactical and operational levels, in the air and maritime environments the focus is much more on the operational and strategic levels.

The Land Domain

The land domain exhibits a number of attributes, including its political importance; its variability; its resistance as a medium; its opacity; and its mutability.

Political Importance

Human beings live upon land, which gives land a profound tangible and intangible significance. Control of territory is central to the physical capacity and viability of states, and to the credibility and legitimacy of governments.[2] Thus, a capacity to take and hold territory is often a crucial index of success or failure in major combat operations. Adolf Hitler was not defeated until Berlin fell; Saddam Hussein was not defeated until Baghdad was taken; France surrendered in 1940 because it no longer had the capacity to prevent the occupation of its territory; and Russia failed in its initial assault on Ukraine in 2022 because it could not secure vital territory, including the cities of Kyiv, Kharkiv and Odesa.

Variability

Land is not a consistent medium. Different combinations of elevation, global position, climate and population density can create great varieties in the operating environment even over relatively small areas. Land is therefore a complex environment in which to operate.[3] In woods and jungles, for example, moving and sustaining heavy forces is difficult; problems with visibility and navigation make coordination a challenge. In the desert, excessive heat and sand pose problems for the reliability of equipment and the stamina of personnel. With few obvious landmarks, navigation is problematic if access to global positioning systems is unavailable. Snow and subzero temperatures can likewise inhibit the capacity of military organisations to function effectively. The challenges of operating in any given terrain can also change radically depending upon variations in season and weather.

Resistance

Land is a more resistant medium that air, water or the electromagnetic spectrum. One effect of this is that the simple act of moving land forces can create all kinds of difficulties, even where there is no actual fighting. Troops become tired; equipment and vehicles become worn; and units become disorganised. Another effect is that it is relatively difficult to move over land the sort of bulk goods that are often essential for the logistics of an army, such as ammunition and fuel. Indeed, in land warfare, the problems of actual combat may be dwarfed by the challenges of moving and sustaining troops in the field. In the period from June to November 1941 during Operation Barbarossa, for example, the German Army lost two-thirds of motor vehicle strength, most of which was lost to wear-and-tear rather than enemy action.

Opacity

Land is rarely truly flat; as Stephen Biddle notes, even on the 'flat' North German Plain, typically 65 per cent of the terrain within 1,000 yards is invisible to an average weapons position.[4] The various obstructions provided by variations in elevation, vegetation and urbanisation can block or inhibit the capacity of firepower and sensors to function. This opacity creates opportunities for cover and concealment. Exploiting terrain gives opportunities to mitigate the effects of sensors and firepower through such techniques as using cover, camouflage and dispersal to either reduce the ability of the enemy to find targets or to apply combat power against them. Guerrilla warfare, for example, is to an extent an exercise in exploiting the cover and concealment provided by land. While the opacity of land can be an important enabler, it also creates challenges. Opacity can make communication and cooperation between friendly forces more difficult, as well as promoting in combat personnel such negative psychological effects as feelings of isolation.

Mutability

Land is mutable: it can be altered through deliberate human activity or accidental effects, impacting on all four of the previous factors. For example, as the Soviets demonstrated in World War Two, it may be possible to move government, industry and population, changing political calculations regarding the value of certain territories. The building of roads, canals or railways may make some land less resistant; alternatively, destroying key communications networks may have the opposite effect. Land can be made less opaque through clearing fields of fire or constructing observation points; or it can be made more so by using camouflage or constructing trenches and fortifications.

Land is thus a politically vital medium: taking and holding it (or threatening credibly to do so) will often be an end in war as well as a means. The challenges of operating on land are shaped by the variety of different land environments and also by the fact that, as an opaque medium, land can be used as a mitigating factor in war. Land shapes, channels, facilitates and mitigates elements in the conduct of warfare. The interaction between the five factors previously outlined means that some land matters more than another; varieties in land can create important avenues of advance, fields of fire, points of observation or such obstacles as steep slopes, rivers or towns. Understanding and manipulating 'ground' (the lie of the land) is often crucial to success in land warfare because terrain can provide not only an important obstacle to operations but also a means of reducing the effect of enemy firepower.

The Attributes of Land Forces

Land forces have a number of fundamental attributes shaped by the demands of land as a medium. In particular, land forces are human-centric, complex, geographically focused, persistent and slow.

Human-centric

Whereas, put crudely, air forces and navies 'man the equipment', armies 'equip the man (and woman)'.[5] While fighting 'platforms' (such as tanks) have become more important since the First World War, armies still place a premium on having a larger number of smaller combat elements.[6] This is necessary to control ground and to manipulate the advantages of terrain through dispersal and camouflage. One key expression of this is the continued importance of infantry.

Complex

Following from the previous point, land forces are complex, not necessarily in terms of technology (which may vary depending upon the army in question), but in terms of numbers of 'moving parts'. This complexity is multiplied by the growing role of specialists in land warfare. Land forces encompass not just combat elements, such as tanks and infantry, but also combat support, combat service support and command support elements. Combat support provides such indirect capabilities as fire support, air defence, reconnaissance and combat engineering, and includes artillery, engineers and air defence units. Combat service support encompasses logistics, supply, administration and medical services. Staff officers, and intelligence and communications personnel provide the command support. While complexity is a functional requirement for armies, it multiplies friction in warfare, particularly in relation to command and control.

Geographically Focused

In operations, the objectives of land forces tend to be geographically focused: they are focused on control of particular physical points. These points may be specific or relative in nature. The former might include sites of military, economic or political significance such as population centres, high ground, choke points or transport hubs. The latter include occupying points relative to the position of the enemy to inflict geographic dislocation upon them: for example, taking up positions on the enemy flanks or rear.

Persistent

Land forces can remain in place for long periods of time. This presence allows land forces to apply continuous fire and surveillance. Land forces can hold ground, whereas air and naval forces cannot. General Norman Schwartzkopf has noted that: 'There is not a military commander in the entire world who would claim he had taken an objective by flying over it'.[7] Physical presence is often a requirement for political control and for the attainment of such broader objectives as providing security for civilians. Without ground forces, military effects can be ephemeral. As one Iraqi pilot noted in 2014 in relation to his attacks against Islamic State forces: 'When we go to bomb a place the ground troops don't accompany us. We bomb a place and kill a few, then Isis disperses but they regroup later.'[8] There is often no substitute for the presence of land forces. For example, although precision-guided munitions (PGMs) are effective in delivering firepower, self-evidently they cannot patrol the streets of a town.

Slow

All other things being equal, land forces tend to be slower than elements in other domains. Data can move almost instantaneously through the electromagnetic spectrum; air platforms can move hundreds (or indeed in terms of **hypersonics** thousands) of miles per hour; and ships can travel hundreds of miles per day. In the Second World War, for example, even over land **mechanised forces** averaged only twenty-one kilometres per day of movement, a figure that dropped to four kilometres per day if they were heavily engaged with an enemy. Equally, armies are also often sluggish when it comes reorienting themselves geographically. A fleet can change direction in minutes; an army, however, might takes days, or even weeks, to change its axis of advance or deployment.

Strengths and Limitations

Collectively, the attributes just discussed create a range of potential strengths and limitations in land forces, the relevance of which will depend upon the context and the way land power is employed.

Versatility

Because land forces are complex and human-centric, they are also adaptable; they are relatively less dependent on technology to define capabilities than air forces or navies. By refocusing such non-technological variables as training and ethos, armies can solve many military problems through new techniques and approaches. One reflection of this is the general utility of land forces across the whole spectrum of war, from peace support operations through to major combat operations. Armies, however, are not infinitely versatile. Land forces may be more versatile, or less so, depending upon their resources, culture, technology, concepts and doctrines. Moreover, land forces are likely to be optimised for particular kinds of warfare and particular physical environments; success or failure in major combat operations is likely to relate in part to the relative capacity of belligerents to adapt to the reality of local conditions.

Resilience

Because land forces are human-centric, they are physically resilient in the sense that the number of combat elements in an army can make them difficult to destroy quickly. At the same time, being less capital-intensive than air forces or navies, it can be easier to replace land forces, although the newer forces might well be less capable. Broadly speaking, as long as a state has the political will to do so, it can keep raising land forces. On the other hand, because they are human-centric, armies display physical fragilities, particularly in terms of human vulnerabilities to extremes in weather, shortages of food and water, and the ravages of disease. In addition, land forces can exhibit psychological fragilities: if their morale breaks, soldiers can hide, quit the field and/or surrender. Casualties from these physical and psychological sources can often be larger than losses suffered from enemy action, and armies are usually defeated psychologically long before they are entirely destroyed physically.

Control

Because land forces can exercise a persistent presence over geographic areas and their populations, they can exert the most meaningful forms of political and physical control. This control provides the basis for the attainment of other goals. On the other hand, this persistent presence can bring powerful costs: physical risk, because prolonged proximity to the enemy gives the latter more opportunities to inflict harm; and political risk, because the deployment of land forces usually puts more national credibility on the line, may alienate local populations, and might, if the terrain under control is another country, challenge the prestige and credibility of the local government.

Decisiveness

Taken together, the strengths previously outlined mean that armies have the greatest *potential* for decision. Land power is 'the strongest among equals. It alone can achieve the greatest strategic and political effect.'[9] Air and naval attacks cannot, by themselves, defeat land forces. Land forces may be made irrelevant; for example, in the latter stages of the Pacific campaign in the Second World War sea control allowed the US to bypass some Japanese island garrisons, simply allowing them to 'wither on the vine'. Firepower delivered from the air or from maritime assets may also inflict considerable damage on and disruption to land forces and their operations. Ultimately, however, only land forces can physically defeat other land forces. Numerous ways exist in which land forces can mitigate the effects of remotely delivered firepower, from greater dispersal and deception through to more effective anti-platform weapons, such as surface-to-air missiles (SAMs). Nevertheless, the extent to which land power is in practice decisive depends on many other factors: the wrong political aims, poor strategy or an insufficiency in means may rob land forces of their effect and may, indeed, make their use counterproductive.

In combination, the characteristics of the land environment and the attributes of land forces have been fundamental to the development of modern land warfare. The political significance of land means that performance in land warfare matters. Yet there are basic difficulties in the effective conduct of land operations. Armies are difficult to move. They are difficult to sustain. They are problematic both to command and to control. On the other hand, these attributes and characteristics also provide features that provide great utility. Armies can occupy and control; they are flexible and adaptable; and terrain can be exploited to great advantage.

Key Developments in Land Warfare

If the characteristics and attributes previously outlined provide a baseline for understanding some of the enduring issues in the conduct of land warfare, the reasons for the evolution of the modern system of land warfare lie in the interaction between those features and a range of key developments that became of decisive importance in the twentieth century.

Scale

The first development was the growing scale of war. The period from the mid nineteenth century through to 1914 saw an enormous growth in the size of armies. Reflecting broader political, social and economic changes, the emergence of 'industrialised people's war' led to a massive expansion in the size of armies.[10] By 1914, European armed forces collectively stood at around 20 million men. One consequence was the prospect of war without flanks: war in which the armies disposed by belligerents were so large that the formation of a continuous front across the whole theatre of battle was possible. Unless a victory could be won quickly, before the enemy's forces had been fully deployed, land warfare was likely to become an exercise in frontal assaults. Once this had become the case by 1915, the onus on the military was to develop ways in which to facilitate frontal breakthroughs of the enemy. Another consequence of the increasing scale of war was the increasing irrelevance of what has been termed the 'Napoleonic **paradigm** of war': the view that war could be won quickly in a single decisive battlefield clash between two main armies. With mass armies, the effect of tactical actions was unlikely to be decisive in isolation, because belligerents possessed more than one army. Thus, the means to win wars would focus more and more on the coordination and sequencing of multiple tactical actions in order to produce a broader effect. This would shape the emergence of operational art.

Firepower

Another key influence on the development of land warfare in the twentieth century was the growth in firepower. Indeed, this is a point of continuing relevance. Between 1900 and 1990, average artillery ranges increased by a factor of more than twenty; small-arms rates of fire increased three or four times; and the weapons payload and un-refuelled range of ground-attack aircraft increased by more than six times.[11] The machine guns, quick-firing artillery and magazine-loaded rifles of the early twentieth century were later augmented by tanks, aircraft and, latterly, PGMs such as laser-guided bombs. The growing lethality of firepower challenged the ability of armies to operate in close formations and in the open. In response, armies moved to consider ways in which to mitigate the effects of enemy firepower. Traditionally, these responses included the use of cover and concealment, and suppressive fire. The extended reach of firepower 'deepened' the battlefield, allowing distinctions to be made between 'deep' and 'close' operations, the latter describing activities near the front line, and the former operations far behind it. Depth created opportunities to use firepower at extended ranges to attack targets behind the enemy front line – to attack reserves, for example, and such critical infrastructure as transport nodes, command-and-control facilities and rear artillery positions. Because of the greater range and accuracy of firepower, if properly coordinated military forces were capable of providing support over greater distances. This permitted additional, if operationally challenging, opportunities for combinations of close and deep attack. This also permitted greater depth to be used in defensive positions. War is of course adversarial, so these opportunities were also, paradoxically, vulnerabilities, since they were open to use by the enemy as well. For example, during the Cold War the doctrines of NATO and the Warsaw Pact both focused on the use of new technology to add greater range and firepower in the attack, while also attempting to incorporate such measures as greater dispersal to reduce their vulnerability to one another.

Command and Control

Developments have also taken place in the command and control ('C2') of armies. C2 can be defined as follows: 'The exercise of authority and direction by a properly designated commander over assigned and attached forces in the accomplishment of the mission.'[12] C2 is, and always has been, fundamental to the effective performance of armies because it is the function through which the activities of land forces are synchronised. Modern C2 has been complicated by a number of developments. One has been the growing complexity of modern armies in terms of organisation, specialisation, size, mobility and dispersal. This has intensified the problems of control and coordination. Another issue has been technological developments in areas such as communications, sensors, data acquisition and information processing. From the use of field telephones and wireless radios at the start of the twentieth century, modern C2 systems are now often reliant on computers, mobile systems, data links and remote sensors. The concept of C2 has therefore been expanded to encompass '**C4I**' (command, control, communications, computers and intelligence). Taken together, these two issues have created the problem of how these systems can be organised and managed effectively, given the increasing volumes of information available.[13] In general, the systems for the C2 of armies have grown in size and complexity over time. 'Personalised' approaches to C2, which have traditionally placed an emphasis on the activities and decisions of a small number of very senior commanders, have been replaced with larger permanent staff systems with formalised structures and procedures. In addition to being more costly, developments in precision firepower have also made command-and-control systems more vulnerable to enemy attack, not least because headquarters have become larger and command-and-control systems more integrated. In 1870, for example, the headquarters of the entire Prussian Army consisted of seventy men. Today, a modern US Army **Corps** alone might have a headquarters staff of more than 600.

Logistics

Logistics are vital to the effectiveness of land forces. Logistics encompass 'planning and executing the movement and support of forces'.[14] The British General Sir Archibald Wavell noted that: 'It takes little skill or imagination to see *where* you would like your army to be and *when*; it takes much more knowledge and hard work to know where you can place your forces and whether you can maintain them there.'[15] The logistics of land warfare became increasingly complex in the twentieth century. In part, this was because of the growing scale of war, with armies become progressively larger. But it was also a reflection of the growing complexity of military organisations and their increasing consumption of the materiel of war, especially ammunition. By 1918, for example, the German Army was expending 300 million rounds of ammunition a month. The industrial revolution shaped important facets of modern military logistics, not least in terms of mass production and new bureaucratic and organisational approaches. These helped to shape the use of one of the most significant logistic developments in land warfare during the period: the military use of railways from the second half of the nineteenth century. This greatly increased the capacity, speed and range of land logistics. Despite their value, especially at the strategic and operational levels, railways also created many challenges. Many areas had no railways, and where they did exist they might be open to enemy attack. Moreover, while railways could supply static forces on railheads, they could not support mobile operations. Once armies left their railheads, they continued to rely on traditional horse-drawn supply. Rail supply was thus inflexible. It was the internal combustion engine that promised to bridge the gap between a mobile army and its railheads. Yet, as experience during and after the Second World War illustrated, motor transport also created its own logistic problems. Generating, sustaining, maintaining and operating the number of motor transport vehicles required for a modern army proved to be difficult and came with associated costs for the flexibility and mobility of an army as a whole (see Figure 4.1). Air transport emerged in the Second World War as another means of logistic support for armies, augmented during the Cold War by helicopters. But while these made a useful contribution to land logistics, adding range, mobility and flexibility, the limited carrying capacity meant that they could only perform a supporting role in the modern logistics effort.

Logistic constraints continue to impinge on the capacity of modern military systems to realise their theoretical potential in terms of such things as mobility.

Figure 4.1 Modern mechanised warfare has created new opportunities but also additional challenges, not least in the sphere of logistics. Here US Marines refuel an M1A1 Abrams tank in Helmand province, Afghanistan, 2011. Depending upon conditions, the Abrams can consume 300 gallons of fuel every eight hours. Source: Courtesy of US Marine Corps; photo by Staff Sergeant Brian A. Lautenslager

Major logistic continuities continue to be imposed by the nature of the land environment. Paradoxically, therefore, modern logistics, which are a crucial enabler, remain an important source of friction in land warfare. During the war in Ukraine, for example, the character of early Russian operations in 2022 was shaped by problems in movement and supply that stemmed from the logistic consequences of an assumption that the fighting would be limited and the war short. Equally, later operations on both sides were significantly affected by shortages in munitions and the challenges of moving supplies forward from railheads to front line units.

Joint and Multi-domain Operations

As will be discussed more fully in Chapter 18, joint – that is, multiservice – operations are not new in land warfare; land operations have often had important riverine or amphibious elements. However, since the early twentieth century, air power has had an increasingly pervasive influence on land warfare. Air power can provide an important means to mass firepower quickly at particular points and at ranges beyond that of land systems. Combinations of air and land forces can produce important synergies because the means used by enemy forces to escape the effects of air power, such as dispersion, are often those things that make them more vulnerable to land attack, and vice versa. Joint operations between land and air forces can be controlled according to a spectrum running from simple deconfliction at one end through to full **integration.** Historically, however, joint warfare (or 'jointery' as it is sometimes termed) has often proved to be problematic. This often stems from a difference in perspective: soldiers have a tendency to see air power as a **shock** instrument for immediate and visible close air support; airmen take a theatre-wide view – many crucial airpower roles are not immediately visible to land forces. In the last decade, joint approaches to land warfare have been overtaken by a focus on multi-domain operations in which land forces must consider integrated activity across a wider canvas. Electronic warfare, cyber operations, information activities, navigation, targeting, and C2: all of these are increasingly vital to land operations, but they are conducted in or through the electromagnetic and space domains. The planning and execution of land warfare must therefore be conducted with even greater integration of effects from other domains.

These key developments have raised recurrent problems for the conduct of land warfare. How does one attack successfully in the face of increasing firepower? How does one manoeuvre swiftly, given the complexity of logistics? How does one maintain control over large, complex army organisations under the stress of combat? Fundamentally, how can one win?

The Principles of Land Warfare

The question of how armies should deal with the consequences of the developments previously outlined has been a recurrent challenge in the twentieth and twenty-first centuries. Based on an assessment of past experience, armies have developed sets of principles designed to express concepts fundamental to the successful application of military art on land. An indicative selection is provided by the US' 'principles of war' (actually better termed 'principles of warfare') (see Box 4.1). Whatever their theoretical merit, however, applying these principles in the real world is often very difficult. The value and application of these principles is a matter of context. For example, surprise can be a key force enabler and has been used routinely throughout history as a way of multiplying the effectiveness of military operations. However, failed attempts to achieve surprise may leave friendly forces far more vulnerable than they would otherwise have been. In the 1944 Battle of the Bulge, for example, the choice by German forces of the difficult terrain of the Ardennes as the avenue of attack contributed to them achieving initial surprise but at a cost of making the subsequent exploitation much more difficult because the lines of advance were narrow and separated, and because the terrain created defensive choke points that could be exploited by US troops.

Indeed, a central problem facing armies in responding to the key agents of change in the modern period has been that land warfare embodies competing demands.

BOX 4.1 THE US PRINCIPLES OF WAR

Objectives: Military operations should be directed towards a defined, decisive and attainable objective that contributes to the broader political and military objectives.

Offensive: Military operations should be proactive rather than reactive. Success in land warfare is more likely if a focus is placed on aggressive operations designed to seize and hold the initiative.

Mass: Military power should be concentrated at the decisive time and place. Success is more likely if a preponderance of force can be gathered for the most significant battles and not dispersed at less important points.

Economy of force: Forces allocated to secondary objectives or positions should be minimised in order to facilitate the concentration of forces at the decisive point.

Manoeuvre: Friendly forces should use movement to place the enemy at a disadvantage. This might involve trying to move onto the enemy's flanks as a way of avoiding a frontal assault, or using combinations of fire and manoeuvre to suppress the enemy and advance on a position.

Unity of command: The forces allocated to a specific operation or purpose should be allocated a single overall commander so that the activities of different elements are properly coordinated.

Security: Friendly forces should be protected from enemy action that might disrupt or harm them. This principle encompasses a wide range of activities, from providing land forces with adequate anti-aircraft protection through to information-security techniques, such as establishing secure communications and aggressive patrolling to inhibit enemy reconnaissance efforts.

Surprise: Military forces should be used in a manner, time or place that is unexpected by the enemy.

Simplicity: Unnecessary complexity should be avoided in preparing, planning or conducting operations. Those factors that create general friction in warfare, such as human involvement, fear, chance and uncertainty, mean that the more complex a military operation is, the more likely it is that something will go wrong.

Prosecuting land warfare effectively involves important trade-offs that comprise competing perspectives on how to relate time, space, fire, movement and protection.[16] The value of any solution may be entirely context-specific: techniques that work in one context may invite disaster in another. Some of the key trade-offs during the period in question include those between attack and defence; manoeuvre and attrition; consolidation and exploitation; concentration and dispersal; and centralisation and decentralisation.

Attack and Defence

Victory in land warfare requires offensive operations. Even where an army conducts prolonged defensive operations to wear down the opposition, a return to the attack is likely to be required in order to exploit this attrition. At the strategic level, the growing scale of war has generated economic and political costs that often place a premium on ending wars as quickly as possible. At the tactical and operational levels, a force that does not attack is likely to cede the initiative to the enemy. In the air and maritime environments, attack is often the stronger form because the physical capacity of air and maritime forces to absorb the effects of modern firepower is limited. This means that victory will often go to the side that finds and attacks the enemy first.

However, traditionally in land warfare it is often more difficult to attack than it is to defend. The frictions associated with such issues as supply, C2, coordination, integration and the application of firepower tend to be magnified in attack because attacking generally requires that forces manoeuvre. Manoeuvre is challenging because armies are complex and because land is difficult to move over and inhibits communication. Defending forces can also use the terrain to multiply the effectiveness of their forces. Defending troops can be concealed or placed in prepared positions as ways of reducing the effect of the attack. The problems associated with offensive operations have been worsened by developments in firepower that have increased the weight and distance of the defensive firepower to which attackers are likely to be exposed. Thus, while armies cannot win without attacking, they are also often most vulnerable when engaging in offensive operations.

Manoeuvre and Attrition

Manoeuvre constitutes the movement of forces relative to the enemy to achieve an advantageous position. It is sometimes viewed as the opposite of attrition, the process of undermining the enemy by killing personnel and destroying materiel, because of the association between attrition and static positional warfare, such as that which characterised the First World War. In reality, attrition and manoeuvre are related concepts. High rates of movement do not necessarily translate into effective manoeuvre. Effective manoeuvre involves placing one's forces in positions of advantage relative to the enemy. This relational element has a spatial and a temporal dimension: it is about being in the required place at the appropriate time. Attrition may enable manoeuvre by opening gaps that friendly forces can move through; manoeuvre may enable favourable attrition by placing forces in positions to fire upon the enemy more effectively or as a means of gaining surprise.

The dynamic qualities inherent in manoeuvre give it the potential for decisive results. Classic forms of manoeuvre include those that focus on placing forces, or threatening to place forces, on an enemy's flanks or rear – namely, turning movements (passing around a flank), **envelopments** (passing around the flank and threatening to move to the rear) and encirclements (trapping forces by blocking movement to the flanks or rear), creating what the Germans termed a *Kesselschlacht* or 'cauldron battle'.

Some of the developments since 1900 have strengthened the capacity for manoeuvre: the internal-combustion engine; air mobility, which has created the capacity for '**vertical envelopment**'; and the shift from such fixed communications as field telephones to wireless radios and digital communications equipment. Against these developments must be set the growing scale of war and, in particular, increases in firepower that have made manoeuvring forces potentially more vulnerable. While methods exist to reduce the effect of firepower on manoeuvring forces, such as dispersal and the use of cover, these counter-measures pose two challenges: first, they reduce the speed of manoeuvre, reducing the tempo of an assault; and second, they are demanding techniques in terms of training, motivation, and C2. Paradoxically, then, while manoeuvre may be the means to avoid unfavourable attrition, it may also, if poorly executed, have entirely the opposite effect by exposing moving forces to the full effect of enemy firepower.

Consolidation and Exploitation

A successful operation leads to a choice between exploitation, pushing on to maximise the initial victory, and consolidation, pausing to reconstitute the attacking forces before moving on at a later point in time. Exploitation is a key means of translating local and temporary successes into broader and more significant gains. The initial victory may leave the enemy disorientated and unbalanced. However, the effects of demoralisation, disorder and shock, while powerful, are often temporary. Exploitation is a means to sustain and magnify these effects. It is one enabler for a high tempo of operations. Tempo describes the rate of activity relative to the enemy. This relational component is significant. Sustaining a high tempo of operations is an important way of keeping the initiative, maintaining surprise and invalidating much of the enemy's decision making. Indeed, Richard Simpkin defines initiative as 'constantly creating new situations to be exploited'.[17] Thus, exploitation can be a key way of encouraging the broader systemic collapse of a portion of the enemy forces. While consolidation is a passive activity, exploitation is active.

Despite its apparent effectiveness as a tool, exploitation can be a double-edged sword. First, successful exploitation is challenging and requires, amongst other things, an ability to identify opportunities and avenues for exploitation. Exploitation requires timely activity. While planned exploitation is important, opportunistic exploitation can be one of the most effective means of exploitation because of its flexibility and speed. Exploitation will often require fresh reserves or **echeloned** forces. Exploitation can be facilitated by simultaneity: seeking to overload the enemy's decision making so that the enemy cannot establish effective priorities. This can be achieved through multiple penetrations, or penetrations whose objectives are unclear and that might threaten several targets. However, multiple penetrations will create significant challenges for the command, control and coordination of attacking forces.

Second, exploitation can bring risks. One purpose of rapid exploitation is to pre-empt battle and avoid counter-attacks. However, in land warfare the relationship between attack and defence is a fluid one. Generally, one of the purposes of defensive operations will be to create the right conditions for a later counter-offensive. Defensive operations can permit economy of force in one area to enable the creation of mass in another; they can allow a pause for the reorganisation or reconstitution of reserves; they can also inflict attrition on the attacking forces and create the conditions for a successful counter-attack. Because exploiting forces will often be advancing rapidly, on a narrow front and without the organised logistic and combat support available for pre-planned assaults, they are vulnerable to aggressive, or 'active', defences, particularly those based upon depth (area defence) or mobile counter-attack (mobile defence). The successful German offensive at Kharkhov in 1943 was a strike at Russian forces overextended by exploitation. While consolidation might be more passive, it is a much easier and less risky task to perform than exploitation.

Concentration and Dispersal

Concentrating one's forces has long been viewed as a desirable element in war. Clausewitz notes, for example, that one key constituent of success in war is 'always *to be very strong*; first in general, and then at the decisive point'.[18] Dispersal can create difficulties in C2 and can make troops vulnerable to being swept away by larger enemy forces. Indeed, differential concentration, accepting weakness in some areas to achieve the necessary mass at the decisive point, has been used routinely as a way of trying to achieve breakthroughs. However, the logic of the dispersed battlefield makes concentration problematic. Progressively greater dispersal has occurred precisely because mass has become increasingly vulnerable to firepower. Moreover, mass cannot substitute reliably for deficiencies in skill. In 1973, the Syrian attack on the Golan achieved a 6:1 superiority over the Israelis by massing on a narrow front three echelons (or waves) totalling five **divisions** and four **brigades**. However, the difference in tactical skill between the two sides stalled the Syrian attack, making the Syrian concentration an effective exercise in Israeli economy of effort.[19] In addition, dispersal, in the form of multiple echelons or lines of forces, deployed successively can bring many advantages. In the attack, for example, the rear echelons, or 'follow-on forces', provide the means to exploit any initial breakthroughs. They allow success to be reinforced. In defence, multiple echelons give great 'elasticity'. The attackers are worn down as they encounter each defensive echelon, and uncommitted echelons provide the means for the defender to counter-attack and regain lost ground.

Centralisation and Decentralisation

Many of the important trade-offs in land warfare involve time. Hasty attacks, for example, trade mass for time; prepared assaults do the reverse. Rapidity can be a telling force multiplier, magnifying the effects of manoeuvre, surprise and firepower. However, the growing complexity of land warfare, in terms of the nature of armies (size, specialisation and potential mobility) and the volume of information available, creates important trade-offs between time and certainty. For example, coordination is crucial in land warfare. Most land warfare involves elements of firepower, movement and decision making, intelligence gathering, processing and dissemination by a multitude of different combat, command and support elements. One way of responding to the uncertainties of complexity is to centralise C2, concentrating certainty at the top. This 'directed command' approach allows commanders to impose more unity of effort and coordination on armies. However, centralisation often trades certainty and order for time. In particular, centralisation may slow decision-making processes down, as decisions need to be referred upwards, and may reduce the initiative displayed by local commanders. This tension can manifest itself in many ways. The complexity of modern logistics, with the associated premium that is often placed on detailed planning, is also at odds with more modern concepts of opportunistic exploitation and mobility. The ability to exploit local successes with reserves is likely to be undermined by centralised decision making.

Decentralised decision making is an obvious alternative. Termed by the Germans *Aufstragstaktik* (**mission command**), this mode of C2 places an emphasis on instilling in subordinates a clear understanding of what needs to be achieved but giving them latitude as to how it is to be done. By devolving decision making downwards, the tempo of operations is increased and the best use can be made of opportunities as they arrive: opportunities for exploitation, for example. Decentralisation accepts less certainty than centralisation but attempts to deal with this by increasing the ability of an army to act faster and thus shape events. Despite its theoretical advantages, however, decentralised C2 carries potential penalties. These include a loss of focus in operations, problems in combined arms and jointery, and overextension in exploitation operations. Effective decentralisation is a fundamentally demanding mode of C2 that requires excellent training, effective communications, a supporting philosophy of command and a significant degree of junior officer initiative. Whatever its theoretical advantages, therefore, decentralised C2 may create risks and simply be inappropriate for many armies.

Conclusion

Modern land warfare has been shaped by the existence of a range of interrelated challenges. Some of these derive from the land environment itself, such as the impact of terrain on operations. Some derive from the characteristics of armies, such as their complexity. Others have emerged because of such key developments in technology, politics and economics as the growing scale of war and the increasing lethality of firepower. Responding to these challenges has been complicated by the wide range of trade-offs that exist in land warfare, which allow for the creation of many different and often conflicting responses. In the next chapter, we examine the consequences of these factors and the development of the modern system in land warfare as the dominant solution to the challenges of land warfare that have been outlined.

RESEARCH QUESTIONS

1. In what ways does the land environment differ from the air and the maritime?
2. In relation to the air and maritime arms, what are the strengths and weaknesses of land forces?
3. How useful are principles of war?
4. Why is joint warfare often so problematic to execute successfully?
5. Looking at the trade-offs previously outlined, which approaches seem best to characterise contemporary Western approaches to land warfare, and why?

FURTHER READING

Angstrom, Jan and J. J. Widen, *Contemporary Military Theory: The Dynamics of War* (London: Routledge, 2015). Chapter 5, 6 and 7 provide an illuminating discussion on the principles of war, joint operations and the interplay between manoeuvre and attrition.

Biddle, Stephen, *Military Power: Explaining Victory and Defeat in Modern Battle* (Princeton, NJ: Princeton University Press, 2004). Biddle explains the development of the modern system of land warfare and its significance as an antidote to such developments as increases in weapon firepower.

Black, Jeremy, *Logistics: The Key to Victory* (Barnsley: Pen and Sword, 2021). Chapter 6–11 provide a wide-ranging analysis of developments in modern logistics that also tries to encompass non-Western perspectives.

Friedman, B. A., *On Tactics: A Theory of Victory in Battle* (Annapolis, MD: Naval Institute Press, 2017). This book engages in a thematic analysis of land warfare, exploring issues such as deception, shock, and C2.

Holmes, Richard, *Acts of War: The Behaviour of Men in Battle* (London: Cassell, 2004). An essential introduction to the experience of land warfare through the eyes of the soldier.

Johnson, Rob, Michael Whitby and John France, *How to Win on the Battlefield: The 25 Key Tactics of all Time* (London: Thames and Hudson, 2013). An easily digestible introduction to such relevant concepts as shock action, attack, envelopment and concentration.

King, Anthony, *The Combat Soldier: Tactics and Cohesion in Twenty and Twenty-First Century Armies* (Oxford: Oxford University Press, 2019). This volume examines small-unit cohesion in land forces. In doing so, it illustrates the human-centric nature of land warfare.

Shamir, Eitan, *Transforming Command: The Pursuit of Mission Command in the U.S., British and Israeli Armies* (Stanford, CA: Stanford University Press, 2011). Investigates the relationship between military change and approaches to C2.

Strachan, Hew, *European Armies and the Conduct of War* (London: Allen & Unwin, 1983). An excellent overview of European warfare from the eighteenth century through to 1945.

Tuck, Christopher, *Understanding Land Warfare* (London: Routledge, 2014). Chapter 1 includes an extended discussion of the issues covered here, and identifies, in particular, the weaknesses inherent in land power.

ONLINE RESOURCES

For a balanced analysis of the strengths and weaknesses of land power, see Milevski, Lukas, '*Fortissimus Inter Pares*: The Utility of Landpower in Grand Strategy', *Parameters* (Summer 2012). *Parameters*, the journal of the US Army War College, also has many other relevant articles, https://bit.ly/47MRZYM.

The US National Defense University publishes *Joint Force Quarterly*, http://ndupress.ndu.edu/JFQ.aspx, which contains many relevant articles. See, for example, Kevin D. Stringer and Katie M. Sizemore, *The Future of U.S. Landpower.*

The Royal United Services Institute (RUSI) has a land warfare theme, with excellent research by Jack Watling and Nick Reynolds, www.rusi.org/explore-our-research/topics/land-warfare. See, for example, 'Stormbreak: Fighting through Russian Defences in Ukraine's 2023 Offensive'.

Military doctrine can provide important insights into land warfare from the practitioner's perspective. Useful Australian and British analyses can be found here: *Land Warfare Doctrine 1: The Fundamentals of Land Warfare* (Australian Army, 2014), ch. 1, https://bit.ly/46brTgP.

Joint Doctrine Publication 0-20, *UK Land Power* (5th ed.) (Shrivenham: Doctrine Concepts Development Centre, 2022), www.gov.uk/government/publications/uk-land-power-jdp-0-20.

Dr Albert Palazzo, *Land Warfare: An Introduction for Soldiers, Sailors, Airmen, and Civilians*, Australian Army Occasional Paper No. 14 (Australian Army Research Centre, 2023), https://bit.ly/4n7LunW

NOTES

1 'Land Warfare Doctrine 1: The Fundamentals of Land Warfare' (Australian Army, 2002), ch. 1, p. 1.
2 Colin S. Gray, *Modern Strategy* (Oxford: Oxford University Press, 1999), p. 213.
3 See Patrick O'Sullivan, *Terrain and Tactics* (London: Greenwood, 1991).
4 Stephen Biddle, *Military Power: Explaining Victory and Defeat in Modern Battle* (Princeton, NJ: Princeton University Press, 2004), p. 36.
5 Gray, *Modern Strategy*, p. 213.
6 Lukas Milevski, '*Fortissimus Inter Pares*: The Utility of Landpower in Grand Strategy', *Parameters* (Summer 2012), p. 11.
7 Quoted in David Lonsdale, *The Nature of War in the Information Age: Clausewitzian Future* (London: Frank Cass, 2004), p. 50.
8 'Iraq Voices Anger as US Air Force Defends Irbil – But Not Baghdad', *The Observer*, 17 August 2014.
9 Milevski, 'Fortissimus Inter Pares', p. 15.
10 See Stig Forster and Jorg Nagler (eds.), *On the Road to Total War: The American Civil War and the German Wars of Unification, 1861–1871* (Cambridge, UK: Cambridge University Press, 2002).

11 Biddle, *Military Power*, p. 30.

12 *Department of Defense Dictionary of Military and Associated Terms* (U.S. Department of Defense, November 2021), p. 40.

13 Martin van Creveld, *Command in War* (London: Harvard University Press, 1985), pp. 1–10.

14 *Department of Defense Dictionary of Military and Associated Terms* (U.S. Department of Defense, November 2021), p. 132.

15 Ibid., pp. 231–2.

16 Jan Angstrom and J. J. Widen, *Contemporary Military Theory: The Dynamics of War* (London: Routledge, 2015), p. 111.

17 Quoted in J. P. Kiszely, 'The Contribution of Originality to Military Success', in Brian Holden Reid (ed.), *The Science of War: Back to First Principles* (London: Routledge, 1993), p. 26.

18 Carl von Clausewitz, *On War*, ed. and trans. Michael Howard and Peter Paret (Princeton, NJ: Princeton University Press, 1976), p. 61.

19 See Michael J. Eisenstadt and Kenneth M. Pollack, 'Armies of Snow and Armies of Sand: The Impact of Soviet Military Doctrine on Arab Militaries', in Emily O. Goldman and Leslie C. Eliason (eds.), *The Diffusion of Military Technology and Ideas* (Stanford, CA: Stanford University Press, 2003).

5 Modern Land Warfare

CHAPTER OUTLINE

KEY THEMES

- Despite debates on the revolutionary impact of such concepts as **blitzkrieg**, modern land warfare has had a strong evolutionary dynamic.
- Modern tactics emerged during the First World War as a result of the need to cope with significant increases in firepower.
- Building on theories developed during the interwar period, the concept of operational art emerged in practice during the Second World War as a means of connecting tactics to strategy.

Introduction

The parameters of how we commonly think about modern land warfare were established by developments in the First and Second World Wars. These developments cover the shift from a mode of warfare characterised in the early part of the twentieth century by linear battle with a focus on tactics to a kind of warfare characterised towards the end of the twentieth century by a focus on mobile, combined-arms warfare at the operational level. These developments have been identified by Stephen Biddle as constituting the emergence of a definable 'modern system of war'. This modern system comprises 'a tightly interrelated complex of cover, concealment, dispersion, **suppression**, small-unit independent maneuver and combined arms at the tactical level, and depth, reserves and differential concentration at the operational level of war'.[1]

By and large, the basis of the modern tactical system of warfare was established by the end of the First World War, as the belligerents struggled to develop the means to cope with the inadequacy of existing tactical concepts in the face of the effects of modern firepower. In the wake of the First World War, this system was refined by belligerents, but the same basic precepts informed tactics and operations in the Second World War and after. Operational art emerged as a response to the demonstrated challenges of converting the tactical-level successes attainable using modern tactics into broader successes at the higher levels of war. The conscious and unconscious focus on operational-level solutions informed Soviet theories on operational art and German blitzkrieg, and formed the basis of operational techniques developed during the Cold War.

The First World War and the Emergence of Modern Tactics

The events of 1914 cruelly exposed the limitations of pre-war concepts on the conduct of land warfare. The severity of the mismatch between the theory and the reality of land warfare in 1914 might encourage the belief that it was the result of incompetence and wilful ignorance with regard to the effects that change, particularly in the scale of war and the increases in battlefield firepower, would have on the character of land warfare. This is not true. Pre-war armies were alive to the new, emerging trends in war; debates on the implications of change were widespread, erudite and rational. It was long recognised, for example, that developments in firepower posed a challenge (see Figure 5.1). The increasing firepower available to armies created an enormous problem in crossing the open ground between two forces, what the French Colonel (later Marshal) Ferdinand Foch (1851–1929), a key pre-war theorist, referred to as the 'zone of death'. The invention in the late nineteenth century of machine guns, quick-firing artillery, magazine-loaded rifles and smokeless propellants had extended and intensified the 'zone of death' between armies. The solutions discussed were rational and, indeed, form a key part of modern tactics. One was dispersal: allowing troops to spread themselves out and to make use of local cover, so making them more difficult targets. Another was a focus on suppressive fire as a way of beating down the defence and preventing them from bringing their firepower to bear. However, both carried their own challenges. Lacking the technology for effective tactical wireless radio communications, dispersed troops were much more difficult to command, control and motivate, threatening a loss of momentum in the attack; and suppressive fire was difficult to coordinate between units, particularly between advancing infantry and their supporting artillery. These problems were multiplied by the general focus placed at the time upon offensive action. Since

Figure 5.1 Modern land warfare has been conditioned by increases in battlefield firepower. While machine guns have had a pervasive impact, mortars, especially, have also proved to be a major source of infantry casualties in war. Here, US soldiers fire their 120 mm mortar during a fire support exercise in Latvia, 28 August 2023. Source: Courtesy of US Army; photo by Army Staff Sergeant Oscar Gollaz

industrialised mass warfare was believed to be unsustainable in the long term, success would have to be achieved quickly, and this could only be done through offensive operations.[2]

The solution was an emphasis on the moral component of war as a means of compensating for technology. Victory was to be attained by dominating the battlefield through a focus on the human will: seizing the initiative and exploiting it by close offensive action to break the enemy's spirit. Defensive operations were viewed merely as a temporary mode in preparation for the attack, or the means of holding in some areas of the battlefield to concentrate the resources for the offensive in the decisive sector. Under such theorists as Foch and Colonel Louis Loyzeau de Grandmaison (1861–1915), offensive action became a cardinal principle in land warfare. Grandmaison, for example, argued that 'the French Army, returning to its traditions, no longer knows any other law than the offensive . . . All attacks are to be pushed to the extreme . . . to charge the enemy with the bayonet to destroy him . . . Any other conception ought to be rejected as contrary to the very nature of war.'[3]

However, the tactical expression of this approach was more sophisticated than might be supposed: an emphasis was placed on both firepower and shock action. Firepower was essential to suppress and weaken the defence; this would prepare the way for the decisive act – closing with the enemy. Infantry would thus infiltrate forwards, using cover and concealment; they would then use small arms in combination with support from quick-firing artillery and machine guns to weaken the defence, before closing with the bayonet. For example, French infantry regulations for 1895 prescribed that the

> Advance is made by successive rushes followed by a quick fire of short duration. The fighting line reinforced by the reserves . . . gradually reaches to within 150 or 200 metres of the enemy. At this distance magazine fire is commenced, and all available reserves . . . close up for the assault. At a signal from the Colonel the drums beat, the bugles sound the advance and the entire line charges forward with cries of '*en avant, à la baionette*'.[4]

The tactical dilemmas facing the armies of the period were evident in their responses to the Boer War (1899–1902). The heavy casualties inflicted on the more closely ordered British troops by their Boer adversaries encouraged experimentation by European armies with looser 'Boer tactics'. But these tactics proved impractical for mass warfare. The German Army found, for example, that approaches based on dispersing troops into skirmish order would spread an infantry **battalion** over a frontage of 3,000 metres, making it impossible for officers to control their troops effectively.[5] By 1903, the German Army had returned to methods in which the basic tactical unit was an infantry **company** of similarly armed riflemen, deployed in a fashion that would allow its officers to maintain close control over their men (see Figure 5.2).

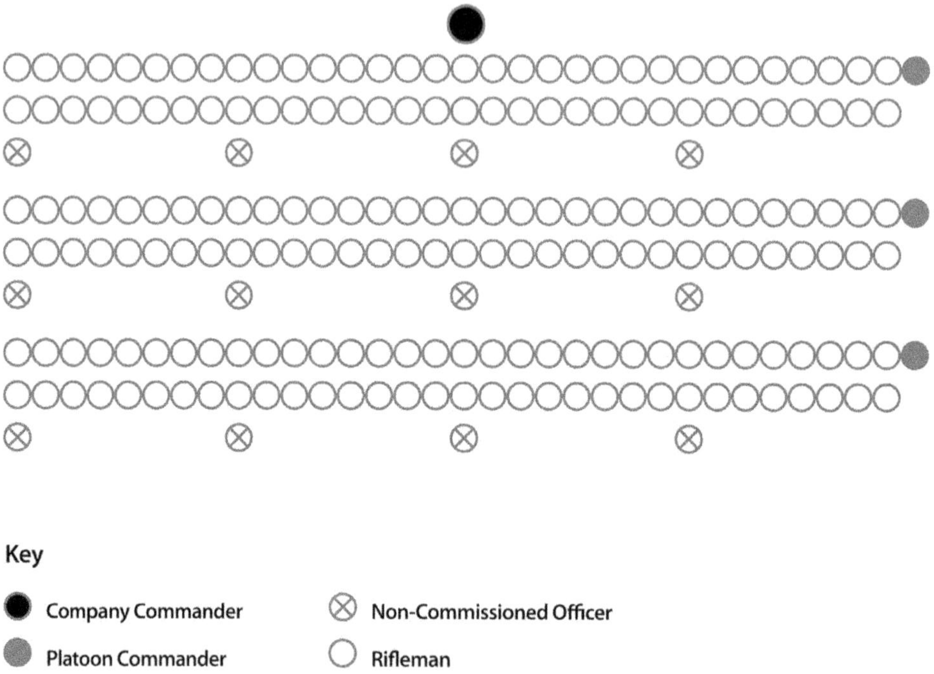

Figure 5.2 1914 infantry company deployed in 'column of platoons'. From Bruce I. Gudmundsson, *Stormtroop Tactics: Innovation in the German Army, 1914–1918* (Westport, CT: Praeger, 1995), p. 9.

It was widely recognised that an offensive approach to land warfare was likely to be costly. This bloody sacrifice was regarded as being the necessary price to pay for achieving rapid and decisive success. Thus, the evidence from conflicts up to 1914, which were in many respects contradictory, tended to be used to reinforce existing orthodoxy. A British observer of the Russo -Japanese War (1904–1905), Sir Ian Hamilton (later the British land commander at Gallipoli), noted in 1910 that: 'War is essentially the triumph, not of the Chassepot over a needlegun, not of a line of men entrenched behind wire entanglements and fire-swept zones over men exposing themselves in the open, but of one will over another weaker will.'[6] By 1914, what had emerged was, in a sense, 'anti-modern' warfare: a misinterpretation of the implications of social and technological change that resulted in a primary focus on enduring human elements of warfare, such as morale, discipline and the offensive spirit.

The first year of the war demonstrated the inapplicability of these approaches. Modern firepower made frontal assaults by infantry brutally ineffective. In August 1914, German forces encountered the British Expeditionary Force at Mons. A British soldier noted that the Germans 'advanced in companies of quite 150 men in files five deep ... The first company were simply blasted away to Heaven by a volley at 700 yards and, in their insane formation, every bullet was bound to find two billets.'[7] The official German account noted that: 'Well-entrenched and completely hidden, the enemy opened a murderous fire ... casualties increased, the rushes became shorter and finally the whole advance stopped. With bloody losses the attack gradually came to an end.'[8] Yet the growing scale of war resulted in the creation of a continuous front that made the obvious alternative, flanking movements, impossible.

Some important adjustments were made relatively quickly. By March 1915, artillery, not infantry, had become the 'Queen of Battle'; the tactical mantra became 'the artillery conquers, the infantry occupies'. By the Somme offensive, which opened on 1 July 1916, artillery was employed in staggering quantities: 1,437 artillery pieces fired 1.5 million shells over the first seven-day period.[9] However, the utility of artillery as an arm of decision was fundamentally undermined by developments in defensive tactical methods – the adoption of the concept of defence in depth – which mitigated the effects of this offensive firepower.

Defence in Depth

Attached to a principle of holding ground through forward defence, the German High Command was appalled at the attrition inflicted on their troops by the battles on the Somme, which seemed to presage the emergence of *die Materialschlacht*, 'the battle of materiel': warfare decided purely by which side could endure attrition the longest. The German Army set about developing the tactical means to counter the firepower of attacking artillery, and the conclusions were reflected in the doctrinal publication *The Principles of Command in the Defensive Battle in Position Warfare*, published 1 December 1916. Four pillars underpinned the new doctrine: depth, increasing infantry firepower, elasticity and initiative.

Depth was achieved by having multiple defensive zones, creating a 'web defence'. By 1917, this might have consisted of up to five successive defensive lines, mixing multiple trench lines and strong points sited for cover and all-round defence. These would include an 'outpost zone' of 500–1,000 metres in depth, which acted as 'tripwire'; a 'battle zone' of two kilometres or more; and an artillery protection zone (see Figure 5.3). Ground was used to mitigate enemy firepower; for example, where possible, defensive lines were placed on the reverse slope of hills to make enemy observation and direct fire more difficult. Forward strong points were often just linked networks of shell holes, making them more difficult to spot. Depth performed a number of functions: it allowed the trading of space for time; it imposed disorder and attrition on the advancing enemy; and it allowed the forward zone, which was the zone that would be saturated by enemy artillery, to be lightly held.

Infantry firepower was enhanced by deploying new technology, including light machine guns; by using smaller, more flexible subunits relying on fire-and-manoeuvre to utilise the advantages of cover; and by improved integration of the artillery into the defence plan. This increased firepower allowed fewer forces to be deployed in the forward areas and yet still allowed them to impose meaningful costs on the advancing enemy.

Elasticity expressed the focus in the new doctrine on rapid counter-attacks. Attackers were always likely to achieve some initial successes, especially against the weaker outpost zone. On the principle that attacking forces were likely to be most vulnerable soon after their attack had broken into the outer defences, defensive units were echeloned for immediate counter-attacks. Through the effective use of terrain, enhanced tactical firepower and local strong points designed to provide economy of force, a larger portion of the defensive manpower could be placed in reserve and allocated to counter-attacking roles.

In order to work effectively, all of these ideas required a greater exercise of tactical initiative by defending forces. Isolated elements in the outpost zones needed to have the motivation to keep on fighting even when cut off; counter-attacks needed to be launched quickly to take full advantage of the disorganisation inflicted on the enemy through the depth and firepower of the defence. This would be achieved by devolving command responsibility and decision making downwards. Local commanders were given command over all of the forces in their area, allowing them to initiate counter-attacks without waiting for orders from above.[10]

The development of defence in depth worsened already existing challenges for the attacker and created for offensive operations a fundamental difficulty: exploitation. The central problem for much of the First World War was not that tactical success was impossible. Far from it: in general, with sufficient artillery support infantry could succeed in taking the first line of the enemy's defences. However, the reliance in the attack on extended artillery barrages could deliver only limited gains. Heavy bombardments destroyed the ground over which the attacking infantry would have to advance and also gave away the point of attack, allowing the enemy to mass reserves in preparation for a counter-attacks. Moreover, even where troops

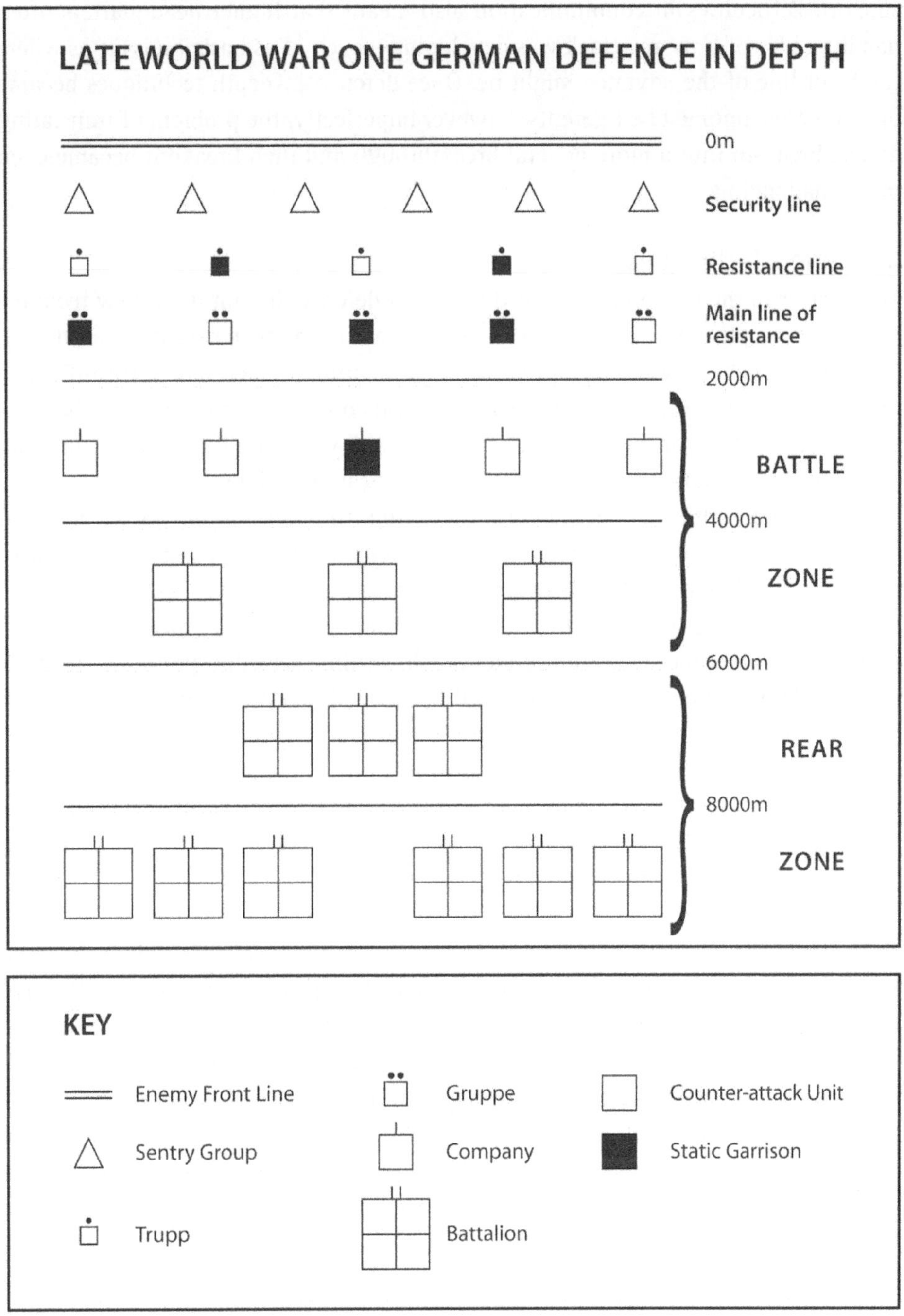

Figure 5.3 Late First World War German defence in depth.

achieved initial successes, other problems would then manifest themselves. Communications relied on field telephones connected by cables. These were static. It therefore proved difficult to coordinate with their reserves the activities of assaulting troops once they had left their trenches (usually disorganised and worn-out by the attack), with other friendly forces on their flanks and with artillery support. Difficulties in communication also meant that higher headquarters often had little idea of how an attack was developing – even of as basic an issue as where the front line of the advance might be. Once defence-in-depth techniques became disseminated amongst belligerents, however imperfectly, the problem of translating a local break-in into a more general breakthrough and then breakout became even more challenging.

Infiltration Techniques

The answer to the predominance of the tactical defence did not lie in new technology. For example, while both aircraft and tanks assumed greater significance during the war, the technology of both was still too immature to exert a decisive influence on the conduct of operations; light payloads and command-and-control difficulties mitigated the effect of the former; unreliability and vulnerability the latter. Instead, solutions were found in the use of new tactical techniques. These techniques emerged from within the belligerent armies often through bottom-up, ad hoc, and informal methods of innovation and adaptation. Importantly, armies also learnt from one another through the competitive pressures of combat and through the transfer or capture of doctrinal publications. Biddle notes that during the war a process of 'convergent evolution under harsh wartime selection pressures' resulted in 'a stable and essentially transnational body of ideas on the methods needed to operate effectively in the face of radically lethal modern weapons'.[11]

To explore the content of these new ideas it is useful to examine developments in the German Army. German adaptation was facilitated, amongst other things, by its lack of a strong tradition of centralised doctrine, an effective system for learning lessons, a robust learning culture and devolved training.[12]

Reflected in such documents as *The Training Manual for Foot Troops* of December 1916 and January 1918 (for battalions and below), and *The Attack in Position Warfare* of January 1918 (for **regiments** and above), the new German offensive techniques placed a priority on two things. First, the objective of offensive operations was to be the disruption of enemy forces rather than their destruction. By focusing on the disruption of the enemy military system, the offensive would paralyse the enemy's ability to respond appropriately. Secondly, the revised German methods were based upon flexible infiltration. Referred to as *Flachen und Lücken*, or 'surfaces and gaps', attacking forces would avoid enemy strength (surfaces) and instead seek to flow through gaps in the defence.

Achieving these two effects depended upon realising a number of principles. One was neutralisation of the enemy. For example, rather than extended, destructive artillery barrages the focus was on heavy but sudden and unexpected attacks facilitated by more scientific gunnery techniques, such as pre-registering fire by map. The technique of 'map shooting' had been developed on the Eastern Front by Colonel Georg Bruchmüller. Targeting focused less on enemy entrenchments than on the broader infrastructure required for the enemy to function and respond, including headquarters, command posts, transport nodes and enemy artillery positions. As Bruchmüller noted, 'We desired only to break the morale of the enemy, pin him to his position.'[13]

A second requirement was depth in the attack. The assault required multiple echelons. The first echelon would bypass centres of resistance, leaving them to be mopped up by follow-on forces. The first echelon would ignore flanks and push on, following routes of tactical success. It would not halt to be relieved. This facilitated continuous offensive action. The speed of offensive action and the depth in the assault maximised the shock against the enemy, provided protection to the vulnerable flanks of the attack and helped to ensure that the defenders did not regain the initiative. Jointery was also a feature, with aircraft used to help interdict the enemy rear areas, adding yet more depth to the attack. Another important principle was effective combined arms. Although, in general, the control of heavy artillery was centralised, pyrotechnics were used to control a creeping artillery barrage, the *Feuerwalze* or 'fire wall', which would facilitate more flexible artillery support for the infantry.

A further means was a focus on independently manoeuvring small-unit infantry teams. The new doctrine eschewed a rigid and inflexible linear advance in favour of greater flexibility and a focus on initiative at lower levels (see Figure 5.4). Specialist 'storm battalions' were organised around assault teams with light machine guns, mortars, flamethrowers and light artillery. These units were used as the cutting edge of the attack. The basic infantry subunit became much smaller: the *Gruppe*, a section with riflemen and a light machine gun. The section manoeuvred around the light machine gun, which acted as a firebase. To enable these changes required improved training and small-unit leadership. In January 1917, for example, the Germans established an infantry division whose sole purpose was to experiment with, and to train in, the new tactics.[14]

These tactical developments began to emerge as early as 1915, and by 1918 they were employed to great effect by all sides. In March 1918, Germany employed them as part of its great spring offensive and achieved impressive tactical successes. In the last year of the war, these techniques appeared to have restored the superiority of offensive over defensive operations: the Germans overran Allied defences three times – at the second battle of the Somme, the battle of Lys River and at the Chemin des Dames. The Allies used similar techniques in their later offensives that ended the war, including the second battle of the Marne in July, Amiens in August and the 100 Days' offensive of September to November 1918. That mobility did not depend upon tanks was illustrated by the great success of General Allenby in Palestine: at Megiddo in 1918, Allenby achieved both breakthrough and exploitation with cavalry in concert with air power. It is important to note, however, that these offensives still involved attrition. The 1918 offensives cost the Germans a million men. British losses from August to November 1918 were greater than in the Passchendaele offensives of 1917. Still, by the end of the war, these new 'modern' tactical techniques of land warfare had restored an element of manoeuvre to the battlefield and had established the basis of techniques that would later be used in the Second World War.

Figure 5.4 US Army Private First Class Robert Parker (2nd from left) provides fire support for his squad members during a live-fire exercise, Iraq, 2010. Squad-level fire and manoeuvre lies at the heart of modern infantry tactics. Fire suppresses the enemy and enables manoeuvre; manoeuvre allows fire to be brought to bear on the enemy more effectively. Courtesy of US Department of Defense; photo by Petty Officer 2nd Class Ted Green.

Thus, the period from 1900 to 1918 saw a shift from what can crudely be termed 'anti-modern' warfare to a form of land warfare that was recognisably modern. In 1900, the response to the material conditions of land warfare had been to place undue emphasis on the moral component of war, expressed through a concentration on linear, close shock action. By 1918, the response was to place more emphasis on the conceptual dimension of warfare, finding new ways to use existing resources, not least combined arms, flexible subunit manoeuvre, infiltration tactics and tactical depth. These techniques spread rapidly, if with varying degrees of rigour, across the combatants through a 'bloody process of mutual education'. The war had produced, as Stephen Biddle notes, a 'stable and essentially transnational body of ideas on the methods needed to operate effectively in the face of radically lethal modern weaponry'.[15] New technology, such as mines and anti-tank guns, would complicate, but not change, the basic tactical principles developed in 1917 and 1918. These principles, including decentralisation, combined arms, fire and movement, dispersal, cover and concealment, and small-unit manoeuvre, continue to be the foundations of tactics today. The military socialist Anthony King argues that by the middle of the First World War 'the outlines of every form of tactical procedure later refined and

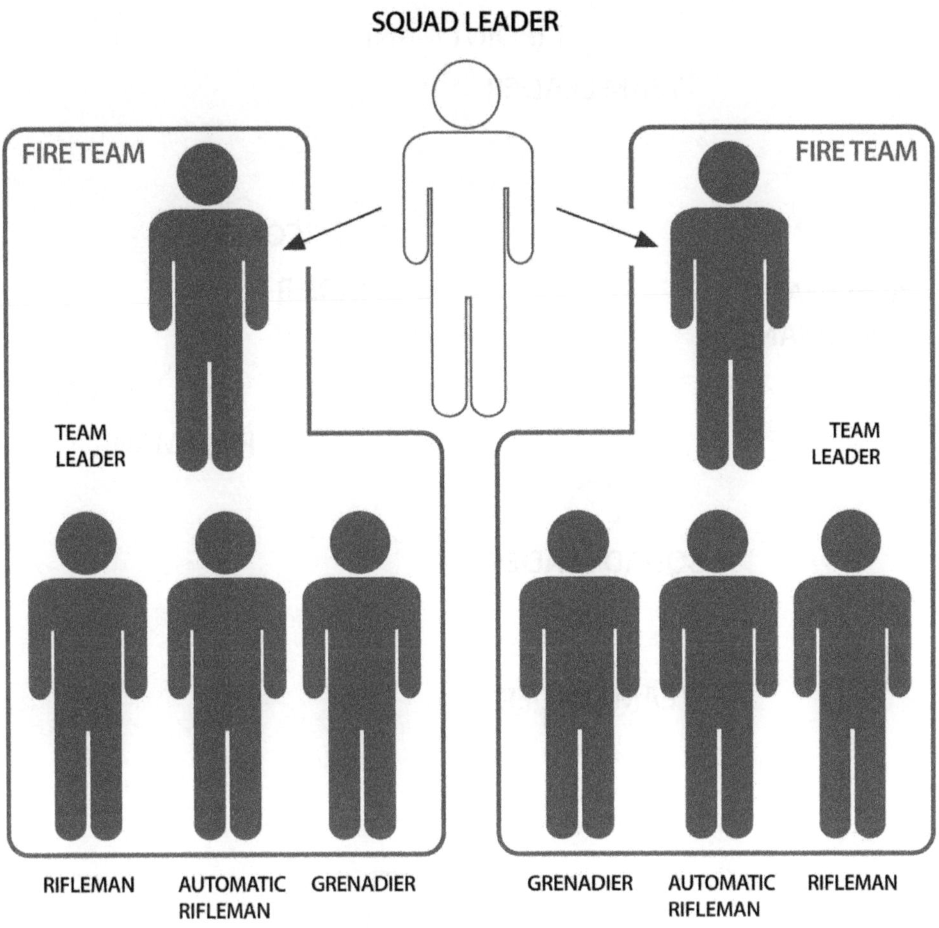

Figure 5.5 A modern infantry squad. The squad is broken down into two fire teams, allowing it to advance by bounds of alternate fire and movement. Adapted from Field Manual 7–8, *The Infantry Platoon and Squad* (Washington, DC: Headquarters of the Army, 22 April 1992).

sophisticated by today's professional army were substantially in place, at least in selected units within the combatant's armies'.[16] Contemporary infantry tactics are founded on the activities of the infantry **squad** or section, which has its own automatic weapons and manoeuvres independently, in a dispersed fashion, combining the activities of its sub-elements, the **fire teams** (see Figures 5.5 and 5.6).

The Second World War and After: The Operational Art

The period after the First World War is commonly perceived as one dominated by the development and execution of blitzkrieg, a form of warfare that for many writers constitutes a definable military revolution. Taking this view, we could argue that, while states other than Germany were mired after 1918 in First World War thinking,

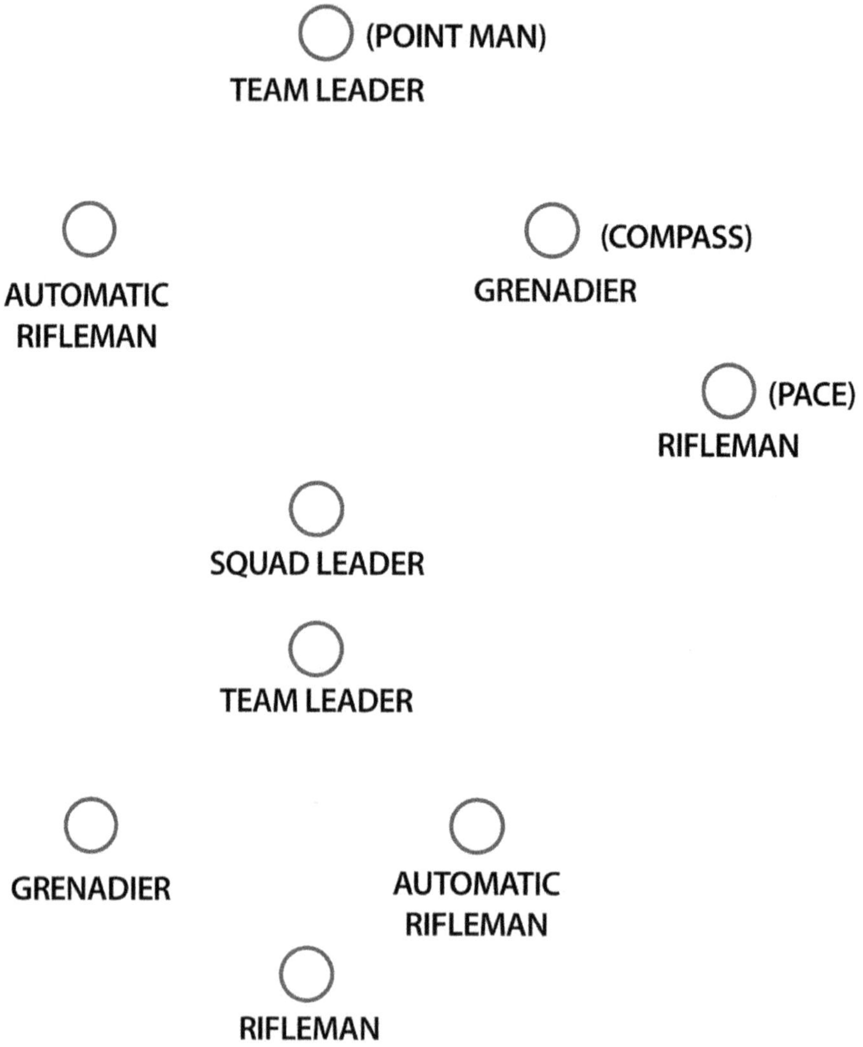

Figure 5.6 Deployment of a modern infantry squad. Compare this with Figure 5.2. Adapted from Field Manual 7–8, *The Infantry Platoon and Squad* (Washington, DC: Headquarters of the Army, 22 April 1992).

German post-First World War techniques represented a 'paradigm shift' that provided the bridge between the static attrition of the Great War and modern mobile land warfare. But the reality is much more complex. As the preceding discussion has demonstrated, warfare had already become more mobile by the end of the First World War, and infiltration tactics provided the basis of tactics used during the Second World War and after. German successes of 1939–1941 did not derive from a revolutionary tactical superiority but from other advantages: but what advantages? The problem experienced in 1918 was how to translate the success of tactical actions into something broader and more decisive. The German spring offensive of that year, for example, had mauled two British armies, but this tactical success had not resulted in broader operational and strategic success: the offensive could not be sustained logistically, and the German High Command lost control over the offensive after five or six days.[17] How could this gap between tactical success and strategic effect be bridged?

Traditional military thought had identified two levels of war: strategy and tactics. Strategy encompassed all those activities tasked with bringing forces to the battlefield with maximum advantage; tactics covered the conduct of forces on the battlefield itself.[18] What was most significant about the period after 1918 was not blitzkrieg itself, but the fact that it expressed the conscious and unconscious reflection of the importance of an intermediate level of war, between strategy and tactics, of which the ideas and practices that informed what later became known as blitzkrieg were a manifestation. The emergence of this level, an operational level that would require the practice of operational art, resulted from material and cognitive developments. In material terms, the growing scale of modern war created new forms of complexity that meant that strategic success could not be delivered through a single decisive battle, but only through the coordination in time and space of multiple tactical actions. As noted in Chapter 1, at a cognitive level some recognition of this had already begun to occur: Jomini, for example, used the term 'grand tactics' to refer to this intermediate level, and the Prussian/German Army had begun to refer to a lower level of strategy using such terms as *Kriegsoperationen* ('war operations') and *operativ* (loosely, 'operational'). The pre-First World War military mindset, with its focus on decisive battle, was not conducive to more systematic thinking about the subject. Von Schlieffen, for example, envisaged his plan for war in 1914 as a giant Cannae, and his attempt to treat the whole massive operation of 1.5 million men as a single choreographed tactical action exceeded the command and logistic realities of the time.[19]

Operational-Level Mobile Warfare

The most systematic thinking in the interwar period regarding this intermediate level of war emerged not from the Germans but from the Red Army. Concluding that, in modern war, one could not defeat the enemy with a single tactical blow, Soviet thinkers began to develop a conceptual framework that would allow the delivery of coordinated, successive attacks against the enemy and so enable local tactical successes to be exploited to produce a larger effect. This focused on operational art (*Operativnoye Iskusstvo*): the theory and practice of preparing for and conducting combined and independent operations by large units (armies and groups of armies). As A. A. Svechin (1878–1938), one of the key Soviet theorists, noted, 'Tactics make the steps from which operational leaps are assembled; strategy points out the path.'[20] For Svechin, 'Operational art governs tactical creativity and links together tactical actions into a campaign to achieve the strategic goal.'[21]

The Soviet perspective emerged from their recognition of the growing importance of depth in the practice of warfare. Experiences in the Russian Civil War (1918–1924) had demonstrated how cavalry corps and cavalry armies could be used to engage in deep penetration well beyond the enemy front line. After the First World War, the maturing technologies of mechanisation and wireless radio seemed to provide new means with which to realise this concept. Mechanised mobile forces would allow 'deep battle' and '**deep operations**'. 'Deep battle' comprised the ambition tactically to penetrate the enemy to their rear artillery line. This would be followed by 'deep operations': exploitation beyond an individual battlefield into the depth of the theatre of operations. Enshrined in the Field Service Regulations of 1936, this doctrine envisaged infantry, cavalry and mechanised forces operating with air support in a two-part battle (see Figure 5.7). First, using artillery fire to suppress the enemy, an echeloned, combined-arms attack would be launched on a narrow front to penetrate the enemy line. Secondly, 'mobile groups' consisting of cavalry and mechanised forces would exploit the initial breakthrough, striking deep and **outflanking** the enemy defences. These mobile groups would encircle the enemy to a depth of 200 or 300 kilometres. Also enshrined in this doctrine was the importance of simultaneity: influencing at the same time the entire depth of the enemy positions by using smoke, deception and air attack. The aim, according to the regulations, was the 'violent development of tactical success into operational success with the aim of the complete encirclement and destruction of the enemy'.

The possibilities promised by new technology were also recognised by other armies. In May 1918, J. F. C. Fuller, a British staff officer, conceived 'Plan 1919', a massive, armoured offensive that he hoped would end the war. Plan 1919 combined tanks and aircraft in a massive joint effort on a narrow front that would rupture the enemy line. Using the mobility of armour and the reach of aircraft, this force would then engage in what was in effect a 'deep battle', exploiting quickly, overrunning enemy command-and-control nodes and completely paralysing the German capacity to respond. Another British military theorist, Basil H. Liddell Hart, argued for a future similar to that of Fuller's; however, whereas Fuller focused exclusively on tanks, Liddell Hart saw the need for a force of accompanying mobile infantry – in effect, mechanised infantry. In 1927, Britain created the Experimental Mechanical Force (EMF), consisting of a mixed force of tanks, motorised infantry and artillery with air support. By 1939, the UK had the only fully motorised army in the world. The US also recognised the possibilities provided by new technologies. In 1928–1929, the US created the Experimental Armored Force, which included small tanks and lorried infantry.[22]

Indeed, the ideas that we commonly associate with blitzkrieg continued to be resisted by significant elements in the German Army and Luftwaffe. Even in the Polish campaign in 1939, tensions existed between such radicals as Heinz Guderian (author of *Achtung – Panzer!)* and conservatives over the proper use of armour and mobile forces. Many in the German Army continued to view armour as primarily an infantry-support weapon. Thus, as late as 1937 and 1938 scarce tanks were allocated to form two infantry-support tank brigades. The Luftwaffe continued to prioritise tasks other than close air support. Not until 1940 did the German Army's regulations focus on the operational-level use of armour. Even afterwards it remained far from being a template that was applied consistently throughout the army.

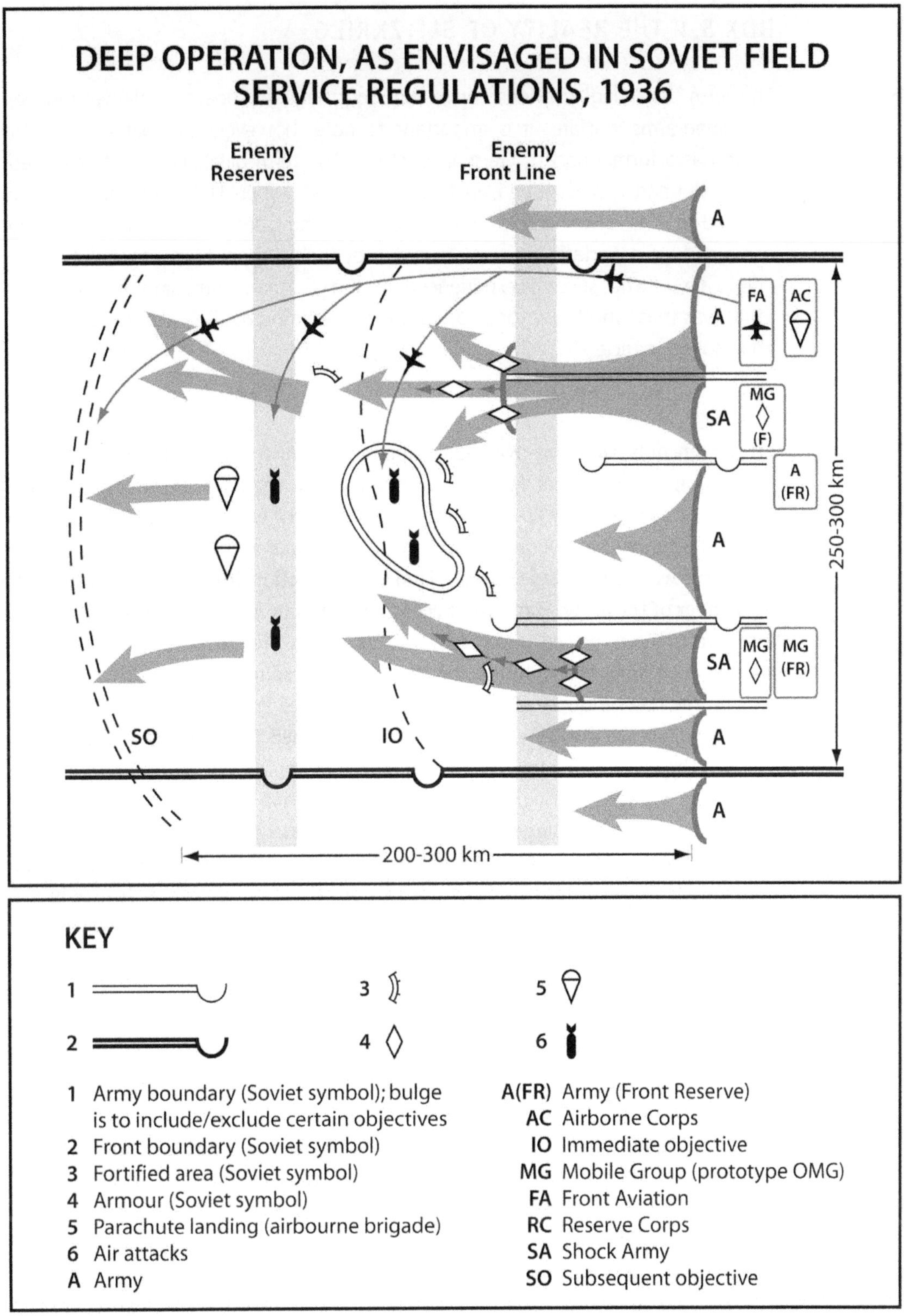

Figure 5.7 Deep operations, as envisaged in Soviet Field Service Regulations, 1936.

BOX 5.1 THE REALITY OF BLITZKRIEG

The term 'blitzkrieg' provides convenient shorthand for operational-level mobile, combined-arms warfare. It is important to note, however, that blitzkrieg never existed as a formal part of German doctrine. The term blitzkrieg was rarely used in the German Army; indeed, in November 1941, when Hitler first heard it, he referred to it as 'a very stupid word'. Moreover, the German principles for mobile combined-arms warfare were not regarded by the German Army as revolutionary. The scale of the success experienced in the German campaign in France in 1940 was thus wholly unexpected, with Hitler referring to the result as 'a miracle, an absolute miracle'.

However, only Germany was as comprehensive in its focus on combined-arms exploitation as the Soviets. Moreover, since the Red Army was thrown into turmoil by political purges in 1937–1938, the German Army was left as the pre-eminent exponent of a form of operational art, even if this was not formally codified in the way that it was in the Soviet Union. Under the direction from 1919 to 1926 of the commander of the army, Hans von Seeckt, the German Army sought to compensate for the restrictions placed upon it by the Versailles Treaty by creating a military machine with superior mobility and flexibility. Despite the popular tendency to focus on the revolutionary character of blitzkrieg (see Box 5.1), the principles from which it was derived were evolutionary and stemmed from the tactical principles extant at the end of the First World War. German approaches applied technologies for mobile warfare through a conscious adaptation of the tactical concepts developed in the latter stages of that war. Thus, the Riechswehr's first Field Manual, the 1921 *Leadership and Combat of Combined Arms* (*Fuehrung und Gefecht der verbundenen Waffen*) and the later *Die Truppenführung*, or 'troop leadership' of 1933, married the infantry assault unit tactics and effective artillery doctrines of the First World War with close air support and the use of tanks.[23] The new doctrine continued to stress flexibility, initiative and exploitation, with a focus on either narrow breakthroughs or encirclement. The essence of the German techniques used in the early part of the war was a surprise attack on a narrow front designed to ensure a penetration of the enemy front line. Swift exploitation would then become the priority, with a focus on the demoralisation of the enemy as much as their physical destruction: multiple columns would exploit the initial penetration by moving to the rear of the enemy, bypassing concentrations and acting as pincers to encircle the enemy. Aircraft would act as flying artillery and, in concert with rapidly moving panzer divisions, would deepen the battle, helping to create operational-scale systemic shock.[24]

Despite the apparent importance of panzer divisions to the German techniques, blitzkrieg was not primarily a tank phenomenon. Indeed, by 1941 the German Army was reducing the amount of armour in panzer divisions and trying to increase the allocation of motorised and mechanised infantry. Combined arms, rather than tanks, was one of the keys to German success. For example, anti-tank guns would be used to protect the vulnerable flanks of the breakthrough. Engineers would be on hand to increase mobility. Combined arms was facilitated by flexible training and command-and-control structures that allowed the use of all-arms **battlegroups** to suit the situation. Blitzkrieg was thus the result of training and doctrine in combined arms, tied to a focus on penetration and manoeuvre.

A key enabler was the recognition of the importance of radio communications in land warfare. Widespread use of wireless radios enabled the effective command and control of more complex, mobile and dispersed forces. From the mid 1920s, for example, the German Army fitted new vehicles with radio mounts, and efforts were made to develop a full range of radios including short-range sets for vehicles and high-power/low-frequency sets for headquarters. There was also acknowledgement of the importance of joint operations. Even before the re-creation of the Luftwaffe in 1933, the German Army maintained a doctrine on cooperation with the air force. This cooperation was reflected also in the development of specific joint assets, especially the JU-87 Stuka dive bomber. The practical reflection of these ideas was the creation of panzer divisions – mobile all-arms formations, built around the tank but including infantry, artillery and other supporting arms. By 1939, two-thirds of the German tank force was concentrated in six panzer divisions.

The German Army achieved startling successes in France and Poland and in the first stages of the attack on Russia. In the battles against France, at least, the operational-level application of concepts of deep battle seemed vindicated.[25] Five days into the attack, for example, German forces were already conducting deep penetration and exploitation, wreaking havoc on Allied command and control and morale. Deep operations, realised through such principles as combined arms, mobility, rapidity, fire-and-manoeuvre, massing at decisive points. decentralised command and control and rapid exploitation, seemed to have restored the capacity to deliver decisive outcomes in land warfare, even if these principles were still being applied in a rather ad hoc fashion.

Operational Defence in Depth

Yet, despite these extraordinary successes, the Second World War came to exhibit a progressively more positional and attritional character. Why did blitzkrieg cease to deliver remarkable victories? One reason for this was that the early opposition facing the German Army provided to an extent a 'best-case' test for operational-level mobile warfare, because armies such as those of the Poles and French were badly deployed and had inadequate reserves. Operation Barbarossa was launched against a Russian opponent suffering from the mutually reinforcing problems of political purges, reorganisation, expansion and inexperienced commanders. Moreover, the Soviet leadership forced ill-chosen offensive and defensive operations on Russian commanders. If Barbarossa had been launched four years earlier, or one year later, it might well have been much less successful.

Logistics imposed other emerging limitations on operational-level manoeuvre. Mobile armoured warfare may have helped solve some tactical problems, but it created new logistical ones. Operational-level mobile warfare required intensive, complex, mobile logistic support if it were not quickly to lose momentum. Whereas a 1914 infantry division required 100 tons of supplies a day, a panzer division required 300 tons and a US division by 1944 required 600 tons.[26] In the Polish campaign of 1939, no German unit advanced more than 150 miles into Poland, yet it still proved difficult to keep front-line units in supplies. In Russia, with supply lines extending up to 900 miles, the problems of supplying the needs of high-intensity mobile warfare often proved insurmountable. Even operating the rail lines was problematic, given freezing weather conditions and incompatible rail gauges; linking railheads to mobile forces was even more difficult, because of the German Army's dearth of motor transport and poor roads, and challenging weather. For example, by November 1941 some of the lead German infantry divisions were operating ninety miles from their railheads, a distance twice that from which they could be supplied effectively.

Exploitation posed a related challenge. In 1940, only one-tenth of the German Army was made up of panzer or mechanised divisions. The rest was reliant on horses for its transport; indeed, the German Army used nearly twice as many horses in the Second World War (some 2.7 million) as it did in the First.[27] Panzer exploitation could often only take place once infantry and logistics had caught up. It is notable that the average daily rate of advance for panzer divisions in Poland was only eleven miles. Quick 'leaps' forward by mobile forces were accompanied by long pauses until the infantry and logistics support caught up. In Russia, this 'mobility gap' imposed delays that reduced the tempo of advance and provided opportunities for Russian counter-attacks. Operational-level mobile warfare also therefore required broad-based mechanisation if effective mobile combined arms was to be achieved. In that sense, the German Army of the Second World War was only 'semi-modern'.

Another difficulty was the vulnerability of attacking forces. Operational-level mobile warfare relied on causing the systemic collapse of the enemy in order to prevent the enemy from launching counter-attacks against vulnerable exploitation forces. If the enemy did not collapse quickly, then the costs of a risk-based exploitation approach were likely to mount. In the Polish campaign, German tank losses amounted to 10 per cent of the initial force. Many units also lost up to 50 per cent of their motor vehicles. The cutting edge of blitzkrieg, the panzer divisions, suffered heavy attrition even in the early stages of the campaign in Russia: from June to November 1941 the German Army lost two-thirds of its motor vehicles and 65 per cent of its tanks. The attrition in motor vehicles compounded the larger logistic problems. From November 1941 to March 1942, the German Army lost another 75,000 vehicles but could only find 7,500 replacements.[28]

However, the central difficulty experienced by Germany was the relational nature of warfare: its enemies adapted. The essence of blitzkrieg comprised the pushing of a mechanised combined-arms force through the enemy front line so that it could penetrate the enemy far into the depth of their defences, causing their systemic collapse. The answer to this lay in the rational development of concepts developed in the First World War, in this case the principle of 'defence in depth', applied at an operational and not just a tactical level. This was not a new idea. The Russian deployment prior to Barbarossa was based on defence in depth, but it was poorly executed. By the middle of the Second World War, as combatants became more experienced, the use of depth had reasserted the strength of the defence. New technology, such as anti-tank guns, complicated combined arms but it also made defence in depth potentially more effective by improving the effectiveness of non-tank forces in fighting armour. At Kursk, for example, the Soviet defences were in places 110 miles deep. Defences this deep were designed not just to inflict losses on the attacker but also to disorganise them and to break down their capacity for combined arms by separating armour from supporting infantry. At points of expected German attack, the defences had 1,500 to 2,000 mines and twenty-five to thirty anti-tank guns per kilometre of frontage. The defence in depth concept also harnessed armoured and mechanised forces. The Soviets held the Steppe Front of five armies in reserve ready for a counter-attack. Depth in defence also helped to mitigate surprise and gave opportunities for defenders to launch counter-attacks.[29] The Germans themselves elevated the mobile counter-attack to an art form through the use of 'manoeuvre on interior lines', using mobile forces based on a central position to counter-attack enemy attempts at encirclement, defeating them sequentially in detail.

This did not mean that the tactical and operational offensive concepts developed since the First World War were irrelevant; far from it. Offensive successes were still possible. For example, in Operation Bagration, which began in June 1944, the Russians smashed Germany's Army Group Centre, destroying seventeen divisions and reducing another fifty to below half strength. The offensive pushed the Germans back 350 miles. Soviet concepts developed from 1943 were illustrative of the techniques created to overcome defence in depth. Reconnaissance elements were strengthened to promote the chances of a breakthrough, transforming time-consuming reconnaissance into the first echelon of the attack designed to seize outposts and 'recce' by fire. Attack groups were made more flexible by dividing them into reconnaissance, blocking, fire and attack subgroups to promote greater flexibility in combined arms. Use was made of tailored assault groups and specialist formations, such as combat engineers. Great emphasis was put on deception to achieve surprise and to facilitate the massing of attacking troops at critical points. To increase the pace of exploitation, the Soviets promoted decentralised command and control: relatively junior officers were encouraged to use initiative and seize targets of opportunity. The size of forward elements and their distance from the main body was increased: by 1944, the lead elements of a tank corps might operate some fifty miles in front of their parent formation, and would often include a combined arms force of a tank brigade and field and anti-aircraft artillery, assault guns and engineers. For important points of exploitation, forward air controllers would accompany the forward units, and dedicated air assets would be allocated for close air support.

Nevertheless, neither Bagration nor other examples of rapid breakthroughs, such as General Patton's advance of 400 miles in twenty-six days that ended the Normandy campaign, induced the general systemic collapse of the enemy forces as blitzkrieg had in 1939 and 1940. These were not the victories envisaged by Fuller and Liddell Hart. Operations from late 1942 onwards were often reminiscent of the First World War with their emphasis on set-piece attacks. Eventual Allied victory depended upon broad, protracted attrition at the strategic level, in which elements of more mobile warfare were interspersed with long periods of positional fighting. In a general sense, this could still be decisive: in two and half years of war, the Soviets drove the Germans from the Volga River to the Elbe. However, Allied breakthroughs depended on attrition first rather than lightning breakthroughs, and this attrition might have been as bad as or worse than that of the First World War. The combined casualties at Verdun in that war were 750,000 suffered over a period of ten months; in Normandy, 637,000 casualties were suffered in eighty days. The breakout from Normandy was enabled by two months of heavy, static fighting that wore the Germans down. Most German infantry units suffered 100 per cent casualties during the campaign.[30]

The Operational Level of War

German and Soviet thinking had focused on the importance of operational art. The operational level of war did not exist for them as a formal concept, and instead lay at whatever level the operational art was practised. Perhaps the most significant post-war developments were (a) the spread of concepts of operational art to English-speaking armies, and (b) the formal doctrinal recognition by the US in the 1980s of a distinct operational level of war.

The essentially evolutionary nature of the development of modern land warfare was sustained during the Cold War despite the great uncertainty caused by the impact of such new technology as nuclear weapons, helicopters and PGMs, and by new strategic ideas including deterrence and limited wars. Nuclear weapons posed a fundamental challenge to existing thinking about land warfare. As the eminent civilian strategist Bernard Brodie noted, 'Thus far the chief purposes of our [the US'] military establishment has been to win wars. From now on its chief purpose must be to avert them.'[31] In the Soviet Union, less emphasis was placed on operational art; in the US, the solution was to prioritise nuclear armed units, emphasising firepower over manoeuvre. By the 1960s, however, it was clear that nuclear war was not inevitable, and that conventional land warfare might still have a vital role to play in future conflict.

From the 1960s through to the 1980s, Soviet military doctrine returned to an emphasis on familiar themes related to operational art, albeit modified to take into account developments in technology and US doctrine. Soviet doctrine noted that 'the possibilities of defeating the enemy in the entire depth of his operation combat formations have increased'.[32] New technology provided the means to supplement ground operations in 'land–air' battle with a 'vertical echelon' delivered by air-mobile forces. Nevertheless, Soviet doctrine continued to stress the need for surprise, attacking the enemy throughout its depth, superiority in numbers and firepower at decisive points, mobility, continuous operations and the importance of maintaining large reserves.

In the US, however, defeat in Vietnam prompted a reassessment of existing doctrine.[33] One conclusion reached was that the defeat there was partly attributable to an over-reliance on firepower and a managerial approach to war that focused on systems and technology. Other factors also influenced this reassessment. For example, the Arab–Israeli Yom Kippur/Ramadan War of 1973 demonstrated the impact of PGMs: in three weeks of fighting, the losses of armour and artillery exceeded the entire US inventory at the time. Modern war appeared to be fought at a high tempo in a fast-moving, complex, all-arms environment, which required excellent command and control. The result of this process of reflection was the emergence of a new doctrinal concept, 'AirLand battle', introduced formally in a new edition of Field Manual 100–5, *Operations,* in 1982. AirLand battle tried to weave into a whole, **close operational** interaction between air–ground forces, combined arms, fire support, electronic warfare, deception, intelligence and manoeuvre. AirLand battle tried to marry firepower with manoeuvre by emphasising four concepts: initiative, depth, agility and synchronisation. The essence of AirLand battle was 'deep battle' and developing the capacity to slow Soviet second-echelon forces while pinning down and destroying the first echelon. Manoeuvre and firepower were treated as inseparable elements.[34] As part of this new approach, the new doctrine identified for the first time a formal operational *level* of war (indeed, it did not mention operational art at all). This operational level of war was defined as:

> Planning and conducting campaigns. Campaigns are sustained operations designed to defeat an enemy force in a specific place and time with simultaneous and sequential battles. The disposition of forces, selection of objectives, and actions to weaken or outmaneuver the enemy all set the terms for the next battle and exploit tactical gains. They are all part of the operational level of war.[35]

Subsequent doctrinal developments since then have formally codified the concept of operational art in the doctrine of the US, and that of its allies, as well as retaining the notion of a formal operational level of war (see Box 5.2).

Manoeuvre Warfare

The formal integration into Western military doctrines from the 1980s onwards of operational art was accompanied, and indeed supported, by the parallel emergence of the concept of **manoeuvre warfare**. Responding to criticisms that the US Army was too attritional in its approaches, advocates of manoeuvre warfare argued for an emphasis instead on attacking the conceptual and moral components of an enemy's fighting power rather than the physical (see Box 5.3). This placed a primacy on undermining the enemy's will, cohesion and decision-making capacity, rather than destruction in a crude attritional struggle. Manoeuvre warfare has been characterised as the capacity to cycle through **OODA loops** (Observe, Orientate, Decide, Act) faster than the opponent, thus invalidating their decision making, robbing them of

BOX 5.2 THE OPERATIONAL LEVEL OF WAR AND OPERATIONAL ART

The operational level

> 'The operational level links the tactical employment of forces to national and military strategic objectives. The focus at this level is on the design, planning, and execution of operations.'
>
> (US JP 3-0, *Joint Operations*, 2017)[36]

> 'The operational level of warfare is the level at which operations are planned, conducted and sustained, to contribute to achieving national strategic aims, as well as synchronising action, within theatres or areas of operation. The operational level provides the bridge between the strategic and tactical levels.'
>
> (UK JDP 0-01, *UK Defence Doctrine*, 2014)[37]

Operational art

> 'The cognitive approach by commanders and staffs – supported by their skill, knowledge, experience, creativity, and judgment – to develop strategies, campaigns, and operations to organize and employ military forces by integrating ends, ways, and means'.
>
> (US JP 3-0, *Joint Operations*, 2017)[38]

> 'The employment of forces to attain strategic and/or operational objectives through the design, organization, integration and conduct of strategies, campaigns, major operations and battles.'
>
> (NATO Glossary of Terms and Definitions)[39]

> '[T]he linking of military-strategic objectives with tactical-level activities'.
>
> (John Kiszeley, 'Thinking About the Operational Level')[40]

> '[T]he mediating and balancing mental interaction between strategic and tactical reasoning'.
>
> (Huba Wass de Czege, 'Thinking and Acting Like an Early Explorer')[41]

The focus of the operational level is the campaign, a series of tactical actions that should be linked by time, geography and a common purpose, so that they serve broader military and grand strategic objectives. Operational art is the employment of military forces at this level

the initiative and promoting systemic collapse. (The OODA loop concept is discussed in more depth in Chapter 10).[42] As exponents of manoeuvre warfare acknowledged, there was nothing strictly new in this approach; instead, it was a systematisation of historical 'best practice'. This evolutionary approach was reflected in a resurgence in

BOX 5.3 MANOEUVRE WARFARE

Manoeuvre warfare is a war-fighting philosophy that seeks to shatter the enemy's cohesion through a variety of rapid, focused and unexpected actions which create a turbulent and rapidly deteriorating situation with which the enemy cannot cope (US Marine Corps publication *MCDP1 Warfighting*, p. 73).

Western armies of the study of the Soviet methods of 1943–1945 and also of German operational art. Some of the key tools associated with manoeuvre warfare drew on German approaches adopted and utilised before and during the Second World War, including *Aufstragstaktik* ('mission command'), *Schwerpunkt* ('focus of effort') and *Flachen und Lücken* ('surfaces and gaps').

Manoeuvre warfare places an emphasis on speed, focus, surprise, disruption and exploitation. It is a demanding philosophy that requires initiative, flexibility, risk-taking, lateral thinking and an ability to cope well with uncertainty. Manoeuvre warfare was reconceptualised by the British in the mid 1990s into the '**manoeuvrist approach**', a philosophy of unorthodoxy and adaptability that was applicable to all forms of warfare.

Conclusion

The preceding discussion demonstrates that there is a strong evolutionary dynamic to the way in which land warfare has developed over time. The infiltration tactics of 1915–1918, blitzkrieg and manoeuvre warfare form much more of a continuum of development than they do radical discontinuities. Modern tactics evolved on the battlefields of the First World War; they embodied the principles of decentralisation, combined arms, fire-and-movement, dispersal, cover and concealment and small-unit manoeuvre. Modern tactics enabled offensives to succeed even under the conditions of the radical increases in the theoretical lethality of battlefield fire-power. Yet, given the growing scale of warfare, there were limits to the extent to which tactics could solve the problem of translating local successes into larger-scale breakthroughs. Modern operational art emerged as a solution. Building on the capabilities provided by mechanisation and radio communications, new concepts emerged to guide the sequencing of tactical actions in time and space in order to meet strategic objectives.

Successful mastery of the modern system of land warfare has enabled armies to mitigate some of the consequences of industrialised people's war, such as firepower, and to harness others, such as new weapons platforms and means of mobility. The use of this system explains why casualty rates have not expanded in relation to theoretical lethality or the speed of modern weapons. Despite increases in firepower technology, in the period between 1900 and 1990 average casualty rates decreased by more than 60 per cent. It also explains why, despite the power of the defence demonstrated in the initial part of the First World War, modern armies have been able to conduct successful offensive operations. But will the modern system of warfare continue to apply in the future? Moreover, if the modern system of warfare is so effective, can we assume that it is the only way of fighting land warfare? To answer these questions we turn now to the final chapter on land warfare.

RESEARCH QUESTIONS

1. In the period 1870–1913, what key factors shaped the nature of the debates on the impact of technology on land warfare?
2. What factors shaped battlefield adaptation and innovation during the First World War?
3. What were the strengths and weaknesses of Soviet operational art during the Second World War?
4. Why did it take so long for operational art to be codified in US military doctrine?
5. How does one know that one is operating at the operational level?
6. How useful is the concept of a distinct operational level of warfare?

FURTHER READING

Citino, Robert M., *Quest for Decisive Victory: From Stalemate to Blitzkrieg in Europe, 1898–1940* (Lawrence, KS: Kansas University Press, 2002). The first five chapters provide a particularly useful analysis of pre-First World War conflicts and the conclusions that were drawn from them by European armies.

Corum, James S., *The Roots of Blitzkrieg: Hans von Seekt and German Military Reform* (Lawrence, KS: University Press of Kansas, 1992). This analyses the sources and nature of the German interwar process of reflection and adaptation.

English, John A. and Bruce I. Gudmundsson, *On Infantry* (Westport, CT: Praeger, 1994). An excellent analysis of the development of infantry doctrine and organisation.

Fox, Aimee, *Learning to Fight: Military Innovation and Change in the British Army, 1914–1918* (Cambridge, UK: Cambridge University Press, 2018). Provides a convincing analysis of British tactical learning in the First World War.

Freiser, Karl-Heinz, *The Blitzkrieg Legend: The 1940 Campaign in the West* (Annapolis, MD: Naval Institute Press, 2005). This book discusses the essentially evolutionary origins of German doctrines for operational-level mobile warfare.

Glantz, David, *Soviet Military Operational Art: In Pursuit of Deep Battle* (London: Frank Cass, 1991). Glantz charts the development of Soviet thinking on operational art from its origins in the 1920s to the doctrines of the Cold War.

House, Jonathan, *Combined Arms Warfare in the Twentieth Century* (Lawrence, KS: Kansas University Press, 2001). A detailed survey of developments in land warfare from the late nineteenth century to the 1990s.

Krause, Michael D. and R. Cody Phillips. *Historical Perspectives of the Operational Art*, Center of Military History (United States Army, Washington D.C., 2005). An excellent overview of the origins and development of operational art, https://bit.ly/41OH1hR.

Leonhard, Robert, *The Art of Maneuver: Maneuver-Warfare Theory and AirLand Battle* (New York, NY: Ballantine, 1991). An introduction to US operational art and manoeuvre warfare and its application to the doctrine of AirLand battle.
Olsen, John Andreas and Martin Van Creveld (eds.), *The Evolution of Operational Art: From Napoleon to the Present* (Oxford: Oxford University Press, 2011). A comprehensive assessment of the theory and development of operational art across different nations.

ONLINE RESOURCES

There is a great deal of tactical military doctrine available online. For example, ATP 3-21.8, *The Infantry Rifle Platoon and Squad* (Headquarters, Department of the Army, April 2016), https://bit.ly/4lNQRri, is worth comparing with First World War era doctrine, including the British 'Instructions for the Training of Platoons for Offensive Action' and English translations of German doctrine, including 'The Attack in Position Warfare', https://tinyurl.com/yerc67b8.

Issues relevant to modern military tactics and operational art are discussed in a wide variety of online sites and publications including: *Joint Force Quarterly* (https://ndupress.ndu.edu/jfq/): *Military Review* (www.armyupress.army.mil/Military-Review/); the Modern War Institute (https://mwi.westpoint.edu/);*War on the Rocks* (https://warontherocks.com/); Defence-in-Depth, https://defenceindepth.co/); and the Strategic Studies Institute (https://ssi.armywarcollege.edu/).

Extant US Army doctrines can be found at https://armypubs.army.mil/ProductMaps/PubForm/ADP.aspx.

Access to older US doctrine, including AirLand Battle, can be found at https://cgsc.contentdm.oclc.org/digital/collection/p4013coll9.

NOTES

1 Stephen Biddle, *Military Power: Explaining Victory and Defeat in Modern Battle* (Princeton, NJ: Princeton University Press, 2004), p. 3.
2 Colin McInnes, *Men, Machines and the Emergence of Modern Warfare, 1914–1945* (Camberley: Strategic and Combat Studies Institute, 1992), p. 4.
3 Quoted in Jay Luvaas, *The Military Legacy of the Civil War: The European Inheritance* (Lawrence, KS: University Press of Kansas, 1988), p. 167.
4 Ibid., p. 167.
5 Bruce I. Gudmundsson, *Stormtroop Tactics: Innovation in the German Army, 1914–1918* (Westport, CT: Praeger, 1995), p. 1.
6 McInnes, *Men, Machines and the Emergence of Modern Warfare*, p. 8.
7 Michael Glover, *Warfare from Waterloo to Mons* (London: Book Club Associates, 1980), p. 248.
8 Ibid.
9 Williamson A. Murray, 'The West at War', in Geoffrey Parker (ed.), *The Cambridge History of Warfare* (Cambridge, UK: Cambridge University Press, 2005), p. 294.
10 Robert T. Foley, 'A Case Study in Horizontal Military Innovation: The German Army, 1916–1918', *Journal of Strategic Studies*, 35(6) (December 2012), 808–12.
11 Biddle, *Military Power*, 28.
12 Ibid., 812–20.

13 Timothy T. Lupfer, *The Dynamics of Doctrine: The Changes in German Tactical Doctrine during the First World War* (Lawrence, KS: Combat Studies Institute, July 1981), p. 45.
14 Ibid., p. 41.
15 Biddle, *Military Power*, p. 28.
16 Anthony King, *The Combat Soldier: Infantry Tactics and Cohesion in the Twentieth and Twenty-First Centuries* (Cambridge, UK: Cambridge University Press, 2018), p. 129.
17 See David T. Zabecki, *The German 1918 Offensives: A Case Study in the Operational Level of War* (London: Routledge, 2009).
18 On the relationship between strategy and tactics see Beatrice Heuser, *The Evolution of Strategy: Thinking War from Antiquity to the Present* (Cambridge, UK: Cambridge University Press, 2010), pp. 3–35.
19 It was at Cannae that Hannibal achieved a successful, and since widely studied, envelopment of a Roman army in 216 BC.
20 Quoted in John Kiszley, 'Thinking about the Operational Level', *RUSI Journal* (December 2005), 38.
21 Jacob W. Kipp, 'The Tsarist and Soviet Operational Art: 1853–1991', in John Andreas Olsen and Martin Van Creveld (eds.), *The Evolution of Operational Art: From Napoleon to the Present* (Oxford: Oxford University Press, 2011), p. 66.
22 For a discussion on interwar theorists, see Allan R. Millett and Williamson Murray (eds.), *Military Effectiveness, II: The Interwar Period* (Cambridge, UK: Cambridge University Press, 2010).
23 Milan Vego, *Joint Operational Warfare: Theory and Practice* (Newport, RI: US Naval War College, 2009), p. I-22.
24 Dennis Showalter, 'Prussian-German Operational Art, 1740–1943', in John Andreas Olsen and Martin Van Creveld (eds.), *The Evolution of Operational Art: From Napoleon to the Present* (Oxford: Oxford University Press, 2011), p. 51.
25 There is still debate as to whether the Polish campaign was really blitzkrieg at all, given that the use of mobile armoured forces was still overwhelmingly tactical in conception.
26 Martin Van Creveld, *Technology and War: From 2000 to the Present* (London: Brassey's, 1991), p. 181.
27 Karl-Heinz Freiser, *The Blitzkrieg Legend: The 1940 Campaign in the West* (Annapolis, MD: Naval Institute Press, 2005), p. 27.
28 For details of the huge logistic problems see David Glantz, *Barbarossa Derailed: The Battle for Smolensk, 10 July–10 September 1941*, vol. I (Solihull: Helion and Company, 2010).
29 See Lloyd Clarke, *Kursk: The Greatest Battle* (London: Headline, 2012), pp. 207– 12.
30 Total casualties (including replacements) as compared with initial strength.
31 Quoted in Michael Evans, *The Primacy of Doctrine: The United States Army and Military Innovation and Reforms, 1945–1995*, Army Occasional Paper No. 1 (Canberra: Directorate of Army Research and Analysis, Departmentt of Defence, August 1996), p. 3.
32 David Glantz, *Soviet Military Operational Art: In Pursuit of Deep Battle* (London: Frank Cass, 1991), p. 38.
33 Richard Lock-Pullan, '"An Inward Looking Time": The United States Army, 1973–1976', *The Journal of Military History*, 69(2)(April 2003), 498–9.
34 Evans, *The Primacy of Doctrine*, p. 20.
35 Justin Kelly and Mike Br Army Staff Sgt, *Alien: How Operational Art Devoured Strategy* (Carlisle, PA: Strategic Studies Institute, 1992), p. 61.
36 Joint Publication 3-0, *Joint Operations*, January 2017, I-13.
37 Joint Doctrine Publication 0-01, *UK Defence Doctrine*, November 2014, 20.

38 JP 3-0, I-13.
39 AAP-06, *NATO Glossary of Terms and Definitions*, 93.
40 John Kiszeley, 'Thinking About the Operational Level', *RUSI Journal* (December 2005), 42.
41 Huba Wass de Czege, 'Thinking and Acting Like an Early Explorer: Operational Art is Not a Level of War', *Small Wars Journal* (14 March 2011).
42 William S. Lind, *The Maneuver Warfare Handbook* (Boulder, CO: Westview, 1985), p. 6

6 Future Land Warfare

CHAPTER OUTLINE

KEY THEMES

- The future form of land warfare is far from certain.
- For some, the future is net-centric warfare, an information and technology-focused view on the changing character of warfare. To meet the demands posed by the changing character of conflict, armies must embrace the theme of multi-domain operations.
- However, history suggests that in the future multiple forms of land warfare are likely to coexist because the practice of land warfare is shaped by many different political, economic, social and cultural contexts.

Introduction

In this final chapter on land warfare, we turn our attention to the future. The two preceding chapters have highlighted the evolutionary underpinnings of the 'modern system' approach to land warfare. Can we assume similarly that future land warfare will look much like that of the past? This is clearly a crucial question for land forces around the world. Governments do not have the luxury of perpetual analysis: given the time taken to generate effective military power, choices have to be made now about the sorts of land forces that will be required for the future – their size, structure, equipment, training and doctrine. But these choices carry risks: while we might hope to be prepared for the right future, history suggests, as the previous chapter has illustrated, that we often do not get the sorts of wars that we expect.

Currently, the debate on the changing character of land operations is dominated by two themes: net-centric warfare, and multi-domain operations (MDO). Many commentators – whether Western, Russian, Indian or Chinese – believe that a new information-based military revolution is underway that will fundamentally change how armies will fight. This chapter explores what net-centric warfare and MDO are and why they have exerted such traction on the debates on future land warfare. However, history demonstrates that we are often poor at predicting the future of war. For this reason, this chapter also examines some of the critiques levelled at these concepts. There are many plausible reasons to believe that the future character of land warfare might be more complex and heterogenous than we think.

Net-centric Warfare

Net-centric warfare is an example of an information-based theory of victory. A 'theory of victory' is an intellectual concept that shows how a military organisation thinks that it will deliver success. For example, counterinsurgency doctrine is a theory of victory.[1] An information-based theory of victory assumes that achieving superiority in information over an adversary provides the decisive foundation for success in warfare. As Jonathan Lindsay comments, this kind of theory of victory assumes that:

> Accurate intelligence sensors connected to precision weapons via common networks and protocols – seeing all, striking all, all together – can improve military performance. Smaller, yet smarter forces that can identify and prosecute targets more quickly can thereby defeat larger but slower enemies.[2]

The Development of Net-centric Warfare

This theory of victory has long had an important impact on debates surrounding the changing character of land warfare. In the 1970s and 1980s, for example, Russian, US and Israeli analysts argued that technological change was in the process of delivering a 'military-technical revolution' or 'revolution in military

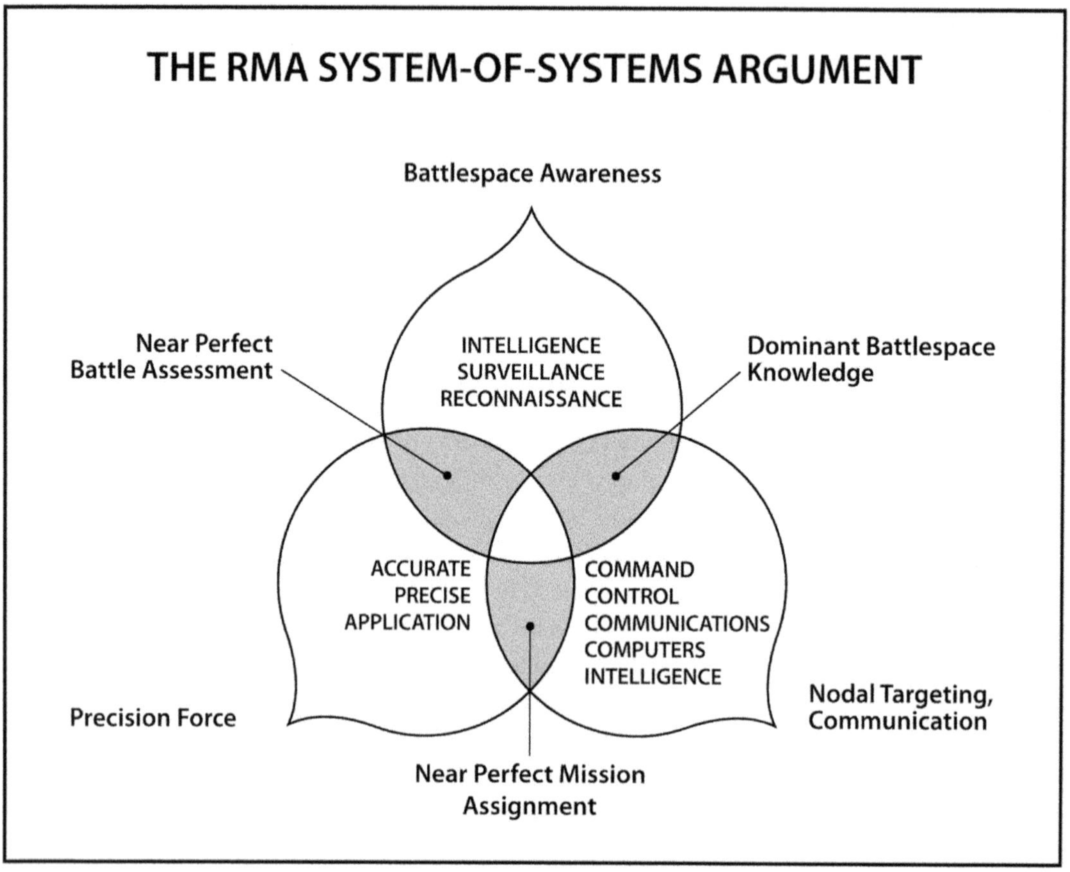

Figure 6.1 The RMA system-of-systems argument. A 'system of systems' is created through intense networking between systems, utilising new technology (especially digital communications) and associated procedures to create a more unified whole out of the distinct elements. This allows information to flow much more quickly and efficiently, which, in theory, dramatically increases the speed at which decisions can be made and the tempo at which operations can be conducted.

affairs' (RMA).[3] Advances in sensor technology, including aerial and space-based systems such as the Global Positioning System (GPS) and optical, thermal and laser systems promised to dramatically enhance the ability to find enemy targets. In parallel, improved means for delivering firepower, such as stealth technology and **cruise missiles**, would allow those targets to be destroyed more quickly, with more precision and at longer ranges. New synergies between these two developments would be achieved through unprecedented networking, enabled by new digital technologies for collecting and processing information, that would connect the sensors to the 'shooter' systems. Through greater integration and the creation of a '**system of systems**', the combination of precision attack, sensors and networking promised to create what were termed variously 'guided-munitions networks' or 'reconnaissance-strike complexes' (see Figure 6.1). Cumulatively, therefore, new technology would succeed in creating a paradigm shift in warfare: a revolutionary new way of fighting that would invalidate many of the verities of the past. Leveraging this RMA would allow armies to attain what the US termed 'full-spectrum dominance', a decisive superiority in military effectiveness across every mode of war and at every level.

The Gulf War of 1990–1991 cast a long shadow over subsequent debates on the character and future of land warfare. The then US secretary of defense, Richard ('Dick') Cheney, asserted that the Gulf War 'demonstrated dramatically the new possibilities of what has been called the "military-technical revolution in warfare"'.[4] Theorists argued that the US military had triumphed in 1991 because it had achieved 'dominant battlespace awareness': a decisive information advantage that had allowed the US to manoeuvre and to apply massive force, quickly and with great precision, while preventing the enemy from doing so. The decisive coalition victory achieved in 1991, achieved rapidly and at minimal cost to the attackers, strengthened the hand of those who argued that the developments of the 1970s and 1980s could be taken further: that in the post-Cold War period, the US had a unique opportunity to use the possibilities inherent in emerging technologies to produce a dramatic leap forward in military effectiveness.

This view led to the development of specific concepts such as network-centric warfare (NCW). This was defined in 1999 by one of its advocates, the prominent Pentagon technical advisor John Gartska, as:

> An information superiority-enabled concept of operations that generates increased combat power by networking sensors, decision makers, and shooters to achieve shared awareness, increased speed of command, higher tempo of operations, greater lethality, increased survivability, and a degree of self-synchronization.[5]

To deliver this information-centric model of the changing character of warfare, the US army prioritised certain themes in its force development. One was to develop a digitally linked force through investment in information technologies. The fruits of this included the Army Battle Command System (ABCS), a digital command-and-control system designed to integrate functions such as manoeuvre, logistics, air defence and artillery into a single 'system of systems'.[6] A feature of this system was Blue Force Tracking (BFT), a capability that allowed commanders access to a 'common operating picture' (COP), which gave troops access to the position of all friendly forces. In equipment terms this resulted in the procurement of next-generation digitally enabled platforms, such as the Stryker, a light, mobile, wheeled armoured fighting vehicle. New autonomous aerial vehicles (UAVs) would enhance the intelligence, surveillance and reconnaissance (ISR) capabilities of land forces, as well as providing new forms of precision fire. Organisationally, the US Army embraced more complex forms of combined arms at lower levels. The most obvious feature of this was the replacement of the division by the brigade as the key army formation. Brigade combat teams (BCTs) would be created by pushing down to the brigade level many of the divisional support assets. Overall, the transformed US army would be smaller but it would be more powerful. This increase in power would be the result of its ability to acquire, process and disseminate digital information across the system of systems. Networked and digitally integrated US forces would have an information advantage over their adversaries. This advantage would make the army more agile and flexible than the enemy; increase the tempo of friendly decision-making and activities; and allow more precise identification and targeting of enemy vulnerabilities. Net-centric approaches in many ways reflected an advanced form of manoeuvre warfare (see Chapter 5).

The US was not alone in the emphasis that it gave to the net-centric model of war. Both Russian and Chinese thinking on the development of warfare in many respects mirrored net-centric assumptions. Soviet and then Russian theorising on the changing character of warfare identified an ongoing 'Information Technology Revolution in Military Affairs'. This view argued that modern warfare would be dominated by reconnaissance-strike complexes (RSCs), the integrated application of sensors and fires in near real time that would result in a dramatic increase in the tempo and lethality of warfare. In China, military reforms from the early 1990s were heavily influenced by the lessons drawn from the Gulf War and later lessons from the conventional phases of the wars in Afghanistan (2001) and Iraq (2003), their study of US thinking, and by the People's Liberation Army (PLA)'s assessment of the growing importance of technology and information in modern war. The result was a progressive modernisation in PLA doctrine, including in 1993 a new strategy called 'Local War Under High Technology Conditions', updated again in 2004 as 'Winning Local Wars under the Conditions of Informationisation'. The PLA believed that information, and associated themes including integration and digitisation, were becoming decisive components in modern warfare.[7] In April 2004, the Indian Army introduced a new doctrine known colloquially as 'Cold Start'. This doctrine also contained many familiar elements: a desire to reshape the structures of the Indian Army from clumsy army corps to smaller 'integrated battlegroups' in order to create forces capable of a faster and less predictable manoeuvre warfare-style approach to operations, and a desire to see much better joint integration.

By the mid part of the 2000s, however, the revolutionary impact of net-centric approaches was being questioned in many quarters. There had always been critics who had argued that the net-centric model misinterpreted the sources of success on the modern battlefield. Some commentators argued that US success in the 1991 Gulf War had very little to do with leveraging a new and revolutionary information-based model of war, and everything to do with the fact that the Iraqis were so poor at modern system warfare. The Iraqis were according to one critic 'one of the worst led, worst fought forces in the history of warfare'.[8] Similarly, the experience of the conventional stages of the wars in Afghanistan and Iraq seemed to show that success on the ground continued to depend on competence in traditional combined arms and joint warfare. Indeed, in Iraq, many of the new net-centric technologies simply did not perform well when confronted with the harsh realities of combat. Networks routinely crashed, situational awareness at the tactical level was often poor and automated logistic systems failed.[9] In addition, as the wars in Afghanistan and Iraq transformed into complex, protracted counterinsurgency and nation-building operations, they absorbed much of the practical and intellectual efforts of Western forces.

Despite these critiques, however, the second decade of the twenty-first century has seen a renewed emphasis on net-centric information-based theories of victory. Why has this been the case?

What Are the Drivers of Military Change?

Renewed enthusiasm for the net-centric model of war has occurred because of assessments of the broader changes taking place in human affairs. These assessments argue that technological developments, especially in the realms of computer hardware and software, evident in the impact of the Internet, AI and machine learning (ML), have been creating effects in human society, economics and governance so profound that a genuine revolution in human affairs is taking place. We are, as some assessments have argued, at 'a historical inflection point': a watershed in human affairs.[10] Since warfare is a societal, human and political activity, this process is inevitably shaping a new military revolution as well. In military circles, a certain consensus has emerged on the key trends driving forwards a new revolution in the character of warfare.[11] These trends consist of a mix of imperatives and opportunities for change.

One dominant trend is the accelerating rate of change. Part of this process of change is geopolitical in character and is linked to the rise of non-Western powers, including India and China. But at the heart of this trend is an accelerating rate of technological development. This technology includes new forms of sensors, firepower, robotics and human augmentation; but AI and ML are key parts of this debate. The US Army's Training and Doctrine Command has argued that:

> [E]merging technologies like artificial intelligence, hypersonics, machine learning, nanotechnology, and robotics are driving a fundamental change in the character of war. . . . the impacts have the potential to revolutionize battlefields.[12]

AI and ML have already been used on battlefields. During Israel's military operations in Gaza that began in October 2023, systems, including those known as Lavender and Where's Daddy, have been used to sift data, generate targets and track their movements with often minimal human involvement.[13] In the Russo-Ukraine war, there has been a significant tilt towards autonomous drones as a way of mitigating the impact of electronic warfare (EW) measures on these platforms.

Second, and as a result in part of technological change, there has been an expansion in the domains of warfare. Space and cyber have moved from being supporting capabilities to fully-fledged warfighting domains; together, they have expanded the manoeuvre space and they have unique characteristics that cannot be exploited effectively by legacy concepts and thinking.

Third, society is becoming increasingly informationalised. Data and networks are the new oil and are increasingly vital to the functioning of our societies, driving an ongoing information-based revolution, a 'fourth industrial revolution', as Mick Ryan has termed it.[14] As a result, the 'pervasiveness of information and rapid technological development have changed the character of war'.[15] Fourth, there is an ongoing equalisation in the distribution of military power. Western militaries have in the past been able to rely on qualitative superiority to offset their quantitative inferiority. Going forwards, this will be less and less the case. China and Russia especially have invested heavily in their military capabilities, creating anti-access/area denial (A2/AD) networks (see Chapter 9): complexes of network-enabled sensors and long-range fires designed to undermine an attacker's capacity for joint and combined warfare. A final trend is hybridisation (see Chapter 20). Processes of technological change are enhancing the effectiveness of the non-kinetic instruments of power and so broadening our definitions of war beyond conventional military activities. Conventional warfare is increasingly likely to be preceded, followed and accompanied by hybrid warfare, demanding greater synchronisation between military and non-military capabilities in both war and peace, and placing greater emphasis on the capacity to influence the cognitive and human dimensions conflict.

What Will the Future Battlefield Look Like?

Taken together, these trends will produce a future battlefield with a range of challenging features. Future battlefields will be increasingly transparent: land forces will be under constant observation, due to improved thermal and optical imaging, penetrative ISR including space and drone capabilities, and the impact of mobile phones and social media. This transparency, combined with the greater range and accuracy of precision firepower and developments in sophisticated real-time targeting systems for ISR, target acquisition and **fire control**, is creating a battlefield that is also much more lethal (see Figure 6.2). As Albert Palazzo has argued: 'On today's battlefield, if it can be sensed it can be killed from afar, often with a single round.'[16] Future battlefields will be hyperactive environments in which things like unmanned systems and automated command and control will drastically increase the tempo of operations. The increased ranges of sensors and firepower will also further expand the size of the battlefield, with forces likely to be open to attack as they assemble in home areas, or as they transit and try and deploy into theatre. Given some of the preceding factors, the future battlefield will also be more dispersed because the massing of forces will expose them to the more lethal enemy firepower. Finally, the future battlefield will be highly decentralised. Traditional linear, sequential approaches to campaigning will not be able to cope with the complexity and agility of future threats; land warfare, like all warfare, is an iterative, time-competitive competition, and greater decentralisation will be the only way to win that competition.

The Inadequacy of Joint Warfare

To survive on the future battlefield, land forces will need to move from episodic synchronisation to continuous integration. Land forces will need to be able to mass effects rapidly and often simultaneously from all five domains of warfare in three different dimensions: the physical (or material) dimension; the information dimension (encompassing all the means, including data and networks, that humans use to communicate); and the cognitive (or human) dimension that encompasses people and the ways in which humans interact. But traditional jointery is judged to be no longer sufficient to achieve this. Traditional approaches comprehend and conduct warfare by deliberately creating horizontal and vertical compartmentalisation. The horizontal divisions are reflected in 'levels of war' thinking, and vertical divisions in terms of things like the existence of single services and multiple domains, and also

Figure 6.2 A High Mobility Artillery Rocket System (HIMARS). With standard Guided Multiple Launch Rocket System (GMLRS) munitions, the HIMARS has a range of more than fifty miles and an accuracy to within three feet of its target. Artillery rocket systems like these have contributed significantly to extending the range and lethality of ground combat.
Source: Courtesy of the US Army

different arms and capabilities within domains. These barriers are institutionalised through single-service and joint command-and-control hierarchies. But while these divisions introduce order into how we conduct warfare, they also introduce frictions, slowing down the ability to synchronise efforts. For critics, the changing character of warfare demands that land forces move beyond increasingly anachronistic solutions like jointery. Ruminating on the challenges posed by the changing character of conflict, the then US chairman of the Joint Chiefs of Staff, General Martin Dempsey, in 2011 posed the question: 'What's after joint?'[17]

MDO

The answer to this question is MDO, which the US Army defines as: 'The combined arms employment of joint and Army capabilities to create and exploit relative advantages that achieve objectives, defeat enemy forces, and consolidate gains on behalf of the joint commander.'[18] MDO emerged in 2018, building on the 2017 concept of multi-domain battle. MDO seeks to create a 'system of systems': a large deeply integrated network that allows land forces rapidly to create tailored force packages integrating elements from any domain and level of war. By being able to create and apply these multi-domain forces at tempo, the US Army would be able to intensify the synergies traditionally achieved by jointery, achieve decision superiority over the enemy and pose insoluble challenges to them. As one US commentator has argued, 'The goal of MDO operations is to create complex, simultaneous dilemmas at once for the enemy.'[19]

To deliver this, the US Army is concentrating its force development on four themes. The first is agility: the ability to move forces and adjust their dispositions and activities more rapidly than the enemy. The second is convergence: the concerted employment of capabilities from multiple domains and levels against combinations of decisive points in any domain to create effects. This convergence would be conducted by headquarters at the divisional level and above, because it is at these levels that headquarters units would have the necessary structures and experience to integrate capabilities from multiple domains and levels. Endurance forms the third theme and requires forces able to conduct operations for extended periods of time, possibly in degraded environments. Finally, future forces would need to be able to operate at depth with an ability to attack the enemy everywhere that they are deployed.

The US Army has recognised that many things will be required to turn the MDO theory into a reality. An absolute requirement for MDO is a reliable and robust digital architecture. As one US official has commented, successful multi-domain warfare 'will depend less on discrete warfighting platforms and more on the networks, data and IT infrastructure that binds them all together'.[20] Organisational reforms to allow multi-domain integration (MDI) at lower levels are another imperative. 'All formations will have to become multi-domain, or they'll be irrelevant', asserted one US general in 2019.[21] The US Army has established a number of multi-domain task forces (MDTFs) to bring together long-range precision fires and effects, and capabilities like cyber. New command-and-control systems, experimental training and wargaming, and changes in single-service culture have also been identified as important foundations for MDO.

Other Perspectives

As the new orthodoxy regarding the changing character of warfare, multi-domain approaches have been widely accepted, although the terms used often vary. NATO has its own concept of MDO; Britain has concepts for both MDO and MDI (see Box 6.1). Neither Russia nor China use the term MDO, but their concepts for land warfare follow the same net-centric logic. Russia has developed its approach to the reconnaissance-strike complex through themes of the 'Reconnaissance-Strike System' and 'Reconnaissance-Fire System'. Both of these ideas presume that building intense networks between **C4ISR** (command, control, communications, intelligence, surveillance and reconnaissance) and precision fire capabilities can produce 'an ecosystem of combined arms, uninterruptedly executing "sensor-shooter

BOX 6.1 MDO AND MDI

'The orchestration of military activities, across all domains and environments, synchronized with non-military activities, to enable the Alliance to deliver converging effects at the speed of relevance.' (NATO definition)[26]

'The combined arms employment of capabilities from all domains.' (British Army definition)[27]

'At their most basic but ideal form, MDO are about maximising fighting power through the merging of current and future technology, updated doctrine and the operational art of the commander and their staff.' (Ian Bowers, *Understanding Multi-Domain Operations*)[28]

'The posturing of military capabilities in concert with the other instruments of national power, allies and partners; configured to sense, understand and orchestrate effects at the optimal tempo, across the operational domains and the levels of war.'
(British government definition of MDI)[29]

loops"'.[22] Russian operations in Syria were used by some as the architype for MDO, with Russia executing the campaign through tight integration between capabilities across domains and allies. Likewise, China's PLA has a current modernisation programme motivated by the belief in an ongoing 'global revolution in military affairs' in which AI, digitisation and integration are regarded as essential foundations for success in what it defines as 'new type' operations. China now places significant emphasis on the space and cyber domains. The PLA also takes the view that the future of war is moving from 'informationalised' to 'intelligentised' warfare, the latter characterised as an AI-enabled net-centric form of war in which autonomous systems will be key.[23] An analysis in the *PLA Daily* argued that:

> In the future intelligentised battlefield, networks of robots on land, sea, and air will be supported by big data and cloud computing. More sophisticated artificial intelligence technology will shift from assisting human operators to replacing them ... This will greatly condense the combat decision cycle of planning operations, allocating tasks, striking targets, and evaluating losses.[24]

MDO therefore reflects the latest orthodoxy on the future character of warfare. US Army doctrine asserts that in the changed conditions of land warfare 'all operations are multi-domain operations'.[25]

The Future of Land Warfare

There are those who believe, however, that the future character of warfare might be less certain than this current multi-domain orthodoxy might imply.[30]

The MDO Debate

One source of scepticism lies with the MDO concept itself, which could be less robust than is assumed. There are, for example, significant differences between the ways in which multi-domain approaches are defined. As Box 6.1 shows, some definitions of MDO are relatively evolutionary in perspective, focusing on an expanded form of combined arms warfare that seeks to bring the space and cyber dimensions into existing approaches. But others are much more ambitious and aim at a form of MDI that extends across government departments, non-military instruments of power and allies. This lack of definitional coherence means that debates about MDO might in practice be debates about very different concepts. It is worth noting that the most ambitious concept, the UK's MDI, was quietly shelved in 2023. Critics have also argued that MDO might be unrealistic. Armies traditionally struggle to execute joint operations effectively; yet MDO is even more complex and poses challenges such as getting buy-in from other organisations and allies; or working out ways of devolving the authorities required for forces to draw on scarce assets from other domains; or developing the expertise within an army to understand how capabilities from other domains should be used properly. These issues multiply the perennial problems of jointery like the impact of single-service cultures. MDO also poses problems of resilience. As a net-centric approach to war, properly functioning networks are vital to MDO. But this makes these networks an obvious target for enemy action. Can multi-domain warfare survive the inevitable frictions of war and perform effectively in degraded environments? Then there are the issues of the relevance of MDO to less conventional scenarios, including counterinsurgency and **stability operations**, given that much of the impetus for the development of MDO has come from the conventional military challenge posed by Russia and China. The campaigns in Iraq and Afghanistan after 2001 demonstrated the very real tensions between a net-centric paradigm featuring smaller forces and the pursuit of quick, decisive success, and the complex, long-term, personnel intensive, and highly political demands of counterinsurgency and nation-building scenarios. Finally, there is the broader question regarding whether MDO, like net-centric approaches in general, might be an exercise in self-delusion: it might be an expression of how armies would like to fight, rather than how they might actually have to fight. This criticism focuses on the ways in which net-centric approaches promise (in the spirit of manoeuvre warfare) that, if they just employ the right military concepts, small but high-quality armies can win quick, decisive, and low-cost victories over larger adversaries. MDO provides an alternative to prolonged attrition. The attraction of this promise to small, but relatively high-quality, Western armies is obvious. But might attrition be inevitable in land warfare?

Aside from issues specific to the concept of MDO, there are two general points worth addressing in a discussion of the future of land warfare. The first of these is the impact of continuities in land warfare. The war in Ukraine provides a useful case study of the interaction between change and continuity. The second is the problem of ethnocentrism.

Continuity and the Character of Land Warfare: A Ukraine Case Study

The debates on the character of future warfare often put insufficient emphasis on the impact of continuity. For the historian David Edgerton, this is because our thinking about the future is clichéd: it is, and has been, blinded by novelty, technology and the search for paradigm shifts. Intellectually, argues Edgerton, 'we still live in a world of grand narratives, of great ruptures, and transitions'.[31] In analyses of the changing character of warfare, these clichés lead to conclusions that privilege the new, and marginalise the relevance of continuity and evolution. For example, assessments of German land warfare in World War Two will often highlight the significance of tanks. Yet most German divisions were infantry divisions, and each of those relied for its mobility and supply on 5,000 horses. German land operations depended to a significant extent on very traditional capabilities.[32]

Evidence for the problems caused by this bias is provided by the current war between Russia and Ukraine, the largest conventional war in Europe since World War Two. While for Ukraine this war began in 2014, with Russia's annexation of Crimea and support for separatists in Donetsk and Luhansk oblasts, the conventional stage of this conflict commenced in February 2022 and it is still ongoing at the time of writing (see Box 6.2).

The war in Ukraine has been aptly described by some commentators as 'a war of old truths and new developments'.[33] For many commentators, there are ways in which the fighting in Ukraine has reinforced some of the consensus surrounding the changing character of war.[34]

From this perspective, the war supports the argument regarding the lethality of the modern battlefield. The character of the fighting has been influenced significantly by fires with greater range and accuracy, within a battlefield that is more transparent, and where firepower can often be applied more expeditiously. Longer-range precision fire systems have exerted a significant impact on the character of the fighting. Whereas conventional artillery has a range of 20–30 miles, equipment such as the High Mobility Artillery Rocket System (HIMARS) and Army Tactical Missile System (ATACMS) have ranges of around 50 and 190 miles, respectively. They have been used by Ukraine to attack logistics hubs, command-and-control centres and troop concentrations. The reach of fires has also been extended by precision-guided missiles, including the Russian Iskander 9M723 and the British Storm Shadow, and drones (UAVs). If they are observed, troops can be struck accurately throughout the operational depth. This has also complicated logistics because much of the supply line from 'factory to foxhole' can be subject to enemy fires.[35]

Battlefield transparency has expanded. At the highest level, satellite imagery has been able to provide significant insights into the distribution of forces and positions in the theatre. Air ISR, whether from fixed-wing drones such as the Russian Orlan-10 or, increasingly, from smaller tactical systems, has played an important part in the detection of enemy troops.[36] Cyber and EW assets have proven vital for identifying forces through their electronic signatures. The proliferation of mobile

BOX 6.2 THE WAR IN UKRAINE

Russia invaded Ukraine on 24 February 2022 with the intention of replacing the existing Ukrainian government with one more amenable to Russian interests. Russian planning evidently presumed that the campaign would be more one of occupation than of conventional fighting. Advancing on concentric axes towards the main cities, Russia expected that Ukrainian resistance would collapse almost immediately. It did not, and in fighting that lasted until early April 2022 Russian forces transitioned to conventional military operations and attempted to fight their way into their objectives. Despite some successes in the south, they largely failed. Russia then withdrew its forces from Kyiv and the vicinity of Kharkiv and focused instead on the Donbas. The extensive Russian use of firepower and attrition forced Ukrainian forces into a gradual withdrawal from some positions and Russia was able to occupy all of Luhansk oblast. From early September to mid November 2022, Ukrainian forces launched two counter-offensives that took back Kherson and considerable territory to the east of Kharkiv. From mid October, Russia had begun missile and drone attacks on Ukrainian infrastructure. It also announced a partial mobilisation on 21 September as well as launching offensive operations in a limited number of places, in particular around the town of Bakhmut on the eastern Donbas front. Utilising heavy firepower and frontal assaults, the Russian offensive slowly made some gains, finally seizing most of Bakhmut in May 2023. In parallel, the Russians created extensive defensive positions in depth along the whole front. At the beginning of June 2023, Ukraine launched a major counter-offensive in the east and south. Thanks to the nature of the Russian defensive systems and weaknesses in Ukrainian planning and execution, this offensive made only limited gains and ended six months later. Since then, and with the exception of a limited Ukrainian offensive into Russia's Kursk oblast in September 20024, the conflict has become an attritional struggle marked by incremental, but persistent, Russian gains, achieved at very high cost.

phones has enabled friendly local populations to provide important HUMINT (human intelligence) on tactical deployments, movements and battle damage assessments. Related to this, SOCMINT (social media intelligence), which involves gathering and analysing enemy social media footage, has also become an important phenomenon in the war.[37] Something else that we have seen during the conflict is the growing importance of open-source intelligence (OSINT): third-party analysis of available satellite, video and social media information made available globally through the Internet.[38]

The war has demonstrated that the relationship between range, precision and transparency has been intensified by the sorts of systems integration that lies at the heart of net-centric perspectives. Chapters 12 and 20 discuss more fully the space and cyber domains, but the Russo-Ukrainian conflict has demonstrated the clear

Figure 6.3 Recce troops from 1 Royal Welsh deploy their ARES aerial reconnaissance drone. Autonomous aerial vehicles are now an often essential component of modern combined arms warfare.

advantages in land warfare that can come from integrating the traditional arms and domains more fully with drones, cyber, space and EW (see Figure 6.3). For example, in Ukraine, EW capabilities conduct three critical tasks: intelligence gathering, in terms of identifying enemy forces; protection of friendly forces; and electronic attack. EW evidently is not only a supporting tool – it may actually drive military planning.[39] Being able to disrupt the connections between units, drones, radar, air defence, data communications, GPS and the Internet has often had major battlefield effects. The evidence from the Russo-Ukraine war is that modern militaries need to invest heavily in EW capabilities, and to have those capabilities available even down to lowest tactical levels.

In terms of this broader integrative dynamic, US Army assessments have noted that Ukrainian cross-domain manoeuvre has been only 'episodic', but that the advantages generated by closer integration of the domains at lower levels of organisation would indicate that a fully modernised force, optimised for multi-domain activities, could create a difficult range of dilemmas for an adversary by broadening the range of options available to friendly forces, increase situational awareness and reduce decision-making times. For example, the impact of precision fires is increased notably by integrating the targeting information from satellites, drones and geolocation.[40] Better integration between precision fires and intelligence has often led to much shorter 'kill chains' and increased pressures on the enemy in terms of their ability to effectively relate time, manoeuvre, and decision-making. Indeed, as Chapter 12 explores in more detail, UAVs have had a pervasive influence on the land campaign. Drones are, as one commentator notes, 'providing unprecedented visibility and sharpening the accuracy of normally inexact artillery fire'.[41]

To survive in this environment has generated additional imperatives to disperse forces and to use mobility to 'shoot and scoot'. As one assessment of the lessons of the war has argued, 'Survival on the battlefield is a function of dispersion, manoeuvrability and acting quickly enough to disrupt the enemy's kill chain.'[42] If forces cannot remain mobile, then the lesson from Ukraine is that they need to have the capability, both in skills and equipment, to provide themselves with hardened cover. Overhead protection, and measures to defeat thermal imaging are important. Only the most hardened targets are proof against many of the precision munitions in use, and those positions that are not hardened, such as open trenches, have proven to be vulnerable even to small drones.

Nevertheless, the war in Ukraine also exhibits many important continuities with past features of land warfare.[43]

One obvious lesson from Ukraine is that land warfare still matters. This is a necessary corrective to some previous views on future war that have been increasingly enthusiastic about the likely role of the new domains. As the then British Prime Minister Boris Johnson commented in 2021, 'Nobody uses tanks anymore, the next wars are going to be all to do with cyber, hybrid warfare, space.'[44] Cyber, hybrid warfare and space matter, of course, but the challenge of defence planning for the future is that they cannot be traded off reliably against conventional capabilities. All domains are relevant in war, '[b]ut the war in Ukraine revolves essentially around capturing, defending and recapturing territory'. Armies play the leading role.[45]

A second observation is that the attributes of the land environment explored in Chapter 1 continue to exert a powerful influence on the conduct of land operations. From the evident vulnerabilities of forces attacking over open ground, through to the importance of trenches and fortifications to mitigate firepower or the impact of wind and rain on the ability to fly drones, the character of land warfare continues to be shaped by factors such as the variety and mutability of terrain. In this regard, as one commentator has noted, 'today's war isn't so very different from the past'.[46]

Another continuity is the continued relevance of older technologies alongside the new. Much of the immediate fire support is provided by older unguided mass fire mortar and artillery tubes. In Ukraine 'simple artillery has been the most prevalent – and necessary – weapon on the battlefield'. [47] Indirect fire from artillery and rockets have been responsible for 70–90% of the casualties inflicted.[48] Large numbers of older Cold War model tanks have been brought out of reserve and deployed on the battlefield. Even weapons from the Second World War have proved useful. Ukrainian troops using an old maxim machine gun with iron wheels commented that, 'It only works when there is a massive attack going on . . . [but] then it really works. So we use it every week.'[49]

A particular point of continuity, given the issues explored in the previous chapter, is that the Russo–Ukraine war shows the continued importance of modern system

Figure 6.4 Abrams and Leopard II tanks, during a live-fire exercise in Poland, 2023. In the context of debates about their obsolescence, the war in Ukraine has demonstrated that a tank's combination of protection, mobility and firepower gives it a continued role in modern conventional warfare. But tactical adaptation has been evident. In Ukraine, tanks are often used at range in a mobile fire-support role. Source: Courtesy of the US Army; photo by Army National Guard Staff Sergeant Matthew A. Foster

warfare. Tactically, combined arms warfare employing infantry, artillery, tanks and other supporting elements in a tightly coordinated manner has been critical in taking and holding ground.[50] Used on their own, tanks have proved to be very vulnerable to anti-tank guided weapons and drones; as part of a combined arms teams, on the other hand, tanks have demonstrated their continued significance in both defensive and offensive operations. As a Ukrainian commentator has noted: 'All speculations on the end of the tank era have been somewhat premature. Main battle tanks continue to serve their typical role: supporting the infantry, spearheading assaults, and exploiting breakthroughs with mechanized infantry following them'[51] (see Figure 6.4). However, their survivability on the modern battlefield continues to depend upon proper combined arms integration so that their vulnerability to such threats as drones and anti-tank weapons are mitigated by other arms and capabilities. Infantry have also demonstrated their continued status as the foundation of combined arms warfare.[52] Indeed, one of Russia's key early problems was a lack of infantry. At a higher level, operational art remains a vital contributor to success. Many of Russia's challenges have been linked to problems in their operational art, and the assumption that it was possible to take approaches that had worked at the brigade-level in Syria, and then just scale them up. Basic errors, such as the lack for the first portion of the operation of an overall commander, have been compounded by a command culture in which battlefield commanders often seem to be reluctant to pass unpalatable truths up the chain of command, leading to faulty situational awareness.[53]

Linked to this, and despite net-centric assumptions that the future character of warfare will feature rapid, decisive, lower-cost mobile operations by smaller, agile forces, the fighting in Ukraine in fact echoes the attritional, positional land warfare of the past, in which mass has been a pivotal issue. Thus far, much of the fighting has involved frontal assaults on entrenched enemy positions supported by the extravagant application of firepower. Casualties have been high, advances often very slow and materiel has been consumed at a prodigious rate. In the first twelve months of fighting, the US estimated that Russia and Ukraine had suffered 189,000–225,000 and 125,000–131,000 casualties, respectively. Over the same period, Russia had lost somewhere between half and two-thirds of its 3,000-strong operational tank force.[54] In the war, drones have had a life expectancy of six days, with an overall attrition rate of 90%. Nevertheless, while losses have been high, the lethality of Ukraine's battlefields is not higher than many of those in the past.[55] One lesson from this is the continued importance of mass in modern conventional warfare. Mass provides the basis for sustainable operations, and '[s]ustainability is a critical prerequisite for military success'.[56] Providing the manpower, equipment, supplies and munitions necessary to fight the war has been a constant struggle for both sides, even with significant external support. Another lesson is that, like experiences in World War One, processes of tactical and operational adaptation and innovation might be just as important as technology in defining the character of warfare.[57]

It is possible to argue, therefore, that the character of land warfare in Ukraine is the result of the interaction between continuity and change, shaped by local context. Indeed, the relevance of this local context brings us to the issue of ethnocentrism and future land warfare.

The Many Characters of Land Warfare

In thinking about the future of war, the problem of ethnocentrism is an expression of the ways in Western states generalise about the future character of land warfare on the basis of their own specific circumstances and beliefs. To put this another way, debates about '*the* changing character of land warfare' imply that there is only one future. In reality, if we look at how land warfare has been fought in the past, we can see that land warfare has had many different characters; why, then, should the future be any different?

That there might exist in parallel many different characters of land warfare is unsurprising. On the one hand, logically there should be an important imitative dynamic in the development of land warfare. War is a serious business. Failure can often be catastrophic for a state. There should therefore be every incentive for armies to imitate the structures, values and practices of other armies that have a demonstrated history of effectiveness. Even where states are not actually at war, examining the experiences of other states that *are* at war may provide important lessons. Over time, particular armies, through noted success in war, may acquire the status of 'paradigm armies' – armies that appear to embody so many of the standards of military effectiveness that they are widely copied. 'Modern war' is therefore 'Western war' because in the twentieth and twenty-first centuries the Western way of warfare, the key tactical and operational features of which have been outlined in the preceding discussion, appears to be uniquely effective, at least in terms of the prosecution of major conventional high-intensity land combat.

However, the processes that have shaped the way states develop and use military power on land (and in other environments, for that matter) are complex. The range of potential responses to military change is broad and can include mixtures of:

- **Imitation**, or the importation and recreation of values and ideas.
- **Innovation**, or the introduction of new techniques or ideas.
- **Adaptation**, or the contextualisation of imported values/ideas.
- **Resuscitation**, or the repair of existing institutions that have fallen into decay.
- **Stability**, or no change at all.

The last of these may be a perfectly rational option, given that the sources of military failure can lie with such factors as poor political choices or mistaken grand strategy: issues over which an army might have little or no control. What mix of these approaches that an army adopts as it develops is a matter of context, not least because this context will be fundamental to answering such basic questions as what 'effectiveness' means. This context may include a state's factor endowments (such as resources, demographics or geography), its political culture, civil military relations, the organisational culture of its armed forces, the desired goals of the government and the outlook of its people. This context, rather than strict military necessity, may play a decisive role in shaping how states fight land warfare. For example, the issue of whether or not a state has a professional or a conscript army may have an important bearing on how it conducts land warfare; yet the choice between the two may have as much to do with broader political and ideational objectives, such as nation-building, as with military-centred definitions of efficiency.

Same Paradigm, Different Responses

In examining the past we can see that, despite the development and diffusion during the First World War of many common military practices, the interwar period was marked by significant differences in approaches to land warfare even between Western states. There were many generic challenges to the 'modernisation' of armies during the period leading up to the Second World War. There was a strong anti-war bias in the politics of many countries during the period, which tended to marginalise the military; economic conditions were often unfavourable to heavy military investment and additional calls on those resources that were available were made by air forces. There was also the effect of peace; notwithstanding the Spanish Civil War (1936–1939), new concepts and new technology could not be extensively tested and validated. Institutional factors also shaped views on modern warfare; for example, the 'cavalry outlook' that had a strong representation in some armies tended to shape the view on the potential uses of mobile forces. Political ideologies, from the revanchism of Nazism to the modernist outlook of Marxism, were also relevant. The point is that these generic political, economic, historical and bureaucratic conditions influenced each country differently. The evidence demonstrates that, even where countries have close military interaction, there may still be significant differences in the way in which they organise and practise land warfare. Even during wartime, these differences may persist. During the Second World War, for example, Britain adopted consistently a more centralised and methodical approach to operations than Germany, with a great emphasis on artillery support. This approach was conditioned by such specific factors as Britain's progressive shortages in manpower.[58]

Moreover, even where armies might plan to fight in a modern-system fashion, political necessity may force armies to fight in conditions that are unexpected and/or not conducive to the application of assumed norms of land warfare (see Figure 6.5). As Lord Kitchener commented, 'We make war as we must, not as we would like.' There is often a tendency for armies to focus on the needs of symmetrical, high-intensity war, because these wars pose the greatest risk to the state and because this task may reinforce accepted norms of military professionalism. As the costs of such wars have grown (and bearing in mind the potential, in some cases, for nuclear escalation), the probability of their occurrence has diminished. After 1945, the number of interstate conflicts declined and the number of intrastate conflicts increased. The need to adapt techniques to meet what, from a Western military point of view, might be regarded as 'peripheral' tasks is complicated by the inherently asymmetric nature of warfare: opponents will tend to adapt their techniques to mitigate their own weaknesses and exploit their strengths. Martin van Creveld notes, for example, that an inverse relationship often seems to exist between the modernity of an army (defined in terms of technology and organisation) and its effectiveness at unconventional operations.[59]

In the Indo-China War (1946–1954), Viet Minh strengths in irregular jungle warfare led the French to adopt elements of static, positional attrition warfare. Used most famously at Dien Bien Phu in 1954, the concept of the *base aéroterrestre*, establishing air-supplied fortified camps on Viet Minh supply routes, was adopted because it was believed, erroneously as it transpired, that French firepower would ensure that the attrition would be inflicted disproportionately on their opponent. During the Korean War of 1950–1953, troop shortages, difficult terrain and enemy tactics forced the UN to drop defence in depth in favour of a thin line of discontinuous strong points on high ground, supported by air power and often huge quantities of artillery fire.

Similarly, the doctrinal focus of the Russian Army in the 1990s was conventional warfare, rooted in the Soviet thinking of the Cold War. Even in 2000, the focus of doctrine was still on high-technology war against external threats. Yet the major combat experience of the Russian Army consisted of urban operations in Grozny in 1994–1995 and 1999–2000 as part of the war in Chechnya. Even if we were to

Figure 6.5 Adaptation in war: British troops are seen here landing on the beaches of Normandy, France on the 6 June 1944. Joint land–sea training had languished during the interwar period. Circumstances dictated that these skills and capabilities would have to be regenerated if the Allies hoped to open up a second front against Germany.

assume, then, that many armies make similar general assumptions about the way to conduct land warfare, we can conclude that there are still likely to be important differences in how operations are conducted, not least because political necessity and adaptive enemies may force armies to fight according to unfamiliar rules.

Multiple Paradigms

A variety in the forms of land warfare is also likely because land warfare, like all warfare, cannot be divorced from its wider context. The modern system is difficult to implement because it carries with it a variety of political, social and economic trade-offs. Effective combined-arms and joint capabilities are expensive and may be beyond the abilities of states to procure. Devolved command and control may be at odds with more authoritarian political systems. This means that states may have modern equipment but not conduct 'modern' warfare, at least by the definition of contemporary Western militaries. This contingent effect of varying context has been extended by some writers into the realms of culture. For example, Victor Davis

Hanson has argued that the 'Western way of war' has demonstrable superiority and that, at its heart, this superiority stems from Western culture. Features of this culture, such as individualism, consensual government and civic militarism, provide the foundation for specific military advantages like organisation, discipline, morale, initiative and flexibility. Williamson Murray has also identified a 'Western way of war' built on 'finance, technology, eclecticism, and discipline'.[60] However, cultural explanations for military behaviour remain controversial, not least because of the difficulty of defining culture and identifying exactly how it shapes actions.

It is not difficult to find evidence of the way that local context has shaped the ability of states to fight land warfare. One example would be the Iran–Iraq War of 1980–1988, in which the character of the fighting was reminiscent of the middle element of the First World War, with a focus on artillery and infantry assaults in the context of static, attritional warfare. Both sides laboured under great difficulties. Command, control and intelligence were a recurring challenge. In part, this stemmed from difficulties at the grand strategic level that cascaded downwards. In Iran, military operations were subject to interference from the mullahs, and serious divisions existed between the army proper and the *Pasdaran*, or Revolutionary Guards. In Iraq, a climate of fear and a focus by Saddam Hussein on loyalty rather than competence stifled enterprise and initiative. There were also basic technical, doctrinal and organisational problems: major failings in intelligence gathering, a lack of effective and secure communications and rigid and slow command chains. There was also a lack of training, leadership and organisation for combined-arms warfare. Reliance on conscripts and high attrition of combat-effective elements reduced the capacity of both sides to formulate, disseminate and implement demanding alternatives. Neither side had the logistic capacity to sustain large-scale mobile warfare; even small increases in logistic lines or relatively minor movements of forces often resulted in disorganisation and disruption.

However, we should resist the tendency to see local context and efficiency as automatic trade-offs. There is a political context. The purposes of armies vary. Some are not designed to fight major combat operations. For example, although Latin American armies have acquired much of the panoply of war for modern major combat operations, in the period we are examining they have been deployed predominantly on internal operations. In other states, considerations of military effectiveness may be traded off deliberately against domestic political priorities; in Saudi Arabia, for example, parallel military structures, consisting of an army and a national guard, have been created to help forestall coups. Jeremy Black argues that Western attempts to develop taxonomies of military change fail to understand the role played by social and political circumstances in shaping the development of armed forces. Many of the things that we regard as essential for military efficiency, such as a focus on professional officers, discipline and training, are culturally conditioned. Thus, Black comments that, 'Modernity, defined in a Western fashion and as a Westernising project, emerged in large part through military forces operating under Western systems of control and discipline.' As he goes on to argue, even where organisation and weapons might converge with

Western practices, this does not imply 'Convergence in terms of the cultural suppositions affecting war, especially understandings of victory, suffering and loss.'[61] Cultural perspectives argue that the legitimacy of a particular paradigm of land warfare cannot be defined solely in terms of military efficiency or organisational interests.

In that vein, the Yom Kippur/Ramadan War of 1973 might be construed as the victory of a Western-style army, the Israeli Defence Force (IDF), featuring a military system based on integration, trust and professionalism, over fundamentally less competent, Soviet-orientated Arab opposition. In actuality, the IDF had developed a style of land warfare that was somewhat at odds with Western norms of war, not least because the IDF placed an emphasis on offensive air and armour operations at the expense of true combined arms. This was the approach that had worked in previous Arab–Israeli wars. In fact, in the early part of the 1973 war, the IDF forces were often poorly handled, an Egyptian general noting that, 'Their sole tactic remains the cavalry charge.' The Syrian and Egyptian Armies certainly suffered from challenges relating to the poor performance of junior officers, problems with combined arms and a lack of flexibility. Many of these issues derived from a deeply embedded culture of conformity, deference and avoidance of shame that often resulted in passivity on the part of officers and a lack of initiative. Recognising these challenges, Egypt deliberately set out to compensate, its president, Anwar Sadat, noting, 'We will simply have to use our talents and our planning to compensate.' The improvement in the effectiveness of the Egyptian Army in 1973 came from methods that might be regarded as 'anti-modern' in terms of the conduct of contemporary land warfare: rigid planning; the exhaustive practising of a very limited number of missions; a focus on consolidation, not exploitation; and an emphasis on defence, not attack. From an Egyptian perspective, the 1973 war was far from being a defeat, and in the sense that Egypt achieved its political objectives it was indeed a successful use of military power.

Another example of the potent impact of differing contexts was the methods used by the Chinese PLA forces in Korea. The PLA response to encountering the conventional forces of the United Nations (UN) encompassed elements of adaptation and compensation. Adaptation stemmed from a basic lesson: large-scale modern land warfare could not be fought against UN forces without adequate logistics and firepower. The Korean War saw the evolution of the PLA from a light, guerrilla war-orientated army to a mirror in some ways of the US Army, with an emphasis on firepower, especially artillery, and on air power, professionalism and logistics. Where they could not adapt, the Chinese compensated tactically. The Chinese often advanced at night, using low ground to bypass strong points and infiltrate. This allowed the Chinese to attack from unexpected directions and to threaten the artillery positions to the rear that were so vital for the support of company positions. If assaults had to be made on positions, the Chinese rarely used crude human-wave tactics. Instead, they would use machine guns and mortars to suppress and pin down the defenders before assault groups crept forward searching for weak points.

In order to counter US air and artillery support, Chinese forces would try and 'hug' US positions.

The history of land warfare in the twentieth century was filled with examples that combine elements of continuity and important elements of variation. The war between Somalia and Ethiopia from 1977 to 1978 over the Ogaden involved tanks, armoured personnel carriers and heavy artillery, and featured the use of tank spearheads, combined arms and air-mobile operations. Yet it was also conditioned by the local context – such as the interaction between guerrilla and conventional warfare, between foreign advisors and indigenous forces and between regular forces and militias – into something very different from the Western European experience of war. Similarly, the 1987 war between Chad and Libya featured Chadian 'Toyota War', using light vehicles to inflict heavy losses on the heavier and less-mobile Libyans. The Indo-Pakistan War of 1971 has been characterised by Robert M. Citino as 'high-tempo manoeuvre warfare' but under South Asian conditions.[62] Victory was achieved very quickly by an Indian Army lacking a significant degree of mechanisation; and rapidity was achieved by capitalising on local advantages, such as support from the population in East Pakistan (who provided intelligence and logistic support), by the use of infiltration tactics and by exploiting the passivity of the Pakistan defences. In the Sino-Vietnam War of 1979, the Vietnamese engaged the Chinese with local and regional forces, manipulating the difficulties in terrain and the Chinese reliance on roads to launch infantry-based irregular attacks while main-force regular units were generally held in reserve.

Similarly, irregular adversaries can display complex adaptive behaviour depending upon local conditions. The 30,000 or so Islamic State (ISIS) militants in Syria and Iraq in 2014 were able to obtain equipment taken from retreating Iraqi forces, including Abrams tanks, armoured fighting vehicles and artillery. In its operations, IS demonstrated the complex fluidity of modern land warfare. In mid September 2014, with air strikes being launched against IS forces in Iraq but not Syria, IS was fighting two kinds of war: in Syria, free from the threat of air attack, the assault on Kobani in Kurdish Syria was launched using tanks, rockets and artillery. Simultaneously, in Iraq, IS adopted more traditional irregular methods to lessen the impact of enemy air power.

Conclusion

Currently, the dominant view on the changing character of land warfare is one of MDO. This perspective reflects net-centric assumptions that information, its collection, analysis and dissemination is the foundation for success in warfare not least because it delivers faster, more relevant decision making and targeting. Driven by conclusions reached regarding the impact of trends such as the accelerating pace of technological change, informationalisation, equalisation, hybridisation and the widening of the domains relevant to warfare, many modern armies have assumed that the future land warfare battlespace will be more transparent, lethal, dispersed, hyperactive and decentralised. MDO, which attempts to fuse together capabilities from all of the domains and levels of war, has been the response.

But whether this view really reflects the future character of land warfare is a matter of debate. For some critics, MDO is a poorly defined concept and difficult to implement effectively, especially given the adversarial nature of war. For others, the net-centric paradigm is an expression of clichéd thinking, especially in terms of the extent to which it privileges novelty and revolution over continuity and evolution. As the Russo-Ukraine war demonstrates, the character of future land warfare might be the product of the interaction between change and continuity, producing forms of land warfare that blend the familiar with the unfamiliar. Moreover, it might be that our assessment of the changing character of land warfare is essentially ethnocentric. The past seems to show that land warfare is a contingent activity powerfully shaped by context. Therefore, even if concepts of MDO come to fruition, they may reflect only one of many different characters of war; and MDO itself might manifest in different ways in different conflicts.

The political significance of land as an environment outlined in Chapter 4 is likely to continue to persist, and so land warfare is highly likely to remain important. But while the land environment will almost certainly remain crucial in wars of the future, it may be that predicting the future is less important than building into land forces the capacity for flexibility: the capacity to adapt to the actual conditions of land warfare faster than an adversary. Amongst other things, this requires creating within armies a culture of flexibility. As the historian Sir Michael Howard has noted, 'No matter how clearly one thinks, it is impossible to anticipate precisely the character of future conflict. The key is to be not so far off the mark that it becomes impossible to adjust once that character is revealed.'[63]

RESEARCH QUESTIONS

1. What are the main factors driving military change?
2. What is MDO? How does it differ from joint operations?
3. What might be the challenges in learning lessons relevant to future land warfare from the war in Ukraine?
4. To what extent can valid lessons for future land warfare be drawn from the Russo-Ukraine War?
5. What are the challenges associated with military imitation?
6. What factors have shaped China's approaches to military modernisation in the last fifteen years?
7. What are the characteristics of military flexibility? What are the issues associated with realising these characteristics?

FURTHER READING

Black, Jeremy, *War since 1945* (London: Reaktion, 2004). An antidote to Eurocentric, Cold War-focused analyses of warfare.

Farrell, Theo and Terry Terriff (eds.), *The Sources of Military Change: Culture, Politics, Technology* (Boulder, CO: Lynne Reiner, 2002). Using historical case studies, this book examines the manifold influences that shape how military organisations change.

Finkel, Meir, *On Flexibility: Recovery from Technological and Doctrinal Surprise on the Battlefield* (Redwood City, CA: Stanford University Press, 2011). Finkel provides a detailed analysis of the nature and importance of military flexibility in coping with unexpected threats.

Howard, Glen E. and Matthew Czejak (eds.), *Russia's Military Strategy and Doctrine* (Washington, DC: Jamestown Foundation, 2019). Examines Russia's military modernisation in terms of both geographic and thematic factors. Available online at the Jamestown Foundation, https://Jamestown.org.

Latiff, Michael H., *Future War: Preparing for the New Global Battlefield* (New York, NY: Vintage, 2018). Latiff explores the impact of technology on the battlefields of the future. He argues that developments such as autonomous systems, enhanced human beings, cyber capabilities and new forms of firepower will change the face of future warfare.

Pollack, Kenneth M., *Arabs at War: Military Effectiveness, 1948–1991* (Lincoln, NE: University of Nebraska Press, 2002). A fascinating case study of the challenges of absorbing Western norms in land warfare.

Saunders, Phillip C., Arthur S. Ding, Andrew Scobell, Andrew N. D. Yang and Joel Wuthnw (eds.), *Chairman Xi Remakes the PLA: Assessing Chinese Military Reforms* (Washington DC: National Defence University Press, 2019). This book provides a comprehensive assessment of China's programme of military reform. It covers not just the PLA combat forces, but also the strategic context and drivers of change, civil-military relations, jointery and logistics.

Sondhaus, Lawrence, *Strategic Culture and Ways of War* (London: Routledge, 2006). Explores cultural contexts and their impact on militaries.

Watling, Jack, *The Arms of the Future: Technology and Close Combat in the Twenty-First Century* (London: Bloomsbury, 2023). In addition to providing an excellent analysis of the technological aspects of future land warfare, Watling also makes a compelling case that how new technology is employed is at least as important as the technology itself in determining the character of the future battlefield.

Williamson, Murray, *The Past As Prologue: America and the Future of War* (Stanford, CA: Hoover Institution, 2017). This is an important critique of the technology and innovation-centric focus of much of the current analysis of future war.

ONLINE RESOURCES

For more on MDO see the web sites of the US Army's Training and Doctrine Command (https://armypubs.army.mil/ProductMaps/PubForm/Details.aspx?PUB_ID = 1022250) and US Army doctrine (https://usacac.army.mil/node/3048).

The lively debates on future war are reflected in contemporary US online military fora, including sites such as *War on the Rocks* (https://warontherocks.com/) and West Point's *Modern War Institute* (https://mwi.westpoint.edu/), which contain blogs, reports, and podcasts. It is also worth looking at US professional journals including *Parameters* (https://press.armywarcollege.edu/parameters/), *Army Times* (www.armytimes.com/news/), the *Marine Corps Gazette* https://mca-marines.org/magazines/marine-corps-gazette/ and *Military Review* (www.armyupress.army.mil/Military-Review/). Relevant material on future war, including topics such as AI, robotics and key trends can be found at a very wide range of think-tanks and policy organisations, including the Center for a New American Security (www.cnas.org/), RAND (www.rand.org/), Congressional Research Service (https://crsreports.congress.gov/), Chatham House (www.chathamhouse.org/topics/defence-and-security) and RUSI (https://rusi.org/).

NOTES

1 Jonathan Lindsay, *Information Technology and Military Power* (Ithaca, NY: Cornell University Press, 2020), p. 21.
2 Ibid., p. 13.
3 See Dima Adamsky, *The Culture of Military Innovation* (Stanford, CA: Stanford University Press, 2010).
4 Quoted in Eliot A. Cohen, 'The Mystique of U.S. Airpower', *Foreign Affairs*, **73**(1) (January/February 1994), 110.
5 David Alberts, John Garstka and Frederick Stein, *Network Centric Warfare: Developing and Leveraging Information Superiority* (U.S. Department of Defense, CCRP, 1999), p. 2.
6 Gregory Fontenot, E. J. Degen and Tommy Franks, *On Point: The United States Army in Operation Iraqi Freedom* (Annapolis, MD: Naval Institute Press 2005), pp. xiii–xiv and 11.
7 See Edmund J. Burke et al., *People's Liberation Army Operational Concepts* (RAND, 2020), www.rand.org/pubs/research_reports/RRA394-1.html.
8 Adrian R. Lewis, *The American Culture of War: A History of U.S. Military Force from World War II to Operation Enduring Freedom* (Abingdon: Routledge, 2007), 321–5.
9 Fontenot *et al.*, *On Point*, p. 408.
10 *Army Futures Command Concept for Maneuver in Multi-Domain Main Battle 2028*, AFC Pam 71-20-1 (Army Futures Command, 2020), p. 10.
11 See, for example, *The Operational Environment and the Changing Character of Warfare*, TRADOC Pam 525-92 (US Army Training and Doctrine Command, 2019), pp. 5–8; *Global Strategic Trends*, pp. 125–45; AFC Pam 525-2, *Future Operational Environment: Forging The Future in an Uncertain World, 2035–2050* (Army Futures Command, 2020) pp. 2–6.
12 *The US Army in Multi-Domain Operations 2028*, TRADOC Pam 525-3-1 (Training and Doctrine Command, 2018), p. i.
13 Natasha Karner, 'Israel accused of using AI to target thousands', *The Conversation*, 11 April 2024, https://rebrand.ly/7r8prs3..
14 See Mick Ryan, *War Transformed: The Future of Twenty-First Century Great Power Competition and Conflict* (Maryland, MD: Naval Institute Press, 2022).
15 Speech, Chief of the Defence Staff, September 2020, www.gov.uk/government/speeches/chief-of-the-defence-staff-general-sir-nick-carter-launches-the-integrated-operating-concept.
16 Albert Palazzo, 'Precision and the Consequences for the Modern Battlefield', *Small Wars Journal* (19 August 2016), https://rebrand.ly/b6dd99.
17 Jeffrey M. Reilly, 'Multi-Domain Operations: A Subtle But Significant Transition in Military Thought', *Air and Space Power Journal* (Spring 2016), https://rebrand.ly/jeffreyreillya461c7.
18 FM 3-0, *Operations* (Washington, DC: Headquarters Department of the Army, October 2022), pp. 1–2.

19 Quoted in Kimber Nettis, 'Multi-domain Operations: Bridging the Gap for Dominance' *16th Air Force*, 16 March 2020, https://rebrand.ly/c86909.
20 Quoted in Billy Mitchell, 'Air Force's Shift to Multi-domain Operations Depends on Networks, *Fedscoop*, 18 September 2019, https://fedscoop.com/multi-domain-operations-air-force-matt-donovan/.
21 Quoted in, 'Army's Multi-domain Unit a "Game-Changer" in Future War', *Defense Systems Information Analysis Center,* 9 April 2019, https://rebrand.ly/dc1172.
22 Dmitry Dima Adamsky, 'The Impact of the Russian Operations in Syria on Hezbollah Operational Art: A Hypothesis', *Studies in Conflict and Terrorism*, 43/5 (2020), 416.
23 See Elsa B. Kania, 'Artificial Intelligence in China's Revolution in Military Affairs', *Journal of Strategic Studies*, 44(4) (2021), 515–42.
24 Lindsay, *Information Technology*, p. 20.
25 FM 3-0, pp. 1–11.
26 'Multi-domain Operations: Enabling NATO to Out-pace and Out-think its Adversaries', NATO Strategic Warfare Development Command, 29 July 2022, https://rebrand.ly/9cbbf7.
27 Army Doctrine Publication, *Land Operations* (Headquarters Land Warfare Centre, 2022), p. 2-2.
28 Ian Bowers, *Understanding Multi-Domain Operations*, CHACR In-Depth Briefing, No. 77, July 2024, p. 2.
29 Joint Concept Note 1/20, *Multi-Domain Integration* (Ministry of Defence, 2020), p. 3.
30 See, for example, David Ellison and Tim Sweijs, 'Empty Promises: A Year Inside the World of Multi-domain Operations', *War on the Rocks*, 22 January 2024. https://rebrand.ly/17f561.
31 David Edgerton, *The Shock of the Old: Technology and Global History Since 1900* (London: Profile, 2019), p. xii.
32 Ibid., p. 35.
33 Frederik Mertens, Bjorn de Heer, Tim Sweijs, Paul van Hooft, and Frank Bekkers, 'Lessons from Land Warfare: One Year of War in Ukraine', *Hague Centre for Strategic Studies*, 20 February 2023, p. 3, https://hcss.nl/report/lessons-from-land-warfare-one-year-of-war-in-ukraine/.
34 See, for example, Katie Crombe and John A. Nagle, 'A Call to Action: Lessons from Ukraine for the Future Force', *Parameters*, 53(3) (Autumn 2023), 19–29.
35 Charles McEnany and Col Daniel S. Roper, 'The Russia–Ukraine War One Year In: Implications for the U.S. Army', *SPOTLIGHT*, 23(1) (March 2023), 8, www.ausa.org/publications/russia-ukraine-war-one-year-implications-us-army.
36 Dan Sabbagh, 'Traditional, Heavy Warfare has Returned to Europe with Ukraine Conflict', *The Guardian*, 6 March 2023, https://rebrand.ly/traditionalheavyf7693b.
37 Claire Press and Svitlana Libet, 'How Russia's 35-Mile Armoured Convoy Ended in Failure', *BBC News*, 22 February 2023, www.bbc.co.uk/news/world-europe-64664944.
38 'Open-Source Intelligence is Piercing the Fog of War in Ukraine', *The Economist*, 13 January 2023, https://rebrand.ly/grpad3t.
39 Mykhaylo Zabrodskyi, Jack Watling, Oleksandr V. Danylyuk and Nick Reynolds, 'Preliminary Lessons in Conventional Warfighting from Russia's Invasion of Ukraine: February–July 2022', *RUSI* (30 November 2022), 61, https://rebrand.ly/63bbdc.
40 McEnany and Roper, 'The Russia–Ukraine War', p. 9.
41 Isabelle Khurshudyan, Mary Ilyushina, and Kostiantyn Khudov, 'Russia and Ukraine are Fighting the First Full-Scale Drone War', *The Washington Post*, 2 December 2022, www.washingtonpost.com/world/2022/12/02/drones-russia-ukraine-air-war/.

42 McEnany and Roper, 'The Russia–Ukraine War', p. 14.
43 See, for example, William F. Owen, 'The False Lessons of Modern War: Why Ignorance Is Not Insight', *British Army Review*, Issue 185 (Autumn 2023), 24–7.
44 Rosie Laydon, 'UK must learn from Ukraine war and boost land warfare strength, Ellwood says', *Forces.Net*, 8 March 2023, https://tinyurl.com/3yc7p5y7.
45 Mertens et al., 'Lessons from Land Warfare'.
46 'Bakhmut: Russian Casualties Mount but Tactics Evolve', *BBC News*, 16 March 2023, www.bbc.co.uk/news/world-europe-64955537.
47 Sabbagh, 'Traditional, Heavy Warfare Has Returned'.
48 Mertens et al., 'Lessons from Land Warfare'.
49 'Bakhmut: Russian Casualties Mount but Tactics Evolve'.
50 Mertens *et al.*, 'Lessons from Land Warfare'.
51 Ilia Ponomarencko, 'How Many Tanks Does Russia Really Have?', The Kyiv Independent, *War Diary of the Ukrainian Resistance* (Cheltenham, Flint: 2023), 263.
52 Alex Horton and Serhiy Morggunov, 'In Eastern Ukraine, Small Assault Teams Quietly Advance against Russia', *The Washington Post*, 12 October 2023.
53 Isabelle Khurshudyan, Paul Sonne, Serhiy Morgunov and Kamila Hrabchuk, 'Inside the Ukrainian Counteroffensive That Shocked Putin and Reshaped the War', *The Washington Post*, 29 December 2022, https://tinyurl.com/38y324nz.
54 Brad Lendon, 'Russia May Have Lost up to Half of Its Operational Tank Fleet in Ukraine, Monitoring Group Says', *CNN*, 9 February 2023, https://tinyurl.com/346hwjy5.
55 Stephen Biddle, 'Back in the Trenches: Why New Technology Hasn't Revolutionized the War in Ukraine', *Foreign Affairs*, September–October 2023, https://tinyurl.com/5dntexnh.
56 Mertens *et al.*, 'Lessons from Land Warfare'.
57 See, for example, Jack Watling and Nick Reynolds, 'Stormbreak: Fighting Through Russian Defences in Ukraine's 2023 Offensive', *RUSI* (2 September 2023), https://tinyurl.com/mwabzbb8.
58 See Stephen Ashley Hart, *Colossal Cracks: Montgomery's Twenty-First Army Group in North-west Europe, 1944–1945* (Mechanicsville, PA: Stackpole, 2007).
59 Martin van Creveld, 'Technology and War II: Postmodern War?', in Charles Townshend (ed.), *The Oxford Illustrated History of Modern War* (Oxford: Oxford University Press, 1997), pp. 311–12.
60 Victor Davis Hanson, *Why the West Has Won* (New York, NY: Faber and Faber, 2002); Williamson Murray, 'The Future of Western Warfare', in Geoffrey Parker (ed.), *The Cambridge History of Warfare* (Cambridge, UK: Cambridge University Press, 2005), p. 417.
61 Jeremy Black, 'Military Organisations and Military Change in Historical Perspective', *The Journal of Military History*, 62(4) (October 1998), 886.
62 Robert M. Citino, *Blitzkrieg to Desert Storm: The Evolution of Operational Warfare* (Lawrence, KS: University of Kansas, 2004), pp. 209–11.
63 Quoted in *Strategic Trends Programme: Future Character of Conflict* (Shrivenham Development, Concepts and Doctrine Centre, February 2010), p. 1.

PART III
Naval Warfare

IAN SPELLER

7 Concepts of Naval Warfare

CHAPTER OUTLINE

KEY THEMES

- Navies tend to have distinctive attributes that result from the unique nature of the maritime operating environment.
- The nature of this environment means that many of the concepts and theories pertaining to military operations on land or in the air do not apply at sea or apply differently. To understand naval warfare, therefore, one must engage with a distinct body of thought known as **maritime strategy**.
- Many of the key ideas about maritime strategy today have their roots in ideas first articulated in their current form over a century ago.

- Despite the many changes that have occurred over the years, these ideas continue to inform thinking about maritime strategy and thus, by extension, about naval warfare today.
- It is important to consider whether these ideas remain relevant today, particularly given the challenge and opportunities presented to navies by the development of new technology.

Introduction

This chapter examines concepts and theories associated with naval warfare. It begins with a discussion of the nature of the maritime operating environment, and the notion that navies have particular attributes that they derive from this. It then introduces traditional theories of maritime strategy, focusing first on the dominant 'Anglo-American' tradition before examining some alternative approaches. The discussion here sets the context for the examination of the conduct of naval warfare over the past century in Chapter 8 and the analysis of current practice and future possibilities in Chapter 9.

The particular characteristics of the sea and of naval forces, discussed later, have led to the development of a series of concepts and principles peculiar to naval warfare. In order to understand naval warfare and, in particular, to understand the thought processes that lie behind much modern naval activity, it is necessary to be conversant with distinctly naval concepts and principles. This, in turn, requires familiarity with the work of the traditional maritime strategists who first articulated and popularised such concepts. The impact of the most notable of these, Alfred Thayer Mahan, was reflected in the 1940s by the former US secretary of war, Henry Stimson, when he complained that the Navy department frequently 'Seemed to retire from the realm of logic into a dim religious world in which Neptune was God, Mahan his prophet and the United States Navy the only true Church.'[1] While this may not now be a fair reflection of Mahan's impact on the US Navy (USN), it is true to say that the concepts that he and others advanced have continued to influence naval thought and practice through to the present day.

It could be suggested that a conceptual approach derived primarily from an analysis of naval warfare during the age of sail, as was that of Mahan and many of his contemporaries, might find itself increasingly challenged given the dramatic changes in ship design and armament and in the tactical conduct of naval operations that have occurred since the nineteenth century. The contention of these chapters is that, while change is a recurring feature at the tactical level of naval warfare, at the strategic and operational levels the established concepts retain much utility. A key reason for this is that the concepts of maritime strategy and power are derived from the nature of the maritime environment and the possibilities associated with the capacity to exploit this environment. Technology may change, and this has an important impact on tactics, but the nature of the environment itself is enduring.

The Maritime Operating Environment

The maritime environment or domain (the term employed in US doctrine) includes the oceans, seas, bays, estuaries and coastal areas in which navies operate. Today it must include the airspace above them and also encompass activity within space, cyberspace and across the electromagnetic spectrum. It is important to remember that the maritime domain is not limited to the sea but also includes that portion of the land that can be used to have a direct bearing on activity at sea and that may be subject directly to influence from the sea. This is commonly known as the '**littoral** region'. As humans live on land and not generally at sea it is inevitable that much naval activity will focus on this region, where land and sea meet. Notwithstanding this important point, it would be fair to say that it is the nature of the maritime domain beyond the low water mark (i.e., out at sea) that gives navies their particular characteristics and that distinguishes naval warfare from its counterparts on land.

The most obvious feature of the sea is its size, covering around 70 per cent of the planet. The size of the oceans, and the ability of ships to traverse them, means that battles and campaigns can occur across hundreds and even thousands of miles. Distance works differently at sea than on land. For example, the Battle of Trafalgar in 1805 was preceded by a British pursuit of the French that took Nelson from the Mediterranean, across the Atlantic to the Caribbean and back again before he finally met and defeated Admiral Villeneuve off Cadiz. The main American base at Pearl Harbor in Hawaii was around 4,000 miles from Japan, but this distance offered no protection against a surprise attack launched by the Imperial Japanese Navy in December 1941. In the 1982 Falklands/Malvinas campaign, the British Royal Navy successfully conducted an unexpected campaign over 8,000 miles from home and 3,500 miles from the nearest friendly airfield. In comparison, note that Moscow was less than 700 miles from German forces when they began Operation Barbarossa in 1941, a distance that proved too far even for the all-conquering Wehrmacht. The requirement for admirals to 'think big', to consider manoeuvres across hundreds or thousands of miles, has led to the suggestion that they tend to be at home at the strategic level.[2]

Equally important is that fact that most of this area is connected. Furthermore, and in stark contrast to the land and the airspace above land (which are criss-crossed by innumerable physical and political barriers), the sea provides a medium that is freely available to all in peacetime and one that is difficult to deny to a superior navy in war. Distant lands that are bounded by the sea are thus connected by what Alfred Mahan famously called a '. . . great highway . . . a wide common over which men may pass in all directions'.[3] This has important implications for military operations. It offers navies the capacity for manoeuvre on a global scale while simultaneously acting as a barrier to those unable to use the sea. It is also critical for economic activity as the connectivity of the sea, allied to the unrivalled bulk transport capacity of ships, ensures that over 80 per cent of global trade travels by sea.[4] The need to protect maritime trade adds an important economic dimension to naval activity.

In addition to being vast, the seas are also inhospitable. One cannot live on them or travel across them without recourse to special platforms designed for this purpose. Naval warfare, therefore, tends to be about the use and the denial of the use of such platforms. These platforms tend to be expensive, meaning that there are relatively few of them, and they are usually hard to replace without delay. Sadly, they can sometimes be destroyed rather quickly and not always by enemy action. Even today it is true that sailors must first fight and survive the environment before they can engage any human opponent. The inhospitable nature of the seas also means that there is no indigenous population. There is no-one to remark on the passing of warships or to object to their presence. Equally, there is no resident population to defend, and very little fixed agriculture or industry. The consequences of declining battle at sea are thus much less serious than on land, making it easier for an inferior maritime force to avoid a superior opponent. Usually the enemy cannot occupy the deserted battlefield in any meaningful way. This means that naval warfare focuses on the use and the denial of use of the sea rather than the physical control of a medium that can be neither occupied nor fortified.

Geography and topography can be important in naval warfare. The presence or otherwise of shore bases can enable or constrain operations. Narrow straits may create 'choke points' that can inhibit operations and ships and submarines cannot travel across land. The particular features of a coastline may offer advantages to one side or another, and the presence of off-shore islands, shoals and reefs can have a notable impact on operations. Nevertheless, in comparison to the land, the sea is essentially featureless. There are fewer natural barriers to observation and there is usually no terrain that can be exploited to the advantage of the defence. A weaker navy has less ability to mitigate qualitative or quantitative inferiority than does its equivalent on land.

Attributes of Naval Forces

It is often claimed that naval forces have distinctive characteristics or attributes that are derived from the forces themselves and from the medium in which they operate. Different navies have expressed this in slightly different ways, see Box 7.1.

What all of these approaches have in common is the notion that the nature of the maritime environment gives navies an opportunity for sustained manoeuvre that they can exploit because of the flexibility and versatility possessed by most warships. This can provide useful options in wartime where the sea can become a key manoeuvre space, a medium for global connectivity or an impenetrable barrier. It also has important consequences in situations short of all-out war. It means that ships can be deployed overseas without having to cross any territorial boundaries. They can be poised in international waters without infringing on any state's sovereignty and without the need to negotiate basing rights. While at sea they are far less visible than their land-based equivalents, both in a literal and a figurative sense. This means that the deployment of naval forces can be less provocative than that of air forces or

BOX 7.1 ATTRIBUTES/CHARACTERISTICS OF MARITIME POWER/NAVAL FORCES[5]

Indian Navy 'attributes of maritime forces':

Access, Mobility, Sustenance, Reach, Flexibility, Versatility, Resilience, Composite Force Packages, Ability to influence events ashore, Maintenance/Refit/Life Cycle.

Royal Netherlands Navy 'characteristics of maritime operations':

Mobility, Access, Influence, Sustained Reach, Versatility.

Royal Australian Navy 'characteristics and attributes of sea power':

Mobility in Mass, Readiness, Access, Flexibility, Adaptability, Sustained Reach, Poise and Persistence, Resilience, Transience, Indirectness, Speed.

UK Royal Navy 'attributes of maritime power':

Access, Poise, Mobility, Persistence, Versatility.

USN 'attributes of naval forces':

Lethal, Mobile, Expeditionary, Agile, Scalable, Sustainable, Versatile.

armies. The routine deployment of individual ships, task groups or even entire fleets into particular regions is generally less likely to excite adverse comment than the deployment of a **squadron** of land-based aircraft or of ground forces, both of which require a footprint ashore that can become the focus for political dissent. Unsurprisingly, there is a considerable body of literature devoted to the analysis of **naval diplomacy**, examining the way in which navies can exploit these attributes in situations of armed peace or limited war. This was addressed in a number of classic works written by the British diplomat James Cable, has continued to be examined by a number of twenty-first century commentators and is reflected in the published doctrine of numerous contemporary navies.[6]

Maritime Strategy

The ability to take advantage of these attributes or capabilities does not come automatically with proximity to the sea. It depends upon a capacity to exploit the maritime environment. Naturally, much of the literature relating to naval warfare is focused on the ways and means of doing this. There is a rich history of such literature dating back to classical times and from many different countries (see Figure 7.1). However, it would be fair to say that the foundations of modern maritime strategy were laid in the last decades of the nineteenth century and the first of the twentieth, with pioneering work undertaken by a number of

Figure 7.1 The Royal Netherlands Navy frigate HNLMS *De Ruyter* and Royal Navy Daring-class destroyer HMS *Dragon* transit the Atlantic Ocean with ships assigned to US Carrier Strike Group 10 in 2019. Modern ships such as these differ greatly from those of previous generations but, it is claimed, the key concepts of naval warfare and maritime strategy are enduring. Source: www.navy.mil/Resources/Photo-Gallery/igphoto/2002362415/

BOX 7.2 ALFRED THAYER MAHAN, 1840–1914

Born in 1840 at West Point, the son of a professor of civil and military engineering at the US Military Academy, Mahan was to become one of the most prolific and influential writers on maritime strategy. In 1856 he joined the US Naval Academy at Annapolis and remained a naval officer until 1896 when he retired with the rank of captain, later benefitting from a 1906 Act of Congress that promoted to rear admiral all surviving captains who had served in the navy in the US Civil War. Unusually for his time and profession he was not keen on service at sea and he is remembered not for his exploits as a commander but rather for a written output that amounted to twenty books and 137 articles before he succumbed to heart failure in December 1914.

Mahan sought to demonstrate the influence of 'sea power' upon history and to affirm that there were enduring principles of maritime strategy that remained valid despite changing technology. Such principles could be discovered through an examination of the past, which revealed them in 'successes and failures, the same from age to age'. Unfortunately his interpretation of the past often lacked the accuracy or detachment of an impartial historian. He wrote to promote the education and instruction of fellow naval officers and his focus on principles must be seen within this context.

The key point of Mahan's work was that maritime power had played a decisive role in the course of history and that strength at sea was key to a state's material prosperity and success in war. He believed that the past showed that maritime preponderance was key to prosperity and success as a great power, focusing in particular on the experience of the British from the seventeenth century. To Mahan, national prosperity, and through it the means to wage war, were dependent on sea-borne trade. Such trade required the protection of a navy. There was therefore a close and beneficial relationship between trade and naval strength. Maritime trade encouraged the development of a navy to protect it and also provided the raw materials (trained manpower, ship building and repair facilities, etc.) to support such a navy. A strong navy could lead to dominance at sea, at the expense of rival countries, which in turn encouraged more trade.[10]

commentators, the most significant and influential of whom were an American, Alfred Thayer Mahan, and a Briton, Sir Julian Corbett; see Boxes 7.2 and 7.3.

Mahan and Corbett were the most prominent writers on maritime strategy in their day and they remain the most influential but they were not the only ones. Many others contributed to what was a vibrant field of study, including Lieutenant-Captain Berezin (Russia), John and Philip Colomb (Britain), Stephen B. Luce (USA), Jurien de la Gravière (France), Stepan Makarov (Russia) and Curt von Maltzhan (Germany).[7] In Japan, Akiyama Saneyuki and Sató Tetsutaró laid the foundations for an approach that was deeply influenced by Mahan.[8] Thus, there

BOX 7.3 SIR JULIAN CORBETT, 1854–1922

Born in 1854 and trained as lawyer, Corbett lectured at the Royal Naval War College at Greenwich from 1900. Like Mahan, Corbett used an examination of the past to identify the important role that maritime power had played in British military and economic success. While recognising the strengths of maritime power, Corbett placed a greater emphasis than Mahan on its limitations. In contrast to Mahan, whose focus tended to be on activity at sea, Corbett emphasised the importance of joint operations involving the coordination of land and sea forces. His work also placed less emphasis on the need to seek battle, something that his critics described as 'sea heresies'. The British Admiralty explicitly disassociated itself from such ideas in their official history of the First World War at sea, inserting a disclaimer to the effect that they did not agree with the author (Corbett). Corbett remained unrepentant asking, in a post-war public lecture, 'What material advantage did Trafalgar give that Jutland did not give?'[11] It is a question that students of strategy today would do well to ponder. In retrospect it would be fair to say that he got more right than did his critics. His historical method was certainly more satisfactory than Mahan's and his conclusions are more nuanced. Nevertheless, he did get some things wrong; most obviously in standing against the introduction of convoys for trade defence during the First World War.

were a considerable number of individuals who wrote on maritime strategy and history and who may, despite their various differences, be said to have formed something of a **'blue water'** school of thought regarding the use of major navies. Focused on the advantages to be gained by securing, maintaining and exploiting **command of the sea**, and usually also emphasising concentration of the **battle fleet** in pursuit of a decisive engagement, they helped to establish the key concepts around which much subsequent debate has focused. Many of these concepts remain relevant today and are referenced in current doctrine and debate[9]; the key points are introduced later.

Command of the Sea

The sea itself cannot be commanded in the same way that the land can be. It is not an environment open to physical control. Command of the sea has therefore tended to be defined as the freedom to use the seas and to deny that use to an enemy. This is frequently portrayed as the most important task for navies in war. Philip Colomb, for example, argued that 'The primary aim of naval war is the command of the sea.'[12] Both Mahan and Corbett recognised the importance of this concept, although Mahan tended not to employ the phrase. Some commentators have portrayed command in absolute terms but most (including Mahan, Colomb and Corbett) recognised that the extent to which one could control activity at sea varied according to circumstance and that total command was unusual. Colomb, for example, wrote of levels that ranged from 'indifference' to 'disputed command' and then 'assured command'.[13] Corbett argued that disputed command was a normal state of affairs, at least in the early stages of any conflict, and that general command of the sea was not a necessary precursor to all operations. Indeed, he suggested that there might well be circumstances when general command of the sea was not the first and overriding priority and that a navy might first seek to exploit a local command to secure some military or political objective.

It is important to stress that, as both Mahan and Corbett identified, command of the sea means command of communications at sea. It does not imply physical control of the environment, as might be the case on land, but rather control of enemy activity. Unlike road and rail communications on land, lines at sea exist only in a notional sense. They can be neither attacked nor defended. To secure **sea lines of communication**, therefore, one does not protect an actual line (as none exists), one protects or attacks those things that attempt to use the lines of communication; usually those things are ships.

Decisive Battle

For Mahan the favoured means of achieving command of the sea was through a decisive battle in which the main enemy fleet was defeated or, better still, destroyed. Examples of such battles might be Trafalgar (1805), Navarino (1827), Tsushima (1905) or Leyte Gulf (1944), all of which, to a greater or lesser degree, removed the main threat posed by the enemy fleet. In truth, however, it is relatively rare for a single battle to be decisive. Often identified as the shining example of a decisive battle, Trafalgar was actually just one of a series of British victories over their French (in this case Franco-Spanish) opponents. Similarly, at Leyte Gulf the USN virtually extinguished the threat posed by the Japanese surface fleet, but this was only the last in a series of impressive American victories. Most frequently the decision is a result of a series of encounters.

It is important also to question the extent to which even a dramatic victory is decisive. A battle may have a significant impact on the war at sea without necessarily having an immediately decisive effect on events ashore. British victory at Trafalgar, for example, could not stop Napoleon from defeating their Austrian and Russian allies at Austerlitz six weeks later. That battle had more immediate significance for the balance of power in Europe than did Nelson's victory, even if British command of the sea (enabled by victories such as Trafalgar) did set the conditions that allowed for eventual French defeat. Of course, had the result of Trafalgar been reversed and the British defeated comprehensively then the impact may have been more decisive as it could have enabled a French invasion of Britain (although, in truth, the obstacles to this would still have remained significant). The point here is that a victory is decisive because of the things that it enables. A narrow success that can be exploited may be of more value than a spectacular rout that cannot. Equally, the potential fruits of victory must be weighed against the costs of any defeat.

BOX 7.4 THE USN AND 'DECISIVE BATTLE' TODAY

In April 2020, the USN issued an updated version of naval doctrine, incorporating numerous changes on the previous iteration, to reflect growing concerns about great power competition and the challenge posed by the emergence of the Chinese Navy as a major peer rival. The new document placed a strong emphasis on the overriding importance of the battle for **sea control**, claiming that 'The course of a war can hinge on the outcome of a single battle.'[14] This is a seductive notion that is reflected in maritime thought and naval practice down through the centuries. In reality, however, wars are rarely decided by any single event, no matter how dramatic, and naval battles can only really be understood if considered in the context of the wider war. Often control can be assured without battle, especially if an adversary can be deterred from engaging through fear of the likely result.

Offensive Action and the Concentration of Force

Mahan's belief in the central importance of gaining command of the sea led him to stress the need for offensive action and the value of concentrating force in pursuit of the defeat of the enemy. In his examination of the various wars between Britain and France he praised the British for recognising this and criticised the French for their failure to consistently focus on the enemy battle fleet; it was a point that many others were keen to emphasise. The German, Curt von Maltzhan, for example, argued that battle was the keystone to the whole system of naval warfare and stressed the importance of the offensive, describing a reluctance to take the offensive and to risk the loss of ships in battle as being a 'cankerworm of decay'.[15] According to this approach battle was at the heart of naval warfare; it proved a seductive concept for navies.

In practice, an imperative towards offensive action might not actually be helpful. The Imperial German Navy, in particular, has often been criticised for its stubborn belief in the centrality of battle and for failing to realise that their main rival, the British, did not need to win a battle in order to prevail. By closing off the exits from the North Sea and the English Channel, Britain could dominate the key maritime communications without seeking battle and without needing to institute a close **blockade**. German failure to recognise this, or to devise a suitable response once the policy became apparent during the First World War, was criticised (during the war and after) by Wolfgang Wegener; see Box 7.5.

Corbett offered a more balanced view on the role of battle and the utility of concentration. He understood the value of both but recognised that sometimes it might not be possible to force battle on an opponent and it also might not be necessary. In some situations it was possible to dominate key maritime communications without necessarily having to fight a battle, as was the case for Britain in 1914. In such circumstances it made no sense to fight on anything other than favourable terms.

BOX 7.5 WOLFGANG WEGENER, 1875–1956

Wolfgang Wegener served in the German Navy before, during and after the First World War, retiring in 1926 as a vice admiral. He criticised German policy during that war, arguing that deference to the German Army's ingrained concepts of land warfare had led the navy to prepare for battle without thinking enough about strategy and, in particular, about the importance of geography and maritime communications. To Wegener, the exploitation of maritime power required a combination of a suitable *fleet* and *position*. Bottled up in the Helgoland Bight, the Imperial German Navy had had the former but not the latter and it was therefore unable to engage the Royal Navy on anything like favourable terms. He favoured the seizure of Denmark (he later added Norway) as one means of improving the navy's strategic position. These ideas were criticised by another German, Herbert Rosinski, who argued that Wegener paid insufficient attention to the issue of material superiority without which victory was unlikely no matter where it occurred. It is ironic that in the Second World War, when Germany secured all the territory that Wegener wanted, and more, it had the position but lacked a fleet strong enough to truly exploit it.[16]

In any case, a weaker fleet was unlikely to accept battle against the concentrated might of its enemy. They would have to be forced to fight in order to protect something that mattered to them. This might imply some level of diversion to tempt them out or the conduct of raids or expeditions that, by threatening a vital interest, would require a response. In addition to this, assets would have to be diverted away from the battle fleet in order to undertake the myriad duties that the navy would have to attend to while it waited for the opportunity to deal with the main enemy force. Concentration could be more difficult in practice than it was in theory.

Fleet in Being

One of the main problems with a policy that revolves around seeking out and destroying the enemy in main battle is the fact that weaker opponents are usually loath to let this happen. It is easier for a navy to decline battle than it is for an army as at sea there are generally no fixed points to be protected, no population or territory to defend. A weaker navy might simply avoid battle or remain within a protected anchorage, maintaining their '**fleet in being**' on the assumption that its mere existence would constrain enemy choices and thus serve a useful strategic purpose even without achieving command of the sea.

Colomb illustrated this concept with reference to the actions of the English Admiral Torrington who, in 1690, faced a superior French fleet in the Channel. Torrington declined to engage it in battle, reasoning that the mere presence of his undefeated force would inhibit the French from conducting an invasion of England as they could not do so without running an intolerable risk. Unfortunately his strategy was not understood ashore and his hand was forced by his superiors who demanded an attack. Torrington had no choice but to comply and was defeated at the Battle of Beachy Head. French indecision and poor weather were all that remained to save England from invasion.

Colomb, who approved of Torrington's initial caution, tended to emphasise the impact that even a markedly inferior fleet in being could effect and, by extension, to stress the value in defeating such a force whenever the opportunity presented itself. Mahan disagreed, arguing that a bold French commander would not have been deterred by the mere existence of Torrington's fleet; his preferred solution remained the defeat of the enemy in battle and he stressed that war could not be fought without taking risks. Corbett's conclusion was that a fleet in being could dispute command of the sea by adopting a defensive attitude, and avoiding a decisive battle, if it actively sought every opportunity for a counter-strike.[17]

Blockade

Blockade was a common response to an adversary that maintained a fleet in being, with an enemy force confined to harbour or unable to sortie without the risk of encountering superior force. Close blockade involves the stationing of forces close inshore, able to intercept the movement of any ships in or out of harbour. While this approach has clear advantages it can be very difficult to sustain and, given the confluence of threats that exist within littoral waters, may be particularly difficult to employ today. Distant blockade, sometimes described as observation blockade or choke point control, does not attempt to stop the enemy from leaving harbour, rather it aims to deny them access to particular areas. As such, they do not require the main force to remain close inshore, although some capacity to observe enemy movements is obviously helpful. Distant blockades have the additional advantage that, in allowing an enemy to sortie, they may give the blockader the opportunity to intercept and to defeat their foe. Today, with the development of remote surveillance and stand-off weaponry, the distinction between the two types could be less obvious. It may be possible for a superior navy to create the effect of a close blockade while keeping most assets at some distance.

Sea Control and Sea Denial

Command of the sea is often portrayed in rather absolute terms. In their published maritime doctrine, the Royal Australian Navy, for example, suggests that 'Command of the sea implies that dominance has been achieved to such a degree that the risk to one's own forces from enemy action is negligible.'[18] Dominance such as this is not the norm historically, at least not in a conflict against a peer rival. There may be some circumstances when positive use of the sea can be achieved without meeting such exacting requirements. Command is usually limited in time, place, extent and consequence. Equally to the point, one cannot actually 'command' the sea in the same way that one can control land; it is not open to territorial conquest. As has been discussed, gaining command of the sea simply means gaining control of sea

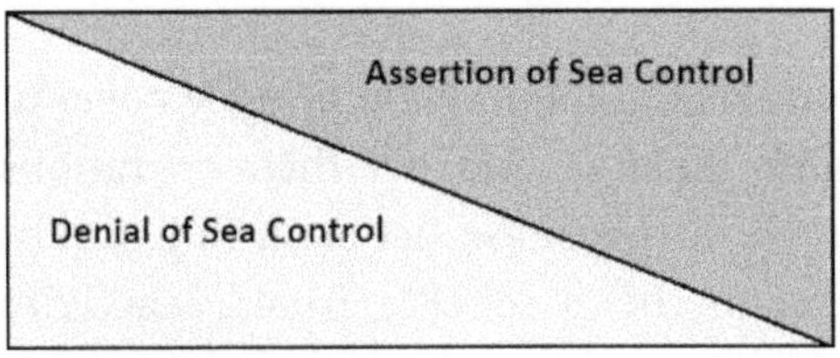

Figure 7.2 Sea control.

BOX 7.6 THE IMPORTANCE OF 'POTENTIAL CONTROL'

Writing in the 1960s, Admiral J. C. Wylie USN discussed the value of 'potential control', by which he meant the clear ability to secure control should the need arise. He believed that this could be a key enabler in both war and peace, so much the better if an adversary did not dare to challenge it.[21] A similar point has been made more recently by the US commentator Robert Rubel, who argues that today 'command of the sea' is best understood as a strength relationship between adversaries where the weaker navy dare not directly challenge the stronger. He uses the term to mean a strategic condition of maritime dominance, akin to Mahan's idea of naval mastery, different from the term 'sea control', which is more relevant at the tactical and operational level to denote control of a specific area.[22]

communications. Defeating an enemy fleet is not an end in itself but rather it is a means of dominating the use of those communications. This is reflected in the modern concept of sea control, which can be defined as the '. . . Condition that exists when one has freedom of action to use an area of sea for one's own purposes for a period of time and, if necessary, deny its use to an opponent.'[19] This concept, which owes much to Corbett's analysis, reflects a realistic understanding of the degree of control that can be achieved and of the role of sea control as an enabler and not an end in itself.

It may often be the case that a navy will not seek control in a particular area, but instead will focus on the more limited task of denying such control to an adversary. **Sea denial** tends to require a lower level of capability than does control and was described by US Admiral Stansfield Turner as being akin to 'guerrilla warfare at sea'. Navies will usually find themselves balancing the need to exert control or to achieve denial, with the emphasis on one or the other differing in time and place. Turner expressed this in the form of a diagram (see Figure 7.2), with navies sometimes emphasising activity to the right of the figure, and sometimes to the left. It is worth noting that the assertion of sea control will also deny control to an enemy (control cannot be shared), but denial of control does not imply that control passes to friendly forces (control can remain in dispute).[20]

Cover

An important function of sea control in one region might be to provide cover to weaker forces or detached units to enable them to conduct their operations unhindered by the main force of the enemy. In this sense the main function of a powerful naval force in one region might be to enable friendly activity hundreds or even thousands of miles away by providing the appropriate cover. In this way the British Grand Fleet at Scapa Flow, by neutralising its German counterpart, provided vital cover for all other Allied activities at sea during the First World War.

Exploiting Sea Control

As has been discussed, sea control is relevant only insofar as it enables other things. There are numerous ways in which it can be exploited to good effect. Both Mahan and Corbett laid great emphasis on the value of an economic blockade, founded on **control of the sea**. This would enable the superior navy to drive enemy trade from the seas, undermining their industry, impoverishing their finances and perhaps also leading to shortages of food and raw materials. At the same time control would provide a necessary foundation on which trade defence could be built. It supplied the necessary cover to allow light forces to protect friendly trade and to hunt down enemy raiders who, operating without control, might sometimes be a nuisance but, it was argued, would never be able to achieve the slow strangulation that was associated with a successful blockade.

Another way in which sea control could be exploited was through the direct projection of power ashore, either through shore bombardment or by landing troops. Corbett paid particular attention to such operations, regarding joint army–navy cooperation as being central to British success in a serious of wars. In 1911 in his most famous work, *Some Principles of Maritime Strategy*, he articulated this in the following way,

> Since men live upon the land and not upon the sea, great issues between nations at war have always been decided – except in the rarest cases – either by what your army can do against your enemy's territory and national life, or else by fear of what the fleet makes it possible for your army to do.[23]

That this now seems to be a statement of the obvious is a reflection both of the perspicacity of Corbett's work and the degree to which his ideas continue to influence modern naval thinking. Views such as this were discomforting for a naval audience in the 1900s whose preferred focus was on battle at sea.

A number of Corbett's contemporaries examined the conduct of **amphibious operations** in some detail (see Figure 7.3). Most notably amongst these was Sir Charles Callwell, an Anglo-Irish officer in the British Army who wrote two impressive studies on the importance of military operations to activity at sea and also on the value of maritime command to land campaigns. Unfortunately, these do not appear to have had much impact in their day. Too often navies succumbed to the

Figure 7.3 Four US Landing Ship Tanks unload men and equipment at Inchon during Operation Chromite in September 1950. The amphibious landings at Inchon helped to reverse the course of the Korean War, demonstrating the value of being able to project power from the sea. Source: https://tinyurl.com/2b5xf35u

tendency to concentrate primarily on operations at sea, and on fighting other navies, and paid scant attention to the challenges presented by the type of joint operations that Corbett and Callwell favoured.[24]

These concepts that have been outlined were derived largely from an examination that focused mainly on the challenges and opportunities facing major 'sea powers'. They have been described as representing an Anglo-American tradition in maritime strategy, although many that contributed to it were neither British nor American.[25] For many commentators this tradition was validated by experience in two World Wars. Thus, for example, after 1918 Herbert Richmond offered analyses that reflected Corbett while Mahan continued to influence many navies, including those of Japan and the USA. Post 1945, Bernard Brodie, Stephen Roskill, Stansfield Turner, Edward Wegener and James Wylie were amongst those who offered perspectives that broadly reflected traditional assumptions about maritime strategy and sea control, updated also to include an understanding of the impact of air power on the established concepts.[26] From the other side of the iron curtain the commander-in-chief of the Soviet Navy, Admiral Sergey Gorshkov, supported the dramatic expansion of his navy from the 1960s with an analysis that (once one strips out the communist rhetoric) was grounded in the same logic as that of Corbett.[27]

Alternative Approaches

It could be argued that the 'Anglo-American' tradition discussed above was not particularly well suited to countries that had an inferior navy or that were ill placed to exploit maritime power in the traditional way. In such situations it might make more sense to devote limited resources to denying the enemy the unfettered use of the sea rather than seeking to gain positive use for oneself. This is particularly true as sea denial can often be achieved with small and relatively unsophisticated forces that today might typically include mines, submarines, anti-ship missiles and land-based aircraft.

The French Jeune École

Even as Mahan was formulating his ideas, an alternative school of thought in France was articulating the utility of an asymmetric strategy of sea denial in any future war with Britain. Known as the 'Jeune École' (Young School), the influence of this group spread beyond France and it had an impact upon all of the major European navies in the 1880s and 1890s, raising important questions about the utility of traditional strategies based upon securing command of the sea with large, expensive **battleships.** The school advocated adopting an asymmetric response to British sea control. Abandoning any attempt to match the British battleship for battleship, it argued instead for relying on coastal defence and small, fast and inexpensive torpedo launches to deny the British the ability to institute a close blockade, releasing fast steam-driven **cruisers** into the Atlantic to prey on British trade in a ruthless 'guerre de course' designed to force Britain to sue for peace. The Jeune École had fallen from favour in France by the end of the century, not least because the strategy that it advocated was unlikely to offer any useful military options in a war against its most likely future opponent, Germany. In any case, the technological developments that made big ships vulnerable to small craft were soon matched by counter-measures that somewhat evened the balance, including the provision of more small craft to defend the battleships.[28]

The Jeune École may have been eclipsed but this did not necessarily invalidate its central argument. Within a few years a new form of technology, that of the submarine, offered a different means of achieving the same result. The unrestricted U-boat campaigns undertaken by Germany in both World Wars were grounded in the same logic as that expressed by the Jeune École (see Figure 7.4). Rather than attempting to gain positive use of the sea, the U-boat campaigns sought to exploit a particular technology in order to deny its use to Britain and its allies. Thus, a number of inter-war German commentators, including Hugo von Waldeyer Hartz and Kurt Assmann, emphasised economic warfare over the battle fleet, based on the

Figure 7.4 In 1919 two US officers inspect U-117, a German minelaying submarine surrendered to the Allies at the end of the war. The use of submarines to attack British merchant shipping presented an acute challenge to the dominant navy, but one that was eventually mastered. Source: https://tinyurl.com/2z9akd4m.

logic that Britain was dependent on maritime communications and could be forced onto the defensive, perhaps even defeated, by a weaker navy not so encumbered.[29] That the German submarine campaigns both failed does not necessarily mean that the idea was not well grounded. For a country able to devote only limited resources to maritime power, and facing an opponent reliant on using the sea, a strategy that focuses on sea denial rather than sea control may indeed make more sense.

The Soviet New School

An emphasis on local sea denial was also apparent in the coastal defence theories developed by the Soviet New School that emerged in the Soviet Union in the late 1920s and early 1930s. Reacting to the paucity of traditional maritime assets, and in light of the experience of maritime **power projection** being applied against the nascent Soviet state in 1919, this school of thought advocated an integrated system of minefields, coastal artillery, submarines and motor torpedo boats instead of a more traditional, balanced fleet. This approach was, however, abandoned by the Soviet Union in the 1930s when greater resources and increased ambition led the navy to emphasise a more traditional approach to maritime power that could extend beyond coastal waters.[30]

The Chinese Navy: Active Defence

Communist China went through a similar process, emphasising the value of 'mosquito fleets' of small defensive coastal craft in the 1950s before moving towards a more traditional interpretation of the role of the fleet once greater resources became available.[31] In the 1950s and 1960s, the People's Liberation Army Navy (PLAN) fought a number of engagements against Nationalist Chinese vessels, using their limited naval assets in support of land-based systems (artillery and aircraft) in local waters. The focus was on hit and run attacks to create local superiority, using superior numbers of smaller vessels to defeat larger and more powerful Nationalist ships. The approach reflected Maoist ideas of guerrilla warfare on land, and was articulated by the first commander of the PLAN, the general turned admiral Xiao Jinguang, as 'sabotage warfare at sea' using deception, surprise, unorthodox methods and an offensive spirit to achieve small incremental victories in local waters. The approach was formally codified as the concept of Active Defence in 1956 and remained in place until the more ambitious policy of 'Near Seas Defence' was introduced in the 1980s.[32]

Following a similar logic, some Western navies – including those of Denmark, Norway and Sweden – emphasised coastal defence during the Cold War, and invested in ideas and capabilities designed to challenge Russia access and control within their littorals. The emphasis tended to be on coastal artillery and missiles, shore-based aircraft, mines, submarines and small missile-armed surface combatants rather than more impressive assets designed to secure and exploit control.[33] The removal of the threat from the Soviet Union in the 1990s prompted a change in policy to focus on ways of making more positive use of the sea, through participation in multinational peacekeeping and humanitarian relief missions. However, the re-emergence of an apparent threat from the East has brought renewed interest in the defence of home waters and investment in the capabilities designed to support this.[34]

Raoul Castex (1878–1968)

While achieving, maintaining and exploiting sea control might represent the main aim for dominant maritime powers, and coastal defence and commerce raiding might be the favoured option of their weaker opponents, it is not immediately clear whether either approach is suitable for a major navy that is still inferior to its main rival. To address this problem it is helpful to refer to the work of a French naval officer, Raoul Castex. Castex was a prolific writer, publishing eighteen major works and over fifty journal articles. His major contribution was the enormous five-volume *Théories stratégiques* (Strategic Theories) published between 1929 and 1935.[35] He recognised the value of gaining what he called 'mastery of the sea', defined as control of sea communications. He also recognised the centrality of battle to its achievement. He was, however, very aware of the problem of achieving this with inferior forces. For those not yet in a favourable position of strength there was a range of things that one could do to improve the situation. At the heart of his theory was the concept of 'strategic manoeuvre'. Such manoeuvre implied exploiting the possibilities of activity such as attacks on commerce, naval raids, amphibious operations or blockades to force an opponent to divert resources. This also implied a diversion of friendly resources, something that Mahan warned against. However, Castex suggested that it was possible to use space and distance to concentrate more rapidly than an opponent, thereby using strategic manoeuvre as a vehicle for creating local superiority of numbers and thus the conditions under which battle might be successfully entertained. To Castex, the guerre de course, including submarine operations, could be a useful way of diverting enemy forces but it could not be decisive on its own. Rather, it had to be integrated into a system of operations whose eventual aim was to contest mastery of the sea. The main target remained the enemy fleet, and the chance of defeating a fleet with inferior numbers was 'almost nil' but one need not passively accept an inferior position.

Conclusion

This chapter has argued that navies tend to have distinctive attributes that result from the unique nature of the maritime operating environment. For this reason the theory and practice of naval warfare is different from its equivalents on land and in the air. The key concepts of maritime strategy, discussed in this chapter, were established over a hundred years ago and were often derived from an examination of the practice of naval warfare over the previous centuries. They are far from new but they continue to have an impact on thought and practice today. This is particularly true of Corbett, whose emphasis on joint operations provides a close fit with the priorities of many contemporary navies. On the other hand, one tends not to find overt positive references to the Jeune École or German U-boat theorists in public policy statements today; few organisations are willing to admit to be preparing to launch ruthless attacks on civilian ships. Of course, it would be foolish to assume that there could never again be a sustained guerre de course; a wise student of strategy soon learns to be wary of the word 'never'. It is certainly the case that many navies today are focused on sea denial at a local, a regional and (for some) a global level, and much debate today focuses on the challenge posed by A2/AD techniques and technologies (see Chapter 9). Given this, and the constant references within naval doctrine and both professional and academic commentary, it seems reasonable to suppose that the traditional concepts retain some currency. The next chapters will test this assumption with an examination of the evolution of naval warfare over the last century (Chapter 8) and of the nature of naval warfare in the twenty-first century (Chapter 9).

RESEARCH QUESTIONS

1. Are the traditional concepts of maritime strategy still relevant in the twenty-first century?
2. How does the nature of the maritime environment influence the characteristics and capabilities of naval forces?
3. Have political, military, economic and/or technological developments eroded the importance of the sea as a 'great highway' over the course of the last century?
4. Do the ideas of the Jeune École offer a useful guide to action for smaller navies today?
5. Is 'command of the sea' the primary aim of naval warfare?

FURTHER READING

Hattendorf, J. N. (ed.), *Mahan on Naval Strategy: A Selection of Essays by Alfred Thayer Mahan* (Annapolis, MD: Naval Institute Press, 1991). This book offers excerpts from Mahan's major works, providing a valuable summary of his ideas.

Holmes, James, *A Brief Guide to Maritime Strategy* (Annapolis, MD: Naval Institute Press, 2019). Holmes provides an introduction to maritime strategy, with a particular emphasis on the continued utility of Mahan's key ideas.

Lambert, Andrew, *The British Way in Warfare: Julian Corbett and the Battle for a National Strategy* (New Haven, CT: Yale University Press, 2021). This book provides a detailed insight into Corbett's ideas, appropriately set within the context in which he wrote.

McCranie, Kevin, *Mahan, Corbett and the Foundations of Naval Strategic Thought* (Annapolis, MD: Naval Institute Press, 2021). An excellent introduction to the work of both Mahan and Corbett, made relevant to modern concerns.

Roksund, Erne, *The Jeune École* (Leiden: Brill, 2007). Roksund provides a detailed and authoritative examination of the ideas developed by the Jeune École.

Speller, Ian, *Understanding Naval Warfare*, 3rd ed. (London: Routledge, 2024). This book addresses traditional concepts of naval warfare and also analyses contemporary practice. It examines the issues raised in this chapter in greater depth and detail.

Sumida, Jon, *Inventing Grand Strategy and Teaching Command. The Classic Works of Alfred Thayer Mahan Reconsidered* (Baltimore, MD: Johns Hopkins University Press, 1997). Sumida provides a clear, accessible and authoritative introduction to Mahan's ideas.

Till, Geoffrey, *Seapower. A Guide for the Twenty-First Century*, 4th ed. (London: Routledge, 2018). Written by one of the most respected commentators on contemporary maritime strategy, this book provides a detailed and wide-ranging examination of the subject.

The US Naval Institute Press has published a series of short books that reproduce some of the lesser-known writings of a number of maritime strategists, including Mahan, Corbett and Gorshkov. With introductions and comments by leading academics, these are interesting and useful works.

It is, of course, always useful to refer to the original texts. Of these the following are of particular interest.

Callwell, Charles E., *Military Operations and Maritime Preponderance: Their Relations and Interdependence* (Annapolis, MD: Naval Institute Press, 1996) with an introduction and notes by Colin S. Gray.

Castex, Raoul, *Strategic Theories* (Annapolis, MD: Naval Institute Press, 1994) edited, abridged and translated by Eugenia C. Kiesling.

Colomb, Philip, *Naval Warfare. Its Ruling Principles and Practice Historically Treated* (Annapolis, MD: Naval Institute Press, 1990) with an introduction and notes by Barry M. Gough.

Corbett, Julian S., *Some Principles of Maritime Strategy* (Annapolis, MD: Naval Institute Press, 1988) with an introduction and notes by Eric J. Grove.

Wegener, Vice Admiral Wolfgang, *The Naval Strategy of the World War* (Annapolis, MD: Naval Institute Press, 1989) introduced, translated and edited by Holger Herwig.

ONLINE RESOURCES

Lambert, N.A, *The Neptune Factor. Alfred Thayer Mahan and the Concept of Sea Power* (Annapolis, MD: Naval Institute Press, 2024) Provides a compelling examination of Mahan's ideas, including reference to his lesser know works.

Original versions of Alfred Mahan's major works, including *The Influence of Seapower Upon History, 1660–1783* (1890) and *The Influence of Seapower Upon the French Revolution, 1793–1812* (1892), and many works of classic naval history and maritime strategy written by other authors (including Corbett and Colomb) are available free online at https://archive.org/ch_7_foot_12.

NOTES

1 Philip Crowl, 'Alfred Thayer Mahan: The Naval Historian', in Peter Paret (ed.), *Makers of Modern Strategy from Machiavelli to the Nuclear Age* (Princeton, NJ: Princeton University Press, 1986), p. 444.

2 Admiral Lord West of Spithead, 'Maritime Warfare and the Importance of Sea Control', in Julian Lindley-French and Yves Boyer (eds.), *The Oxford Handbook of War* (Oxford: Oxford University Press, 2014), p. 437

3 Alfred Thayer Mahan, *The Influence of Sea Power Upon History 1660–1783* (Boston, MA: Little Brown, 1890), p. 25

4 UNCTAD, *Review of Maritime Transport 2022* (New York, NY: United Nations Publications, 2022).

5 JDP 0-10. *British Maritime Doctrine*, 5th ed. (2017), pp. 2-1–2-6. *Australian Maritime Doctrine: RAN Doctrine 1* (2010), pp. 86–94. Indian Navy, *Naval Strategic Publication 1.1. Indian Maritime Doctrine* (2015), pp. 70–2. US Navy, *NDP1. Naval Doctrine* (2020),

p. 5–6. Ministry of Defence (Netherlands), *Fundamentals of Maritime Operations: Netherlands Maritime Military Doctrine* (2014), pp 91–2.

6 In particular see James Cable, *Gunboat Diplomacy 1919–1979: Political Applications of Limited Naval Force*, 3rd ed. (Basingstoke: Macmillan, 1999); Ken Booth, *Navies and Foreign Policy* (London: Croom Helm, 1977); and Edward Luttwak, *The Political Uses of Sea Power* (Baltimore, MD: Johns Hopkins University Press, 1975). For useful recent studies see Hervé Coutau-Bégarie, *Le Meilleur des ambassadeurs: Théorie et pratique de la diplomatie navale* (Paris: Économica, 2010); Christian Miere, *Maritime Diplomacy in the Twenty-First Century. Drivers and Challenges* (Abingdon: Routledge, 2014); and Kevin Rowlands, *Naval Diplomacy in the Twenty-First Century: A Model for the Post-Cold War Global Order* (London: Routledge, 2020).

7 Geoffrey Till, *Seapower. A Guide for the Twenty-First Century*, 4th ed. (London: Routledge, 2018), ch. 3.

8 Sadao Asado, *From Mahan to Pearl Harbor: The Imperial Japanese Navy and the United States* (Annapolis, MD: US Naval Institute Press, 2012), ch. 2.

9 For example, see Robert C. Rubel, 'Command of the Sea. Redux', in *US Naval War College Review*, **75**(2) (Spring 2022) and Hu Bo, *Chinese Maritime Power in the Twenty-First Century: Strategic Planning, Policy and Predictions* (London: Routledge, 2019).

10 See Jon Sumida, *Inventing Grand Strategy and Teaching Command: The Classic Works of Alfred Thayer Mahan Reconsidered* (Baltimore, MD: Johns Hopkins University Press, 1997).

11 N. A. M. Rodger, 'Naval Strategy in the Eighteenth and Nineteenth Centuries', in Geoffrey Till (ed.), *The Development of British Naval Thinking: Essays in Memory of Bryan Ranft* (London: Routledge, 2006), p. 31. Also see Andrew Lambert, *The British Way in Warfare: Julian Corbett and the Battle for a National Strategy* (New Haven, CT: Yale University Press, 2021).

12 Philip Colomb, *Naval Warfare: Its Ruling Principles and Practice Historically Treated* (Annapolis, MD: Naval Institute Press, 1990) first publ. 1891, p. 1.

13 Ibid., 204–12.

14 Department of the Navy, *Naval Doctrine Publication 1. Naval Warfare* (2020).

15 Curt von Maltzhan, *Naval Warfare*, transl. by John Combe Miller (London: Longmans, 1908), p. 46.

16 Vice Admiral Wolfgang Wegener, *The Naval Strategy of the World War*, trans. and ed. Holger Werwig (Annapolis, MD: Naval Institute Press, 1989 [1929]). Herbert Rosinski, 'German Theories of Sea Warfare', in B. Mitchell Simpson, III (ed.), *The Development of Naval Thought: Essays by Herbert Rosinski* (Newport, RI: Naval War College Press, 1977).

17 John B. Hattendorf, 'The Idea of a "Fleet-in-Being" in Historical Perspective', *Naval War College Review*, **67**(1) (Winter 2014), 43–60.

18 *Australian Maritime Doctrine* (2010), p. 71.

19 *British Maritime Doctrine*, p. 289.

20 Stansfield Turner, 'The Naval Balance: Not Just a Numbers Game', in *Foreign Affairs*, **55**(2) (January 1977) and 'Missions of the US Navy', *Naval War College Review* (Mar–Apr 1974). Also see Christofer Waldenstrom, 'Sea Control Through the Eyes of the Person Who Does It: A Theoretical Analysis', in *US Naval War College Review*, **66**(1) (Winter 2013), 77–100.

21 J. C. Wylie, *Military Strategy: A General Theory of Power Control* (Annapolis, MA: Naval Institute Press, 1987), first publ. 1967, p. 155.

22 Robert C. Rubel, 'Think Differently About Naval Presence', in *Proceedings of the US Naval Institute*, December 1921, pp. 28–33. Robert C. Rubel, 'Command of the Sea Redux', in *US Naval War College Review*, **75**(2) (Spring 2022).

23 Julian S. Corbett, *Some Principles of Maritime Strategy* (Annapolis, MD, Naval Institute Press, 1990) first publ. 1911, p. 16.

24 Sir Charles Callwell, *The Effect of Maritime Command on Land Campaigns Since Waterloo* (London: Blackwood, 1897) and *Military Operations and Maritime Preponderance: Their Relations and Interdependence* (London: Blackwood, 1905). Also see Sir George Aston, *Letters on Amphibious Wars* (London: John Murray, 1911) and George Furse, *Military Expeditions Beyond the Seas*, two vols. (London: William Clowes, 1897).

25 See Speller, *Understanding Naval Warfare*, ch. 1.

26 Bernard Brodie, *A Guide to Naval Strategy* (New York, NY: Praeger, 1965); Sir Herbert Richmond, *Seapower in the Modern World* (Oxford: Bell, 1934); Stephen Roskill, *Strategy of Seapower* (London: Collins, 1962); Edward Wegener, 'Theory of Naval Strategy in the Nuclear Age', in *US Naval Institute Proceedings*, May 1972; James Wylie, *Military Strategy: A General Theory of Power Control* (Annapolis, MD: Naval Institute Press, 1989), first publ. 1967.

27 Sergei Gorshkov, *Navies in War and Peace* (Annapolis, MD: Naval Institute Press, 1974) and *The Seapower of the State* (London: Pergamon, 1979). Also see Kevin Rowlands (ed.), *Twenty-First Century Gorshkov. The Challenge of Sea Power in the Modern Era* (Annapolis, MD: Naval Institute Press, 2017).

28 See Eric Roksund, *The Jeune École* (Leiden: Brill, 2007).

29 B. Mitchell Simpson III (ed.), *The Development of Naval Thought: Essays by Herbert Roskinski* (Newport, RI: Naval War College Press, 1977), pp. 15–17. Herger H. Holwig, 'The Failure of German Sea Power, 1914–1945: Mahan, Tirpitz, and Raeder Reconsidered', in *The International History Review*, **10**(1) (February 1988), 95.

30 Bryan Ranft and Geoffrey Till, *The Sea in Soviet Strategy* (London: Macmillan, 1983), pp. 85–88.

31 Bernard D. Cole, 'The History of the Twenty-First Century Chinese Navy', in *Naval War College Review*, **67**(3) (Summer 2014).

32 Martin H. Murphy and Toshi Yoshihara, 'Fighting the Naval Hegemon: Evolution in French, Soviet and Chinese Naval Thought', in *US Naval War College Review*, **68**(3) (Summer 2015), 13–39.

33 See Jacob Borresen, 'Coastal Power: The Sea Power of the Coastal State and the Management of Maritime Resources', in Rolf Hobson and Tom Kristiansen (eds.), *Navies in Northern Waters, 1721–2000* (London: Frank Cass, 2004), pp. 249–75. C. Nils Ove-Jansson, 'The Baltic: A Sea of Contention', in *US Naval War College Review*, **41**(3) (Summer 1988), 47–61.

34 Niklas Granholm, 'Small Navies and Naval Warfare in the Baltic Sea Region', in Robert McCabe, Deborah Sanders and Ian Speller (eds.), *Europe, Small Navies and Maritime Security* (London: Routledge, 2019).

35 Raoul Castex, *Strategic Theories*, ed. and transl. by Eugenia Kiesling (Annapolis, MD: Naval Institute Press, 1994).

8 The Evolution of Naval Warfare

CHAPTER OUTLINE

KEY THEMES

- The techniques of naval warfare have been subject to many changes over the past two centuries.
- Technology has also changed and this has had an impact on all forms of naval activity. However, to understand technology one must place it within an appropriate context. It is not an independent variable.
- Despite such changes there have also been some notable continuities and these suggest that the concepts articulated in the previous chapter retain considerable relevance.

Introduction

The previous chapter suggested that there has been a considerable degree of continuity in thinking about naval warfare; concepts and principles articulated in the nineteenth century continue to be employed in the twenty-first. Over the same period there have been many obvious changes in the conduct of naval warfare, particularly in the tactics adopted and in the technology used. No navy today maintains a fleet of wooden sailing ships similar to those employed by Admiral Nelson in 1805 nor do any possess pre-**dreadnought** battleships akin to those used to good effect by Admiral Togo a century later. No modern commander would deploy their fleet in battle in the same way that either Nelson or Togo did and to do so would be to invite disaster. It is legitimate therefore to question whether principles articulated in Togo's era, which were often derived from an examination of Nelson's, are still useful today when platforms, weapons and sensors have changed so much and where the general strategic context has been transformed. This chapter will address that question.

Unfortunately there is not the space here to provide a detailed history of the evolution of naval warfare over the past century; still less can we examine the very rich history before this period. The readers are fortunate that there are numerous good books that already do precisely this and some of these are introduced in the 'Further Reading' guide at the end of this chapter. The aim here is not to present a comprehensive history but rather to illustrate some of the ways in which naval warfare has changed over time, and also some of the continuities. There will be a particular focus on the past 150 years, roughly the time at which steam, steel and shellfire replaced the 'wooden ships and iron men' of Nelson's era. This should offer some context within which the concepts and principles articulated in the previous chapter can be assessed and will also provide a useful foundation for the next chapter, which addresses naval warfare today.

From Fighting Sail to Steam, Steel and Shellfire

In the century between the battles of Trafalgar (1805) and Tsushima (1905) there were dramatic changes in naval technology and also in the conduct of naval warfare at the tactical level. The most obvious technological changes revolved around the transformation of warships from wooden sailing vessels armed with short-range cannon firing solid shot to armoured steel vessels powered by steam engines, armed with much longer ranged heavy weapons firing armour-piercing shells and (by the 1900s) equipped with radio. The adoption of steam propulsion was particularly significant and brought costs and benefits. It provided greater speed and offered ships the ability to manoeuvre without relying on the vagaries of the wind. This was particularly useful when operating on rivers or inshore areas, places where sailing ships had been at a disadvantage. Steam power also increased the potential to provide reliable logistic support to overseas expeditions. On the other hand, whereas sailing ships had enjoyed almost unlimited endurance, steam power relied on coal (later oil) and the requirement to restock with this fuel limited the endurance of warships, making possession of overseas coaling stations of particular importance. This factor favoured the British who possessed a string of bases at key points throughout the world. They also gained strategic advantage from their dominance of the network of under-sea telegraph cables that, in the second half of the century, began to make possible strategic direction of forces in different parts of the world.

The wooden three-decked ship of the line was eventually replaced by steam-powered ironclads and then by modern-style battleships that were steam powered, built of iron (later steel), armoured, armed with heavy guns mounted in revolving turrets on the centreline of the ship and with numerous medium- and small-calibre guns added as a secondary armament. HMS *Victory* and HIJMS *Mikasa*, Nelson and Togo's flagships at Trafalgar and Tsushima, are preserved at Portsmouth and Yokosuka (respectively) and reflect the technological advances of a century. However, the obvious differences between these vessels do not disguise an important element of continuity. They were both designed to do broadly the same thing, namely to fight and defeat other warships in battle. They were not the only warships of their time but they were understood to be the most powerful vessels, the key measure of naval strength and the ships that would determine victory in battle. To use a twentieth century term, they were the **capital ships** of their eras and the major navies (and some minor ones) were willing to expend vast sums on their construction and upkeep.

Even as the battleship emerged as the new capital ship, a number of developments promised to threaten its ascendancy. These included the explosive sea mine, first employed during the Crimean War (1854–1855) and used to good effect by the Confederacy in the US Civil War (1861–1865). Such weapons posed a serious threat to even the most powerful vessels and the Union Ironclad USS *Cairo* was the first warship to be sunk by a mine in 1862. A generation later, mines accounted for the loss of three battleships and a number of cruisers in the Russo-Japanese War (1904–1905). They were used on a large scale by all sides in the First World War, and to notably good effect by Ottoman Turkey during their defence of the Dardanelles in 1915.

The self-propelled torpedo, first developed in the 1870s by Robert Whitehead, was another relatively cheap weapon that could sink the mightiest warship if it could be delivered accurately. The threat posed to big ships by these weapons and by the small fast torpedo boats that carried them led to the development of a new kind of ship, torpedo boat **destroyers** (later known simply as destroyers), to protect the bigger ships and, if possible, launch their own torpedo strikes. Pioneering work with submarines resulted, by the turn of the century, in vessels that had considerable military potential. Powered on the surface by diesel engines and by electric motors when submerged, and armed with torpedoes (and usually also a light gun on deck), submarines added yet another dimension to naval warfare. Such weapons, in addition to long-range shore-based artillery, promised to make enemy coastal waters a dangerous place to be.[1]

Inevitably in a period of technological change, the second half of the nineteenth century saw a considerable degree of experimentation in ship design and also in tactics. In the age of sail the effective range of the cannon mandated that battle would usually be decided at distances of 200 metres or less, with the British in particular favouring encounters at point-blank range where their superior gunnery would usually prevail. If ships could be laid alongside each other boarding operations were possible, providing an opportunity to capture vessels that were notoriously difficult to sink using solid shot.[2] Explosive shells, deployed at sea from the 1830s, made wooden ships easier to sink but armour redressed the balance, to the point where the USS *Monitor* and CSS *Virginia* were unable to sink each other in the first ironclad versus ironclad engagement at Hampton Roads (1862) (see Figure 8.1).[3] Experience during the US Civil War, and Austrian success in ramming and thus sinking the Italian flagship at the battle of Lissa (1866), prompted an interest in

Figure 8.1 Officers from the USS *Monitor* relax on deck after the engagement with the CSS *Virginia* at the battle of Hampton Roads, 1862. (Courtesy of Naval History and Heritage Command, US Navy, NH 61923). Source: https://tinyurl.com/mt8eyv82

a rather ancient weapon, the naval ram, until improvements in the range, accuracy and lethality of naval guns ensured that combat would no longer take place at such close range. At the Battle of the Yalu, fought between the Japanese and Chinese in 1894, most fire occurred at a range of around 2,000 metres. Ten years later, at the Battle of the Yellow Sea, the Japanese opened fire at 11,000 metres and both they and their Russian opponents were fully engaged at 9,000 metres.[4] In such circumstances the long-range heavy guns of the battleship were the dominant weapons and tactics involved manoeuvring the heavy ships into a superior firing position and, where possible, launching torpedo attacks with cruisers and **flotilla** craft (see Box 8.1 and Figure 8.2).

While the tactics and technology of naval warfare certainly changed over the course of the century, there were some notable continuities at the operational and strategic levels. There had been numerous major naval battles in the decades leading up to Trafalgar, but there were few in the century that followed. Those battles that did occur – including, for example, at Navarino (1827), Sinope (1854), Lissa (1866),

BOX 8.1 'CROSSING THE T'

'Crossing the T' was a tactic in naval warfare, where one fleet manoeuvred to cross in front of the line of enemy vessels, allowing its ships to concentrate fire from guns at the front and the rear of each vessel while only receiving fire from the forward guns of the leading enemy ships. In essence this placed the friendly fleet in the position of the losers at Trafalgar, with the enemy bearing down on them in line ahead, although the increased range, accuracy and lethality of naval gunfire meant that the result would likely be rather different. The Japanese successfully 'crossed the T' at Tsushima (1905) and the British did so twice at Jutland (1916). In the last ever battleship versus battleship engagement, the Battle of the Surigao Strait (1944), US battleships crossed the Japanese T and devastated their opponents with accurate radar-guided fire at long range.

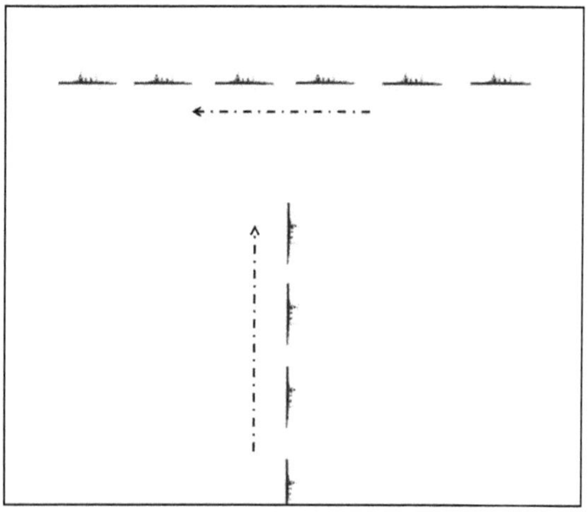

Figure 8.2 'Crossing the T'.

the Yalu River (1894) and Santiago de Cuba (1898) – tended to be on a smaller scale and did not feature clashes between the leading navy (the British) and its main rivals. Some, such as the battles of Hampton Roads (1862) or Iquique (1879), revolved around duels between individual ships. This did not diminish the potential significance of victory or defeat. The battles for sea control in the War of the Pacific (1879–1883), for example, were on a much smaller scale than the Anglo-French wars of the previous century but the consequences remained familiar. Thus, the Peruvian victory at Iquique lifted the Chilean blockade of that town but subsequent defeats at the second Battle of Iquique and the Battle of Angamos (also in 1879) gave Chile control of the sea and opened up Peru and Bolivia to invasion and eventual defeat. The battles may have been small, but the consequences were not.[5]

Steam propulsion enhanced a navy's ability to project power ashore, through **expeditionary operations** or through riverine operations such as those undertaken during the First Anglo-Burmese War (1824–1826) and the First Opium War (1838–1842). Protected by armour, powered by steam and equipped with heavy guns, rockets and/or mortars, navies could also conduct effective strike operations against coastal fortifications. This was illustrated in a variety of actions, and was forcefully demonstrated by successful maritime power projection during the Crimean War (1854–1855) and the US Civil War (1861–1865). The land could fight back, using mines and coastal fortifications to protect vulnerable targets and exploiting the potential for rail links (and much later also motor transport) to rapidly concentrate forces to contain any landings. Nevertheless, evidence in these two wars suggested that the advantage was, for the time being at least, tipped in favour of the maritime force.[6]

In the early years of the new century, the battle of Tsushima (1905) provided a classic example of an engagement in which the main force of one side (Russia) was decisively defeated by another (Japan). For some this reaffirmed the centrality of battle in naval warfare. However, the dramatic nature and scale of that victory should not hide the reality that the war revolved around more than one battle and that, while battle at sea was important, this was only one element in eventual Japanese success. Japanese torpedo boats and mines, for example, sank or damaged a number of Russian ships. Critically, of course, the war was joint in nature and the Imperial Japanese Navy was required to land and support the army ashore and also received support from that army (which destroyed Russian ships hiding in besieged Port Arthur). Thus, while Tsushima was taken by many as an affirmation of the importance of battle, others, such as Corbett, reflected on the importance of joint cooperation for eventual success.[7]

Into a New Century

The launch by the British in 1906 of HMS *Dreadnought* revolutionised battleship design. Heavily armed and armoured, the 21,850 ton *Dreadnought* was notable for new steam turbine engines that provided an impressive top speed of twenty-one knots and for an all-big-gun armament of ten twelve-inch guns. Making all existing battleships obsolete, *Dreadnought* lent its name to a new generation of capital ships designed along similar lines, albeit in progressively greater size and strength. The British also pioneered a new type of vessel, the battlecruiser. These ships carried dreadnought-type guns but sacrificed heavy armour for improved speed. The number and quality of dreadnought battleships was the measure by which navies judged themselves prior to 1914 and rival dreadnought construction set the terms for the pre-war Anglo-German naval race. The prestige associated with possession of such ships, and their potential to dominate any battle at sea, led to the construction or purchase of dreadnoughts by all the major navies and by many navies of second or third rank, including those of Argentina, Brazil and Chile.

The all-big-gun armament adopted by dreadnought battleships improved the accuracy of long-range gun fire. Fire control was much easier if all the guns were the same calibre, firing in salvoes that could be corrected until the enemy ship was straddled and then hit by shell-fire. By 1910, continuous aim fire and director control had replaced local gun-laying, further improving long-range accuracy (and making effective fire-control equipment and procedures as important as superior guns). Battle could now occur at very long range. At Jutland in 1916 the engagement began when the battlecruisers on both sides opened fire at around 16,000 yards (14,600 metres). In the last ever battleship versus battleship engagement, at the Surigao Strait in October 1944, US gunfire was aided by radar-guided fire control and the battle-line opened fire at 26,000 yards (23,700 metres), over twice the range at Tsushima forty years earlier.[8]

Battleships may have been the 'capital ships' of the age, but they were not the only vessels that navies required. By the end of the nineteenth century the major fleets were made up of a mix of vessels that included battleships designed to secure control of the sea by engaging and defeating other warships, cruisers able to exercise that control by protecting or attacking trade and projecting power ashore through gunfire or naval landing parties, and flotilla craft required to conduct inshore work, carry despatches, land troops and, increasingly, protect larger vessels from attack by other flotilla craft. Successful fleet tactics involved coordinating the activity of multiple ships of different types and could be considered to be analogous to the combined arms tactics of land warfare.

It was very difficult to control a large fleet containing many ships with different roles and capabilities. Communications remained dependent on flag signalling until the 1900s when wireless telegraphy began to be deployed at sea. The latter did not solve the problem, and in some senses it served to compound it, tempting some commanders to centralise too much control in their own hands and stifling initiative amongst their subordinates. Use of radio did provide a means for dispersed ships to communicate, greatly assisting the process of **scouting** and providing shore-based admiralties a means to support (or interfere with) commanders at sea. Unfortunately, however, radio transmissions could be detected, betraying the presence of enemy vessels and, if your codes were broken, allowing much useful information to be gathered by the enemy. For this reason, ships at sea often maintained radio silence, continuing to communicate by flag signals and searchlight flashes.[9]

The Test of War, 1914–1918

The dangers facing battleships in enemy coastal waters led the Royal Navy to adopt a distant rather than a close blockade of Germany once war broke out in 1914. This robbed the Germans of the chance that they had been counting on to whittle down British battleship strength to the point at which the smaller German fleet might engage them with some prospect of success. As a result, the German **High Seas** Fleet spent the war imprisoned in the Baltic and North Seas. On occasion it was able to bombard towns on the east coast of England and to threaten the Scandinavian

BOX 8.2 THE BATTLE OF JUTLAND, 31 MAY 1916

There were a number of naval battles during the war, notably at Helgoland Bight (28 August 1914), Coronel (1 November 1914), the Falkland Islands (8 December 1914) and Dogger Bank (24 January 1915). However, the caution exercised by both sides in the use of their big ships and their reluctance to fight when outnumbered meant that the main fleets clashed only once, at the Battle of Jutland, on 31 May 1916. Typically, the battle occurred as a result of a German attempt to tempt out and then ambush a detachment of the British fleet. Forewarned by signals intelligence, the British, on the other hand, sought to exploit a rare opportunity to engage the main enemy force. With 250 vessels employed and no significant contribution from either submarines or aircraft, the resulting engagement stands as the largest surface-only engagement of modern times and the only major battle of the dreadnought era. The much anticipated clash proved to be an unsatisfactory experience for the British, who suffered a greater material loss than the Germans. The latter managed to avoid annihilation through a mixture of skill, luck and the caution of their enemy and arrived home badly battered but largely intact. Despite this, the battle merely confirmed the defeat already being inflicted on a navy that could find no way to use its surface fleet to achieve meaningful strategic effect. That the German high command recognised this was reflected in the shift of priority away from the big ships and towards submarines.[10]

convoys and, once, at the battle of Jutland in May 1916, to assault its jailor; see Box 8.2. The realisation of how close the High Seas Fleet had come to annihilation in the latter case led its leadership to be more circumspect in future. In the meantime the British blockade cut off German trade, isolated its colonies and slowly strangled its people. By neutralising the High Seas Fleet, the dreadnoughts of the British Grand Fleet set the conditions for Allied sea control beyond the North Sea. The cautious way in which these vessels were employed should not be allowed to hide the importance of this role. The control provided by the Grand Fleet allowed other vessels to engage in trade protection, amphibious operations and a variety of other tasks unmolested.

Reliance on the sea represented a vulnerability for Britain, a country whose industry was dependent on the import of raw materials and whose people would starve without imported foodstuffs. The Germans, like the French before them, recognised this vulnerability. Pre-war plans had envisaged the use of surface ships in a traditional *guerre de course*. In the event, a small number of German light cruisers and converted merchant ships attacked British trade before being sunk or interned in neutral ports. Despite causing considerable alarm and disruption, their effect on the British war effort was limited. The submarine campaign against shipping heading towards British ports had a far greater impact. Once German

U-boats (submarines) were released by their government from the requirement to operate within the bounds of international law, and were allowed to sink ships without warning and with no consideration for the safety of civilian passengers and crew, British losses mounted alarmingly. Given the primitive state of submarine detection equipment and anti-submarine weapons, it was fortunate that the first such exercise of unrestricted U-boat warfare, in 1915–1916, was curtailed due to the international outrage that it caused. The second attempt, begun in February 1917, came close to success before the British adopted suitable counter-measures, primarily through the introduction of convoys; see Box 8.3. Unfortunately for Germany, the campaign contributed to the US decision to declare war in 1917, adding the American fleet to the Allied inventory. The U-boat campaign demonstrated the vulnerability of a state dependent on seaborne communications to a sea denial strategy but (as Mahan would have expected) the impact that it had on British life and economy failed to match that of the Allied blockade on Germany.[11]

The absence of any dramatic victory at sea during the First World War and the magnitude of the horror of the land campaigns can mislead some into neglecting the importance of naval activity in that war. Allied sea control provided a necessary precondition for eventual victory over the Central Powers. Sea control kept Britain safe from invasion. It enabled Britain to deploy its armies to France and to sustain them there through four harrowing years of war. It allowed Britain and France to mobilise the resources of their global empires, to conduct operations and campaigns

BOX 8.3 CONVOYS

The use of convoys – whereby ships travel to their destination in groups under naval guidance or protection – was a traditional way of protecting trade. Unfortunately convoys are a very inefficient way of moving ships. They take time to assemble, sail at the pace of the slowest vessel and may swamp the reception facilities of a port once they arrive. They can also be difficult to maintain, with some merchant ships struggling to keep station. They have the additional problem of placing rather a lot of 'eggs in one basket', raising fears that a raider might overpower the escort and then devour all in the convoy. They do, however, have numerous advantages. Convoys may be protected by escorting warships; with appropriate intelligence they may be re-routed to avoid known danger areas; and gathering ships together into one group makes them much harder to find in the vastness of the oceans. If they are found and attacked, then the escort may drive off the attacker or, if it is unable to do so, may at least buy time for the merchant ships to flee. Convoys were often employed during the age of sail and were to prove equally effective in both world wars despite the ill-founded misgivings expressed by Corbett. Indeed, not only did they serve a vital defensive function in protecting ships from attack, they also served an offensive function; the best place to find and then attack a raider was usually in the vicinity of their prey.

overseas and to seize isolated German colonies. It set the context within which Britain could meet the U-boat challenge and eventually enabled the US to deploy its armed forces across the Atlantic. It also allowed the Allies to trade with the rest of the world, giving them access to resources that were denied to the Germans. With sea control Allied victory was possible; without it defeat would have been inevitable.[12]

One area where the Allies were not able to exploit sea power as effectively as they would have wished was that of power projection. Indeed, their failure to exploit fully the potential for maritime power projection denied the Allies the full fruits of their naval superiority. They did conduct numerous shore bombardments and the British even launched small-scale carrier airstrikes against targets ashore. A small number of amphibious operations were tried, including a failed expedition to Tanga in German East Africa (1914) and the raids on Zeebrugge and Ostend (1918). The largest and most famous operation, the assault on Gallipoli in 1915, succeeded only in securing a tiny lodgement that was later abandoned in the face of determined opposition and severe logistical problems. The advantage, it seemed, had shifted in favour of the defender. Ironically, while the initial assault in April 1915 and a subsequent landing in August were characterised by muddle and lost opportunities, the evacuation, staged between December 1915 and January 1916 and conducted under the noses of the Ottoman Army, was a masterpiece of careful planning and effective joint cooperation. The Germans had rather more success in landings conducted to seize islands in the Gulf of Riga in 1917, exploiting local sea control to good effect although the circumstances there were more benign than they had been at Gallipoli.[13]

From Arms Control to World War, 1918–1945

The end of the war in 1918, and the scuttling of the captive High Sea Fleet at Scapa Flow the following year, did not bring an end to naval rivalry. In the years that followed there were, however, attempts to manage this through arms control agreements that sought to limit the size and number of major warships. The Washington Treaty of 1922 was successful in halting, or at least delaying, a potential American, British and Japanese naval arms race, but this, and the later London Treaties of 1930 and 1936, could not long remove the root causes of naval rivalry. By the limits that they set, the treaties influenced the design and construction of warships, and led to the creation of a new type of vessel, the heavy cruiser of up to 10,000 tons. The 'building holiday' that was imposed on capital ship construction hit the British hardest as the Royal Navy was generally equipped with older vessels than its rivals. Limits on battleship size and armament also worked against the British who, unlike their future adversaries, abided by these limitations. The 1930 London Treaty established limits on the numbers of cruisers that were determined by the relative strength of the major navies and not by their likely tasks, again disadvantaging the British who were unique in having a global empire to protect. Typically, restrictions on the use of submarines against merchant ships, contained in the London Treaties and also in the 1936 Anglo-German Naval Agreement, proved to be worthless in wartime.[14]

Despite the attempts at arms control, navies continued to try to adapt techniques and technologies for future conflict. Notable technological advances included the development of ASDIC (now called **sonar**), a device that used sound-waves to detect submerged submarines and also of radar that, when deployed at sea, could be used to detect enemy vessels/aircraft and assist in fire control. Improved sensors, signals intelligence and the ability to conduct reconnaissance by air reduced the opacity of the sea somewhat, leading to the evolution of what one commentator has described as 'picture centric warfare'. Having a superior picture might mean more than having superior guns, and weapons were worthless unless information could be gathered and then processed in a timely and efficient manner. The need to link sensor to shooter, to manage multiple friendly forces and to counter numerous enemies simultaneously saw the development of manual and then automated means of gathering and managing information, evolving in the Second World War into an early form of the current Combat Information Centre/Operations Room, the nerve centre of a modern warship.[15]

Despite the relative lack of success of amphibious operations during the First World War, the Americans, British and Japanese all studied ways of undertaking such operations in the future. A lack of priority retarded British progress, although much useful theoretical work was undertaken and prototype landing craft developed. With more obvious use for amphibious forces in a conflict between themselves, the Japanese and Americans made better progress. Japanese capabilities were in advance of all others, prompted by the use of amphibious forces in their war with China.[16] However, it was to be American and British techniques and capabilities that would, during the Second World War, solve the problems of conducting landings on an enemy-held shore and by 1943–1944 offer the Allies the ability to land hundreds of thousands of troops, plus all of their supporting equipment and logistics, over open beaches in the face of enemy opposition. Amphibious forces had finally come of age.[17]

One area where technologies developed significantly was in the use of aircraft. The potential for aircraft to have an impact on war at sea was evident even prior to the First World War. During that conflict both fixed-wing heavier-than-air aircraft and lighter-than-air rigid and non-rigid airships played a role in reconnaissance, anti-submarine operations and bombing. After years of experimentation the Royal Navy commissioned HMS *Argus* in September 1918, the first true aircraft carrier (with a full flight deck from bow to stern and a hangar below deck for the carriage and maintenance of aircraft). By this time the British were planning to launch a strike by carrier-based aircraft against the German High Seas fleet in harbour although the end of the war brought the cancellation of such plans. Twenty-two years later they would demonstrate the ability of carrier-based aircraft to strike at ships in harbour when just twenty-one Swordfish biplanes flying from HMS *Illustrious* sank one Italian battleship and damaged two others at Taranto on the night of

BOX 8.4 THE BATTLES OF THE CORAL SEA (4–8 MAY 1942) AND MIDWAY (4–7 JUNE 1942)

The Battle of the Coral Sea is significant as it was the first engagement between fleets at sea decided entirely by air power. Indeed, the surface ships of both sides were never even close to being within visual or weapons range of each other. The battle resulted in one US aircraft carrier sunk and another damaged in exchange for one small Japanese carrier sunk and two others damaged. In all cases the damage was inflicted by enemy carrier aviation. Although tactically indecisive, the battle resulted in the Japanese abandoning an attempted invasion of Port Moresby in New Guinea. The Battle of Midway resulted from a Japanese attempt to draw out and destroy the remaining US carriers by attacking the US base at Midway Atoll. Forewarned by successful intelligence, and assisted by a degree of luck, the US fleet was able to surprise the larger Japanese force, sinking all four Japanese carriers present for the loss of only one of their own. Once again, neither fleet was ever within range of the other's guns. Despite their losses, the Japanese still possessed a large superiority of gun-armed surface forces but in the face of US control of the skies, were compelled to withdraw. The battles illustrated the growing importance of aircraft carriers in naval warfare.[19]

11–12 November 1940. A year later, on 7 December 1941, the Imperial Japanese Navy improved on this, sinking four battleships and damaging many other warships in a pre-emptive strike on the US Pacific Fleet at Pearl Harbor.[18]

Although expected initially to play a role subordinate to the guns of the battle fleet, carrier-based aircraft were to prove themselves in the Second World War to be the decisive arm in naval warfare. Carrier-based aircraft – and, when in range, land-based aircraft – could fulfil a variety of roles at sea including reconnaissance, spotting for gunfire, bombing and torpedo attack, air defence and anti-submarine operations. They could act in support of traditional surface-oriented action, as at the Battle of Cape Matapan in the Mediterranean in March 1941. They could also threaten naval vessels independently. Allied experience off the coast of Norway and at Dunkirk in 1940 and in the Mediterranean from 1941 demonstrated the vulnerability of warships to attack by land-based aircraft and showed the need for appropriate anti-aircraft weapons, tactics and, above all else, fighter cover. Too often land-based air forces proved unable to provide the latter, leaving their naval colleagues dangerously exposed. The most radical developments occurred in the Pacific War, where the true potential of carrier-based aircraft was shown in the attack on Pearl Harbor and in subsequent operations. At the Battles of the Coral Sea in May 1942 and again, on a greater scale, at the Battle of Midway in June that year, the USN and the Imperial Japanese Navy fought major battles in which their surface vessels were never within sight of each other or within range of their big guns. The outcome was decided in both cases by the action of carrier-based aircraft resulting, at Midway, in a major defeat for the Japanese (Box 8.4).

In contrast to the First World War, where the vital contribution of maritime power to Allied success was overshadowed by the dramatic events on land, the struggle at sea in the Second World War was obviously central to the eventual outcome. Within Europe, Allied naval power set the limits to Axis expansion, sustained Britain during the dark days of 1940–1942 and eventually provided the means for a counter-offensive across the Mediterranean, into Italy and France and then the Third Reich itself. Once again German surface raiders and U-boats attempted to cut Allied sea-borne communications, this time aided by long-range aircraft and German possession of Norway and French Atlantic ports. Once again the Allies were able to overcome the threat, with a combination of convoys, escorts and, of increasing importance, air support. Aircraft, either shore or sea based, proved to be one of the most effective means of defeating submarines. The anti-submarine campaign in the Atlantic also illustrated the importance of intelligence and of good **operational analysis**. The ability of US industry to replace lost shipping was also critical. On the other side of the world, from 1942 the US initiated a submarine campaign against Japanese shipping that was as ruthless as its German counterpart but that, given woeful Japanese counter-measures, had, by 1945, destroyed Japan's merchant fleet.[20]

It should be noted, of course, that the war in Europe was not won at sea but, as Corbett would have been quick to comment, by armies on land. In the case of the Western Allies these armies were landed from the sea and, given their continued reliance on seaborne supplies, may justly be regarded as an expression of maritime power. In the east, the Soviet Union absorbed, contained and then destroyed the main German armies. It was aided in this process by the diversionary effect of Allied maritime power, ensuring that the Germans could never concentrate their entire strength against it, and also by the provision of vital supplies by convoys fighting their way through to Murmansk.[21]

The Pacific War, fought over a vast expanse of ocean was, from the perspective of the Western Allies, primarily maritime in nature but one should note the importance of land-centric campaigns in Burma, China and eventually also Manchuria that represented the main focus for the Japanese Army and that also played a key part in eventual Japanese defeat; the maritime war was one part of a wider conflict. After an initial surge of success that was halted at Midway in June 1942, the progressive destruction of the Japanese fleet, and in particular its aircraft carriers and naval aviators, set the conditions for Allied victory at sea. In the process the USN grew into a force of unprecedented size and capability, dwarfing all of its rivals and relegating the British, for the first time in centuries, to a navy of the second rank. In a series of engagements fought across the Central Pacific between 1942 and 1945, the USN shattered the Imperial Japanese Navy, opening up Japanese-held islands to assault by ground forces (Figure 8.3). To the south, naval forces supported operations by US and Australian troops that liberated New Guinea and the Philippines. By 1944 the Japanese position had become so desperate that they resorted to using Kamikaze attacks, attempting to fly explosive-laded aircraft directly into ships.

Figure 8.3 Ships of the US Third Fleet and the British Pacific Fleet off the coast of Japan in 1956. The battleship USS *Missouri* is in the foreground. Source: https://tinyurl.com/55wxzwmj

This seriously complicated the problems of air defence, as it was now no longer enough to distract or deter a pilot; the aircraft had to be destroyed. In this sense the kamikazes presaged the problems that would face navies during the missile era. In any case, US maritime power had, by summer 1945, brought Japan to its knees. The atomic attacks on Hiroshima and Nagasaki, with bombs transported by sea and dropped by aircraft operating from islands seized from the sea, forced the Japanese leadership to accept this fact. They also threatened to pose a fresh set of problems for navies.[22]

Navies in the Nuclear Age

The experience of war between 1939 and 1945 could be taken to have validated established thinking about naval warfare. The Pacific campaign, in particular, certainly lent weight to those whose vision of maritime power was informed by Mahan, with a series of major battles setting the conditions for successful and decisive US power projection. Typically, in 1947 Admiral Chester Nimitz USN submitted a report to Congress that restated the validity of the traditional principles, with an additional focus on how airpower had enhanced the reach and role of navies.[23] In the years that followed, navies continued to focus on their traditional roles. However, the devastating potential of nuclear weapons posed challenges that were both tactical and strategic. At the tactical level, the destructive potential of such weapons posed serious questions over the future viability of concentrated naval forces. Navies could (and did) point to their potential for manoeuvre and also dispersal as effective defensive counter-measures in addition to the value of the air defence and counter-strike potential provided by their aircraft carriers. Unfortunately, some maritime operations required a degree of concentration that would render them highly vulnerable. These included important activities that had been central to Allied success in the Second World War, such as large-scale amphibious operations and the delivery of convoys to congested ports. Over time, warship design adapted to make these vessels and their crew less vulnerable to the side effects of nuclear attack and also to attack by chemical and biological weapons. The deployment of nuclear weapons (including bombs, missiles, depth charges and torpedoes) by some navies certainly enhanced their offensive potential. Nevertheless, the widespread use of nuclear weapons against maritime forces and their supporting infrastructure would have posed serious questions as to their ability to perform traditional duties, or indeed any coordinated role. The same, of course, applied to armies and air forces and was denied as vociferously by generals and air marshals as it was by admirals.[24]

While questions remained about the role of navies in any major war, their value in situations short of all-out-war soon became apparent. Western naval forces, in particular, fulfilled a variety of vital roles in the numerous lesser conflicts that characterised the Cold War. That the traditional roles of power projection and naval diplomacy remained as important as ever was demonstrated in a series of conflicts and crises from the Korean War in 1950 to Vietnam in the 1960s, the various Arab–Israeli disputes, the Malvinas/Falklands Conflict in 1982 and the Gulf War of 1990–1991. Somewhat belatedly the Soviet Union came to recognise the value of this role and from the late 1960s developed both the size and reach of its navy. The presence of Soviet ships became a feature in waters that had previously been the preserve of the US and its allies. Notably, for example, the US, Soviet and some European navies all deployed warships to the Persian Gulf during the Tanker War in the 1980s, coexisting within the same operational space in a manner that was uncommon on land (Box 8.5).

BOX 8.5 THE 1980S TANKER WAR

The Tanker War occurred during the Iran–Iraq War (1980–1988) when Iraqi air attacks on Iranian oil terminals eventual prompted Iranian strikes against ships heading to Kuwait (which provided Iraq with its only access to the sea). By 1987 the situation was sufficiently bad for the US, Soviet Union and a number of European countries to have deployed warships to protect shipping operating in this vital area. The threat to shipping was posed by aircraft, missiles and unconventional fast craft armed with rockets and small arms. The dangers of operating in a war zone were illustrated when the USS *Stark* was hit by two Exocet missiles fired at a range of around thirty-five kilometres by an Iraqi aircraft. (Thirty-seven crew were killed.) Iranian mine laying posed a particular danger and resulted in serious damage to the cruiser USS *Samuel B. Roberts* and to numerous merchant ships. In retaliation the US launched a number of offensive operations to degrade Iranian mine-laying capabilities and to punish the regime for its activities. In the midst of one such operation, the USS *Vincennes* accidentally shot down a civilian airliner, with the loss of 290 innocent lives. By the end of the conflict around sixty western warships and twenty-nine Soviet ones had been deployed to the region. Despite this it is estimated that 411 merchant ships were hit over the course of the Tanker War, with around a quarter lost. Nevertheless, neither side succeeded in cutting the flow of oil from the other.[25]

The years after 1945 saw the final demise of the battleship, most of which had been retired from active service by the 1960s. A handful of battleships remained in periodic service with the USN until 1992, providing shore bombardment with their sixteen-inch guns and, after a refit in the 1980s, with Tomahawk cruise missiles. Cruisers, destroyers and **frigates** remained important surface combatants although, by the 1970s, the gun was being replaced as the primary weapon system by missiles for anti-air and anti-surface warfare in addition to improved torpedoes, depth charges, rockets and mortars for anti-submarine warfare. The potency of anti-ship missiles was demonstrated in 1967 when the Israeli destroyer INS *Eilat* was sunk by Soviet-built Styx missiles fired by Egyptian missile boats. Israel was to gain revenge in successful missile exchanges with Egyptian and Syrian vessels in the 1973 War. The offensive potential of anti-ship missiles was also illustrated by successful Indian attacks on Pakistani shipping in the port of Karachi in 1971 and Indian sea control isolated the main theatre in East Pakistan (Bangladesh) from reinforcement by West Pakistan.[26]

The 1982 Falklands/Malvinas conflict provided a rare example of a limited war in which a sustained battle for sea control represented the key to eventual success or failure. The Argentine surface fleet was neutralised at an early stage after the loss of the cruiser ARA *General Belgrano* demonstrated a critical vulnerability to British nuclear-powered submarines. Argentinean submarines proved incapable of launching any effective attacks on the British task force or their vulnerable lines of supply and one of their three operational boats was disabled and captured off South Georgia. Mines could have posed a serious challenge, but none were deployed to the critical waters in Falkland Sound. The major battle for sea control was, therefore, between land-based aircraft, operating from the mainland approximately 400 miles to the west of the islands, and the ships and aircraft of the British task force. The British lost one destroyer and a merchant ship sunk by Exocet anti-ship missiles and three warships and one auxiliary sunk by conventional bombs. Numerous other vessels were damaged. These losses, while not surprising given the nature of the operation and the inadequacy of some of the British equipment, highlighted the continued requirement for effective air defence and, ideally, for a large aircraft carrier able to gain local air superiority. In the event, the Argentinean Navy and Air Force were unable to disable any mission critical assets (most obviously the light carriers HMS *Hermes* and *Invincible* or the two landing platform docks HMS *Fearless* and *Intrepid*) and the Royal Navy secured enough control over the battle-space in order to land and support the military force in its successful campaign to liberate the islands. However, in many respects it was a close run thing.[27]

The Falklands Conflict reaffirmed the utility of aircraft carriers, particularly in operations beyond the range of friendly land-based fighters. Even before 1945, aircraft carriers had replaced the battleship as the capital ship of the future in the sense that they represented the most potent, and therefore the most desirable, symbol of maritime power. They provided a more flexible platform and more effective options for air defence, sea control and land attack than did the battleship. Unfortunately, they, and their associated air complements, were also more expensive to operate meaning that by the end of the century only the USN could afford to deploy the largest and most capable vessels. Numerous other navies maintained smaller carriers and the value of these was enhanced by the introduction of short-take-off and vertical-landing (STOVL) aircraft like the AV8B Harrier or the F-35B Lightening (which are able to operate from a smaller vessel and do not need the assistance of a catapult to launch). Unfortunately light carriers tend to embark a relatively small air group. The 27,000 ton Italian aircraft carrier *Cavour*, for example, can accommodate around twenty aircraft (helicopters and AV-8B Harriers). The 70,000 ton British *Queen Elizabeth* class can embark an air group more than twice this size while the 100,000 ton USS *George H.W Bush* can accommodate ninety aircraft; clearly size matters. Nevertheless, and as was demonstrated by the two light carriers deployed by Britain to the South Atlantic in 1982, a small air group can sometimes achieve rather a lot. Often (as was the case in 1982) the choice may be between this or no air group. The point seems to have been taken by the Chinese Navy, who invested considerable resources in the development of a new carrier capability after the commissioning of their first such vessel in 2012 (Figure 8.4).

The employment of helicopters at sea has helped to increase dramatically the range and flexibility of even small vessels. Helicopters are useful for a variety of tasks including surveillance, reconnaissance, search-and-rescue, boarding operations, anti-surface and anti-submarine warfare, the insertion of special-forces

Figure 8.4 The UK Carrier Strike Group led by HMS *Queen Elizabeth* joins Japanese Maritime self-defence forces led by JS *Ise* and US carrier strike groups led by USS *Ronald Reagan* and USS *Carl Vinson* in the Philippine Sea, 2021. Capable of a range of operations across the spectrum of conflict, these ships have power and versatility that reflects the advantages accrued by the ability to take air power to sea. Source: www.navy.mil/Resources/Photo-Gallery/igphoto/2002868802/

and the conduct of amphibious operations. Their use in large numbers operating from converted aircraft carriers and later from specialist helicopter assault ships helped to transform the conduct of amphibious operations from the 1950s. They also help to make modern amphibious ships, such as the *Canberra*-class ships deployed by the Royal Australian Navy or the Chinese Type 075 (Yushen) class, extremely versatile assets with utility in a wide range of scenarios including humanitarian assistance and disaster relief (HA/DR). Large helicopter-capable vessels also have utility in anti-submarine operations (a task for which helicopters are particularly suited) and they can also provide a sea base for attack helicopters, as did HMS *Ocean* and the French helicopter carrier *Tonnere* during the 2011 NATO operation in Libya.

In the 1990s with the end of the Cold War and the removal of the threat posed by the Soviet Navy, most Western navies moved away from strategies designed to cater for a major war in Europe to focus on more limited contingencies. These ranged from crisis response, sanctions enforcement and peace support operations through to power projection in limited war, expeditionary warfare and maritime strike. This change in priorities was reflected in the policy of the USN, in medium-sized navies such as the French and British, and even, on a smaller scale, in the coastal navies of Denmark, Norway and Sweden. However, this shift to what were sometimes called 'post-modern' naval considerations, revolving around collaborative endeavours to deal with transnational threats to maritime security, was impacted by a resurgence of great power rivalry at sea in 2010 as the USN began to focus more explicitly on the challenge posed by Chinese naval expansion and its European allies switched back to the apparent threat posed by Russian aggression. Naval policy in the 2020s thus bore more than a passing resemblance to that of the Cold War.[28]

As ever, while some navies focused on sea control and power projection, others concentrated primarily on sea denial. Existing weaponry such as mines, torpedoes, coastal artillery and land-based aircraft have been subjected to incremental improvements and in the 1960s were supplemented by anti-ship missiles. Small, cheap, fast attack craft armed with such weapons have sometimes appeared likely to fulfil the prophesies of the Jeune École. These vessels pack a powerful punch but are, like nineteenth century torpedo boats, vulnerable to enemy counter-measures. The fate of Iraqi fast attack craft in 1991, destroyed with ease by Coalition aircraft, may be instructive. Indeed, during that conflict it was a very old weapon, traditional sea mines, that posed the greatest threat to Coalition activity at sea, badly damaging the cruiser USS *Princeton* and the amphibious assault ship USS *Tripoli*. Ironically *Tripoli* was, at the time, acting as flagship for the aviation minesweeping operations taking place in the northern Gulf. Mines had been used extensively by all sides in both world wars and have continued to pose a challenge to navies and merchant ships through to the present day.[29]

Below the surface submarines advanced considerably from those employed during the Second World War. By the end of that conflict the Germans had introduced snorkel equipment that allowed their boats to run on diesel engines without having to surface, greatly reducing their vulnerability to air attack. More recently, the development of air-independent propulsion (AIP) systems for diesel-electric submarines (SSKs) further reduces the vulnerability of these boats, making them more like true submarines rather than the submersibles of the two world wars. Advances in submarine technology have made SSKs quieter and thus more difficult to detect, significantly enhancing their potential, particularly in shallow water where large nuclear-power boats are at a disadvantage. The USN developed the first nuclear-powered submarines (SSNs) in the 1950s. Such vessels boast high speed, unlimited endurance and have no requirement to surface in order to replenish batteries. Equipped with torpedoes, anti-ship missiles and, in some cases, land attack cruise missiles, they are extremely potent weapons platforms. It is significant that the British have given their SSNs old battleship names. However, being larger and noisier than SSKs, they are less well suited to shallow, coastal waters. They are also more expensive and technologically demanding than SSKs meaning that, unlike diesel-electric boats that are now widely available, only a few navies currently possess this capability. Ballistic missile submarines (SSBNs) have proved to be an ideal means of deploying a nuclear deterrent due to their relative invulnerability to a pre-emptive strike.[30]

Conclusion

Even from this brief survey, it is clear that there have been many changes in the tactics and technology of naval warfare since the nineteenth century. No doubt there will be many more in the years ahead. Despite this it is still possible to identify continuities across the decades. If he were transported into the present, Admiral Togo would probably be astonished to inspect a modern fleet and he might struggle to adjust to the range and tempo of operations enabled by modern systems and sensors. Nevertheless, he would probably recognise the continued importance of the battle to secure, maintain or challenge sea control and also the requirement to do something useful with such control once you have it. The manner in which battle is conducted has evolved, and will continue to do so, but the importance of achieving domain dominance remains. The things that one can do with such dominance and the range at which one can do this has expanded considerably with the advent of long-range artillery and missiles, organic aircraft and modern amphibious forces. However, a commander from the Russo-Japanese War would be well placed to recognise the value of joint operations and be surprised only by the expanded range and scope of twenty-first century naval capabilities. The next chapter will focus on such capabilities, and on the challenges facing navies today and tomorrow.

RESEARCH QUESTIONS

1. What did the battle of Trafalgar achieve that Jutland did not?
2. How important is technology as a driver of change in naval warfare?
3. To what extent has air power enabled or inhibited naval operations since the First World War?
4. Is it true to say that, while tactics and technology have changed, the broad principles of maritime strategy remain valid?
5. Have modern 'anti-access' technologies, such as hypersonic anti-ship missiles, changed the way that navies will need to operate in the future? Is there any point in studying the past?

FURTHER READING

Black, Jeremy, *Naval Power: A History of Warfare at Sea from 1500 Onwards* (Basingstoke: Palgrave, 2009). As the title suggests, Black provides a brief study of the history of war at sea over the past 500 years. The book offers a useful introduction to the relevant history.

Heck, Timothy and B. A. Friedman (eds.), *On Contested Shores: The Evolving Role of Amphibious Operations in the History of Warfare* (Quantico, VA: Marine Corps University Press, 2020). A collection of over twenty short essays that explore a range of amphibious operations, including many that are not well known.

Mawdsley, Evan, *The War for the Seas: A Maritime History of World War II* (New Haven, CT: Yale University Press, 2019). This history addresses the topic with reference to all of the major combatants and provides an excellent introduction to the conduct and impact of maritime activity during the Second World War.

Murfett, Michael, *Naval Warfare 1919–1945: An Operational History of the Volatile War at Sea* (Abingdon: Routledge, 2009). Murfett provides a valuable single-volume history of war at sea from 1919 until the end of the Second World War.

Sondhaus, Lawrence, *Naval Warfare 1815–1914* (Abingdon: Routledge, 2001). This is a short but authoritative survey of the evolution of navies and of naval warfare from the Napoleonic Period to the First World War.

Till, Geoffrey, *Understanding Victory: Naval Operations from Trafalgar to the Falklands* (Santa Barbara, CA: Praeger, 2014). Till examines four major battles/campaigns from the last 200 years in an attempt to assess whether there emerges any consistent set of factors that help to explain victory and defeat. His conclusions are original and insightful.

Vego, Milan, *Operational Warfare at Sea: Theory and Practice* (Routledge: London, 2010). Vego offers an analysis of the planning and conduct of naval campaigns and operations from the Napoleonic period to the present day.

ONLINE RESOURCES

- The US Naval History and Heritage Command website includes a range of useful resources relating to the history of the USN, www.history.navy.mil/.
- Naval History Online provides a wide variety of links to records, documents and commentary relating to naval history (and with a particular emphasis on the British Royal Navy), www.naval-history.net/index.htm.
- The archives of the US *Naval War College Review* offer articles on a wide range of historical topics, https://digital-commons.usnwc.edu/nwc-review/.
- The online *International Journal of Naval History* includes articles on a range of historical topics, www.ijnhonline.org/.
- The University of Exeter Centre for Maritime Historical Studies has created an online resource that provides a guide to naval records at the UK National Archives, www.exeter.ac.uk/research/centres/maritime/resources/naval_records/.

NOTES

1 For an overview of developments during this period, see Lawrence Sondhaus, *Naval Warfare 1815–1914*, (London: Routledge, 2001) and Robert Gardiner (ed.), *Steam, Steel and Shellfire: The Steam Warship, 1815–1905* (London: Conway Maritime Press, 1992).

2 See Richard Harding, *Seapower and Naval Warfare 1650–1830* (London: Routledge, 1999).

3 For an interesting collection of essays on the battle see Harold Holzer and Tim Mulligan (eds.), *The Battle of Hampton Roads: New Perspectives on the USS Monitor and the CSS Virginia* (New York, NY: Fordham University Press, 2006).

4 Sondhaus, *Naval Warfare 1815–1914*, pp. 171, 189.

5 William F. Sater, *Andean Tragedy: Fighting the War of the Pacific, 1879–1884* (Lincoln, NE: University of Nebraska Press, 2009), esp. chs. 4 and 5. Also see Charles Callwell, *The Effect of Maritime Command on Land Campaigns Since Waterloo* (London: William Blackwood & Sons, 1897), pp. 311–28.

6 Craig L. Symonds, *The Civil War at Sea* (Oxford: Oxford University Press, 2012). Andrew Lambert, *The Crimean War: British Grand Strategy Against Russia, 1853–1856*, 2nd ed. (Farnham: Ashgate, 2011).

7 For a classic analysis of this war see Julian S. Corbett, *Maritime Operations in the Russo-Japanese War 1904–1905* (Annapolis, MD: Naval Institute Press, 1994).

8 Sondhaus, *Naval Warfare*, ch. 7. Paul Halpern, *A Naval History of World War 1* (London: UCL Press, 1994), p. 318. Samuel Eliot Morison, *Leyte. June 1944–January 1945* (Edison, NJ: Castle Books, 1958), pp. 223–4.
9 Norman Friedman, *Network Centric Warfare: How Navies Learned to Fight Smarter Through Three World Wars* (Annapolis, MD: Naval Institute Press, 2009), esp. ch. 1.
10 John Brooks, *The Battle of Jutland* (Cambridge, UK: Cambridge University Press, 2016). Also see Nicholas Jellicoe, *Jutland the Unfinished Battle* (London: Seaforth, 2018).
11 Lance E. Davis and Stanley L. Engerman, *Naval Blockades in Peace and War: An Economic History* (Cambridge, UK: Cambridge University Press, 2006), ch. 5.
12 See Halpern, *A Naval History of World War 1*; Lawrence Sondhaus, *The Great War at Sea* (Cambridge, UK: Cambridge University Press, 2014); and Norman Friedman, *Fighting the Great War at Sea: Strategy, Tactics, Technology* (Annapolis, MD: Naval Institute Press, 2014).
13 Tristan Lovering (ed.), *Amphibious Assault: Manoeuvre from the Sea* (Woodbridge: Seafarer Books, 2005), chs. 2–4.
14 For an overview of this period see Michael Murfett, *Naval Warfare 1919–1945: An Operational History of the Volatile War at Sea* (Abingdon: Routledge, 2009).
15 Friedman, *Network Centric Warfare*, passim.
16 For further details see Williamson Murray and Allan R. Millett (eds.), *Military Innovation in the Interwar Period* (Cambridge, UK: Cambridge University Press, 1996).
17 Ian Speller, *The Role of Amphibious Warfare in British Defence Policy 1945–1956* (Basingstoke: Palgrave, 2022), ch. 1.
18 David Hobbs, *Taranto and the Naval Air War in the Mediterranean, 1940–1945* (Barnsley: Seaforth Publishing, 2020). Alan D. Zimm, *The Attack in Pearl Harbor: Strategy, Combat, Myths, Deceptions* (Havertown, PA: Casemate Publishers, 2011).
19 Samuel Eliot Morison, *History of US Naval Operations in World War II. Coral Sea, Midway and Submarine Actions. May 1942–August 1942* (Boston, MA: Little Brown & Co., 1949); Craig L. Symonds, *The Battle of Midway* (Oxford: Oxford University Press, 2011).
20 See Clay Blair Jr, *Silent Victory: The US Submarine War Against Japan* (Annapolis, MD: Naval Institute Press, 2001). Craig Symonds, *World War Two at Sea* (Oxford: Oxford University Press, 2018), pp. 391–8, 588–95. Evan Mawdsley, *The War for the Seas: A Maritime History of World War Two* (New Haven, CT: Yales University Press, 2018), ch. 17.
21 Mawdsley, *The War for the Seas*, pp. 264–70.
22 Samuel Eliot Morison, *History of United States Naval Operations in World War II*, fifteen vols. (New York, NY: Little Brown and Co., 1947–1962). For a more concise account see Samuel Eliot Morison, *The Two-Ocean War* (Boston, MA: Little Brown and Co., 1963). Also see Symonds, *World War Two at Sea* and Mawdsley, *The War for the Seas*.
23 Admiral Chester Nimitz, 'Report to the Secretary of the Navy', December 1947.
24 For contemporary discussion of these issues see Sir Peter Gretton, *Maritime Strategy* (London: Cassell, 1964) and Lawrence Martin, *The Sea in Modern Strategy* (London: Chatto and Windus, 1967).
25 Martin S. Navias and E. R. Hooton, *Tanker Wars: The Assault on Merchant Shipping During the Iran Iraq Conflict, 1980–1988* (London: I.B. Tauris, 1996).
26 Frank Uhlig, *How Navies Fight: The US Navy and Its Allies* (Annapolis, MD: Naval Institute Press, 1994), pp. 352–62; Vice-Admiral G. M. Hiranandani, *Transition to Triumph: Indian Navy, 1965–1975* (New Delhi: Lancer Publ., 2000), ch. 10.

27 See Admiral Sandy Woodward and Patrick Robinson, *One Hundred Days: The Memoirs of the Falklands Battle Group Commander* (London: Harper Press, 2012).
28 See Ian Speller, 'Modern Maritime Strategy and Naval Warfare' in Ruxandra-Laura Boşilcă, Susana Ferreira and Barry J. Ryan (eds.), *Routledge Handbook of Maritime Security* (London: Routledge, 2022), ch. 4.
29 For example, see Scott C. Truver, 'Taking Mines More Seriously: Mine Warfare in China's Near Seas', *US Naval War College Review*, **65**(2) (Spring 2012).
30 For an analysis of current capabilities, see the annual *IHS Jane's Fighting Ships* (London: Jane's Information Group).

9 Naval Warfare in the Twenty-First Century

CHAPTER OUTLINE

KEY THEMES

- The political, economic and military importance of the sea appears to have been enhanced rather than diminished by recent developments. In particular, the importance of maritime transportation to the globalised world economy has prompted recognition that states have a shared interest in the security of the global commons.
- The dynamic noted in the previous point has been reflected in heightened awareness of the importance of maritime security operations, and of the importance of multinational cooperation to deal with transnational threats. This has encouraged collaboration between navies.
- Notwithstanding the previous point, it is evident that states (and others) seek to use the sea for competitive as well as cooperative purposes. Competition may often be low-intensity, asymmetric or hybrid in nature but it is dangerous to assume that navies will not have toat least entertain the possibility of state versus state violence.
- The resurgence of peer-to-peer superpower rivalry at sea reflects a key dynamic in current maritime strategy. However, it is important to remember that the significance of this varies dramatically. For some navies it is a key issue, while for others it may seem barely relevant.
- It is best today to think of naval warfare within a joint context that acknowledges the impact of all warfighting domains (land, sea, air, space and cyber) on activity at and from the sea.

Introduction

The previous chapters explored concepts of naval warfare and maritime strategy and addressed the evolution of naval warfare in modern times. It was suggested that – despite very significant changes in tactics and technology, and also in the wider context within which naval operations happened – there was still considerable continuity in terms of general principles and also the roles that navies fulfilled. For this reason, it has been argued, that the traditional concepts of maritime strategy may still apply. This is a point accepted by very many navies, and one that is reflected in their published doctrine and strategy statements. However, it is important to question this assumption. It may be the case that things have changed, due perhaps to some technological development or to a radical change in the wider strategic environment. It is possible that naval roles may change to reflect political, economic, social or technological developments; certainly there are many who argue that this will be the case. Even if existing roles remain, navies may be forced to change their forms in order to meet future challenges. New roles may evolve (and old ones disappear) in the face of new challenges while alternative means may be needed to sustain those roles that remain. Sadly, it seems unlikely that the need for navies will be removed by any lack of threats within the maritime environment. Given the nature of the contemporary security environment, it appears likely that navies will be called upon to meet a variety of complex challenges across the full spectrum of conflict, and today, after a considerable hiatus since the end of the Cold War, this includes the reality of great power naval competition between major peer rivals. This chapter will address these issues and will explore the nature of naval warfare today and into the future, before discussing the key features that characterise contemporary naval policy.

Naval Warfare: Changing Roles?

During the Cold War Ken Booth argued that people were interested in using the sea for three general reasons: the passage of goods and people; the passage of military resources; and the exploitation of the resources in and under the sea.[1] An analysis of current maritime thought and practice suggests that, if anything, each of these three factors is now more important than they appeared in the past. The globalised world economy is entirely reliant on maritime trade. The viability of the system and the prosperity and stability of the states that comprise it depend on the timely arrival of goods that can only be carried in sufficient bulk by sea, a point emphasised by the disruption to global patterns of trade by the temporary blockade of the Suez Canal caused by the *Ever Given* incident in March 2021 (see Box 9.1) or by Houthi attacks on shipping off the coast of Yemen. Additionally, the sea remains a vital source of food and of raw materials (notably oil, gas and rare minerals) for many peoples; it is certainly not declining in importance economically.[2] This implies that navies will continue to have a role in protecting economic interests at sea.

BOX 9.1 THE EVER GIVEN INCIDENT, 2021

In March 2021 the large container vessel *Ever Given* ran aground in the Suez Canal, blocking the channel for six days. Data from Lloyds List suggested that the blockage was holding up an estimated US$9.6 billion of goods each day.[3] Hundreds of ships were forced to wait to transit through the canal or to take the longer, slower and more expensive route around Africa. The incident had an immediate effect on global supply chains, causing a major disruption whose impact lasted for months. The incident demonstrated the vulnerability of the globalised world economy to disruptions in maritime trade, whether by accident (as happened here) or through malicious intent. In this case naval intervention was not required to clear the canal as the blockade was not caused by military action. In contrast, however, note that in 1984 an international force including twenty-six ships from six countries undertook mine counter-measure operations in the Red Sea approaches to the Suez Canal to make it safe for shipping after seventeen merchant ships had been damaged by mines laid covertly by an unknown actor (commonly supposed to have been Libya).[4]

The sea remains an avenue available for the projection of military force in peace and in war and in the **grey zone** that lies between. Thus, for example, NATO used the sea to launch strikes against Libya in 2011, and both the US and Russia engaged in sea-based missile and carrier strikes against targets in Syria during the Civil War in that country (although Russian carrier strikes were limited by the inadequacies of their one ageing ship and aircraft generally operated from ashore). The Russian government also used the sea as an avenue to support attacks on Georgia in 2008 and against Ukraine in 2014 and 2022, and in the latter case suffered notable losses. It is not only major navies that can exploit this avenue. For example, in March 2008 African Union troops conducted an amphibious landing to secure control of the rebel Comoros island of Anjouan.[5] Similarly, in September 2012 Kenya troops conducted an amphibious landing close to Kismayo in Somalia as part of an operation to seize control of that city from Al Shabaab.[6] The 2008 attacks on Mumbai demonstrate that a maritime approach can also be exploited by terrorists and other non-state groups.[7]

Evidently, the sea continues to be a medium that can be used to attack others. Such attacks can involve direct action, as in the examples noted above, or could be more indirect, as with attempts to disrupt the movement of shipping. These may include hit and run strikes designed to inflict costs on an adversary and to deny them the free use of a maritime space, as with recent Houthi drone, rocket and missile attacks on shipping off the coast of Yemen (See Box 9.2).[8] They may be designed to send a political signal about power and control or be part of a wider strategy of coercion or intimidation including incidents such as the Iranian seizure of two tankers in the Gulf of Oman and the Strait of Hormuz in April and May 2023,

BOX 9.2 ATTACKS ON SHIPPING IN THE RED SEA, 2023–2024

In November 2023, in apparent response to Israeli military action in Gaza, Houthi forces in Yemen began to launch drone and missile attacks on merchant shipping offshore and particularly in the narrow Bab-al-Mandab Strait. This threatened a major shipping route through the Red Sea and the Suez Canal, and soon many shipping companies were routing vessels on the longer and more expensive route around Africa. In response the US initiated Operation Prosperity Guardian in December, a multinational mission to protect ships in the region, and they also launched land- and sea-based airstrikes against Houthi missile and drone sites ashore, supported by British air strikes from Cyprus. As Houthi attacks continued, the European Union (EU) launched its own mission, EUNAVFOR Aspides, in February 2024 and also deployed naval forces to the region. The European mission focused solely on the defence of shipping and had no mandate to conduct strikes against forces ashore, but within the first few weeks of Aspides German, Italian and French ships found themselves subject to attack and, in common with US and British ships under Prosperity Guardian, shot down incoming drones and missiles.[12]

apparently in retaliation for the US seizure of the tanker *Suez Rajan,* which had been carrying Iranian crude oil in contravention of unilateral US sanctions.[9] The value of naval patrols, as a protective measure, was illustrated later that year, in July, when, according to the USN, Iranian attempts to stop two commercial tankers in the Gulf of Oman were thwarted by the arrival of the destroyer USS *McFaul,* supported by a MQ-9 Reaper drone and a P-8 Poseidon patrol plane. Iranian naval vessels had approached the tankers, ordering them to stop, and even fired upon one, inflicting minor damage, but in both cases they withdrew with the arrival of the USN, responding to distress calls from the ships. The value of presence, which enabled the destroyer to intervene before the ships could be seized, and the capacity of that ship to offer a balanced and scalable response, if needed, was evident (see Figure 9.1).[10] European concern about Iranian activity was reflected in the establishment of Operation Agenor, in 2020, a mission designed to enhance maritime situational awareness within the Strait of Hormuz. By 2024 a total of twenty-five ships from nine different nations had contributed to Agenor, supported by French maritime patrol aircraft and Italian Reaper UAVs for aerial surveillance.[11]

Naval forces may be employed to stop the movement of specific goods to a regime in support of national aims or at the behest of an international organisation such as the UN. An example of the latter is EU Operation Irini, initiated in 2020, employing air, satellite and maritime assets in an attempt to enforce the UN arms embargo on Libya.[13] Ultimately, of course, a maritime blockade can be imposed for military advantage and/or to inflict economic costs on an adversary. Here the impact usually tends to be slow and often those hit hardest are the weak and the poor. Thus, the air and naval blockade of Yemen by a Saudi-led coalition from 2015 prompted

Figure 9.1 Fast attack craft from the Iranian Islamic Revolutionary Guards approach the Panamanian-flagged oil tanker *Niovi* as it transits the Strait of Hormuz, 3 May 2023. This was the second tanker to be taken and forcibly brought to Iran that week. While some navies may seek to challenge the free movement of shipping, others will seek to meet that challenge. Source: www.navy.mil/Resources/Photo-Gallery/igphoto/2003214619/

considerable international opposition due to the impact that it had on innocent civilians.[14] Blockade, as a weapon, has always brought diplomatic complications as it can impact heavily on neutral third parties. Russian moves to blockade Ukraine in 2022 threatened to cause hunger in many developing countries who lost access to Ukrainian grain. As staple food prices rose globally the UN warned that 44 million people in thirty-eight countries were facing 'emergency levels of hunger'. The diplomatic fall-out, including amongst countries that were generally sympathetic to Russia, resulted in an agreement to allow safe passage for grain vessels through an agreed Black Sea corridor.[15] Russia exploited for diplomatic effect discussions about the maintenance and renewal of this agreement, before withdrawing from the agreement in July 2023, announcing that ships approaching Ukraine would be considered legitimate targets regardless of flag, and then launching a series of attacks on Ukrainian grain storage facilities and export infrastructure. This all suggests that blockade, a rather old form of naval warfare, remains relevant in the twenty-first century.

Despite some concerns about creeping territorialisation, the seas remain a medium conducive to free movement in a way that is not analogous to the land or the airspace above it, where rights of passage can lawfully be denied. This makes the seas particularly valuable for the deployment of military force for diplomatic purposes and other situations short of war. Navies, and other maritime agencies, continue to use the sea to foster friendship and goodwill, to support allies and partners or to coerce potential adversaries. Such activities were examined in detail during the Cold War, often under the rubric of '**gunboat diplomacy**', most famously in the work of James Cable.[16] Recent scholarship, including works by Christian Le Mière and Kevin Rowlands, demonstrates the continued relevance of such activity, which may as often be supportive as coercive and which may also frequently involve maritime agencies that are not navies.[17] Indeed, in some respects non-naval forces, like coastguards, may have a particular advantage in appearing less belligerent than naval vessels, which may suit the narrative in a situation where an actor does not wish to appear overtly aggressive. On other occasions, of course, the whole point is to illustrate military potential, and the expansive air and sea manoeuvres by Chinese forces off the coast of Taiwan in August 2022, in response to the visit to Taipei of US House Speaker Nancy Pelosi, provides a good case in point.[18]

In addition to the above, the many ongoing disputes over sovereignty at sea appear to suggest that navies will continue to have a role protecting or challenging rights of passage and use of the sea and in supporting national claims of jurisdiction. Thus, for example, the numerous disputes over sovereignty and jurisdiction in the East and South China Seas have seen the navies and other maritime law enforcement agencies (MLEAs) of many of the claimants engaging in posturing, confrontation, acts of violence and intimidation, and even occasional bouts of limited armed conflict. At the more extreme end of the scale, in 1988 the Chinese navy fought and sank three Vietnamese vessels at Johnson Reef in the Spratley Islands. More typically, China has used its maritime militia, coastguard and also the navy to block and harass vessels belonging to the other littoral states within the region and to challenge so-called 'Freedom of Navigation' cruises by the US and its allies, designed to demonstrate the continued right and ability of warships to transit through areas that China considers its own. The Chinese militarisation of islands and reefs within the South China Seas, including major construction programmes to develop what were previously uninhabitable places, has been one of the key security dynamics in the region, as has been the refusal of Beijing to accept the conclusions of the International Court of Arbitration when its rulings support the claims of others. Less powerful states, including Vietnam and the Philippines, have also sought to use maritime forces to protect their rights, but do so in a situation where they must move carefully in the shadow of a superpower. Similar issues are evident in the East China Seas, and both Japan and China have used their naval forces proactively to support their conflicting claims to the Diaoyu/Senkaku islands.[19.] The problem is not limited to Asia, and disputes over sovereignty and jurisdiction occur in many regions, including Europe. Often politics combines with economics and strategy as sovereignty of rocks and islands promises jurisdiction over wider sea areas and the resources within them.

Writing during the Cold War, Ken Booth and Eric Grove argued that naval roles could be defined broadly as being military, diplomatic and constabulary.[20] This remains a useful way of thinking about naval warfare, or at least of identifying and categorising naval activities. The Royal Australian Navy has adopted a version of this 'trinity' in its public pronouncements, listing a span of maritime tasks that ranges from the benign to the coercive. It is important to remember that the boundaries between these categories are porous and rather arbitrarily drawn. There is considerable overlap between them. The dividing line between coercive diplomacy (diplomatic) and power projection (military), for example, can sometimes be hard to spot. Many of the tasks identified in Figure 9.2 fit traditional assumptions about the

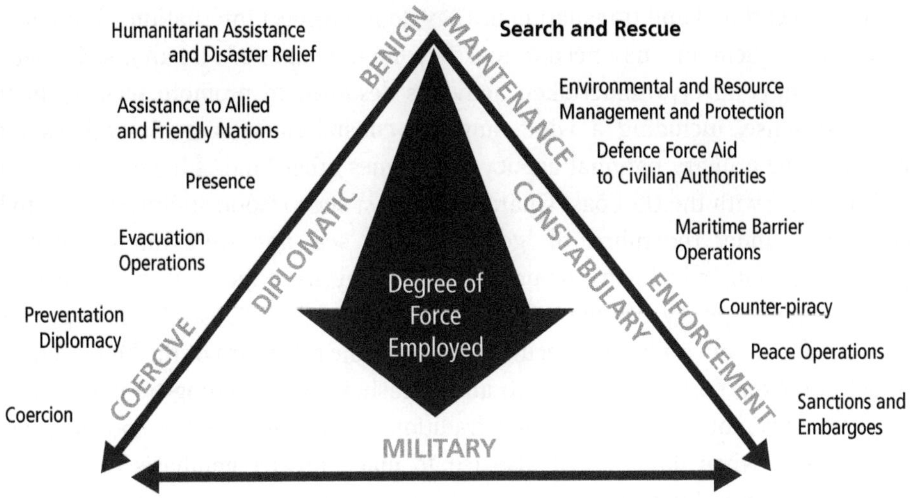

COMBAT OPERATIONS AT SEA

- Intelligence Collection and Surveillance
- Cover
- Maritime Strike and Interdiction
- Containment
- Blockade
- Barrier Operations and Defended Areas
- Layered Defence
- Advance Force Operations
- Protection Of Merchant Shipping

COMBAT OPERATIONS FROM THE SEA

- Maritime Mobility (Sea Lift)
- Land Strike
- Support to Operations on Land and in the Air
- Amphibious Operations

Figure 9.2 The span of naval tasks

roles of navies; others, such as HA/DR or environmental protection, appear rather new. In truth most 'new' tasks are far from unprecedented historically but it is fair to say that many navies now place a greater emphasis on these than was once typical.

One of the features of recent discourse on naval policy has been the focus on broader security challenges posed by potential disorder at and from the sea and on the need to protect and police the global maritime commons. As a policing operation, this is quite a task given that the seas cover over 139 million square miles and provide a medium that is opaque and underregulated. Threats may arise as a result of terrorist or criminal activity at sea or ashore. They include the challenge of piracy, an ancient problem that refuses to go away. Challenges to good order at sea may be linked to poor maritime practice and include environmental pollution and resource degradation (especially of fisheries). They may often involve the transportation of illegal cargo, including narcotics, arms or people, and the need to counter illegal immigration by sea is a notable task for many maritime agencies. These challenges are unconventional and transnational. They do not respect international boundaries and to solve them one may need to look beyond the pages of Mahan and Corbett.[21]

Navies have always undertaken activities designed to promote security in the broadest sense, including a wide range of constabulary roles. Sometimes they represent the primary national agency, sometimes other MLEAs have the lead role, as is the case with the US Coast Guard. In the past such responsibilities tended to be considered under the rubric of 'good order at sea' and were rarely given the prominence (either in theory or practice) that they have received in recent years. An upsurge of piracy off the coast of Somalia in the 2000s, allied to growing concern about non-traditional security threats in the aftermath of the '9/11' terrorist attacks on New York in 2001, led to an increasing understanding by navies of the need to focus more attention on non-traditional challenges, and to cooperate with other navies when doing so. It also led to much greater emphasis on maritime security concerns by policymakers, and also by academics. A number of states issued maritime security strategies or plans to articulate their response to the perceived challenge, as did multinational organisations that included the EU, the African Union and the Association of Southeast Asian Nations (ASEAN).[22] As a result, it is fair to say that 'maritime security' is now a much more mainstream concern than was once the case (see Box 9.3).

Maritime security may be most commonly used as a term to describe non-traditional security roles; however, these do not exist in a context entirely divorced from more traditional naval activities and many navies now define maritime security operations (MSO) in a way that blurs the lines between the military, diplomatic and constabulary roles. MSO go beyond traditional constabulary tasks, such as resource protection within national waters, to include a wider spectrum that, according to British maritime doctrine, may include operations from 'defence (short of war fighting) through to security to development and relieving human suffering

BOX 9.3 DEFINING 'MARITIME SECURITY'

Different organisations have defined 'maritime security' in different ways. The ASEAN Regional Forum Work Plan identified that there were traditional security threats, such as military threats and state sovereignty concerns, and also 'non-traditional challenges' that included 'piracy and armed robbery against ships, people smuggling, terrorism, money laundering and terrorist financing, illicit drugs and illicit small arms trafficking, and human trafficking' while noting also the need for international cooperation to handle 'search and rescue, illegal, unreported and unregulated (IUU) fishing, natural disasters, climate change and understanding and protecting the marine environment'.[23] The term 'maritime security' is most commonly used to refer to these non-traditional challenges, and the current focus on such roles provides a useful reminder that naval roles extend far beyond war fighting, in a way that is not closely analogous to air and land forces.

by utilising the full spectrum of maritime forces'.[24] These may thus involve robust enforcement actions, including those required to support peace operations. They may be more coercive than traditional approaches to the good order at sea. The emphasis is often as much on promoting good order *from* the sea as it is on activity *at* sea.

The above reflects a belief that there are no sharp dividing lines between naval roles nor is the difference between peace and war as clear cut as it may sometimes have seemed in the past. There is now widespread appreciation that armed forces, including navies, must be able to operate across a spectrum, sometimes described as a 'continuum of conflict', that ranges from cooperation through rivalry to confrontation and potentially also armed conflict. In many cases, armed forces will collaborate to deal with common challenges as was the case in the various multinational anti-piracy initiatives off the coast of Somalia or in collaborative exercises designed to boost the maritime security capabilities of West African nations, such as the US-led Africa Partnership Station. On other occasions, they may be required to deter or challenge potential adversaries.

In recent years there has been much literature on the threat posed by 'hybrid warfare' and by activity within the 'grey zone' between war and peace, where actors can conduct covert and special operations, often exploiting plausible deniability to achieve leverage just below their adversary's threshold for armed response. The sea provides an environment conductive to hybrid attack, and always has done, although in the past commentators did not think to attach such a snappy title to these activities. Thus, for example, note covert deniable attacks launched by Italian submarines on shipping heading to Republican Spain during the Spanish Civil War, or the deployment of mines to the Red Sea by an unknown party (likely by Libya) in 1984. More recently, Western commentators have accused China of exploiting grey zone operations in the South China Seas, and Russian activity against Ukraine in the period between 2014 and the outright invasion of that country in 2022 also fits the pattern.[25] In such circumstances navies may require a balanced range of capabilities, able to meet challenges across the continuum and to deny potential opponents the luxury of believing that they can prevail within or beyond the grey zone.

In reality, of course, it has never been the case that military, diplomatic and constabulary roles could be separated into different categories. Often maritime security tasks require at least rudimentary military capabilities to be carried out, and some missions, such as counter-piracy operations, may depend on a range of capabilities that only the military can provide. Diplomatic efforts to coerce or support may depend for their impact on perceptions about potential military capability while military actions in peace and in war can impact on diplomacy and wider non-military security. It may be better, therefore, to consider the three roles more as overlapping spheres than as a triangle with discrete edges (see Figure 9.3). As ever, some navies will concentrate more on one sphere than the other and will tailor their approach accordingly. It is usually the case, though, that even navies with a particular emphasis on constabulary roles retain some focus on the military

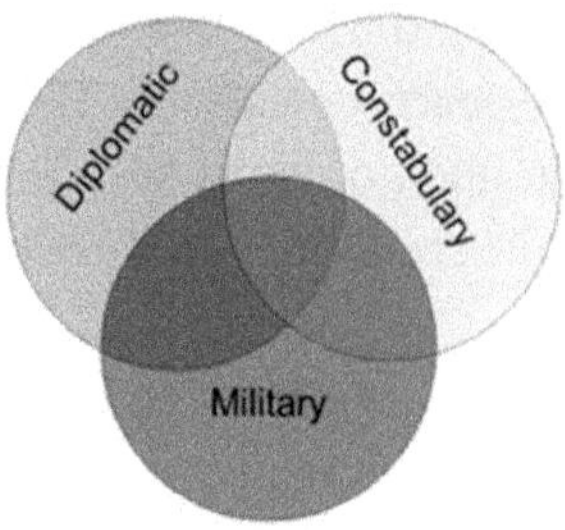

Figure 9.3 Overlapping naval roles.

mission, which represents the defining characteristic of a 'navy' and the thing that distinguishes them from coastguards and other maritime agencies.

Naval Warfare: Changing Forms?

While one can argue that despite significant shifts in emphasis and priority there has been a considerable degree of continuity in the general roles that navies undertake, even a cursory glance through history demonstrates that navies have had to change their forms in order to meet new challenges or to seize opportunities. To be a successful naval officer in the modern period has required the ability to adjust to change. Thus, while navies today have access to, and are challenged by, a range of capabilities radically different from those that existed in previous generations, change has long been the norm in naval warfare. Debates today about the impact of drones, hypersonic missiles or anti-ship ballistic missiles reflect the novel capabilities of new technology, but sit within a long tradition of similar debates such as those in the 1930s that were focused on the impact of airpower on naval operations, or from the 1970s and 1980s about the challenge posed by anti-ship cruise missiles (ASCMs).

Change can be the result of many factors. Technology may be significant, but so also are a wide variety of other things. Changing societal values, for example, may influence decisions about whether, when and how to use force and, of course, about which technologies to develop. Changes in threat perception can be important as shifting priorities may imply different approaches and new force structures even in the absence of any radical technological advance. Such advances do occur, but they have tended to be evolutionary rather than revolutionary in their impact and are often less about the technology per se than about changes in the ways that technology is understood and used. It is wise to be sceptical of the all-too-frequent claims by some commentators that this or that new technology has changed everything. It may be true, but it almost never is. Nevertheless, of course, it is important to understand that change does occur. Its sources and its impact can be hard to predict and there may be severe costs associated with a failure to adapt to it in ways that are timely and appropriate.

One of the developments that has excited particular attention recently has been the proliferation of advanced technology designed to enable adversaries to deny access to and/or to restrict freedom of manoeuvre within an operational area. It is apparent that the former Western lead in high-technology weapons and systems has gone, at least in some areas, and today some high-technology weapons systems, previously available only to major powers, have become more widely accessible to others. The successful attack on the Israeli **corvette** INS *Hanit* off the coast of Lebanon, conducted by Hezbollah in 2006 using a Chinese-designed anti-ship missile, showed that even substate groups can now gain access to effective sea-denial weaponry, a point reinforced more recently by successful Houthi attacks on shipping in the Red Sea using relatively low-technology rockets and drones. The Ukrainian ability to challenge Russia control of the northern Black Sea and the successful sinking of numerous Russian warships using land-based anti-ship missiles, drones and sea drones further reinforces the point. Indeed, within the first two years of the war, Ukraine may have succeeded in destroying around a third of the pre-war Black Sea Fleet; the April 2022 sinking of the Russian flagship, the cruiser *Moskva*, was a particularly notable success.[26]

Thus, while challenges to control are as old as naval warfare itself, the concern now is that a combination of advanced systems and the innovative use of cheaper low-technology capabilities might allow a wide range of potential adversaries to deny the seas to even the most powerful navy. For some this represents a major problem; for others it is an opportunity. For those wishing to use the sea as a platform for their global presence it is the latter rather than the former that applies. Western commentators and navies have focused particular attention on what are often described as A2/AD capabilities as a key challenge (see Box 9.4). The Chinese, who are often identified as being the major challengers, tend to write instead of 'counter-intervention' techniques and capabilities but, whatever language is used, it is clear that navies will face a multidimensional threat when operating within range of adversary denial forces.

New and emerging technology may exacerbate the threat, particularly to surface forces, by enhancing the ability of sensors to detect assets at sea and thus to cue attacks by a new generation of fast, stealthy and accurate weapons that may be increasingly difficult to detect, defeat or destroy. It seems probable that new missiles will evolve to become smaller, faster, smarter, stealthier and more deadly at greater range. The introduction of hypersonic missiles and of anti-ship ballistic missiles will challenge the capacity of existing defences to track and defeat them. Mines may become more discriminating and harder to detect. Old-fashioned contact mines will continue to be cheap and easy to deploy but will remain deadly and difficult to clear quickly. There will continue to be a battle between submarine and anti-submarine technology, and the advent of large underwater drones will give new possibilities for stealthy deployment into contested zones. A growing number of states may deploy nuclear-powered vessels, giving their submarine forces enhanced speed, range and endurance, and this is reflected in moves by medium-sized navies – including those of Australia, Brazil and India – to develop this capability in collaboration with international partners. Torpedoes will continue to pose a deadly threat, and may gain yet more speed, range and accuracy. Enhanced ISR will make the sea less opaque than

BOX 9.4 ANTI-ACCESS/AREA-DENIAL (A2/AD)

'Anti-access' refers to actions and capabilities, usually long range, that are designed to slow or prevent opposing forces from entering an operational area. 'Area-denial' relates to shorter-range measures that are designed to limit freedom of action within the operational area. There are a wide range of actions and capabilities that can be employed. The threat comes not just from new technology but also in the ability of adversaries to adopt innovative tactics, often using older technologies, to maximise their strengths and to exploit enemy weaknesses.

Anti-access approaches might include long-range air, drone and missile attacks to strike at forces or support infrastructure, and the use of submarines to interdict sea lines of communication. These may be supported by long-range reconnaissance and surveillance systems that can enable targeting. New hypersonic missiles and anti-ship ballistic missiles may pose huge challenges to existing air defence systems at great range from the launch site. Mounting bases and support infrastructure might be subject to cyber-attacks and to strikes by special forces. Key space-based systems (important for command and control, communications, navigation, surveillance and targeting) could suffer attack by kinetic and non-kinetic anti-satellite systems including attacks on ground stations.

Area denial may involve sophisticated air defences to deny air superiority or use of ships, missiles or submarines to deny sea control. Naval mines may be used to close straits or to deny a stretch of coastline, and landmines could be used to inhibit operations ashore. Within the littoral land-based rockets, mortars and artillery may pose a threat to inshore operations and also to landing forces. Low-technology threats (such as armed and explosive-laden small boats and craft) add another challenge, particularly if they are able to exploit cluttered or restricted waters to 'sneak up' on an adversary. Divers equipped with explosive charges may pose a threat to ships at anchor. Small, fast, rocket-armed vessels and drones may exploit swarming tactics to swamp an adversary's defensive systems. Chemical or biological weapons could be used to degrade operational efficiency within a given area.

previously, opening up possibilities for targeting and attack, and increasing the need for robust counter-measures. Aircraft will continue to pose a deadly danger, particularly when equipped with the latest anti-ship missiles and supported by effective sensors. Uninhabited systems have become more common and more capable and are certain to feature more prominently in future combat on, above and under the seas, providing new options for persistent surveillance and for covert attack. Enhanced AI may create new options for fully autonomous drones and will likely have applications across the full spectrum of naval activity, from logistics through to combat.

Of course it is important to remember that developments in one area are likely to be matched by others elsewhere. For example, more effective anti-ship missiles may be countered by an enhanced capacity for long-range strike, designed to take out the missile sites or supporting infrastructure before they can be used against friendly assets. Equally, of course, just as anti-ship cruise missiles led to the deployment at sea of effective systems designed to jam, spoof or shoot down incoming threats, it may be the case that emerging challenges, such as those posed by hypersonic missiles, will be met by equivalent countervailing measures. Significant progress has been made in recent years developing powerful directed-energy weapons (lasers) for use against surface and air targets, with obvious potential to significantly enhance the defensive armoury of warships in the near future. Lasers have the advantage of being much cheaper to fire than missiles (as little as US$1 to US$10 per shot) and also of offering unlimited 'shots' as long as the ship generates sufficient electricity. This suggests that they will be ideal weapons for dealing with swarming attacks designed to swamp defences and deplete missile stockpiles. Current ship-borne lasers lack the beam power to destroy anti-ship missiles but can be effective against drones and small boats and thus may contribute to the fight against missiles by allowing a ship to use fewer of its own missiles against UAVs and more of them against ASCMs.[27] It is not unreasonable to suppose that future generations of ship-borne lasers will have the beam strength to deal with a much wider range of targets, including incoming missiles, and many navies now include laser weapon systems as integral to their plans for future warships (see Figure 9.4).[28]

The evolution of anti-ship ballistic missiles has also promoted increased investment in ship-based ballistic missile defence (BMD), although the challenges here are significant. The USN has been at the forefront in developing BMD capabilities, using the advanced Aegis-combat system, and plans to have fifty-three BMD-capable ships operating by 2024.[29] Other navies have followed suit, including those of Britain, France and Italy, who have announced plans to deploy a BMD variant of the Franco-Italian Aster 30 missile at sea on their air-defence destroyers.[30] In future they may need such defences to protect the fleet, to help protect deployed forces ashore and also to provide more general defence for their homeland and for that of allies. It is notable, for example, that NATO has refocused its own emphasis on BMD to include the protection of civilian infrastructure as well as for fielded forces, influenced by the widespread Russian use of missiles and drones to attack civilian targets in its war against Ukraine.[31]

Just How Radical Are These Changes?

The notion that the challenge to sea control could become global as well as regional may be an uncomfortable realisation for some navies, including the most powerful, but it is not something that will surprise any historian. The requirement to fight to achieve domain dominance is nothing new even if, from a Western perspective, until recently the threat had tended to be both limited and localised. Great power competition at sea represents the historical norm. What may be new is that in future a combination of technology and innovative techniques will give weaker adversaries defensive options that are much more effective than those available in the past, and this may affect all military domains. Of particular concern is the notion that

Figure 9.4 The amphibious transport dock USS *Portland* tests a new laser weapon against a surface target in the Gulf of Aden, December 2021. The development of new laser weapons may provide ships with a powerful new self-defence capability against surface and air threats. Source: www.navy.mil/Resources/Photo-Gallery/igphoto/2002909430/

major surface ships might become critically vulnerable to new and cheaper weapons systems. This has been a recurrent theme in thinking about warfare for the past century (and before). Typical of such approaches was the lament, over two decades ago, by two American commentators who argued that '[T]he US Navy is making a few well-armoured knights and they will face a forest full of peasants armed with longbows.'[32] One could note the similarities between perspectives such as these and the ideas of the *Jeune École* in the nineteenth century. Today, while the USN plans to keep its 'armoured knights' in the years ahead, it also aims to increase its own force of 'peasants' more suited to fighting in forests.

To date, claims that advances in weapons technology have made surface vessels obsolete have proven unfounded. A balanced naval task force, containing a mix of anti-submarine, anti-surface and anti-air assets, represents a powerful offensive and defensive force with relevance across the spectrum of warfare. The sheer utility of large surface ships suggests that major navies will continue to need them to fulfil a variety of roles and that they will therefore invest heavily in their protection. If the US, Chinese or any other navy were to abandon their large ships they would also have to abandon many roles; they have shown no willingness to do either. Perhaps a more reasonable response to the challenge would be the recognition that there are some places that one cannot safely send major surface vessels, or at least not until major operations (across all domains) have significantly degraded enemy capabilities. Once again, this is the norm historically.

The diffusion of sophisticated A2/AD capabilities may require navies to be more circumspect in their use of large, expensive and mission-critical vessels. It may increase the desire to keep assets such as cruisers or aircraft carriers further offshore, operating over the horizon, where threats may be more manageable. Of course, enhanced anti-access capabilities may push the notional 'horizon' much further back than it has been previously. This will raise the value of more covert capabilities, including submarines, that are able to operate closer to the source of the danger. It will enhance the utility of uninhabited systems whose loss could be tolerated (see Box 9.5). It may also imply an increasing reliance on smaller and cheaper ships whose vulnerability might be compensated for by increased numbers and by a reduced investment (human, military and economic) in each individual platform. The ship itself might be a relatively basic host for a variety of more sophisticated remote weapons systems (including unmanned air, surface and underwater vehicles), with investment focused on the systems rather than the ship. The threat suggests a need for vessels to be as stealthy as possible, and therefore to reduce emissions, and also on the need to be able to integrate the offensive and defensive potential of multiple platforms, across all relevant domains, as seamlessly as possible in a manner that allows the whole to represent more than the sum of its parts. Such ideas underpin current US ideas about Distributed Maritime Operations, where dispersed forces can be networked together, creating offensive and defensive synergies within a high threat environment. It remains to be seen how well the idea will stand up to the test of combat against a peer adversary.[33]

It is not impossible that new technology allied to new techniques will pose such a threat that navies will be forced to change their form in some way; note for example US plans to greatly increase the emphasis placed on uninhabited vessels in future (see later). This is not unprecedented. The evolution of the submarine and the torpedo, of aircraft at sea and on land, the development of anti-ship guided missiles and so on have all prompted navies to adapt, developing new weapons, systems or even entirely new ship types, and abandoning others, to meet new challenges or to seize new opportunities. One should also remember that navies have often had to fight for control, sometimes against peer rivals and sometimes against an asymmetric threat. Indeed this could be viewed as one of the defining characteristics of naval warfare. That fight must now be multidimensional with navies facing challenges in all of the war-fighting domains (land, sea, air, space and cyber). These challenges can only be met if navies cooperate effectively with joint forces, and particularly with land-based air forces, hence the focus today on integration across all domains (see Chapter 18). Once again, however, while the methods may have changed the principle is not new at all. An examination of the battle of the Atlantic or of the Solomon Islands campaign in the Second World War, for example, would reveal the need for joint integration to achieve cross-domain synergies in order to defeat enemy anti-access and area-denial capabilities.

BOX 9.5 UNINHABITED MARITIME SYSTEMS/DRONES

For many years UAVs have played an important part in air operations, including over maritime spaces. In recent years great progress has been made in the development and use of uninhabited surface vehicles (**USVs**) at sea, and also in uninhabited underwater vehicles (**UUVs**). Together these systems are commonly described as 'drones'. Often these can be relatively unsophisticated, such as those USVs employed by Houthi rebels in Yemen to attack shipping close offshore or those used by Ukraine in attacks on Russian warships in the Black Sea. However, major investment by many navies has also resulted in more sophisticated systems with utility for persistent ISR, for mine clearance and also for offensive strikes. Much smaller than traditional naval craft (and therefore more stealthy), drones can be used in places where one would hesitate to risk human life, giving them obvious utility in contested seas. Removing the human element from the vessel should also make them much cheaper to operate than traditional ships, while also making them less versatile. This is undoubtedly an area that will see continued development in future. Note, for example, US plans to develop and deploy large uninhabited surface vessels (LUSVs) and also to create vessels that might be optionally crewed.[34]

Ukrainian success using drones against Russian warships in the Black Sea prompted some speculation about this representing a dramatic change in the very nature of naval warfare. One should note that the same claim was made for a variety of other new technologies in the past (torpedoes, aircraft and missiles). Clearly both sea and air drones have been employed to good effect by Ukraine and there is a clear cost–benefit advantage to using relatively cheap drones to sink vessels that cost many millions and take years to build. On the other hand, the ability to launch asymmetric attacks against ships at sea and in harbour is hardly new, even if the specific form of technology is relatively so, and the Ukraine war has also shown that such drones are vulnerable to counter-measures even by an adversary (Russia) that may not be as competent or well-equipped as some other navies. Drones are very likely to figure prominently in the future maritime battlespace, but as yet there appears little reason to believe that they have on their own fundamentally transformed the nature of naval warfare.

Contemporary Naval Policy

As was discussed in Chapter 7, to understand naval policy properly one must recognise that there is no set template that applies to all navies. Naval activity is set within the context of maritime strategy, which itself must reflect national strategy. This will be different for all states not least because different states have different aims and objectives, and their will and capacity to meet these objectives, and the strategies by which they will chose to do this, will also differ. As a result, it can be difficult to make generalisations about the policies and priorities of all navies and it would take a book much longer than this one to adequately explore all the world's navies although, of course, such books do exist.[35] Here the aim is merely to give some insight into the more important trends that are evident today and that seem likely to impact policy in the near future.

The Return of Great Power Rivalry

One of the main features of current discourse on naval policy has been debate surrounding the impact of the recent increase in the size, capability and ambition of the Chinese Navy and of the re-emergence of great power rivalry at sea. The USN had become accustomed to a position of naval dominance, lacking any serious peer rival after the demise of the Soviet Union in the early 1990s, but this is no longer the case. Sustained investment by Beijing in the PLAN, in land-based air and missile forces, and in space-based systems able to support long-range intelligence, surveillance, reconnaissance and targeting has transformed the situation. The PLAN is no longer a small force optimised only for local defence in seas dominated by its adversaries.

US sources suggest that by 2020 the PLAN already had more vessels than the USN, with approximately 340 platforms including major surface combatants, nuclear-powered submarines, a large number of amphibious ships and two aircraft carriers. This figure does not include around eighty-five patrol combatants and craft that can carry ASCMs. The US Department of Defense has argued that the battle force of the PLAN is due to grow to 400 ships by 2025 and to 440 by 2030. In contrast, the USN had 294 battle force ships at the end of fiscal year 2021 and its budget submission for fiscal year 2024 outlined plans for a force of 290 by 2030.[36] It is important to remember, however, that such figures can be deceptive. The USN still has a larger number of the most capable naval vessels and likely also has a significant qualitative edge in terms of major surface combatants and nuclear-powered submarines; certainly Chinese aircraft carriers and their associated air groups currently cannot match the size and capability of their US counterparts. The USN also has far more experience in terms of complex operations and long-term overseas deployment. Few would argue that China could match the US in naval operations outside home waters and here one should also note that the US might benefit from the support of numerous allies who also possess significant naval capabilities, including Australia, Britain, France, Japan and South Korea. However, within East and Southeast Asia the PLAN would be supported by numerous small ships and craft belonging to the China Coast Guard and Maritime Militia, by systems based on the plethora of small islands currently being militarised by China in this region and also by very substantial land-based air and missile systems. Indeed, the latter may provide the greatest threat to adversary forces at ranges that extend to hundreds and potentially even thousands of miles from the shore, depending on the reach and range of anti-ship missile systems and the surveillance and targeting capabilities required to make such systems effective.[37]

Within their reach and range, Chinese 'counter-intervention' capabilities could pose a major challenge to a navy accustomed to achieving dominance wherever it sails. It may be that in any future conflict the USN might have to keep its big ships well clear of this danger, at least until the threat has been diminished by substantial shaping operations (such as strikes against shore-based missile and control systems). Current US Naval Doctrine continues to emphasise the importance of offensive action and of battle as the key to achieving sea control in a manner that is redolent of Mahan.[38] It might be wise to remember that Mahan wrote from the perspective of a nation that was not (yet) dominant at sea. Corbett offered a view from the nation that was, and put far less emphasis on the importance of battle, which might or might not be useful depending on circumstances. In Corbett's time geography allowed Britain to win the war at sea without having to approach the German coast, meaning that the onus was on Germany to find a way of defeating an enemy that refused to risk big ships carelessly amidst the mines, submarines and torpedo boats in the one place in the world where the Germans wanted to fight them. The result may be instructive.

Geography is no more benign for China than it was for Imperial Germany. Access to the open ocean is restricted by a chain of islands that runs from Korea, through Japan, Taiwan, the Philippines, Borneo and Indonesia to Singapore (the First Island Chain). Beyond that a 'Second Island Chain', running through the Bonin, Mariana and Caroline islands in the western Pacific, provides an additional barrier and houses the major US base in Guam. This suggests that the US and its allies could use this position to restrict the PLAN to the East and South China Seas, using land-based forces, local allies and stealthy US vessels (especially drones and submarines) to challenge Chinese control here, while chasing down Chinese forces in the seas beyond and seizing Chinese bases, much as Britain did to Germany in the First World War. Chinese commentators certainly appear acutely aware of their vulnerability to blockade through the First Island Chain, often described as their 'Malacca problem' given the high percentage of maritime exports and imports that transit the Strait of Malacca between Singapore and Indonesia.[39]

On the other hand, the analogy with 1914–1918 is not entirely satisfactory. Britain could generally keep clear of the southern North Sea and the Baltic without compromising any key mission or abandoning any ally, in a way that is not similar to the US position in Asia. In that region the physical presence of US ships in peace and in the build-up to any potential conflict might represent an important signal of support to friends and allies whose willingness to take sides in any future fight might be directly influenced by the presence (or otherwise) of allied ships. These are not waters that the Americans can abandon without cost. In addition, a strategy based on land-based systems must cater for the acute vulnerability of immovable bases and airfields to long-range ballistic missile attack. Moreover, one must be aware of the potential for an adversary to reduce the constraints posed by geography through alliance formation or through offensive military action, as did Germany in 1940.

In response to these challenges, the USN has articulated a desire for a new force structure that retains present strengths in terms of major surface combatants (still necessary for a broad range of tasks) but that places new emphasis on significant numbers of smaller, stealthy, less expensive assets, including large uninhabited surface and subsurface vessels, able to contest control in a high-threat environment.[40] It has also developed the concept of Distributed Maritime Operations, designed to allow dispersed naval forces to be networked into a cohesive whole, which includes land-based joint forces, to enhance defensive options and pose novel challenges for any adversary. Within this context the USMC has initiated a major review, to refocus away from traditional expeditionary operations within a relatively benign maritime environment and to emphasise a new Expeditionary Advanced Base Operations concept designed to use small, agile and dispersed forces ashore to support the battle for sea and air control/denial within contested waters. For the time being at least, forward presence remains the cornerstone of the US position in Asia.[41]

Here one should emphasise that the US response to contested access is avowedly joint, with a heavy emphasis placed on the need to conduct so-called Joint All-Domain Operations (JADO) designed to ensure a convergence of effects across multiple domains (land, sea, air, space and cyber) to create windows of opportunity within a complex contested environment. The navy is not expected to fight its battle alone. It is significant, for example, that the 2022 update to the army's key doctrine included (for the first time) a chapter focused on operations within the maritime environment, noting the role that land-based systems might play in the battle to achieve, deny or exploit sea control.[42] These issues are explored in greater depth in Chapter 18.

It is important to remember that Chinese naval expansion may be prompted primarily by defensive concerns, and this is certainly how it has been portrayed from Beijing. Prior to Communist victory in 1949, China suffered over a century of humiliation and depredation inflicted by adversaries who arrived by sea. Its interest in maritime strategy is understandable. As an emergent superpower, China may be no more willing to accept a subservient position at sea than was the US a century ago. Unfortunately, of course, changes in the relative balance of power require an adjustment in posture and attitude by all parties that can sometimes be hard to achieve peacefully. China's rather expansive vision of its own maritime rights and sovereignty, and Beijing's evident dissatisfaction with some of the existing laws and norms within the maritime domain, at least as they are interpreted by the US, suggest a potential for tension that has often been reflected in events, and in the naval action, within the region.[43]

As discussed in Chapter 7, in the past China focused on local defence where generally inferior forces would contest control through a form of guerrilla warfare at sea. This matured into the concept of 'Offshore Waters Defence' and in 2015 expanded to include 'Open Seas Protection', as the growing navy catered for greater ambition. Recast in 2019 as 'Near Seas Defence' and 'Far Seas Protection', the latter appears to include the western Pacific and the Indian Ocean. Here, beyond the immediate support of most land-based systems, the PLAN is likely to find itself outmatched by its rivals in any conflict, but the capacity to deploy forces further afield in peacetime gives Beijing greater military reach and influence than was previously the case, and the development of a string of overseas facilities should enable it to support an enhanced global presence in future. That it should wish to do so may make some established navies uncomfortable, but it should not surprise them. Closer to home, the combination of land- and sea-based systems, supported by satellite ISR, may give China the capacity to challenge even the most powerful navy. Lower down the spectrum, Beijing has proven adept at using its Coast Guard and Maritime Militia in support of expansive claims for Chinese sovereignty and resource extraction offshore.[44]

What About Everyone Else?

Many navies are influenced profoundly by the dynamics of great power rivalry. Sometimes this is because they believe themselves threatened directly or indirectly by one of the major powers, and the naval policy of Iran (with reference to the USA) and most Southeast Asian countries (with reference to China) must take account of this. The Australian decision to pursue the development of nuclear-powered submarines through the AUKUS partnership with the US and UK must be considered within this context. Middle-ranking Asian navies, including those of Japan and South Korea, have obviously been influenced by the challenge of China, the desire to cooperate with the US and, in the case of South Korea, by the need to worry about the behaviour of their neighbour immediately to the north. The requirement for Taiwan to be concerned about Chinese military expansion is more obvious still. Slightly further afield, the Indian Navy has reacted to an apparent need to respond to growing Chinese presence within the Indian Ocean and Chinese support for the navies of Bangladesh, Pakistan and Sri Lanka.[45]

Within Europe most of Russia's neighbours have, for many years, expressed concerns about policy designs in Moscow and this has had a major impact on naval policy in the Baltic region and Scandinavia where there has been a pronounced refocus back on 'traditional' matters of denial and control at sea and within the littoral. More widely, NATO, who for a period lacked any serious challenger at sea, is focused once again on the challenge that Russia may pose within the European littoral, within the high north and also the threat that it may pose to maritime communications in the Atlantic. The challenge may not be as acute as it was during the height of the Cold War, as Russia lacks the power and status of the Soviet Union, but recent events in Ukraine demonstrate the danger presented by Moscow and the need to cater for the threat of military adventurism. The re-establishment of a NATO Atlantic command (Joint Force Command, Norfolk) in 2020 and the US reactivation of their Atlantic-focused Second Fleet in 2018 reflects this renewed focus on Atlantic security and the threat posed by Russia.[46]

From a Russian perspective, the changes to European security architecture prompted by its invasion of Ukraine will only reinforce the sense of isolation and encirclement that appears to obsess decision makers in Moscow and that was reflected in the 2022 edition of the Maritime Doctrine of the Russian Federation.[47] The Russian navy has provided only limited support for ground forces during its war in Ukraine, and at heavy cost. (See Box 9.6.) However, naval deployments will

Figure 9.5 The aircraft carrier USS *Gerald R. Ford* and the Turkish amphibious ship TCG *Anadulo* transit the Mediterranean in August 2023. In their different ways, both ships are flexible and versatile assets with relevance across the spectrum of conflict. Source: www.navy.mil/Resources/Photo-Gallery/igphoto/2003287460/

continue to provide a means to support distant allies, notably Syria, and of conducting exercises and other diplomatic activity with friends and partners, including the Chinese Navy. It seems likely that the submarine arm will continue to be prioritised and to represent the most capable part of the fleet. That this navy retains a capacity to launch long-range cruise missile strikes is evident, as is the potential to pose significant challenges to NATO control, particularly within the Baltic region, where land-based aircraft, drones and missiles could combine with mines and submarines to pose a significant threat. Here Russian aggression in Ukraine has had the unfortunate (for Russia) effect of encouraging neutral Finland and Sweden to join NATO, further shifting the balance in that sea towards that alliance while also generating new responsibilities for the West. Within the Black Sea it remains to be seen what will happen in the war with Ukraine, and the ultimate fate of Crimea (and the naval base at Sevastopol) will have an important bearing on the future balance there.

Within the Middle East, policy and practice reflects immediate concerns and also the reality of external interest and intervention. In the former case this includes sometimes intense local rivalry and dispute and the reality of conflict, notably in the case of the Saudi-led intervention in Yemen. It has also seen cooperative activity, including with many extra-regional navies, to address the challenge presented by

BOX 9.6 THE RUSSIAN INVASION OF UKRAINE, 2022

In 2022 Moscow invaded Ukraine across its extensive land border. Russia apparently expected an easy victory, but its armies were halted and then driven back before a bloody stalemate ensued that endured into 2025. The tiny Ukrainian Navy was all but wiped out in the first days, and Russia used its dominance at sea to launch missile strikes against the land, to provide logistical assistance to forces ashore and to conduct minor landings, such as the seizure of Snake Island. There the outmatched Ukrainian defenders gained world fame by responding to Russian demands to surrender with the memorable signal '*Russian warship go f##k yourself*'. The island fell, but proved too hot for Russia to hold in the face of persistent Ukrainian strikes, and it was abandoned and retaken by its legitimate owners in June. Despite their lack of a navy, Ukraine contested Russian sea control and achieved some notable successes using drones and missiles, sinking a number of patrol boats, support vessels and amphibious landing ships. Notable successes include the sinking of the Russian flagship, the cruiser *Moskva* (April 2022) and damage to the frigate *Admiral Makarov* (October 2022) that put the ship out of action until summer 2023. Russian moves to blockade Ukrainian grain exports threatened to impact significantly the supply of food to many third parties, resulting in agreements to allow shipment through agreed corridors until Russia withdrew from these in July 2023. Geography mandates that the war is driven primarily by a land-based context, but the sea has been far from irrelevant.

Supported by increasing access to Western missile systems, such as the British-supplied Storm Shadow cruise missiles, Ukraine has launched a number of successful attacks on naval assets and infrastructure in occupied Crimea, including attacks in September 2023 that appear to have disabled the Kilo class submarine *Rostov-on-Don* and a *Ropucha*-class amphibious ship in dry dock, and that badly damaged the headquarters of the Black Sea Fleet. In response Russia was forced to relocate many ships to the port of Novorossiysk, further to the east, in order to reduce its vulnerability to such attack. Despite this, Russian losses continued to accumulate. Ukrainian successes included drone attacks on Russian ships sheltering in Novorossiysk and the apparent sinking of the Russian patrol ships *Tsezar Kunikov* and *Sergey Kotov* by naval drones off the coast of Crimea in February and March 2024. By Spring 2024, it was estimated that the Russian Black Sea Fleet had lost a third of its pre-war strength.[48]

piracy in the Gulf of Aden. Iran has used regular naval forces, and those of the Revolutionary Guards, to harass commercial shipping, or to protect Iranian interests, depending on how one views such things, and the region remains an important area of interest for the USN, and for others including the UK, China, and France who, like the US, retain basing rights and local support facilities to help sustain their presence in a region far from home.[49]

For very many navies worldwide, the issues of great power competition described previously are not obviously relevant. Most African navies focus limited capabilities on the protection of offshore sovereignty and resources, and maritime security matters dominate.[50] Within Latin America the emphasis also tends to be on maritime security, notwithstanding possession by many navies of assets capable of contesting or exploiting control offshore. Brazil possesses the largest and most capable navy within the region, maintaining a balanced fleet with a significant amphibious capability that includes the helicopter carrier *Atlântico* and the Foudre-class LPD *Bahia*. It is a force capable of fulfilling a wide range of military, diplomatic or constabulary roles. Thus, in addition to national duties in home waters, the navy contributed vessels to support the UN Interim Force in Lebanon (UNIFIL) mission to Lebanon, from 2011 to 2020, and in 2022 marines from the navy achieved the highest certification under the UN Peacekeeping Readiness Certification System. Brazilian moves to enhance its submarine arm and to develop nuclear powered boats, in collaboration with France, suggests an interest in very traditional missions to secure or contest control beyond the littoral.[51] With much more modest means the neighbouring Uruguayan Navy focuses on maritime security challenges within local waters, including fisheries law enforcement, smuggling, counter-narcotics and border control.[52] As noted, different navies focus on different things for different reasons.

Conclusion

The discussion in this chapter suggests that navies continue to fill roles that might broadly be defined as military, diplomatic and constabulary, but that these are not entirely separate categories. As one might expect, different navies will emphasise different roles and the priorities of individual navies will change and adapt in response to perceived challenges. For some, military contingencies will dominate while for others constabulary tasks may be their main role. There is nothing new or unusual about this. There has been much commentary and debate recently on the challenges associated with Sino-American rivalry at sea, and this represents one important issue relating to the future of naval warfare. For some navies such concerns may be dominant, while for others they may seem barely relevant. Inevitably, evolving technology will impact what navies can do at and from the sea, how they do it and how others try to stop them. It is not impossible that some radical new technology will emerge to make irrelevant the entire body of thinking about naval warfare, and to sweep navies from the surface of the sea, but that has not happened yet and it does not appear entirely probable; it is a big surface to sweep clean. What does seem likely is that navies will have to continue to adjust the roles that they fulfil, and the ways that they fulfil them, in order to remain relevant. In doing so they will need to work ever more closely with other forces and agencies, whether it be in low-intensity maritime security operations or in high intensity combat. In complexity of contemporary security challenges and the multidimensional nature of the twenty-first century, battlespace demands closer joint (or multi-domain) integration, as does the requirement for cost-cutting synergies. Such issues are discussed in more detail in Chapter 18. What does seem clear is that the ability to use or to deny the use of the sea will continue to be important in a wide range of circumstances and that navies therefore will remain important tools of policy in peace, war and all the complex stages between. The conclusion here remains the same as in previous editions of this book, that an understanding of naval warfare remains as important today as it was in the past.

RESEARCH QUESTIONS

- Is the sea any more or less important to global prosperity and security today than it was when Mahan first wrote on the subject?
- In what ways will new and emerging technology impact traditional naval roles? To what extend will technology inhibit or enhance the activities of navies?
- How should the US respond to the growing power and ambition of the Chinese Navy?
- How can China best use its developing strength at sea to advance national interest?
- In what ways can navies and other maritime law enforcement agencies cooperate to deal with transnational security challenges such as piracy, drugs smuggling and illegal, unregulated fishing?

FURTHER READING

Bo, Hu, *Chinese Maritime Power in the Twenty-First Century: Strategic Planning, Policy, Predictions* (London: Routledge, 2019). Provides a very interesting insight into maritime thought and practice from the perspective of a Chinese commentator.

Erickson, Andrew S. and Ryan David Martinson, *China's Maritime Grey Zone Operations* (Annapolis, MD: Naval Institute Press, 2023). This book provides a useful analysis of Chinese maritime activity in the 'grey zone' below the threshold for outright military conflict.

Hill, Alexander & Timothy Stapleton (eds.), *African Navies: Historical and Contemporary Perspectives* (London: Routledge, 2023). This edited volume provides a useful perspective that stands outside the dominant narrative focused on major navies.

Kennedy, Grey and William de Sousa Moreira (eds.), *Power and the Maritime Domain: A Global Dialogue* (London: Routledge, 2023). This edited collection offers a series of interesting perspectives on maritime power today approaching the topic from a multidisciplinary perspective.

Kennedy, Paul and Evan Wilson (eds.), *Navies in Multipolar Worlds: From the Age of Sail to the Present* (London: Routledge, 2021). The essays in this collection address the challenges of multipolarity in the past and also include a number that address twenty-first century concerns.

Patalano, Alessio and James A. Russell (eds.), *Maritime Strategy and Naval Innovation: Technology, Bureaucracy and the Problem of Change in the Age of Competition* (Annapolis, MD: Naval Institute Press, 2021). In this volume a variety of authors address the challenges posed by naval innovation in the past through to the present.

Speller, Ian, *Understanding Naval Warfare*, 3rd ed. (London: Routledge, 2024). This book explores in greater depth all of the issues raised in this chapter.
Stohs, Jeremy, *European Naval Power: From Cold War to Hybrid Wars* (Basingstoke: Palgrave, 2024). The author provides a detailed examination of European naval policy over a period of profound change, from the Cold War to the present.

ONLINE RESOURCES

A number of navies – including those of Australia, Britain, India, Sri Lanka and the US – have made their key doctrine and/or strategy publications available online. In particular, see the following:

- Australian Maritime Operations (2017), www.navy.gov.au/media-room/publications/australian-maritime-operations-2017.
- Netherlands Military Maritime Doctrine (2014), https://tinyurl.com/4fdssyxa.
- Russia, *Maritime Doctrine of the Russian Federation* (2020), available in English, https://tinyurl.com/54n7mrpp..
- Sri Lanka. *SLN BR1. Maritime Doctrine of Sri Lanka. To Nurture a Stable Environment at Sea* (2020), www.navy.lk/assets/img/doctrine/sln_br1_ctp.pdf.
- USN. *Naval Doctrine Publication 1. Naval Warfare* (2020), https://cimsec.org/wp-content/uploads/2020/08/NDP1_April2020.pdf.
- USN, *Advantage at Sea. Prevailing with All-Domain Naval Power* (2020), https://media.defense.gov/2020/Dec/16/2002553074/-1/-1/0/TRISERVICESTRATEGY.PDF.

UK Ministry of Defence, *UK Maritime Power*, (2017), https://tinyurl.com/52eum79r.

NOTES

1 Ken Booth, *Navies and Foreign Policy* (London: Croom Helm, 1977), p. 15.
2 See UN Conference on Trade and Development, *Oceans Economy and Fisheries*, https://unctad.org/topic/trade-and-environment/oceans-economy.
3 Mary Ann Russon, 'The Cost of the Suez Canal Blockade', *BBC News*, 29 March 2021, www.bbc.com/news/business-56559073.
4 Richard A. Mobley, 'Revisiting the 1984 Naval Mining of the Red Sea: Intelligence Challenges and Lessons', *Studies in Intelligence*, **66**(2) (June 2022).
5 Mark Tran, 'African Union Troops Invade Rebel Island', *The Guardian*, 25 March 2008. Simon Massey and Bruce Baker, 'Comoros: External Involvement in a Small Island State', *Chatham House. Programme Paper AFP 2009/1*, July 2009.
6 Clar Ni Chonghaile, 'Kenyan Troops Launch Beach Assault on Somali City of Kismayo', *The Guardian*, 28 September 2012. David M. Anderson and Jacob McKnight, 'Kenya at War: Al-Shabaab and its Enemies In Eastern Africa', *African Affairs*, **114**(454) (January 2015), 1–27.
7 See Peter Lehr, 'No Princes of the Sea: Reflections on Maritime Terrorism', in Joachim Krause and Sebastien Bruns (eds.), *The Routledge Handbook of Naval Strategy and Security* (London: Routledge, 2015), ch. 15.
8 See Havard Haugstvedt, 'Red Sea Drones: How to Counter Houthi Maritime Tactics', *War on the Rocks*, 3 September 2021, https://bit.ly/46gxZf0.

9 Felicity Schwartz, Stefanie Palma and Christ Cook, 'US Expected to Begin Unloading Oil from Seized Iranian Tanker', *The Financial Times*, 11 June 2023. Maziar Motamedi, 'Iran Seizes Second Oil Tanker in a Week Amid US Confrontation', *Al Jazeera*, 3 May 2023, https://tinyurl.com/32ad84n4.

10 'Navy: Iran Tried to Seize 2 Oil Tankers Near Strait of Hormuz and Fired Shots at One of Them, US Navy says', *Associated Press*, 5 July 2023, https://tinyurl.com/293pase7.

11 EMASoH – Agenor Website, www.emasoh-agenor.org/.[10 Jan 2024].

12 US Department of Defense, 'Statement from Secretary of Defense Lloyd J. Austin III on Ensuring Freedom of Navigation in the Red Sea', 18 December 2023. EEAS, *EUNAVFOR Operation Aspides*, www.eeas.europa.eu/eunavfor-aspides_en?s = 410381.

13 European Council Press Release, 'EU launches Operation Irini to Enforce Libya Arms Embargo', 31 March 2020, https://bit.ly/4g20zFe.

14 For example see UNICEF, 'United Nations Leaders Call on the Saudi-led Coalition to Fully Lift Blockade of Yemeni Red Sea Ports', December 2017, https://bit.ly/4g74Szc. Aziz El Yaakoubi, Jonathan Landay and Raya Jalabi, 'Under Pressure Over Yemen Blockade, Riyadh Seeks US Help with Defences', *Reuters*, 27 October 2021.

15 UN, 'Black Sea Grain Initiative Joint Coordination Centre', www.un.org/en/black-sea-grain-initiative. 'What is the Ukraine Grain Deal?', *BBC News*, 19 May 2023, www.bbc.com/news/world-61759692.

16 For example see James Cable, *Gunboat Diplomacy 1919–1979: Political Applications of Limited Naval Forces*, 3rd ed. (Basingstoke: Macmillan, 1999).

17 Christian Le Mière, *Maritime Diplomacy in the Twenty-First Century: Drivers and Challenges* (London: Routledge, 2014). Kevin Rowlands, *Naval Diplomacy in the Twenty-First Century: A Model for the Post-Cold War Global Order* (London: Routledge, 2019).

18 Martin Quin Pollard and Yimou Lee, 'China Military "Completes Tasks" Around Taiwan, Plans Regular Patrols', *Reuters*, 11 Aug 2022, https://bit.ly/4mI9oXi.

19 See Le Mière, *Maritime Diplomacy in the Twenty-First Century*. Also see Andrew S. Ericksen, *Maritime Gray Zone Operations. Challenges and Countermeasure in the Indo-Pacific* (London: Routledge, 2023).

20 Booth, *Navies and Foreign Policy*, p. 16; Eric Grove, *The Future of Sea Power* (Annapolis, MD: Naval Institute Press, 1990), pp. 232–6. Note that Booth used the term 'policing' in preference to 'constabulary'.

21 See R. Boslica, S. Ferreira and B. J. Ryan (eds.), *The Routledge Handbook of Maritime Security* (London: Routledge, 2022).

22 US Govt, The National Strategy for Maritime Security, Washington, DC, 2005. African Union, *2050 Africa's Integrated Maritime Strategy*, 2012. EU *Maritime Security Strategy*, 2014. *ASEAN Regional Forum Work Plan for Maritime Security*, 2018–2020, 2018.

23 *ASEAN Regional Forum Work Plan for Maritime Security.*

24 JDP 0–10, *British Maritime Power*, 5th ed. (2017), p. 52.

25 See Ericksen, *Maritime Gray Zone Operations*. Also see Admiral James Stavridis USN (retd.), 'Maritime Hybrid Warfare is Coming' in *Proceedings of the US Naval Institute*, 142 (12) (December 2016).

26 Viktoriya Fedorchak, *The Russia–Ukraine War: Towards Resilient Fighting Power* (London: Routledge, 2024), ch. 7.

27 Congressional Research Service, *Navy Shipboard Lasers: Background and Issues for Congress*, 21 April 2023, https://sgp.fas.org/crs/weapons/R44175.pdf.

28 For example see George Allison, 'Britain's New Type 83 Destroyer to be Armed with Laser Guns', *UK Defence Journal*, 29 June 2023, https://tinyurl.com/3jzjzv24.

29 Congressional Research Service, *Navy Aegis Ballistic Missile Defense (BMD) Program: Background and Issues for Congress*, 20 April 2023, https://sgp.fas.org/crs/weapons/RL33745.pdf.

30 Xavier Vavassseur, 'France and Italy Ink MoU for the MLU of Horizon Destroyers', *Naval News*, 20 June 2023, https://tinyurl.com/ajuhe7ry. Naval News Staff, 'UK Type 46 destroyers set for BMD upgrade', *Naval News*, 25 May 2022, https://tinyurl.com/4e3ac87z.

31 NATO, *Ballistic Missile Defence* 28 November 2022, www.nato.int/cps/en/natohq/topics_49635.htm.

32 Joseph Gattuso and Lori Tanner, 'Set and Drift: Naval Forces in the New Century', *Naval War College Review* (Winter 2001).

33 For a discussion of these issues, see Dmitry Filipoff, 'Fighting DMO', in *CIMSEC*, 20 February 2023, https://tinyurl.com/ypvrfff4.

34 Congressional Research Service, *Navy Large Unmanned Surface and Undersea Vehicles: Background and Issues for Congress*, 17 April 2023, https://sgp.fas.org/crs/weapons/R45757.pdf.

35 For the most detailed information see the annual publication *Jane's Fighting Ships* produced by Jane's Information Group. Also see the annual *Seaforth World Naval Review*, currently edited by Conrad Waters.

36 Congressional Research Service Report, *China Naval Modernization: Implications for U.S. Navy Capabilities – Background and Issues for Congress*, Updated 15 May 2023, https://crsreports.congress.gov/product/pdf/RL/RL33153/267.

37 Ian Bowers and Sarah Kirchberger, 'Not So Disruptive after All: The 4IR, Navies, and the Search for Sea Control', *Journal of Strategic Studies*, **44**(4) (2021). Also see Stephen Biddle and Ivan Oelrich, 'Future Warfare in the Western Pacific. Chinese Anti-Access/Area Denial, US Air Sea Battle and Command of the Commons in East Asia', *International Security*, **41**(1) (Summer 2016).

38 US Navy, *Naval Doctrine Publication 1. Naval Warfare*, April 2020.

39 For example, see Hu Bo, *Chinese Maritime Power in the Twenty-First Century: Strategic Planning, Policy, Predictions* (London: Routledge, 2019).

40 Chief of Naval Operations, Chief of Naval Operations Navigation Plan 2022, July 2022, https://bit.ly/3HEpNwK.

41 See the Department of the Navy & HQ Marine Corps, *Tentative Manual for Expeditionary Advanced Base Operations*, February 2021.

42 Headquarters, Department of the Army, *FM 3-0. Operations*, October, 2022.

43 See Michael McDevitt, *China as a Twenty-First Century Naval Power: Theory, Practice and Implications* (Annapolis, MD: Naval Institute Press, 2020) and Toshi Yoshihara and James Holmes, *Red Star over the Pacific, China's Rise and the Challenge to US Maritime Strategy*, 2nd ed. (Annapolis, MD: Naval Institute Press, 2018).

44 Weston S. Konishi, 'China's Maritime Challenge in the South China Sea', *Chicago Council on Global Affairs*, January 2018. Also see Andrew S. Ericksen (ed.), *Maritime Gray Zone Operations: Challenges and Countermeasures in the Indo-Pacific* (London: Routledge, 2023).

45 Howard M. Hensel and Amit Gupta (eds.), *Maritime Security in the Indian Ocean and Western Pacific Heritage and Contemporary Challenges*, (London: Routledge, 2023).

46 Conrad Waters, 'Europe and Russia' in Conrad Waters (ed.), *World Naval Reviews 2023* (Seaforth Publishing: Barnsley, 2022), pp. 92–111.

47 *Maritime Doctrine of the Russian Federation*, July 2022. Also see Andrew Monaghan and Richard Connolly (eds), *The Sea in Russian Strategy* (Manchester: Manchester University Press, 2023).

48 James Bosbotinis, 'Naval Aspects of the Russo-Ukrainian War', in Conrad Waters (ed.), *Seaforth World Naval Review 2023* (Barnsley: Seaforth Publishing, 2022), pp. 12–21. George Allison, 'Images Show Storm Shadow Damage to Russian Submarine', *UK Defence Journal* 18 September 2023, https://tinyurl.com/5cnwer6n. Fedorchak, *The Russia–Ukraine War*, ch. 7.

49 Conrad Waters, 'Asia and the Pacific' in Conrad Waters (ed.), *Seaforth World Naval Review 2023* (Barnsley: Seaforth Publishing, 2022).

50 See Alexander Hill and Timothy Stapleton, 'African Navies in the Twenty-First Century', in Timothy Stapleton (ed.), *African Navies: Historical and Contemporary Perspectives* (London: Routledge, 2023).

51 Nelza Oliveira, 'Brazilian Navy Receives Unprecedented UN Certification', *Dialogo Americas*, 31 May 2022, https://tinyurl.com/489ynnkm.

52 US Embassy in Uruguay, 'U.S. Supports Uruguay Navy's Fleet Modernization with $8.69 million Protector Class Donation', November 2022, https://uy.usembassy.gov/protectorclassvessels/.

PART IV
Air and Space Warfare

DAVID JORDAN

10 Concepts and Characteristics of Air and Space Warfare

CHAPTER OUTLINE

KEY THEMES

- The air and space environments are complex. This is reflected in the sustained and vigorous debates on the roles, use and utility of air and space power.
- Air and space power, while potent and flexible, are subject to limitations that can reduce their effectiveness. Technology has helped to offset a number of obstacles to the efficacy of air and space power.
- Air power has become a vital factor in most forms of modern warfare. Some degree of control of the air is required for armies or navies to perform effectively. Air power creates powerful synergies in combination with surface forces.
- The 'strategic effect' that air power can deliver is much broader than the simple delivery of firepower against targets beyond the battlefield. Air power is a flexible tool, although this flexibility can be undermined by trying to impose its use on a single conceptual model.

Introduction

There is an understandable perception that air power originated with the development of the first practical aeroplane by the Wright brothers in December 1903, but the brothers' success marked the end of a long period in which humankind had sought to fly. During the period where humans attempted to conquer the air, a number of thinkers began to ponder the question of how the air might be exploited for military purposes. This means that a number of the key concepts of modern air warfare have their roots in the late eighteenth century. Some of the premises regarding modern air power come from concepts within the institutional memory of armies and navies (even if the memories were rather dim), while some other basic notions underpinning modern air power thinking are closely related to long-standing principles of war itself, rather than being revolutionary and completely new. The First World War saw a pronounced quickening of aviation technology, and by its end in 1918 the fundamental roles and missions of air services had been established. The success of aircraft in the conflict – particularly in the vital role of correcting the fire of artillery, the dominant weapon in a war of static lines – also led to deeper thinking about military aviation, and from this stemmed a range of controversies and disputes over the fundamental purpose of air power, many of which remain relevant today.

Despite – or perhaps because of – its relative youth compared with land and sea power, air power is a contested area. The 1920s and 1930s saw intense debate as to its precise utility and its political, ethical and technological dimensions, a discourse complicated by contending perspectives regarding the degree of subservience or otherwise of air services to surface forces. This was further complicated by arguments between those air power theorists who argued that air forces could be the decisive factor in conflict with little or no involvement of the other services and those who thought such ideas ludicrous. The picture was further complicated by subtle variations in the views of the leading air power thinkers and the fact that some nations – notably France and Germany – took different views from these theorists with regard to their own air services. (See Box 10.1.)

While these controversies began in the immediate aftermath of the First World War, not all have been resolved, despite technological advances and different perceptions about the nature of war itself. Debate – often heated – has ebbed and flowed over the ensuing decades, as practitioners, politicians and analysts use the most recent conflict to espouse a particular view of air power and the 'right way' to use it. Such contentions are influenced by service loyalties and the dictates of the prevalent fiscal climate – often inextricably linked factors as armed services fight for limited funding. Endeavouring to understand air power in modern war can, therefore, sometimes be a challenge, and comprehension can be made more difficult without understanding conceptual debates from air power's early years. Inherent in any assessment of the evolution of air power is the constant of technological development. From the start, this has driven air power theorists to postulate views

BOX 10.1 AIR POWER DEFINED

There are a number of ways of defining air power. These began with relatively broad views of the exploitation of the air; the leading American air power theorist 'Billy' Mitchell defined air power as 'The ability to do something in the air. It consists of transporting all sorts of things by aircraft from one place to another.'

Nearly sixty years later, two senior British airmen, Air Vice-Marshal Tony Mason and Air Marshal Sir Michael Armitage, interpreted air power as 'The ability to project military force by or from a platform in the third dimension above the surface of the earth.'[1] Moving into the twenty-first century, we can see a growing emphasis placed on space and the notion of 'aerospace power'. In 2012, the Indian Air Force definition of air power stated:

> Air power, in a classic sense is defined as the total ability of a nation to assert its will through the medium of air. It includes both civil and military aviation, existing and potential. In the modern sense, air power which has evolved into aerospace power is defined as the product of aerospace capability and aerospace doctrine. Air power is the strength of an air force as opposed to an attendant capability.

Ten years later, most of that definition remained intact, but space power had been given a greater emphasis, with 'aerospace power' as the basis of the service's thinking.[2]

Although separated by almost ninety years, the three definitions encompass the wide range of activities that can be conducted by the exploitation of the air environment, all of which have, at their heart, issues of national power and its expression from aerial platforms, along with the often-forgotten elements (personnel, organisation, engineering and manufacturing facilities and technology) that support them.

of revolutionary or near-revolutionary changes to the nature of warfare, even if their calculations have often depended on nascent technology working perfectly from the outset, something that has rarely occurred.

Notions that air power and its associated technology have rendered the views of 'traditional' theorists such as Carl von Clausewitz obsolete have all too frequently been disproved when subjected to Clausewitz's ideas of 'friction' and 'the fog of war'. This, in turn, has meant that cynics have been far too willing to criticise the quality of advocacy for air power, reducing often complex issues to simplistic sound bites.

This chapter examines the development and refinement of the basic principles of air power and the imperatives underpinning their ideas. We should note that as a result of interwar thought and the Second World War, 'air power' has often become associated with aerial bombardment to the point that the term 'strategic air power' has come to be seen as meaning bombing rather than the use of air power to attain strategic ends.

This chapter addresses some of the areas where air action not involving bombing has been important strategically. Air power has been vital when employed in conjunction with surface forces (used here as shorthand for armies and navies). It could be argued that the views of the theorists regarding the strategic application of air power have been disproved by the successful application of air power in the land and maritime environments, but such contentions have often been based on a simplistic analysis of events.

While the major concepts of control of the air (and space), strategic air operations and operations in conjunction with other forces remain valid, theory and practice has evolved considerably. This has made air power a particularly dynamic environment in its short history. The chapters here analyse these factors, beginning with an examination of the notable characteristics of the air and space power environments before considering the key concepts of air and space power and the way in which they have been employed since the First World War. Finally, Part IV of this book concludes with some considerations regarding air and space power in the twenty-first century, raising some of the major issues that have arisen to date, and that are likely to present challenges for policymakers and those involved in delivering air and space power in a bid to achieve the political and strategic objectives laid down for them.

The Air Environment

The air is perhaps the most challenging environment in which humans can fight. As altitude increases, thinner air means that the supply of oxygen decreases to the point where the ability of a human being to function declines progressively until unconsciousness and then death ensue. The drastic fall in temperature as altitude increases adds to the problems of survival. Aircrew in the First World War operated aeroplanes that could, by the conflict's end in 1918, reach heights of approximately 20,000 feet. The bitter cold experienced even at relatively low altitudes could be partially overcome by wearing heavy clothing, but this hampered movement and dexterity, making the aircraft more difficult to fly. The cold and a lack of oxygen meant that operating at above 10,000 feet was a deeply fatiguing experience.

These physiological effects were soon recognised by doctors; by the outbreak of the Second World War, most – although by no means all – military aircraft were provisioned with an oxygen system, with the aircrew supplied through a face mask. As technology advanced, pressurisation systems were developed for certain military aircraft to keep the pressure experienced in the cockpit or passenger area at that experienced several thousand feet lower than the actual altitude at which the aircraft flew. A further challenge facing aircrew, and one not regularly encountered by sailors or soldiers, is that of gravitational force. As an aircraft manoeuvres, *g*-forces may increase. Blood drains from the pilot's head, increasing the risk of unconsciousness. If *g* is sustained for any length of time, 'blackout' may follow. If the pilot fails to recover quickly, the aircraft can depart from controlled flight and crash. In combat, a semi- or unconscious pilot is highly vulnerable to attack. The crews of high-performance military aircraft are at risk of so-called *g*-induced loss of consciousness (GLOC). This factor has led to the need to provide aircrew with equipment to mitigate the effect of *g*, in the form of garments that inflate as *g*-force increases, compressing the lower limbs to restrict the flow of blood away from the head and reducing the onset of the loss of consciousness.

Physiological challenges presented by temperature and altitude are not the only issue. Aircraft need to be designed to meet the challenges of operating at a variety of altitudes and speed ranges. As a generalisation, it may be said that basic physics and aerodynamic principles complicate the design process for military aircraft rather more than for the equipment to be found in the other two environments. A further consideration for military aircraft designers is the need to provide the crew with the means of escape should their aircraft be fatally damaged or suffer a mechanical failure. After the First World War, air forces began to issue their pilots with parachutes to provide them with a chance of escaping from a fatally damaged aeroplane. The jet age further complicated crew escape. The increasing speeds of aircraft and thus the power of the air current over the cockpit made escape more difficult, leading to the development of the ejection seat. Even this presented challenges, since the force required to expel the seat from the aircraft is such that it can cause spinal compression, while there is a risk of traumatic limb amputation caused by wind blast should the pilot be compelled to eject at particularly high speeds.

While these factors may not appear, at first glance, to have a great deal of relevance to understanding modern air warfare, they are of importance. Unlike sailors and soldiers, military aviators operating combat aircraft that fly at altitude require an array of personal survival equipment simply to ensure that they stay alive, whether or not they encounter the enemy.

The Attributes of Air Power

The challenge of the environment itself is not air power's only distinct characteristic. Proponents of maritime power sometimes note that 70 per cent of the earth's surface is covered by water. Airmen are not averse to responding that *all* the earth's surface is covered by their operating environment.[3] Air forces can, at least in theory, range across the entire globe, giving air power one of its main characteristics – *reach*.

Reach

The movement of armies can be hindered by terrain, while navies have historically been unable to attack deep into the heart of enemy territory, constrained by the need for navigable waterways for their warships. Aircraft are unaffected by such vagaries and can engage the enemy at depth, through strikes against rear-echelon forces or by attacking war industries or communications infrastructure. This characteristic has influenced much thinking about air power. It underpinned the concept that strategic bombardment could win wars without surface forces and played a broader part in the consideration of operational art – perhaps best evinced by the examples of Soviet thoughts on air power's part in deep battle, the German use of air power with land forces in blitzkrieg and NATO's development of the AirLand [sic] battle doctrine in the 1970s and 1980s.

'Reach' is also relevant in terms of the range over which air and space power can operate. It has permitted the employment of aircraft (and space-based platforms) for the purpose of gaining information about opponents during both war and peace, and for the deployment of both air and land forces for the purpose of crisis response. This has included the dispatch of forces in a bid to deter opponents or to contain a situation, such as in response to the Iraqi invasion of Kuwait in 1990 and the subsequent deployment of a large multinational force to Saudi Arabia, or to deliver humanitarian assistance (such as the use of aircraft to deliver food during the Ethiopian famine of 1984). In terms of air power, 'reach' is significant because of the speed with which aircraft can be employed in response to an emerging crisis situation – that is to say, the *rapidity* of air power is a key complementary factor to *reach.*

Rapidity

In general, aircraft can generally deploy more quickly to a trouble-spot than either ships or vehicles. Where a swift response to a crisis is required, aircraft enable the deployment of troops and equipment. This can be of vital importance at a strategic level, since the ability to engage a desired target within a matter of hours as opposed to a matter of days may be critical in shaping an adversary's behaviour.

Cases in point include the rapid reinforcement of Saudi Arabia in 1990 after Iraq's invasion of Kuwait. Following Saudi Arabia's formal request for military assistance in the face of a perceived threat from Iraq, Operation Desert Shield was launched. Although an international response, the vanguard of this deployment came in the form of American fighter and attack aircraft, followed by warplanes from other nations. Desert Shield also saw the delivery of large numbers of troops and equipment, increasing the strength of the defences in Saudi Arabia within the space of a few days. Had Saddam Hussein decided to invade, though, his numerical superiority in terms of both troops and aircraft would have made defence difficult. Only when shipping carrying heavy armour and other equipment too large to be carried in meaningful numbers by air arrived in Saudi Arabia did the balance swing decisively in favour of the defences. Thus it is important to note that while air power offers reach and rapidity, this is not a panacea to all crises, as the military forces and materiel that can be delivered in this manner are relatively limited in their fighting power, in terms of both the weight of their equipment and the supplies that may sustain them. While aircraft may reach a trouble zone quickly, if they are to operate from the area, and their supporting equipment does not arrive, they will swiftly cease to be able to contribute.

Furthermore, the concepts of reach and rapidity of action do not apply exclusively to land-based air power, since the ability to project air power from the sea has been a significant factor in warfare. **Aircraft carrier** operations began in the First

World War, but carrier-based air power came into its own during the Second World War, most notably in the Pacific theatre. The Pacific War began with the projection of Japanese air power from its carrier fleet against the US naval base at Pearl Harbor, and ended in 1945 with targets in Japan being attacked from American and British carrier-based aircraft.

More recently, the importance of combining ships and aircraft was seen in the Falklands Conflict of 1982. Long-range air power from land bases in the form of transport operations, air-to-air refuelling and reconnaissance played a significant, and usually underrated, part in that operation, while the carrier-based Sea Harriers of the Royal Navy provided the fleet with the necessary measure of protection against Argentine attacks on shipping, and a small number of Royal Air Force (RAF) Harriers aboard the carriers provided air support for British forces once they had landed upon the islands. Without the carriers it would have been impossible for fighter aircraft to cover the fleet and support the landings, since there were no land bases within range that could be used for this purpose. The difficulties facing the use of land-based air power were demonstrated in attacks by a single Vulcan bomber against the runway and Argentine positions around Port Stanley airfield. The attacks achieved much of the effect desired by the British chiefs of staff in inflicting damage sufficient to guarantee that the airfield could not be used by the most advanced aircraft within the Argentine inventory and in communicating intent to the Argentines, but at a price. It took more than a dozen air-to-air refuellings to get a single aircraft to and from the only available airfield on Ascension Island, and this ensured that the air-to-air refuelling of maritime patrol and transport aircraft supporting the naval task force sent to retake the islands could not be carried out. The chiefs of staff regarded this as a price worth paying, demonstrating that the provision of air power – its *apportionment* – is a difficult business, with planners having to decide upon the correct prioritisation of often-scarce assets. These long-range attacks on the Falklands (known as Operation Black Buck) also highlighted the fact that the aircraft carriers were essential; without them operating fighter aircraft would have been impossible, ceding control of the air to the Argentine forces. As discussed later, being forced to grant an opponent almost guaranteed freedom of action in the air is regarded as one of the most dangerous positions to be in, with often-disastrous consequences resulting in instances where this has occurred.

Although the Falklands campaign was a prime example of the limits to air power's reach (even with air-to-air refuelling), the conflict served to demonstrate a number of critical aspects of air power. Most notable was the importance of air power to the success of joint operations. As discussed later, numerous instances exist of the contribution of air power to the efforts of the surface forces, either by *shaping* the conditions in which they operate, or through direct support of their operations, be that on land or at sea. The *flexibility* of air assets, combined with the rapidity with which they can reach the required part of the battle area, enables commanders to concentrate air power and exploit the synergies from coordinating air and surface units to maximise the psychological and material impact upon the enemy.

While air power can operate independently, the evidence suggests that synergising operations with surface forces dramatically increases the effect that can be achieved.

This conflicts with the views of the classic air power theorists and raises considerable debate amongst commentators, and is considered in more detail in the next chapter.

Height

A further critical attribute of air and space power is that of height, or elevation.[4.] Air and space craft can operate far above the surface of the earth, with space platforms being even higher, outside the earth's atmosphere. This provides significant ability to observe activities across the surface of the globe. Aircraft are constrained by international law, preventing overflight of territory without permission, but this does not apply to satellites, which can be placed in orbit so that they can provide imagery of a particular target of interest in territory, which would otherwise be impossible to survey.

The development of Surface to Air Missiles (SAMs) in the 1950s meant that altitude could no longer be regarded as a defence as aircraft became vulnerable. The most obvious illustration of this was the destruction of the U-2 reconnaissance aircraft flown by Francis Gary Powers while it was carrying out a sortie gathering intelligence over the Soviet Union in 1960. The challenges presented by air defences were to be partly offset by the development of long-range sensors that could survey an area of interest obliquely without the need for overflight, and in the case of one aircraft type, the Lockheed SR-71, through the use of extremely high speed to make it almost impossible for defence systems to track and acquire the aircraft on their fire-control radars, creating almost insuperable difficulties for SAMs in reaching it. Even so, the use of SR-71s for overflight was limited, and stand-off and space-based systems were much preferred.

The combination of air-breathing craft and satellite systems enables extensive imagery of areas of interest to be obtained. It should be noted that aircraft and satellites complement one another, since the predictability of satellite orbits and the challenges inherent in changing them at short notice mean that it is possible for those knowing that they are under surveillance to cease or camouflage their activities when a satellite passes overhead. They may also use counters such as ground-based lasers to dazzle optical sensor systems on satellites. This relates to another key characteristic of air and space power, namely *flexibility*.

Flexibility

Air and space power can be used in a variety of ways to achieve a number of desired outcomes or *effects*. This can range from applying force – often referred to as 'kinetic activity' – through the gathering of information to the delivery of supplies and/or personnel. Air and space power may either be the mechanism through which these desired outcomes are achieved directly, or *enablers* that either create the conditions that permit the achievement of the desired result or provide key elements of support without which land or maritime forces would be less likely or even unable to achieve the intended outcome, otherwise known as the desired *end-state*. This flexibility is not, of course, unique to air and space power, since (for instance) an army unit might find itself conducting combat operations, gathering intelligence and providing humanitarian assistance all in the space of a day's operations, or even one patrol. While not unique, flexibility is a significant *force-multiplying* aspect of air power. A flight of combat aircraft might be employed to attack a pre-planned target, then to carry out reconnaissance and finally to support a unit of troops on the ground during a sortie, with each of these tasks being carried out with many miles between the locations at which the aircraft perform these tasks. It is the ability to conduct several different tasks over a considerable area during a single sortie that is perhaps the most notable – but not only – feature of the flexibility of air power. Flexibility can be seen, then, as the result of synergy between the characteristics of reach and rapidity.

The above characteristics may all be seen as positive aspects of air and space power, but as with all forms of military power there are limitations as to what can be achieved. Without understanding the limitations of air and space power, it is impossible to accurately comprehend what air power can and cannot achieve, or to make nuanced analysis of what air and space power has been used to do in previous conflicts and with what degree of success.

Impermanence

The most significant limiting factor is that of impermanence. Aircraft are incapable of occupying ground, which means that there are very few instances in which troops will not be required, unless a campaign is conducted in which the seizure or occupation of territory is not necessary. Aircraft cannot stay aloft permanently, despite the development of air-to-air refuelling. Technical limitations, such as the finite amount of lubricants that can be carried aboard an aircraft to keep its engines functioning, will necessitate an aircraft's return to base, while the physiological challenges of flying fast-jet combat aircraft mean that unless spare crew members and/or suitable rest facilities are provided (an impossibility on a tactical combat aircraft because of the compromises this would impose on aircraft performance), the endurance of a crewed aircraft of this type is limited. Even in the case of larger aircraft with greater capacity for fuel, lubricants and extra crew members and/or rest facilities, fatigue becomes an issue in the endurance of an aircraft. This, of course, means that the presence of aircraft over a battlefield or an area of interest can only be guaranteed if there are sufficient numbers of them to enable continuous coverage. Even in the days of the Second World War, when the major powers had thousands of aircraft, such coverage proved impossible.

In the main, this was the result of a lack of aircraft numbers. Although the US produced over 200,000 combat aircraft during the course of the Second World War, even this was insufficient to furnish enough aircraft to provide theoretical permanent air cover.[5] The practicalities were even more formidable. Visually identifying surface targets in darkness was, of course, extremely difficult, while poor weather not only made visual acquisition of targets more difficult but also often prevented aircraft from flying at all. Technological developments since the end of the Second World War increased the ability of tactical aircraft to operate in night and in poor weather conditions, but brought about increased costs – which in turn limited the number of aircraft that could be purchased, bringing the issue of numbers to the fore once again.

Impermanence thus gives an enemy the opportunity to gain respite from attack as aircraft return to base to rearm. Given the likelihood that it will be impossible to provide sufficient aircraft numbers to keep an aerial presence overhead, such lacunae in air coverage may reduce the shock effect of an air attack. This can, however, be offset by closely coordinated action with the other components to ensure that the effect upon the enemy achieved by air action, be it physical or psychological, is exploited to the full. During the Normandy campaign in 1944, for instance, air attacks against German positions caused considerable psychological disturbance to German troops, frequently leading to the abandonment of vehicles and emplacements as the air attack was followed up by the advance of ground forces.[6]

It is not just in the realms of attack that impermanence matters, since the absence of reconnaissance aircraft permits enemy forces to move with a reduced risk of being detected and thus targeted; this was, for instance, a notable factor in the success of North Korean and Chinese forces in moving supplies during the Korean War, who threw temporary bridges across rivers during the hours of darkness to move men and supplies before disassembling and concealing them prior to daylight and the reappearance of reconnaissance aircraft.

Technology, though, has brought about a number of changes that may have profound implications for this particular limitation to air and space power. The development of remotely piloted air systems (RPAS), more popularly known as 'drones', has permitted both aerial reconnaissance and attack sorties to be conducted by an air system that has long endurance unconstrained by human factors.

Operated from 'cabins' at air bases often thousands of miles away, RPAS have demonstrated an ability to keep an area under near-continuous surveillance and, if armed, have been able to conduct attack operations against fleeting targets that would otherwise have been impossible because of the delay that would have been caused by the need to dispatch combat aircraft to 'prosecute' the target. RPAS operations are controversial (as discussed later), but the rise of this type of aircraft is, at time of writing (2024), apparently changing one of the key characteristics of air power. The ability to procure large numbers of small, expendable drones with cameras and/or light explosive ordnance attached to them has been particularly notable in the war in Ukraine since 2022. Many hours of video footage of drones, particularly those of the Ukrainian armed forces, have become available, and the palpable sense that the battlefield is always under surveillance in daylight has grown.

At their technological sophistication increases, RPAS have become more robust, making them less fragile and prone to accidental loss, but the proliferation of cheap systems that are regarded as expendable – the Armed Forces of Ukraine accepting a loss rate of up to 90% of their cheaper drone systems – has made a profound difference to the way in which we think about the impermanence of air power. The employment of larger remotely piloted systems has begun to include those sometimes referred to as high-altitude pseudo-satellites (HAPSs). These may be powered by solar energy and operate just below the edge of space; in some instances, they may operate almost autonomously, with human oversight from a control centre. Their endurance is considerable; the Airbus Zephyr system conducted a trial flight of sixty-four days' duration in 2022. While these systems are seen as having considerable utility for commercial purposes such as communication and environmental monitoring, their potential for military uses is particularly notable. HAPSs may have very low radar, thermal and sound signatures, making them difficult to detect, even if their lack of manoeuvrability would leave them vulnerable to engagement by a suitable weapons system.

Environmental characteristics therefore have significant implications for the effectiveness of air power in warfare. Some of the limiting or adverse characteristics can be mitigated by design, technological development and close coordination with the other services, while the positive characteristics, such as reach, speed and flexibility, allow air power to be employed to telling effect. The best means of exploiting these characteristics are, however, a source of controversy. These debates and the manner in which air and then space power have been employed are discussed in the next chapter, but before we analyse the practical application of air and space power it is useful to explore the key concepts that underpin much air and space power thinking and that have influenced their employment.

It is fair to say that early conceptual thought often lacked rigour, not least because those conducting the thinking were doing so from an almost non-existent knowledge base. Nevertheless, there was a general appreciation within armies and navies that using aircraft could be of great utility in war within a decade of the Wright brothers' first flight in December 1903. The First World War represented the first opportunity for testing the pre-war speculation about the use of aircraft (in the term's widest sense, meaning both aeroplanes and dirigibles/airships). As the war progressed, a number of key concepts either emerged or evolved from their nascent pre-war state. It is worth noting here that today's key concepts relating to air and space power can all be traced back to an era when the basics of aerodynamics and flying were not fully understood.

Concepts

Control of the Air

Perhaps the most important aspect of air power is the need to ensure that air forces have the freedom to operate in the face of hostile activity. Without having at least

Figure 10.1 Perhaps the ultimate exemplar of control of the air, the F-22 Raptor highlights the fact that immense capability comes at great cost.

some degree of freedom of action, air forces are unable to function properly, and this has serious effects upon surface forces. In the absence of air defence, enemy aircraft can attack targets almost at will. Control of the air may be defined in general terms as possessing the ability to ensure that the enemy is unable to use its air forces, or enemy ground-based air defences are unable to prevent one's own activities in the air or to use the air to prevent the successful operations of friendly surface forces (see Figure 10.1).

As noted above, the first role that air power undertook came in the form of reconnaissance and observing for artillery. Both these functions were of critical importance in the First World War, and these functions had to be carried out if armies were to function effectively, particularly once the war bogged down into static, trench warfare. It then became necessary for the warring sides to attempt to deny their opponent the ability to utilise their air assets effectively, which led to the development of air fighting.

Although we will examine the evolution of control of the air later, it is useful to note here one particular way in which the First World War helped to develop a critical element of thinking within the concept, namely the use of air power in an offensive role. It became obvious that fighter aircraft could not mount a truly effective defence of their own forces if they waited for the enemy to come to them. Early warning of the approach of enemy aircraft was limited because of the lack of any systems designed to achieve this. Unless aircraft were airborne, mounting standing patrols, defensive fighters were required to take off and to climb to height within a very short space of time, often requiring speeds and altitudes beyond the capabilities of even the best-performing fighters of the war.

The head of the French air service, Paul du Peuty, and his British counterpart, Hugh Trenchard, both came to the view that the offensive use of air power was most effective. This required patrols of fighters well over enemy-held territory seeking to dominate the airspace and preventing adversaries' fighter aircraft from interfering with operations. The sheer scale of airspace over the Western Front meant that it was impossible to prevent German aircraft from crossing the line and attacking French and British ground positions, particularly during the battle of Verdun during 1916. Protests from French ground units led to du Peuty being ordered to carry out far more defensive patrols, with the result that even more German aircraft came over French lines. Trenchard, already a proponent of offensive air action, became possibly the leading early advocate of offensive air power as a whole (as discussed later), particularly in gaining control of the air. Although early-warning technology enabled a much more effective defence to be conducted, as we shall see, the basic principle of offensive air power as an integral part of control of the air, as established by du Peuty and Trenchard, was proven to be valid even if the initial approach was relatively unsophisticated. It was further adopted and adapted, notably by the American theorist William 'Billy' Mitchell, in thinking about the use of air power in war.[7] Although he would later downplay the role of fighter aircraft – or 'pursuit' in the American lexicon of the time – Mitchell was clear about the value of the offensive in the gaining of control of the air:

> Our aviation doctrine should be to find out where the hostile air force is, and to destroy it as rapidly as possible ... Pursuit aviation ... is the kind designed to take and hold the offensive in the air against all hostile aircraft, ... it is with this branch of Aviation that **air supremacy** is sought and obtained.
>
> Pursuit squadrons are essentially an offensive element, and to enact their role successfully, they must take and maintain the offensive. They should seek the enemy and wherever found, attack and destroy him.[8]

It is not unfair to suggest that such thoughts provide much of the conceptual underpinning of the concept of control of the air today. By the end of the First World War, British and French fighter squadrons proved remarkably effective in keeping German fighters away from friendly aircraft conducting artillery-spotting and reconnaissance missions, with a concomitant benefit to the operations of the British and French armies, suggesting that the advocates of offensive action had a point.

The early experiences of the First World War have been replicated ever since. Nations and coalitions that have been at a serious disadvantage in the air – or, in the case of non-state actors such as insurgents, without any air power of their own – have struggled to succeed.

It is important, though, to make a distinction between nation states and the alliances in which they fight and insurgents. The characteristics of an insurgency (as described in Chapter 13) mean that, while possessing the freedom of action to exploit air assets is of great utility to counterinsurgents, it does not represent the difference between success and failure. This is because the complex, multifaceted elements of a COIN campaign extend well beyond the military domain and its contribution to its outcome. Finally, although control of the air is a vital part of modern military operations, it is important to remember that it is rarely, if ever, an end in itself, but rather a critical enabler for other air operations and the prosecution of operations by surface forces.

Strategic Air Operations

The notion that air power can have an effect at the strategic level of conflict stems from before the First World War and remains a source of considerable debate today.[9] Matters are complicated by the fact that the term 'strategic air power' is open to many interpretations, most revolving around the use of aircraft to bomb targets that are generally not to be found on the battlefield or at sea but within the enemy homeland (see Figure 10.2). The use of bombers to try to affect the strategic levels of war during both the First and Second World Wars has created an overgeneralised concept of what strategic air power is.

Figure 10.2 Originally designed at the height of the Cold War to deliver nuclear weapons against targets in the Soviet Union by penetrating sophisticated air defences, the USAF's B-1B bomber fleet came to the fore in delivering conventional munitions in the wars of the early years of the twenty-first century.

BOX 10.2 AIR POWER AND SECURITY

More central to the study of international security is the question, often conflated with the preceding one, of whether air power facilitates offence as a whole – whether investment in air power tends to make aggression and conquest easier to a greater degree than it protects against them – and of whether it encourages aggression as a result. Air power can certainly be a potent offensive instrument, and during the inter-war years longer-range aircraft, and bombers in particular, were prominently cited as likely tools of aggression whose restriction or elimination would help avert war.[10]

Strategic air power is broader than attacking key targets in enemy territory, rather it is the employment of air power to achieve an effect against the opponent at the strategic level of war. This may not involve fighting at all and in fact may *prevent* conflict (see Box 10.2). Complicating the picture is the fact that some thinking about strategic air power owes much to the concept of using air power offensively, an idea originally associated with gaining control of the air.

A further, and important, consideration is that 'strategic bombing' as understood in the context of the First and Second World Wars is associated with attacks on cities and thus civilian targets, giving rise to serious questions about the legality and ethical use of air power. This is a complex area, and a work of this nature can only address the matter in broad terms. Those wishing to understand the use of air power for strategic attack against targets that may lie within cities, or in close proximity to areas where large numbers of civilians may live, have to consider this issue in great depth. It forms an integral part of the modern process of targeting – a process profoundly influenced by the experience of the Second World War – and considerations about the use of new technology in air power such as RPAS and autonomous air systems that are able to make targeting decisions through the use of artificial intelligence and sophisticated programming.[11.]

More importantly, as discussed below, air and space power have demonstrated an ability to achieve effects at the strategic level without recourse to the use of force, but while much air power thinking recognises this, there remains a tendency to suggest that bombardment of enemy targets at depth is the sole strategic function of air power.[12] This ignores the powerful *deterrent* and *coercive* effects that the mere threat of the use of air power may have on an adversary. This is, of course, particularly applicable when one thinks of the role of the US, Soviet, British and French air forces as part of national deterrence during the Cold War, but the potency of conventional air attack, particularly in using guided weapons, deserves consideration. Conventional deterrence, a useful tool in *coercive diplomacy*, draws upon the characteristics of reach and rapidity to help shape adversary thinking, something considered in the following chapters.[13.]

Offensive Air Power and Morale Bombing

Although the Italo-Turkish War (1911–1912) saw the first offensive use of air power the idea was not fully articulated until September 1916, by the commander of the British Royal Flying Corps (RFC) in France, Brigadier General Hugh Trenchard. He produced a memorandum entitled 'Future Policy in the Air', outlining the key principles for gaining and maintaining control of the air.

Trenchard sought to address concerns from ground units that they should enjoy direct protection from their air service, which meant friendly aircraft remaining overhead at all times. This concern remained a factor throughout the twentieth century, and air forces have often been subjected to complaints that they pay inadequate attention to the demands of surface forces in pursuit of operations well beyond the immediate battle area. For Trenchard, such complaints ignored the fact that it was much better to prevent enemy aircraft from reaching friendly forces in the first place than having to engage them while they were in the process of attacking or, worse still, after they had completed their attack. Trenchard argued: '[A]n aeroplane is an offensive and not a defensive weapon . . . The aeroplane is not a defence against the aeroplane; but it is the opinion of those most competent to judge that the aeroplane, as a weapon of attack, cannot be too highly estimated.'[14]

This not only underpinned the approach that Trenchard and the RFC (and from 1 April 1918 its successor, the RAF) would employ for the remainder of the war but helped to form wider views on the way in which air power could be best exploited. As well as taking the view that air power was best employed offensively, Trenchard added his voice to those who had suggested that one of the effects of air power might be psychological:

> The mere presence of a hostile machine in the air inspires those on the ground with exaggerated forebodings with regard to what the machine is capable of doing . . . The sound policy then which should guide all warfare in the air would seem to be this: to exploit this moral effect of the aeroplane on the enemy, but not to let him exploit it on ourselves. Now this can only be done by attacking and continuing to attack.[15]

This line of thought was not Trenchard's alone, and two strands of thought emerged amongst air power thinkers during the 1920s and 1930s. The first believed that the enemy's rear areas and even homeland should be bombarded from the air. The second strand was that the psychological effects of air power could be exploited to bring about the collapse of enemy morale, and thus resistance. When Trenchard was called upon to put such theories into action with his appointment in spring 1918 to command the so-called Independent Force that was specifically tasked with bombing Germany, he was singularly unimpressed, believing that this was a diversion of effort away from the crucial arena of war, the Western Front itself.[16] However, as chief of the air staff in Britain from 1919 to 1929, Trenchard took the idea of carrying air power to the enemy's homeland as the core building block that would maintain the RAF's independence from the other two services. Trenchard offered the British government two distinct reasons for maintaining the RAF as an independent force. The first was that of policing the British Empire, which he claimed – correctly, as it transpired – could be done at less cost if aircraft were employed in some regions to support locally raised forces instead of garrisons of British troops. The second reason was to concentrate on bombing the enemy in a major conflict, although it was hoped that the mere thought of devastating air attacks on the enemy's key industry and other so-called 'vital centres' would deter war. It must be remembered that Trenchard and other air power visionaries believed that air power could prevent major wars through *deterrence*, and that, if that failed, aerial bombardment would bring swift victory with far fewer casualties than had been seen during the First World War.

Information Dominance

The role of air and space power in joint operations has been a key concept since aircraft were employed in support of land and maritime forces during the First World War. The primary function between 1914 and 1918 was to obtain information about the enemy through both visual and photographic reconnaissance. As technology evolved, it became possible to garner intelligence through the use of aircraft with equipment that could intercept radio traffic and signals and process electronic signatures given off by equipment:signals intelligence (SIGINT) and electronic intelligence (ELINT), a form of intelligence-gathering that could not only be of value to the maritime and land components but also be of significance at the strategic level as it permitted analysis of and reasonably accurate conjecture about the capabilities of potential adversaries – notably the Soviet Union – during the Cold War period, approximately 1945–1990. This is an excellent illustration of the way in which air power has developed from providing support at a purely tactical level to using the generic capabilities of gathering information to inform political decision-making. As technology has evolved in armies and navies, the use of detailed information for the purposes of targeting the enemy, or gaining *information dominance*, enabling detailed and effective planning of military operations to be conducted, has become critical, particularly in terms of the precise targeting of military force from air, land and sea – the construct of *network-centric warfare*. The rise of space power and intelligence-gathering platforms in orbit has only added to the importance of air and space power, both in joint operations and at the political level.

Joint Operations

Air power, though, quickly developed to provide more than just information for land and maritime forces. The protection offered by fighter/pursuit aircraft, as noted previously, was an important function above the battlefield, and in terms of

BOX 10.3 THOUGHTS ON AIR POWER AND JOINT OPERATIONS

There is much that air power can do to enable the ground element of joint operations to succeed. But for those tasks that require friendly forces to be continuously up close and personal to people – enemy, allies and the undecided – one needs soldiers present. Sensibly understood, air power does not aspire to perform all strategic missions unaided in all forms of warfare.[17]

protecting a fleet from enemy attack, particularly from the air (see Box 10.3). Furthermore, the use of aircraft to attack enemy targets grew in importance; the use of *air-delivered fires* (terminology for the use of weapons by aircraft against ground or sea-surface targets) as a means of bringing greater firepower to bear against an opponent, or to shape the battlefield, has become of critical importance, perhaps best exemplified in the use of air power in a preparatory role prior to Operation Desert Storm in 1991. The concepts here are very straightforward, although, as will be seen in the next chapter, a debate about the most efficacious means of providing firepower in support of the land component has been ongoing since the end of the First World War. Put simply, armies seek the provision of **close air support**, whereby aircraft are called in to deliver weapons against enemy positions blocking an advance, that are bringing down fire on friendly forces, or otherwise presenting a clear risk that cannot be dealt with by the use of land-based systems such as artillery. Air forces, on the other hand, prefer to employ **air interdiction**, where aircraft operate at depth, attacking enemy supply dumps, troop concentrations and targets such as railheads or bridges, aiming to destroy or inflict serious attrition upon opponents before they reach the battlefield, rendering them much less effective. Furthermore, air interdiction is conducted away from friendly forces, thus reducing the risk of *fratricide* as a result of confusion over where enemy positions are and the accidental targeting of one's own side.

Command and Control

The command and control (C2) of air power has been a lively subject for debate since the dawning of air power. A concept often encountered in discussion of air power is that of its 'indivisibility', where all military aircraft should be under the C2 of air forces, rather than armies and navies having their own air arms as an integral part of their orders of battle. This is a controversial claim that has not gained wide acceptance. In the first years of the RAF's existence, particularly during the 1920s, both the Royal Navy and British Army argued vigorously for the disestablishment of the new service and the division of air assets between the two of them.[18] This was partly because of a genuinely held belief that air power was subordinate to maritime and land power with its primary purpose being to support surface units (thus rendering the existence of a separate service nonsense), and partly because the existence of a third service meant that the reduced amount of funding available for defence purposes was even more thinly divided. The counter-argument held that the division of air forces between services and their subjection to the C2 structures of the navy and army led to the 'penny packeting' of aircraft, reducing the ability to use them flexibly or to concentrate them at a decisive point.

The RAF ultimately lost the practical argument over the concept of indivisibility in its purest form with the decision to place the Fleet Air Arm under the control of the Royal Navy (in 1937), followed by the creation of an Army Air Corps (1957), and many – but far from all – nations now have their own air forces along with air arms under the direct control of their armies and navies. The most potent example of this, of course, is in the US, with US Army Aviation, US Naval Aviation and USMC air elements being amongst the biggest air forces in the world in their own right. Another aspect of C2 related to notions of indivisibility, but with rather less associated controversy, is that of *centralised control and decentralised execution.*

This concept may be understood in simple terms by examining British and American doctrine from the Second World War. The comparison is useful because the US did not have an independent air service at the time, although the US Army Air Force (USAAF) might be said to have enjoyed a degree of autonomy that made it appear on occasion to be an independent service in all but name. While British airmen argued strongly for all air power to be placed under the central control of an air force officer, the US Army's doctrine did not accord with this principle. Following the serious reverse at the battle of the Kasserine Pass (February 1943) in which it became clear that the way in which the USAAF had been employed had been deficient, the US urgently issued Field Manual 100-20, *Command and Employment of Air Power,* which held that:

> The inherent flexibility of air power is its greatest asset. This flexibility makes it possible to employ the whole weight of the available air power against selected areas in turn; such concentrated use of the air striking force is a battle winning factor of the first importance. Control of available air power must be centralized and command must be exercised through the air force commander if this inherent flexibility and ability to deliver a decisive blow are to be fully exploited.[19]

The implications of this were considerable, not least since the doctrine went on to make clear that only in exceptional circumstances were air forces to be placed under the command of ground forces and that a *joint* approach to command was necessary. The air force commander, held to be best-placed to effectively apportion aircraft against competing demands from the ground forces, would be responsible to the overall commander in the operational theatre. Such a step would ensure that a sufficient concentration of air assets was available to gain and maintain control of the air and to deliver appropriate attacks against enemy formations.[20] Not without reason has this been described as the USAAF making a 'declaration of independence', a separation that was to be realised in 1947 with the creation of the US Air Force (USAF).[21]

The US was not alone in this view; the idea that army commanders should seek to exercise command of air force units was strongly deprecated by Field Marshal Bernard Montgomery as a result of his experiences in North Africa. Montgomery argued: 'I hold that it is quite wrong for the soldier to want to exercise command over the air striking forces. The handling of an Air Force is a life-study, and therefore the air part must be kept under Air Force command.'[22]

Montgomery's contention lay in his concern that if army officers, unfamiliar with the complexity of the air environment, attempted to exercise close control of their air forces, then it would see a dilution of effort ('penny packeting') and a reduction in the flexibility that could be obtained through the use of the air environment.[23] Although Montgomery's relationship with his air commander, Air Vice-Marshal Arthur Coningham, eventually collapsed in acrimony, Coningham concurred with Montgomery's analysis, noting that the complexity of warfare in a technological age meant that it took years 'for a sailor, soldier or airman to learn his profession'.[24]

This convergence of opinion has remained key to concepts of C2 within the field of air power. It is complemented by decentralised execution, which grants subordinate commanders the authority to decide upon the best way in which to carry out the task(s) assigned to them. This approach means that in a joint operation air assets will fall under the C2 of air force officers working under the overall direction of the theatre-level commander (the Joint Force Commander or 'JFC' in modern parlance, who may themselves come from the air force), with the senior air officer – the Joint Force Air Component Commander (JFACC, pronounced 'Jay-Fac') – overseeing the integration of all air assets. This construct has not been without challenge, as we shall see later, but in its broadest sense remains valid. Finally, concepts of C2 are those that draw together the other key air-power concepts highlighted in this chapter when they are employed on operations. The way in which this has been done, as air and space power have evolved, is where we turn next.

RESEARCH QUESTIONS

1. To what extent have commentators taken the concept of control of the air for granted?
2. Why has effective cooperation between the air, land and maritime been so difficult?
3. Have the early air power theorists been vindicated in their belief that the nature of air power is inherently strategic?
4. Evaluate the view that air power can only ever be subordinate to armies and navies.
5. To what extent has space power been overlooked as a key factor in modern strategy?

FURTHER READING

Biddle, Tami Davis, *Rhetoric and Reality in Air Warfare: The Evolution of British and American Ideas about Strategic Bombing, 1914–1945* (Princeton, NJ: Princeton University Press, 2002).

Biddle, Tami Davis, *Air Power and Warfare: A Century of Theory and History* (Carlisle Barracks, PA: United States Army War College Press, 2019, https://press.armywarcollege.edu/monographs/378/.

Cox, Sebastian and Peter Gray, *Air Power History: Turning Points from Kitty Hawk to Kosovo* (London: Frank Cass, 2002).

Cooling, Benjamin Franklin, *Case Studies in the Development of Close Air Support* (Washington, DC: Office of Air Force History, 1990), https://media.defense.gov/2010/Sep/24/2001309649/-1/-1/0/AFD-100924-035.pdf.

Cooling, Benjamin Frankling, *Case Studies in the Achievement of Air Superiority* (Washington: Air Force History and Museums Program, 1994).

Dolman, Everett C., *Astropolitik: Classical Geopolitics in the Space Age* (Abindgon: Frank Cass, 2002).

Douhet, Giulio, *Command of the Air* (Tuscaloosa, AL: University of Alabama Press, 2009 [1921]).

Gray, Colin, *Airpower for Strategic Effect* (Maxwell, AL: Air University Press, 2012).

Haun, Phil, Colin Jackson and Tim Schultz (eds.), *Air Power in the Age of Primacy: Air Warfare Since the Cold War* (Cambridge University Press, 2021).

Jordan, David, 'Sir Hugh Trenchard', in Matthew Hughes and Matthew Seligman (eds.), *Personalities in Conflict* (Barnsley: Pen and Sword, 2000).

Kometer, Michael W, *Command in Air War: Centralized versus Decentralized Control of Combat Air Power* (Maxwell, AL: Air University Press, 2007)

Meilinger, Phillip S. (ed.), *Paths of Heaven: The Evolution of Air Power Theory* (Maxwell, AL: Air University Press, 1997).

Mitchell, William, *Winged Defense* (Tuscaloosa, AL: University of Alabama Press, 2010 [1925]).

Olsen, John Andreas (ed.), *A History of Air Warfare* (Dulles, VA: Potomac Books, 2010).

Warden III, John A., *The Air Campaign: Planning for Combat* (London: Brasseys, 1989).

ONLINE RESOURCES

Aether: A Journal of Strategic Air Power & Spacepower (US): https://www.airuniversity.af.edu/aetherjournal/.

Air and Space Power Journal (US): www.airuniversity.af.edu/ASPJ/.

(Indian) Centre for Air Power Studies: https://capsindia.org/.

Freeman Air & Space Institute (UK): www.kcl.ac.uk/research/freeman-air-and-space-institute.

Joint Force Quarterly (US): http://ndupress.ndu.edu/JFQ.aspx.

RAND Project Air Force: www.rand.org/paf.html. Royal Air Force Centre for Air & Space Power Studies (UK): www.raf.mod.uk/what-we-do/centre-for-air-and-space-power-studies/.

Royal Australian Air Force Air Power Development Centre: http://airpower.airforce.gov.au/.

US Air Force Historical Support Division: www.afhistory.af.mil/.
(US) Air University Press: http://aupress.maxwell.af.mil/.

NOTES

1 William Mitchell, *Winged Defense: The Development and Possibilities of Modern Air Power – Economic and Military* (New York: G. P. Putnam's Sons, 1925), p. xii; M. J. Armitage and R. A. Mason, *Air Power in the Nuclear Age* (London: Macmillan, 1983), p. 2.

2 Indian Air Force, *Basic Doctrine of the Indian Air Force, 2012* (New Delhi: Air War Strategy Cell, 2012), p. 5; Indian Air Force, *Doctrine of the Indian Air Force* (New Delhi: Directorate of Operations, 2022), p. 75.

3 See the UK's former joint air and space power doctrine publication, *AP3000: British Air and Space Power Doctrine*, 4th ed. (Shrivenham: Ministry of Defence, 2009), p. 16.

4 See Phillip S. Meilinger, 'Ten Propositions Regarding Air Power', www.airuniversity.af.edu/Portals/10/ASPJ/journals/Chronicles/meil.pdf.

5 See USAAF Office of Statistical Control, *Army Air Forces Statistical Digest: World War II* (1945), p. 112, https://apps.dtic.mil/sti/pdfs/ADA542518.pdf.

6 See Ian Gooderson, *Air Power at the Battlefront: Allied Close Air Support in Europe 1943–1945* (Abingdon: Frank Cass, 1998) for extensive coverage of the effectiveness of air-launched weapons against German armour in terms of destruction and psychological effect.

7 See, for instance, Arthur Gould Lee, *No Parachute* (London: Jarrolds, 1969); David Jordan, 'The Army Cooperation Missions of the Royal Flying Corps/Royal Air Force 1914–1918' (unpublished PhD thesis, University of Birmingham, 1997); James Pugh, 'The Conceptual Origins of the Control of the Air: British Military and Naval Aviation, 1911–1918' (unpublished PhD thesis, University of Birmingham, 2014); Air Vice-Marshal Peter Dye, 'France and the Development of British Military Aviation', *Royal Air Force Air Power Review*, 12(1) (Spring 2009), 1–13; Richard P Hallion, *Control of the Air: The Enduring Requirement* (Washington, DC/Bolling Air Force Base: Air Force History and Museums Program, 1999).

8 William Mitchell, Testimony to Congress, 'Statement Regarding the Necessity of the Air Service', January 1921; William Mitchell, Staff Paper, 'Air Service Tactical Application of Military Aeronautics', 5 January 1919; William Mitchell *Memoirs of World War I: From Start to Finish of Our Greatest War* (New York: Random House, 1928), p. 82.

9 See, for example, Anon., 'Air Power', *Naval Review*, 1(2) (1913), 57–75; Brett Holman, *The Next War in the Air* (London: Ashgate, 2014); Michael Paris, *Winged Warfare: The Literature and Theory of Aerial Warfare in Britain 1859–1917* (Manchester: University of Manchester Press, 1992).

10 Karl P. Mueller, 'Air Power'. www.rand.org/content/dam/rand/pubs/reprints/2010/RAND_RP1412.pdf, p. 6.

11 For wide-ranging discussion of the legality and ethics of bombing, see, inter alia, Mark Clodfelter, 'Aiming to Break Will: America's World War II Bombing of German Morale and its Ramifications', *Journal of Strategic Studies*, 33(3) (June 2010), 401–35; Anthony C. Grayling, *Among the Dead Cities: The History and Moral Legacy of the WWII Bombing of Civilians in Germany and Japan* (London: Bloomsbury, 2007); Stephen A. Garrett, *Ethics and Airpower in World War II: The British Bombing of German Cities* (London: Palgrave Macmillan, 1993); W. G. Sebald, *On The Natural History of Destruction* (London: Hamish Hamilton, 2003); Peter R. Faber, 'The Ethical-Legal Dimensions of Strategic

Bombing during WWII: An Admonition to Current Ethicists', Paper to Joint Services Conference on Professional Ethics XVII Washington, DC, 25–26 January 1996;Ronald Schaffer, *Wings of Judgment: American Bombing in World War II* (Oxford: Oxford University Press, 1985); Louis A. Manzo, 'Morality in War Fighting and Strategic Bombing in World War II', *Air Power History*, 39 (Fall 1992); Hermann Knell, *To Destroy a City: Strategic Bombing and Its Human Consequences in World War II* (Cambridge, MA: Da Capo Press, 2003); Matthew Evangelista and Henry Shue (eds.), *The American Way of Bombing: Changing Ethical and Legal Norms, from Flying Fortresses to Drones* (Ithaca, NY: Cornell University Press, 2014).

[12] See Richard Lock-Pullan, 'Redefining "Strategic Effect" in British Air Power Doctrine', *RAF Air Power Review*, 5(3) (Autumn 2002), esp. 60–3, for consideration of this (despite the title, the article is applicable to all air forces, particularly the USAF).

[13] See Mueller, 'Air Power', pp. 6–8.

[14] The National Archives (TNA), Air 1/718/29/1, 'Future Policy in the Air', 22 September 1916.

[15] Ibid.

[16] David Jordan, 'The Battle for the Skies: Sir Hugh Trenchard', in M. Hughes and M. Seligmann (eds.), *Leadership in Conflict 1914–1918* (Barnsley: Leo Cooper, 2000), p. 85.

[17] Colin S. Gray, *Airpower for Strategic Effect* (Maxwell, AL: Air University Press, 2012), p. 314.

[18] There is voluminous literature on the fight for the survival of the Royal Air Force between 1919 and the early 1930s: H. Montgomery Hyde, *British Air Policy between the Wars, 1918–1939* (London: Heinemann, 1976); Malcolm Smith, *British Air Strategy Between the Wars* (Oxford: Oxford University Press, 1984); Neville Parton, *The Evolution and Impact of Royal Air Force Doctrine, 1919–1939* (London: Continuum, 2013) all offer useful insights.

[19] Field Manual 100-20, *Command and Employment of Air Power* (USAAF, 1943), p. 1:2.

[20] Ibid. For a full discussion of the evolution of US doctrine in terms of the development and application of centralised command and decentralised execution, see Daniel R. Mortensen (ed.), *Air Power and Ground Armies* (Maxwell, AL: Air University Press, 1998), esp. David R. Mets, 'A Glider in the Propwash of the RAF?', pp. 30–63.

[21] See Richard P. Hallion, *Strike from the Sky: A History of Battlefield Air Attack 1910–1945*, 2nd ed. (Tuscaloosa, AL: University of Alabama Press, 2010), p. 173.

[22] Montgomery made this point, albeit sometimes with different wording, in a number of short pamphlets he issued during his command of British Eighth Army and later 21st Army Group; see, for instance, *Some Notes on High Command in War* (Tripoli, 1943).

[23] David Syrett, 'The Tunisian Campaign', in Benjamin Franklin Cooling (ed.), *Case Studies in the Development of Close Air Support* (Washington, DC: Air Force History Office, 1990), p. 173. Vincent Orange, *Coningham* (London: Methuen, 1990), pp. 181, 194–210.

[24] Syrett, 'The Tunisian Campaign', p. 173.

11 The Evolution of Air and Space Power

CHAPTER OUTLINE

KEY THEMES

- Air power has evolved rapidly, with enormous technological advances.
- Much early air power thinking was overly optimistic, placing too much faith in what could be achieved by aerial bombardment. Some proponents of air power claimed that air forces would swiftly make armies and navies irrelevant in future war.
- Technology was insufficiently advanced to allow aerial bombardment to be conducted precisely. This led to 'area' bombing of cities during the Second World War, raising profound moral, legal and ethical issues about targeting. Despite the development of precision weapons, concerns about targeting remain. The development of remotely piloted air systems and the way in which they are used has created further concern.
- The concentration on bombing by leading proponents of air power often obscured the part air power played in other roles and in conjunction with land and maritime forces.

- The exploitation of space has had a profound effect on modern life. As a result, theories of space power have evolved, but international treaties have, to date, limited the prospect of out-of-atmosphere combat operations. The use of space for intelligence gathering and navigation has grown exponentially.

The Evolution of Control of the Air

By the end of 1914, the First World War had developed into a war of static lines. Gathering intelligence about the enemy was no longer possible using traditional means such as scouting patrols, placing an importance on aerial observation that remained throughout the course of the war. Denying the enemy the ability to conduct aerial reconnaissance missions was essential, and all the air services involved realised this: the challenge was how to achieve this. Aircraft were not routinely armed at this point, and although pilots and observers equipped themselves with rifles, pistols and hand grenades to give them a chance to attack the enemy, none of these methods was effective – aiming weapons was not an easy task. Although the obvious answer was to fit a machine gun (or guns) fixed to the aircraft and firing forward, the problem of preventing the bullets from the gun hitting the propeller created a challenge. Some 'pusher' fighters such as the British DH2 solved this by placing the engine behind the pilot, allowing a nose-mounted machine gun a clear field of fire, but these aircraft, while competitive in 1915 and 1916, were never going to be better performers than the so-called 'tractor' design with the engine at the front of the aircraft. This meant that the tractor aircraft was better, but the unreliability of machine guns in freezing temperatures meant that they needed to be placed not in or on the wings, but close to the pilot so that they could be cleared when they jammed. Initially, this left mounting them above the top wing of a biplane as the answer.

This was inconvenient, making reloading difficult, and the most effective form of machine gun, fed by a belt containing several hundred rounds of ammunition rather a weapon such as the Lewis gun, fed by a drum containing either forty-seven or ninety-four rounds, was too heavy to be mounted in this way. Initially, this had to do, but after a variety of attempts, interrupter gear solved the problem. This was first fielded by the Germans in 1915, but the French and British swiftly followed suite, making air fighting at scale a viable proposition. By 1918, the supposed – and entirely false – 'glamour' of air combat gave rise to the impression that air fighting was an end in itself, rather than part of the critical struggle to control the air and enable the gathering of information by friendly forces and denying that to the enemy.

The fact that the technology of the interrupter gear gave the German air service the ability to dominate the airspace above the Western Front to the extent that the period from June 1915 through to early 1916 became known as 'the Fokker Scourge' in which French and British operations were hindered severely was a lesson not lost on any of the warring parties, or those who came to think about air power in later years. While brief, the period of the Eindekker's dominance marked the point at which control of the air could be thought of as a proper dynamic contest with implications for the success or failure of air operations, and potentially of those operations on the ground that aircraft were trying to support.

The experiences of the First World War have been replicated ever since. Without control of the air, the operations of surface forces become ever more difficult. In the opening rounds of the Second World War, the Luftwaffe enjoyed considerable success against Allied forces, their efforts contributing to German successes between 1939 and 1941. Even so, there were warning signs for the Germans that they could not guarantee maintaining control of the air. In 1940 at Dunkirk, the RAF gained some degree of temporary, localised control from the Germans, preventing full-scale attacks on the evacuation beaches and the ships withdrawing the British Expeditionary Force and parts of the French Army from the encircled port.

The subsequent Battle of Britain ended in failure for the Luftwaffe. Unable to defeat a well-organised force supported with radar, the Luftwaffe could not establish control of the air, preventing an effective coercive bombing campaign to bring the British to terms, and denying what had been set as an essential precondition for an invasion. It must be said that an invasion would have been a difficult proposition at the best of times, but in 1940 – thanks to the Royal Navy – it would have almost certainly been one of the most spectacular disasters in military history. RAF Fighter Command ensured that coercive bombing failed to create conditions where considering capitulation never entered the minds of the British War Cabinet in 1940, as well as providing sufficient protection for ports, factories and other vital centres to prevent the German air attacks from crippling Britian's industries or war capability.

The Germans themselves realised the dangers of losing control of the air over one's homeland in the face of the Allied strategic air offensive. The overconfident head of the Luftwaffe, Hermann Goering, once told the German public that no enemy aircraft would fly over the Reich but was soon proved incorrect. While the British bomber offensive moved to night operations to reduce losses to fighters, the American philosophy of attempting highly accurate bombing required daytime operations, leading to large-scale air battles. The bombers suffered heavy losses, but from late 1943 a shift in emphasis saw American bombing raids being used to wear down the Luftwaffe fighter force as well as to inflict damage on key targets. The Germans could not ignore the challenge posed by the escorted bomber formations and were forced to engage. This meant that on the Western Front the focus of German fighter efforts was over Germany itself. This militated against the deployment of large numbers of fighter aircraft to the occupied territories in Western Europe, and the pressure imposed by fighting against the numerically superior Soviet air forces in the East meant that the Luftwaffe was unable effectively to oppose Anglo-American air operations in North-West Europe from June 1944 onwards.

The same pattern was followed in the Pacific War. Initial Japanese successes were transitory. The US' ability to produce vast numbers of aircraft and the men to fly them eventually overwhelmed the Japanese air forces. The battle of Midway marked the point at which American carrier-based air power came to the fore. The Americans inflicted heavy and ongoing attrition upon the Japanese, as did long-range USAAF fighters. The nadir for the Japanese came in June 1944 with the American assault on the Marianas Islands, in which the Japanese Army and Naval Air Forces suffered crushing losses in what became known as the 'Great Marianas Turkey Shoot'. The inability to provide effective air support to the army from this point onwards placed the Japanese at a grave disadvantage during the last year of the war. Allied aircraft, by contrast, became particularly important in adding to the striking power of land forces, while gaining control of the air enabled the use of transport aircraft to support advancing Allied forces, particularly in Burma, where the ability to resupply troops in the jungle proved a critical factor in the defeat of the Japanese in this theatre.

Once the Americans had captured island bases from which their B-29 bomber force could attack Japan itself, the importance of defending against air attack was brought home to the Japanese leadership, just as it had been to their German counterparts (see Figure 11.1). Although the Japanese tried, they could not stop the raids. The B-29s inflicted massive damage to Japanese cities, with the ultimate demonstration of what could occur when control of the air over the homeland was lost coming in August 1945, when atomic weapons were dropped on Hiroshima and Nagasaki: both attacks occurred without the interference of Japanese aircraft. While the importance of control of the air had been established beyond any doubt by 1945, the development of nuclear weapons had an interesting effect upon conceptions of air superiority during the Cold War. Initially the only means of delivering nuclear weapons was from aircraft. This prompted both sides in the Cold War to invest in their air defence assets. In the US, this led towards a concentration upon fighter aircraft that could engage the enemy at long range using guided missiles, and the traditional fighter aircraft, designed to win control of the air over the battlefield, fell out of favour. The limitations of such a policy were seen in Vietnam and, most notably, in the Middle East. The success of Israeli pre-emptive strikes on Egyptian airfields in the 1967 Six Day War and the subsequent freedom of operational manoeuvre this granted the IDF highlighted the fact that being able to fight and win against enemy fighters that were designed for combat with similar types remained as important as it had always been. The initial reverses suffered in the 1973 war by the Israeli Air Force to SAMs highlighted a new factor – the need to suppress the enemy's air defences on the ground as well as in the air. The first signs of this had been seen in the RAF bomber offensive over Germany in the Second World War, but it was only in Vietnam and then, particularly starkly during the 1973 war, that the extent of the threat became clear, as noted below. The Israelis went on to demonstrate this again in 1982 in their invasion of Lebanon, ensuring that they destroyed the Syrian integrated air defence system in the Bekka Valley as a precursor to operations as well as engaging and defeating the Syrian Air Force in the air.

Figure 11.1 The ultimate in strategic bombardment during the Second World War, the B-29 Superfortress was the world's first nuclear-capable bomber and the backbone of the American bomber fleet in the immediate post-war era. Source: https://media.defense.gov/2009/Jun/25/2000536926/-1/-1/0/090625-F-1234K-159.JPG

Post–Cold War Aspects of Control of the Air

Despite the constant reminders of the importance of maintaining control of the air, a debate about the concept emerged in the aftermath of the Cold War. Coalition operations against the Iraqi Air Force in 1991 highlighted yet again the possibility that lesser powers might adopt an asymmetric approach towards control of the air, using ground-based systems rather than fighters. The North Vietnamese used SAMs and anti-aircraft artillery (AAA) extensively, and the 1973 Arab–Israeli Yom Kippur/Ramadan War had a clear strand of asymmetric thinking by the Egyptians, who relied upon SAMs against the Israelis to offset enemy air superiority.[1] The Israelis seriously damaged the Egyptian Army once it moved beyond the protection of its SAM coverage, but the lesson here was that the nature of control of the air had changed: the enemy would no longer seek to engage only in attritional air battles but would use a variety of different techniques to achieve the desired aim. The examples of making a limited air effort against the enemy before falling back on the use of SAMs reinforced the importance of another dimension to control of the air, namely suppression of enemy air defences (SEAD). The Americans made a start in Vietnam with 'Wild Weasel' fighter-bombers fitted with additional electronic equipment and anti-radar missiles duelling with SAM sites in a bid to protect strike packages.[2]

In 1991, the Iraqi response to the overwhelming dominance of coalition air power was to keep its combat force on the ground unless absolutely necessary, and to then try to send it to sanctuary in Iran when the coalition used PGMs to strike the Iraqis' aircraft in their shelters.

The change was further shown during Operation Allied Force, NATO's response to the Kosovo crisis in 1999. After initial attempts to resist the NATO air strikes led only to losses of Yugoslavian aircraft and none for NATO, the burden of the Yugoslavian air defence effort switched to a small, but capable, SAM force, which was never fully suppressed, even shooting down an F-117 'stealth' fighter. In 2003, the Iraqi Air Force chose not to fly at all in the face of the invasion by the US-led coalition. Operation Enduring Freedom, the response to the terrorist attacks on New York on 11 September 2001 (9/11), was conducted against a state (Afghanistan) that had no credible air force at all. These experiences gave rise to a debate amongst some commentators as to whether control of the air remained as important as it once did. As discussed in the next chapter, more recent events have brutally exposed the limitations of this line of thought.

Strategic Air Power

The huge losses caused in static land warfare between 1914 and 1918 led to a determination that the experience should not be repeated. This made the notion of exploiting the potential reach of bombers to carry the war to the enemy's homeland and in effect bombing the enemy population into a rapid surrender highly attractive. The degree of destruction envisaged from bombing (which the Second World War showed to be wildly optimistic in terms of both the precision that could be achieved and the effect on civilian morale) also served as a deterrent.[3] Three key theorists – who might equally be termed visionaries – led the way in this school of thought.

The Italian Giulio Douhet's book *Command of the Air* argued it was necessary to control the air, but by relying not upon the fighters but heavily armed 'battleplanes'. Douhet proposed that bombing population centres would shatter the enemy's will, bringing rapid surrender. Douhet further contended that it was impossible to defend effectively against bombing. Control of the air would be achieved by attacking logistic and manufacturing centres for enemy air power. 'Battleplanes', capable of defending themselves against interception, would destroy the opposing air force's fighting power at the outset of war, preventing an enemy counterstroke; the enemy, its air manufacturing capability destroyed and unable to re-equip its air force, would be at the mercy of the nation with extensive bomber forces and thus quickly vanquished. Douhet's apocalyptic – and profoundly ethically and legally questionable – vision was flawed. In his mind, every bomber would find and hit its target, with every bomb detonating. This was simply unrealistic in the inter-war period and challenges remain today, even with much greater technology.

In contrast to Douhet, Hugh Trenchard, Chief of the Air Staff (CAS) in the UK between 1919 and 1930, felt that directly targeting civilians was unjustifiable. Undermining enemy morale came by targeting not people, but 'vital centres', such as the factories that employed them and the transport network that took them to and from work. The fact that civilians would undoubtedly be casualties of such attacks was viewed as regrettable, but awareness that this might call into question the legitimacy of the approach meant that what came to be known as 'collateral damage' was not often discussed. Trenchard's tenure as CAS saw the production of several doctrine manuals, the most important of which was Air Publication (AP) 1300, *Royal Air Force War Manual.* AP1300 suggested: 'Objectives should be selected the bombardment of which will have the greatest effect in weakening the enemy resistance and his power to continue war.'[4] The manual noted that it was important there was a full understanding of the enemy country.[5] Without such knowledge, identifying the key targets for attack would be difficult. This raised a difficulty: it might be that the British conception of what was an enemy 'vital centre' was not the same as that of the opponent, and striking something that the enemy did not value would not be effective. This applied, of course, not only to the British, but to all air forces – could they be sure that they were bombing the right targets to affect enemy morale? Air power thus required more than just bombers; intelligence and cultural understanding were also needed. It must be said that whether this has ever been fully achieved is open to doubt.

Trenchard's outlook was dominated by considerations of the offensive; he accepted that it was necessary to retain a small fleet of fighters largely to maintain the morale of the civilian population, even if the majority of funding for the RAF should be spent on bomber aircraft. Overinvestment in fighters would be like an Association Football team packed with defenders: an air force so-configured would 'certainly not win, nor would they stop the attack on their goal from continuing.[6]

This was in keeping with the notion that air power could not have a truly strategic effect if used purely for defensive purposes. It was also wrong, particularly once defences could use radar to gain early warning to launch fighter aircraft against incoming attacks – as demonstrated in the Battle of Britain.

The debate was no less heated in the US where Colonel William 'Billy' Mitchell and US Army Air Corps (USAAC) and the Air Corps Tactical School (ACTS) developed US air doctrine. Following the First World War, 'pursuit' (fighter) aviation was seen as the main effort of the USAAC, since its duty was to maintain air superiority. From the mid 1920s, though, the USAAC saw bombardment as its most important task. Pursuit aviation remained significant, being employed to escort friendly bombers or to carry out sweeps against the enemy fighter force. By the early 1930s, the position had changed yet again. The development of high-speed bombers convinced many USAAC officers that bombers would be almost impossible to intercept in a future conflict. Advocates of pursuit aviation, notably Captain

Claire L. Chennault, felt that this faith in the bomber was misplaced, but were ignored.[7]

The USAAC developed a concept of targeting key elements in the enemy's war economy. The precision needed to do this would be delivered by sophisticated bombsights, while careful understanding of the enemy would allow a list of targets to be drawn up. This was the 'key-node' approach through which the USAAC (later the USAAF) developed thoughts about strategic air power. Like Trenchard, the USAAC's bomber advocates saw the erosion of enemy civilian morale through attacking vital centres combined with physical destruction, bringing rapid victory. When war came again in 1939, 'strategic' air power did not deliver in the way in which the inter-war theorists had envisioned.

Theory, Practice and Controversy

The nature of air bombardment in the Second World War is the source of much controversy. The extensive debate can obscure some of the key issues; certainly, it can suggest that strategic air power is only that delivered by bombers. Although there are dangers in compressing the analysis of such a huge subject into a few sentences, some key conclusions regarding the strategic bombing campaign can be made. First, the *nature* of the Second World War did not meet theorists' expectations. Surface forces were heavily engaged from the outset, while the financial constraints of the inter-war years meant that the British and American bomber fleets needed to conduct the sort of bombing campaign that did not exist. Second, capability was lacking; the early years of the war were marked by a lack of navigational and bombing accuracy, driving the RAF to an 'area' policy of attacking German cities, increasing the chance of striking industrial targets; the corollary of this, of course, was that no discrimination could be made between civilian housing and industrial areas. Despite the introduction of navigation devices and improved bombsights, the commander of RAF Bomber Command, Sir Arthur Harris, remained convinced that area bombing would bring success, refusing to change target sets. Bomber Command *did* strike targets other than cities in the latter part of the war, but the Air Staff found it extremely difficult to persuade Harris to launch his forces against these alternative targets.

The USAAF's daylight bombing policy gave some accuracy, but despite the sophistication of the Norden bombsight the degree of precision desired could not be achieved. There were several reasons for this, including the depredations of German fighters, anti-aircraft fire and bad weather, which meant that it was often impossible to see the targets through heavy cloud. Bombers had to release their ordnance using radar targeting, which was inaccurate, making the realisation of key-node targeting theory impossible.

Weather conditions in the Pacific were better, but the dispersal of Japanese industry was such that firebombing of area targets – with enormous civilian casualties – resulted; the bombing concluded with the use of two nuclear weapons, which could hardly be said to fit in with the notion of precise targeting of key nodes. The USAAF remained committed to the notion that it should seek to target key elements of the enemy's war-making capability, exemplified by the dispute in 1944 over the employment of the bomber forces in the run-up to the invasion of Europe. While General Eisenhower, as Supreme Allied Commander, supported the concept of targeting German transportation put forward by several senior airmen, General Carl Spaatz, commander of the American bombing forces, argued vehemently for attacking oil production, knowing that the Germans had always been painfully short of oil. Spaatz was overruled, with the proviso that oil might become a major target once Allied forces were established ashore. The end result was to intensify the debate regarding 'strategic' air power.

The failure of the bomber offensive to achieve the vision of inter-war theorists damaged the credibility of air power in the eyes of many observers, who felt that the view that air power was best used in direct support of ground and naval forces had been vindicated. However, the atomic bomb meant that conceptions of air power operating in a strategic role had to be rethought. The Americans and Soviets established large forces of bomber aircraft to carry nuclear weapons, while the British and French developed smaller bomber forces to carry their own nuclear deterrent.

The appearance of nuclear weapons was particularly important in the US, since it helped convince the Truman administration that, while the US Army should still have its own air power, the bulk of American combat aircraft should be under the auspices of an independent air force, leading to the creation of the USAF in 1947. The USAF remained wedded to the notion that air power could win wars alone, a perspective articulated through the refinement of two concepts that defined the nature of considering strategic air power, but which remain controversial. Building upon theories pertaining to nuclear strategy, air power thinkers developed the concept of employing air power for coercive purposes; this was then followed by attempting to take the oft-expressed idea that strategic air power had 'effect' and defining what, exactly, constituted effect at the strategic level, and the means by which it could be achieved. We shall return to the issue of coercion shortly.

One of the other problems that arose from the Second World War lay in the fact that the use of the term 'strategic' came to be associated with bombing, but this was a misnomer. Air power showed that it could have effect at the strategic level without a large-scale bombing offensive. The battle of the Atlantic was of great importance to Britain, which was reliant upon shipping to bring in vital supplies; Churchill remarked that the German submarine threat was the one thing that truly worried him during the war. The efforts of RAF Coastal Command and US naval aviation, in conjunction with surface units escorting convoys, defeated the U-boat threat; this, surely, was the use of air power to achieve strategic ends? It came in conjunction with surface forces but could not be said to have been a case where air power was somehow subordinate to them, not least since the maritime patrol aircraft were used for far more than carrying out convoy escort. Some bombing of targets related to the U-boat force was also carried out, and if we piece together the events of the battle of the Atlantic we begin to see that there is a danger in 'stove-piping' considerations of air power; attempting to define air power by roles such as bombing or air fighting ignores the overlap that occurs between these functions, and they cannot be easily pigeonholed into categories such as 'independent' or 'subordinate' action. The whole point was that air power was used as a critical tool to achieve a vital strategic end-state. Some air operations may have been independent of Allied naval units, but they were never independent of the strategic purpose for which they were applied.

An additional illustration of air power's strategic effect beyond simply bombing came in 1948 with the Berlin Airlift. Soviet aspirations to bring about revisions in the control of Berlin through blockade were thwarted by the massive airlift conducted by the Western allies to sustain the city (see Figure 11.2). This was a huge strategic success, enabled by air power and without a shot being fired or a bomb dropped. We might also cite the use of reconnaissance over Cuba in 1962. This revealed the construction of Soviet missile sites on the island and set off the events that brought about the removal of these weapons. Once again, this was an example of air power achieving a strategically significant role, but in this case illustrating the overlap with surface forces, with USN ships enforcing a blockade. This in fact suggested a point that has been curiously ignored – that air power is in fact part of an array of resources that nations can use to attain their desired ends, either by using them independently or in combination. In the third decade of the twenty-first century, we now speak in terms of 'multi-domain operations', but this concept is nothing new, even if it was not articulated as precisely as it might have been. The key is to use the full array of resources, in which air and space power now play an indispensable role, to achieve a series of *effects* that either defeat the adversary in battle or compel modification of behaviour, by deterring action in the first place or making the opponent change course or desist from actions that have brought about the use of force.

Coercive Air Power

Coercion is a complex and multilayered concept (as described in Chapter 3), but Robert A. Pape – drawing upon Thomas Schelling and Robert J. Art – provides a good definition:

> Coercion is like deterrence in that both focus on influencing the adversary's decision calculus. However, coercion differs from deterrence in that deterrence is concerned with maintaining the status quo by discouraging an opponent from changing his behaviour, while coercion seeks exactly the opposite: to force change in the opponent's behaviour.[8]

The Johnson administration attempted to do this between 1965 and 1968, seeking to use air power against North Vietnam to coerce the Hanoi government into ending support of the insurgency in South Vietnam conducted by the National Liberation

Figure 11.2 The use of transport aircraft such as the Douglas C-54 Skymaster to break the Soviet blockade of Berlin was perhaps the most strategically effective use of air power during the twentieth century. To some extent, the airlift has been overlooked as an example of air power having strategic effect as a result of the tendency towards assuming that strategic air power must equate to the bombardment of key enemy targets deep behind the battle-front. Source: https://media.defense.gov/2009/Jun/25/2000536926/-1/-1/0/090625-F-1234K-159.JPG

Front (better known as the Viet Cong – see Figure 11.3). This coercion, through the bombing campaign Operation 'Rolling Thunder', failed. The North Vietnamese remained resolute in their defiance of American efforts. There were several reasons for this.

The American approach applied air power in an incremental fashion, with the threat of greater destruction in subsequent attacks being seen as the means to make the North Vietnamese modify their behaviour.[9] This had no persuasive effect. The targets chosen for attack by the US administration were not essential to the North Vietnamese ability to continue prosecuting the war; indeed, targets that might have

Figure 11.3 F-105D Thunderchief aircraft during a mission over Vietnam. The Thunderchief bore the brunt of the USAF's air efforts over North Vietnam during Operation Rolling Thunder, suffering heavy losses.

made a difference such as Haiphong Harbour were 'off limits' for fear of provoking a military response by the Soviet Union or People's Republic of China. The Americans also overlooked the determination of the government in Hanoi and the insurgents in the south of the country to bring about national unification. They were quite prepared to wait until the US tired of the conflict, which in turn meant that Vietnamese resilience was greater than anticipated.

Rolling Thunder came to a dismal close in 1968. Four years later, coercive air power had more effect. Hanoi's 1972 Easter Offensive against the South saw the Nixon administration launch Operation Linebacker, a much less restrained employment of bombing against targets throughout the North. The culmination of Linebacker II – a short, brief assault against key targets in December 1972 – came with the signing of the Paris Peace Accords enabling the US to disengage from the war.

Air power proponents contend that Linebacker demonstrated that if air power had been employed against key targets without the political constraints and gradual escalation seen in Rolling Thunder, the result of the conflict might have been different. The alternative perspective contends that this ignores the fact that the war had changed by 1972, since the Tet Offensive in 1968 saw enormous losses amongst the Viet Cong, forcing Hanoi to embark upon a more conventional form of warfare.

Bombing would still not have succeeded against an insurgency, even without the constraints under which Rolling Thunder was conducted. The shift to conventional operations made the North Vietnamese vulnerable to air power, as demonstrated by the telling effect of air attack on their forces during the invasion of the South during spring 1972. Targets chosen for attack in the Linebacker campaigns were important to the sustenance of a conventional army. Mining Haiphong harbour ensured that the North Vietnamese Army began to run short of supplies.[10] Whether the application of Linebacker-like force in 1965 would have brought about Hanoi's capitulation or not is impossible to prove, not least since it was ground combat that devastated the Viet Cong in 1968, causing the change to a more conventional form of war in which air power could play to its strengths.

The debate over the employment of air power in Vietnam highlighted several issues. The first was the long-understood need to know the enemy, to allow effective targeting. The second was public opinion, both national and international. A key legacy of the Second World War was awareness of air attack's destructive capacity, creating aversion within Western societies towards anything that had the appearance of targeting civilians. Allegations that American bombing was wilfully targeting civilians not only gave the Soviet Union a propaganda weapon but contributed to undermining public support for the war in the US.

The air campaign in Vietnam led to much introspection on the part of the Americans, and considerable thought about air power generally. The Cold War paradigm in which 'strategic' meant the use of nuclear weapons began to unravel as the USAF looked at how it operated.

The introduction of AirLand battle doctrine during the mid 1970s led to a brief period during which the view that air power was simply a supporting arm to surface forces returned; this did not last long, as new perceptions of strategic air power developed. The new thinking drew heavily upon ideas postulated by Colonel John Boyd, a retired USAF officer, taken to a new level by Colonel John A. Warden III (see Box 11.1).

As noted earlier, air power theorists have been loath to concentrate upon the utility of air power in support of the surface battle, often for fear of the implications that this might be perceived to have on the validity of the existence of independent air forces. This has led to practical problems, with air forces and armies almost wilfully choosing not to cooperate as closely as they might (while complaining about the attitude of the other service) when the two services have been required to cooperate in wartime.

Conducting the decision cycle more quickly than the adversary meant that the opponent would lose situational awareness and become confused; as confusion mounted so would enemy uncertainty to the point where they would become paralysed and unable to resist. Warden built upon these ideas during the 1980s and was presented with an opportunity to articulate them following the Iraqi invasion of Kuwait in August 1990. Warden's concept of strategic air power envisaged the use of air forces to attack targets vital to the enemy's ability to prosecute war without having to engage the enemy army, a concept that Mitchell

BOX 11.1 JOHN BOYD AND JOHN A. WARDEN III

Boyd's thought was not designed with air power alone in mind. He developed the notion that wars would be won through 'decision cycle dominance'. The decision cycle laid out by Boyd of the 'OODA loop', made clear the aim of dominance being achieved through 'getting inside the opponent's OODA loop' (see Figure 11.4).

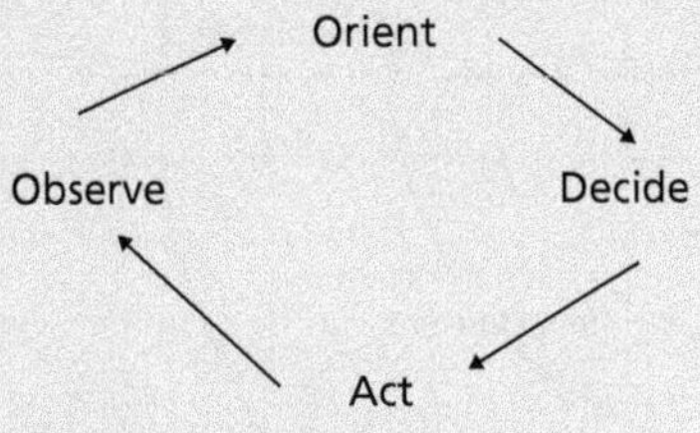

Figure 11.4 Boyd's OODA loop.

and Douhet would have recognised. Warden did not consider the enemy's fielded forces completely irrelevant, since they formed one of the five key target sets in his conception. The target sets were represented visually by a series of concentric rings. Leadership lay in the centre of the rings, moving outward through key production, infrastructure and the population to the outer ring, military forces. This representation demonstrated Warden's view that the enemy state could be regarded as a system – or a 'system of systems' – all aspects of which were equally vulnerable to attack by air power at any time (see Figure 11.5).

While Warden's vision might seem a simple refinement of earlier thinking, his concept of air power was enabled by technological developments. The visions of destruction held by the early theorists fell foul of the apparently insuperable problems of accurate weapons delivery and navigation to the target, particularly in poor weather. While technological development meant that poor weather could be mitigated and navigation carried out more precisely by the 1960s, aiming weapons against ground targets remained problematic.

The solution came through guided weapons. Their development began in the 1920s, and there had been limited use of such bombs during the Second World War, although they had not enjoyed a high success rate. Further work in the US led to the creation of the Paveway series of laser-guided bombs and electro-optically guided ordnance. These demonstrated their worth in the Vietnam War, notably in attacking bridges in North Vietnam. By the late 1980s, the range of PGMs available meant that it was possible to have confidence in the ability of a relatively small number of aircraft not only to locate their targets but also to be able to attack them with a high probability of success. With technology obviating the need to send large bomber fleets against individual key targets, a range of targets could be attacked simultaneously, giving air power the ability to cause the strategic paralysis that Boyd and Warden advocated. The 'parallel warfare' that simultaneity of targeting

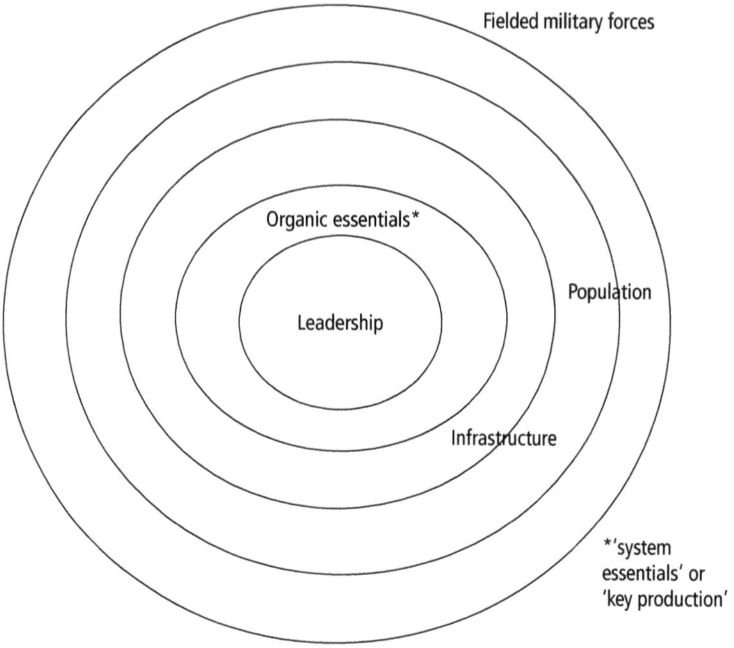

Figure 11.5 Warden's 'five ring' model.

through the use of PGMs permitted appeared to offer the tantalising prospect that the long-held vision of air power bringing about swift victory without the need to engage hostile fielded forces might be realised.

Despite this, it cannot be denied that air power's greatest contribution has been not operating independently of other forces, but as part of a joint overall effort. This might involve air operations independent of surface forces on occasions, and operating in close concert with them on others, depending upon the effects that are desired to contribute towards achieving the *desired end state.*

The Rise, Fall and Rise Again of Joint Effort

The desire of aviators to stress the importance of their contribution to modern warfare means that there has always been a tendency for air power proponents to downplay roles that might be seen as 'supporting' and thus – in theory – that could be conducted by air services controlled by a navy or an army. While this has been important in highlighting that air power's potential can be hindered if totally subordinate to surface forces with assets assigned in 'penny packets' and not easily brought together to provide combat mass, some of the advocacy has been unhelpful.

This can be seen through the lens of the RAF and its work during the inter-war period. Despite its published doctrine extolling the key role of air power being that of bombardment, the RAF expended much effort in colonial policing, working in conjunction with ground forces. The fact that 'boots on the ground' – to employ a now familiar, if over-used, phrase – mattered in such operations was in fact recognised by the RAF but simply not well publicised to avoid compromising the message of the importance of independent air power.[11] The USMC made much use of air–land cooperation during its inter-war operations, although given the nature of the USMC as a potentially self-contained force with its own supporting arms this was only to be expected. The use of air power in these situations also saw the effective use of aircraft in transport and liaison roles, all of which contributed to the effect that was achieved. This continued as a key theme after 1945. While the ground component was of key importance in a counterinsurgency, the role of air power was significant, if sometimes undersold.[12]

The use of transport aircraft and helicopters grew in importance, particularly in such campaigns as the Malayan Emergency (1948–1960) and in Algeria (1954–1962). The value of air transport has remained constant, particularly in fighting insurgencies in areas with limited communications – as seen in the importance placed on such activity by the Soviets and then the anti-al-Qaeda/Taliban coalition in Afghanistan. Air transport has been used to rapidly deploy troops to areas almost inaccessible by land, enhancing the capability of ground forces and in evacuating wounded personnel. This was as true in Malaya in the 1950s as it was in the campaigns in Afghanistan and Iraq in the early twenty-first century

Aerial reconnaissance has also been essential. It was particularly valuable for the French when fighting FLN in the Algerian countryside, but once the insurgency moved into the cities its value lessened as the insurgents exploited the cover provided by an urban environment – exactly the same issue that had affected the RAF in Palestine in the 1920s and 1930s. The development of 'drones', discussed in the next chapter, has perhaps changed the equation again in urban areas.

It was not just in terms of COIN where considerations of 'independent' air power did not apply across the board. In the inter-war years, the French air service remained dedicated to supporting the land component. The Soviets saw aeroplanes as an integral part of the land battle, with air power conducting deep attack rather than independent air action being an important part of their doctrine. The Germans, meanwhile, assessing the reasons for their defeat in 1918, concluded that it was impossible for land forces to function against a serious opponent without air power and developed doctrine with heavy emphasis on supporting ground forces, although suggestions that they abandoned notions of strategic bombardment entirely are inaccurate. In simple terms, the Germans aimed to achieve effects that would deliver the desired end-state. This required control of the air, interdiction of supplies and attacks on war production as well as aircraft acting as 'aerial artillery' supporting troops on the ground.

This was key to German success in the early part of the Second World War. The British and French failed to develop an effective counter to this, leading to disaster in 1940. Complaints by the British Army regarding the inadequacy of air support grew louder in the face of defeats by the German Afrika Korps in the desert campaigns, but by this point steps were in hand to overcome the difficulties. The RAF, initially through an ad hoc approach by local commanders rather than centrally formulated doctrine, fell back on the lessons learned in 1914–1918. The quality of air–land integration improved immeasurably as close liaison was developed between air and ground formations at all levels, most notably between senior commanders. Similar improvements occurred as the USAAF developed and refined its own doctrine for air support. The Afrika Korps commander, Erwin Rommel, complained that his forces could not compete in the face of coordinated action by enemy air and land forces. Lessons from North Africa were taken to the Italian campaign, and then to Western Europe after D-Day.

The system of air–land support was particularly significant, if not perfect. Heavy bombers, employed above the battlefield, did not always have the desired effect, and often caused 'friendly fire' incidents.[13] Yet air power was effective. It dented the morale of German soldiers, while the Allies' control of the air reduced the number of German air attacks on their own forces. The campaign to interdict German supplies was highly effective, thus denying the Germans the ability to respond as rapidly to the Normandy invasion as might otherwise have been the case. Attempted counter-attacks were halted by Allied air power before enemy units had reached their starting point for the attack.

A similar situation pertained on the Eastern Front, where the Soviets used air power on a massive scale to support land operations. Careful coordination of air attacks in support of the objectives of the various Red Army fronts as they advanced meant that a combination of firepower from both land and air, combined with sheer weight of numbers, first rebuffed the Germans and then forced them into retreat. It was notable that the Soviet Air Force was seen as another part of the overall land war, with attacks at depth being part of the overall conception of deep battle rather than a nod to independent activity. This approach has influenced Russian thinking on air power to this day.

In the Far East, transport aircraft were critical to success in the China–Burma–India (CBI) theatre of operations. The lack of communications infrastructure in many of the locations in which campaigning was conducted meant that aerial resupply was the only means by which rapid transport of men and supplies could be guaranteed, particularly given the considerable geographical area the CBI theatre covered. Air supply was essential during the battles of Kohima and Imphal, for although the Japanese successfully cut off the British positions there, the regular delivery of supplies from the air and evacuation of casualties meant that controlling the land communications links was not as significant as it might have been; incapable of gaining control of the air, the Japanese were unable to prevent supplies from getting through. The commander of the British XIVth Army, Viscount Slim, observed that the victory in Burma belonged as much to the air forces involved as to the troops who had fought on the ground.[14]

In the maritime environment, the importance of combined air–maritime interaction was demonstrated on numerous occasions. The Royal Navy's air attack on Taranto in 1940 played a significant part in the maritime campaign in the Mediterranean. Conversely, the Japanese attack on Pearl Harbor in December 1941 failed to destroy American aircraft carriers, and this gave the Americans the opportunity to strike a devastating blow six months later at Midway. The Americans went on to employ their maritime air power to telling effect in the advance on the Japanese home islands, notably in the destruction of the last real vestiges of Japanese air power during the Marianas campaign in June 1944 and in the provision of close air support to invasion forces as the 'island-hopping' campaign progressed.

Joint Air Power in the Nuclear Age

Although the post-war period was dominated by nuclear weapons and the creation of the strategic air forces that would employ them, air–surface cooperation remained an essential part of modern warfare. As noted above, for all the talk of independent air action, it was combined effort that mattered. The Korean campaign (1950–1953) was notable for the 'hard slogging' of the troops on the ground, reliant upon air support to contain the North Koreans and then offsetting the numerical superiority of Chinese forces. Marshal of the Royal Air Force Sir John Slessor (Chief of the Air Staff 1950–1952) observed that there would be 'more Koreas', implying that visions of air power winning wars swiftly and independently were misplaced.[15] The Vietnam War strengthened the notion that air power was inextricably linked with land and maritime power, a combination of American air-mobile tactics, aerial resupply and close air support by USAF, US Naval and USMC aircraft playing a critical part in the conflict, even if historians later concentrated upon Rolling Thunder and Linebacker as exemplars of the air war. Israel's employment of air power in support of land forces was a significant – although sometimes overstated – factor in their successes in 1967 and, after heavy casualties, in 1973. In both wars, air power delivered considerable support to the Israeli army, both in the form of protection from air attack, and through the effects of close air support and interdiction.[16] The original function of air power, namely the gathering of information, remained critical throughout – and in an era where precise, proportionate targeting is required, information has become a vital area. The gathering of information has been transformed by the rise of space-based platforms, and it is now necessary to consider the evolution of this critical component of air and space power.

Space Power

Space power is still a relatively new form of military power with its origins in the late 1950s, yet is now of great significance to modern life as a whole, enabling precision timing vital to banking and finance, and revolutionising navigation through the use of the GPS, to note but two. Its importance to national security for major powers has given rise to a ready stream of doctrinal thinking as to how space power may be exploited in the future and the creation of military formations dedicated to its use. The first Trump administration's creation of the US Space

Force (USSF) was met with a mixture of criticism and satire (even inspiring a television series), but the pace at which space has become integral to life on earth, and thus a critical part of many nations' infrastructure, has tended to validate the decision. The UK chose to create a Space Command within the RAF's structure, although this is a joint organisation covering all three armed services; at the time of writing in 2024, Space Command is led by a British Army major general. Other air forces – for example the Russian and French services – now refer to themselves as 'aerospace' or 'air and space' forces, highlighting the integral nature of space to modern warfare.

There is some debate as to whether space power should be considered an adjunct of air power or whether it should be regarded as a completely separate entity altogether. Attempting to produce a universal definition of space power is difficult but the following premise put forward by David E. Lupton in his book *On Space Warfare: A Spacepower Doctrine* remains amongst the best: 'Spacepower is the ability of a nation to exploit the space environment in pursuit of national goals and purposes and includes the entire astronautical capabilities of the nation.'[17]

Like air power, space offers the characteristics of height, speed and reach discussed in the previous chapter, although at different orders of magnitude. The vantage point enjoyed by aircraft pales into insignificance in comparison with the field of vision from 100 miles above the earth. The speed at which space-based assets move is far greater than that of conventional aircraft. Depending on a space platform's orbit and/or propulsion system, it is possible for it to travel around the world several times in twenty-four hours, providing regular coverage of an area of interest, or for the space asset to be moved above such an area from its extant orbit. Space power has become an increasingly important aspect of military planning and operations, and the potential of the operating environment is considerable. It does, perhaps, suffer from problems of perception, since notions of military operations from space seem to be almost inevitably coloured by perceptions drawn from the *Star Trek* television series (and associated franchises) and George Lucas's *Star Wars* series of films. This perhaps obscures the fact that space technology, while not as advanced as portrayed on screen, has evolved rapidly and cannot be divorced from the military operations conducted by major industrialised powers today, as we will see in the next chapter. While some commentators deny the very existence of a concept of space power, this is flawed, fallacious thinking overtaken by the reality of developments that have accelerated in the twenty-first century.

The Development of Space Power

Space power's origins lay very much in the Cold War, the so-called 'space race' between the US and the Soviet Union being a display of the two nations' rivalry as each sought to demonstrate the superiority of its technology – and perhaps subliminally the supremacy of the political system that had developed it.

Yet although the launch of the Soviet Sputnik satellite in 1957 and the subsequent 'race' to the moon, which ended with the Apollo 11 mission in 1969, were important, and have tended to disguise the way in which space power has evolved.

From the early 1960s, both the Soviets and the Americans placed satellites in orbit to obtain information about their adversary. This meant that the dangers of overflight by reconnaissance aircraft were removed; whereas the loss in 1960 of the U-2 flown by Gary Powers led to a diplomatic crisis and the shooting down of both crewed aircraft and RPASs increased tension, satellite imagery could deliver most of the information desired, without any of the risk.

Although satellites could be placed in a geostationary orbit (that is to say, remaining over a fixed point, rotating at the same speed as the earth), early satellites could not provide the twenty-four-hour coverage given by this approach, because they recorded their information on film cartridges that had to be jettisoned over friendly territory for subsequent analysis by intelligence services. This demanded a geosynchronous orbit, with the satellite circling the earth frequently so as to cover a wide area of the earth's surface with its sensors. Technological improvements made it possible transmit the information gathered to an operating centre, where the 'product' could be interpreted and disseminated to the agencies that required them. Throughout the Cold War, increasingly sophisticated reconnaissance satellites were developed. These employed a range of imaging capabilities, including radar, infrared and photography, while the resolution and clarity of images obtained became almost legendary.

Satellites provided large amounts of information about the disposition of opposing forces, but such information was carefully controlled as it was a vital form of intelligence and thus limiting circulation for security purposes was important. This secrecy meant that the wider military application of space power was relatively limited in scope, if not in scale. During the Vietnam War, satellites were predominantly used for the purpose of weather forecasting and communications, with some navigational information transmitted in addition. Although the utility of space platforms became widely recognised, the high-security classifications applied to their use meant that the potential was not fully understood, nor was it integrated effectively into the wider military environment. By the late 1980s, the US held a commanding lead in military space power – but much of the American military remained unaware of the capabilities that were on offer. The American interventions in Grenada (1983) and Panama (1989) saw the exploitation of information from satellites being used to inform military operations, even though the high levels of classification pertaining to the intelligence product obtained from space again meant that there were difficulties in ensuring that information gained from space assets was provided to those who needed to know about it in a timely manner. This was firmly driven home by experience of the 1991 Gulf War, sometimes seen as the 'first space war'.

An Air and Space Power Revolution?

The end of the Cold War changed the world's strategic landscape, leaving the US as the world's one true superpower. Optimistic talk of a 'new world order' with democracy and peaceful cooperation being the norm was common.[18.] In Western nations, politicians seized upon what became known as the 'Peace Dividend', imposing large cutbacks in defence spending; as aircraft were (and are) amongst the most expensive items of equipment to buy and operate, air forces suffered considerable cuts.[19] Unfortunately, the envisaged stable, more peaceful, world did not materialise. The first challenge arrived when Saddam Hussein invaded Kuwait on 2 August 1990. The nature of the air and space power contribution to the eviction of Iraqi forces from Kuwait led to suggestions that an air power revolution had occurred; when the role of space power was appreciated some years later, it was suggested that this domain, too, had undergone revolutionary change.

Saddam's invasion gave rise to fears that he might not stop with Kuwait and move on to attacking Saudi Arabia. This prompted a number of nations, notably the US and the UK, to respond to a request for military assistance from Riyadh using air power as the opening step. A huge airlift of troops and the deployment of an array of combat aircraft – notably US F-15 fighters and A-10 attack aircraft – to Saudi Arabia and other Gulf nations sent a powerful message to Saddam Hussein that any ideas he might have had about attacking Saudi Arabia should be abandoned. The Soviet Union, with greatly improved relations with the West, sought to use its position as a long-standing ally of Iraq to broker a settlement, but Saddam was intransigent, possibly seeing withdrawal from Kuwait as a humiliation that might threaten his regime. He chose to stand fast, and a UN Security Council Resolution gave Saddam until 15 January 1991 to withdraw his troops from Kuwait. If he did not, UN member states were permitted to use 'all necessary means' to bring about the withdrawal. This set the stage for war.

The rapid movement by air of troops and combat aircraft to deter further Iraqi aggression was followed by the arrival by sea of armoured forces, notably from the US and the UK, as thoughts turned to how to evict Saddam's forces from Kuwait. Initial planning drew upon AirLand Battle concepts designed for fighting the Soviet Union, but it was at this point that the ideas of John Warden outlined previously came to the fore.

Warden believed that the application of overwhelming air power against multiple target sets would bring about the decisive defeat of Iraq. Creating an informal planning cell known as 'Checkmate' in the USAF's Air Staff Plans Directorate, Warden on his own initiative designed plans for an American aerial response. This coincided with demands from General Norman Schwarzkopf, commanding US Central Command (CENTCOM, the American command leading the anti-Saddam coalition) that the air force do just this. Warden's planning team and its ideas came to the fore. Their plan, 'Instant Thunder', was the antithesis of Rolling Thunder, envisaging an air campaign enabled by air supremacy and directed against C2 facilities in Iraq, power stations and communications infrastructure. We see here echoes of the inter-war era and the idea of decisive air attack aimed at vital points of the enemy's infrastructure. Although Schwarzkopf was enthused, the air component commander, Lieutenant General Charles Horner, was unconvinced. He thought Warden's approach impractical, with its focus upon targets in Iraq rather than upon the Iraqi units occupying Kuwait. Horner's director of Campaign Plans, Brigadier-General 'Buster' Glosson, was even less persuaded, describing the overall concept of victory through air power alone in nine days or fewer in most unfavourable terms. Horner and Glosson were concerned that Warden was over-optimistic and needed to recognise that there would be a land campaign. Warden demurred and was returned to Washington, but key members of his team, notably Colonel (later Lieutenant-General) David Deptula remained, ensuring that air power was a critical part of the ultimate campaign plan.

This final plan had four key phases: attacking strategic targets; a campaign against Iraqi air forces in Kuwait; neutralising the Iraqi Republican Guard and cutting off Iraqi forces in Kuwait; and finally supporting the coalition ground assault into Kuwait that would follow once Iraqi forces in Kuwait were reduced to no more than 50 per cent combat effectiveness by air attack. When the war began on 17 January 1991, the opening air campaign was considered a spectacular success.

The first three phases of the campaign occurred simultaneously, the concept of *parallel air operations*. The use of PGMs and the F-117 'stealth' aircraft which surviving Iraqi radars found almost impossible to locate, let alone track, enabled multiple targets to be struck. The Iraqis all but abandoned the use of fighters to contest control of the air after multiple engagements with coalition fighters (overwhelmingly USAF F-15s), and it ended in comprehensive defeat and without loss to the American fighters. The Iraqis instead turned to their huge network of SAMs and AAA; while this did have a notable impact on the air war, the ground-based air defences (GBAD) shot down a number of coalition aircraft. After six weeks of air attacks, the ground war was launched, driving Saddam's forces out of Kuwait in a little over 100 hours of combat. Air power was held by many observers to have been the decisive factor, but some disagreed; a few observers made the point that not all of Saddam's C2 network had been destroyed, but it was difficult to deny that the damage inflicted was extensive and dislocated Iraqi C2 efforts.[20] Furthermore, there was an unexpected element to the air campaign of strategic significance, namely what became known as 'the great Scud hunt' in the Iraqi Western Desert.

Saddam Hussein sought to break the coalition by detaching its Arab members by bringing Israel into the war against him. He did so by firing SS-1 'Scud' ballistic missiles (and Iraqi-built derivatives) into Israel. The Israelis were dissuaded from responding by a mixture of diplomatic pressure from the US and the application of a considerable amount of effort into tracking down the mobile Scud launchers and the deployment of Patriot SAMs to intercept missiles fired at Israel. Satellites were used to detect the infra-red signature of a missile launch 'bloom', allowing the Patriot systems to be forewarned and prepared for action. Although the SAMs did not destroy as many Scuds as first thought (a number of the Iraqi-built weapons broke up in the final stages of flight), the strategic effect of keeping Israel out of the war was significant. Yet this was part of a joint effort in which coalition Special Forces sought to locate the surface-to-surface missiles; even if relatively few missiles and their launchers were destroyed, the Iraqi campaign was seriously dislocated by the coalition efforts.

Yet there were some negative implications for air power. First, the erroneous attack on the Al Firdos bunker led to the deaths of several hundred civilians. The coalition had correctly identified the bunker as an Iraqi C2 facility but had not detected that it had been abandoned and was in use as an air raid shelter, leading to tragedy. A reminder of air power's destructive capability was also seen on the Basra Highway as coalition aircraft attacked retreating Iraqi units. The destruction was so great that coalition aircrews reported their concerns to their commanders, and the fear of turning a rout into a massacre of a defeated force that posed little threat contributed to the decision to end the ground war. At the end of the conflict, the coalition had achieved its aim of liberating Kuwait and had done so sustaining casualties that were almost unbelievably low. Fears of tens of thousands of coalition deaths that had been raised in the later months of 1990 did not transpire; the coalition sustained 345 fatalities, some to 'fratricide', and around 1,000 wounded. The Iraqis, by contrast, were thought to have suffered somewhere between 30,000 and 100,000 casualties.

With air power playing such a prominent role in the coalition's success, and with regular press briefings showing the accuracy of PGMs, an impression was created that an air power revolution had indeed occurred, and the idea that air power might be the dominant form of major warfare (as opposed to peacekeeping and counterinsurgency) began to be aired. As will be discussed in the next chapter, this view was far too simplistic. Air and space power were integral to the success of the coalition's liberation of Kuwait, but it was the way in which they were employed and the effects achieved in the pursuit of a coherent joint strategy that brought about success.

Conclusion

Air power evolved rapidly during the First World War, and the rate of development in terms of the application of technology to aircraft and their systems has not slowed since. From the late 1950s, the exploitation of space became an important element in military power (see Figure 11.6), leading to the rise of a number of theories and concepts as to how to exploit this domain for military use, albeit within the constraints of a number of international treaties. Nevertheless, the fundamental roles of air power remained. Air power did not render land or maritime power obsolete, instead making major contributions to the way in which warfare was

Figure 11.6 A Delta II rocket launches with an earth-observing satellite payload, January 2015. The exploitation of space for both military and civilian purposes makes it a critical aspect of modern security and defence thinking.

conducted. In peacetime, air power was an important instrument of strategy, delivering important outcomes during the Berlin Airlift and the Cuban missile crisis. The ability to deliver success both independent of surface forces (Berlin) and in conjunction with them (Cuba) was clear.

The evidence of numerous conflicts suggests that although air power evolved considerably in terms of the capability of the aircraft employed and the degree of accuracy that could be obtained in weapons delivery, its utility in supporting the land and maritime components was undiminished; if anything, it became an important enabler to both environments. Yet despite this clear evidence of air power's contribution to warfare, shown in conflicts ranging from the global conflagration of 1939–1945 through a variety of insurgencies to the 1991 Gulf War, it was impossible to dismiss the idea that air power offered policymakers an extra dimension, being able to deliver rapid effect at a strategic level without necessarily being involved in the support of the other components. Events since the end of the 1991 Gulf War have not resolved this tension, and it is to the modern era that we now turn.

RESEARCH QUESTIONS

1. Why has strategic bombardment retained such an important position in thinking about air power, despite extensive evidence that it is simply part of the wider-ranging contribution of air power to military operations?
2. To what extent was cooperation between armies, air forces and navies driven by the circumstance of war and then forgotten after 1945?
3. Analyse the view that the Vietnam War demonstrated enduring limitations of air power that no amount of technological advancement will overcome.
4. To what extent has the rise of space as an operating environment marked a revolution in military affairs?
5. Evaluate the idea that the use of air power since its earliest days has demonstrated that its strategic significance lies not in any particular role, but in its key characteristics of reach, flexibility and rapidity and the way in which these are applied to achieve objectives.

FURTHER READING

Biddle, Tami Davis, *Air Power and Warfare: A Century of Theory and History* (Carlisle, PA: US Army War College Press, 2019).

Bowen, Bleddyn, *War in Space: Strategy, Spacepower, Geopolitics* (Edinburgh: Edinburgh University Press, 2020).

Bowen, Bleddyn, *Original Sin: Power Technology and War in Outer Space* (London: Hurst, 2022).

Clodfelter, Mark, *The Limits of Air Power: The American Bombing of North Vietnam* (New York, NY: The Free Press, 1989).

Fedorchak, Viktoriya, *British Air Power: The Doctrinal Path to Jointery* (London: Bloomsbury, 2019).

Gray, Colin S., *Airpower for Strategic Effect* (Maxwell, AL: Air University Press, 2012).

Haun, Phil, *Tactical Air Power and the Vietnam War* (Cambridge, UK: Cambridge University Press, 2024).

Johnson-Freese, Joan, *Heavenly Ambitions: America's Quest to Dominate Space* (Philadelphia, PA: University of Pennsylvania Press, 2009).

Klein, John J., *Space Warfare: Strategy, Principles and Policy* (London: Routledge, 2006).
Meilinger, Phillip S. (ed.), *Paths of Heaven: The Evolution of Air Power Theory* (Maxwell, AL: Air University Press, 1997).
Olsen, John Andreas, *John Warden and the Renaissance of American Air Power* (Dulles, VA: Potomac Books, 2007).
Olsen, John Andreas (ed.), *A History of Air Warfare* (Dulles, VA: Potomac Books, 2010).

ONLINE RESOURCES

See Chapter 10.

NOTES

1 Shmuel L. Gordon, 'The Air Force and the Yom Kippur War: New Lessons', *Israel Affairs*, 6(1) (1999), 221–37.
2 See Bernard C. Nalty, *Tactics and Techniques of Electronic Warfare: Electronic Countermeasures in the Air War against North Vietnam* (Washington, DC: Air Force History Office, 1977).
3 See Brett Holman, *The Next War in the Air* (Farnham: Ashgate, 2014); the same author's 'World Police for World Peace: British Internationalism and the Threat of a Knock-out Blow from the Air, 1919–1945', *War in History*, 17(3) (2010), 313–32; George H. Quester, *Deterrence before Hiroshima* (New Brunswick: Transaction Publishers, 1986).
4 Phillip S. Meilinger, 'Trenchard and Morale Bombing', in Phillip S. Meilinger, *Air War: Theory and Practice* (London: Frank Cass, 2003), p. 49.
5 Ibid.
6 TNA, AIR 19/92, Minutes of a Meeting in Chief of the Air Staff's Room, 19 July 1923.
7 Ibid., p. 78.
8 Robert A. Pape, 'Coercive Air Power in the Vietnam War', *International Security*, 15(2) (Fall 1990), 106.
9 Mark Clodfelter, *The Limits of Air Power* (New York, NY: Free Press, 1989), pp. 45–72.
10 Ibid., p. 196.
11 Air Ministry, *Air Staff Memorandum 46: Notes on Air Control in Undeveloped Countries* (1930).
12 See, for example, Harry Kemsley, 'Air Power in Counter-insurgency: A Sophisticated Language or Blunt Expression?' and David Jordan, 'Countering Insurgency from the Air: The Post-War Lessons', both in *Contemporary Security Policy*, 28(1) (2007), 96–111, 112–26; Andrew Mumford, 'Unnecessary or Unsung? The Role of Air Power in Britain's Colonial Counter-insurgencies', *Small Wars and Insurgencies*, 20(3/4) (2009), 636–55; James S. Corum and Wray R. Johnson, *Airpower in Small Wars: Fighting Insurgents and Terrorists* (Lawrence, KS: University of Kansas Press, 2003).
13 Ian Gooderson, 'Heavy and Medium Bombers: How Successful Were They in the Tactical Air Support Role during World War II?', *Journal of Strategic Studies*, 15(3) (1992), 367–99.
14 Field Marshal Viscount Slim, *Defeat Into Victory* (London: Pan, 2012 [1956]), p. 624.
15 Quoted in David MacIssac, 'Voices from the Central Blue: The Air Power Theorists', in Peter Paret (ed.), *Makers of Modern Strategy: From Machiavelli to the Nuclear Age* (Princeton, NJ: Princeton University Press, 1986), p. 644.
16 See Kenneth M. Pollack, 'Air Power in the Six-Day War', *Journal of Strategic Studies*, 28(3) (2005), 471–503.

17 David E. Lupton, *On Space Warfare: A Spacepower Doctrine* (Maxwell, AL: Air University Press, 1988), p. 7.

18 See, amongst others, George H. W. Bush and Brent Scowcroft, *A World Transformed* (New York, NY: Alfred A. Knopf, 1998); 'New World Order Galloping Into Position', *Washington Post*, 25 February 1990; Odd Arne Westad, *The Global Cold War: Third World Interventions and the Making of Our Times* (Cambridge University Press, 2007); T. V. Hall and John A. Paul, *International Order and the Future of World Politics* (Cambridge, UK: Cambridge University Press, 1999). The concept of 'New World Order' is not new: President Woodrow Wilson spoke of one during the First World War.

19 As an example, the Royal Air Force ended the Cold War with thirty squadrons of fighter and attack aircraft. At time of writing (mid 2014) it has six. This reduction was not matched with a reduction in the number of commitments to conflicts.

20 John Andreas Olsen, *Strategic Air Power in Desert Storm* (London: Frank Cass, 2003), pp. 269–74.

12 Air and Space Power in the Contemporary Era: 2000–2040

CHAPTER OUTLINE

KEY THEMES

- The contested concept of air power as a revolution in military affairs.
- Technology as a key enabler for air power to achieve effect.
- Air and space power's role in the post-Cold War world and the early twenty-first century.
- The importance of maintaining access to space and the growing threat to space platforms.

Introduction

As the preceding chapters have shown, the development of air and space power has been swift. In little more than a century of heavier-than-air flight, aircraft have moved from being capable of spending little more than five minutes in the air to possessing the ability to spend more than a day aloft; the speeds that military aircraft can attain have gone from under 100 miles per hour (160 kilometres per hour) to over 2,000 miles per hour (3,218 kilometres per hour) and the loads they are capable of carrying have increased dramatically.[1] By the end of the Vietnam War, it was possible for fighter aircraft to routinely engage enemy aircraft with missiles (although the success rate of such weapons in Vietnam was low), while attack aircraft with PGMs could use one weapon to destroy a target when it might have previously taken several aircraft using over a dozen bombs to achieve the same result. Between the early 1900s and 1989, air and space power had a clear role, directed against potentially hostile nation states or alliances, with regular diversions into 'small wars'. It became something of a mantra, particularly after Vietnam, to note that high-speed fighter-bombers and attack aircraft, designed to fight a possible Third World War, were not best-suited for this sort of 'brushfire' war, not least since their speed and relative lack of endurance over a target area meant that it was difficult for aircrew to locate targets. Although a prominent and repeated charge – and not without reason, particularly in the 1950s and 1960s, prior to the development of targeting pods and PGMs, as well as technology that allowed ground troops to accurately direct aircrews' attention to the target that needed to be struck – the fact that air transport and reconnaissance were critical contributions to such campaigns often went unremarked. The constant fear of a major state-on-state war, notably between NATO and the Soviet Union, meant that the development of high-technology fighter aircraft largely went unquestioned. When doubts were raised in the 1970s as the result of the escalating cost of combat aircraft, the solution (aircraft such as the General Dynamics – now Lockheed Martin – F-16 and McDonnell Douglas – now Boeing – F/A-18) came in the form of aeroplanes designed to be as light and as cheap as possible, but as more technology was added to these designs, they too became sophisticated and costly weapons systems in their own right. The evolution of 'stealth' aircraft, typified by the Lockheed F-22 Raptor and the same manufacturer's F-35 Lightning II (often referred to by its original programme name of 'Joint Strike Fighter, or 'JSF') highlighted the continuing belief that there was a place for high technology to allow for the dominance of airspace to enable success in military operations (see Figure 12.1).

The 1991 Gulf War appeared to validate this approach to a large degree, although there was considerable misapprehension about the nature of the air war. As noted in the last chapter, the use of precision weapons, while highlighted in the coalition's regular media briefings, was far lower than assumed: video footage of bombs and missiles hitting their targets with remarkable accuracy did not convey the full picture. Numerous unguided weapons were expended, making up the bulk of the coalition's weapons expenditure. Also, the seeming invulnerability of the F-117 'stealth' aircraft, perceived as cutting through Iraqi air defences as though it was invisible before delivering laser-guided bombs with devastating accuracy, was a misleading point of view. Neither the manufacturer, Lockheed, nor the USAF claimed that the F-117 could not be detected by enemy radar systems; the idea behind the 'stealth' aircraft was that locating and tracking it would be incredibly difficult, making it far harder for the

Figure 12.1 A trio of F-35A fighter aircraft. The F-35 programme represented the first truly international '5th Generation' fighter programme, with a combination of stealth and cutting edge avionics making it perhaps the most sophisticated combat aircraft to yet be produced at great scale.

opponent to destroy the aircraft. After-action reports suggested that, contrary to the public's perception, not every guided bomb had hit the target either. These two facts did not surprise those familiar with air warfare but created a more general view that air power had now 'come of age' with revolutionary new capabilities, and could at last deliver the sort of decisive effects that the early theorists had postulated (see Figure 12.2). As ever, the situation was far more complicated than that (see Box 12.1).

The Age of Air Power?

For all the success of air power in the 1991 Gulf campaign, it was the overall effects of combat operations, intelligence gathering, air transport and air-to-air refuelling that demonstrated the efficacy of air power, pointing not to independent operations but the carefully planned application of air power as part of an overall joint campaign plan being the means of achieving success. Nonetheless, the short duration of the 1991 ground war and relatively low coalition casualties meant that air power became the preferred tool of choice for Western politicians throughout the 1990s; other nations, while not intervening in conflicts in the same way that the Western powers did, also took note of the possible effects that could be achieved by air power.

The collapse of Yugoslavia and the bitter civil war that ensued as the state broke into new, independent nations after 1992 saw much use of air power, first in attempts at supporting UN peacekeepers who struggled in the face of there being no peace to keep. The UN's reluctance to use force meant that there was much

Figure 12.2 An RAF Eurofighter Typhoon FGR4. A major international collaborative effort, the Eurofighter programme overcame initial difficulties to produce a high-quality '4.5 Generation' fighter aircraft that has become the mainstay of nine different air forces.

BOX 12.1 A PRECISION REVOLUTION?

The 1991 Persian Gulf War came to be seen in the media, and later in some historical accounts, as a war dominated by the use of precision-guided munitions. In reality, the war was far from a precision revolution. Only 9 per cent of the weapons dropped were PGMs; the rest were unguided ('dumb' bombs and rocket projectiles). Although the degree of accuracy that could be achieved in 1991 with an unguided weapon was greater than it had been in any previous war thanks to the weapons aiming systems on aircraft, the degree of precision achieved was far lower than that of the PGMs. One of the key factors in the relative lack of use of PGMs lay in the fact that only 10 per cent of the American strike aircraft involved were capable of using these weapons, while, of the other air forces engaged, only the RAF could match this – but used two of the three strike aircraft types deployed (the Tornado GR1 and Jaguar GR1) to deliver, for the most part, unguided weapons, with the Tornado moving to the use of PGMs only after Buccaneer S2 aircraft arrived in-theatre in February 1991 to provide designation for the Tornados' laser-guided weapons as well as employing their own PGMs.

BOX 12.1 (cont.)

The Kosovo campaign was presented as another precision war in the media, but again, the figures are instructive; while the amount of PGMs used was unprecedented, 71 per cent of the weapons released by NATO aircraft were unguided.[2]

It was not until the 2003 war against Iraq that most of the aircraft weapons used could be considered precision guided. Not only did their use make air power more effective but it also meant that targeting could be carried out with a much higher level of confidence that unintended casualties amongst the civilian population could be reduced, although notions that there ought to be none were fanciful. The risk of errors inputting target coordinates, weapons failure or releasing the weapon from the aircraft at the wrong time could all lead to bombs 'going wild'. Bombs fitted with larger aerodynamic control surfaces to allow for greater precision could, if their guidance system broke or one of the control surfaces malfunctioned, miss the target by some distance. Furthermore, the blast from the guided bombs might, despite careful targeting, inflict casualties or strike buildings that were never intended to be hit, leading to the development in the early 2000s of so-called 'low-collateral' weapons – precise, but with smaller warheads that would still achieve the desired destructive outcome if the target were hit, but with less risk to civilians. Such weapons became increasingly important during the insurgencies in Afghanistan after 2001 and Iraq after the major combat operations ended in April 2003. By the time of NATO's operation against the Libyan dictator Muammar Gaddafi in 2011, the use of precision weapons in the form of GPS-guided ordnance, laser-guided weapons and long-range cruise missiles such as the Storm Shadow/SCALP were to the fore; the European operators of the F-16 (Belgium, Denmark, Norway and the Netherlands) used only precision weapons, while the only unguided weapons used by the British were in the form of rockets fired by Apache attack helicopters.

While it appeared that air forces had become almost exclusively focused on using guided weapons, this was not true of the USAF or other nations; the Americans continue to have the option of delivering unguided bombs in the form of cluster munitions and the old-fashioned 'iron' bomb, often delivered by the B-1B and B-52 bomber forces. The Israeli air force has made use of 750 lb bombs of a design dating back to the 1950s in attacks on targets in Gaza in its campaign following the Hamas raids on Israel in October 2023, while unguided munitions have been an integral feature in the fighting in Ukraine following the 2022 Russian invasion. While it might be said that there has indeed been a precision revolution of sorts in the use of air power, it is not universal and is unlikely to be so for years to come, if ever (see Box 12.2).

BOX 12.2 STEALTH AIRCRAFT

The growing sophistication of air defences long-exercised air commanders, who recognised the need to find some means to defeat them to permit attack aircraft to operate. The first attempts came during the Second World War, using the electromagnetic spectrum to jam or 'spoof' enemy radar systems. This was built upon with the development of the SEAD role during Vietnam. Another approach considered during the Second World War was that of making aircraft less visible to the human eye, particularly through the use of devices known as Yehudi lights, which reduced an aircraft's luminance against the sky.[3] These measures in fact built on early – and largely unsuccessful – experiments in the First World War. They were not implemented in production but not forgotten.

As technology developed, it became possible to envisage the prospect of developing aircraft with an extremely low radar signature, through the use of radar-absorbing material (RAM) and shaping an aircraft's structure so that radar energy was not reflected in such a manner as to make it obvious that the radar had detected an approaching aircraft. The reduction of the aircraft's radar cross-section (RCS) was but one approach to what became known as 'stealth' or, more precisely, low-observable (LO) aircraft.[4]

The US, with its considerable research and development capability, led the way in this field, and by the early 1970s it became possible to consider the production of an LO aircraft, with the main aim being to penetrate Soviet air defences. In 1975, Lockheed began a programme known as 'Hopeless Diamond', to develop a technology demonstrator; this in turn gave rise to the Advanced Technology Bomber (ATB) programme from 1979. The Hopeless Diamond project ultimately led to the F-117 Nighthawk, while the ATB became the B-2 Spirit.[5]

The F-117 gained fame during Operation Desert Storm thanks to its successful penetration of Iraqi air defences and the use of laser-guided bombs against an array of key targets; no aircraft were lost. Some of the claims for the success of the F-117s were later challenged by the US General Accounting Office, but the public perception of 'stealth' aircraft, invisible to radar and delivering their weapons with absolute precision, was set.[6]

In fact, 'stealth' aircraft are not invisible; as the term 'low observability' suggests; such aircraft are more difficult to detect rather than impossible to locate. The cost of stealth aircraft is prodigious, because of the technology involved in terms of both design and the RAM used to build them.[7] The cost makes such aircraft controversial, a particular feature during conflicts post 9/11, where critics argue that the stealthy properties of this type of aircraft have not been required. It is also argued that stealth is a wasting advantage as detection technology increases; proponents counter that non-stealth aircraft would be at an even greater risk of detection and destruction.[8]

BOX 12.2 (cont.)

This remains a contentious point and it is noteworthy that the People's Republic of China and Russia have sought to develop their own stealthy aircraft such as the J-20 (China) and Su-57 (Russia), while the Korean KF-21 Borame has recognisable LO features. The UK, Japan and Italy have embarked upon the Global Combat Aircraft Programme, aiming to place an LO 6th Generation fighter type in service by 2040. Awareness of the growing potency of ground-based missile defences, illustrated by the war in Ukraine with both sides making extensive use of SAMs, has largely quelled the suggestion that reducing the observability of combat aircraft is an expensive luxury, with most commentators now feeling that 'stealth' features are essential to the operational viability of any aircraft, drone or long-range missile system (apart from true hypersonic missiles whose speed presents the defender with immense challenges).

frustration amongst peacekeeping troops who felt that the UN was more concerned with not provoking the warring parties – particularly the forces of the Republika Srpska – than protecting the peacekeeping forces.[9] By 1995, frustration in Western capitals had increased to the point that a mortar attack by the Republika Srpska forces led to Operation Deliberate Force; NATO air units conducted a short punishment bombing campaign against the Serbians, and, in conjunction with an offensive by Croatian forces, the attacks helped to bring forward peace talks that led to the Dayton Accords, which ended the civil war in 1995. The conflict was not at an end, a point brought home in 1999 with Operation Allied Force, the bid to bring about the end to the ethnic cleansing campaign against Kosovar Albanians by the Federal Republic of Yugoslavia, led by President Slobodan Milosevic.

The campaign was conducted by NATO against a backdrop of considerable concern from certain alliance members over the wisdom of the operation and considerable opposition from Russia. Political concerns saw the prospect of an invasion by NATO troops being ruled out, and air power was employed as the means to bring about Milosevic's compliance with international demands for a settlement of the Kosovo crisis.[10]

There were expectations, even within the US administration, that the campaign would last a few days, rather than the seventy-eight it actually took, although media reports suggesting that it was expected to last only three days were mistaken; the political limitations imposed upon those planning the campaign meant that their list of permissible targets would be exhausted in seventy-two hours, after which permission to expand the target list would need to be granted by the governments involved.

Without the presence of a credible ground threat to Slobodan Milosevic's regime, air power shaped the political conditions by which Milosevic felt it necessary to capitulate to NATO's demands to end ethnic cleansing in Kosovo. The air campaign was hindered by initial confusion over targeting and bad weather, which militated against the use of laser-guided weapons. NATO's Supreme Allied Commander Europe (SACEUR), General Wesley K. Clark, argued that the air campaign should be conducted against fielded forces in Kosovo itself. His air component commander, Lieutenant General Michael Short, disagreed, contending that air power should 'go for the head of the snake', in keeping with classic strategic air-attack theory. Clark's view – in fairness, a perhaps more politically aware one than Short's – prevailed initially, and the combination of bad weather and poor results from targeting forces in Kosovo led to a re-evaluation of the campaign.

The strategic target sets that Short had advocated began to be attacked, particularly targets that were of significance to supporters of the Milosevic regime. This 'crony attack' approach undermined support for Milosevic, while the apparent ability of NATO air assets to attack almost at will created an impression within the Serbian regime that the weight of bombing could leave Serbia utterly devastated if the government failed to comply with the demands of the international community.[11] Combined with the realisation that expected support from Russia would not be forthcoming, indictment as a war criminal and growing talk of a credible threat of an invasion, Milosevic chose to capitulate. The perceived success of air power in Kosovo enhanced consideration of the use of air attack to bring about rapid victory, through use of precision weapons. Once again, though, there was a need for caution. While critics of the air war could be found proclaiming that something other than air power was responsible for victory, it seems reasonable to conclude that, without the air campaign, Milosevic would not have been forced to accede to the demands of the international community.[12] Yet even allowing for this, there were questions about targeting. The Chinese embassy was bombed after it was misidentified, causing considerable political difficulties for NATO, while the headquarters of the state broadcaster in Yugoslavia were bombed, with the death of a number of journalists. This was a controversial attack, held by a number of commentators to be a violation of international law, although the International Criminal Tribunal established to deal with war crimes in the former Yugoslavia disagreed.[13] Furthermore, the appalling weather meant that it was difficult to employ laser-guided weapons, as laser designators could not be used to 'paint' the target to produce the reflected 'basket' of laser light that laser-guided weapons need to strike their target accurately.[14] Casualties caused amongst the civilian population by cluster bombs and unguided weapons increased political pressure to move to a more precise form of weaponry and demands for a ban on cluster munitions.[15]

As the twenty-first century began, it seemed that air power might become the 'weapon of choice' in future conflicts, at least for Western powers, anxious to avoid the political risks that casualties amongst ground troops might bring in what were referred to as 'wars of choice'.[16] In addition to the prospect of using air power in short, decisive conflicts, the ongoing containment of Saddam Hussein through the use of 'no-fly zones' added to the view that air power would become the dominant mechanism of crisis intervention. This dynamic changed on 11 September 2001.

Air Power in an Age of Insurgency

The attacks on the US on 11 September 2001 led to a US-led intervention in Afghanistan, initially in a bid to bring Osama bin Laden, leader of the Al-Qaeda (AQ) terrorist organisation to justice and to remove the Taliban government that was hosting him. After the removal of the Taliban regime was complete, the US and many of its allies embarked upon the reconstruction of Afghanistan, but against a backdrop of continued resistance from AQ and Taliban fighters in what became a protracted and deadly insurgency. In the opening phases of the campaign, carrier-based attack aircraft and USAF bombers supported the anti-Taliban Northern Alliance (aided by Western special forces) with considerable success. There were several controversial incidents involving targeting errors (particularly against parties of civilians mistaken for insurgents), but the support from air power was of great value in removing the Taliban.

As the number of conventional troops in Afghanistan increased to meet the growing insurgency, a number of issues relating to air power became apparent. During an operation in the Tora Bora mountains – Operation Anaconda – there was considerable consternation created when it appeared that Bin Laden had managed to slip away during particularly heavy fighting in which a number of American soldiers were killed. This created some inter-service tension, particularly when senior US Army officers criticised the USAF for failing to provide adequate support; the air force, irritated, criticised the army for failing to include it fully in the planning process. This prompted a swift review and the development of improved procedures to enable better cooperation between the air and land components.[17]

As well as Afghanistan, the US, now led by President George W. Bush, became increasingly focused upon the matter of Saddam Hussein. Although largely contained by the use of no-fly zones over the north and south of Iraq, Saddam remained a regional problem, particularly since he refused to make clear whether or not he had disposed of his WMD as required after the 1991 war. His behaviour had seen a number of air strikes made against him as a result, notably the four-day Operation Desert Fox in 1998, in a fruitless bid to make him comply with a weapons inspection regime.[18]

Operation Iraqi Freedom

The Bush administration's decision-making over Iraq after 2000 has been the source of enormous controversy, outside the scope of this book. For our purposes, though, it is worth noting that air power was to play a critical role even though the desired result of removing Saddam from power would require the use of a large invasion force.

The role envisaged for air power during what became known as Operation Iraqi Freedom (OIF) was based upon the evolving concept of 'Rapid Dominance'. This required air power to play a key part in overwhelming the enemy with great rapidity. The authors of the 'Rapid Dominance' concept presaged the final version of their study with a pamphlet called *Shock and Awe*, a title that became closely associated with air power in OIF.[19] John Warden's ideas of targeting the enemy leadership were taken a stage further, with time-sensitive intelligence information used to launch an attack on the Dora Farm complex, where Saddam was thought to be, on the night of 19 March 2003.[20] Saddam was not killed in the attack, but this was the first of a number of time-critical air attacks against enemy C2 systems with the aim of quickly achieving the desired level of dominance over the Iraqi regime, with another (equally unsuccessful) example of 'time-sensitive targeting' applied against Saddam on 7 April.[21]

The 'shock and awe' concept was poorly articulated in public, however, and television coverage of attacks on leadership targets in the middle of Baghdad were taken – erroneously – by some sources as a sign that air power was being used in an indiscriminate fashion. Once again, a failure to explain the complexities of air power, particularly the exceptionally detailed targeting process that requires estimates of (amongst other things) potential 'collateral damage', the legality of the choice of target and the proportionality of the use of force against it, laid air power open to criticism because of the visually spectacular nature of many of the attacks on key targets. The concentration of the media on the bombing in and around Baghdad obscured the fact that air power was being used in other ways.

Battlefield mobility was enabled by the use of both fixed- and rotary-wing aircraft, while a number of types of reconnaissance aircraft, in conjunction with space-based platforms, delivered vast amounts of information for commanders, providing 'information dominance' over the Iraqi forces, even when they were blanketed by sandstorms that they thought gave them protection from coalition air attack. The sheer threat presented by the opposing fighter aircraft, coupled with psychological warfare operations against its commanders, prompted the Iraqi air force to remain on the ground, leaving the opposition to coalition air action to come from SAMs.[22] Air power's most notable effect was arguably in terms of providing close air support and interdiction; in the latter role, coalition aircraft inflicted devastating levels of damage and disruption upon Iraqi forces.[23] An effective combination of air and land power brought about enormous, combined effects against the enemy, just as had been expected and predicted by Bernard Montgomery in his observations about air–land integration during the Second World War.

Although air power had been of great utility in bringing about the desired initial outcomes in both Afghanistan and Iraq, the challenge that now faced those thinking about and delivering air power came not from state-on-state warfare, but insurgencies. In both cases, the long insurgencies suggested that notions of rapid dominance and swift victory were consigned to the past; coupled with the Israeli experience in Lebanon, it seemed that it might be the case that air power's role was to be not dissimilar to that in the First World War, namely supporting troops on the ground. Superficially, this appeared correct but this was to overlook the exceptional force-multiplying effects of air power and, crucially, to ignore the possibility that insurgencies were not the only sort of wars that Western nations would have to fight.

The Age of Insurgency

As noted in previous chapters, air power has often been seen as a peripheral factor in counterinsurgency campaigns, there to provide support to troops on the ground. This remained largely true during the campaigns in Iraq (2003–2011) and Afghanistan (2001–2014), since air mobility was of critical importance in moving troops around both countries in the face of extremely dangerous road conditions created by improvised explosive devices (IEDs). Helicopters in particular were used for this task, and were not invulnerable, but their presence enabled movement that would otherwise have been conducted on the ground to be carried out at lower risk; it was, of course, impossible for air mobility to replace the need for troops on the ground.

The use of air power to deliver fire support to troops remained controversial, even though the majority of casualties amongst the civilian population in both Iraq and Afghanistan were inflicted by the insurgents, and then by heavy weapons such as artillery, rather than by air attack. The use of air-delivered fires, exploiting precision weapons in a manner not previously seen in COIN operations, made a considerable contribution to ground operations, although there were suggestions that an over-reliance upon air power had crept into land-component thinking, even though the new American COIN doctrine, FM3-24, gave little detailed coverage to the use of air power in its first edition.[24] In contrast, Lieutenant General Karl Eikenberry, commander of the Combined Forces Command Afghanistan, was absolutely clear on air power's contribution:

> Without air and space power, 500,000 to 600,000 troops would be needed in Afghanistan to achieve the same effects as the 40,000 soldiers, sailors, marines and airmen we have there today. Air and space power provides the asymmetric advantage over the Taliban such that no matter where they choose to fight, coalition forces can bring to bear overwhelming firepower in a matter of minutes. Moreover, putting 5–600,000 troops into the country may achieve the same military effect, but it could also have a negative impact on the population; such numbers could appear as an occupying force rather than a security assistance force. In short, there is no substitute for effective air and space power.[25]

Air power was also a source of controversy because of the dramatic increase in the use of RPAS, particularly to conduct attacks against targets over the Afghan border in Pakistan. These attacks, conducted by remotely piloted aircraft operated by the Central Intelligence Agency (CIA), struck at supposed Taliban and AQ safe havens, but the implications for Pakistani national sovereignty, as well as frequent alleged instances of civilian casualties alongside the individuals targeted, has been a source of great controversy.

This has created a number of difficulties for air forces using RPASs, with criticisms of 'drone wars' conflating CIA operations with those of regular forces. RPAS have provided regular persistent surveillance over large areas of Iraq and

Afghanistan, and their extended endurance has been critical in allowing the development of detailed intelligence pictures. 'Weaponised' RPAS such as the MQ-9 Reaper, have added an extra dimension in terms of their ability to provide overwatch for ground forces and fire support when required, often ensuring immediate support has been provided rather than seeing troops have to wait for aircraft to be called in to deliver an attack. RPASs also offer a greater opportunity for the crews to increase their situational awareness before deciding to release weapons, reducing – but not eliminating – the danger of collateral damage or mistakes in identification that might occur if the decision to release has to be made by aircrew travelling at notably higher speeds in a jet.[26]

The importance of air power, both as a force multiplier and as a means of providing critical support to the land component, may have been overlooked and sometimes misrepresented in popular reporting, but a study of the evidence means that it is difficult to disagree with Anthony H. Cordesman's analysis:

> Much of the reporting on the Iraqi and Afghan wars focuses on the ground dimension . . . The fact remains, however, that Iraq and Afghanistan are air wars as well, and wars where air power has also played a critical role in combat.[27]

Air Power in a Post-Afghanistan World?

The drawing down of coalition forces in Afghanistan took place against another change in the strategic context in which air power has been used. The idea that states would not fight against other states, popular in the mid 2000s, came to be replaced by an understanding that the types of conflict in which air power might be used would be just as varied as before, but likely to be more complex. This was exemplified by the NATO-led operation to enforce UN Security Council Resolution 1973, aimed at protecting the population of Libya from the efforts of Colonel Muammar Gaddafi's regime to quell an insurgency against his rule. The operation was notable for the relative lack of American participation beyond critical enabling capabilities such as air-to-air refuelling and heavy attacks upon the Libyan air defence system during the opening phases of the campaign. Air power was used to destroy Libyan regime targets, since Gaddafi had been identified as the centre of gravity of the whole Libyan effort – reducing his power over his own forces and his prestige through attacks on targets closely associated with Gaddafi. A further apparently novel feature came in the use of air power to support indigenous Libyan forces, aided by a small number of special forces soldiers from the wider anti-Gaddafi coalition; this created complications in terms of air–land integration, but it is perhaps worth reflecting upon the fact that air support to indigenous units is not entirely new, being a feature (albeit to a much lesser extent) in the colonial policing operations of the inter-war period.

Tensions between NATO and Russia, particularly after Russia's illegal annexation of Crimea in 2014, coupled with an increase in the number of long-range flights by the Russian air force requiring interception and escort by a number of NATO air forces, suggested that the need to consider wider possibilities than COIN campaigns remained valid. Any doubts about this were completely assuaged by Russia's invasion of Ukraine in February 2022. This is discussed further later, but the war represented a clear demonstration of the ways in which both air and space power have become an integral part of modern warfare. Much of the pre-invasion intelligence for Ukraine and Russia was derived from use of space-based systems, many of them commercially owned rather than under the control of the state, while the US and its NATO allies were able to observe the build-up of the invading force making use of visual and signals intelligence gained from satellite overflight, using both government-controlled systems and information from commercial sources.

The Expansion of Space Power

The evolution of the way in which space power came to be seen as a military and strategic tool beyond that of military- or government-owned space-based systems began with the end of the Cold War. Iraq's invasion of Kuwait changed the way in which the US sought to exploit space power, since when Operation Desert Shield began in August 1990 the Americans were notably unprepared to use space power to full effect. While there was some extant doctrine regarding effective integration between space assets and terrestrial-based forces C2 of space assets, hampered by the over-classification of intelligence product derived from space systems, it did not function as well as it might. National command authorities were provided with much useful information from space platforms, but General Schwarzkopf, as theatre commander, did not receive information that would have been extremely useful.

Nevertheless, space power played a vital role. Approximately 80 per cent of communications to and from CENTCOM came via space-based communications assets. The GPS, a relatively new piece of technology, proved an essential asset to the coalition, giving precise navigational coordinates to army formations manoeuvring across featureless deserts. Aircrews purchased their own hand-held GPS terminals and attached them in their cockpits with Velcro, preferring to trust GPS ahead of the less accurate navigation equipment fitted to their aircraft. This began a trend which more than 30 years later has seen GPS become almost ubiquitous in military aviation; by the 2010s, some aviators complained that the risk of GPS jamming, coupled with a reduction in training in traditional aerial navigation methods, meant that there was a real risk of technological dependency reducing effectiveness.

Multispectral sensor information (that is to say, using radar, infra-red and electro-optical sensors) provided an array of highly detailed images that aided in battle damage assessment (BDA), although there were complaints that BDA details that would have been of considerable utility in planning failed to reach those in the operational theatre who would have most benefitted from the information the most. Perhaps most importantly, space power's most dramatic contribution to Desert Storm came with its use in the campaign against the Iraqi Scud missile attacks against Israel. Satellites with infra-red sensors were employed to detect the heat 'bloom' generated by the firing of the Scuds' rocket motors. From this information, which provided the coordinates of the launch site, it was possible to make a rough calculation as to where the missile was heading. This information was then sent to the USAF's Space Command in the US, which passed the information directly to the crews manning Patriot SAMs based in Israel and Saudi Arabia, bringing them to alert so that they could use their own radar systems to search for and detect the incoming missile. As Gregory Billman observes, the 1991 Gulf War 'Provided space power with its first large-scale opportunity to demonstrate its capabilities.'[28]

The Americans reflected deeply upon the use of space power in Desert Storm and made amendments to the way in which space assets were tasked and information disseminated. The significance of GPS increased dramatically after Desert Storm as the USAF pursued the development of GPS-guided munitions, notably with the Joint Direct Attack Munition (JDAM) series of weapons, where a GPS guidance kit is fitted to standard unguided bombs. The need for such a system was illustrated during the NATO operation against Slobodan Milosevic's regime in 1999, when many aircraft sorties had to be aborted because bad weather prevented aircrew from seeing the ground, preventing them from designating targets for their laser-guided weapons. The JDAM set a trend for nations around the world to develop their own GPS-guided weapons, such as the Chinese Fei Teng family of precision munitions.

Space Vulnerabilities

The increasing importance of space power during the 1990s in terms of both GPS and information gathering created new concerns about the exploitation of space. These are particularly acute in the US, which relies upon space assets like no other nation; in turn, many of America's allies are dependent upon US space systems for their militaries – for instance, the RAF now employs the 'Enhanced Paveway' series of bombs, which combine laser and GPS guidance to make the weapons employable in all weathers. The concern stems from the fact that it is evident that an adversary may seek to deny the Americans (and thus their allies) the use of space assets in future conflict. It is possible for GPS signals to be jammed, but this may be a double-edged sword for some nations given their own GPS-guided munitions. As well as the Chinese Fei Teng family mentioned above, India's arsenal includes the Gaurav glide bomb; Israel makes use of the Spice (in fact an abbreviation for 'smart, precise impact, cost-effective'), while Russia employs its equivalent of GPS, the GLONASS system, to provide information for a series of air-to-ground munitions such as the KAB-500S-E. Degrading the navigation system, or denying it entirely by either jamming or use of anti-satellite weapons, thus becomes a factor for consideration, and a number of systems now employ dual guidance. The Spice, for example, uses electro-optical guidance to allow the weapon to be steered onto the target by a crew member in an attacking aircraft, while the Gaurav utilises an inertial navigation system (INS).

The potential for adversaries not just to jam satellite signals is not the only challenge that nations with a space capability now face. It is possible for nations or groups of non-state actors (or even, potentially, individuals) to obtain commercial satellite images for reconnaissance purposes, while the risk of interference through the electromagnetic spectrum, or cyber-attacks against the terrestrial locations controlling these systems has to be considered. So much of modern life, from banking, timing and basic navigation in road vehicles, is dependent upon space-based systems that there are grounds for concern over the possible risk to space assets, either from hostile action or, potentially, from collisions in orbit between satellites or 'space junk' striking a satellite and rendering it inoperative.

In Operation Desert Storm, the coalition made sure that the Iraqis were unable to make use of the French commercial SPOT (*Système probatoire pour l'observation de la terre*) imaging satellite system, which might have given Saddam information about the disposition of coalition forces; in the insurgency in Iraq after Saddam's deposition, and in the intervention in Afghanistan, concerns have been expressed about the ability of insurgents to use packages such as Google Earth to gain images of the layout of coalition bases, enabling them to make effective indirect fire attacks on the most vulnerable parts of those facilities. To an extent, this was addressed by Google Earth responding positively to requests to obscure the imagery of bases, but commercial concerns offering similar services may not be so accommodating in future. The use of commercial satellite imagery by both Ukraine and Russia has played a notable part in targeting during the Russo-Ukraine war, with the ability to exploit space-based platforms removing risk from aircraft facing strong enemy air defence systems as they seek to obtain information.

Furthermore, it is possible that adversaries with access to suitable technology may seek to 'blind' satellites with the use of ground-based laser systems that dazzle the satellite's equipment. A US Army test in 1997 employing a low-powered laser blinded a USAF satellite flying 300 miles above the earth's surface.

Subsequently, there have been suggestions that the Chinese, embarking upon a space programme of their own, may have employed low-powered laser blinding devices to deny the US intelligence information about sites of interest in Chinese territory. Another threat may emanate from adversaries launching a cyber-attack on space-based platforms, interrupting communication between the control room and the platform itself. Such an attack could be used to render the space asset useless, either by sending it tumbling out of orbit or shutting down key systems. Russia hinted at the prospect of using a system employing a nuclear warhead to degrade or destroy the satellites of adversaries – although it is not clear whether this was anything more than coercive bluster – and the US and India have both demonstrated the ability to hit satellites using missiles launched from the surface of the earth.

Space Control and Force Application

American concerns about such developments have increased discussion of the concept of space control. Like control of the air, this seeks to ensure freedom of action of friendly assets without interference from the enemy, while denying the opposition access to the benefits provided by space. This represents a horrendously complex issue for the US, since blinding or destroying a civilian-owned, -launched and -operated satellite system if the owner refuses to ensure that either information product or communications facilitation provided by their space asset is unavailable for enemy exploitation is fraught with legal difficulties. The Americans developed an air-launched anti-satellite (ASAT) weapon in the 1980s for use by the F-15 Eagle fighter aircraft. The system was successfully tested before the project was cancelled over concerns that it violated international treaties. A Chinese test of an ASAT in 2007 caused considerable consternation, particularly in the US, while the Indian ASAT launch in 2019, under the code name of Mission Shakti, led to considerable criticism of the Indian government for creating more space debris by testing the weapon. US military war games have illustrated the threat posed by an adversary capable of employing ASAT or blinding technologies. As a participant noted at the end of one such war game, '[The enemy] took out most of our space-based capabilities. Our military forces just ground to a halt.'[29] Observers suggest that the only means by which the US can guarantee space control is not only to invest in anti-satellite capabilities deployed from earth-based locations but also actively to fight for control in space itself; the US Space Commission report of 2001 concluded that the threat to American space capability was a 'virtual certainty', making the need to invest in some form of space control technology seem even more important. The degree of space control considered necessary by some proponents would involve placing weapons in space, an issue of considerable political sensitivity. Weaponisation of space, even for defensive purposes, is controversial; the Soviets fitted a 30 mm cannon to the Salyut-3 space station in the 1970s, with the aim of protecting the station from a possible attack by an American platform, but such was the sensitivity about placing weapons in orbit that this was not revealed at the time, details emerging only as the result of information provided from those who served aboard Salyut-3. This makes another potential space concept, that of force application, an even more controversial area.

The concept of **space force application** takes the possibility of weaponising space a stage further, in that it would see the development and use of weapons systems against terrestrial targets. Such a step would involve the use of directed-energy and kinetic-energy weapons (that is to say, lasers and ultra-high-speed projectiles that destroy the target through their kinetic energy rather than with a warhead) against both missiles and enemy ground targets; enemy targets on earth might also be attacked using space-based conventional weapons. The value of the kinetic-energy weapon from space against such targets as hardened bunkers would be that the energy inherent in such a weapon descending from space would be far greater than anything that could be obtained by a conventional weapon launched from within the earth's atmosphere.

The Ultimate Frontier

While space power is still, in many ways, a nascent form of warfare, the critical nature of space-based platforms means that there is a widespread belief that issues of space control and the weaponisation of space will need to be addressed, even if not in the short term.[30] Space power shares many features of air power, notably in the way in which it is a key enabler for operations. The former commander-in-chief of both North American Aerospace Defense Command and the USAF's Air Force Space Command, General Howell M. Estes III, has observed: 'The potential of aircraft was not recognised immediately. Their initial use was confined to observation ... until one day, the full advantage of applying force from the air was realised, and the rest was history. So too with the business of space.'[31]

While Estes's view may involve too linear a description of the way in which the utility of using air power for the projection of military force was realised, the comparison with air power (and arguably land and naval power) is valid. As soon as the value of the operating environment was realised, it became clear that future conflict between powers of roughly comparable technical proficiencies would involve the struggle for control of that environment. This has become the underpinning rationale of air power, and it appears that space power will increasingly be subjected to the same dynamics, albeit only as long as the competing powers possess an approximately symmetrical degree of technical advancement and aptitude. For asymmetric operations, where one power enjoys overwhelming technological superiority against the opponent, the value of space power as a key enabler remains unchallenged, hence the notion that 'space superiority has joined air superiority as a *sine qua non* of global reach and power'.[32]

It is difficult to overstate the importance of space power to modern societies; positioning, navigation and timing (PNT) systems are integral to financial services, communications, agriculture and the generation of power and are all dependent on the functioning of satellites. The risk of loss of PNT is a major concern for many governments. The risks are plentiful. The most difficult to legislate for and mitigate come in the form of 'space weather' – events such as coronal ejections, geomagnetic storms and solar winds – degrading the operations of satellites and 'space junk' where objects travelling at extreme high speed collide. Such collisions might see functioning satellites rendered inoperable by those that remain in orbit but that are no longer under control from ground stations. Debris from previous collisions or, as noted above, ASAT tests, might also have catastrophic effects if they collide with space-based PNT systems.

The challenges presented by a potentially deliberate assault by an adversary upon a nation's space assets could be enormous. The risks might come via cyber-attacks upon space operations centres on earth, or deliberate attacks on satellites. Such steps undertaken by a space-faring nation might create a scenario analogous to MAD, associated with nuclear weapons during the Cold War, with the risk of 'Space-MAD' potentially dissuading warring powers from interfering with their enemy's access to space lest retaliation have hugely deleterious effects not only on military operations but also on the functioning of key elements of civic society. The challenges of denying space access to nations drawing upon commercial or third-party sovereign capability also present many challenges, prompting efforts to regulate and create international norms that would be stronger and more efficacious than the 1967 Outer Space Treaty, which has been overtaken by technological developments. In such a climate, it is unsurprising that some air forces have rebranded themselves as 'aerospace forces' (for example, Israel and France), while the US chose to create the USSF as a separate service; although satirised, USSF performs a vital function in providing space assurance and examining how best to protect this critical part of American national infrastructure, both civilian and military. While not rebranding as an aerospace force, the UK chose to create a new Space Command within the RAF (in fact a 'joint' organisation housed at RAF headquarters, with the second of its commanders being a British Army general officer). Whatever the preferred approach, the growing seriousness with which nations have engaged with space power issues illustrates just how important space has become.

The risks of interference with space assets are of great concern, although musing by Russia in 2024 on the subject of placing a nuclear-armed anti-satellite capability in orbit (a potential retaliation for American and European military aid to Ukraine) saw considerable criticism and concern expressed by Russia's opponents and friends alike – highlighting the growing pervasiveness of space in global affairs. The importance of PNT is now matched by the use of systems such as Starlink for communications, for both civilian and military purposes. Starlink has been employed to considerable effect by the Ukrainian Armed Forces in their fight against Russia, while some evidence has emerged of the system being drawn upon by the Russians. The ability or otherwise of the third party owning a capability such as Starlink to limit or deny access to the system highlights a further challenge to nation states without their own systems – they may find themselves at the whim of a corporation's shareholders, or with a reasonably technologically adept enemy 'piggybacking' off systems that are not fully secure. Also, as discussed later, the use of space to enable the operation of uncrewed air systems – 'drones' – is of ever-growing importance as we enter the second quarter of the twenty-first century, while the information derived from satellites for targeting, BDA and navigation of both aircraft and long-range weapons systems is critical to the operations of air, land and maritime forces.

Air and Space Power in Modern Wars

The rise of technology and its integral part in operations in both the air and space environments is marked by issues over costs. This has been an increasing challenge for the traditional, mainly Western, air power nations. Also, many states now have growing access to sophisticated equipment. The days when countries had to accept downgraded 'export' versions of combat aircraft, equipped with previous-generation missiles, bombs and lower-quality avionics are long gone. Advanced Russian aircraft such as the Su-27 are readily available to those who have the money to purchase them, along with advanced air-to-air missiles and PGMs.

China, in its bid to develop air forces that contain a large number of high-quality aircraft, rather than relying simply on mass, has produced aircraft that are attractive to export partners; the JF-17 'Thunder', while not in Chinese service, has been the subject of an enthusiastic partnership programme with Pakistan to replace some of its obsolete aircraft with the JF-17, as well as providing its Chinese J-10 fighter, again armed with a panoply of advanced weapons. Long-range missiles such as the PL-15 add to the potential ability of the PLAAF to conduct effective operations against so-called high-value assets (HVAs) such as airborne early warning and electronic intelligence (ELINT) aircraft, which could operate with a high level of impunity by standing off the adversary's territory; the ability to engage such aircraft at hundreds of miles range makes planning the operation of HVAs more challenging than ever before. For many smaller nations with at best few HVAs of their own, access to long- and ultra-long-range missiles increases their ability to challenge numerical or capability superiority of their opponent.

Although it seems unlikely that the Chinese J-20 'stealth' fighter will be exported in the near future, the possibility of it entering service with nations unfriendly towards Western (and particularly American) interests is a source of possible concern. Nations generally well-disposed to the traditional air powers, such as Qatar and the United Arab Emirates (UAE), have small but exceptionally well-equipped air forces; the F-16s employed by the UAE are probably the best in the world, their avionics surpassing those currently fitted to the F-16s in use by the USAF (see Figure 12.3).

The Democratisation of Air Power?

The growing ability of nations to obtain effective air power that was previously only available to industrialised nations means that air power has become much more of a factor than even some of the early theorists might have supposed. There is a further important consideration about the availability of systems that can be used for everything from reconnaissance to attack, which is that it brings air power, even if in only a basic form, within the reach of non-state actors and individuals. In the Middle East, Hamas and Hezbollah have acquired both drones and missile systems and have targeted Israel with these systems since the early 2000s, while more recently the Houthi rebels in Yemen have attacked shipping in the Red Sea and launched weapons against Israel, provoking retaliation against both the Houthis and their major supplier, Iran. Groups able to obtain weaponised drones represent a particular challenge. The threat of the use of swarms of drones against infrastructure targets has become a particular concern for many nations with weaponised, commercially available systems potentially being used to attack high-value targets (see Figure 12.4).

The temptation to adopt this approach does not only reside with non-state actors but is also attractive to nations that wish to boost their air power, especially if they cannot afford a large fleet of combat aircraft; the drone provides a means of 'force multiplication'. The small size of many drones and their relative low costs means that, while systems such as the MQ-9 Reaper and KVD002 may represent the current 'ideal' for drones, it is possible to obtain considerable capability through commercial means, particularly if the funding or desire exists to be able to obtain a regular supply, making the loss of drone systems palatable. Whereas in the past only a few nations might be able to afford drones and relatively sophisticated missile systems, this is no longer the case and drones may present both an air and a space threat.

Figure 12.3 Illustrative of the way in which the Western dominance of high-technology aircraft has been eroded, the Chengdu J-20 fighter represents the Chinese approach to '5th Generation' combat aircraft, including a two-seat variant to control uncrewed collaborative combat aircraft.

Capable combat aircraft and long-range missiles have also been supplied to nations that, in the 1970s, would have found their wish to purchase such systems blocked by one of the two superpowers. The spread of air power technology creates what might be termed the democratisation of air power, in making it more accessible to nations that otherwise might find themselves at a serious disadvantage.

The Ukrainian approach to the use of drones during the war with Russia is instructive in this regard. The extensive use of both imported and domestically built drones has been dramatic. Drones provide enormous amounts of reconnaissance information to both sides but represent a particular force-multiplying effect for Ukraine. As well as providing reconnaissance and targeting information for other weapons systems, the Ukrainians have made use of drones to conduct long-range attacks against Russia, complementing missiles such as the Storm Shadow and being used to overwhelm the Russian air defences with sheer numbers. A combination of so-called 'kamikaze drones' fitted with explosives or the ability to release ordnance and other drones fitted with electronic warfare equipment to confuse or overburden enemy air defence radars and reporting systems and missiles – increasingly fitted with their own defensive aids to defeat enemy missile attacks – makes the work of defenders far more difficult. As part of their ongoing conflict, the Ukrainians have developed a series of domestically produced drones of

Figure 12.4 The XQ-58 Valkyrie experimental collaborative combat aircraft. Part of the US 'Skyborg' programme, the XQ-58 is representative of the new era in air power with uncrewed systems working in close cooperation with more traditional combat aircraft types.

varying sizes that have become almost ubiquitous over the battlefield and provide a great deal of footage of Russian forces in combat with the Ukrainian defenders. The 'Seth' drone uses autonomous targeting, which means that the traditional 'human in the loop' (controlling the drone and any release of weapons) approach has been superseded by the 'human on the loop', where an operator can monitor and intervene to prevent a drone from releasing weapons, or can retask the drone. In a highly contested electromagnetic environment, the challenge of communicating with drones is extremely high, and autonomy creates the means by which enemy interference can be reduced significantly. This approach, though, raises some serious ethical issues about targeting, particularly if used against enemy troops, since machines become the arbiters of whether to take human life or not. In an existential conflict, such considerations may be less relevant to those at risk of destruction, but the increased ability of drones to operate without human input is significant.

It is not just nations aiming to make up for a lack of combat aircraft that have shown interest in drones; major powers such as the US made use of drones from the late twentieth century. The ability to use satellites to control a drone operating thousands of miles away from the controllers was most obviously seen in operations by the US, UK and their allies in Iraq and Afghanistan, but the sometimes-overlooked conflict between Armenia and Azerbaijan in 2020 also illustrated the way in which drones could act as significant force multipliers both in terms of increasing the number of attack and surveillance assets available and their endurance over a battlefield as long as enemy defences were weak or incapable of engaging effectively. In Iraq and Afghanistan, drones such as the MQ-9 Reaper could operate with almost complete impunity, while in the Armenian–Azerbaijani conflict, careful planning and Armenia's difficulties in tracking drones meant that the Azerbaijanis were able to achieve impressive results against important Armenian targets, particularly air defence sites and armoured formations.

Furthermore, the drones available by the early 2020s range from the sophisticated types such as the MQ-9, through to the less-costly Turkish TB-2 Bayraktar. The latter system gained early fame in the Russo-Ukrainian war when it inflicted serious damage on Russian troops, but a combination of effective ground-based air defences and electronic warfare enabled the Russians to mitigate and for some time obviate the threat of the TB-2. Undaunted, the Ukrainians made use of thousands of small first-person view (FPV) drones, more commonly associated with hobby drone flying prior to the war. Fitted with cheap but effective video cameras and weaponised with relative ease, the Ukrainian FPVs have become an almost-pervasive feature of the battlefield. The ease of production of such systems and their relatively low cost makes them expendable – it was at one point in 2023/24 estimated that Ukraine was suffering 90% attrition of its FPV-type drones, but this was entirely sustainable given the resilience of production facilities and output. The notion that being able to accept 90% loss rates on air operations would be sustainable would have astonished the air power theorists of the 1920s and 1930s. It is, therefore, no coincidence that larger powers are developing their own low-cost, high-volume drone capabilities to complement their crewed aircraft and more sophisticated, longer-endurance drone systems.

Conclusion

As has been discussed over the last three chapters, air power has grown from being purely subordinate to surface forces to playing a significant part in the delivery of military power; the rise of space power has only added to this. The air is a complex operating environment, and visions over how it might best be exploited have led to considerable debate. Nowhere has this discussion been more heated in terms of the potential contribution of air power at the strategic level, through attacks against targets deep in the enemy heartland. As has been shown, limiting consideration of air power's possible strategic effect to 'kinetic' operations has been short-sighted; also, the critical point that air, maritime and land power are all subordinate (or at least should be) to national strategic objectives is sometimes in danger of being missed, often for parochial reasons as service chiefs seek to promote the value of their arm in the seemingly constant struggle over budgets.

Despite this debate as to where air power is best employed, a few general observations can be made. No army or navy can operate truly effectively in the absence of some form of control of the air, particularly over the course of a long conflict. Possessing control of the air for a limited period of time or in a limited area may be all that is required for the success of a particular operation, but prolonged activity in the face of enemy air superiority makes the achievement of success increasingly unlikely. That said, control of the air is an enabler for operations rather than an end in itself.

A second key point is to note how important air power is to surface operations. The Second World War demonstrated that surface forces could not function to full effect in the face of enemy air superiority and that the efficacy of their operations was greatly enhanced by being able exploit the key characteristics of air power discussed in the first section of this chapter so as to project power beyond the range of the surface forces. Synergy between air and surface units greatly enhances the effect of what can be achieved, particularly in an era when precision weaponry enables targets to be attacked with considerable discrimination. The value of intelligence gained from air and space platforms has become a fundamental part of military planning in Western nations, while some space technology, such as GPS, has become so embedded in the conduct of day-to-day operations that it is difficult to envisage how Western militaries might operate without it.

Air and space power's attributes make it essential to conducting modern conflict. Now that the veil of secrecy of the Cold War era has been lifted and some of the mystique of what space-based assets can achieve, it is difficult to argue against the view that air and space are critical enablers to the prosecution of modern war. While the time has perhaps not yet arrived for air and space to be blended seamlessly into a concept of 'aerospace power', it is evident that the synergies of air and space power, and the way in which these contribute to modern war, make them vital to the business of war. The rise of drones as a vital weapon of modern war, both in terms of their capabilities and the ability to build them in large numbers that permits high loss rates to be tolerated, changes the character of aerial warfare in ways that might not have seemed possible even at the start of the twenty-first century. The importance of seeking to control airspace to enable operations, and to attempt to deny this privilege to the enemy, is at least as important now as it ever has been, with nations that had fondly assumed that the end of the Cold War meant that investment in air and space power could be reduced finding that an arrange of aerial capabilities and ground-based defences is of vital importance to national security.

Although these chapters have sought to give an insight into the complex realm of air and space power, it is worth ending with a caveat – and this is that air and space power are immature forms of warfare. They have proved their worth in a comparatively short space of time and are still developing. Colin Gray suggests:

> The grand strategic historical narrative of air power is complete in the record to date, but it is seriously unfinished. Air power is still in the process of becoming something different in character, though not in nature.[33]

This sage observation is a useful point to draw our considerations to an end: air and space power have developed at a tremendous rate, enabled by technological advancement of which early aviators could not have dreamed. Yet while technology has perhaps enabled some of the early visions of key air power thinkers to come to fruition in limited ways, we are nowhere near witnessing the end of air and space power development. Claims that the age of air power is drawing to a close could not be further from the truth.

RESEARCH QUESTIONS

1. To what extent has the development of RPAS('drones') revolutionised air power?
2. Evaluate the view that space has become so important that we should now talk about aerospace power rather than talking about air and space power as separate environments.
3. Do the wars in Afghanistan and Iraq demonstrate that air forces should be configured to perform COIN operations as their main role, or that they should be configured so as to enable intervention without 'boots on the ground'?
4. Does the proliferation of high-technology equipment mean that the advantages traditionally enjoyed by Western air power will inevitably come to an end by the end of the twenty-first century?
5. To what extent is the value of close cooperation between air forces, armies and navies an enduring lesson of air and space power history? And why has this cooperation been so difficult to achieve?

FURTHER READING

Antal, John, *Seven Seconds to Die: A Military Analysis of the Second Nagorno-Karabakh War and the Future of Warfighting* (Haverstown, PA: Casemate, 2022).

Bowen, Bleddyn E., *War in Space: Strategy, Spacepower, Geopolitics* (Edinburgh: Edinburgh University Press, 2022).

Corum, James S. and Wray R. Johnson, *Airpower in Small Wars* (Lawrence, KS: University of Kansas Press, 2003).

Davis Biddle, Tami, *Airpower and Warfare: A Century of Theory and History* (Carlisle, PA: US Army War College Press, 2019).

Gray, Colin S., *Airpower for Strategic Effect* (Maxwell, AL: Air University Press, 2012).

Hallion, Richard P., Roger Cliff and Phillip C. Saunders, *The Chinese Air Force: Evolving Concepts, Roles and Capabilities* (Washington, DC: National Defence University, 2012).

Henriksen, Dag and Bronk, Justin (eds.), *The Air War in Ukraine: The First Year of Conflict* (Abingdon: Routledge, 2025).

Lambeth, Benjamin S., *The Unseen War: Allied Air Power and the Take Down of Saddam Hussein* (Annapolis, MD: Naval Institute Press, 2013).

Lambeth, Benjamin S., *Airpower in the War Against ISIS* (Annapolis, MD: Naval Institute Press, 2021).

Meilinger, Phillip S. (ed.), *Paths of Heaven: The Evolution of Air Power Theory* (Maxwell, AL: Air University Press, 1997).

Olsen, John Andreas (ed.), *Global Air Power* (Dulles, VA: Potomac Books, 2011).

Olsen, John Andreas (ed.), *European Air Power: Challenges and Opportunities* (Dulles, VA: Potomac Books, 2014).

Pape, Robert A., *Bombing to Win: Air Power and Coercion in War* (New York, NY: Cornell University Press, 2006).

Sadeh, Eligar (ed.), *Space Strategy in the Twenty-First Century: Theory and Policy* (London: Routledge, 2012).

Sheehan, Michael, *The International Politics of Space: No Final Frontier* (London: Routledge, 2007).

Singer, P. W., *Wired for War: The Robotics Revolution and Conflict in the Twenty-First Century* (New York, NY: Penguin, 2009).

Strawser, Bradley J., *Killing by Remote Control: The Ethics of an Unmanned Military* (New York, NY: Oxford University Press, 2013).

ONLINE RESOURCES

www.airuniversity.af.edu/CASI/: China Aerospace Studies Unit.

www.airuniversity.af.edu/AetherJournal/: *Æther: A Journal of Strategic Airpower & Spacepower.*

www.kcl.ac.uk/research/freeman-air-and-space-institute: Freeman Air and Space Institute.

https://ciasp.scholasticahq.com/: Contemporary Issues in Air and Space Power.

www.raf.mod.uk/what-we-do/centre-for-air-and-space-power-studies/: RAF Centre for Air and Space Power Studies.

www.airuniversity.af.edu/: Air University.

www.defense.gouv.fr/air: Armée de l'air et de l'espace (French Air and Space Force).

NOTES

1 The maximum speed of combat aircraft has, in fact, decreased since the retirement of the Lockheed SR-71 'Blackbird' reconnaissance aircraft, which reached a top speed of just over 2,000 miles per hour, three times the speed of sound (Mach 3). Experience from the Vietnam War demonstrated that supersonic speed was useful but rarely reached in combat, and the fastest aircraft since that time have a maximum speed of around 2.5 times the speed of sound.

2 Benjamin S. Lambeth, *NATO's Air War for Kosovo* (Santa Monica, CA: RAND, 2001), p. 88, www.rand.org/pubs/monograph_reports/MR1365.html.

3 Office of Scientific Research and Development, *Visibility Studies and Some Applications in the Field of Camouflage*, esp. ch. 6,www.loc.gov/item/2009655226.

4 An excellent brief survey can be found in Arend G. Westra, 'Radar versus Stealth: Passive Radar and the Future of U.S. Military Power', *Joint Force Quarterly*, 55 (4th Quarter 2009), https://apps.dtic.mil/sti/tr/pdf/ADA515506.pdf.

5 For the development of stealth aircraft, see Thomas Withington, *B-2 Spirit Units in Combat* (Oxford: Osprey, 2006), pp. 6–29; Paul F. and Alison J. Crickmore, *Nighthawk F-117 Stealth Fighter* (St Paul, MN: Motorbooks, 2003); Steve Pace, *B-2* Spirit (New York, NY: McGraw Hill, 1999).

6 See US General Accounting Office, *Operation Desert Storm: Evaluation of the Air Campaign* (Washington: GAO, 1997), www.gao.gov/products/nsiad-97-134. The GAO was renamed the Government Accountability Office in 2004.

7 GAO, *B-2 Bomber Cost and Operational Issues* (Washington: GAO, 1997), www.gao.gov/assets/230/224502.pdf. RAM also costs more to maintain than conventional aircraft

construction materials such as metals and composites, although as technology evolves the cost differential has declined.

8 Jan van Tol et al., *AirSea Battle: A Point of Departure Operational Concept* (Washington: Center for Strategic and Budgetary Assessments, 2009) makes the case for the value of stealthy platforms, and not just aircraft.

9 The Republika Srpska should not be confused with the current Republika Srpska, which forms one of the two entities of Bosnia Herzegovina; the historical Republika Srpska was an unrecognised and self-proclaimed quasi-state.

10 See Ivo H. Daalder and Michael E. O'Hanlon, *Winning Ugly: NATO's War For Kosovo* (Washington, DC: Brookings Institution, 2000) for a contemporary analysis and David L. Phillips and Lawrence Burns, *Liberating Kosovo: Coercive Diplomacy and U.S. Intervention* (Cambridge, MA: MIT Press, 2012).

11 Julian H. Tolbert, 'Crony Attack: Strategic Attack's Silver Bullet?' (Master's Thesis, School of Advanced Air and Space Studies, 2002), https://apps.dtic.mil/sti/html/tr/ADA462291/index.html; Stephen T. Hosmer, *Why Milosevic Decided to Settle When He Did?* (Santa Monica: RAND, 2001), p. 75, www.rand.org/pubs/monograph_reports/MR1351.html.

12 As an extreme example, shortly after the end of the campaign, the author was told by a British Army officer that the talk of a land option had been the cause of Milosevic's capitulation, thus proving that land power is *always* the decisive factor in war, and showing air power's strategic irrelevance. Even with the benefit of a much greater evidential base today, this seems excessively parochial.

13 Human Rights Watch, 'The Crisis in Kosovo', www.hrw.org/reports/2000/nato/Natbm200-01.htm and 'Final Report to the Prosecutor by the Committee Established to Review the NATO Bombing Campaign against the Federal Republic of Yugoslavia' (ICTY, June 2000), paras. 71–8, www.icty.org/x/file/Press/nato061300.pdf.

14 Michael Russell Rip and James M. Hasik, *The Precision Revolution: GPS and the Future of Aerial Warfare* (Annapolis, MD: Naval Institute Press, 2002), pp. 210–11.

15 Human Rights Watch, 'The Crisis in Kosovo'.

16 The phrase was first used in 1982 by the Israeli prime minister, Menachem Begin – a 'war of necessity' being one fought to maintain a state's existence, or where a vital national interest could only be defended by the use of force.

17 Benjamin S. Lambeth, *Air Power against Terror: America's Conduct of Operation Enduring Freedom* (Santa Monica: RAND, 2005), pp. 204–31, www.rand.org/content/dam/rand/pubs/monographs/2006/RAND_MG166-1.pdf.

18 Mark J. Conversino, 'Operation DESERT FOX: Effectiveness with Unintended Effects', *Air and Space Power Journal, Chronicles Online Journal* (July 2005), www.airuniversity.af.edu/Portals/10/ASPJ/journals/Chronicles/conversino.pdf.

19 Harlan K. Ullman *et al.*, *Shock and Awe: Achieving Rapid Dominance* (Washington, DC: National Defense University, 1996); Harlan K. Ullman and James Wade, 'Rapid Dominance: A Force for All Seasons', *RUSI Whitehall Paper Series*, 43(1) (1998).

20 Donald Rumsfeld, *Known and Unknown: A Memoir* (New York, NY: Sentinel, 2011), pp. 459–61.

21 Anthony H. Cordesman, *The Iraq War: Strategy, Tactics and Military Lessons* (Washington, DC: Center for Strategic and International Studies, 2003), p. 281.

22 Lt. Col. Stephen Collins, 'Mind Games', *NATO Review* (Summer 2003), www.nato.int/docu/review/articles/2003/06/01/mind-games/index.html.

23 Carl Conetta, 'Catastrophic Interdiction: Air Power and the Collapse of the Iraqi Field Army in the 2003 War', www.comw.org/pda/fulltext/0309bm30.pdf; David E. Johnson,

Learning Large Lessons: The Evolving Roles of Ground Power and Air Power in the Post-Cold War Era (Santa Monica, CA: RAND, 2007), pp. 105–36.

24 Lara M. Dadkhah, 'Close Air Support and Civilian Casualties in Afghanistan', https://tinyurl.com/yc8xkm4w; Phillip S. Meilinger, 'Airpower and Collateral Damage: Theory, Practice and Challenges', www.ausairpower.net/APA-EMEAC-2013-02.html.

25 'NATO's Future Joint Air And Space Power', NATO Joint Air Power Competence Centre, April 2008, p. 4, https://tinyurl.com/26c6erwm.

26 Damian Killeen and David Jordan, 'RPAS: Future Force or Force Multiplier? An Analysis of Manned/Unmanned Platforms and Force Balancing', *RAF Air Power Review*, 16(3) (Autumn/Winter 2013), 10–29, https://tinyurl.com/2h5ksh5e.

27 Anthony H. Cordesman, 'Air Combat Trends in the Afghan and Iraq Wars', Center for Strategic and International Studies, March 2008, https://tinyurl.com/3a53zupn.

28 Gregory Billman, 'The Inherent Limitations of Space Power: Fact or Fiction?', in Bruce M. DeBlois (ed.), *Beyond the Paths of Heaven: The Emergence of Space Power Thought* (Maxwell, AL: Air University Press, 1999), p. 511.

29 Benjamin S. Lambeth, *Mastering the Ultimate High Ground: Next Steps in the Military Uses of Space* (Santa Monica, CA: RAND, 2003), p. 101.

30 Ibid., p. 118.

31 Ibid.

32 Department of the (US) Air Force, *Global Reach – Global Power* (Washington, DC: Department of the Air Force, 1992), p. 8.

33 Colin S. Gray, *Airpower for Strategic Effect* (Maxwell, AL: Air University Press, 2012), p. 315.

PART V
Irregular Warfare

JAMES D. KIRAS

13 Key Concepts and Terms of Irregular Warfare

CHAPTER OUTLINE

KEY THEMES

- Irregular warfare is primarily about politics and organisation. Violence plays a role in irregular warfare, as in all forms of war, for political purposes. The immediate purpose of violence is to demonstrate the political ineptitude of the ruling government and as a tool to intimidate and coerce populations.
- The ultimate goal of irregular warfare, regardless of its type, is political power for the purposes of political, social, economic and/or religious change.
- The character of irregular warfare is dynamic but its nature, outlined previously, is not. This character is shaped by social, environmental and technological factors. Insurgents, terrorists and revolutionaries have adopted irregular warfare methods for a key pragmatic reason: to offset their military and organisational weaknesses.
- Insurgency and terrorism will likely continue to be the most prevalent forms of irregular warfare now and in the future for a number of reasons.

Introduction

The withdrawal of Western military forces from Afghanistan, followed by the collapse of the sponsored Government of the Islamic Republic of Afghanistan, occurred in rapid succession from July 2020 through August 2021. These events – which capped twenty years of operations in the country at a cost of more than 70,000 dead, including just over 3,500 from the US and coalition forces – surprised some. Video of Afghans clinging to the side of departing C-17s called to mind footage of American helicopters leaving Saigon hurriedly in 1975, leading to political finger-pointing domestically. Accompanying the withdrawal were uncomfortable questions, prompted by reports or investigated incidents of legal, moral and ethical excesses by Western military forces most associated with irregular warfare and special operations forces (**SOF**), leading to comprehensive reviews, ongoing inquiries and investigations, and the disbanding of specific units.

The withdrawal, however, came as a source of relief to others. Irregular warfare distracted from other policy priorities and shifts occurring the West. From 2018 onwards there was a growing realisation of the expansion of Russian and Chinese military power. To address it, Western militaries focused their attention on 'great power' and **strategic competition.** Decades of operations in Iraq and Afghanistan had atrophied conventional military skills and equipment. Resources expended on Afghanistan, estimated at between US$800 million and US$2.4 trillion, could be allocated instead to competition and preparing for conflict with the Russian Federation and the People's Republic of China.[1] Continuing developments related to irregular warfare passed largely without notice. For example, Department of Defense Instruction, which outlined the significant role played by conventional forces in irregular warfare, was published late in September 2025 but is unknown and overlooked.

The focus on great power conflict has led to two efforts amongst those concentrating on irregular warfare. The first attempts to couch irregular warfare as the norm in great power competition. Supporters argue that hidebound military officers and organisations continue to organise, train and equip for conventional wars that are increasingly unlikely and anachronistic. They add that Western militaries have a long tradition of fighting irregular opponents and irregular warfare has been the norm, rather than the exception historically, comprising as it does a set of 'new rules' for conflict.[2] Irregular warfare is fundamentally different from conventional warfare, such advocates charge, in that force plays a greatly diminished role compared with security, development and governance. More effective approaches to irregular warfare begin with understanding local political dynamics within the 'human terrain' that occupies a central position (see Figure 13.1). The second stems from the fear of a recurrence of a historical pattern amongst Western militaries. This pattern, identified by several scholars and practitioners, finds militaries immersing themselves completely in the conduct of irregular warfare, developing new capabilities and understanding, only to purge hard-won knowledge and experience in the

Figure 13.1 Understanding the 'human terrain' in irregular warfare often is the difference between success and failure. Obtaining sufficient understanding quickly enough, particularly local information about insurgents or terrorists, is often the greatest challenge for external powers assisting host nations and their security forces in dealing with internal threats. This photo depicts the complexity of this terrain on modern battlespaces. During Combined Joint Task Force–Operation Inherent Resolve, forces conducting a patrol to protect key terrain and natural resources encountered a hostile pro-Syrian regime militia at a checkpoint near Qamishli, Syria, 12 February 2020. After coalition troops issued a series of de-escalation attempts and warnings, the patrol was attacked by a barrage of stones, small-arms fire, and arson from nearly 10 militia men. Coalition forces returned fire in self-defence, killing an adult male combatant. The incident is under investigation. One US service member received a superficial injury during the engagement and since returned to duty. The coalition operates in Eastern Syria to partner with Syrian Democratic Forces to defeat ISIS remnants and protect critical infrastructure.

pursuit of the next craze. Ignoring irregular warfare at their peril, successive generations are condemned to repeating a frenzied 'boom–bust cycle' of recovering lost knowledge in the midst of fighting the latest unconventional threat only to lose it once more.[3]

The Russian invasion of Ukraine in March 2022 seemingly rendered discussions of irregular warfare moot. Despite their previous success in annexing Crimea using irregular means – including a mixture of SOF, proxies and local militias in just three short weeks in 2014 – Russian leaders opted for a conventional invasion of the country eight years later, employing air assaults, armoured columns and heavy firepower. Many observers fixated on capturing lessons learned in the first modern conventional conflict by a great power in almost two decades, including the changes in the character wrought by drones and social media. They also revived debates about the viability of tanks and mass formations on current and future battlefields.[4] Largely overlooked were a series of irregular successes, particularly in the preparations for resistance activities across a swath of the Ukrainian population quickly mobilised to detect and stymie Russian advances.[5]

Events from 2023 onwards have served as a reminder of the continuing relevance yet misunderstanding of irregular warfare. After a long gestation period and considerable debate, the US Joint Staff released a new definition of irregular warfare more in line with daily competition activities: 'A form of warfare where states and non-state actors campaign to assure or coerce states or other groups through indirect, non-attributable, or asymmetric activities.'[6] Removing the qualifier 'violence' from the definition has led to less clarity about irregular warfare and its boundaries. Any doubts about what it might be were erased on 7 October 2023 when Hamas conducted a series of activities under Operation Al-Aqsa Flood from the Gaza Strip into Israel. What distinguished Hamas' operation from others was the attacks against massed non-combatant targets, including kibbutzes and a concert venue, for two specific purposes: the shock value of a coordinated attack by land and air captured and distributed on social media, and the killing and seizing of as many Israelis as possible. Shortly thereafter, Yemeni Houthi proxy militias began a campaign attacking shipping in the Red Sea, having previously attacked targets in Saudi Arabia and the United Arab Emirates. These attacks, as well as Hamas' offensive, have been termed as an Iranian-sponsored irregular warfare campaign by proxy.[7]

Do the conflicts in Ukraine, Palestine and Yemen signal a return to irregular warfare? What are the boundaries between irregular warfare and other forms of conflict? Is irregular warfare an artifact of the twentieth and early twenty-first centuries? Why are the armed forces of democracies, which have a well-demonstrated ability to project combat power, seemingly powerless in the face of irregular adversaries? The three chapters on irregular warfare in this volume suggest the rationale for adopting irregular warfare is understandable and pragmatic.

In order to demystify irregular warfare, this chapter first defines and distinguishes between its key terms of reference. This straightforward task is much more difficult than it first appears. Much of the confusion related to irregular warfare results from the misunderstanding and misapplication of its core terminology. With the core terms and concepts firmly in hand, Chapter 14 surveys various theories of irregular warfare from the perspective of those who seek to exploit insurgent and terrorist violence. The key theme of this review is that irregular warfare methods themselves have rarely been sufficient to achieve meaningful change. Historically, insurgents and terrorists have taken one of two approaches depending on the specific context of the conflict. The first is to outlast and force the eventual withdrawal of an occupying adversary, often by increasing costs or exhausting them morally and materially. The second approach has been to translate internal support from the population, as well as external support from sponsors, into political and military capabilities that overwhelm the forces of its adversaries. Chapter 15 looks differently at the challenges confronting those who seek to defeat irregulars. The 'science' of countering irregulars has been established historically through a number of well-known and, some might argue, self-evident principles. Difficulties in counterinsurgency and counterterrorism, as in all other forms of warfare, lie largely in attempting to apply such principles thoughtlessly without accounting for the unique context and changing circumstances of the conflict – in other words, failing to grasp the nature of the struggle at hand or the 'art' of strategy.

Definitions

Irregular warfare

Defining irregular warfare, much less its component elements, is no easy task. Several problems plague attempts to define irregular warfare clearly and concisely. In some cases, authors are inclined to lump everything together under a concept to the point where a term describes everything but explains nothing. One recent example includes 'information operations (including psychological operations and propaganda), cyber operations, support to state and non-state partners, covert action, espionage and economic coercion'.[8] At the other end of the spectrum are scholars and soldiers who create categorical definitions as they try to separate the terminology of irregular warfare with etymological and mechanical precision, such as the canon of US Joint Doctrine. Such definitions suit the purposes of specialised disciplines but have little recognition or application outside of their specific communities. In addition, new terms are created or revived to capture the realities of the most recent manifestations of violence. For example, preferred terms have changed over a century to describe exactly the same phenomenon: partisan warfare, unconventional warfare and resistance, or the mobilisation and arming of segments of a populus, with or without military support, to struggle against an incumbent government. Organisations, professional communities and influential individuals become wedded to terms that describe their understanding of a phenomenon and reflect their functional focus or preferences. What the social scientist terms 'civil wars' the military professional understands as counterinsurgency or counterterrorism. Both describe internecine violence within a population. As a result, the use of seemingly innocuous language can lead to either misunderstanding, vociferous disagreement in policy and planning circles or confusion amongst allied nations. Some object to the term 'irregular warfare' while others embrace it.[9]

Language, and in particular specific terms, presents other challenges in attempting to define irregular warfare. The two most daunting obstacles are the changing connotations of specific terms and the subjective and often emotional qualities associated with them. For example, Bruce Hoffman has charted the evolution in meaning behind the term 'terrorism' from state violence against the population to the violence used by substate groups for political purposes.[10] Insurgency was first used to describe insurrections, or violence with limited aims and duration, but the term now conveys motivation, organisation and a degree of popular support. Although this might appear to be an exercise in definitional hair-splitting, words have meanings that in turn can influence how and what actions are taken. For several months after the fall of Baghdad in 2003, senior leaders within the office of the US Secretary of Defense forbad the use of the term 'insurgency' to describe the violence lest it appear to be anything more threatening than the last vestiges of a dead regime. More recently, the national security debate has shifted the frame of reference of irregular warfare from non-state actors to state behaviour and activities of sponsored proxies.[11] The subjective value associated with specific terms can also lead to misunderstandings and disagreement over collective action that should be taken between governments or agencies. Differences of opinion over what should be labelled 'terrorism' have nothing to do with the form of violence employed. What colours perceptions is the fact that innocent civilians are often the victims of indiscriminate violence that strikes an emotional chord. As debates wracking university campuses over Hamas' attacks and Israel's response to them suggest, scholars and decision makers are likely to disagree over whether such violence should be rationalised and legitimised. One consequence has been an inability to forge meaningful consensus on what constitutes terrorism that, in turn, has impeded attempts to proscribe it internationally, which continues despite two decades of concerted effort against it regionally and globally.

One method of defining irregular warfare and its associated concepts relates to the purpose for which the violence, regardless of its form, is used. Ultimately, irregular warfare has at its core a cause based on grievances. The range of potential grievances and motivations behind them are numerous and can include ethnic and religious persecution, foreign occupation or domination, economic disparity and other forms of injustice that are real or merely perceived. Bard O'Neill has offered a comprehensive categorisation of types of causes for which groups are willing to commit violence. He categorises these types of insurgencies as:[12]

- Anarchist
- Apocalyptic-Utopian
- Reformist
- Egalitarian
- Pluralist
- Preservationist
- Traditionalist
- Secessionist
- Commercialist

As these categories suggest, some groups conduct irregular warfare to weaken the existing order and destroy it (anarchists), or profit from chaos (commercialist) or prefer to break away from the existing order and establish one of their own (secessionist). Others believe the existing order can be saved (reformist) or changed to serve traditional norms (traditionalist) or privileges (preservationist). Still others believe a more just and equitable society (egalitarian) can be created, while some believe that they are anointed to mete out religious rewards or punishments (apocalyptic-utopian). Groups can espouse a single cause, blend together one or more of the above and shift from one cause to another over time. Almost all groups seek to change the existing system whether on a national, regional or global basis. The only way for most groups to change the status quo is establish their own territory, or seize control of the existing system by some means and redistribute power or remake society according to their ideology. For the Taliban in Afghanistan and ISIS, control means enacting Sharia law along strict Wahhabi lines and replacing local tribal normative frameworks and traditional power structures. Power and control are ultimately political objectives. The violence within irregular warfare is far from random in nature. Instead, it should be suborned to a political purpose to the maximum extent possible.[13]

Another trait that irregular warfare has in common with other forms of warfare is the idea of dynamic resulting from the struggle between adversaries. On a theoretical level, each adversary is seeking to impose its will upon the other while avoiding having another will imposed upon them – what Clausewitz termed 'polarity'. What distinguishes war in theory from war in practice is the dynamic that exists within and between adversaries and other actors, the level of information available to each and other contextual variables that give each war its own unique traits and characteristics, as well as influential audiences engaged in the struggle or observing.[14] The interaction between adversaries, in turn, creates friction, chance and uncertainty that influences the outcome of events and disrupts even the soundest and most elegant strategy.[15] Within irregular warfare, the role played by friction, chance and uncertainty is magnified due to the political nature of the struggle, the character it takes and the resources involved.

The key distinction between irregular and other forms of warfare, and different types of irregular warfare, rests on resources and the ability to translate them into effective capabilities and effects. These resources can be physical or psychological, technological or social, or a combination. Groups conducting irregular warfare are attempting to defeat or overcome adversaries that possess significantly more powerful and numerous resources. Most often, substate groups are fighting against a state that not only possesses superior resources but also a legitimate monopoly on violence within its borders. In order to have a reasonable chance of success in any type of irregular warfare, groups must keep their activities hidden from their adversary for as long as possible so as not to be detected, tracked and destroyed.[16] Those who conduct irregular warfare rarely do so as a matter of preference or because they find a semi-clandestine and potentially dangerous lifestyle appealing. Most groups adopt irregular warfare because other, more decisive, forms of political violence are unavailable to them. If given a choice, some insurgent or terrorist leaders would prefer to have the nuclear or conventional resources and capabilities of their adversary to achieve their objectives without the need for a prolonged struggle.[17]

To some extent, the appeal of a group's cause with and the access to a particular support base determines the resources it has available to it. Groups can also forge alliances with others to pool together their resources, as well as seek out state sponsors willing and able to finance, train, equip and support them.[18] Yet few groups are coordinated, sophisticated or competent enough, at least in the early stages, to turn resources into capabilities that can overwhelm or coerce their adversary. Due to the nature of their cause, or extremist views, other groups are unable to translate their call for social justice into anything more than a handful of fanatical supporters and modest resources. The quality and quantity of resources a group enjoys have a significant bearing on the type of irregular warfare it can wage, the character of the violence employed and the time it takes to achieve its objectives.[19] Within the framework of great power competition, it is important to note that the best-sponsored groups are not always the most successful and often become predatory on the population they need to win over.[20] To sum up, *irregular warfare* is defined as the use of violence by substate actors, groups within states or state actors working by, with or through their proxies, for the political purposes of achieving power, control and legitimacy, using unorthodox or unconventional approaches to warfare contrary to prevailing norms, due to a fundamental weakness in resources or capabilities or the desire to limit the escalation of conflict. Other definitions of irregular warfare are contained in Box 13.1.

BOX 13.1 DEFINITIONS OF IRREGULAR WARFARE

The term 'irregular warfare' is only one of many coined to describe conflict between those fielding conventional forces and capabilities against an opponent who refuses battle, uses hit-and-run tactics and even targets non-combatants indiscriminately in order to achieve their objectives. W. E. D. Allen wrote on the subject of irregular war prior to the Second World War and his definition is shaped and limited by his studies and experience gained while serving with Lieutenant Colonel Orde Wingate in 1941. Wingate and Allen advised, trained, equipped and fought with Abyssinian irregulars against occupying Italian regulars. The other definition develops an 'umbrella' term to mobilise various US departments and agencies to compete more effectively against Russian, Chinese and Iranian irregular warfare.

> Irregular war is in fact as old as the hills which offer it its best terrain; older, clearly, than 'regular' war which has grown out of it, as the city grew out of the village. It would be difficult to define precisely where irregular war ends and regular war begins. It would be possible to say that irregular war is warfare carried out by forces other than the regular armies of a belligerent power. But this definition is not exact . . . Irregular and regular war are clearly two aspects of the same activity, but it should be taken as axiomatic that irregular action in the field should always be ancillary to parallel regular action . . . in no instance have guerrilla operations proved ultimately successful without the regular forces of a friendly power. (W. E. D. Allen, *Guerrilla War in Abyssinia* (New York, NY: Penguin, 1943), p. 18.)

BOX 13.1 (cont.)

[I]rregular warfare refers to activities short of conventional and nuclear warfare that are designed to expand a country's influence and legitimacy, as well as to weaken its adversaries. It includes numerous tools of statecraft that governments can use to shift the balance of power in their favor: information operations (including psychological operations and propaganda), cyber operations, support to state and nonstate partners, covert action, espionage, and economic coercion. Many of these tools, such as information operations, can be used for both irregular and conventional warfare. They are simply a means. In irregular warfare, however, a country designs and uses those tools to undermine its adversaries as part of balance-of-power competition without engaging in set-piece battles. Other government officials have used different terms – such as 'political warfare,' 'hybrid warfare,' 'grey zone activities,' '**asymmetric warfare**,' and 'the indirect approach' – to capture some or all of these activities. (Seth Jones, *Three Dangerous Men* (New York, NY: W. W. Norton & Co., 2021), p. 11.)

Types of irregular warfare

The types of irregular warfare dictated by resources can be broken down into five main categories or forms: coup d'état, terrorism, revolution, insurgency and civil war. Each is explored according to its centre of gravity, mechanism for success, strategic and tactical orientation and duration. Table 13.1 summarises the key attributes of the different types of irregular warfare.

Coup d'état

As a form of irregular warfare, coups d'état are conducted to change the system by overthrowing key facilities of governments as quickly and with as little initial bloodshed as possible. Coups tend to be instigated by small numbers within the system to ensure the secrecy of the plot and prevent its discovery. For these reasons, conducting a coup d'état requires nerve, timing, planning and luck but little in the way of additional resources, as the seven recent coups in Africa from 2021 to 2023 suggest.[21] Often the instigators of coups d'état come from the officer corps, as the military is the one government institution that can quickly crush such acts of rebellion. Those who conduct coups seek to gain power in order to change national policies or correct ethnic or religious exclusion – and gain wealth in the process – with even odds of success, at least in Africa.[22] In some cases, coup plotters seek the active support or tacit approval of other state leaders before they conduct their actions, often to achieve tacit approval or access key resources such as funding, equipment or intelligence.

Table 13.1 Attributes of types of irregular warfare∗

Type	Resources	Centre of gravity	Mechanism	Strategic orientation	Tactical orientation	Duration
Coup d'état	Few	Elites (organise)	Seizure of power	Offensive	Offensive	Immediate
Terrorism	Few	Elites (influence)	Coercion or provocation	Offensive	Offensive	Lengthy
Revolution	Vanguard, growing to many	Population∗∗ (stimulate)	Popular support (provocation and uprising)	Defensive	Defensive	As quickly as possible
Insurgency	Varied, but often significant	Population (control)	Denial leading to victory over or withdrawal of opponent	Defensive, switching to offensive	Offensive given local superiority	Lengthy
Civil war	Varies, positive correlation of forces	Population (mobilisation)	Denial or negotiated settlement	Varies	Varies	Most often Lengthy

∗ I freely acknowledge the intellectual debt I owe to Arial Merari for this chart. His comparison of forms of insurgency provided the inspiration for my own analysis that differentiates between forms of irregular warfare. See Merari, 'Terrorism as a Strategy of Insurgency', *Terrorism and Political Violence*, 5(4) (Winter 1993), 220.

∗ I use population throughout in its most general sense, which can include specific segments or diasporas of like-minded groups of individuals bound by cultural, political, economic and/or religious ties.

Terrorism

Terrorism also involves small numbers of individuals, operating in cells and groups, with relatively few resources to function. Groups or cells face resource constraints for several reasons, including effective security services that constrain group members' freedom of action and causes that appeal only to a slim minority within a population. Acts of terrorism deliberately target the non-combatant civilian population and other symbols associated with the state (military and police forces, government buildings, monuments, etc.) or the ruling government's power base to spread fear disproportionate to the damage it causes. Groups choose terrorism as a means of using the severely limited resources at their disposal in unorthodox and dramatic attacks, which often are accompanied by self-generated or external media reports, in order to compel or persuade one or more target audiences. Against adversaries, terrorism in its various forms can convince a target population and its leadership that the stakes of a conflict are not worth the current and potential future costs through coercion given their willingness to conduct wanton acts of mayhem and destruction.[23] For domestic audiences, sympathisers and supporters, including states, acts of terrorism demonstrate a group's power, reach and competence, and can facilitate access to resources or even ownership of a particular cause between competing terrorist groups, as was the case between Hamas and Fatah in Palestine in between 2005 and 2006.[24] In addition, acts of terrorism can influence or coerce segments of the domestic population into either action (fleeing or overreacting) or inaction, as was the case with the publicised AQ and later ISIS beheadings. Terrorism often ends in one of the following ways: decapitation of the terrorist leadership; a negotiated settlement; success of the terrorist campaign in achieving its objectives; failure by terrorist groups imploding, provoking a backlash or becoming marginalised; repression; or reorientation of their goals.[25]

Revolution

Revolution bears many similarities to a coup d'état, in that it requires an intellectual or technological elite or 'vanguard' to organise and guide its ultimate success, but it also possesses crucial differences. The primary goal of most revolutions is to paralyse and collapse or overthrow an existing government and redistribute power and resources. There are two critical components to a revolution: a cadre of political organisers that work within a population, and a population that is oppressed, exploited and frustrated enough that it just might turn to protest or violence if the right spark is provided. The cadre of organisers, under the direction of the vanguard, seeks to demonstrate the incompetence of the existing regime, conduct political agitation overtly and covertly and elevate the consciousness of the oppressed population. At the appropriate time, or perhaps as the result of an action either by the revolutionaries or the regime overreacting in response, a critical mass of the population will rise up, overpower the control elements of the regime and allow the vanguard to assume power. Without a sufficient mass of the population behind it, revolutions are doomed to fail. If the vanguard does not impose control should revolution succeed, the result is often prolonged insurgency or civil war between competing factions. Further confusing matters, some try to distinguish between 'insurrection' and 'revolution' when they are in fact indistinguishable. Characterising the 6 January 2021 as an 'insurrection' has been contentious politically yet it serves a pragmatic function: it is defined and can be prosecuted and punished legally.[26]

Insurgency

Partly due to expansion of the term, but mostly as a consequence of the outcome of Iraq and Afghanistan, the term 'insurgency' is unfashionable. The characterisation of various violent Islamic extremist groups as a 'global insurgency' contributed to this state and suggested to critics justification for perpetual conflict externally. Some authors suggest that our concept for this type of irregular warfare requires substantial revision and rethinking given the change in context in which insurgencies now occur.[27] Insurgency shares a number of characteristics in common with other forms of irregular warfare. Successful revolutions place primary emphasis on organising, educating and proselytising amongst the population to prepare it for the inevitable conflict against the system. Maoist and other agrarian-based insurgencies, for example, also stress the need to develop a 'shadow government', or parallel political structure, which controls the rural population and extracts resources without alienating its crucial support base. The level of support required for insurgencies to sink roots and operate successfully is context-specific, as in the case of clan- or tribal-based societies, in which these social units can be self-supporting. Insurgencies of this type may not require the support of the general population, but rather the spreading of enough instability, uncertainty and fear to prevent the population from assisting the insurgents' adversaries.

While theorists agree that the centre of gravity for an insurgency is popular support, a fundamental difference between revolutions and insurgencies is how resources mobilised or obtained from the population or other sources are utilised. Insurgencies harness resources in order to conduct attacks using guerrilla tactics that are designed to inflict ever-increasing losses on government or occupying forces and tip the balance of forces in the insurgents' favour. Such tactics include hit-and-run raids, ambushes and, more recently, remote attacks using mortars, rocket launchers and improvised explosive devices. Guerrilla tactics are conducted by small units organised along conventional military lines, such as squads, platoons or companies, on a scale and intensity designed to achieve operational or strategic effects over time: the weakening of the resolve of their political adversaries and the withdrawal of competing, occupying and/or government forces. The insurgent political structure fills the subsequent vacuum and attempts to consolidate its hold over the population by a mixture of intimidation, coercion, co-option or terror. Insurgent groups also recruit amongst the population, levy taxes and convince the local residents that the government or other groups cannot protect them and it is in their best individual and collective interest to support the insurgents actively or passively. Successes for insurgent groups allow them to translate support into larger militias and battalions, regiments and divisions of guerrillas with which to conduct even more widespread and ambitious attacks. These attacks further put their adversaries on the tactical, operational and even strategic defensive. Should the circumstances permit, insurgent groups translate time and resources into conventional or other capabilities that assume the strategic offensive to escalate the conflict into a civil war and end the conflict once and for all.

Insurgency is also one of the most forgiving and flexible forms of irregular warfare. Local and even regional defeat of guerrilla forces does not spell the end of most insurgencies. Mao's theory of prolonged war, discussed in detail in Chapter 14, acknowledges the possibility of backsliding out of necessity. The insurgent shadow network structures embedded within the population, including a confederation of informers and supporters, mean that even if government or other forces return the insurgent threat and presence remains. For example, the Taliban and ISIS distributed leaflets clandestinely to specifically identified locals in Afghanistan and East Jerusalem, respectively, warning them of future consequences. Time and space, as well as an external sanctuary such as Pakistan for the Taliban, can allow insurgent groups to recover and recoup their losses. Given the time it takes to weaken its adversaries to the point of collapse, or to tip the balance of forces and translate resources into meaningful capabilities, insurgencies are almost always prolonged in nature. The character of and popularity of the cause championed by insurgent leaders, as well as willingness to compromise on their desired goals, is often critical in determining an insurgency's duration and likelihood of success. Where adversaries are unwilling or unable to compromise or negotiate, the insurgency is almost always likely to end only after one of them submits, is eradicated or collapses.

Civil war

Civil wars differ from other forms of irregular warfare in that they occupy a space between the boundary of conventional and irregular warfare. Within civil wars the struggle is between competing and roughly matched factions within a territory for the control, recognition and legitimacy to govern a state. What makes these wars difficult to categorise is their wildly varying causes, scope and scale. Factions may espouse any one or a number of the causes that Bard O'Neill suggests (see Table 13.1): for example, within societies over differences in policies (the American Civil War, 1861–1865) and form of governance (the English Civil War, 1642–1651 or the Syrian Civil War, 2011–2024); a desire for self-governance (Eritrea from Ethiopia, 1974–1791); or disagreement over a negotiated settlement to a conflict (the Irish Civil War, 1922–1923). The scope and scale of civil wars are also diverse; a few last for short periods of time while most stretch over several decades, and casualties can range from tens of thousands into the millions. In some cases former insurgents fight one another, whereas in the most devastating civil wars factions fielding large armies fight more or less conventionally to impose their control upon one another through the destruction of their adversary's fielded forces. Some reject civil wars as a form of irregular warfare for this reason; others object to its categorisation as such because the adversaries possess nearly the same capabilities. The key distinguishing aspect of civil wars is geographic in nature; such wars exist within identifiable territories between two or more factions that may or may not employ civilian militias, paramilitaries and unorthodox tactics. A contemporary illustration of the problem is Afghanistan, where the Taliban are engaged in an ongoing conflict with members of ISIS–Khorasan Province as well as other Salafist groups and local warlords.

Conclusion

In order to avoid potential confusion and bound the review of the subject, subsequent chapters focus on two forms of irregular warfare: insurgency and terrorism. One reason for doing so is historical in nature. Revolution, for example, has largely fallen out of favour as a form of irregular warfare over the last half century, the events of the Arab Spring notwithstanding, due to changes in the international economic and political system. Stripped of their former political ideological impetus, and desire to provoke a conflict within the state, the vast majority of revolutions over the past two decades have been largely non-violent in nature.[28] While some consider disinformation, trolling and election interference by Russia and China as irregular warfare, there is little concrete evidence that such activities directly influence outcomes, much less inspire political violence. Organising and maintaining a clandestine mass movement for several years is exceptionally difficult, but this has been mitigated, to a degree, by the use of social media, cell phones and peer-to-peer networks. The ideologies that fuelled the bulk of the revolutions over the past three centuries – egalitarianism and Marxism – have either been discredited or discarded partially due to the collapse of their sponsors but also as a result of political and economic progress and reform. Right-wing movements, another possible contender, have suffered from cohesion and more widespread appeal problems, specifically racial- or ethnic-based civil wars. Revolutions remain opportunistic in nature and rely heavily on chance and an ability to exploit the unfolding situation. The group that prevails is the one that is sufficiently organised and that is supported either by enough of the population or by force of arms to seize and consolidate its power base.

The second reason to focus on insurgency and terrorism, as opposed to other forms of irregular warfare, is related to time and geographic scope. Coups d'état occur quickly if they are properly organised, and luck favours the plotters. There is little that potential intervening powers can do to halt a coup that is taking place. If the plotters succeed, they become the de facto legitimate governing authority of the state and should be dealt with according to international rules and norms. If the plotters fail, they are likely to be executed by the state as both traitors and a potential future threat. Although morally repugnant to some, coups d'état are viewed by many outside political and business leaders pragmatically as a source of stability in troubled states when military leaders assume power. Civil wars, in contrast, are difficult to identify for many of the reasons outlined above. As suggested previously, they vary so wildly in geographic and military scope, scale and cause as to be problematic as a definable category of irregular warfare. Most often, civil wars feature an incumbent regime and an insurgent (a single or many groups) vying for power and control. One method of exploring the complexities and identifying the continuities of irregular warfare, to make sense of the present and the future, is to look at its theory and practice throughout history, which is the subject of the next chapter.

RESEARCH QUESTIONS

1. What differentiates irregular warfare from conventional or nuclear warfare? Does this differentiation matter?
2. Are terrorism and insurgency unique and separate phenomena or are they related? If so, how? If not, why?
3. Can terrorism form the basis of a strategy or is it merely a tactic?
4. Why is legitimacy such an important concept in irregular warfare – and to whom?
5. Should civil wars be considered a type of irregular warfare or are they sufficiently unique?

FURTHER READING

Hoffman, Bruce, *Inside Terrorism*, 3rd ed. (New York, NY: Columbia University Press, 2017) remains the best single-volume treatment of various aspects of terrorism, including definitions, motivations, forms of violence and the role of the media.

Kalyvas, Stathis, *The Logic of Violence in Civil War* (Cambridge, UK: Cambridge University Press, 2006) offers a powerful analysis, as well as several theoretical frameworks across different levels of analysis, to determine where selective and indiscriminate violence are most effectively applied in irregular warfare.

O'Neill, Bard E., *Insurgency and Terrorism: From Revolution to Apocalypse*, rev. ed. (Washington, DC: Potomac Books, 2005) remains one of the best single-volume analyses of the difference between forms of irregular violence and the factors that shape its character, conduct and response.

Ucko, David and Marks, Thomas, *Crafting Strategy for Irregular Warfare: A Framework for Analysis and Action,* 2nd ed. (Washington, DC: NDU Press, 2022) offers frameworks for both evaluating irregular threats, including those outlined in the typology above, and developing responses to them.

ONLINE RESOURCES

The Center for Irregular Warfare and Armed Groups (CIWAG) website (https://tinyurl.com/3fhazx25) features a number of useful resources and links, including a number of informative case studies and reports.

The RAND Corporation website (www.rand.org/) has a searchable index of reports on various aspects of irregular warfare, including insurgency and terrorism, going back to 1948. Most contemporary reports are available free for download in several formats optimised for mobile devices.

The US Army Special Operations Command's Assessing Revolutionary and Insurgent Strategies (ARIS) website, now defunct but archived, (https://

publicintelligence.net/usarmy-revolution-insurgency-studies/) offers a number of classic and contemporary studies and reports to download in eBook form, including the two-volume 'Casebook on Insurgency and Revolutionary Warfare', 'Human Factors Considerations of Underground in Insurgencies', and 'The Palestinian Arab Insurgency (1890–2010).

The online *Small Wars Journal* (https://smallwarsjournal.com/) and *Long War Journal* (www.longwarjournal.org/) feature news updates, short articles and blog postings by subject matter experts and practitioners on rarely covered facets of irregular warfare.

NOTES

1 'Estimated Cost to Each U.S. Taxpayer of Each of the Wars in Afghanistan, Iraq and Syria', Department of Defense Comptroller, unpublished table, June 2022, https://tinyurl.com/3z662rrs.

2 Sean McFate, *The New Rules of War: Victory in the Age of Durable Disorder* (New York, NY: HarperCollins, 2019), pp. 28–30.

3 See Dennis Drew, *Recapitalizing the Air Force Intellect: Essays on War, Airpower, and Military Education* (Maxwell AFB, AL: Air University Press, 2008), pp. 37–9 and, more recently, David Maxwell and Deak Roh, 'Breaking the Boom–Bust Cycle of Irregular Warfare', Irregular Warfare Institute podcast, 18 December 2020, https://mwi.westpoint.edu/breaking-the-boom-bust-cycle-of-irregular-warfare/.

4 See for example Mykhaylo Zabrodskyi, et al., *Preliminary Lessons in Conventional Warfighting from Russia's Invasion of Ukraine: February–July 2022* (London: Royal United Services Institute, November 2022).

5 Oren Liebermann, 'How Ukraine Is Using Resistance Warfare Developed by the US to Fight Back against Russia', *CNN News*, 27 August 2022, www.cnn.com/2022/08/27/politics/russia-ukraine-resistance-warfare/index.html.

6 The Joint Staff, Joint Publication 1, vol. 1: *Joint Warfighting* (Washington, DC: The Joint Staff, 27 August 2023).

7 Helene Cooper and Erik Schmitt, 'How a Ragtag Militia in Yemen Became a Nimble U.S. Foe', *The New York Times*, 24 January 2024.

8 Seth Jones, *Three Dangerous Men: Russia, China, Iran, and the Rise of Irregular Warfare* (New York, NY: W.W. Norton & Co, 2021), p. 11.

9 David Ucko and Thomas Marks, *Crafting Strategy for Irregular Warfare: A Framework for Analysis and Action*, 2nd ed. (Washington, DC: NDU Press, 2022), pp. 8–19.

10 Bruce Hoffman, *Inside Terrorism*, 3rd ed. (New York, NY: Columbia University Press, 2017), pp. 3–20.

11 Department of Defense, *Summary of the Irregular Warfare Annex to the National Defense Strategy* (Washington, DC: Department of Defense, 2020), p. 2.

12 Adapted from Bard E. O'Neill, *Insurgency and Terrorism: From Revolution to Apocalypse*, rev. ed. (Washington, DC: Potomac Books, 2005), pp. 19–29.

13 See esp. ch. 10, 'Intimacy', in Stathis Kalyvas, *The Logic of Violence in Civil War* (Cambridge, UK: Cambridge University Press, 2006).

14 This point is unfortunately misconstrued by Emile Simpson in his otherwise exceptional work. See Simpson, *War From the Ground Up*, pp. 54–66.

15 Carl von Clausewitz, *On War*, ed. and trans. Michael Howard and Peter Paret (Princeton, NJ: Princeton University Press, 1976), pp. 89, 119–21.

16 James Kiras, 'Irregular Warfare: Terrorism and Insurgency', in John Baylis *et al.* (eds.), *Strategy in the Contemporary World*, 2nd ed. (Oxford: Oxford University Press, 2007), p. 179.
17 Osama bin Laden repeated the desire to obtain legal sanction for and acquisition of nuclear weapons. See, for example, 'Jihad against Jews and Crusaders' first published in *al-Quds al-Arabi* in London, 28 February 1998 (www.fas.org/irp/world/para/docs/980223-fatwa.htm) as well as the 2003 fatwa cited by bin Laden. Nasir Bin Hamd Al-Fahd, 'A Treatise on the Legal Status of Using Weapons of Mass Destruction against Infidels' (May 2003).
18 Daniel Byman does justice to this exceptionally difficult subject in *Deadly Connections: States that Sponsor Terrorism* (Cambridge, UK: Cambridge University Press, 2005).
19 Weinstein concludes resource-rich rebels are likely to abuse local populations because they can afford to do so. See Jeremy Weinstein, *Inside Rebellion* (Cambridge, UK: Cambridge University Press, 2006).
20 Jeremy Weinstein, *Inside Rebellion: The Politics of Insurgent Violence* (Cambridge, UK: Cambridge University Press, 2006), pp. 310–30.
21 Megan Duzor and Brian Williamson, 'Coups in Africa: By the Numbers', *VOA News*, 3 October 2023, https://projects.voanews.com/african-coups/.
22 Rebecca Schiel, Jonathan Powell and Christopher Faulkner, 'Mutiny in Africa, 1950–2018', *Conflict Management and Peace Science*, 38:4 (2021): 481–99.
23 Robert Pape, *Dying to Win* (New York, NY: Random House, 2005), pp. 20–3.
24 Mia Bloom, *Dying to Kill* (New York, NY: Columbia University Press, 2005), pp. 76–85.
25 Pathways identified and explored in Audrey Kurth Cronin, *How Terrorism Ends* (Princeton, NJ: Princeton University Press, 2009).
26 18 U.S. Code § 2383 – Rebellion or insurrection.
27 See Mackinlay, *The Insurgent Archipelago*; David Kilcullen, *The Accidental Guerrilla* (Oxford: Oxford University Press, 2009), esp. 1–38.
28 Examples include Czechoslovakia's 'Velvet Revolution' (1989), Serbia's 'Bulldozer Revolution' (2000), Georgia's 'Rose Revolution' (2003), Ukraine's 'Orange Revolution' (2004–2005), Lebanon's 'Cedar Revolution' (2005), the various revolutions of the 'Arab Spring' (2010) and, most recently, the abortive Hong Kong 'Umbrella Revolution' (2014).

14 The Historical Practice of Irregular Warfare

CHAPTER OUTLINE

KEY THEMES

- Understanding the continuity and differences between historical rationale and practice, and not just the most recent era of lessons learned, is the key to success in current and future irregular wars.
- Striking a balance between gaining the willing and demonstrated support of the population, versus simply controlling and coercing it, is a consistent theme historically. Brute force has been effective in the short term, but its use creates more problems than it solves.
- Traumatic events for those conducting or countering it, particularly failure, are often the catalyst for reflection and an upsurge in interest in and writing on irregular warfare.
- The most effective practitioners of irregular warfare historically accurately assess the subjective and objective conditions for success within its specific context, or provide a comprehensive roadmap that links tactical action to strategic purpose.

Understanding Modern Irregular Warfare through the Lens of the Past

The study of irregular warfare historically presents a number of unique challenges. Although the history of irregular warfare, in the form of bandit raids or other unconventional tactics, arguably existed long before more organised, conventional warfare by fielded armies, there are relatively few memoirs, much less theories of violence, by those conducting irregular warfare against militarily superior opponents prior to the nineteenth century. Classic texts on ancient warfare from across the globe – including Maurice's *Strategikon* (Byzantium), Sun Tzu's *The Art of War* (China) and Kautilya's *Arthasastra* (India) – addressed unconventional methods of fighting such as raids, ambushes, stratagems and ruses as a method of gaining an advantage over an opponent prior to or during battle.[1] Other ancient texts, including epic poems, theological texts and historical narratives, suggest that irregular tactics were used to overcome formidable defences. The most famous example remains the Trojan Horse in Homer's *Iliad*, but far more accounts describe a common subterfuge: taking walled cities by using traitors inside to open gates for armies waiting outside.[2] In addition, some texts discuss the specific fighting qualities, or what scholars now call 'strategic culture' or 'way of war', of irregular or barbarian opponents.[3] Indeed, some scholars have gone so far as to suggest that civilisations have distinct styles of fighting, either as a result of geography or as an explanation for their political and economic success.[4] Ancient and medieval texts, however, must be approached with caution. Amongst their problems are author bias, hearsay or fabricated evidence, lack of supporting evidence and, in many cases, few other surviving corroborating or contradictory accounts.[5] Scholars and practitioners are forced to either read between the lines of existing accounts and manuals on the art of war or make inferences from histories of powers that were confronted by and defeated irregular threats.[6] With the benefit of hindsight and contemporary knowledge, authors are also inclined to interpret portions of ancient texts as evidence of the historical practice and theoretical continuity of irregular warfare. For example, contemporary scholars suggest that the public and dramatic assassinations conducted by Jewish Zealots against leading Roman citizens and subjects, or by the Nizari Ismaili Assassin sect against medieval Christian and Muslim rulers, were not just acts of terrorism but the first recorded acts of suicide terrorism.[7] Not only was the context of such attacks completely different but so too were the targets and intended effects. It is crucial not to cast modern connotations onto ancient texts without explaining key differences and providing sufficient background information.

Out of necessity, this chapter will survey the most important developments in irregular warfare theory or doctrine historically. Works by a number of other authors provide comprehensive surveys of irregular warfare campaigns and thinkers.[8] For the purposes of this chapter, irregular warfare as it is understood in the modern context begins with the end of limited war in the West in the eighteenth century. A number of social, economic, political and military changes spurred the development of irregular warfare from the eighteenth century until the end of the Second World War. The first change, associated with the ideas of the Enlightenment, was the desire to replace feudal monarchies with a more representative, equitable and just form of government. Western armies during the early and mid eighteenth century were comprised of limited numbers of professional, uniformed soldiers, organised into battalions and regiments, whose drill, tactics and battlefield manoeuvres were highly stylised and scripted, and little had changed since the first manual-of-arms for pike, harquebus and musket was published in 1607.[9] Monarchs feared arming the citizenry, which was comprised largely of peasants. This fear was based on the thought that armed peasants would reject the status quo, organise and overwhelm the small standing forces of the monarchs. Such philosophers as John Locke questioned the moral and ethical basis of non-representative forms of government including monarchies. Locke's libertarian ideas influenced thoughts on democracy amongst revolutionaries such as Alexander Hamilton and Thomas Jefferson, amongst others. Hand in hand with the development of the idea of representative government, such as a democracy, was the rise of one of the most potent forces to mobilise the population for war: nationalism. The rise of nationalism, and threats to nascent revolutionary governments in the American colonies and in France in the late eighteenth century from standing professional armies, led in turn to the development of conscription and the concept of 'the nation in arms'.

The American Revolutionary War (1775–1783) is important in the modern history of irregular warfare. The details of this war, including the role that the citizen-soldier militia of 'Minutemen' played in securing victory, are well known.[10] Most Americans are familiar with the basic details of the conflict but time, popular culture and national myth have shaped the public understanding. The war had its fair share of brutality, including massacres committed by Continental and British forces alike.[11] Some firebrands at the time claimed that the British should have been more brutal in dealing with the upstart colonial population.[12] The war featured elements of irregular warfare familiar to the modern reader: unorthodox tactics used by colonial troops that had been shaped in fighting against native American tribes and in the North American theatre during the Seven Years War against the French (1756–1763)[13] and unconventional campaigns, including the pivotal insurgency conducted in South Carolina by partisan leaders such as Andrew Pickens and the most famous guerrilla leader during the campaign, Francis Marion.[14] These aspects of the American Revolutionary War are not what make it unique. Indeed, the Austrian Hapsburg Empire fought campaigns against irregulars on its eastern borders. The English and French, as well as the Austrians, developed light infantry and other skirmishing forces almost a century prior to the American revolutionary war, and Robert Rogers established 'Standing Orders' for his famed irregular Rangers in 1759.[15] What marks the American Revolutionary War as unique is the mark the fighting left on a Hessian officer, Johann Ewald.

Johann Ewald and Partisan War

Johann Ewald served as an officer in an elite *jäger* regiment recruited to fight on the side of the British Crown against the rebels. *Jäger* were light infantry skirmishers who operated in advance or independent of main force combat units and were responsible for **screening** their movements, gathering information and conducting probing attacks and raids against enemy camps and units. The fighting in British North America made a deep impression on many officers during the conflict, including the remarkably introspective Ewald.[16] Upon his return to Cassel in 1784, Ewald penned his *Abhandlung über den kleinen Krieg*, or *Treatise on Partisan War*, one of the first manuals, or what we would call today 'doctrine' (see Box 14.1), on the unique character of and requirements for conducting and countering irregular warfare in the context of his day. This work, as well as Ewald's other published works, including his diary, offer considerable insights into both the continuities of and changes in modern irregular warfare from the eighteenth century until today.[18]

As in works by other officers of his generation, Ewald offers a number of prescriptions on how to prepare and organise for, and conduct, partisan operations. However he insists that different skills and a different mindset and approach are necessary to succeed in partisan warfare. Anticipating critiques of British performance in Iraq and Afghanistan over the past decades that could equally be applied to their fellow contemporary Americans, Ewald suggests that British troops 'Were not really suitable for the small war, because they did not have sufficient patience for this difficult and laborious kind of warfare.'[19] Unlike the conventional units of his day, partisan leaders require independent thought and action in order to identify and seize opportunities, prevent ambush, retain mobility and make the best possible use of the terrain.[20] Although Ewald's advice was bound by the norms and codes of conduct of his day, many of his recommendations at the tactical level for light infantry or special operations forces commanders either still ring true in modern doctrine or remain applicable today, including the commander's need to identify

BOX 14.1 WHAT IS DOCTRINE?

Scholars agree on the purpose of doctrine, but not on its form. The purpose of doctrine is to transmit and share 'best practices' or 'lessons learned' about the conduct of warfare. But how are these practices and lessons codified, understood and transmitted? Andrew Birtle suggests that US Army counterinsurgency doctrine does not have to be published but can consist instead of 'Custom, tradition, and accumulated experience that was transmitted from one generation of soldiers to the next through a combination of official and unofficial writings, curricular materials, conversations, and individual memories.'[17] This chapter suggests that doctrine must be written down and published to be considered as such.

patterns in rebel attacks and quickly adapt and develop innovative countermeasures against them.[21]

Ewald differs from his contemporaries in his passing discussions on the nature of irregular warfare. The revolutionary ideals that inspired the American colonists had a significant impact on their operations. For example, Ewald was amazed when he observed the suffering American forces were willing to endure, and the minimal supplies they required to fight effectively, for the cause of 'Liberty and Independence'.[22] As colonial powers were to discover after the end of the Second World War, and the US and its coalition partners discovered in Iraq, ideals such as nationalism and self-determination are potent motivating forces and extremely difficult to defeat unless one is willing to either apply relatively unrestricted force or provide an equally powerful, contrasting set of ideas. On the use of force and relations with the local population, Ewald's works highlight the dilemma that confronts all powers fighting irregular wars. To suggest that Ewald discusses 'winning the hearts and minds' of the population is to read too much into his observations and prescriptive advice. The dilemma confronting Ewald is how to gain potentially valuable support, including information about local irregular forces, from the population without alienating it. His works are filled with references and incidents where acts of kindness towards the population, even known revolutionary leaders, yielded valuable information about the condition or location of American forces.[23] Trusting the population blindly, without verifying information gained through reconnaissance and other sources, was a formula for potential betrayal and disaster.[24] But Ewald also did not shirk from using force against the population – 'The place was ransacked and plundered because all the inhabitants were rebellious-minded' – either to punish known rebel sympathisers or when necessity dictated.[25] He understood, however, that force used out of necessity came at the cost of alienating support from segments from the population that either had supported or were willing to support his forces at the time.[26] The need to strike a balance between gaining the willing and demonstrated support of the population, versus simply controlling and coercing it, is a consistent theme historically that separates those who have succeeded in irregular warfare and those who have failed.

The history of irregular warfare from the end of the eighteenth century until the First World War (1914–1918) is filled with considerable political, social, economic and military change. The most violent episode in Western history during the nineteenth century, the Napoleonic Wars (1798–1815), saw the concept of 'the nation in arms' lead inexorably to much more destructive, total warfare and the harnessing of popular sentiment in raising armies against the occupying armies of Napoleon. The combination of weather, inadequate French supplies, vast geographic space and the incessant attacks by partisan forces in Russia under the command of such leaders as Denis Davidov led to the decimation and retreat of Napoleon's *Grande Armée*.[27] In Spain, French forces faced a more favourable climate and small geographic space that contained much more rugged terrain and a population that had grown weary of and exceptionally hostile to French looting, reprisals and other depredations. The subsequent campaign waged by Spanish irregulars or *guerrilleros*, operating in the countryside while French field armies were occupied with garrison duties and contending with a small British expeditionary force, harassed and bled the army of Marshal Nicholas Soult while in a campaign noted for its duration and brutality.[28] It is from this conflict that the term 'guerrilla' was derived.

Other significant changes in the history of irregular warfare at this time include a number of revolutions and the development of theories of violence, followed by colonial conquest and writings reflecting on pacification campaigns and experience throughout Africa, Asia and America. The most noteworthy revolutions during this period were the French Revolution (1789–1798) and events during the so-called 'Year of Revolutions', which swept Europe and parts of Latin America in 1848. The leaders of the French Revolution sought to change from a monarchy to a more equitable form of government, a republic. Republican ideals were ultimately corrupted by personal power and institutional paranoia, which both set the stage for Napoleon's rise to power and contributed to the lexicon of irregular warfare, the term 'terrorism', which was first used to describe systemic and deliberate violence by the state to instil fear and preserve order amongst its citizenry.[29] The range of causes that spurred the Year of Revolutions relates to societal change stemming from the economic revolution in modes and means of production associated with the Industrial Revolution, which figure prominently in the theories of Karl Marx and Louis Auguste Blanqui. Although the theories of both are largely footnotes to history today, the disagreements between them over the mechanism and methods for success of the revolution are worth exploring for one key reason. The intellectual points of departure between Blanqui and Marx have been echoed by Latin American revolutionaries such as Che Guevara and Carlos Merighella, and, most recently, between radical Salafist terrorist authors such as Ayman al-Zawahiri and Abu Musab al-Suri, as the next chapter suggests.

Karl Marx, Louis Auguste Blanqui and Socialist Revolution

From the perspective of those seeking to overthrow the existing political system using irregular violence, the writings of Karl Marx and Louis Auguste Blanqui provided two contrasting yet related rationales for violence. Marx, who was decidedly the more intellectual of the two writers, contributed the theory of 'historical materialism', the central tenets of which are well known but have also been misconstrued. Capitalism, according to Marx, contained internal contradictions that would lead to its own collapse. The pace of economic change outstrips the ability of the capitalist system controlling society to adjust to such change; the class inequalities inherent in the capitalist system and the social disruption caused by cycles of economic growth and collapse would impel those in control of the means of production, the workers, to revolt. In addition to this objective condition inherent in the system, Marx also wrote about the need to develop the subjective conditions for revolution. In particular, Marx saw the Socialist Workers' party as performing two vital tasks. The first task was to educate the masses of workers, or proletariat, about the inequities in the system through pamphlets, speeches and other means so that the party could exploit crises and foment revolution. The second task was to build the party infrastructure to organise the workers, increase the size of the organisation and seize the initiative and power when the revolutionary moment presented itself. Revolution, in Marx's mind, was a historical inevitability that could be exploited by the revolutionary. The key to success in Marx's mind, however, was organisation and, above all else, patience that the internal contradictions would lead to revolution.[30]

Although Louis Blanqui largely agreed with Marx on the economic foundations of revolution, he differed in opinion on its social and organisational aspects. That the workers were exploited was unquestionable. However, Blanqui believed that the workers would rebel anyway and, as a result, they could not be educated and should not be informed of the plans for revolution. Only the vanguard, or the intellectual elite that was freed from class bonds and formed into its own general staff, could truly understand the purpose and direct the course of the revolution. The best method for organisation, therefore, was the creation of secret societies that would be difficult for the state security apparatus to monitor and track. Proper organisation, thorough planning, a correct reading of the conditions and boldness of action in the right place and time would create the subjective conditions for revolution.[31] In addition, Blanqui urged his co-conspirators to read about military tactics and organisation so that revolutionaries understood their purpose during the insurrection, organised the masses and fought in a more cohesive manner.[32] When the conditions were deemed ripe, the vanguard would lead the attacks against the key organs of the state. Revolutionary ideals were a necessary precondition but not sufficient to guarantee success of the insurrection. The oppressed masses would not only follow the example set by the insurgents but also their revolutionary zeal could be harnessed in an effective military manner against any counter-attacks by the remaining forces of the state.[33] It was up to the leaders of the vanguard to organise the masses once they were committed to the struggle. Put simply, according to Blanqui's scheme the insurgent vanguard could create and manipulate the subjective conditions so that the revolution could succeed. Once the time had arrived for insurrection, the vanguard must not wait and continue to talk about revolution: it must seize the initiative and lead the revolution to victory.[34] Although Blanqui's technique for insurrection grew more sophisticated after each unsuccessful attempt, his appreciation for and assessment of the social and economic factors of revolution remained virtually unchanged. In fact, one author has concluded that 'parts of Blanqui's thinking were frustratingly vague and immature' and his understanding of socialism was 'ideological chop suey'.[35] As Blanqui and those who followed after him, such as Mikhail Bakunin, were to discover, perceiving that the conditions are right, assessing the chances for success objectively and accounting for differences in the context of irregular warfare are not easy tasks when revolutionary fervour colours one's perceptions.

Given the broad range and diverse perspectives that characterised socialist theories of revolution throughout the nineteenth and early twentieth centuries, it is surprising that there was relatively little by way of theory, doctrine or treatises written about how to counter the threat of irregular warfare. Indeed while the leading military theorists of the nineteenth century, Carl von Clausewitz and Antoine Henri de Jomini, acknowledged the underlying power of and difficulties associated with facing a people in arms, they nevertheless paid scant attention to the subject in their works.[36] With the possible exception of Clausewitz, who grappled with a theoretical understanding of the nature of war and the place that battle played within it, the vast majority of military officers who put pen to paper were concerned less with irregular warfare than with fighting and winning conventional battles decisively to win wars quickly. At their worst, works on 'strategy' and 'the art of war' were tedious studies on lines of manoeuvre and battlefield formations.[37] Other works provided historical narratives of battles past, often those conducted with such skill by Napoleon, to illustrate principles of war and other maxims.[38]

In addition to divining the secret of decisive battle, military writers during this time were preoccupied with the changes to the art of war that technology was rendering. In 1815, the accurate range of a smoothbore musket was less than 100 yards and cannons fired solid iron shot at targets in their line of sight. Lack of accuracy meant commanders relied on mass to make up for the difference. Over the next century, the range of rifles increased almost tenfold due to the development of rifling, cartridges, primers and the cylindro-conoidal bullet. The introduction of smokeless powder made the source of rifle fire difficult to pinpoint. Accurate fire and breech loading meant men could disperse, seek cover and still inflict numerous casualties. Advances in metallurgy and engineering led to the development of the first automatic weapons that could sustain rates of fire of several hundred rounds per minute, making the ground in front almost impassible, as well as long-range, breech-loading, indirect-fire artillery. Artillery could also fire hollow shells designed to burst upon impact, increasing their lethal radius. Breech loading and powder cartridges allowed for high rates of sustained fire.[39] All of these advances created a 'storm of steel' on the battlefield, in which the number of casualties grew significantly, and against which frontal assaults were all but suicidal.[40]

Charles Callwell and Imperial Soldiering

In addition to significant advances in the range and lethality of military weapons, the nineteenth and early twentieth centuries were characterised by the race by European powers to secure overseas colonies at the expense of the local population throughout Asia and Africa. Although the sheer range of campaigns makes generalisations about them difficult, they all shared one thing in common. Nationalism, combined with feelings of divine purpose and a sense of racial or ethnic superiority, led military commanders from a number of nations to consider that they were fighting opponents who were mere 'savages' and therefore undeserving of the courtesies and treatments due their civilised opponents. While some concepts and ideas from this era continue to be discussed in the current context of counter-insurgency – such as the oil-spot or ink-blot theory of French officer Joseph-Simon

Galliéni (whereby the territorial control of adjacent garrisons combines and spreads like blots of ink on a sheet of paper) – the brutality with which some of these campaigns were waged seemed reasonable to the participants at the time but appears cruel and inhuman today.[41] In South-West Africa, for example, German General Lothar von Trotha waged a vicious campaign over three years (1904–1907) that sought to annihilate the Heraro tribe.[42] Occasionally 'savages' inflicted significant defeats on imperial armies, as occurred during the disastrous First Afghan War (1839–1842) fought by the British or at Little Big Horn in 1876, but defeats on this scale were a rarity.[43] A more common scenario involved small numbers, relative to the local population, of European or American forces conducting operations against the natives and relying on a combination of discipline, firepower, pluck and superior will to turn the tide of the campaign (see Figure 14.1). More often than not, 'savage armies' obliged them by making mass charges against Western forces armed with rifle, artillery and, in some cases, machine guns. Perhaps the defining incident of this type of warfare was the battle near the town of Omdurman in the Sudan on 2 September 1898. British forces and auxiliaries, numbering no more than 25,000, were confronted by an Ansar, or dervish, army of some 50,000. The Ansar army believed that their spiritual leader, Abdullah al-Taashi, was the Mahdi or imam prophesied to return and restore justice and greatness according to the Shi'ite interpretation of Islam. The results of the battle confirmed that religious zeal and courage, combined with primitive weapons and tactics, was no match for modern firepower in a set-piece battle. Almost half of the Ansar army was killed or wounded, while the British and their auxiliaries suffered just over 400 casualties.

Although military handbooks, or doctrine, largely reflected preoccupations with decisive battle in the face of destructive, modern technology, imperial and colonial campaigns in far-off lands were bound to make their presence felt within the literature. Irregular warfare, especially against tribes, was nevertheless largely considered as either an adjunct to major war at best or an aberration fraught with danger but with little opportunity for honour or glory. As is often the case in the history of irregular warfare, events that cause national trauma and reflection provide the catalyst for an upsurge in interest and writing in the subject. In Ewald's time, it was the defeat inflicted upon the British forces and their Hessian allies despite the tactical prowess and success of the *Jäger*. The defining irregular war of the end of the nineteenth and the beginning of the twentieth century was fought against Dutch farmers, or Boers, who were living in what is now called South Africa.

The Second Boer War (1899–1902), in common with other irregular wars, contained numerous different forms of war in different phases. The pretext for war was a failed coup d'état in 1895 backed by British immigrants and mine owners, including the prime minister of the Cape Colony, Cecil Rhodes. The goal of the failed coup was the overthrow of the Boer government in the Transvaal. After four years of uneasy truce, during which time Boer governments in the Transvaal and the Orange Free State made preparations for war, British demands and ambitions, and the rejection of Boer concessions, led to the issuing of ultimatums. The war officially

Figure 14.1 Religion, zeal and numbers were no match for Western technology and military discipline at the close of the nineteenth century. In this popular depiction of imperial soldiering from 1900, greatly outnumbered US Marines fight against rebel Chinese 'boxers' while attempting to relieve besieged legations in Peking.

began on 11 October 1899 with mixed results. The initial Boer offensive got bogged down with sieges of Kimberley, Mafeking and Ladysmith, but nevertheless the Boers were able to inflict significant defeats on British forces especially during 'Black Week' (10–15 December 1899) at the battles of Stormberg, Magersfontein and Colenso. The arrival of British reinforcements from throughout the Commonwealth resulted in the relief of the besieged towns. Faced with the defeat of their army, Boer leaders shifted to a mobile guerrilla-warfare phase, which the authors of the British official history of the war labelled as 'The gadfly of regular armies, finding its natural prey in railways, convoys and isolated posts, and born exponents in the horsemen of the Free State.'[44] Operating in independent commandos, small numbers of Boer farmers used horses for mobility and relied on accurate fire using the latest magazine-fed Mauser rifles to conduct hit-and-run raids against isolated British detachments. The guerrilla phase lasted until the end of the war on 31 May 1902. Initially British commanders, including Horatio Herbert Kitchener, had difficulty dealing with Boer tactics. The combination of tactics intended to deny the Boers mobility and support, including forced resettlement of the Boer population into concentration camps, the destruction of Boer farmsteads, the construction of reinforcing blockhouses and the use of mobile columns to intercept Boer forces once detected, led to British victory, but not without domestic and international criticism. The Second Boer War was one of the first irregular wars that featured the prominent impact of timely media reporting and battlefield photography. The reporting of aspects of the war related to moral issues, augmented by photographs of dead British soldiers and emaciated Boer civilians, shocked and outraged the British public at how the war had been handled.[45]

In addition to calls for reform of the British Army's outdated commissioning, officer development and training regimens, the Second Boer War stimulated public and professional interest in irregular wars. As a result, a number of handbooks and manuals were published on the subject. They ranged from Ernest Swinton's innovative and practical *Defence of Duffer's Drift*, designed as a primer for junior officers to works that described functional dimensions of irregular warfare, illustrated by examples such as Thomas Miller Maguire's *Guerrilla or Partisan Warfare* and William Heneker's *Bush Warfare*.[46] The most detailed and influential work, however, was written by Colonel Charles Callwell in 1896 with updated editions appearing in 1899 and 1906. What sets *Small Wars: Their Principles and Practice* apart from other contemporary works is Callwell's attempt to analyse comprehensively the realm of irregular warfare and present this assessment in a logically consistent manner, including classes of campaigns, types of adversaries and the influence of different types of terrain upon operations, amongst other matters. Some of his advice is dated and can be offensive to modern readers, especially on the subject of the pacification of local inhabitants. Callwell suggests that harsh punitive measures against villages, crops and livestock are required as a way of 'Bringing such foes to reason ... for they understand this mode of warfare and respect it.'[47] One must appreciate that Callwell's work was a product of its time and to dismiss it outright on these grounds would be remarkably short-sighted. He was one of the first authors to recognise the need for conventional forces to use their advantages against the key strengths of irregulars. For example, Callwell appreciated that irregular opponents did not have to fight decisively in order to win. Irregulars possessed the strategic advantages of time, manoeuvre, intelligence, limited supply requirements and the initiative to accept battle at the time and place of their own choosing.[48] In addition, Callwell also identified that irregular warfare was not limited to tribes who preferred such fighting culturally but was adopted by enemy commanders as a form of warfare out of either choice or necessity.[49] In any event, he understood the stresses that guerrilla war imposed upon conventional forces, including the requirement to fight accordingly to methods that ran contrary to well-established military principles and maxims such as mass and never dividing one's force. Although now taken as common sense, Callwell struck upon a key dimension of irregular warfare in 1896: 'The more irregular and the less organised the forces of the enemy are, the more independent do they become of strategical rules.'[50] In other words, irregular enemies organise and fight according to their own preferences and not according to yours. Conventional forces could defeat irregular adversaries but not by trying to fight them in a conventional manner. Such adversaries preferred to fight protracted campaigns and Callwell also recognised that a number of 'preventable causes' might allow conventional forces to play into their adversary's hands, such as:

> Bad organization or they may follow from insufficient preparation . . . lack of zeal among subordinates, or they may be due to want of energy in high places. But one of the commonest causes of operations being unduly prolonged, is to be found in their having been allowed to drift into a desultory form of warfare, and this is a question of strategy and tactics.[51]

Fighting irregular enemies required flexibility on the part of the commander, constant vigilance and self-assessment, as well as an understanding of the enemy's preferences and the practical difficulties associated with irregular warfare – considerations that field commanders confronting irregular enemies now and in the future would do well to adopt.

The period marked by the close of the nineteenth century until the start of the First World War saw a number of developments in the field of irregular warfare but little in the way of theory or doctrine development. Having quickly and decisively defeated Spanish forces in Cuba and the Philippines for the ostensible reason of freeing the local populations from Spanish oppression, the US found itself engaged in struggles against local insurgents in the Philippines instead. Led by Emilio Aguinaldo, the Philippine insurgents fought a guerrilla campaign with the goal of prolonging the conflict long enough to influence the peace lobby in the US. Instead of achieving this goal, guerrilla attacks led to the deployment of more troops and the adoption by the US forces of harsh tactics and policies very similar to those adopted by the British in South Africa.[52] The US declared the war over with the capture of Philippine General Miguel Malvar in 1902. As in Britain, the harsh conduct of military forces against the civilian population, including charges of wartime atrocities, was reported in the press (see Figure 14.2). Such reports led members of Congress to form the Lodge Committee in January 1902 to investigate the charges, although little came of the proceedings. Throughout Europe, the socialist revolutionary movement saw numerous debates, disagreements and schisms between rival claimants over when to take action, the form that action should take and who should be allowed to join each specific national social democrat political party. The more radical elements, dubbed anarchists, believed in 'propaganda by the deed' against the state and its supporting elements.[53] Although some of the tactics used by such groups in Britain, France and Russia were already well established, such as kidnapping and assassination, anarchists were amongst the first to conduct bombings using stable, high-yield explosives for their attacks. The successful assassination of Russian Tsar Alexander in 1881 by Russian anarchists prompted other groups to imitate their success, a pattern that would be repeated amongst various Marxist–Leninist terrorist groups throughout the 1960s and 1970s and amongst terrorist and insurgent groups today.

Figure 14.2 Popular notions of the noble aspects of imperial soldiering, such as civilising 'savage' races, were challenged during the Second Boer War (1899–1902) and Philippine War (1899–1902). Newspaper reports of atrocities by British and American soldiers, and graphic photographs taken by reporters and soldiers that were subsequently published, drove home the brutal realities of irregular warfare to the public. According to the original caption, this photograph is of 'insurgent dead just as they fell in the trench near Santa Ana, 5 February 1899'.

The First World War, Paul von Lettow-Vorbeck and T. E. Lawrence

Although it is a historical stretch to suggest that an act of terrorism started the First World War more than a century ago, there is little doubt that the assassination of Archduke Franz Ferdinand and his wife by members of a Serbian nationalist group provided the pretext for the event that would set the chain of mutual defence pacts and mobilisation orders in motion and led to German troops violating Belgian neutrality. Once the front lines between armies stabilised in the West and East in 1915, there was little scope for irregular warfare on the Eurasian continent. British and German military and political leaders concocted a number of schemes designed to draw enemy attention and resources by conducting irregular warfare by proxy in each other's various colonial possessions or the territory of their enemy's allies. Some schemes seemed sound in theory but were executed ham-fistedly or were simply impractical. Amongst these were German attempts to foment *jihad* and other plans against Egypt. These attempts were designed to threaten British control of the Suez Canal, and without exception they failed for reasons of national chauvinism, inadequate resources, insufficient knowledge and competing local and national interests.[54] Other independent rebellions took place. In the case of Ireland, the uprising in Dublin during Easter Week 1916 failed to achieve the objectives envisioned by the leaders of the Irish Republican Brotherhood but paved the way for the more successful urban insurgency planned and led with daring and skill by Michael Collins from 1918 to 1921.[55]

Other irregular campaigns during the First World War were driven by necessity or were accidental in nature. For example, the guerrilla campaign led by Paul von Lettow-Vorbeck in East Africa resulted from conventional victories that significantly depleted his force despite their success. For the next four years, Lettow-Vorbeck and his initial force of 3,000 Germans and 11,000 native *askaris* threatened the British East Africa Protectorate (Kenya) and largely gave battle at the time and place of their choosing while evading Commonwealth forces on a trek through Portuguese Mozambique, German East Africa (Tanzania) and British Rhodesia.[56] Three features of Lettow-Vorbeck's campaign stand out in particular. First, Lettow-Vorbeck and his officers conducted the campaign in mobile columns with a mixed force of Germans and Africans that retained a high level of unit cohesion until the end of the war, which is evident in the almost equal rates of casualties the force suffered.[57] Secondly, Lettow-Vorbeck's force largely subsisted off the land and captured supplies from 1916 onwards. Thirdly, and perhaps most importantly, Lettow-Vorbeck and his force managed to frustrate a Commonwealth force that contained a number of South Africans who fought the British during the Second Boer War, demonstrating that even those well versed in irregular warfare face much greater challenges when trying to defeat an insurgency.[58] As impressive as Lettow-Vorbeck's achievements were, they were eclipsed by the actions of a British officer fighting as part of the Arab Revolt in the Transjordan.

Thomas Edward Lawrence, better known by his sobriquet 'Lawrence of Arabia', can be considered as the progenitor of modern irregular warfare in the West. This consideration is based on his ability to assess objectively the conditions that existed within his theatre of operations, intuit the strength of the Arab forces and the weaknesses of the Turks, and understand the local culture to the extent he did. Nowhere are these qualities exhibited more than in his account of the Arab Revolt published in the inaugural edition of the *Army Quarterly*. This account is stripped of both the prose and literary pretensions that fill his other accounts of the campaign, *Seven Pillars of Wisdom* and its abridged version, *Revolt in the Desert*. In 'The Evolution of a Revolt', Lawrence provides a brief background sketch of the Arab Revolt and the reasons for its early setbacks.[59] In particular, Lawrence suggests that British attempts to force the Arabs to fight according to modern European battlefield practices ran contrary to their cultural strengths and was doomed to fail. While recovering from an illness Lawrence claims to have discovered a formula to assess the Arab Revolt strategically. This formula consisted of the following factors: the algebraic, or the area of the terrain and number of Turks required to control it; the biological, or the resources that the Turks needed to sustain their forces; and the psychological, or the morale of both the Turks and the Arabs.[60]

The weakest link in the Turkish garrison chain was the biological factor and, using superior Arab mobility in the desert where the Turks rarely ventured, Lawrence sought to stress it even further. Rather than battle Turkish forces in outposts or attempt the liberation of the holy city of Medina, he believed that the Arabs should strike against Turkish supplies: 'Our cards were speed and time, not hitting power, and these gave us strategical rather than tactical strength.'[61] Tactically his forces would fight 'tip and run, not pushes, but strokes'.[62] Lawrence also discriminated the strategic purpose for the violence – namely, forcing the Turks to abandon the Transjordan and freeing the Arabs from Turkish rule – from the tactical limitations and motivations of the tribes that were to conduct the operations. Individual tribes would fight their neighbours just as easily as the Turks. In order to solve this problem, Lawrence adopted two solutions. The first, and base motivation, was personal gain, and he secured sums of gold with which to maintain the loyalty of tribal chiefs even though some of the funds were diverted and payment did not necessarily guarantee numbers for duty.[63] As much as Lawrence waxed eloquently about Arabs fighting for the idea of freedom, wealth and plunder sustained the Arab Revolt throughout the campaign. The second solution was to use a number of tribes individually so that they formed a 'ladder' on the way to Damascus.[64] To increase the range and destructiveness of the Arabs, and by extension the pressure that the tribes could put on Turkish supply lines, Lawrence secured modern rifles, machine guns, explosives and experts trained in their use and tinned rations.[65]

Whether or not Lawrence deserves the laurels piled at his feet is a matter for debate. Lawrence remains an enigma to this day, filled with contradictions, not beyond pranks, and not always absolute with the truth.[66] Whether or not Lawrence could have succeeded in forcing the Turks to withdraw by guerrilla action alone is also a matter of conjecture. As it was, Lawrence's Arab forces secured the right flank of the three corps comprising the Egyptian Expeditionary Corps under the command of General Edmund Allenby and continued to harass Turkish supply lines, drawing off manpower to guard and repair them.[67] Yet Lawrence continues to be held in high esteem by modern irregular warfare specialists as worthy of emulation by design or accident. One counterinsurgency specialist imitated Lawrence's famous '27 Articles' as a method of transmitting important information to company commanders who deployed to Iraq.[68] A white paper entitled 'One Tribe at a Time', written by an American Special Forces officer and circulated with great fanfare in 2009, offered a strategy for success in Afghanistan that bore a number of striking parallels with Lawrence's approach in Arabia.[69] Lawrence was one of the first authors to outline how to conduct a successful unconventional campaign against a conventional opponent as well as emphasise the psychological dimensions of irregular warfare over battle. Lawrence's written account of the objective and subjective conditions in Transjordan in 1916, regardless of whether it was real or fabricated after the fact, serves as one of the few examples of how such conditions can and should be accurately assessed.

Mao Zedong and Protracted People's War

One of the few socialist theorists who also read the subjective and objective conditions strategically after early failure was Mao Zedong (Tse-Tung). As with Lawrence, a number of Mao's claims about the revolution and his role in it are open to question.[70] A rival socialist predecessor of Mao, Vladimir Ilyich Ulyanov or Lenin, had written extensively on revolution, including partisan warfare. But his impact on the revolution in Russia in 1917 had more to do with chance, support from the Imperial German government at a crucial juncture of his exile and the incompetence of the Tsarist regime than reading and influencing the subjective conditions within the country.[71] As a young revolutionary dedicated to the socialist cause, Mao slavishly attempted to follow the then-accepted formula for Leninist proletariat revolution in his native China in 1921. Its failure, primarily due to the lack of meaningful numbers of oppressed urban workers fuelling the machine of capitalism, caused Mao to reflect upon the nature of revolution in China. Over the course of the next sixteen years, Mao succeeded in consolidating his hold on power of the Chinese Communist Party and expanding its base amongst the rural peasantry, despite aggressive attempts by the Chinese Nationalists to crush it. In 1937, however, the Japanese invaded China, and nationalists and communists were faced with a hostile, competent adversary that initially swept away all attempts to stop it. The following year, Mao produced two complementary works on irregular warfare: the pamphlet entitled *Yu Chi Chan*, or 'On Guerrilla War', and a series of lectures at the Yenan Association for the Study of the War of Resistance against Japan, one of which was entitled 'On Protracted War'. No work by an author on or practitioner of irregular warfare has before or since so accurately read most the subjective and objective conditions for success within its specific context, or provided a comprehensive roadmap that links battle to revolutionary victory, as Mao did in 'On Protracted War'.

As with most other significant military theorists, including Clausewitz, Mao's ideas are quoted, cited and too often utterly mischaracterised. For example, Mao's metaphor of the guerrilla fish swimming in the sea of the population is well known, and variations of it were cited in early speeches related to the Global War on Terrorism.[72] Glibly citing the metaphor and understanding the difficulties and problems associated with isolating guerrillas from the population are two completely different things, as most counterinsurgency practitioners understand. Mao's three-phase plan for revolutionary victory, for example, has been rigidly interpreted to provide the foil to advance arguments for why approaches to counterinsurgency plans for Iraq were in need of significant revision.[73] Part of the reason Mao has been misinterpreted is that his theory of warfare, like Clausewitz's, is descriptive rather than prescriptive. And like Clausewitz, Mao provides a framework for understanding the often contradictory relationship that exists between battles and campaigns in achieving the overall political aim of the war.

In 'On Protracted War', Mao sets out to prove that notions of quick victory are impossible and maintaining a line of tactical defences against the Japanese would only result in defeat of Chinese communist forces. The Japanese are simply too well equipped and trained to be fought conventionally. Much like Lawrence, Mao understands that there are too few Japanese troops to conquer and occupy China.[74] China's strengths are its vast geographic space and size of its population.[75] These strengths alone, however, are insufficient to defeat the Japanese. The Chinese peasants must be educated, trained, organised and equipped to fight, and this process takes time. In order to buy the required time, Mao suggests trading geographic space and conducting offensive action at the tactical level instead of slavishly trying to blunt every Japanese offensive and prevent the occupation of major Chinese cities.[76] Trading space, however, does not imply retreating before the Japanese. Tactical offensive action would take place in the spaces occupied by the Japanese in a 'war of jigsaw pattern' designed to threaten their supply lines.[77] In order to deal with such threats, the Japanese would be confronted with a dilemma: cede territory in their rear area to the guerrilla cadres, who would exploit the situation to recruit amongst the population, or divert units to garrison towns and secure supply lines, weakening the strategic offensive and making such units tactically vulnerable to attack and annihilation.[78] Mao states much of what is obvious and intuitive in irregular warfare at the tactical and strategic level: cause the enemy to disperse his forces, strike where the enemy is weak and inflict casualties, avoid pitched battles unless you have overwhelming force, time is a weapon that favours the guerrillas, etc.

Three related features distinguish 'On Protracted War' and its companion work for the communist cadres, *On Guerrilla Warfare*, from other volumes on irregular warfare. The first feature is Mao's distinction between tactical action and its relationship to the overall strategic effort. Mao's discussion is aimed at those who rigidly advocate all-out offence or all-out defence. Both views, in Mao's estimation, are wrong and what is required instead is a more nuanced appreciation of the relationship between offence and defence at the tactical and strategic levels of war. The second unique feature of Mao's theory is his framework for victory, which places tactical actions into an overall plan for victory. The three phases outlined by Mao – strategic defensive, stalemate and strategic offensive – outline an achievable vision of victory provided the members of the Chinese Communist Party are patient and diligent enough.[79] Unlike other irregular-warfare theorists before or since, Mao grasped that tactical guerrilla actions alone, however cleverly executed or destructive, were insufficient to drive the Japanese from China. Guerrilla action was not only designed to weaken the Japanese forces, improve the quality of Chinese forces in the 'university of war' and lead to the balance of forces tipping in the favour of the Chinese communists but also to allow the development of more large-scale military units to conduct mobile warfare in more conventional offensives.[80]

The third and final distinctive feature of Mao's theory of irregular warfare, related to the last point, is the primacy of politics and the role that military action plays in support of it. Guerrilla action was designed not just to achieve military objectives. Such action first and foremost shielded the political activities of the communist cadres, providing them with the breathing-space to organise and receive the support of the population. Mao devotes a portion of both works to the object of war, the role that politics plays and the need to mobilise the population for the war.[81] In order to do this, the population must be educated about why they are fighting and how victory will improve their lives. In addition, the Chinese communists must demonstrate their moral superiority over the Japanese in deed and in action by following Mao's 'Three Rules and Eight Remarks'.[82] In this way the local peasants would see that the Chinese communists were worthy of support. Military action alone could not achieve victory unless a critical mass of the Chinese population actively and willingly sustained and swelled the number of the guerrilla forces. The pivotal role that the population plays in irregular warfare, outlined so clearly by Mao, has figured prominently in almost all modern theory and doctrine, but the relationship between violence, ideology and politics continues to remain elusive, misunderstood and open to disagreement.

The Second World War

Although there were a number of other important irregular wars and incidents prior to 1939, including the Russian (1918–1922), Irish (1922–1923) and Spanish (1936–1939) Civil Wars, US Marine interventions in the so-called 'Banana Wars' in Central and South America, the wave of anarchist terrorism spurred by the invention of dynamite (1880s–1920) and Arab and Jewish guerrilla and counter-guerrilla warfare in British-mandated Palestine, these events were overshadowed historically by a seemingly unstoppable string of German and Japanese victories at the start of the Second World War. Within Britain, the prospect of German invasion appeared all too real by the late summer of 1940. The British Army had lost most of its equipment earlier that year in battle or on the beaches of Dunkirk. To defend the island nation, Prime Minister Winston Churchill approved plans to create a cadre of civilian irregulars eventually labelled the 'Home Guard'. Amongst those selected to train the volunteers were Tom Wintringham and Bert Levy, who had fought together in the Spanish Civil War on the Loyalist side.

Both Wintringham and Levy wrote short, mass-produced works designed as tactical training aids for civilian irregulars based on their experiences in Spain. Wintringham's *New Ways of War* and Levy's *Guerrilla Warfare* discussed guerrilla history, organisation, propaganda requirements, ambush techniques and methods to defeat German panzers.[83]

The German invasion of Britain was postponed and then later cancelled, and Wintringham and Levy's techniques were not put to the test there. The populations of other countries in Europe and Asia were not so fortunate. Harsh German and Japanese policies within the countries they had occupied, including brutal reprisals against villages suspected of supporting guerrillas or partisans, dealt with a tactical military problem but strategically proved ruinous. As the true nature of the German and Japanese occupations were revealed, a percentage of the local population in countries as diverse as Poland, Czechoslovakia, France, the Soviet Union, Malaya and French Indochina conducted active and passive resistance in response. Reprisals and indiscriminate sweeps, especially by German and other national auxiliaries behind their lines on the Eastern Front, did not cow locals into submission but instead swelled partisan ranks.[84] For the Allied Powers, resistance, guerrilla and partisan movements in occupied Europe and Asia were a potential source of offensive support to plans to liberate countries, particularly given the power ascribed to so-called 'Fifth Column' efforts as an explanation for the rapid Axis conquests.[85] The actual contribution made by partisan and resistance movements, operating with the assistance of the British Special Operations Executive, the American Office of Strategic Services and the Soviet STAVKA, remains controversial due to lost or missing records, inflated claims by partisan and resistance groups and the difficulties in assessing the impact of subversion, sabotage and ambush as a drain on the German and Japanese war effort.[86] What is certain, however, is that the ideals articulated by the Allies set the stage for the next chapter in modern irregular warfare.

RESEARCH QUESTIONS

1. Why are there so few theories of irregular warfare by practitioners?
2. Why have theorists disagreed historically on how to conduct irregular warfare?
3. Why were so few insurgent campaigns successful during the nineteenth century? Did this change during the twentieth century and, if so, why?
4. What is the relationship of social context and technology to the theory and practice of irregular warfare?
5. Do Mao and Lawrence deserve the praise for their thoughts on insurgency and guerrilla warfare? If so, why? If not, why?

FURTHER READING

Asprey, Robert, *War in the Shadows*, rev. ed. (New York, NY: Little, Brown & Co., 1994) continues to be the most comprehensive and accessible survey of irregular warfare from ancient to modern times.

Beckett, Ian F. W., *Modern Insurgencies and Counter-insurgencies* (London: Routledge, 2001) is the most lucid and condensed single-volume survey on insurgency and counter-insurgency from 1750 until 2000.

Boot, Max, *Invisible Armies* (New York, NY: Liveright, 2013) is the most recent narrative history of guerrilla warfare from ancient times until the present.

Neuberg, A. (pseud.), *Armed Insurrection* (New York, NY: St Martin's, 1970) is a translation of a 1928 manual for insurrection from a Marxist perspective. The work remains useful for its relative accessibility and insights into Marxists on the role violence plays to achieve political effect.

ONLINE RESOURCES

The Marxist Internet Archive website (www.marxists.org) provides a veritable treasure trove of online primary source documents, including the writing and correspondence of all the major – and most of the minor – theorists, leaders and luminaries of socialist thought, including Blanqui (www.marxists.org/reference/archive/blanqui/index.htm) and Mao Zedong (www.marxists.org/reference/archive/mao/index.htm).

The US Navy Department library has posted, on a single page, the entire text of one of the best-known handbooks of colonial soldiering, Charles Callwell's *Small Wars* (https://tinyurl.com/mwey5jwu), including the original margin headings. The work is useful for both its practical observations and insights on how colonialists viewed those they sought to conquer or repress.

The Ike Skelton Combined Arms Research Library guide on irregular warfare in great power competition (carlcgsc.libguides.com/c.php?g = 1234377&p = 9033069) features two useful sets of resources. One is set of links to other websites and their resources in Canada, Ireland, the UK and the US. The second are links to more than fifty studies and reports on various historical and contemporary analyses on various subjects in irregular warfare.

NOTES

1 See, for example, Maurikios, *Maurice's Strategikon: Handbook of Byzantine Military Strategy*, trans. George T. Dennis (Philadelphia, PA: University of Pennsylvania Press, 1984), pp. 52–7, 93–105; Harro von Senger, *The Book of Strategems: Tactics for Triumph and Survival*, ed. and trans. Myron Gubitz (New York, NY: Viking, 1991); *The Seven Military Classics of Ancient China*, trans. Ralph Sawyer (Boulder, CO: Westview, 1993). The ancient Indian text by Kautilya, *Arthasastra*, provides little guidance on the tactics of fighting as it was meant to be a manual on statecraft. Like Sun Tzu's *The Art of War*, Kautilya places some emphasis on spies, intelligence networks and using proxies in enemy states to foment unrest. See T. N. Ramaswamy, *Essentials of Indian Statecraft: Kautilya's Arthasastra for Contemporary Readers* (New York, NY: Asia Publishing House, 1962), pp. 55–8, 60–1.

2 See, for example, acts of treachery during the Peloponnesian Wars in Robert Strassler (ed.), *The Landmark Thucydides: A Comprehensive Guide to the Peloponnesian Wars* (New York, NY: The Free Press, 1996), pp. 33, 250, 303, 515; Paul Bentley Kern, *Ancient Siege Warfare* (Bloomington, IN: Indiana University Press, 1999), pp. 21, 33–4,59–60,119.

3 Maurikios, *Maurice's Strategikon*, pp. 113–26.

4 Archer Jones, *The Art of War in the Western World* (New York, NY: Barnes and Noble, 1987), pp. 54–7; Victor Davis Hanson, *Carnage and Culture* (New York, NY: Doubleday, 2001).

5 In particular, Flavius Josephus's works, including his account of the Jewish uprising in 70 AD, *The Jewish War*, have been the subject of considerable scholarly inquiry and criticism. See, for example, S. J. D. Cohen, *Josephus in Galilee and Rome: His Vita and Development as a Historian* (Leiden: E. J. Brill, 1979); Tal Ilan and Jonathan Price, 'Seven Onomastic Problems in Josephus' "Bellum Judaicum"', *The Jewish Quarterly Review*, 84 (2/3) (October 1993–January 1994), 189–208.

6 Robert Asprey, for example, begins his historical exploration of guerrilla warfare from the Persian empire under the rule of Darius in 531 BC; John Ellis, in contrast, goes back even further to the actions of the Israelites against the Hittites as described in the Book of Joshua in the Bible. Asprey, *War in the Shadows*, rev. ed. (London: Little, Brown and Co., 1994), pp. 3–4; Ellis, *From the Barrel of a Gun: A History of Guerrilla, Revolutionary and Counter-insurgency Warfare, from the Romans to the Present*, rev. ed. (London: Greenhill, 1995), p. 17.

7 Such works include Bruce Hoffman, *Inside Terrorism*, rev. and expanded ed. (New York, NY: Columbia University Press, 2006), pp. 83–4; Robert Pape, *Dying to Win* (New York: Random House, 2005), pp. 12–13. Critical scholarly treatments of the Zealots and Assassins are Martin Hengel, *The Zealots: Investigations into the Jewish Freedom Movement in the Period from Herod I until 70 AD*, trans. David Smith (Edinburgh: T&T Clarke, 1989); Farhad Daftary, *The Assassin Legends: Myths of the Isma'ilis* (London: I. B. Taurus, 1995).

8 See, for example, Asprey, *War in the Shadows*; Ellis, *From the Barrel of a Gun*; Walter Laqueur, *Guerrilla: A Historical and Critical Study* (Boston, MA: Little, Brown and Co., 1976); Anthony James Joes, *Guerrilla Conflict Before the Cold War* (Westport, CT: Praeger, 1996); Max Boot, *Invisible Armies* (New York, NY: Liveright, 2013).

9 Christer Jörgensen et al., *Fighting Techniques of the Early Modern World: Equipment, Combat Skills, and Tactics* (New York, NY: St Martin's, 2006), p. 25.

10 Mark Kwasny, *Washington's Partisan War, 1775–1783* (Kent, OH: Kent State University Press, 1996).

11 For details of Indian raids and massacres, see John Ferling, *Almost a Miracle* (Oxford: Oxford University Press, 2007), pp. 203, 436–7, 495–6.

12 Ibid., pp. 400–2.

13 See Fred Anderson, *Crucible of War: The Seven Years' War and the Fate of Empire in British North America, 1754–1766* (New York, NY: Knopf, 2000).

14 For details of Marion's exploits, see Daniel E. Fitz-Simons, 'Francis Marion the "Swamp Fox": An Anatomy of a Low Intensity Conflict', *Small Wars and Insurgencies*, 6(1) (Spring 1995), 1–16. To put the 'Swamp Fox's' exploits in the context, see Walter Edgar, *Partisans and Redcoats* (New York, NY: Perennial, 2003).

15 Rogers's 'Standing Orders' consist of nineteen aphorisms and common-sense advice such as 'Don't forget nothing' and 'If we strike swamps, or soft ground, we spread out abreast, so it's hard to track us.' The Standing Orders continue to form part of the heritage of the American 75th Ranger Regiment, which draws its lineage from Rogers's Rangers, and are posted on numerous websites. See https://lrrpranger.org/unitlineage/rgrcreed.html.

16 Laqueur, for example, summarises the 1789 work by Andreas Emmerich entitled *The Partisan in War or the Use of a Corps of Light Troops to an Army*. Walter Laqueur, 'The Origins of Guerrilla Doctrine', *Journal of Contemporary History*, 10(3) (July 1975), 344–5.

17 Andrew Birtle, *U.S. Army Counterinsurgency and Contingency Operations Doctrine, 1860–1941* (Washington, DC: U.S. Army Center of Military History, 1998), p. 5.

18 Johann Ewald, *Diary of the American War*, ed. and trans. Joseph Tustin (New Haven, CT: Yale University Press, 1979).

19 Walter Laqueur, 'The Origins of Guerrilla Doctrine', *Journal of Contemporary History*, 10(3) (July 1975), 346.

20 Ewald, *Treatise on Partisan Warfare*, pp. 68, 80, 114, 183. J. F. C. Fuller provides a concise summary of, and considerable praise for, this work in J. F. C. Fuller, *British Light Infantry in the Nineteenth Century* (London: Hutchinson, 1925), pp. 137–51.

21 See, for example, Ewald, *Diary of the American War*, pp. 57–8.

22 Ibid., pp. 355, 341.
23 See, for example, Ewald, *Treatise on Partisan Warfare*, pp. 69, 70, 76, 78 and the anecdote about the Reverend Dr William Smith related in Ewald, *Diary of the American War*, pp. 92–3.
24 Ewald, *Treatise on Partisan Warfare*, p. 88.
25 Ewald, *Diary of the American War*, p. 57.
26 Ibid., pp. 335–6.
27 See Denis Davidov, *In the Service of the Tsar against Napoleon*, ed. and trans. Gregory Troubetzkoy (London: Greenhill, 1999), pp. 83–161.
28 Ellis, *From the Barrel of a Gun*, pp. 73–6.
29 Hoffman, *Inside Terrorism*, pp. 3–4.
30 Marx's seminal works on the subject remain *Das Kapital* and the volume he penned with co-author Friedrich Engel, *The Communist Manifesto*. This section draws upon Tucker's work that separates the wheat from the Marxist intellectual chaff. Robert Tucker, *The Marxian Revolutionary Idea* (New York, NY: Norton, 1969).
31 Samuel Bernstein, *Auguste Blanqui and the Art of Insurrection* (London: Lawrence and Wishart, 1971), p. 309.
32 Auguste Blanqui, 'Manual for an Armed Insurrection', trans. Andy Blunden (1866) (www.marxists.org/reference/archive/blanqui/1866/instructions1.htm).
33 Bernstein, *Auguste Blanqui and the Art of Insurrection*, pp. 309–10.
34 Auguste Blanqui, 'Manual for an Armed Insurrection'.
35 Bernstein, *Auguste Blanqui and the Art of Insurrection*, p. 299.
36 See, for example, Clausewitz, *On War*, pp. 479–83 and Antoine Henri de Jomini, *The Art of War*, ed. and trans. G. H. Mendell and W. P. Craighill (Westport, CT: Greenhill, 1971), pp. 31–6.
37 Illustrations of the type of diagrams that Clausewitz scorns are contained in Jomini, *The Art of War*, pp. 188–94 and J. B. Wheeler, *A Course of Instruction in the Elements of the Art and Science of War* (New York, NY: Van Nostrand, 1879), pp. 16–18, 92, etc.
38 See, for example, the discussion of the three principles of war and nine maxims contained in the Sandhurst primer by P. L. MacDougall, *The Theory of War*, 3rd ed. (London: Longman, Green, Longman, and Roberts, 1862), pp. 51–2, 98–115.
39 For details see Trevor Dupuy, *The Evolution of Weapons and Warfare* (Fairfax, VA: HERO Books, 1984), pp. 190–202.
40 The phrase from the title of Ernst Junger's memoir, Ernst Junger *Storm of Steel* (London: Chatto and Windus, 1930).
41 Douglas Porch, 'Bugeaud, Galliéni, Lyautey: The Development of French Colonial Warfare', in Peter Paret (ed.), *Makers of Modern Strategy* (Princeton, NJ: Princeton University Press, 1986), pp. 376–407.
42 Von Trotha's statements reproduced in Gil Merom, *How Democracies Lose Small Wars* (Cambridge, UK: Cambridge University Press, 2003), pp. 36–7.
43 For the First Afghan War, see Patrick Macrory, *The Fierce Pawns* (New York, NY: Lippencott, 1966), esp. pp. 241–90.
44 Frederick Maurice and Maurice Grant, *History of the War in South Africa, 1899– 1902*, vol. III (London: Hurst & Blackett, 1908), p. 93.
45 For details on media reporting of the war, see Denis Judd and Kevin Surridge, *The Boer War* (New York, NY: Palgrave Macmillan, 2003), pp. 251–6.
46 Swinton's work remained in print until 1991, which is a testament to its quality and utility. Ernest Swinton, *The Defence of Duffer's Drift* (London: Leo Cooper, 1991). See

also T. Miller Maguire, *Guerrilla or Partisan Warfare* (London: Hugh Rees, 1904); W. C. G. Heneker, *Bush Warfare* (London: Hugh Rees, 1907).

47 Charles Callwell, *Small Wars: Their Principles and Practice*, 3rd ed. (London: HMSO, 1906), p. 41.

48 Ibid., pp. 85–107.

49 Ibid., pp. 126–7.

50 Ibid., p. 52.

51 Ibid., p. 99.

52 For details on the guerrilla war, see Brian Linn, *The Philippine War, 1899–1902* (Lawrence, KS: University Press of Kansas, 2000), pp. 185–321.

53 The phrase has been attributed to a number of anarchists, including Carlo Pisacane, Mikhail Bakunin and Paul Brousse. The latter used the phrase as the title for an article published in 1887. Paul Avrich, *Anarchist Portraits* (Princeton, NJ: Princeton University Press, 1988), p. 244.

54 German strategic objectives are from Tilman Lüdke, *Jihad Made in Germany: Ottoman and German Propaganda and Intelligence Operations in the First World War* (Münster: Lit Verlag, 2005), pp. 33–8, 90–105. See also Hew Strachan, *The First World War, I: To Arms* (Oxford: Oxford University Press, 2001), pp. 700–4.

55 On the rationale for violence and the conduct of the campaign, see Michael Collins, *The Path to Freedom* (Boulder, CO: Roberts Rinehart Publishers, 1996), pp. 63–74.

56 Paul von Lettow-Vorbeck, *My Reminiscences of East Africa*, 6th ed. (Nashville, TN: Battery Press Reprints, 1990), p. 72.

57 When Lettow-Vorbeck's force surrendered on 25 November 1918, it numbered 155 Germans and 1,156 *askaris*. Charles Miller, *Battle for the Bundu: The First World War in East Africa* (London: Purnell Book Services, 1974), pp. 325–6.

58 Byron Farwell, *The Great War in Africa: 1914–1918* (New York, NY: Norton, 1986), pp. 80–1.

59 T. E. Lawrence, 'Evolution of a Revolt', *Army Quarterly*, 1 (October 1920), 55–6.

60 Ibid., pp. 59–62.

61 Ibid., p. 63.

62 Ibid., p. 64.

63 A summary of monies paid early in the revolt is contained in 'Sherif Hussein's Administration', in Malcolm Brown (ed.), *Secret Dispatches from Arabia and Other Writings by T. E. Lawrence* (London: Bellew, 1991), pp. 61–4 (originally in *Arab Bulletin*, 26 November 1916).

64 Lawrence, 'Evolution of a Revolt', p. 63.

65 Ibid., pp. 63, 65–6.

66 See, for example, the assessments contained in Linda Tarver, 'In Wisdom's House: T. E. Lawrence and the Near East', *Journal of Contemporary History*, 13 (1978), 585–608; Lawrence James, *The Golden Warrior: The Life and Legend of Lawrence of Arabia* (New York, NY: Paragon House, 1993); Suleiman Mousa, *T. E. Lawrence: An Arab View* (New York, NY: Oxford University Press, 1966).

67 Matthew Hughes, *Allenby and British Strategy in the Middle East, 1917–1919* (London: Frank Cass, 1999), pp. 77–8.

68 David Kilcullen, 'Twenty-eight Articles: Fundamentals of Company-level Counter-insurgency', (March 2006), https://d-n-i.net/fcs/pdf/kilcullen_28_articles.pdf.

69 Major Jim Gant, *One Tribe at a Time* (Los Angeles, CA: Nine Sisters Imports, 2009).

70 Jung Cheng and Jon Halliday, *Mao: The Unknown Story* (New York, NY: Knopf, 2005), pp. 233, 243.

71 V. I. Lenin, 'Partisan Warfare', in Franklin Mark Osanka (ed.), *Modern Guerrilla Warfare* (New York, NY: Free Press, 1962), pp. 65–79.

72 Mao Tse-Tung, *On Guerrilla Warfare*, trans. Samuel B. Griffith (New York, NY: Praeger, 1961), p. 93. A variation of Mao's metaphor, 'draining the swamps', was used by senior Department of Defense officials in speeches just after the 11 September 2001 attacks.

73 Steven Biddle, 'Seeing Baghdad, Thinking Saigon', *Foreign Affairs*, 85(2) (March/April 2006), 2–14.

74 Mao Tse-Tung, 'On Protracted War', in *Selected Military Writings* (Peking: Foreign Languages Press, 1966), pp. 196–7, www.marxists.org/reference/archive/mao/selected-works/volume-2/mswv2_09.htm.

75 Ibid., p. 201.

76 Ibid., p. 255.

77 Ibid., pp. 219–22.

78 Ibid., pp. 248–50.

79 Ibid., pp. 210–19.

80 Mao, *On Guerrilla Warfare*, p. 73.

81 Mao, 'On Protracted War', pp. 226–31, 257–61; Mao, *On Guerrilla Warfare*, pp. 88–93.

82 Contained in Mao, *On Guerrilla Warfare*, p. 92.

83 T. Wintringham, *New Ways of War* (Harmondsworth: Penguin, 1940); Yank' Levy, *Guerrilla Warfare*, 2nd ed. (Boulder, CO: Panther, 1964). The other work used by the Home Guard at this time was S. J. Cuthbert, *We Shall Fight in the Streets*, 2nd ed. (Boulder, CO: Panther, 1965).

84 See Ben Shepherd, *War in the Wild East* (Cambridge, MA: Harvard University Press, 2004), amongst others.

85 Explored in Louis de Jong, *The German Fifth Column in the Second World War* (Chicago, IL: University of Chicago Press, 1956).

86 A point emphasised in Gordon Harrison, *Cross Channel Attack: The United States Army in World War II* (Washington, DC: US Army Center of Military History, 1989), p. 207.

15 Current Irregular Warfare

CHAPTER OUTLINE

KEY THEMES

- Given their resource constraints and the character of irregular warfare, insurgents and terrorists have relatively few choices regarding the organisation or strategies they pursue. There is more continuity in insurgent strategy and organisation than there is change.
- Doctrine for countering insurgency, whether historical or contemporary, agrees in kind but differs only in preferred terminology, degree or specific approach. The principles of countering irregular warfare, therefore, are largely immutable. What matters regarding doctrine, however, is the ability of organisations and their leaders to adapt to the environment, learn faster than their opponent and connect their actions to the overall strategic effort, and not become the strategy itself.
- Irregular warfare is a complex phenomenon that is difficult to understand as different types of violence can be used individually or simultaneously. This can

lead to confusing the method or tactics of irregular warfare for its strategy or its purpose. Fixating on the tactics of violence, or improving one's own performance, as opposed to tackling your opponent's organisation and rationale, leads to operational frustration and strategic failure.

- Although irregular warfare conforms to the characteristics of the nature of war, its highly political essence make it challenging to understand. This essence is evident in the terms used to characterise irregular warfare, their politicisation and paradoxical influence on opponents, and the agency of local populations, proxies and host nation partner governments.

Introduction

The current era of irregular warfare starts at the conclusion of the Second World War and decolonisation or, rather, had its genesis during it. American President Franklin Roosevelt and British Prime Minister Winston Churchill could not possibly have known how truly strong and problematic the future whirlwind would be when they issued the Atlantic Charter in August 1940. Although most of its points appeared innocuous, the third point – the right of all peoples to self-determination – would cause the greatest difficulties. In particular, the leaders of socialist or nationalist movements in colonial territories interpreted the Atlantic Charter as the basis for declarations of independence once the war was over. The most famous example occurred in French Indochina in September 1945, where Ho Chi Minh declared Vietnam independent using language borrowed from the US Declaration of Independence.[1] Within the first three years of the end of the Second World War, France, the Netherlands and Britain were fighting insurgent groups that used guerrilla and terrorist tactics in their colonies including Malaya (Malaysia), Palestine, French Indochina (Vietnam, Laos and Cambodia) and the Dutch East Indies (Indonesia).[2] In other cases, the struggle for post-war predominance between different groups raged during the war in former monarchies such as Yugoslavia. In the case of occupied Greece, the struggle for supremacy between a number of rival nationalist and socialist factions started as early as 1942 and developed into a civil war that concluded only in 1949.

To outside observers, and within the broader context of the Cold War between the West and the Soviet Bloc, the majority of groups waging guerrilla or terrorist campaigns appeared to be communist-inspired or -directed. This observation, combined with increasing tensions with and territorial gains by the Soviet Union, suggested that the wave of irregular warfare was part of a vast, socialist conspiracy to defeat the West. In addition, both the Western and Soviet powers were looking at ways to compete with one another and expand their own influence in ways that would limit the possibility of escalation of conflict into conventional or nuclear war. One way to expand this influence was by providing support to proxies, including friendly states and insurgent or other groups. Nikita Khrushchev's speech in January 1961 implied Soviet support for those groups fighting 'wars of national liberation' and this speech only cemented the idea of a global conspiracy. Arguably the perception of a global communist conspiracy was a key element in the American decision to intervene in Vietnam.

Insurgent Strategies after Mao

Up to the American commitment of combat troops to Vietnam in 1965, irregular wars conducted against colonial powers, newly independent governments or other 'puppet' regimes followed four basic strategic approaches regardless of the group's political or religious ideology. In some cases, groups used these approaches independently, in parallel or in sequence depending on their success (or lack thereof). The first attempted to imitate Mao's success in China by following his advice in 'On Protracted War'. The success of Mao's approach was based on the assumption of large geographic space and a sizeable rural peasant population. Vietnamese General Vo Nguyen Giap is the most famous student of Mao who applied the formula to great success against the French. Giap oversaw the growth of a large Viet Minh army that contained regular forces and guerrillas. The siege and defeat of the French base at Dien Bien Phu in 1954, although not precisely Mao's envisioned strategic offensive phase, was enough to convince the political leaders in France that the war could not be won.[3] Since Vietnam, several insurgent groups have also attempted to apply Mao's ideas in their own country. Although Maoist-inspired insurgencies continue to be waged to this day in India and Turkey, the formula has been less successful in countries such as Thailand, Sri Lanka, Peru and the Philippines as groups have emphasised the military aspects of the campaign, including acts of terrorism, at the expense of political considerations.[4]

The second approach that irregular groups used involved attempts to convince the colonial power that the costs of maintaining their hold over the country were unacceptable without fighting major battles. In most cases, geography dictated this choice; this is especially true where population density was high and massed guerrilla movement was impractical or unwise. Zionist groups in the British-mandated Palestine, for example, conducted independent operations and some coordinated attacks ranging from pipeline sabotage and assassination to car bombings. Two incidents in particular characterised the type of attacks conducted by groups that included the Palmach, Lehi, the Stern Gang and Irgun: the bombing in July 1946 of King David Hotel, which housed numerous British-mandate offices including that of the Secretariat and the Criminal Investigation Division, and the kidnapping and hanging of two British sergeants in reprisal for the death sentences carried out against three Irgun members in July 1947.[5] Factors that contributed to the British decision to turn the territory over to the UN included awkward questions in the British parliament about the costs of operations within the mandated territories; media reporting of significant incidents and the loss of credibility after security measures led to an increase in attacks in circumstances (which also occurred in Iraq in 2006 and Afghanistan in 2021); and their shocking nature.

The third strategic approach was to seek diplomatic resolution because the conflict had reached a stalemate. Insurgent groups prevailed upon outside parties and sought to gain the attention of the member states of the UN in the hope their cause would be raised as an issue for resolution by the General Assembly. The leaders of the Algerian FLN, for example, which was losing ground militarily against French forces, sponsored a general strike in 1957, as well as bombings and other attacks, timed to maintain interest within the General Assembly on the subject of Algeria's future.[6] Indonesian leaders routinely prevailed on outside powers, including Britain, the US and the UN to resolve their on-again, off-again war to secure their independence from the Dutch (1945–1949).

The fourth and last strategic approach was something entirely different and recalled the nineteenth-century anarchist motto of 'propaganda by the deed'. Writers including Ernesto 'Che' Guevara, Regis Debray and Carlos Marighella made a fundamental break with established socialist revolutionary theory by suggesting that action take the place of organisation. Guevara and Debray, for example, suggested that the objective conditions within Latin America were ripe for revolution and guerrilla action by a revolutionary vanguard could itself create the subjective conditions.[7] Guevara's experience in the Cuban Revolution (1956–1958) only confirmed this.[8] The peasants and workers did not need to be educated or enlightened; the actions of a few would inspire, awaken and attract the masses to join in the insurgency. Marighella, on the other hand, suggested that urban guerrilla action would reveal to the masses the true nature of the ruling regime. Urban guerrillas could find all of the resources they needed within cities, including money, arms, media outlets and targets, to attack. The regime would have difficulty locating the guerrillas. The vain attempts by the regime to do so would only demonstrate its incompetence as the guerrillas continued their assault, leading to reprisals and security measures that would impose hardships upon the population.[9] The rural population would eventually be involved in the struggle but Marighella was vague on precisely how.[10] In their zeal, Guevara and Marighella convinced themselves of their own revolutionary prowess. Guevara, for example, failed to take his own advice about when one should not attempt guerrilla warfare when he departed for Bolivia in 1966: 'Where a government has come into power through some form of popular vote, fraudulent or not, and maintains at least an appearance of constitutional legality, the guerrilla outbreak cannot be promoted since the possibilities of peaceful struggle have not yet been exhausted.'[11] Considered the 'Guerrilla Enemy Number One' by the US, perhaps even the Osama bin Laden of his generation, Guevara was tracked down by Bolivian Rangers and killed in October 1967. Although both Guevara and Marighella were killed by state security forces, their writings and example inspired a generation of Marxist–Leninist terrorists from 1967 until the collapse of the Soviet Union.

Developments in Counterinsurgency and Counterterrorism

The current generation of irregular warfare experts drew much of their early knowledge from the classic works written between 1960 and 1973 by Filipino, British, French and American authors with first-hand experience in the Philippines, Malaya, Kenya and Algeria.[12] Works by such authors as Robert Thompson, Frank Kitson, David Galula, Roger Trinquier, Napoleon Valeriano and Edward Lansdale are still read for their insights.[13] After President John F. Kennedy officially made counterinsurgency a high national priority in 1962, most of these authors shared their experiences in sponsored conferences and written works or acted as advisors to the US government.[14] French Lieutenant Colonel David Galula, for example, produced both of his written works, *Pacification in Algeria* and *Counterinsurgency Warfare*, while sponsored by the RAND Corporation and Harvard's Center for International Affairs in 1963 and 1964.[15] Robert Thompson, considered one of the foremost experts on pacification during the Malayan Emergency and author of works including *Defeating Communist Insurgency*, served as head of the British Advisory Mission in South Vietnam from 1961 until 1965 and later as a personal advisor on counterinsurgency to President Richard Nixon.[16] Until Abu Ghraib, French Colonel Roger Trinquier's work, *Modern Warfare*, was the preferred text in American staff and war colleges given his focus on decisive results and characterisation of irregular violence as terrorism best dealt with through counter-terror. Much of what these authors have to say is still useful today provided its context is understood (see Figure 15.1). Given their range of experience and the quality of the works that these authors produced, it is not surprising that this era, which began with the Malayan Emergency in 1948 and ended in Afghanistan in 2021 with the withdrawal of NATO and US forces, can be considered as the 'golden age and renaissance of counterinsurgency and counterterrorism'.

Doctrine

This 'golden age and renaissance' was marked by two significant developments in modern irregular warfare: an explosion and revival of doctrinal publications and the creation, recreation and expansion of specialised forces to counter irregulars. As the previous chapter has outlined, authors as far back as the American Revolutionary War had attempted to distil lessons learned in fighting irregular adversaries for the benefit of officers faced with this threat in the future. Interest in partisan and small wars waxed during such conflicts but waned as military officers focused their efforts on problems of conventional warfare on land, sea and, later, in the air. Given the wealth of experience that French, British, Dutch and American officers had accumulated, it is surprising how few formal attempts were made to capture hard-won lessons in doctrine.[17] The mere existence of doctrine, however, does not guarantee success. Doctrine provides guidelines for leaders to review, digest, use and modify provided it is read and understood. If used improperly and unimaginatively, doctrine can instead be misconstrued as a set of inviolate rules never to broken, becoming a

Figure 15.1 The French experience with irregular warfare in Indochina and Algeria led Roger Trinquier and David Galula to different conclusions about how to combat irregular foes. Here French Foreign Legionnaires, backed by US-supplied tanks, conduct large-scale and ineffective sweeps against guerrilla Viet Minh forces in the Red River Valley in the year of the French defeat at Dien Bien Phu, 1954.

set of intellectual handcuffs. The absence of doctrine, however, places an undue burden on theatre and local commanders to improvise and make up techniques and procedures as they go along. As David Galula lamented, the lack of common doctrine to pacify regions in Algeria led to completely different practices being followed even in neighbouring regions, and these often changed as officers came and went.[18] The same situation existed on a much larger scale, for different reasons, within and between the various geographic regional commands in Afghanistan prior to General Stanley McChrystal's appointment as commander of the International Security Assistance Force (ISAF) in 2008.

Published American doctrine on irregular war had existed as early as 1921 and was refined into a work that is still useful today: the Marine Corps' 1940 *Small Wars Manual.*[19] Amongst the lessons incorporated into this manual, which had to be relearned recently, were the need for liaison with diplomats (US State Department officials), the role played by aviation in small wars and guidelines for disarming the population, holding elections, establishing local security forces and withdrawing forces.[20] A quarter of a century after the release of the *Small Wars Manual*, the Department of the Army and Headquarters, USMC released a catalogue of field manuals and pamphlets from 1963 until 1973, which included: FM 31-15, *Operations Against Irregular Forces*; FM 31-16, *Counterguerrilla Operations*; DA-PAM 550-100, *US Army Handbook of Counterinsurgency Guidelines for Area Commanders: An Analysis of Criteria*; DA-PAM 550-104, *Human Factors Considerations of Undergrounds in Insurgencies*; FMFMRP 12-40, *Professional Knowledge Gained from Operational Experience in Vietnam 1965–1966*; and FMFM 8-2, *Counterinsurgency Operations.* As Colin Gray has noted, the American defence community has a short attention span, is captivated by the most recent intellectual fad and is largely ahistorical in its outlook, particularly with irregular warfare.[21] A decade after the withdrawal of US forces from Vietnam, and with the refocusing of defence priorities back on problems of potential conflict with overwhelming Warsaw Pact forces in Europe, most of these doctrinal publications were shelved and forgotten. Their lessons had to be revived and relearned in 2006, at the height of the Iraq insurgency, with the unprecedented public rollout of combined Army and Marine Corps doctrine, FM 3-24/MWCP 3-33.5, *Counterinsurgency,* which in a modified form as a joint doctrine publication in 2013. This was followed a year later by the first doctrine, in any form, to combat terrorism, JP 3-26, *Counterterrorism.*

Organisational Adaptation

Doctrine, no matter how prolific, is only as useful as the soldiers who put it into practice. As Johann Ewald noted, soldiers who excelled at conventional warfare had difficulties in adapting to the less rigid, more individualist style of fighting in irregular war. To help address this problem, authors including Ewald, Charles Callwell and William Henecker suggested conventional forces should be augmented by forces skilled in partisan and guerrilla methods. Not surprisingly, this era saw the formation or development of a number of specialised military units skilled in guerrilla methods. The British in Malaya had developed the Ferret Force and the Malaya Scouts, the latter of which evolved into a revived[22] Special Air Service Regiment. The French in Indochina in turn fielded the *Groupement de commandos mixtes aéroportés* (GCMA), in which French commissioned and non-commissioned officers led groups of local tribesmen. The commanding officer of the GCMA during the battle of Dien Bien Phu was Roger Trinquier.[23] Within the US, President Kennedy elevated the status of the fledgling US Army Special Forces, or Green Berets, as the tip of America's spear in the fight against communist insurgencies and stimulating the creation of Navy SEAL and Air Force 'air commando' units. With the rise of transnational terrorism after Vietnam, enterprising enlisted and junior officers advocated for the creation of specialised hostage rescue forces such the American Delta Force and the British Special Projects Teams. As with doctrine, the uniquely qualified personnel of such SOF could not overcome military and political hesitance, incompetence or misuse at the operational and strategic level.[24]

The Principles of Counterinsurgency

The legacy of the 'golden age and renaissance of counterinsurgency and counter-terrorism' continues to be a blessing and a curse for those facing current irregular threats. Most doctrine or works from the era – such as Thompson, Kitson, Galula, Trinquier, Valeriano or Lansdale – agree in kind on counterinsurgency but not on the degree or specific approach. These works have led to a set of fairly well-understood principles of countering irregular warfare. For countering insurgents, principles incorporate aspects of, but are not limited to:[25]

- Controlling the population and tracking their movements through the use of checkpoints, identification checks, forced relocation and/or intimidation and coercion.
- Gaining the support of the most important population, which is often expressed in the phrase 'winning the hearts and minds', and can mean their active participation in local government, self-defence militias and providing information to authorities, usually by providing local security and stability; at the very least, the population should be prevented from supporting insurgents and terrorists (see Figure 15.2).
- Obtaining precise information on the organisation and location of insurgent and terrorist groups so they can be killed, captured or turned against their comrades.
- Creating or improving the quality and quantity of military and paramilitary forces and law enforcement bodies so that they are competent enough to provide local security and stability, with limited outside assistance, as well as deny the insurgents and terrorists sanctuary; these forces must be able to accomplish these objectives in such as manner as to not be perceived by the population as tools of government oppression.
- Developing, or assisting in the development of, just and responsive governance and coordinated responses across all government agencies at the local, regional and national levels to address the political, social and economic conditions that led to violence in the first place and inform ongoing and future actions against the insurgents and terrorists.

Figure 15.2 The support of the population – which can include providing information on insurgents, terrorists and revolutionaries or taking direct action against them – is based in part on effective local governance. Such governance must be credible, responsive, honest and based on intricately linking local needs with available resources. Such understanding often requires specific cultural information that can only be provided by direct contact with the population. A member of the Afghan National Army Special Forces shakes hands with a local elder during a presence patrol with Afghan National Police and coalition force members to escort a district governor in Helmand province, Afghanistan, 17 March 2013.

Counterterrorism doctrine suggests its activities are consistent with the principles of other joint operations but places a special emphasis on the following:

- Ensuring operations are perceived as legitimate by various important audiences, domestically and abroad.
- Focusing on obtainable objectives that yield decisive results.
- Guaranteeing unity of effort across various government departments and agencies, not only to ensure unity of effort but also to not burn out finite counterterrorism resources.
- Balancing offensive and defensive activities to maintain the initiative but that do not take on a life of their own and undercut campaign goals.
- Conducting precise, or 'surgical' operations that are proportionate to the threat and in the employment of violence to preserve legitimacy.[26]

As with doctrine and forces trained in defeating terrorists and insurgents, knowledge of such principles alone is insufficient. The curse of these eras, which lasted from 1945 and continues through to today, can be summed up in two main problem areas: the 'big idea' and stressing performance over politics.

The first problem area, the 'big idea', begins while searching for solutions to deal with irregular threats. Practitioners rediscover, repackage or are introduced to campaign narratives and analysis, the details of a specific historical programme or works from the previous generations. For example, several of the doctrinal publications mentioned in a previous section from the Vietnam era were amended or republished as part of the Assessing Revolutionary and Insurgent Strategies (ARIS) project.[27] Such analogues are appealing as they appear to provide the answer to the current questions. For example, the iconic 'success' story of this era, the British campaign in Malaya from 1948 until 1960, was mined for lessons of victory in counterinsurgency applicable today. Most practitioners drifted away from Malaya, given its unique contextual attributes of that conflict such as a racially distinct ethnic-minority insurgent group and the existence of an integrated, functioning colonial civil administration. They shifted their focus to the failed French campaign in Algeria (1954–1962). Algeria was appealing in that the works of Trinquier and Galula are accessible and the conflict featured a tapestry of religious and cultural elements similar to those found in Iraq, Afghanistan and elsewhere.[28] Also 'rediscovered' was Alastair Horne's narrative of the Algeria war, *A Savage War of Peace*. While there is a sizeable body of literature on the subject from this period that was rediscovered, other conflicts for which there are few published details or accounts that occurred after 'the golden age of counterinsurgency' are apt to be overlooked. The various 'bush wars' of Africa and counterinsurgency and counterterrorism campaigns in Central and Southern America during the 1970s and 1980s are rich with insights about insurgent and counterinsurgent adaptation, organisational learning and the interactions between adversaries at the level of policy and strategy that changed the character of those wars.[29] More recent 'big ideas' to which future practitioners may be drawn, in the historical cycle of interest in and abandonment of counterinsurgency, are the much-publicised and lengthy doctrine manuals, such as the US Army Field Manual 3-24, *Counterinsurgency* and British Army Field Manual Volume 1, Part 10, *Countering Insurgency*, as well as the works of various noteworthy practitioners including David Petraeus, Rupert Smith, Peter Mansoor, H. R. McMaster, David Kilcullen and John Nagl, amongst others.

As several scholars have pointed out, reasoning by analogy and looking to history for answers to contemporary problems are fraught with pitfalls.[30] One such pitfall is simplifying the past. In reviewing works produced during this time, those looking for answers are apt to take the principles, insights and conclusions they find at face value. What may be overlooked is the specific context of the conflict in which the works were written.[31] More recently, the attempt to apply the template for success in Iraq from 2007 onwards, embodied in 'The Surge', proved problematic when transferred to Afghanistan from 2008 onwards. Some of this can be put down to time and resource constraints, excessive haste or intellectual laziness. More often than not other errors are based on sins of omission or commission by the original authors or architects. Some authors – including Thompson and Kitson, and more recently David Petreaus and Stanley McChrystal – compressed significant details and omitted nuances and the complexities of the campaigns to save space and ease readability. Contemporary accounts also suffered because participants often related the details of the conflict as they knew and understood them from their specific vantage point or the subjects painted themselves in a positive light. Sins of commission include deliberately playing down negative aspects or contrary evidence of the concepts and ideas put forth. Such accounts are often distilled down even further as they are read for the immediately applicable or 'actionable' wisdom contained within. Kitson's and Thompson's works, in particular, depict a version of counterinsurgency that appears kinder and more humane than that painted by their French counterparts, Trinquier and Galula. More recent scholarship on British counterinsurgency challenges the traditional image of 'winning hearts and minds' and suggests 'where they won they did so by being nasty, not nice, to the people' through harsh, coercive methods.[32]

In simplifying the past, other details can be overlooked as well. For example, the most basic depiction of irregular warfare identifies three primary actors: the insurgent or terrorist group, the population and the government (i.e., counterinsurgent or counterterrorist) forces. The insurgent or terrorist group and the government seek to influence the population to gain their support. On a conceptual level, this is understandable. But for reasons that Clausewitz well understood, what separates war in theory from war in reality, regardless of the form it takes, are the details, frictions and interactions between actors. Few campaigns during the 'golden age and renaissance of counterinsurgency and counterterrorism' involved monolithic irregular groups, populations or governments. Petty jealousies, rivalries and struggles for predominance between competing factions, shifting allegiances and indifference and incompetence between all three, as well as the practical difficulties of comprehending these much less deal directly with them, is the stuff of irregular warfare. What is often difficult for outsiders to understand in contemporary irregular wars, such as Syria, Iraq and Afghanistan, is that the purpose of seemingly brutal and discriminate violence actually reflects the complex tapestry of motivations and uses of political violence at the organisational and local level between numerous competing groups, for which there are no clear-cut or easy solutions (see Figure 15.3).[33] Those directly dealing with Mali, Syria, Iraq and Afghanistan have been faced by a range of difficulties, such as competing functional and political requirements, minimising their own casualties, dealing with local tribal and militia leaders, focusing on different problems (insurgent or terrorist groups as in Mali, or corruption in Afghanistan) and making decisions based on incomplete information in areas that have no clear moral dividing line.

The labels 'complex' and 'difficult', however, can be applied to all irregular wars during this era. The war in Vietnam was not a simple 'us versus them' conflict, with the population in between that could have been resolved by invading the North and destroying its alleged centre of gravity, its army. As Harry Summers points out, this 'purely military' option was completely divorced from political reality and therefore unwise and impractical.[34] The war in Vietnam was comprised of a number of nested and interrelated problems spiced with the vested interests of various groups. These groups included the US military, whose leaders acted according to their own

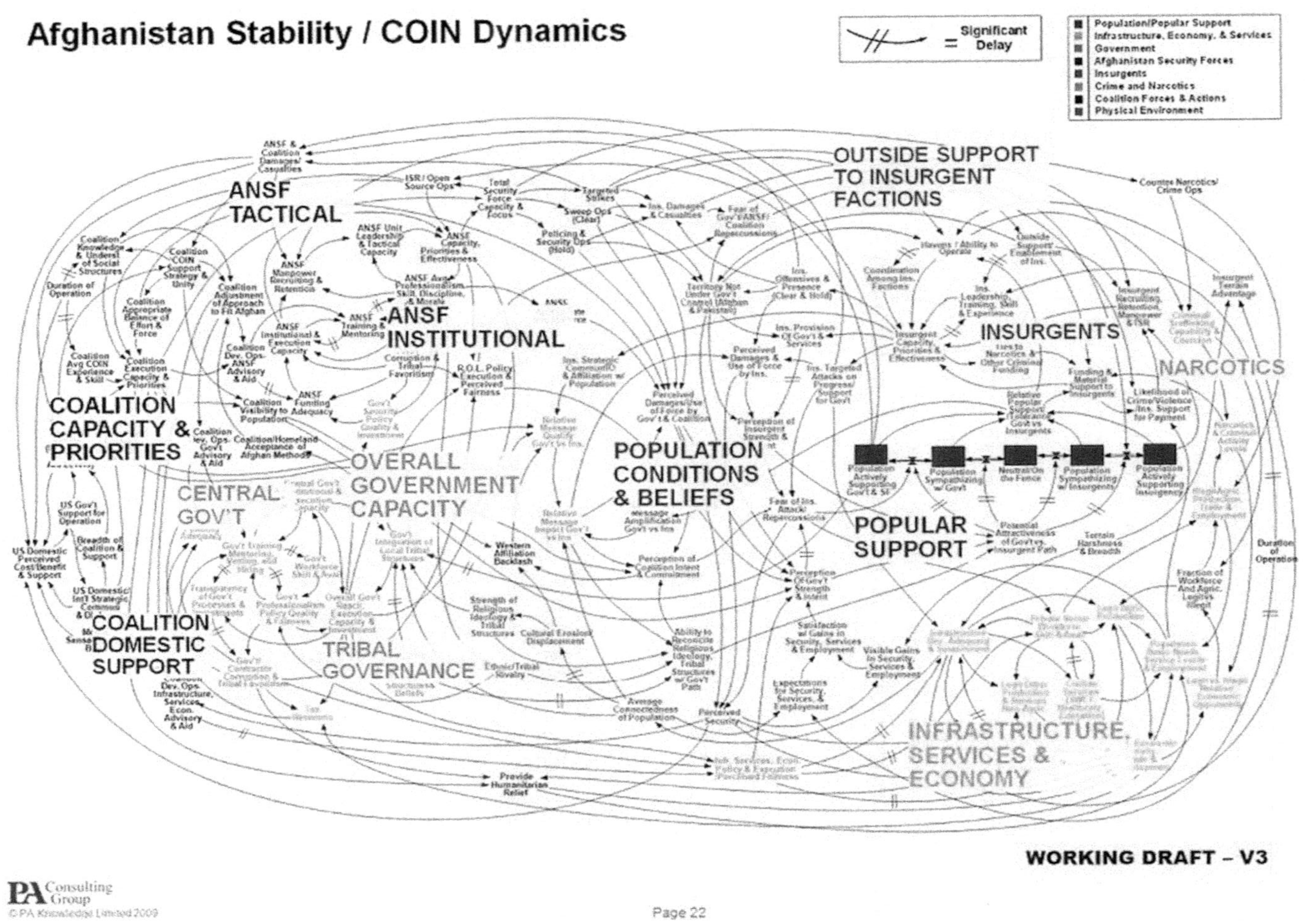

Figure 15.3 No single graphic better depicts the complexity of the operating environment in Afghanistan than the so-called 'spaghetti chart' produced in the ISAF Headquarters and circulated in 2010. For its supporters, the chart demonstrates the complex web of connections among the many actors characteristic of an irregular warfare environment. For its detractors, however, the chart was a perfect illustration of bureaucratic process run amok (demonstrating in particular the negative influence of software tools such as Microsoft PowerPoint on strategic thinking) or the ultimate futility associated with bringing stability to Afghanistan.

individual and organisational imperatives, as well as competing social, political, economic and religious elements within South Vietnam such as the Montagnard hill tribes, an influential Buddhist minority and a social elite of Catholic Vietnamese. Deciding which groups to support first during the Syrian Civil War and later against ISIS was complicated by the volume of armed groups and organisations involved in the conflict, which were estimated from the hundreds to more than 1,500 in total.[35] For decades, oversimplified assessments talked about 'the Taliban' as if was a unified organisation, when in reality activities more likely reflected local political vendettas allied conveniently as part of a dynamic 'caravan' of local and regional opportunists taking advantage of circumstances.[36] Another aspect of oversimplification in the face of complex problems is jumping to snap judgements that the defeat of major powers in irregular wars is inevitable.[37]

The second and final problem associated with learning from the era can be summarised as the tendency to learn military lessons at the expense of political ones. All of the coalition members involved in the campaigns of Iraq and Afghanistan learned from and adapted to their adversaries. Future practitioners looking back into the 'golden age and renaissance of counterinsurgency and counterterrorism' will look back to Afghanistan and Iraq, to identify potential techniques and tricks of the trade to improve their overall performance (see Figure 15.4). Reaching back to the past is laudable, especially if it saves lives and defeats the irregular threat. The more

Figure 15.4 Technology collects remarkably precise information that improves the conduct of military operations but also contributes to the illusion of knowledge and understanding. Those used during the renaissance of counterinsurgency and counterterrorism provided a quantum leap in the quality and quantity of data collected but offered few insights towards what really matters in irregular warfare: local, regional and national politics. Here a sensor provides an 'unblinking eye' over ISIS leader's Amir Muhammad Sa'id Abdal-Rahman al-Mawla compound prior to a SOF raid resulting in his death on 2 February 2022.

recent trend, however, stresses improving the performance of the means used (counterinsurgent or counterterrorist forces) while divining little about the ends to be achieved – elevating the conduct of the campaign to the level of strategy by losing sight of the political goal. Countering irregular warfare has little to do with fighting more effectively against insurgents and terrorists oneself, as the principles outlined previously suggest, but rather assisting local forces to create the conditions for security and stability from the bottom up while assisting the host nation government in its ability to govern credibly from the top down. Studying Nixon's policy of 'Vietnamisation' for potential political insights applicable to Iraq or Afghanistan, for example, is not to equate the latter with the former. The end result, the collapse of the Army of the Republic of Vietnam, was not due primarily to the removal of US air power from the equation. The policies of Vietnamisation, Iraqisation (the 2008 US–Iraq Status of Forces Agreement), and Afghanisation (Accelerated Departure) were sound, but their assumptions and execution left something to be desired.[38] In every case the host nation – South Vietnam, Iraq and Government of the Islamic Republic of Afghanistan – neither possessed military forces competent or trustworthy enough to protect the nation nor did it have an equitable system of governance worth defending. And yet, as Harry Summers related to a North Vietnamese colonel years after the fall of Saigon: 'You know you never defeated us on the battlefield', to which the response was '[T]hat may be so . . . but it is also irrelevant', echoes of which haunt Western capitals more recently.[39] As experience shows, first in Iraq in 2014 and later in Afghanistan in 2020, large portions of the military evaporated in the face of irregular offensives by the ISIS or the Taliban. Military success in both countries could not offset a fundamentally untenable political situation – inadequate power-sharing by the incumbent government between different religious, ethnic and tribal groups within the country.

Why Is Modern Irregular Warfare so Difficult?

Teasing out the details of prior irregular wars can be challenging even after such conflicts end. While the start and end dates of specific conflicts are tied to crucial events, with the benefit of hindsight, the specific details of conflicts are often obscured by a number of research-related pathologies, including favouring one side in the conflict over another, mistaking war for peace, privileging urban elite perspectives, selection bias and abstracting away detail.[40] When faced with irregular conflicts now and in the future, however, blurred lines or uncertain understanding between competition and conflict may lead to knee-jerk reactions and undesired escalation. The cardinal error a political leader or military commander could commit, according to Clausewitz, is misunderstanding the type of conflict about to be undertaken and ensuring that the means applied are suitable to desired ends.[41] Problems occur for the political leader and military planner in contemporary irregular warfare for four related reasons: mistaking the means, forms and types of violence for its purpose; politicising irregular warfare in the pursuit of institutional objectives; overestimating and 'mirror imaging' opponents; and overlooking the agency of irregular actors.

Misunderstanding the Method and Purpose of Irregular Warfare

At the risk of repeating a claim made throughout this work, even the most cursory reading of military history and strategy conveys the clear message that all conflicts are unique to and shaped by their specific context. The Chechens, for example, have fought three irregular wars against Russia over more than 150 years. Although the geography was the same in each case, the character of each conflict was shaped by changes in society, technology, culture, information and a host of other factors. In order to understand the root causes and motivations behind irregular conflicts, some scholars suggest that cultural and language studies are crucial. Few would dispute this sound advice. Unfortunately, other authors have interpreted this to mean that cultural and religious reasons alone explain violence, irregular or otherwise, as an end in and of itself. The implication of this conclusion is clear and disturbing: there is no room for negotiation or bargaining with those for whom violence forms an integral part of their religion and/or culture. Violence serves a purpose that suits the social context – a reflection of a 'sacred value' – that makes bargaining or negotiation exceptionally difficult.[42] When cultural or religious warriors fight professional soldiers, the former are willing to adopt methods that the latter cannot or will not embrace. This advantage is crucial in explaining why militias, tribes and others using irregular tactics have frustrated and defeated more powerful adversaries with professional modern armies.

The kernel of truth behind such claims mistakes individual and group motivation, organisation and fighting style – in other words the technique of violence – for its purpose. Irregular warfare is no different from its regular counterpart in terms of the intended outcome. Those who adopt irregular means are looking to obtain power or extend their influence over others. That power is political in nature and its possession allows the wielder to achieve influence or control for the purpose of systemic change incrementally or suddenly, locally, regionally or globally. The purpose of violence, and the rationale for its use, has been remarkably similar, from Auguste Blanqui to the current generation of state and non-state efforts employing irregular warfare. Not much separates the ultimate purpose of today's irregulars from those who struggled decades or centuries ago. The leaders of ISIS, for example, sought territorial control in order to impose their belief structure on the population, use state power to repress despised ethnic minorities, and implement their ascetic version of Sharia law—while also taking the trappings of political power, including bureaucratic departments, tax collection and revenue generation and the issuance of passports.

Irregular warfare can be difficult to understand due to its character, or the means and methods of violence used. There is a tendency to equate the type of irregular violence according to the methods and means used while overlooking the purpose it is designed to achieve. Put simply, the tactic is mistaken for its strategic utility and purpose of the violence (see Figure 15.5). For example, there is a common

Figure 15.5 In an effort to grasp the nature of the war in which one is involved, there is a danger of oversimplifying complex aspects of irregular warfare such as confusing means used by insurgents, terrorists and revolutionaries for the ends they are trying to achieve. Those who conduct irregular warfare are first and foremost pragmatic opportunists when it comes to using resources at hand. Viet Cong leaders, for example, paid little mind to the conceptual distinction between acts of terrorism or insurgency during the bombing campaign they conducted in the city of Saigon against a multi-storey US officers billet in Saigon, 4 January 1966, which killed four Vietnamese and three Americans.

misperception that insurgents only use guerrilla tactics. Acts of terrorism, such as bombings, assassinations, hijacking and kidnapping, are strictly the realm of terrorists. Noteworthy theorists, including Mao Zedong (Tse-Tung) and Ernesto 'Che' Guevara, would rail against such simplistic assessments of the use of violence within an insurgency. Both authors acknowledged the role that terrorism, as a tactic, can play in their overall campaign.[43] Other methods and techniques such as sabotage, subversion and passive resistance, which have considerable tactical utility but are exceptionally difficult to identify and evaluate, have been confused as unique forms of irregular warfare with their own purpose.

More recent characterisations of irregular warfare seek to change its frame of reference from the non-state level to state-sanctioned activities and behaviour. Power continues to be exercised most effectively at the state level in the international system, and irregular warfare is a means of exerting state influence and accomplishing desired goals. State leaders have a legitimacy that substate leaders and groups do not; irregular warfare now provides a means of competing on the margins of legality and legitimacy. The most recent Joint Staff definition removes violence from the definition of irregular warfare: its scope now is assurance and coercion. The form of activities is what make it 'irregular', characterised by the following attributes: indirect, asymmetric and non-attributable. Opening the aperture this broadly permits a range of state activities to be considered irregular warfare: subversion, sabotage, espionage, influence and psychological operations, narcotics trafficking, and the list goes on. In eroding the boundaries thus all competition short of conflict constitutes irregular warfare. Its purpose is seeking continuous competitive advantage and avoiding conflict crossing the thresholds of conventional or nuclear warfare.

Assessments along similar lines occurred after 1961 but gained momentum with speeches and policy decisions made by President John F. Kennedy. They were accompanied by an outpouring of assessments, including new terminology, that sought to characterise irregular warfare as a competitive activity against the adversary's system of governance. One author depicted irregular warfare, which he termed 'unconventional warfare', in the following manner:

> A weapons system [and] disintegrative weapon, for it seeks to destroy the links which bind together the political, economic, and military organism of the enemy. But it poses no threat of destruction to the lives of millions or to their resources . . . it is a weapon which depends not only on physical forces but on a wide variety of psychological moral factors which cannot be produced and stockpiled at will.[44]

Compared with a 2021 definition of irregular warfare, found in Box 15.1, they are eerily similar:

> [I]rregular warfare refers to activities short of conventional and nuclear warfare that are designed to expand a country's influence and legitimacy, as well as to weaken its adversaries. It includes numerous tools of statecraft that governments can use to shift the balance of power in their favor: information operations (including psychological operations and propaganda), cyber operations, support to state and nonstate partners, covert action, espionage, and economic coercion.

Both are guilty of a sin identified by Samuel Huntington: developing terms outside of a general theory of armed conflict, one that makes 'the distinction between *types of war* and *forms of warfare*' (italics in original).[45]

Politicising Irregular Warfare

Over the past quarter century, military and political leaders misunderstood the character of irregular warfare by parsing it too finely according to subordinate forms, at the expense of a more holistic understanding. In consequence, they tended to view irregular warfare in absolute or static terms, each with 'prescribed' solutions, including insurgency, terrorism or civil war. Such solutions privileged military responses, which only addressed part of a complex phenomenon with social, economic and political dimensions. Now the problem is that irregular warfare is viewed too expansively, within the structure of geopolitical competition whose outcome is dominance over the global (and beyond) order of political and economic system. Doing so inflates irregular warfare beyond its reasonable boundaries by making all activities up to the conventional and nuclear threshold part of it: subordinate forms become subsumed in the continuous quest for advantage.

Expanding frames of reference often begins for sound reasons. More often than not, it starts with observations about contemporary conflict that are irreconcilable with existing ones for war and conflict. The terms 'fourth generation warfare' and 'hybrid warfare', for example, were coined to extrapolate the future of warfare based on identifiable megatrends as well as the outcomes of the Gulf War (1990–1991), Kosovo (1999), Gaza and Lebanon (2006). Writers in the West, Russia and China grappled with the seeming blurring of boundaries between types of warfare and the declared or demonstrated willingness of actors to exploit existing norms and conventions to their advantage through the conduct of 'lawfare' – using legal constraints to one's own advantage. Recent state activities seem to confirm its increasing use: from Russia's exploitation of democratic norms and proxies to annex Crimea in 2014 to Hamas' seizure of Israeli citizens and use of legally protected structures, such as hospitals, as a shield against airpower and to exploit for informational purposes, in 2023–2025

New terms or the reframing of previous ones such as irregular warfare are not problematic in their own right. Problems occur when they are mobilised as part of political discourse to suit institutional purposes. At the height of the 'hybrid warfare' craze after the annexation of Crimea in 2016, alarmist narratives about Russia's prowess and Western unpreparedness called to mind previous social and political scares. These included one surrounding Imperial German subversion in Britain and throughout its empire prior to the First World War and communist collusion and revolutionary warfare prior to and following the Second World War. Initial political rationales driving such narratives may seek positive outcomes, such as prodding NATO member states to uphold their collective security obligations, as was the case from 2014 to 2018. Such narratives, however, become contorted in the pursuit of specific institutional objectives over time, as happened with hybrid and now irregular warfare.[46] In his recent alarmist work, Seth Jones seeks to make Congress and the American public aware of Russian, Chinese and Iranian irregular warfare activities. Many of the sources he quotes are former military and intelligence officials, a high percentage of them from the special operations community, which is seeking to cement its authorities and budget for great power competition given the twilight of counterterrorism.[47] In pursuing institutional agendas, actors constructing political narratives extend original concepts far beyond their original remit with additional consequences.

Overestimating and 'Mirror-imaging'

Narratives also contribute to policymakers and military planners misunderstanding or overestimating the capabilities and skills and 'mirror-imaging' their state and non-state irregular adversaries. Part of the reason for this is understandable. If irregular warfare is undertaken for a purpose, then surely the leaders of such movements must have a plan to translate tactical action into achieving stated ends.

It is easy to be convinced of a 'master plan' guiding it in Beijing, Moscow, Tehran, Raqqa and elsewhere. In a curious paradox, the evidence quoted from irregular sources in support of mobilising narratives has a boomerang effect. This effect, in essence, validates the concepts, ideas and approaches of irregulars and legitimises them. Unfortunately, translation and interpretation mistakes ascribe inaccurate and misleading characteristics to irregular opponents, turning them into seemingly unassailable monoliths, a historical pattern noted earlier. Several Western authors misread the purpose of Russian General Valeri Gerasimov's 2013 article 'The Value of Science Is in the Foresight'. Several employed selective portions of his article in bolstering their claims about a new Russian way of war, one irregular or hybrid in nature. In reality, Gerasimov had two less dramatic purposes: attempting to explain how the West and the US were able to set the conditions for victory long before force was used via their own version of irregular warfare, and even more importantly to spur Russian military scientific thinking that had atrophied in his estimation.[48]

Practitioners from Lawrence to Mao through to Valeri Gerasimov and Qassem Soleimani have developed concepts of operations that takes the current context into account. The inferred superiority of irregulars belies very real problems inherent in the practice of strategy. Revolutionary theorists often disagree on the appropriate method or mechanism for success in irregular warfare. These debates continue to rage amongst irregulars. The debates encompass almost all aspects of strategy, including who to fight (the 'near' enemy, where the violent Islamic extremists reside, or the 'far' one, including the US and the West), as well as when and how. Following the 7 October 2023 attacks, Hamas leaders took the extraordinary step of publishing a narrative rebuttal of Israeli claims and Western media reports, in which they acknowledged, 'Maybe some faults happened during Operation Al-Aqsa Flood's implementation due to the rapid collapse of the Israeli security and military system, and the chaos caused along the border areas with Gaza,' implying a loss of control and disagreements within the group.[49]

Irregular writers and organisers such as Abu Mus'ab al-Suri (born Mustafa Setmariam Nasar), a former member of the Syrian Brotherhood with ties to Zarqawi's al-Qaeda in Iraq, have argued that the violent Islamic extremists conduct what was once labelled 'propaganda by the deed' in an entirely decentralised and independent manner. Victory will eventually result from the cumulative effects of such activities.[50] Other writers argue that a more focused, sequential plan of action is necessary. Abu Bakr Naji outlines an approach that, in keeping with the principles and practices of irregular war, emphasises both the political and military dimensions of the struggle:

> This plan requires: A military strategy working to disperse the efforts and forces of the enemy and to exhaust and drain its monetary and military capabilities; A media strategy targeting and focusing on two classes. [The first] class is the masses, in order to push a large number of them to join the *jihad*, offer positive support, and adopt a negative attitude toward those who do not join the ranks. The second class is the troops of the

enemy who have lower salaries, in order to push them to join the ranks of the mujahids or at least flee from the service of the enemy.[51]

A core component of Naji's vision of success is a hierarchy of highly capable administrators who guide and manage the revolutionary masses, harking back to the earlier generation of socialist revolutionary theorists.[52] Irregulars are not immune to the same squabbles and incompetence as their opponents, nor can they escape the logic of organisation or strategy.

Agency and the Illusion of Control

Disagreements within organisations contribute to the friction Clausewitz identified within the nature of war, regardless of its form or type. Another factor that makes irregular warfare vexing is the agency various actors have that upsets conventional notions about power and control. Control is a central concept within most military theories–land, sea, air, space and cyber. Within the human terrain of irregular warfare, control relates specifically to populations and the need of state authorities to guarantee their security and stability. Technology occasionally alters the power balance between those who govern and those ostensibly under their control. Audrey Kurth Cronin argues that, during periods of open technological innovation, disruptive technologies allow this to occur. Historically, such technologies have included stable high explosives such as dynamite, cheap widely proliferated assault rifles like the AK-47 and, she posits, autonomous, swarming air, sea and ground vehicles. These emerging technologies are not only 'cheap equalisers' but have the potential to 'scramble the balance of power equation', she concludes.[53]

While technology is an underappreciated aspect of irregular warfare, the most impactful agency is political in nature. Two forms bedevil control for the West: the agency of local populations and that of proxies, including armed groups and militias as well as host nation governments. Of these two, the agency of local populations is the most troublesome and disturbing. What potentially turns the power balance between local populations, irregulars and intervening Western forces on its head is the value of highly specific information its members possess. With this information, members of the local population can denounce and identify irregulars or government collaborators, ensuring their demise. Without a level of almost absolute control, the population is free to point out such people to whoever exerts control over an area at a time, using the latter's ignorance of local conditions to solve previous feuds or disputes unrelated to the overall political objective.[54] This issue, termed 'the local of agency' by Stathis Kalvyas, has ominous implications: unless state authorities or insurgents can assert sovereign control over an area, ensuring that the information it receives is completely accurate and punishes disobedience accordingly, they are prone to serving unrelated local political agendas as opposed to national ones. Rather than helpless victims in need of rescuing, local populations can be devious and manipulative in their own politics.

A variation of this theme occurs in the control of proxies. Armed groups and host nations conducting or countering irregular warfare on a state's behalf have their own political goals. Although convenience aligns the group's goals with those of the sponsoring state, the former is not above operating independently when it suits its political purposes or conditions change. In an example after the Battle of Mosul against

> The threat of [ISIS] marginalized and the Iraqi security forces self-confident, the government of Iraq reoriented on the Kurds. In September 2017, Iraqi Kurdistan, under the tutelage of Marzoud Barzani, voted for independence from Iraq. Al-Abadi, unwilling to accept Kurdish independence, launched a limited offensive in mid-October 2017 to thwart the movement. Sidestepping his coalition partners, al-Abadi's Kurdish operation was unilateral.[55]

Proxy leaders understand Western commitments are uncertain and subject to change. In consequence, they often try and extract as many concessions and resources as possible unconditionally for as long as they can using a form of 'reverse leverage' – comprehending their strategic value to the sponsoring state.[56]

SOF and Irregular Warfare Myths

The 2018 National Defense Strategy outlined during the first Trump Administration succeeded in 'pivoting' focus from the irregular warfare problems of the Middle East to the problems of a rising and increasingly assertive China. Military focus would shift away from irregular warfare but return to conventional core competencies such as combined arms warfare or cross-domain warfare, outlined in Chapter 18. The frustrations of irregular warfare would fade into memory in pursuit of new technologies and cracking new conceptual problems such as projecting conventional power inside China's 'A2/AD weapons engagement zone (WEZ)'. Political leaders, as well as the domestic political base, have little apparent stomach or enthusiasm to counter irregular warfare or tackle nation-building on the previous scale of Iraq and Afghanistan. While terrorist groups such as AQ and Al Shabaab continue to threaten the West or Western interests, their capabilities remain limited and they are largely in a 'rebuilding' phase.[57] Counterterrorism has largely returned in the West to the state it occupied prior to 11 September 2001 – a crime best dealt with by law-enforcement agencies.

For Western nations, the economical solution to address the current irregular threat of terrorism and 'big idea', as during the 'golden age of counterinsurgency', was to counter them with irregulars of their own: SOF. Comprised of highly motivated, specially selected, designated and equipped operators, SOF were appealing strategically for a variety of reasons, including their ability to access or threaten remote regions, conduct risky operations with a high likelihood of success, operate across and between legal authorities, experiment and innovate on a small scale and resolve problems economically and quietly compared with other military forces (see Figure 15.6). The selection of special operators, however, comes at the price of limited numbers, and therefore an inability to mass or sustain strategic

Figure 15.6 Special operations forces (SOF) lower political risk for decision-makers through their high degree of tactical performance based on their specialised selection, designation, equipment and joint training. SOF assume higher personal and tactical risk than conventional forces, although their bias for action and agency can create political and strategic problems. Here a Burkinabe soldier retrieves a video drone during Exercise Flintlock 2019 at base camp Zagre, Burkina Faso on 24 February 2019. Exercise Flintlock 2019 brought together African and Western partner nations in order to improve interoperability and prevent terrorism.

effects for long periods of time.[58] To add numbers or mass, or as a prerequisite for access, SOF have worked by, with and through others, which can include conventional forces or other government agencies, as well as proxies such as host-nation armed or security forces or local militias and armed groups. SOF have been most successful when they improve the operational performance and strategic effectiveness of other forces or proxies through their unique skills and training and access to equipment and information, or utilise their connections to other forces or agencies.[59]

SOF's appearance as the cheap solution to the seemingly intractable problems of irregular warfare created problems of their own for Western nations. For political leaders or other military forces, to place the burden of countering irregular threats exclusively on the shoulders of SOF is to miss several of the problems attendant to irregular warfare. First, SOF can often achieve immediate results in pressing irregular problems but this is akin to curing the immediate symptom at the expense of treatment of the underlying disease. Secondly, SOF act as enablers for other forces by enhancing their performance strategically or operationally over time. One of the greatest challenges about working with host-nation forces, or through proxies, is the inability to control them in the direction you prefer strategically, much less politically. Thirdly, by operating across and between legal authorities, SOF lower political risk at the expense of greater legal and ethical risk. In order to pursue irregular opponents who flaunt international norms and laws, SOF often operate in normative and legal grey areas that can be morally hazardous, especially in the covert or clandestine realm. These hazards and risks were realised in investigations into criminal activity and human rights abuses by special operators from Canada, Australia, the UK and the US, some of which remain ongoing. While SOF are best suited to tackle immediate irregular non-state threats, they only establish the conditions for the future success of others to exploit and are not a solution to irregular warfare in and of themselves. Given the difficulties inherent in irregular warfare, the proposed solution may seem appealing and cheap now but such preferences are apt strategically to miss the contextual forest for the trees.

The *Summary of the Irregular Warfare Annex to the National Defense Strategy* recognised these facts (see Box 15.1). Using forthright language, its authors attempted to deflate a myth surrounding SOF and irregular warfare. SOF's limited numbers cannot possibly address all irregular threats; doing so requires conventional forces, proxies and other government departments and agencies. While SOF may be cost-effective and responsive, they cannot be decisive. To assist others in grasping this reality, the *Annex*'s authors stated the myth in a simple tautology: 'IW is CT – CT is SOF – SOF is IW (IW, irregular warfare; CT, counterterrorism).'[60] Just as SOF became an 'easy button' for policymakers against global terrorist threats, irregular warfare now appears to be the answer to great power competition. Given the four problems identified in the previous section, another link in the myth can be added, that 'irregular warfare is normal state behaviour'. Restoring the boundaries of irregular warfare by focusing on violence, relinking it theoretically to forms and types and war, will place it in its appropriate strategic context.

BOX 15.1 *IRREGULAR WARFARE* ANNEX CENTRAL IDEA AND ACTION ITEMS

Receiving little attention when it was initially published in late 2020, the short unclassified *Summary of the Irregular Warfare Annex to the National Defense Strategy* outlines clearly a central idea and six prescribed action ideas to ensure it is realised. They reinforce a number of themes in these chapters:

> The Department must institutionalize irregular warfare [IW] as a core competency for both conventional and special operations forces, sustaining the ability to impose costs and create dilemmas for our adversaries across the full spectrum of competition and conflict. To accomplish this vision, the Department will:
>
> - Break the reactive cycle of investment in IW capabilities by institutionalizing lessons learned from past conflicts, and preserving a baseline of IW-focused expertise and capabilities.

BOX 15.1 (cont.)

- Sustain IW as a core competency for the entire Joint Force, not just Special Operations Forces.
- Ensure widespread understanding and sufficient expertise in IW.
- Ensure its approach to IW becomes more agile and cost-informed by developing and employing resource-sustainable IW capabilities.
- Seize the initiative and use IW capabilities proactively to expand the competitive space, defeat our adversaries' competitive strategies, and prepare for an escalation to conflict, if required.
- Organize to foster and sustain unified action in IW with interagency partners as well as key allies and partners.

Summary of the Irregular Warfare Annex to the National Defense Strategy (Washington, DC: US Department of Defense, December 2020), p. 3

Conclusion

To sum up these three chapters, irregular warfare is difficult to understand for a variety of reasons. One reason is the belief that irregular violence takes unchanging, absolute forms. Those conducting irregular warfare ultimately have to be pragmatic about the violence they use in order to survive, and leaders choose the violence that best suits the local conditions at the time. Different forms of violence can be used simultaneously, or in sequence, in an overall national or global campaign. The purpose of the violence can also change over time. Another reason why irregular warfare is difficult to understand has to do with confusing the method of violence employed for its purpose. This creates enough problems on its own, but intuiting the overarching purpose of groups conducting irregular warfare, much less the competing groups and agendas, is not as simple as it may appear. Insurgent and terrorist leaders may not reveal true goals at the time to their followers or in statements. In addition, published and available statements are often contradictory and the message can change based on the intended audience or over time. Finally, some mistake the complexity of irregular wars for changes in the nature of war. The very character of irregular wars can change as enemies adapt to one another, alliances are forged, rifts form between leaders and groups or proxies join in the fight. In other words, irregular warfare is difficult to understand for precisely the reasons that Carl von Clausewitz suggested make all wars difficult: 'The consequences of the nature of War, how ends and means act in it, how in the modifications of reality it deviates sometimes more, sometimes less, from its strict original conception, fluctuating backwards and forwards.' To this, Clausewitz added an important qualifier. No matter which form war takes, or how puzzling it appears to be to the participant and observer, war cannot escape its nature: 'Always remaining under that strict conception [the nature of War] as under a supreme law.'[61] Despite its complexities and changes, these three chapters have argued that many aspects of irregular warfare have remained and will remain remarkably consistent due the nature of all wars that Clausewitz so keenly deduced almost two centuries ago.

RESEARCH QUESTIONS

1. Is irregular warfare primarily a problem of resources, organisation or information? For whom is the specific problem most acute and why?
2. What changes and what stays the same in irregular warfare? What drives change in irregular warfare, and what are its future boundaries?
3. How do those confronting irregular warfare avoid the traps of 'the big idea' and 'mirror-imaging'?
4. How should those conducting or countering irregular warfare address issues of agency?
5. What fits within the box of irregular warfare, with normal state behaviour, and where might they overlap?

FURTHER READING

French, David, *The British Way in Counter-Insurgency, 1945–1967* (Oxford: Oxford University Press, 2011) provides a useful corrective, based on solid research and scholarship, to a number of the myths associated with the British operations during the 'golden age of counterinsurgency'.

Galula, David, *Pacification in Algeria, 1956–1958*, MG-478-1 (Santa Monica, CA: RAND, 2006). Unlike Galula's more famous analysis of what succeeds and fails against insurgents, *Counterinsurgency Warfare*, this reprinted monograph provides a battalion-level view of the practical challenges associated with putting counterinsurgency theory into practice. In particular, Galula offers insights into the moral hazards and other problems small-unit leaders face when they conduct irregular warfare.

Hackett, Jonathan, *Theory of Irregular Warfare* (Jefferson, NC: MacFarland, 2024) is a recent attempt by a former practitioner to bridge the formidable gap between social science theory, and its often impenetrable lexicon, with military practice, resulting in an intriguing theory based on conditions, elements and a dialectic process.

Shapiro, Jacob, *The Terrorist's Dilemma: Managing Violent Covert Organizations* (Princeton, NJ: Princeton University Press, 2013) builds on the author's prior work with the West Point's Combating Terrorism Center into a fascinating theory, based on principal/agent problems, of the very real, very mundane bureaucratic problems facing extra-normative actors.

Simpson, Emile, *War From the Ground Up*, rev. ed. (Oxford: Oxford University Press, 2018) is a thoughtful, insightful but perhaps excessively postmodern attempt by a recent practitioner to place his experiences in a broader theoretical and philosophical context. Simpson stresses the need for pragmatism, as well as consistency and coherence between narrative and action, from the tactical level up to the strategic.

Trinquier, Roger, *Modern Warfare: A French View of Counterinsurgency* (New York, NY: Praeger, 1964) is a concise monograph written after the author's experiences leading partisan forces in Indochina and combating insurgents and terrorists in Algeria. This work remains influential for two reasons: the author's argument that the character of modern warfare demands a pragmatic, modern response and no other work better captures the practitioner's expression that the ends justify the means, regardless of their consequences.

ONLINE RESOURCES

The 125-page ARIS bibliography on irregular warfare (https://tinyurl.com/sjs2p9md) is organised into four sections (foreign internal defence, counter-terrorism, unconventional warfare and counterinsurgency) as well as annotated for the reader's convenience.

The Irregular Warfare Initiative (https://irregularwarfare.org/) – a non-profit organisation and information clearing house partnered with West Point's Modern War Institute and Princeton University's Empirical Studies of Conflict (ESOC) – features expert podcasts, articles and special projects on different facets of irregular warfare, including space, cyber, maritime, Europe, proxies and partners and the grey zone.

The Combating Terrorism Center at West Point website (https://ctc.westpoint.edu/) offers several useful and informative resources, including an online journal (the *CTC Sentinel*) as well as several worthwhile reports on different aspects of regional and global terrorism. Many of the reports are based on captured and translated documents, making its insights exceptionally valuable.

The Joint Special Operations University Press website (https://jsou.edu/Press/Publications) hosts reports published since 2005, some 123 monographs, eleven edited volumes, annual research topic lists, and twenty-five occasional papers related to irregular warfare and special operations.

NOTES

1 The text of the speech is available online through a number of websites, including https://historymatters.gmu.edu/d/5139/ and www.fordham.edu/halsall/mod/1945 vietnam.html.

2 An accessible historical survey and analysis is available in Ronald Spector, *A Continent Erupts: Decolonization, Civil War, and Massacre in Postwar Asia, 1945–1955* (New York, NY: W. W. Norton & Co., 2022).

3 For details see Martin Windrow, *The Last Valley* (London: Weidenfeld and Nicolson, 2004); Bernard Fall, *Hell in a Very Small Place: The Siege of Dien Bien Phu* (Philadelphia, PA: Lippencott, 1967), esp. pp. 415–25.

4 A conclusion reached by Thomas Marks in *Maoist Insurgency since Vietnam* (London: Frank Cass, 1996), pp. 285–9.

5 Menachim Begin, *The Revolt: The Story of the Irgun*, trans. Samuel Katz, 7th ed. (Jerusalem: Steinmatzky, 1977), pp. 212–37, 283–90. For a recent analysis see Bruce Hoffman, *Anonymous Soldiers: The Struggle for Israel, 1917–1947* (New York, NY: Knopf, 2015).

6 Alistair Horne, *A Savage War of Peace: Algeria, 1954–1962* (New York, NY: Penguin, 1985), pp. 245–7.

7 Brian Loveman and Thomas Davies, Jr, *Che Guevara: Guerrilla Warfare*, 3rd ed. (Lanham, MD: SR Books, 2004), pp. 52–5.

8 Regis Debray, *Revolution in the Revolution? Armed Struggle and Political Struggle in Latin America* (London: Pelican, 1968), pp. 22–5.

9 Carlos Marighella, 'Minimanual of the Urban Guerrilla' (unknown publisher, 1969), www.marxists.org/archive/marighella-carlos/1969/06/minimanual-urban-guerrilla/.

10 Carlos Marighella, *For the Liberation of Brazil*, trans. John Butt and Rosemary Sheed (Harmondsworth: Penguin, 1971), pp. 49–50.

11 Loveman and Davies, *Che Guevara*, p. 51.

12 The year 1960 marked the end of the Malayan Emergency while 1973 marked the withdrawal of US forces from Vietnam.

13 Works include Frank Kitson, *Low Intensity Operations: Subversion, Insurgency, Peace-Keeping* (London: Faber and Faber, 1971); Roger Trinquier, *Modern Warfare: A French View of Counterinsurgency* (New York, NY: Praeger, 1964); Napoleon Valeriano and Charles Bohannan, *Counter-Guerrilla Operations: The Philippine Experience* (New York, NY: Praeger, 1962); Edward Lansdale, *In the Midst of Wars: An American's Mission to Southeast Asia* (New York, NY: Harper and Row, 1972).

14 See, for example, the list of participants at a symposium hosted by RAND in 1962. The report from the symposium has been recently reissued. See Stephen Hosmer and Sibylle Crane, *Counterinsurgency: A Symposium, April 16–20, 1962*, R412-1-ARPA (Santa Monica, CA: RAND, 2006), www.rand.org/content/dam/rand/pubs/reports/2006/R412-1.pdf.

15 David Galula, *Counterinsurgency Warfare: Theory and Practice* (New York, NY: Praeger, 1964) and *Pacification in Algeria, 1956–1958*, MG-478-1 (Santa Monica, CA: RAND, 2006).

16 Robert Thompson's most noteworthy published works include *Defeating Communist Insurgency: Experiences in Malaya and Vietnam* (London: Chatto & Windus, 1966) and *Revolutionary Warfare in World Strategy, 1945–1969* (New York, NY: Taplinger, 1970). The subtitle of Thompson's autobiography gives some idea of his sense of self-worth. *Make for the Hills: The Autobiography of the World's Leading Counterinsurgency Expert* (London: Leo Cooper, 1989).

17 The exceptions occurred in but were specific to the conflict in Malaya: 'Despatch 5, Intelligence Summary: Lessons of the Malayan Emergency' and 'The Conduct of Anti-terrorist Operations, Malaya' or 'ATOM'. A summary of the development of these documents and their contents is contained in Tim Jones, *Postwar Counter-Insurgency and the SAS, 1945–1952: A Special Kind of War* (London: Frank Cass, 2001), pp. 134–7.

18 Galula, *Pacification in Algeria*, pp. 64–8.

19 Headquarters, United States Marine Corps, *Small Wars Manual* (Washington, DC: Government Printing Office, 1940),.5https://apps.dtic.mil/sti/tr/pdf/ADA421035.pdf. For details on the development of Marine Corps irregular warfare doctrine, see Keith Bickel, *Mars Learning: The Marine Corps' Development of Small Wars Doctrine, 1915–1940* (Boulder, CO: Westview Press, 2001).

20 HQ, USMC, *Small Wars Manual*, chs. IX, XI–XIV.

21 Gray's assessment of the American way of war is both keenly insightful and disheartening at the same time. Colin Gray, *Irregular Enemies and the Essence of Strategy: Can the American Way of War Adapt?* (Carlisle Barracks, PA: Strategic Studies Institute, 2006), pp. 30–49.

22 Details of these units are recounted in Alan Hoe and Eric Morris, *Re-enter the SAS: The Special Air Service and the Malayan Emergency* (London: Leo Cooper, 1994).

23 For details, see Howard Simpson, *Dien Bien Phu: The Epic Battle America Forgot* (Washington, DC: Brassey's, 1994), pp. 170–1; Roger Trinquier, *Les Maquis d'Indochine: Les missions spéciales du service action* (Paris: Albatros, 1976).

24 A problem discussed in depth in James Kiras, *Special Operations and Strategy: From World War II to the War on Terrorism* (London: Routledge, 2006), pp. 58–82. As for why hostage rescue teams were not used prior to 11 September 2001, see Richard Shultz, Jr., 'Showstoppers: Nine Reasons Why We Never Sent Our Special Operations Forces after al Qaeda before 9/11', *The Weekly Standard*, 26 January 2004, pp. 25–33.

25 Anthony James Joes, for example, suggests a much more comprehensive list of principles and practices in a phased plan in *Resisting Rebellion: The History and Politics of Counterinsurgency* (Lexington, KY: University Press of Kentucky, 2004), pp. 232–55.

26 The Joint Staff, JP 3-26, *Counterterrorism* (Washington, DC: The Joint Staff, 2014), pp. II-1–II-2.

27 See the ARIS website for details, https://publicintelligence.net/usarmy-revolution-insurgency-studies/.

28 For more detail, see Terrence Peterson, *Revolutionary Warfare: How the Algerian War Made Modern Counterinsurgency* (Ithaca, NY: Cornell University Press, 2024).

29 Such works include John Cann, *Counterinsurgency in Africa: The Portuguese Way of War, 1961–1974* (Westport, CT: Greenwood, 1997); Jose Bracamonte and David Spencer, *Strategy and Tactics of the Salvadoran FMLN Guerrillas: Last Battle of the Cold War, Blueprint for Future Conflicts* (Westport, CT: Greenwood, 1995); David Spencer, *From Vietnam to El Salvador: The Saga of the FMLN Sappers and Other Guerrilla Special Forces in Latin America* (Westport, CT: Greenwood, 1996).

30 Peerless works on the subject remain Richard Neustadt and Ernst May, *Thinking in Time: The Uses of History for Decision Makers* (New York, NY: Free Press, 1988); Yuen Foong Khong, *Analogies at War: Korea, Munich, Dien Bien Phu, and the Vietnam Decisions of 1965* (Princeton, NJ: Princeton University Press, 1992).

31 This obvious, but often overlooked point, is the basis of David Kilcullen, 'Counter-Insurgency Redux', *Survival* 48(4) (Winter 2006–7), 111–30.

32 David French, *The British Way in Counter-Insurgency, 1945–1967* (Oxford: Oxford University Press, 2011), p. 251.

33 Stathis Kalyvas, *The Logic of Violence in Civil War* (Cambridge, UK: Cambridge University Press, 2006), pp. 146–72.

34 See Harry Summers, Jr, *On Strategy: The Vietnam War in Context*, 4th ed. (Carlisle Barracks, PA: Strategic Studies Institute, 1983), p. 75.

35 Christopher Blanchard et al. *Armed Conflict in Syria: Overview and U.S. Response*, Report RL33487 (Washington, DC: Congressional Research Service, October 2015).

36 Robert Crews and Amin Tarzi, eds., *The Taliban and the Crisis of Afghanistan* (Cambridge, MA: Harvard University Press, 2018), pp. 28–9; Simpson, *War From the Ground Up*, pp. 77–8.

37 Dale Walton does an exceptional job of outlining the strategic roads open to, but ultimately left unchosen by, US decision-makers during the Vietnam War in *The Myth of Inevitable U.S. Defeat in Vietnam* (London: Frank Cass, 2002), pp. 151–8.

38 For a comprehensive assessment of the policy see James Willbanks, *Abandoning Vietnam: How America Left and South Vietnam Lost its War* (Lawrence, KS: University Press of Kansas, 2004).

39 Summers, *On Strategy*, p. 1.

40 Identified by Stathis Kalyvas, *The Logic of Violence in Civil War* (Cambridge, UK: Cambridge University Press, 2006), pp. 35–51.

41 Carl von Clausewitz, *On War*, ed. and trans. Michael Howard and Peter Paret (Princeton, NJ: Princeton University Press, 1976), p. 89.

42 Scott Atran, *Talking to the Enemy* (New York, NY: Ecco, 2011), pp. 373–401.

43 See, for example, Mao Tse-Tung, *On Guerrilla Warfare*, trans. Samuel B. Griffith (New York, NY: Praeger, 1961), pp. 21, 87; Loveman and Davies, *Che Guevara*, pp. 60–1. It should be noted that Mao does not refer to terrorism specifically but his statements on how to deal with traitors, collaborators and other counter-revolutionary elements, couched with euphemisms, suggest his intent.

44 Slavko Bjelajac, 'Unconventional Warfare: American and Soviet Approaches', *The Annals of the American Academy of Political and Social Science*, 341 (May 1962), 75.

45 Samuel Huntington, 'Guerrilla Warfare in Theory and Policy', in Franklin Mark Osanka, ed., *Modern Guerrilla Warfare: Fighting Communist Movements, 1941–1961* (New York, NY: Free Press, 1962), p. xv.

46 Ofer Fridman, *Russian Hybrid Warfare: Resurgence and Politicisation* (Oxford: Oxford University Press, 2018), pp. 120-123.

47 Jones, *Three Dangerous Men*, pp. 8, 17, 66–7.

48 Valeri Gerasimov, 'The Value of Science Is in the Foresight: New Challenges Demand Rethinking the Forms and Methods of Carrying out Combat Operations,' *Military Review* (January–February 2016), 25, 29.

49 Hamas, 'Our Narrative: Operation Al-Aqsa Flood', Hamas Media Office, 2023, p. 8.

50 al-Suri is perhaps best known for his 1,600-page manual, the title of which is roughly translated as 'The Call to Global Islamic Resistance'. Murad Batal al-Shishani, 'Abu Mus'ab al-Suri and the Third Generation of Salafi-Jihadists', *Terrorism Monitor*, 3(16) (11 August 2005), 1–3.

51 Abu Bakr Naji, *The Management of Savagery: The Most Critical Stage through which the Umma Will Pass*, trans. William Cants (West Point, NY: Combating Terrorism Center, 2006), p. 21, https://tinyurl.com/45rwcnte.

52 Ibid., pp. 23–36.

53 Audrey Kurth Cronin, *Power to the People: How Open Technological Innovation is Arming Tomorrow's Terrorists* (New York, NY: Oxford University Press, 2020), p. 230.

54 Kalyvas, *The Logic of Violence in Civil War*, pp. 379–86.

55 Amos Fox, 'Time, Power, and the Principal-Agent Problems: Why the U.S. Army is Ill-Suited for Proxy Warfare Hotspots', *Military Review* (March–April 2019), 35.

56 Walter Ladwig III, *The Forgotten Front: Patron–Client Relationships in Counterinsurgency* (Cambridge: Cambridge University Press, 2017), pp. 60–2.

57 Catrina Doxsee, Alexander Palmer and Riley McCabe, *Global Terrorism Threat Assessment 2024* (Lanham, MD: Rowman & Littlefield, 2024), pp. 22, 49.

58 For details see Kiras, *Special Operations and Strategy*, pp. 58–82.

59 James Kiras, 'Special Operations and Strategies of Attrition', *Infinity Journal*, 2(4) (Fall 2012), 18–21.

60 *Summary of the Irregular Warfare Annex to the National Defense Strategy* (Washington, DC: US Department of Defense, December 2020), p. 4.

61 Carl von Clausewitz, *On War*, trans. J. J. Graham (London: Routledge and Kegan Paul, 1956), vol. I, p. 45.

PART VI
Weapons of Mass Destruction

C. DALE WALTON

16 Weapons of Mass Destruction: Radiological, Biological and Chemical Weapons

CHAPTER OUTLINE

KEY THEMES

- WMDs are treated as distinct from 'conventional' weapons, and their stockpiling and use are particularly controversial.
- WMDs are divided into four general types: radiological, biological, chemical and nuclear weapons.
- For a well-equipped modern military, the battlefield utility of radiological and current biological weapons (BWs) is modest. Nonetheless, terrorists might find such weapons useful in inciting fear and causing economic and other damage.
- There are effective defences against chemical and biological attack, but these measures impose considerable operational challenges and inefficiencies on a military force employing protective measures.
- There is an existing norm, accepted by the great majority of states, against the stockpiling and use of chemical and biological weapons (CBWs). However, this norm could break down in the future.

Introduction: Defining WMDs

While most of the chapters in this book focus chiefly on how warfare is conducted, and only address weapons within that context, any discussion of 'WMDs' must have a somewhat different focus. This is because these weapons have been placed in a special category, marking the weapons themselves as being extraordinary and making their use uniquely controversial. Indeed, the term 'conventional weapons' is telling, as it implies that such weapons are normal and thus usable, unlike their WMDs counterparts.

Any recounting of the overall WMDs 'story', therefore, should address *why* these weapons have not been used in various situations where they would have promised military advantage. This is critical because, in general, one should expect that a weapon that is likely to yield military advantage will be used in warfare, and that its use will not be limited or prohibited by international agreement. Nor, it should be noted, have these limits only been legal in character. The legality of the use of nuclear weapons under international law is debatable, but a reasonable case could be made that, if used against military targets (particularly ones well removed from substantial civilian populations), their use might be lawful, at minimum for those states recognised as 'legitimate' nuclear possessors by the Non-Proliferation Treaty. However, despite the numerous wars fought by nuclear-armed states, none has used these weapons in combat since 1945. (Possible reasons for this are addressed in the next chapter.)

Even the term 'weapons of mass destruction' is problematic, as it describes a wide variety of weapons and there is no single, authoritative definition of what constitutes WMDs. However, the term generally is used to describe all nuclear, chemical, biological and radiological weapons (see Figure 16.1), contrasting such devices with 'conventional' weapons – which essentially are all weapons that are *not* WMDs. Nonetheless, WMDs vary enormously in their characteristics and destructive capabilities.

The term WMDs itself can be deceptive, as the phrase 'mass destruction' evokes images of devastation over a broad area. Some WMDs, certainly, are capable of inflicting such cataclysmic damage; thermonuclear warheads, for example, can have a lethal radius measured in kilometres, with a large area around ground zero (the point where the warhead is detonated) being utterly destroyed, buildings obliterated and humans and animals instantaneously killed. However, a canister of mustard gas (a chemical weapon) is also considered a WMD. Yet a modest quantity of mustard gas, even if released on a busy city street, possibly would kill no one (although a fair number of people likely would be hospitalised, with some being grievously injured); moreover, there would be no structural damage to the buildings near the point of release.

Similarly, in late 2001, WMDs were used in terrorist attacks in the US; anthrax toxin (a biological weapon) was mailed to several targets, including various media outlets and the Capitol Hill offices of then-Senate Majority Leader Tom Daschle. Five individuals died and numerous others were hospitalised, but no other direct damage was inflicted, although a thorough cleaning of certain locations through which the anthrax had passed was required. Of course, the damage inflicted by these WMDs terrorist attacks was far smaller than that inflicted a short time before in the September 11 terrorist attacks, which involved no WMDs (at least as the term generally is used).

Figure 16.1 US Navy sailors during an exercise in which yellow smoke is used to simulate exposure to chemical, biological or radiological weapons.

This chapter examines, in turn, three major categories of WMDs, in approximate order of their general tactical utility in warfare between states in the current era, beginning with the militarily least-useful WMDs, radiological weapons. Nuclear weapons will be addressed separately and in greater detail in the next chapter, because those uniquely ominous strategic tools have profoundly shaped international politics since the end of the Second World War and can be expected to continue to do so for decades to come.

Radiological, Biological and Chemical Weapons: A Brief Primer

Radiological Weapons

Until relatively recently, radiological weapons were the 'forgotten' WMDs category. However, after the September 11 terrorist attacks in the US, public discussion of radiological weapons increased greatly.

The first thing that one must understand in any discussion of radiological devices is that they are *not* nuclear weapons, even though they do contain radioactive materials. Unfortunately, many press accounts use the phrase 'dirty nukes' to describe radiological weapons – or, even worse, interchangeably to describe both radiological weapons and relatively crude nuclear devices. Actual nuclear weapons use fissile material, such as Uranium-235 or Plutonium, to create a nuclear reaction and resulting explosion.

In a radiological weapon, no nuclear explosion occurs. A radiological device simply is a bomb that uses a conventional explosive to scatter radioactive material. This material is not necessarily fissile material, which is expensive to produce and extremely difficult for terrorists and similar actors to acquire. More likely, the radioactive matter in question would be something such as Cobalt-60, which is used for cancer radiotherapy and other legitimate purposes worldwide. Radioactive isotopes have a wide variety of uses in medicine, food processing and packaging (using radiation to kill bacteria) and other industries.

It should be noted that different radioactive substances have enormously varied levels of radioactivity. Even the slightest exposure to very 'hot' – that is, highly radioactive – material can result in fatal radiation poisoning. On the other hand, exposure to low levels of radiation might not adversely impact an individual's health. Indeed, human beings constantly receive small doses of 'background radiation' from their surroundings – sunlight, radioactive elements naturally present in soil and water, and so forth.

Depending on the materials used and their quantity, exposure to the nuclear material scattered by a radiological bomb would present a variable health risk. Given that stealing (or otherwise surreptitiously obtaining) and handling extremely radioactive materials is very difficult, while less radioactive – though still dangerous – materials are used in medicine and industry throughout the world, often with few safeguards to prevent their theft, it seems most likely that a terrorist group's radiological weapon would present only a limited threat to the population of a targeted city. Exploding a conventional bomb is a far-from-optimal way to scatter radioactive material, and most likely only a small area would be very dangerously contaminated. Depending on the circumstances, the actual number of fatalities directly attributable to a radiological device could be quite small, even zero, although those close to the explosion possibly would face long-term health risks, such as a greatly increased likelihood of developing cancer. However, tiny quantities of radioactive material would be spread over a much wider area, which raises the prospect of public panic and likely long-term economic consequences related to cleaning up contaminated areas.

While radiological weapons might present a danger in the hands of terrorists, they generally are of little use to a traditional military force. During the Cold War, the US and the Soviet Union demonstrated little interest in radiological weapons, as there essentially was no military task that could not be better performed by nuclear weapons.

Today, no state is known to maintain a radiological arsenal. Thus, there have been little international efforts to create and implement treaties banning these weapons; there is not much point in creating legal agreements to prevent the stockpiling of weapons that states have no interest in possessing. However, terrorists might find such weapons very useful for furthering their goal of inflicting political and economic damage on a targeted society. Given their simple design and the very real possibility that a terrorist group would be able to acquire radioactive material suitable for use in such a device, at some point in the future terrorists may mount one or more radiological attacks, most likely, as discussed above, in densely populated urban areas.

Biological Weapons (BWs)

Although BWs as we know them today are a comparatively recent innovation, disease and poison have been used in warfare for millennia. For example, poisoning wells by throwing animal or human corpses into them is a very old (and sometimes devastatingly effective) practice in warfare. Yet, in many cultures such an action is seen as very wicked, and therefore as violating a taboo. There are many reasons why such a taboo may develop – the indiscriminate fashion in which communicable disease strikes both warriors and non-combatants, the fear engendered by epidemics, and so forth. In any case, 'war by disease' has unquestionably been held in disrepute in many times and places, and this certainly influences perceptions of BWs.

The intense fear that communicable disease can create was powerfully demonstrated during the height of the Covid-19 pandemic. Indeed, many people believed, and still believe, the virus to have been a biological weapon; there is, however, a paucity of evidence for this supposition. Although Covid-19 certainly does not appear to be a weaponised virus, its dreadful economic and social impact was obvious. A communicable disease that was weaponised and released might conceivably cause even more damage globally.[1]

The most significant modern attempt to use BWs was undertaken by Japan in the Second World War, and it largely was aimed at the Chinese civilian population. This included the activities of the infamous Unit 731, based in Manchuria. Unit 731 conducted horrific experiments on human test subjects and devised various means to spread disease, such as the release of fleas infected with bubonic plague.

In essence, BWs include a living pathogen of some type – a virus, for example – or a toxin produced by living organisms. Toxins invented by humans generally are treated as chemical weapons (CWs). Weapons including a living pathogen tend to be more difficult to store and deliver than toxins, because measures must be taken to ensure that the pathogen does not die before its intended target is exposed to it. In any event, the robustness of the agent is important; a living virus that will die very quickly when exposed to sunlight, for example, probably would have little utility as a biological weapon.

Another important characteristic of a BW agent is infectivity. Most actors using BWs would want even a very tiny quantity of an agent to be capable of infecting individuals; the smaller the amount of agent required to infect an individual, the higher its infectivity. Closely related to this is pathogenicity, which relates to the percentage of individuals who actually will manifest the symptoms of a disease to which they have been exposed. A BWs user would desire very high pathogenicity, with the overwhelming majority of individuals manifesting disease symptoms after a bioattack. Similarly critical is virulence, essentially the severity of a particular disease. Biological weapon designers generally would desire great virulence, although, in some cases, they might not want the agent to kill exposed individuals, preferring instead to incapacitate them for a time with symptoms severe enough to render them unable to perform military or other duties. (The section on the use of chemical warfare addresses many of the issues that a force defending against either chemical or BWs must confront.)

The incubation period of a particular disease is another key characteristic of a biological weapon. In military operations, a shorter incubation period usually is more desirable, as one would wish to disable or kill enemy troops as quickly as possible. A terrorist group, however, might prefer a longer incubation period, as this could allow a communicable disease to spread far, infecting a great number of people, before public health authorities became aware of the attack (see Box 16.1).

Effective delivery of BWs presents many challenges. Most critically, a biological agent generally must be dispersed over a wide area, if it is to be used effectively. In general, the most effective way to deliver BWs is in the form of an aerosol (for a liquid) or a dust cloud (for a solid). However, under combat conditions, releasing BWs in this fashion could prove extremely difficult, as the most plausible delivery vehicles for the agent would be relatively slow-moving and low-flying aircraft, which are extremely vulnerable in a modern battlespace. In addition, targeted troops might possess protective gear that would guard them against exposure. The civilian residents of a city at peace, on the other hand, would be far more likely to fall victim to such a mode of delivery. In such an environment, ground vehicles also could also be used to disperse an agent, albeit far less efficiently.

As noted previously, not all BWs must be intended to kill; it is possible to develop biological agents intended to cause temporary incapacitation, but not death. For example, tularaemia (commonly called 'rabbit fever') is a highly infectious, but generally not fatal, illness that can be weaponised. However, *all* BWs intended for use against humans are banned by the Biological Weapons Convention (BWC), which was opened for signature in April 1972; non-lethality is irrelevant to legality under the convention. Similarly, the use of non-lethal chemical agents in warfare is banned under the Chemical Weapons Convention (CWC), which was opened for signature in January 1993. This creates some intriguing ethical questions: one might ask whether it is reasonable that chemical and biological weapons (CBWs), having temporary incapacitating but generally non-fatal effects, are banned. After all, use of such agents in a military operation could decrease the number of deaths and debilitating wounds suffered by combatants, which generally would be considered to be ethically desirable.

In any case, though, most offensive BWs research over the years has been aimed at the development of lethal agents. Indeed, high lethality generally is considered a critical characteristic of BWs. It is, however, very easy to exaggerate the potential effectiveness of these weapons. This is because tiny quantities of most such substances are fatal. Thus, one sometimes sees statistics indicating that a small quantity of a given BW could kill the entire population of the earth. While, in a literal sense, such a statement might be true, such a calculation assumes the efficient delivery of that agent to every person on earth – a practical impossibility, of course.

BOX 16.1 BWS AND TERRORISM

Preparation for the possibility of BWs terrorism presents states with numerous challenges. Where the next bioterrorist attack will occur and which agent will be used obviously remains unknown. Nevertheless, if governments are to be prepared properly for biological terrorism, they must decide long before an attack how much money and effort they will devote to defensive measures and how they are going to spend those resources (see Figure 16.2). Choices concerning public health infrastructure and the stockpiling of vaccines, which diseases will be vaccinated against universally and many other decisions are made in the hope that they will prove to be adequate if a bioterrorist attack did occur.

When assessing the threat of a BW attack by terrorists, one should consider their level of sophistication and financial resources, the agents that might be used, how those agents might be dispersed, what the incubation time and level of pathogenicity and lethality are for the disease caused by the agent and whether effective treatments exist for that disease. Potentially most important of all is whether the biological weapon in question causes a communicable disease and what the characteristics of that disease are, as an uncontrolled outbreak of a very dangerous communicable disease could have worldwide effects and cause many millions of deaths.

Figure 16.2 Italian firefighters participating in a WMDs exercise. They are standing near a container suspected of carrying WMDs.

Conversely, one should not forget that BWs are indiscriminate. When they are actually used in military operations, users must be careful to ensure that their own troops are not placed in danger. Depending on the weapon, this may require injections of a protective vaccine, and some vaccines, such as the anthrax and smallpox vaccines, have a non-negligible rate of serious side effects. Of course, if there is no vaccine or other effective method to create immunity for a given infectious disease, most potential BWs users – apocalyptically minded terrorists being a critical exception – would regard that disease as unsuitable for use in biological warfare.

BWs and States

BWs do have potential military utility in some circumstances, but no states currently acknowledge possession of them. However, it is near-certain that several countries do possess a biological arsenal – although precisely *which* states have BWs remains a matter of contention.

The aforementioned problems with effective dispersion of BWs, protection of one's own troops and other issues go far in explaining why BWs have not played a major role on the modern battlefield. Thus, when President Richard Nixon decided in 1969 unilaterally to renounce US stockpiling and use of BWs, his declaration created relatively little controversy: most Western observers of military affairs agreed that there were no critical roles in which BWs would be superior to other weapons, particularly nuclear ones, and therefore that there was little need to maintain a biological arsenal.

Under international pressure because of the US abandonment of BWs, the Soviet Union also announced that it would destroy its biological stockpile, and both countries eventually acceded to the BWC. The BWC bars states from researching or stockpiling BWs for offensive purposes. However, it does not forbid research focused on improving defences against BWs, and thus states may create very small quantities of biological agents for research purposes. Some critics, however, contend that this provision allows states to skirt the BWC's ban on offensive research, as the line between offensive and defensive research can be hazy, given that even defensive research may yield knowledge useful to the development of BWs (see Box 16.2). Various states – including North Korea, Iran and Syria – are considered likely to have a research programme and/or a BWs arsenal, and even such major powers as China and, as noted, Russia (see Box 16.3) may possess these weapons. At present, given the difficulties involved and the international opprobrium that would accompany their use, it would seem unlikely that a major power will soon use BWs in warfare. However, future use by less powerful states, either against an outside enemy or in an effort to commit genocide against some segment of its own population, is much more plausible.

Chemical Weapons (CWs)

CWs are the only form of WMDs to be used with some regularity in warfare during the twentieth century. Although most of that century's wars saw no use of CWs,

BOX 16.2 'SUPER-BWS'?

Unfortunately, the world may be on the cusp of a technological revolution that would exponentially increase the military utility and lethality of BWs. The discussion in this chapter mainly addresses 'known' BWs – those that have been or almost surely could be created using current technology. However, in recent years there has been an explosion of knowledge in the life sciences. Of particular importance to the current discussion is the rapidly advancing field of genetics and the related development of biotechnology.

Increasing knowledge about the human body and how it counters disease should bring about great advances in medicine in coming years, but, unfortunately, the ongoing biotechnological revolution also creates a very real possibility that BWs far more dangerous than those fielded today may be created. For example, it may be possible to create weapons that cause new and extraordinarily lethal diseases against which there is no current medical defence; there has even been speculation concerning the possible creation of 'ethnic bioweapons' tailored to attack individuals of a particular ancestry. Indeed, it eventually might be possible even to craft a biological agent intended to harm only a specific individual.[1]

Although such grim possibilities are purely speculative at this point, they should be kept in mind when considering the possible future of BWs. If it clearly became feasible to develop 'super-BWs', powerful states might re-examine their decision to dismantle their biological arsenals. Also, of course, if such weapons ever should come into the possession of bioterrorists, either provided by a state sponsor or developed by the terrorists themselves, the results could be catastrophic.

BOX 16.3 CHEATING ON ARMS CONTROL: THE SOVIET UNION AND THE BIOLOGICAL WEAPONS CONVENTION (BWC)

Although the Soviet Union was one of the original signatories to the BWC, Moscow proceeded to break that agreement in spectacular fashion, running a biowarfare industry which produced enormous quantities of BWs. Nevertheless, for decades Moscow was fairly successful in keeping these efforts secret, though many outsiders suspected that it was maintaining a BWs arsenal, especially after a strange incident in the town of Sverdlovsk, where numerous residents died of anthrax poisoning. The Soviets claimed that the epidemic was caused by anthrax-contaminated bone meal in livestock feed and the consumption of meat from infected animals. However, after the fall of the Soviet Union it was confirmed that the deaths were, in fact, the result of an accidental discharge of weaponised anthrax. It was not until Kenneth Alibek (Kanatjan Alibekov), a major figure in the Soviet BW programme, moved to the United States in 1992 and openly

BOX 16.3 (cont.)

discussed it that substantial evidence of its size became available publicly. To this day, however, there are significant questions about the programme; particularly troubling is the fact that the Soviet BWs programme was clearly very advanced – almost certainly the most sophisticated in the world – and although Moscow claims to have fully disclosed the details of its programme and to have ceased all research into offensive BWs, some critics doubt this.

The Hague Convention of 1899 banned 'the use of projectiles the object of which is the diffusion of asphyxiating or deleterious gases'.[2] However, less than two decades later, in 1915, Germany – seeking a military 'edge' that would allow it to break the tactical deadlock on the Western Front – began using chlorine gas; this quickly was followed by the use of CWs by other belligerents. In total, probably less than 100,000 troops, most of them Russian (poison gas fatalities on the Western Front actually were relatively small), were killed by CWs during the war. However, a much greater number of soldiers – probably over 1 million – were wounded by CWs. Interestingly, the survivors of chemical attack included a then-obscure corporal, Adolf Hitler, who was blinded temporarily by mustard gas in 1918.

these weapons were employed in the First World War, as well as some subsequent conflicts.

The horrible effects of the CWs used in the First World War – including death by asphyxiation and, for many survivors, terrible burns, long-term severe lung damage and other debilitating problems – resulted in deep revulsion for CWs. However, this did not prevent CWs use between the World Wars. Notably, during its conquest of Abyssinia (modern Ethiopia) in the mid 1930s, the Italian military used considerable quantities of CWs against its opponents, including by aerial bombardment.

Techniques for delivery of CWs are generally similar to those used for BWs. During the First World War, these included artillery shells and CWs projectors (essentially mortars that fired a canister filled with a chemical agent); chemical artillery shells continue to be stockpiled by some countries. Chemical warheads also can be placed on cruise and ballistic missiles. Effective dissemination of a chemical agent using such techniques does, however, present major challenges. When explosives are used to aerosolise and disperse a liquid chemical agent, they tend to destroy much of the agent; moreover, some agents are flammable and may catch fire, destroying them. For safety and other reasons, many devices for the delivery of CWs are 'binary'. Rather than the agent itself, a binary device – such as an artillery shell or bomb – will contain two or more chemical precursors, which are separated from each other while the weapon is in storage. After the munition is fired, the precursors mix together, creating the deadly chemical agent.

Difficulties in effective dispersion are one of the key disadvantages of both BWs and CWs. Regardless of how CBWs are delivered, climatic factors, particularly wind direction and speed, are critical to their effective diffusion. Indeed, on many occasions during the First World War, troops were exposed to chemical agents dispersed by their own side when the wind direction changed, blowing the CWs back to their lines.

During the Second World War, both Axis and Allied forces maintained CWs stockpiles and declared their willingness to retaliate in kind against enemy use of such weapons. In the European theatre both sides refrained from military first-use of CWs, although Germany did seriously consider their use against Allied troops. (There was, however, substantial use of CWs by Japan in China.) While the Third Reich did not use CWs against Allied troops, however, it did practise another, even more repellent, form of chemical warfare: using CWs to facilitate genocide.

Saddam Hussein's Iraq repeatedly used CWs as a terror weapon against civilian populations. In the Iran–Iraq War of 1980–1988, Iraq launched missiles armed with CWs against Iranian cities; Iran is alleged to have retaliated with its own chemical attacks on Iraqi forces. In the latter part of that conflict, Iraq also employed CWs against Iraqi Kurdish civilians as part of a genocidal campaign against them.

During the Cold War, the US and the Soviet Union amassed large CWs stockpiles, and both superpowers were prepared to use them during a Third World War, although CWs were decidedly less important in military planning than were nuclear weapons. As with BWs, there were serious questions concerning how great the military utility of these weapons would be, especially given the unpredictability of their dispersion and, again like BWs, there were few military missions for CWs that would not have been better performed by nuclear weapons.

Nevertheless, CWs may be judged as having real potential military utility under the right circumstances.[3] While they also have important shortcomings, against a poorly prepared opponent modern CWs may be devastating, combining high lethality with rapidity of action. This in practice means that some types of CWs are likely to be far more useful on a battlefield than are currently available BWs. There are five main classes of chemical weapon: choking (or pulmonary), blood, blister, nerve and non-lethal agents.

The first modern chemical weapon used in combat, chlorine, was a choking agent, as was phosgene, which caused far more fatalities in the First World War than did any other chemical weapon. Choking agents cause damage to the lungs, and exposure to phosgene may result in pulmonary oedema – a build-up of fluid in the lungs that can be fatal. In general, the choking agents are regarded as obsolescent, but nonetheless have been used against both civilians and poorly equipped fighters in recent years. Most notably, chlorine gas has been used extensively in the Syrian Civil War by pro-government troops. Also, as chlorine has many legitimate uses (such as in sewage treatment), it is a readily available chemical that has been used in attacks by both Syrian and Iraqi insurgents.

Blood agents prevent the body from utilising oxygen properly, causing suffocation. (The term 'blood agent' is somewhat confusing, as the agent does not actually poison the blood; rather, it is distributed throughout the body by the blood.) Hydrogen cyanide and cyanogen chloride (generally referred to as CK) initially were used on the battlefield in the First World War. During the Holocaust, hydrogen cyanide, commonly known by the German trade name Zyklon B, was used in the mass murder of prisoners at Auschwitz and other camps. Like the choking agents, blood agents generally are considered obsolescent CWs, but present a danger to civilians and unprepared military forces.

Blister agents, as the name implies, have gruesome effects on human skin, with exposure causing blistering and burns; if inhaled, they damage the respiratory system. Of the blister agents, mustard is by far the most well known, and, although it caused relatively few fatalities in the First World War, it was perhaps the most feared chemical weapon because of the excruciatingly painful wounds that it inflicted on victims. During the 1930s and 1940s, Japan made extensive use of choking and blister agents in China. Several countries are likely to have CWs arsenals that include blister agents.

Nerve agents currently are the most advanced CWs known to exist. These weapons attack the human nervous system, causing rapid death unless the victim receives an antidote such as atropine. Older classes of nerve agent include the G- and V-series. The first of the G-series agents GA (more commonly referred to as tabun) was developed by German scientists in 1936, and the last of them, GF (cyclosarin), was initially synthesised in 1949. The even more advanced V-series agents were invented somewhat later, with the first and best-known of them, VX, being developed by the UK in 1952.

Later still, the Soviet Union secretly developed the even more sophisticated *Novichok* nerve agents in the 1980s and early 1990s; the existence of these weapons was not publicly known until 1992, when the programme was exposed in the Russian media. Notably, Russia had not previously informed the US of the existence of the *Novichok* agents despite the existence of a 1989 agreement between the two countries, known as the Wyoming Memorandum of Understanding (MOU), to share information of their respective CWs programmes. Moreover, a Russian scientist who 'blew the whistle' on the programme subsequently was prosecuted for releasing state secrets, although charges against him eventually were dropped.

Because of their relatively late development, nerve agents have been used less frequently than have other lethal CWs. However, they were used extensively by Iraq during the Iran–Iraq War, as well as against Iraqi Kurds. More recently, sarin gas has been used several times during the Syrian Civil War, most notably in an attack near Damascus, at Ghouta in 2013. While the Syrian government disputed responsibility, the US and the EU, amongst others, contended that the attack was undertaken by pro-government forces.

Military Use of CWs

While they present some of the same difficulties as BWs, such as ensuring that the agent is dispersed properly and protecting one's own troops from exposure, most CWs quickly impact the health, and thus military effectiveness, of exposed individuals; an agent such as sarin can kill within minutes of exposure. Protecting troops against CWs may require that they wear bulky and uncomfortable protective gear, which impedes their capability to conduct military operations effectively. The same is true of operating in areas where BWs may be, or have been, used (an environment heavily contaminated with the radioactive by-products of nuclear weapons use presents even greater challenges). Chemical/biological protective gear is bulky, uncomfortable – particularly in warm climates and/or when a mask is worn – and makes it more difficult for troops to perform tasks ranging from fighting to equipment maintenance. However, when such gear is used properly, it is highly effective in protecting individuals from exposure to dangerous agents.

Given the challenges relating to the use of protective gear, one of the most important effects of CBWs is the inconvenience created by these arms. Such weapons create a hostile physical environment that presents special operational problems. Thus, even if CBWs have little direct effect in terms of casualties, a relatively weak state facing a much stronger opponent may be tempted to use these weapons. Indeed, simply by possessing (or being presumed to possess) such weapons, a state complicates its enemy's operational and tactical planning. For instance, in both the Persian Gulf War of 1991 and the 2003 invasion of Iraq, the US and its allies took careful measures to protect troops from possible CBWs exposure. It is notable that one of the great difficulties for commanders confronting possible use of CBWs is determining how much emphasis should be placed on defensive preparations, as time and energy devoted to possible CBWs attack could be spent on other important tasks.

Advanced militaries spend considerable resources and valuable training time on chemical (and biological) defence, and much can be done to hamper the lethality of chemical warfare. For example, detection and early-warning devices, as well as masks, suits and other protective gear, can be made available to units, and training time devoted to proper use of such equipment; vehicles can be outfitted with air filtration systems that protect occupants from contaminated air; a naval vessel can be constructed so that there is a capacity to 'pre-wet' the ship so as to prevent agents from settling, while the ship's core is a 'citadel' with filtered air (see Figure 16.3). Additionally, it should also be noted that the sort of defences that protect military forces from chemical and biological exposure also are useful in guarding against nuclear contamination. Indeed, one of the few things that the various WMDs share in common is that they all present unusual and difficult contamination problems that require substantial forethought and planning if they are to be addressed successfully.

As the above indicates, even though CWs have considerable potential military utility, battlefield defence against such weapons is quite feasible. Like BWs, CWs potentially are most effective not against well-equipped advanced military forces, but as a terror weapon aimed at civilian populations. However, the fact that CWs do not spread a communicable disease is an important one. While, hypothetically, an epidemic resulting from the use of certain BWs could cause hundreds of millions of deaths, only individuals directly exposed to CWs are at risk. With that said, however, if a large quantity of a highly lethal agent was dispersed in a suitable

Figure 16.3 The guided-missile destroyer USS *Boxer* performs a test of the ship's countermeasure water wash-down system, which coats the ship with water to prevent chemical, biological or radioactive materials from settling.

fashion, it could inflict tens of thousands of fatalities in a compact and densely populated area.

Why States Acquire and Retain CBWs Today

As noted above, the possession, much less the use, of CBWs is banned outright by the CWC and BWC Conventions, treaties that a strong majority of countries have signed and ratified. About a dozen states currently are not party to the BWC and fewer still are not party to the CWC. However, as noted above, not all parties to these conventions obey their treaty obligations – and this group may include one or more of the great powers.

Why, one might ask, are CBWs regarded as different and their use, presumably, somehow less ethical than purportedly conventional weapons, even though, in total, the weapons lumped in the latter category have killed an enormously greater number of human beings? Indeed, the conventional arsenals of many of the more militarily sophisticated states now include devastating devices such as high-yield thermobaric weapons and the (non-thermobaric) US GBU-43, nicknamed the 'Mother of All Bombs', a behemoth filled with 8,500 kilograms of high explosive. Such a weapon would seem to merit placement in the WMDs category far more than, for instance, chlorine gas. Yet, the most powerful states have made it clear that they do not intend to reclassify such weapons, much less remove them from their arsenals.

Despite the disapproving attitude towards CBWs, some countries see them as offering advantages significant enough to justify spending significant sums obtaining and maintaining a stockpile of such armaments. A particularly notable example is provided by Iraq. As part of the armistice agreement ending the 1991 Gulf War, Iraq agreed to surrender its CBWs arsenal (as well as end its effort to obtain nuclear weapons) and submit to UN inspections that would ensure that its WMDs stockpile was destroyed and its capability to make further weapons dismantled. For more than a decade thereafter, an elaborate game ensued in which Iraq would sometimes appear to cooperate partially with inspectors but would also seek to thwart their efforts and stymie their investigations. Many governments, intelligence agencies and other observers worldwide believed that Iraq was secretly maintaining a CBWs arsenal; seizing Saddam Hussein's supposed arsenal of WMDs was a major motive for the 2003 American-led invasion.

Iraq, however, had surrendered the overwhelming majority of its CBWs arsenal in the months following the end of the 1991 conflict and never rebuilt a significant production capability. Saddam Hussein's chief motive apparently was fear of Iran and belief that a CBWs arsenal was critical to discouraging Iranian military aggression against an Iraq weakened by UN sanctions remaining in place after the 1991 Persian Gulf War.[4] The Iraqi leader hoped to 'bluff' potential enemies into believing in a non-existent CBWs arsenal while not so flagrantly violating the

1991 ceasefire that the UN Security Council (UNSC), or a US-organised coalition acting without UNSC authorisation, would invade Iraq. Eventually, of course, the Iraqi dictator lost his dangerous wager, but the fact that it was made is indicative of how important a leader might believe a CBWs arsenal to be.

The Iraqi example highlights a characteristic notable in regard to all WMDs (and, for that matter, conventional weapons): their psychological impact on leaders and populations. States desire particular weapons for their direct military potential (i.e., what they would do on the battlefield) but also for what they indirectly promise, which can include many factors, including intangible ones, such as prestige and a weapon's value as a 'statement' of national greatness.

These factors may be of greatly varying importance depending on the weapon under consideration, and every government will weigh them according to its own unique calculus. In the case of CBWs, unlike nuclear weapons, 'prestige value' presently is quite low. Repudiated formally by the great powers, today CBWs mainly are seen as the weapons of relatively weak actors. CBWs – unlike aircraft carriers and nuclear warheads – are distinctly 'unfashionable'. They do, however, evoke fear very effectively, and a sizeable CBWs arsenal potentially can be acquired for less than the cost of a single fifth-generation fighter aircraft.

Clearly, a simple distinction between 'good' and 'bad' weapons is insufficiently nuanced to explain fully why countries acquire, or do not acquire, CBWs. Given the broad assortment of pressures and threats present in the international security environment, as well as the variety of strategic cultures worldwide, it is hardly surprising that diverse states demonstrate a broad range of attitudes concerning CBWs acquisition, retention and use.

Conclusion: CBWs in the Present and Future

It is difficult to realistically ascertain how great the threat presented by BWs is to global security. Today, interest in BWs *appears* to be minimal in most of the world's major and medium powers, but one or more states may maintain secret research programmes that, potentially, will bear deadly fruit – a new generation of BWs that overcomes the limitations of the agents of previous decades. Given the opacity of several technologically sophisticated powers, China and Russia in particular, it is a possibility that cannot be dismissed summarily.

States that are currently both strongly suspected of fielding BWs and possessed of an apparent willingness to use them are few. Merely by maintaining their arsenals they risk the censure of the international community – particularly since most such states have acceded to the BWC. In any case, BWs clearly are a poor substitute on the battlefield for nuclear or even, in most cases, CWs. BWs do, however, appear far more potentially threatening as a terrorist tool against civilians. However, the number of fatalities that would occur as a result of a major bioterror attack would vary by several orders of magnitude, depending on variables including the biological agent used, how the terrorists attempted to spread the agent and how successful they were in doing so, the level of preparedness of public health officials, and so forth.

While the danger presented by BWs is largely speculative, the fact that CWs remain 'on the battlefield' in some conflicts has been established clearly in recent years. Thus far, the use of CWs has been relatively limited, and confined to international outlaws and semi-outlaws: rogue regimes, as well as terrorists and insurgents who either are in dire straits or actually desire to shock global opinion. There appears to be little prospect that CWs will be openly possessed and used by 'respectable' states in the medium-term future. However, it is conceivable that the norm against the use of CWs in combat could break down altogether, most likely as a result of either of two general circumstances.

First, a great power actor might be presented with an opportunity or danger so large as to justify, in the minds of its policymakers, risking loud and prolonged international outrage. For example, if Beijing were ever to conclude that Taiwan *must* be reabsorbed militarily within a specific time frame, the use of CWs against Taiwanese forces might appear to be little more than a 'diplomatic footnote'. After all, the risks, including war with the US, would be grave even if China avoided CWs use, and the economic and political consequences would be serious even if China won. If CWs appeared to offer a significant prospect of speeding the consolidation of control over the island before US forces arrived in large numbers, the temptation to use them might prove irresistible to Beijing. Secondly, the (presumably secret) development of a new generation of CWs whose characteristics radically enhanced their utility on the battlefield might convince the state possessing such weapons to revise its doctrine and 'normalise' the powerful new weapons.[5] Of course, the combination of both of these conditions would maximise the likelihood of a breakdown in the anti-CWs norm.

RESEARCH QUESTIONS

1. How might terrorists use radiological weapons, BWs and/or CWs as a tool to obtain their political objectives?
2. How great a threat do radiological weapons, BWs and CWs present to the global security environment? How does this threat compare to that presented by nuclear weapons?
3. Did the rather minimal international response to the use of CWs in the Syrian Civil War significantly weaken the international norm against the use of such arms?
4. How likely is it that the norm prohibiting CBWs possession will survive even if future technological developments make these weapons more useful militarily to major states?
5. On balance, should we regard the efforts to prevent the stockpiling and proliferation of CWs as essentially successful? Why or why not?

FURTHER READING

Barenblatt, Daniel, *A Plague upon Humanity: The Secret Genocide of Axis Japan's Germ Warfare Operation* (New York, NY: Harper, 2004). A detailed history of the Japan's BWs research programme of the 1930s and 1940s, and the extensive use of such weapons against civilians by its military.

Koblentz, Gregory D., *Living Weapons: Biological Warfare and International Security* (Ithaca, NY: Cornell University Press, 2011). Discusses the dangers posed by BWs in the context of the global security environment.

Kortepeter, *Inside the Hot Zone: A Soldier on the Front Lines of Biological Warfare* (Washington, DC: Potomac Books, 2020). An autobiographical account by a retired US military officer that presents a detailed description of research into defences against biological warfare.

Leitenberg, Milton and Raymond A. Zilinskas, *The Soviet Biological Weapons Program: A History* (Cambridge, MA: Harvard University Press, 2012). A carefully researched academic history of the Soviet BWs programme that provides a summary of publicly available knowledge about that effort.

Smith III, Frank L., *American Biodefense: How Dangerous Ideas about Biological Weapons Shape National Security* (Ithaca, NY: Cornell University Press, 2014). An informed critique of the US Department of Defense's attitude and policy regarding BWs defence.

Spiers, Edward M., *Agents of War: A History of Chemical and Biological Weapons*, 2nd expanded ed. (London: Reaktion Books, 2021). An overview of the history and dangers presented by CBWs.

Tu, Anthony, *Chemical and Biological Weapons and Terrorism* (Boca Raton, FL: CRC Press, 2017). A detailed guide to the threats presented by CBWs by a leading expert on the 1995 chemical attack on the Tokyo subway.

Tucker, Jonathan, *War of Nerves: Chemical Warfare from World War I to Al-Qaeda* (New York, NY: Pantheon, 2006). A history of the development and use of CWs, with a particular focus on nerve agents.

Zubay, Geoffrey, *Agents of Bioterrorism: Pathogens and their Weaponization* (New York, NY: Columbia University Press, 2012). A detailed examination of thirteen potential BWs agents t assesses the dangers that each would pose if used in a terrorist attack.

ONLINE RESOURCES

Organisation for the Prohibition of Chemical Weapons (OPCW) (www.opcw.org). The website for the OPCW, the implementing body for the CWC, contains information about that treaty, as well as on practical steps for control of chemical agents.

United Nations Office for Disarmament Affairs (UNODA) (https://disarmament.unoda.org/en). The website contains information of UN counterproliferation activities regarding WMDs of all types.

Center for Arms Control and Non-Proliferation (https://armscontrolcenter.org). An American 'think-tank' that studies proliferation and counterproliferation of WMDs, with a particular emphasis on US government policymaking.

James Martin Center for Nonproliferation Studies (https://nonproliferation.org/). Combating the spread of WMDs with training and analysis. The website of this organisation, which is part of the Monterey Institute of International Studies, includes a variety of videos and other resources related to WMDs of all kinds.

The EU Non-Proliferation Consortium (www.nonproliferation.eu). This organisation includes many think-tanks located in a variety of countries, and its website contains a variety of resources organised by topic.

Nuclear Threat Initiative – NTI Education Tutorials (https://www.nti.org/). This website includes brief tutorials of a variety of WMD-related topics.

NOTES

1 On US preparations for both future pandemics and biological attacks, see *National Biodefense Strategy and Implementation Plan: For Countering Biological Threats, Enhancing Pandemic Preparedness, and Achieving Global Health Security*, October 2022, https://tinyurl.com/mwhau5dt.

2 *Hague IV, Declaration II: Declaration on the Use of Projectiles the Object of Which is the Diffusion of Asphyxiating or Deleterious Gases, 29 July 1899*, accessed from the University of Minnesota Human Rights, https://hrlibrary.umn.edu/.

3 On the US military's counter-CBWs capabilities, see Department of Defense Chemical and Biological Defense Program, *Department of Defense Chemical and Biological Defense Annual Report 2020*, March 2020, https://tinyurl.com/2mttmtac.

4 Glenn Kessler, 'Saddam Hussein Said WMD Talk Helped Him Look Strong to Iran', *Washington Post* online ed., 2 July 2009.

5 On possible future developments in CWs, including the 'merging' of biological and chemical warfare technologies, see Jonathan B. Tucker, 'The Future of Chemical Weapons', *The New Atlantis*, 26 (Fall 2009/Winter 2010), 3–29, www.thenewatlantis.com/wp-content/uploads/legacy-pdfs/20100316_TNA26Tucker.pdf.

17 Weapons of Mass Destruction: Nuclear Weapons

CHAPTER OUTLINE

KEY THEMES

- There are two distinct types of nuclear proliferation. When the number of states possessing nuclear weapons increases, this constitutes horizontal weapons proliferation. An increase in the number of nuclear weapons is vertical proliferation.
- Capability, credibility, severity and surety are vital factors in determining the success or failure of a deterrence threat.
- Given the increasing number of states possessing nuclear weapons and the diversity of their strategic cultures, the 'deterrence lessons' of the Cold War may be of limited applicability in the future.
- Every leader is unique, and individual personalities inherently play a role in the making of nuclear decisions.
- It is not probable that terrorists will obtain one or more nuclear weapon in the medium-term future, but the likelihood of such an outcome is not negligible.

Introduction: The 'Nuclear Club'

The Nuclear Non-Proliferation Treaty (NPT) restricts legal possession of nuclear weapons to just five states – China, Britain, France, Russia and the US. All other signatories to the NPT legally renounce the right to build or possess nuclear weapons. However, some of these signatories, such as Iran, may be attempting to break the Treaty's restrictions. Moreover, three countries that never signed the NPT are known to possess nuclear weapons (India, Pakistan and Israel), while North Korea – which has conducted several nuclear tests and possesses a nuclear arsenal – is a former party to the Treaty but withdrew from it in 2003. Indeed, even though the number of states that actually possess these weapons is small, the three most populous states in the world all have them; altogether the nuclear powers are home to billions of people – so, at least in this respect, nuclear possession is not unusual.

Chemical, biological, radiological and nuclear weapons all are viewed negatively, but perceptions of the last of these, as the previous chapter noted, are decidedly mixed. Although many voices worldwide denounce the very possession of nuclear weapons as being immoral, it is also clear that enormous numbers of people – both leaders and regular citizens – associate these devices with international standing and great-power status. Indeed, notwithstanding their diplomatic and economic repercussions, the 1998 nuclear tests by India and Pakistan were popular domestically in both countries. Millions of Indians and Pakistanis saw their country's successful nuclear tests as proof of their technological prowess and status on the world stage – in short, as a source of national pride.

Clearly, great numbers of people worldwide regard nuclear weapons differently from other WMDs. While there is a general view that nuclear devices are morally problematic – and it is obvious that the effects of their use can be horrifying – they are far from universally despised. Rather, this 'absolute weapon', as Bernard Brodie famously dubbed the atomic bomb,[1] is feared and hated for its killing power but, at the same time, seen as granting a special status in the international community. (If nuclear weapons solely brought disrepute upon a state, it is difficult to see why Britain and France, neither of which is likely in the foreseeable future to face critical security threats of the sort that can be addressed by nuclear possession, and both of which, in any case, are members of NATO and therefore protected by the American 'nuclear umbrella', do not surrender their small and expensive national arsenals.) The nuclear club is an exclusive one, even if it is growing.

Nuclear Weapons

The first nuclear devices developed were the type known as fission weapons – the ultimate products of the secret US Manhattan Project undertaken during the Second World War. The first, and thus far only, nuclear weapons used in warfare were deployed on 6 and 9 August 1945, against, respectively, the Japanese cities of Hiroshima and Nagasaki.

The period of American nuclear monopoly was brief. Even before the first nuclear test, Soviet intelligence had already infiltrated the highly secret US nuclear development programme and was using stolen technical data to advance the Soviets' own secret nuclear effort. In August 1949, the Soviets exploded their own atomic device.

A few years later, the next major development in nuclear weapons technology occurred when the US conducted the first test of a thermonuclear weapon, in October 1952. Thermonuclear weapons use an initial fission explosion to create the conditions for nuclear fusion. Thus, thermonuclear weapons sometimes are called fusion or, more accurately, fission–fusion devices; these weapons often are referred to as 'hydrogen bombs' or 'H-bombs'.

Nuclear weapons' yield is measured in kilotons and megatons. A kiloton is equal to the explosive force of 1,000 tons of TNT; a megaton is the equivalent of 1 million tons of TNT. Nuclear weapons have been created with an enormous range of yields. The largest nuclear device ever tested (nicknamed the 'Tsar Bomba' in the West) was a Soviet warhead with a yield of at least 50 megatons. By contrast, some tactical nuclear weapons have a yield measured as a fraction of a kiloton.

It is important to understand that nuclear weapons can vary enormously not only in yield but also in many other essential characteristics. Weapons designers are tasked with creating warheads that can accomplish particular military objectives, and those objectives, in turn, are shaped by the political goals of a state and its military doctrine. In general, nuclear devices have become progressively smaller in yield over the decades as accuracy has improved. This, of course, is because when a warhead lands on, or very close to, a target, that target is exposed to much more explosive force than when the warhead misses by a considerable distance.

Nuclear weapons often are divided into two major categories: tactical nuclear weapons (TNWs) and strategic nuclear weapons. The distinction between the two can be fuzzy but, in general, it would be accurate to say that TNWs are delivered at shorter ranges and are intended for battlefield use. Possible means of delivery for TNWs include tactical aircraft (such as fighter aeroplanes), artillery shells, short-range missiles, cruise missiles and so forth. The US and the Soviet Union even developed nuclear torpedoes and depth charges for use in naval warfare.

Strategic nuclear warheads generally have a larger yield and are delivered at long range, using intercontinental ballistic missiles (ICBMs), submarine-launched ballistic missiles (SLBMs) or heavy bombers. These three means of delivery together constitute the classic Cold War triad. The basic logic underlying the triad is that it is desirable for a nuclear state to possess multiple methods of delivering its strategic nuclear warheads, as this helps to ensure that it may do so reliably, particularly if it is the victim of a devastating first strike inflicted by a nuclear-armed enemy. Each of the three 'legs' of the Cold War triad was developed because it possessed specific advantages.

Bombers were the first means used for nuclear delivery. Originally, bombers carried simple, unguided (and thus relatively inaccurate) gravity bombs, such as those dropped on Hiroshima and Nagasaki, but nuclear-armed bombers now can carry advanced weapons systems, such as cruise missiles, with highly accurate modern guidance systems. Importantly, bombers may be recalled before their

Figure 17.1 The YB-52, a prototype version of the B-52 bomber, lands on a dry lake at Edwards Air Base, 1953. The B-52 is still used today by the US Air Force to carry nuclear weapons.

mission is completed. Thus, for example, if a state believes that a nuclear attack may be imminent and sends bombers out with the intent of delivering a retaliatory strike, its leaders may cancel the bombing mission if they soon thereafter discover that the attack will not, in fact, occur. Using a ballistic missile is more akin to firing a pistol: once the trigger is pulled, the bullet cannot be recalled (see Figure 17.1).

The great advantage of SLBMs is the difficulty that an enemy is likely to encounter in locating and sinking the ballistic missile submarines (colloquially known in the USN as 'boomers') on which they are placed. A single ballistic missile submarine may contain many nuclear warheads. For instance, US *Ohio* class ballistic missile submarines originally were designed to carry twenty-four Trident II SLBMs, each with up to fourteen warheads (the number of launch tubes and warheads subsequently has been reduced because of US–Russian arms control agreements). For decades, ICBMs enjoyed a great advantage over SLBMs in their accuracy, as measured by circular error probability (CEP), which essentially is the size of the circle surrounding a target in which half of the weapons fired at that target may be expected to land. (For example, if 50 per cent of the warheads fired at a target fell within 100 metres of it, but 50 per cent landed more than 100 metres from it, then the CEP would be 100 metres.) However, the development in recent decades of very precise SLBM warheads has eroded enormously the accuracy advantage previously associated with ICBMs (see Figure 17.2).

Ballistic missiles (either land- or sea-based) and the warheads that they carry are comparatively difficult to destroy. This is especially true of long-range ballistic missiles after the initial boost phase of their flight. Nevertheless, a variety of countries have deployed BMD systems with the capability to intercept long-range missiles, and it is likely that many additional states will acquire BMD defences. It also should be noted that the speed with which ballistic missiles deliver their weapons payload would be a particularly important factor in a first strike, as the targeted country would have only a very brief period to make critical strategic decisions before the warheads struck.

During the Cold War, the US and the Soviet Union developed enormous nuclear arsenals; by the late 1970s, they possessed tens of thousands of tactical and strategic warheads. The sheer destructive power of these arsenals, and the fear that they would actually be used in warfare, resulted in a very strong emphasis throughout the Cold War on deterrence theory.

Nuclear Deterrence

Deterrence is not a concept unique to the nuclear era; indeed, deterrence has been practised throughout human history. At its core, the concept is a simple one: using threats, explicit or implicit, to prevent a potential foe from doing something undesirable, such as starting a war over a disputed piece of territory. In order to prevent the 'deteree' from starting a war, the 'deterer' must convince the deteree that doing so is likely to be unprofitable.[2]

There are two main ways in which the deterer may do this. First, it may try to impress upon its counterpart that any war launched by the latter to gain the territory would be unsuccessful. This is deterrence by denial: if the deterrence attempt is successful, the deteree believes that its goals would not be achieved, and thus will not launch a war. Alternatively, the deterer may attempt to convince the deteree that, even if the latter did achieve its goals, it would pay a prohibitive price to do so: it may win the territory, but it would be a victory costing more than it is worth. This is deterrence by punishment. These two forms of deterrence are not mutually exclusive, and, indeed, the most potent deterrence threats generally combine aspects of each. For instance, the deterer may try to convince its opponent that it would both fail to gain the disputed territory *and* pay a high price – in military, financial and/or other losses – for its failed effort.

The flip side of deterrence is compellence, convincing an opponent to perform an action, even though the latter believes it not in their best interests and, thus, would not agree to do so except under duress. Both deterrence and compellence are forms of coercion.[3] If deterrence or compellence is successful, the deterred or compelled party will shape its behaviour so that it is in accordance with the demands placed

Figure 17.2 A Standard Missile Three (SM-3) is launched from the US Navy Aegis cruiser USS *Lake Erie* in a ballistic missile defence test.

upon it. In either case, the state whose behaviour is to be shaped may refuse to cooperate – and in such a case deterrence or compellence has failed. At that point, the would-be coercing power must either carry out its threat – which, in any scenario involving nuclear armaments, carries many dangers, including the possibility (or, depending on what the deterrence or compellence threat was, even the certainty) of catastrophic violence – or 'back down', accepting that it has failed to coerce its opponent.

While deterrence has always been a key aspect of international politics and diplomacy, during the Cold War the concept was absolutely critical; scholars and policymakers obsessed over how to ensure that neither superpower would make a misstep that would result in a Third World War. As a result, a sophisticated body of deterrence theory soon developed.

Because nuclear weapons are capable of inflicting overwhelming damage and can be delivered very rapidly, they presented policymakers with novel problems. While states always had to worry about surprise attacks, technological limitations placed constraints on the ability of aggressors to launch speedy and devastating assaults. Moreover, geography provided many states with a substantial degree of protection. However, the ability of aircraft and, particularly, ballistic missiles to deliver nuclear weapons could make geographic factors almost irrelevant in preventing, or even slowing, offensive success. A nuclear war could be fought, and a state or states utterly destroyed, in an afternoon.

How easy, or difficult, it will be to deter a given country is a matter of conjecture, not an exact science. The deterred party must 'agree' to deterrence – that is to say, it has the option of accepting the possible consequences of its action and of *not* being deterred. Thus, the success of deterrence can never be guaranteed. However, key factors – including credibility and capability – are likely to impact the success of a specific deterrence threat (see Box 17.1). Credibility, in turn, is determined largely by the past actions of the would-be deterer and the perceived appropriateness of the threat to the situation at hand.[4] Thus, a state with a long record of blustering, making extravagant but idle threats that are not carried out, is likely to have much less credibility than one with a reputation for always carrying out threats if the demands that it puts forth are not met.

Capability is a relatively simple concept: a state either has or does not have the ability to carry out a threatened action. In some cases, capability is not at issue, and the would-be deterer clearly has the ability to inflict a particular punishment, the only question being whether it has the will to do so. Sometimes, however, capability may be questionable. This is particularly notable in regard to second-strike deterrence threats. The purpose of such threats – which played a very large role in Cold War deterrence – is to deter a foe from attempting a nuclear first strike. Essentially, the state threatening a second strike is trying to convince its potential foe that even a very well-organised nuclear first strike would not eliminate its ability to retaliate. Thus, a first strike would be a 'murder–suicide', with the attacked state, even as it was in its death throes, lashing out at its aggressor.

BOX 17.1 NUCLEAR THREATS AND THE RUSSO-UKRAINIAN WAR

During the Cold War, both Washington and Moscow tended to be very cautious in their public references to nuclear arms. In the wake of Russia's invasion of Ukraine in February 2022, however, Russia has demonstrated a very different attitude regarding threats of nuclear use. While Vladimir Putin personally has publicly only made vague nuclear threats, other high-level figures – including Dmitry Medvedev, a former Russian president and prime minister – have been far more lurid, employing rhetoric that implies an almost casual willingness to escalate to nuclear use, even possibly against NATO.

The question of how seriously such threats should be regarded has been a controversial one within NATO. However, as of the time of writing, the alliance has demonstrated little willingness to bend to Moscow's will. NATO's minimal response likely indicates that most alliance leaders judge Russian threats as lacking credibility for various reasons, including that use of even one nuclear weapon against any target would cause international outrage, alienating states that currently are friendly toward Russia – including, most importantly, China.

Clearly, such a threat can have a high credibility: a state that had suffered a nuclear strike presumably would wish to take revenge on its enemy. However, whether it could actually do so would depend on many factors. A successful first strike would enormously damage the nuclear arsenal, communications network and other relevant assets of the victim state. Thus, to preserve second-strike capability, the Cold War superpowers spent vast sums building and maintaining large and diverse arsenals, as well as highly robust command, control and communications networks, each hoping to ensure that its peer believed that even a cataclysmic first strike would not prevent devastating retaliation.

Credibility and capability are central to deterrence because of their influence over severity and surety of punishment. Deterrence is, ultimately, based on threatened punishment, and in order to succeed the would-be deterer must issue a threat that is properly 'balanced'. The punishment threatened must be severe enough to dissuade the other party from an action but not be so severe as to be implausible. Thus, the more centrally a deterring state's interests are threatened – particularly if its population, form of government, territory and other most vital assets are placed in danger – the more severe a punishment may be while still remaining credible. The greater the severity and surety of punishment is, the greater is the likelihood of deterrence success; if one of these critical factors is missing – the threatened punishment is too minor or it seems unlikely that the threat actually would be carried out – deterrence can be expected to fail.

As noted previously, however, it is the would-be deteree who ultimately casts the deciding vote in the success or failure of a deterrence threat. If a leader is risk-averse and places a high value on the avoidance of punishment, deterrence threats are likely to succeed. If, however, that leader is reckless and places a much higher value on potential gains than on potential losses, successful deterrence is much more questionable. Moreover, if the leader in question simply believes that there is some overriding imperative – religious, ethical, political or otherwise – that makes it utterly and totally unacceptable to do as the would-be deterer wishes, deterrence failure is certain.

The Cold War and Beyond: Past and Future Possibilities for Conflict

Nuclear Conflict in a Cold War Context

The phrase 'nuclear war' often is used casually to mean an essentially unlimited conflict: a straightforward exchange of warheads, with combatants showing no regard for civilian life and property, whose ultimate outcome is, inevitably, the destruction of the human species, or at least a very great portion of it. This, indeed, is one possible type of nuclear engagement, and during the Cold War the prospect of such a conflict – not unreasonably – aroused fear worldwide. A full-scale nuclear exchange between the superpowers could have involved tens of thousands of warheads, with major cities targeted in Asia, Europe, North America and perhaps elsewhere, and globally devastating environmental damage. However, this sort of clash is only one type of nuclear war.

At the other extreme, nuclear weapons could – at least in theory – be used in a fashion that would cause no civilian casualties and only minimal, mostly local, environmental consequences. For example, use of a relatively low-yield tactical nuclear weapon against a command bunker located in a very rural area or a ship at sea fits into this category. Of course, given the international response that would surely follow even the most discriminating use imaginable of a nuclear weapon (and the less-discriminate nuclear retaliation that might follow if a nuclear-armed state were attacked), there are relatively few plausible scenarios in which such limited nuclear use might occur.

In discussing nuclear conflict, it is useful to make a distinction between counterforce and countervalue targets. The first category includes targets of military/political value to a government, such as military forces (including, even especially, nuclear forces), certain government facilities, communications networks, the leadership itself and similar targets. The second is composed of things that a government would value for their own sake, aside from their military value, such as the population, industrial and transportation infrastructure and so forth. It should be noted that the two categories are not mutually exclusive: many things – such as the leadership and the communications network, for example – may be considered both counterforce and countervalue targets. However, speaking generally, most counterforce targets are of a military/political character, while countervalue ones are not. A carefully constrained nuclear attack would therefore probably be focused on counterforce targets, avoiding collateral damage insofar as possible.

A variety of possible conflicts exist between the most extreme and limited types of nuclear warfare. It is certainly possible to imagine conflicts involving only the limited use of nuclear weapons, perhaps even to send a 'signal' to the opponent. During the Cold War, the US and Soviet Union contemplated many possible warfighting scenarios involving a limited use of nuclear weapons, although whether a nuclear conflict would have remained limited is, fortunately, a speculative question.

The concept of extended deterrence is critical to understanding the NATO nuclear deterrence problem of the Cold War, as well as many possible future crises involving rogue states or other actors. The primary deterrence objective of the US during the Cold War was not to protect its own homeland against Soviet attack. Rather, Washington was trying to protect its NATO allies from invasion, and a potential foe is always likely to question a state's willingness to risk a nuclear strike. Thus, maintaining a high level of credibility was critical. It was feared that, if Soviet leaders became convinced that the US would never accept profound damage to its territory, they would proceed to invade Western Europe. NATO's European members, in turn, worried that the US would desert them in their time of need, accepting, at least temporarily, a Soviet victory in exchange for being spared the danger of an attack on its own homeland.

If, however, the US did not quickly abandon its European allies, it would then have confronted all the problems described previously in regard to managing escalation, including the very real possibilities either of accidentally allowing the escalation process to slip out of control, the result being a massive nuclear exchange, or of failing to escalate quickly and boldly enough to convince Soviet leaders (assuming, of course, that they could be convinced) to abandon their invasion and evacuate NATO territory.

The vision of precisely how nuclear weapons would be used in the defence of Europe, however, changed over time, and it should be emphasised that there was never an entirely concrete, unalterable vision of what form a nuclear defence would take. Over the course of the Cold War, the US had a succession of 'nuclear doctrines' which all approached deterrence somewhat differently. All of these doctrines, however, had to grapple with the problems presented in convincing the potential foe that US nuclear threats were backed by a high degree of credibility and capability.

The evolution in US thinking about nuclear weapons reflected the difficulties inherent in attempting to build a coherent strategy that accounts for both deterrence and possible warfighting. Risks accompany any nuclear strategy; each possible nuclear doctrine involves trade-offs, some dangers being lessened and others increased, and nuclear weapons do not offer a simple solution to all of a state's security needs. Moreover, it should be noted that the great swings in American thinking about nuclear war occurred in the relatively stable security environment of the Cold War, and decisions were made primarily in reference to a single potential foe, the Soviet Union. In the comparatively freewheeling security environment of the twenty-first century, with its great variety of actors, including potentially

BOX 17.2 THE NIGHTMARE OF NUCLEAR TERRORISM

Particularly since the 9/11 attacks, there has been enormous concern about the possibility that terrorists might acquire nuclear weapons. Certainly, terrorist acquisition of a nuclear device would present a 'nightmare scenario'. As noted in the preceding chapter, certain chemical or biological agents could be used by terrorists to inflict grave damage, although there is considerable reason to doubt whether a terrorist group would be able to deliver an agent in a fashion efficient enough to result in huge numbers of casualties. However, if a nuclear weapon were smuggled into the centre of a major urban area and detonated, it would certainly cause devastation. Acquiring nuclear weapons has, however, thus far proven prohibitively difficult for terrorists. It is improbable that even a wealthy and sophisticated group would be able to build a nuclear device, assuming it somehow acquired the necessary fissile material (which itself would be an exceedingly difficult feat). The basic principles underlying the construction of a nuclear warhead are well known, but building one would require advanced engineering, which presumably would be beyond a terrorist organisation's capabilities. Thus, the more likely route for terrorist nuclear acquisition would be obtaining an already existing nuclear weapon, either by theft or by gift.

It is very difficult to estimate with precision the number of casualties that might be inflicted by a nuclear terrorist attack, as these would vary greatly depending on the explosive yield of the weapon, the layout and population density of the urban area in which it was detonated, and many other factors; meteorological conditions such as wind speed and direction and post-attack rainfall are important in determining the spread of radioactive fallout. Clearly, though, any such attack would be a monstrous event with massive international political repercussions.

unpredictable rogue states and terrorist groups, the creation of a satisfactory nuclear doctrine may prove to be even more challenging (Box 17.2).

Nuclear Weapons Today and Tomorrow

There are two basic forms of nuclear proliferation. When weapons proliferate horizontally, the number of states possessing nuclear weapons increases, but when vertical proliferation occurs, the total number of nuclear weapons increases. In general, the Cold War era was one of relatively modest horizontal proliferation; the number of states possessing these weapons grew slowly over the decades. However, the total number of nuclear weapons increased dramatically during the early decades of the Cold War because both Washington and Moscow engaged in rapid vertical proliferation. In more recent decades, however, the number of nuclear weapons on earth has decreased, with 'vertical de-proliferation' as Russia and the US allowed their nuclear arsenals to constrict in size. This trend, however, seems to be reversing, as several countries are known to be building additional warheads; China appears to have particularly ambitious plans for nuclear expansion.

In addition, horizontal proliferation is proceeding, albeit slowly. It is impossible to say how many, if any, new possessors of nuclear weapons will appear over the next few decades, but there are some reasons to believe that it could be a substantial number (Box 17.3).

BOX 17.3 THE 'LIBYA QUANDARY'

Over his decades in power, Libyan dictator Muammar Gaddafi had an unsavoury international reputation. Libya's combination of a small population and substantial oil revenues, however, provided revenue sufficient to permit Gaddafi to remain in power, as he combined domestic terror with ample financial support to favoured tribal leaders. This prevented the formation of a domestic coalition capable of overthrowing the mercurial and sadistic autocrat. Relatively late in his reign, however, Gaddafi attempted to improve relations dramatically with the West. While he began to inch in this direction in the 1990s, after the 9/11 attacks on the US his efforts became more serious. Fear that the US might invade Libya was a key factor motivating this foreign policy shift.

The G. W. Bush administration presented Gaddafi with a stark choice in the negotiations regarding his 'rehabilitation': part of the price would be prompt and complete disclosure of all Libyan WMD programmes.[5] He agreed in late 2003, and subsequent disclosures shocked observers globally. Libya's documentation made it clear that the country – which was not believed to have a truly serious nuclear weapons programme – was surprisingly close to achieving a nuclear capability.

For a time, Gaddafi enjoyed the benefits of an enhanced international standing, but when the Libyan Civil War began in February 2011 he was surprised that Western states, including the US, soon came to support the rebellion against his rule. By March an air operation was launched by NATO and several non-NATO states, with most of the combat sorties flown by a combination of France, Britain and the US. The foreign intervention soon proved decisive, and Gaddafi was captured and killed by rebels in October 2011.

While NATO intervention in the Libyan Civil War was eminently defensible from a humanitarian standpoint, it was questionable from a counterproliferation perspective. Gaddafi's surrender of his WMDs ultimately did not buy protection from outside intervention and left him in a weakened position when fighting the war itself – while of limited utility against a sophisticated military, the Libyan chemical arsenal might have been devastating against rebel forces, particularly in urban combat. If Libya had obtained a known nuclear capability by 2011 – a believable outcome, if not for the 2003 agreement – NATO intervention in Libya would have been extremely improbable. Repressive authoritarians who observed Gaddafi's downfall may have drawn some very unhelpful lessons regarding the desirability of obtaining WMDs in general, and nuclear weapons in particular.

First, it should be kept in mind that nuclear weapons have now existed for over three-quarters of a century. Basic nuclear weapons technology is not, in any reasonable use of the term, 'cutting edge'. There are many thousands of individuals on earth who possess at least some of the knowledge and skills required to build a nuclear device, and many of them are citizens of – or simply are willing to work for – states that may desire nuclear weapons.

Secondly, if one or more states obtain, or appear to be close to obtaining, nuclear weapons, this may convince certain other states that they should build nuclear weapons. We have seen this phenomenon to a limited degree in the past – for example, India's determination to have a nuclear capability was clearly a major driver of Pakistan's nuclear programme, while India's own nuclear efforts were largely driven by its concern about China's nuclear arsenal – and we may see more extreme cases of it in the future. For instance, there has been speculation that future Iranian acquisition of nuclear weapons might drive several other Middle Eastern states, possibly including Saudi Arabia, Turkey and others, to seek nuclear weapons.

Thirdly, and most importantly, nuclear weapons continue to have great utility both on and off the battlefield. Diplomatically, nuclear weapons bring (potentially considerable) benefits in terms of prestige, ability to practise nuclear deterrence and coercion and in other areas. Indeed, a nuclear-armed state may be able to dissuade a more powerful opponent even from taking military action against it. Many observers, for example, have argued compellingly that, if Iraq had possessed nuclear weapons when it invaded Kuwait in 1990, the US-led force that eventually liberated Kuwait would never have been assembled. Indeed, it is even conceivable that an elderly Saddam Hussein might still be alive, in office, and more affluent and powerful than ever.

Conventional warfare as practised by the US and other militarily advanced states places opponents with technologically outmoded equipment and minimally trained personnel in an undesirable position. Under current conditions, and regardless of whether one is fighting at land, on sea or in the air, quality of personnel and equipment generally trumps quantity. If, however, nuclear weapons are brought into the equation, the situation can be radically altered, and even an otherwise weak force may be able, at least temporarily, to enjoy a critical advantage over a far more powerful enemy.

Nuclear Conflict: Future Possibilities

Unfortunately, the occurrence of a limited nuclear conflict somewhere in the world remains entirely possible. Most critically, there would be the issue of what is targeted. It is possible, as previously noted, that nuclear weapons might be used – probably out of desperation – in a strictly battlefield role, and perhaps it would be possible to limit a conflict to tactical nuclear use.

Alternatively, however, it is possible that a state may use its nuclear arsenal in a much different manner, perhaps even undertaking a first strike intended to maximise civilian casualties. Such an action would not fit the Cold War vision of how nuclear escalation would likely unfold, but as an increasingly varied group of states

BOX 17.4 DIFFERENT LEADERS, DIFFERENT GOALS

Leaders may vary enormously in what they most value, what risks they are willing to take and other attitudes relevant to WMDs use. Even leaders within the same broad political tradition have diverse priorities and beliefs; George W. Bush, Barack Obama, Donald Trump and Joe Biden are all recent US presidents, but they are quite distinct personalities. The differences between leaders from very dissimilar political and strategic cultures – for example, a US president and a North Korean despot or Iranian supreme leader – may be so great that it is difficult for each to comprehend accurately what motivates the other. The possibility for misunderstanding, missed signals and other communication breakdowns is high when two such leaders are interacting.

This is especially the case when leaders engage in 'mirror-imaging'. That term, which came into common use during the Cold War, relates to the tendency to assume that another individual shares one's own general value hierarchy, reasons in a similar fashion and is otherwise quite similar to oneself. Western diplomats and other leaders often, and arguably quite justifiably, were criticised for tending to mirror-image Soviet leaders, paying insufficient attention to the specifics of Marxist–Leninist ideology and the Russian–Soviet historical experience and culture. Of course, there nonetheless was no US–Soviet nuclear conflict, and thus no instance of catastrophic deterrence failure. This, however, provides no guarantees regarding deterrence reliability in the future.

Leaders – like any other human beings – ultimately decide what they value, and those choices will not always appear reasonable and responsible to outside observers. One can think of many historical examples of states, even great powers, whose leaders had unsavoury or bizarre goals – Hitler's Germany is an obvious twentieth-century example, but Stalin's Soviet Union and Mao's China also both acted murderously towards perceived internal enemies and pursued various objectives that were in line with an extreme, even deranged, state ideology. If great powers can act so radically, one can easily imagine how smaller states like North Korea might behave in a surprising fashion.

acquires nuclear weapons, there is no guarantee that this will continue to be the case (see Box 17.4).

While the probability of a globally devastating nuclear war is, hopefully, extremely low in any given year, the possibility of a nuclear war occurring *somewhere* in the world probably is much higher than it was during most of the Cold War. Some of the reasons for this are obvious, such as the fact that more states possess nuclear arms and, presumably, the more nuclear-armed actors there are, the greater the likelihood that one of them will decide to use its weapons. However, there also are more subtle reasons: the actors involved may have radically different world-views and values.

Ultimately, what we know about the avoidance of nuclear conflict is based on the behaviour of a small sample of actors over, historically speaking, a rather brief time. We do not have a sufficiently large body of historical evidence to make highly trustworthy predictions about the future use, or non-use, of nuclear weapons. With that in mind, however, it does appear that horizontal proliferation is a continuing trend. While there was considerable optimism immediately after the Cold War that a 'nuclear-free' world was possible, most observers now treat this as, at best, a distant hope. There is substantial reason to suspect that the nuclear club will continue to increase in numbers over time, although the rapidity with which it will grow is uncertain.

Given this unclear, and possibly quite hazardous, international security environment, BMD likely will become progressively more important in the future. The architects of ambitious Cold War-era missile defence schemes, particularly the Reagan Administration Strategic Defence Initiative (SDI) program, were faced with the daunting task of building a highly reliable defensive shield that would destroy the great majority of many thousands of nuclear warheads. Even with today's vastly more advanced computer-processing power and other technological advances, this would be an extraordinarily difficult and expensive task. However, against the small arsenals of most of the current and likely future nuclear states, missile defence might prove quite feasible, and missile defences could enormously complicate nuclear war planning. When a state launches a nuclear attack on a country with effective BMD, the attacker cannot know which of its warheads will break though the defence and land on target; when the attacking country has only a small number of nuclear weapons, they might all be intercepted by the defence. Given these potential defensive advantages, and their utility against non-nuclear threats as well, an increasing number of states may be expected to acquire advanced BMD in the coming years.

Of course, the possibility of nuclear conflict does not preclude the possible use of CBWs. It is likely that we will again see the use of CBWs by states that are not nuclear-armed. Indeed, it is even possible that the use of CBWs may be the catalyst for the next use of nuclear weapons, as a nuclear-armed state could decide to retaliate to a CBWs attack with nuclear weapons. Some nuclear-armed states implicitly or explicitly maintain the option to retaliate in this fashion.

Overall, given continuing horizontal proliferation and the military usefulness of nuclear weapons, it is likely that the norm prohibiting nuclear use will be broken at some point. Although some authors believe that there genuinely is a strong taboo that will prevent nuclear weapons from being used again in warfare,[6] it is notable that since the invention of these devices no nuclear power has been confronted with a situation in which *not* using nuclear weapons would have immediate and catastrophic consequences. For instance, no nuclear-armed state has chosen to allow its military to be destroyed in conventional battle, much less permitted conquest by a foreign invader, rather than resort to the use of nuclear weapons. Such extreme situations would provide real tests of whether the norm against nuclear use truly is strong enough to be described as a taboo. Moreover, as discussed previously, there is no guarantee – especially given the continuing horizontal proliferation of nuclear weapons – that all future leaders of nuclear-armed powers will have a very high threshold for nuclear use.

The occurrence of one nuclear conflict would not ensure that there would be many such wars. However, the possibility of a progressive 'normalisation' of nuclear weapons usage should not be dismissed out of hand. Perceptions concerning the military usability of nuclear weapons are shaped continuously by the behaviour of the actors possessing such weapons; if a number of state and non-state entities prove willing to use nuclear weapons, it may be that the high 'wall' separating conventional weapons from nuclear weapons will break down, leading to an increasing willingness to use the latter in combat.

Conclusion: Nuclear Weapons in the Present and Future

At present, nuclear weapons are 'dormant' in regard to actual warfighting, having remained unused since the Second World War. They do, however, play an important role in shaping the international security environment, and their existence, and particularly the possibility of nuclear proliferation, drives many political events. For example, the nuclear activities of North Korea and Iran have created two of the most significant ongoing diplomatic predicaments facing the UNSC, amongst other bodies.

Concerning nuclear weapons, the period from the end of the Cold War to the present might reasonably be described as a transitional stage. The Cold War was defined by an icy standoff between two heavily armed superstates, with humanity's fate largely resting on the decisions made by the two opponents. The present era, by contrast, surely will not have such a simple, straightforward narrative. Rather, an assortment of relationships amongst states possessing nuclear weapons will be significant, and various scenarios may unfold in different parts of the world. In some cases, countries likely will use nuclear weapons to menace their less well-armed neighbours, with a regionally destabilising effect; however, other states that obtain nuclear arms will use them in a more defensively orientated manner. Sometimes, one or more great powers – whether or not acting under the aegis of the UN – may choose to use force to prevent a specific instance of proliferation; on other occasions, proliferation will proceed without meaningful interference by outsiders. Some of the states that today are at odds with each other may find that mutual possession of devastating weapons 'cools the passions', and their leaders will find it prudent to seek compromise and the diminishment of tensions rather than military victory. Other states might not be so accommodating, and proceed down a path leading to a nuclear war.

RESEARCH QUESTIONS

1. How strong is the norm against nuclear weapons amongst states? Could it survive the severe 'weight' of, for example, a devastating CB terrorist attack on a major American or British city, even if intelligence indicated strongly that the CBs in question had been provided to the terrorists by a state actor?
2. Was the invention and vertical proliferation of nuclear weapons the key reason why the Cold War did not become a Third World War?
3. If the number of nuclear powers were to increase greatly, how would this impact the international security environment?
4. Do the advantages accompanying membership in the nuclear 'club' still outweigh the disadvantages for France and Britain?
5. Would the continued proliferation of BMD make nuclear weapons potentially less useful as a strategic instrument, especially for states with small arsenals?
6. Would further reduction in the nuclear stockpiles of states belonging to the 'NPT Five' significantly enhance the global security environment?

FURTHER READING

Barnaby, Frank, *How to Build a Nuclear Bomb: And Other Weapons of Mass Destruction* (New York, NY: Nation Books, 2004). Explains in accessible language the steps that a state or terrorist group must take if it is to build WMDs.

Cirincione, Joseph, *Bomb Scare: The History and Future of Nuclear Weapons* (New York, NY: Columbia University Press, 2007). A history of nuclear weapons.

Croddy, Eric A., Jeffrey A. Larson and James J. Wirtz (eds.), *Weapons of Mass Destruction: The Essential Reference Guide* (Santa Barbara, CA: ABC-CLIO, 2018). Contains information on a variety of topics and issues related to nuclear armaments and other WMDs.

Freedman, Lawrence, *Nuclear Deterrence: A Ladybird Expert Book* (New York, NY: Penguin, 2018). A brief and highly readable introduction to nuclear deterrence and related issues.

Freedman, Lawrence and Jeffrey Michaels, *The Evolution of Nuclear Strategy: New, Updated, and Completely Revised*, 4th ed. (New York, NY: Palgrave MacMillan, 2019). Offers an excellent, detailed discussion of how the nuclear strategy of various states has developed over time.

Futter, Andrew, *The Politics of Nuclear Weapons: New, Updated, and Completely Revised*, 2nd ed. (New York, NY: Palgrave MacMillan, 2020). Provides a detailed discussion of many issues and views related to nuclear arms.

Langewlesche, William, *The Atomic Bazaar: The Rise of the Nuclear Poor* (New York, NY: Farrar, Straus and Giroux, 2007). Discusses many of the key issues related to nuclear proliferation, particularly the possibility that terrorist groups will obtain nuclear weapons.

Sagan, Scott D. and Kenneth N. Waltz, *The Spread of Nuclear Weapons: An Enduring Debate*, 3rd ed. (New York, NY: W. W. Norton, 2012). Two scholars of international relations debate what the likely impact of the spread of nuclear weapons will be on the global security environment.

ONLINE RESOURCES

https://fas.org/: The Federation of American Scientists (FAS) is an American group opposed to nuclear weapons and other WMDs. Its website contains information on WMDs of all kinds.

www.acq.osd.mil/ncbdp/nm//NMHB2020rev/: The *2020 Nuclear Matters Handbook (Revised)* was put together by the US Department of Defense as a resource for US government professionals working on issues related to nuclear weapons.

https://nonproliferation.org/: Combating the spread of WMDs with training and analysis. The website of the James Martin Center for Nonproliferation Studies, which is part of the Monterey Institute of International Studies, includes resources related to nuclear and other forms of WMD.

https://wagingpeace.org/: The Nuclear Age Peace Foundation, which favours global nuclear disarmament, maintains this website. It includes various resources on nuclear weapons.

https://armscontrolcenter.org: The website of the Center for Arms Control and Non-Proliferation, a Washington-based think tank, includes fact sheets and other resources about WMDs, including nuclear weapons.

www.nti.org/: The website of the US-based Nuclear Threat Initiative, which focuses on the prevention of proliferation of WMDs of all kinds, includes a variety of resources.

NOTES

1 Bernard Brodie, *The Absolute Weapon: Atomic Power and World Order* (New York, NY: Harcourt, Brace, 1946).

2 On nuclear deterrence, see Stephen J. Cimbala, *The Past and Future of Nuclear Deterrence* (Westport, CT: Praeger, 1998); Stephen J. Cimbala (ed.), *Deterrence and Nuclear Proliferation in the Twenty-First Century* (Westport, CT: Praeger, 2000); Herman Kahn, *On Thermonuclear War*, new ed. (Edison, NJ: Transaction, 2007 [1960]); Herman Kahn, *On Escalation: Metaphors and Scenarios* (Westport, CT: Greenwood Press, 1986 [1965]); Thomas C. Shelling, *Arms and Influence* (New Haven, CT: Yale University Press, 1966).

3 The concept of coercion – particularly non-nuclear coercion – is addressed in detail in Robert A. Pape, *Bombing to Win: Air Power and Coercion in War* (Ithaca, NY: Cornell University Press, 1996).

4 On the concept of credibility, see Daryl G. Press, *Calculating Credibility: How Leaders Assess Military Threats* (Ithaca, NY: Cornell University Press, 2005).

5 On the negotiations leading to the surrender of Libya's WMD programme, see Robert G. Joseph, *Countering WMD: The Libyan Experience* (Fairfax, VA: National Institute Press, 2009).

6 See John Mueller, *Atomic Obsession: Nuclear Alarmism from Hiroshima to Al-Qaeda* (New York, NY: Oxford University Press, 2009).

PART VII
Current and Future Challenges

18 Joint Warfare

IAN SPELLER

CHAPTER OUTLINE

KEY THEMES

- Joint operations, integrating activity across different warfighting environments, have been important throughout history. In the past such integration tended to revolve around the land and maritime interface until a third dimension (air) was introduced in the twentieth century. Today effective joint integration includes activity in the land, maritime, air, space and cyber domains.
- The requirement to integrate activity across different domains and to coordinate the activity of different services provides particular challenges, adding together the difficulties inherent in single service operations and then multiplying them. Proficiency in such operations does not come about by accident but must be worked at.

- There was a tendency in the past for individual services (army, navy and air force) to focus primarily on their own needs and concerns, often to the detriment of joint capabilities. That this might undermine the national defence effort was not always appreciated by those whose vision was influenced most heavily by their own service loyalties.
- Today it is widely understood that for armed forces to survive and prosper within a high threat environment joint forces must be able to integrate and cooperate as seamlessly as possible. Modern technology creates additional opportunities in this respect, and also significant challenges.

Introduction

It is traditional to think of warfare as occurring within three distinct physical environments, on land, sea or in the air, and this distinction is reflected in the institutional structure of most armed forces, which are divided into separate services (armies, navies and air forces) designed primarily to operate within these different environments. More recently the ability to operate in space has prompted many militaries to consider this to represent a fourth environment and some now also list cyberspace as a fifth. This has been reflected in the institutional structure of many; for example, in 2019 the US established a Space Force as a service branch of the US armed forces and the German Bundeswehr have created a Cyber and Information Domain Service which became operational in 2017. However, it is important to remember that military activity often crosses environmental and institutional boundaries and that operations tend to occur on land, sea *and* air, not land, sea *or* air; today there are few operations in any of these environments that are not impacted by the capacity (or incapacity) to use space and cyber capabilities. Successful military operations, therefore, tend to require some degree of joint (meaning inter-service) cooperation to coordinate capabilities across all relevant environments in support of unified purpose and action.

Joint warfare has been important throughout history, as will be explored below, but has become even more salient today as the ability of forces in one environment to influence activity in the others has grown substantially in recent years. Since the end of the Cold War, in particular, most advanced militaries have focused a great deal of time and attention on the need to enhance joint cooperation. Moreover, in recent years there has been a growing tendency for some to think of warfare not so much as occurring within different physical environments but rather as occurring across different domains, with an emphasis on the value of being able to achieve better cross-domain synergy. This is sometimes articulated as representing an evolved form of 'jointery', taking the focus beyond institutional cooperation towards more seamless all-domain integration.

This chapter addresses these issues. It builds on the foundation laid earlier in this book, where war was discussed within traditional environmental boundaries, and examines the character of joint warfare in the more traditional sense of that term before then addressing evolving concepts about MDO and integration. It concludes with a brief discussion of the dynamics associated with contemporary combined (meaning multinational) operations. As will be seen, this is an important topic and one that is key to understanding the way in which most operations today will be planned and fought.

What Is 'Joint Warfare'?

According to NATO, the word 'joint' is an adjective used to describe 'activities, operations and organizations in which elements of at least two services participate'.[1] Thus, in the past the US Armed Forces defined joint warfare as 'team warfare' designed to tie together the activity of different agencies.[2] Today the adjective 'joint' is applied very widely to all sorts of military concepts, doctrine and organisations, reflecting the understanding that team activity across service divides can be key to success across the spectrum of conflict. That dynamic is not new; indeed it has existed through all recorded history, but it was not always well appreciated in the past by practitioners and commentators who preferred to focus on single service priorities. Even today, the proliferation of the term 'joint' across many military organisations may not always be matched by action, and understanding that transcends parochial institutional barriers.

Before proceeding, it would be useful to make a distinction between joint strategy and joint operations. The latter involve forces from different services working together within an operational context. The former might include such operations, but might also involve services operating separately but yet contributing to a coordinated strategy linking actions across different domains. Thus, for example, an army might fight an adversary ashore while the navy attacks their shipping and blockades their ports. Strategically the effort here might be joined up but the two elements might never actually cooperate closely. This is not usually what is meant by the term 'joint warfare', which most commonly is applied to situations where the services actually work together at the operational and tactical levels, requiring a greater degree of cooperation, coordination, understanding and compromise than is required when services are operating separately towards a joint end.

Much contemporary discussion about joint warfare focuses on the operational level, as it is here where inter-service activity is most commonly coordinated and this is also the level at which joint command is most likely. Events at the tactical level are often profoundly influenced by joint activity; indeed there would be little point in the latter if this were not the case. However, at the tactical level, training and organisation are more commonly defined by traditional service boundaries, except in those units specifically designed to meet a defined joint need. Even here, the members of such units are usually first trained by one or other service, and will usually return to that service at some point. In such circumstances, single service loyalties and identities dominate at the tactical level, and service-specific proficiency at this level is generally recognised to be a vital prerequisite for joint competence at the operational level. Joint forces cannot fight well together unless they are good at their own core business.

As already noted, 'joint operations' are usually defined as those operations that involve forces from more than one service (army, navy or air force). The term 'joint forces' is often defined in more specific terms, to refer to a force composed of significant elements from more than one service operating under a single commander. This represents a very particular type of organisation, where forces are under control of a dedicated 'joint force commander'.[3] This definition does not encompass situations where different services fight together without such an arrangement, as was most commonly the case before the mid twentieth century and still often occurs today. It is therefore important to remember that when some militaries refer to 'joint forces' they mean something more developed than just inter-service operations but also that joint operations might often be conducted by forces that would not match the definition of 'joint forces' as it is meant here.

The above represents an institutional understanding of joint warfare, focusing on the challenge of integrating activity involving different services. It is important to note that many of the challenges of joint warfare could apply in situations where there is only one service employed. For example, it is easy to understand that an amphibious operation conducted by the army, air force and navy working in unison would be inherently joint, whatever the command arrangements. However, can that term still be applied to an operation undertaken by the navy, employing a naval landing force supported exclusively by naval aircraft? Here the operation would involve only one service, but would cross the same environmental boundaries and hence experience many of the same challenges as the mutiservice operation. In this sense the operation might be described as being 'functionally joint' even if it were not institutionally so. It could be the case that coordination between the different elements might prove easier when conducted by only one service but this may not always be so. A land force commander from the naval service (a marine) might be as likely to disagree with the naval commander offshore as would a colleague from the army. Put simply, there may be an inherent tendency for those with responsibility for different force elements to pull in different directions, whatever the colour of their uniform. Events at Guadalcanal in 1942 offer a case in point, see Box 18.1.

Of course, joint operations are not relevant in all contexts; armies, navies or air forces might sometimes be able to achieve success on their own, although perhaps not as frequently as their more ardent supporters sometimes believe. Thus, for example, it would be fair to say that joint capabilities were not central to the expansion of the Mongol empire in the thirteenth century; it was the proficiency of their horse warriors that mattered most. Similarly, Prussia prevailed in the wars of German unification from 1866 to 1871 through the strength of the German Armies. Joint operations were not very relevant to Prussia as victory was attained in short, decisive land campaigns against adversaries who shared a common border. On the other hand, even land-oriented powers such as the Mongols often found cause to attempt joint operations, as with their ill-fated efforts to invade Japan in 1274 and

BOX 18.1 GUADALCANAL, 1942

The Battle for Guadalcanal began on 7 August 1942 when US forces landed on the Japanese held island. With the initial land force ashore the USN decided to withdraw its aircraft carriers, on the night of 8 August, to protect them from the threat of Japanese naval and air attack. This, and the defeat of Allied naval surface forces at the Battle of Savo Island on the night of 8–9 August, forced the withdrawal of the amphibious transport group, leaving the marines marooned ashore without their heavy artillery, without the reserve marine regiment and without much of their ammunition, medical support and logistics. The land force commander (a marine) objected, but his objections were not heeded. Here, facing a genuine challenge to sea and air control, the admirals offshore did what their training and experience suggested was correct, and prioritised the safety of their ships. This may have been the correct decision, but it was not one likely to appeal to the marines ashore who now faced the danger of defeat by enemy land forces. In this event, they were able to hold on until reinforcement arrived, but the incident illustrates the potential for imperatives in one environment to impact on the others. In this situation the land force commander (General Vandegrift) was subordinate to the naval task force commander (Admiral Fletcher) and the amphibious force commander (Admiral Turner), an arrangement which may not have facilitated a balanced approach to the consideration of joint matters.[4]

1281. Very often those victorious on land found eventual need to develop joint capabilities or to accept that their dominium ended where the waves lapped the shore, as did the German Army in 1940. Moreover, for around a century now, success in land or maritime operations has generally depended, at least to some degree, on successful joint cooperation with air forces and, despite the claims of some, air forces have generally also been most impactful when integrated into a joint context. With the additional need today to account for activity within space and cyberspace, it is much harder to conceive of entirely single service operations than it was in the past.

Joint Warfare in History

Joint operations have occurred throughout all of recorded history. It does not require particular strategic insight to understand that the capacity to coordinate activity across different warfighting domains can provide strategic, operational and/or tactical advantage depending on circumstances. The value of a joint approach was evident as early as the twenty-fourth century BC when Sargon of Akkad exploited strength at sea and on the land to build an empire in Mesopotamia. Eight hundred years later the Egyptian Pharoah Kamose undertook joint operations in his campaign against the Hyksos in the Nile Delta, coordinating action between land and maritime forces. A thousand years after this Athens achieved great success and also devastating failure in its conduct of joint operations during the Peloponnesian War (431–404 BC).[5] There is no space here to give even a brief account of such operations through the ages; to do so would require a multivolume history. It is sufficient to note that joint operations continued to be important in the centuries that followed, in multiple different contexts. Note, for example, those undertaken by Pompey the Great in 67 BC in his campaign against pirates in the Mediterranean, by the Japanese in the Genpei Civil War (1180–1185) or by Chinese admiral Zheng He in the 1411 invasion of Sri Lanka. The joint expeditions undertaken by Zheng He between 1405 and 1433 extended Ming China's influence across the Indian Ocean, suppressed piracy and returned much treasure to China, before they were halted by a dynasty that turned its back on the sea; a decision that was to cost China dearly in the centuries ahead.

The adoption of gunpowder added another element to joint cooperation, greatly extending the range and impact of those things that could be fired from sea to shore, and vice versa. Thus, for example, in 1347 the English employed sea-based artillery to bombard the shore during the siege of French-held Calais. Two centuries later, at the Battle of Pinkie in 1547, English ships fired on the flank of the Scottish army, helping to disorder their left wing and thus made a significant contribution to the victory of the English Army ashore. In the 1940s, German Army commanders had good cause to lament the difficulty of conducting mobile operations within range of the guns of Anglo-American naval forces. They had even more cause to regret the potency of Allied air support for surface forces. The advent of military aviation in the early years of the twentieth century added an important new element to the conduct of joint operations, and one that no sensible admiral or general could afford to ignore.[6] More recently, the need to account for operations in space and cyberspace has added further complexity to the overall equation.

When exploring the history of joint warfare one must be careful to avoid the idea of steady progress and development. As Stuart Griffin has perceptively noted, the idea of any such 'evolution' is misplaced as periods of competence have very often been followed by neglect; levels of understanding and proficiency wax and wane over time.[7] Thus, for example, the British justly gained credit for their very effective exploitation of joint operations in the Seven Years War (1756–1773), with the capture of Quebec and Havana in 1759 standing as good examples of effective army and navy cooperation. It should be noted, however, that British successes towards the end of this war were preceded by some notable early failures and their record in the wars that followed was decidedly mixed. Impressive American performance in joint operations at Vera Cruz in 1847 and by the Union during the Civil War (1861–1865) did not translate into a similar level of proficiency during the Santiago campaign in the Spanish American War (1898). The same dynamic of progress and regression was evident in the twentieth century. British expertise in air–ground cooperation developed during the course of the First World War was largely lost before the start of the Second. The remarkable development of American and British joint knowledge and capabilities in the Second World War represented one of the key factors in eventual success against both Germany and Japan, but this did not stop the retreat back into single service parochialism that characterised the experience of both once hostilities ended.

Of course, this can be true of all military activity and reflects a range of factors relating to the ways in which the lessons from experience are captured and communicated and also the level of priority given to different types of activity. A particular problem for joint operations has often been that these were rarely seen as the first or most important responsibility of individual services whose primary focus and loyalty would be concentrated on their own interests. In the absence of formal joint institutions, which are largely a late twentieth century phenomenon, it was difficulty to ensure that joint considerations were given due weight unless the need was obvious and immediate.

Joint operations were central to success and failure on all fronts during the Second World War, a point that was recognised by all but the most obtuse observers (see Figure 18.1). The same was true of many of the wars and minor conflicts that characterised the Cold War, although here sometimes the importance of joint cooperation was made most evident by its absence. The US experience in Vietnam, for example, demonstrated that the American armed forces were less capable of

Figure 18.1 US troops wade ashore from an LCVP at Omaha Beach in Normandy on 6 June 1944. The D-Day landings and the successful campaign that followed were possible only because of the extraordinary proficiency in joint and combined operations that had been achieved by Anglo-American forces at this stage of the war. Source: https://tinyurl.com/3crptnyh

effective joint cooperation than had been the case twenty years earlier. This, and a series of embarrassing failures in subsequent operations, prompted a much stronger emphasis, from the mid 1980s, on creating mechanisms to enhance joint cooperation amongst US forces and this was later matched by similar developments in many other armed forces. Today the importance of joint warfare is very widely recognised, and this has been reflected in the development of joint doctrine, institutions and organisations (see later discussion). It is also reflected in the conduct of operations and even in situations where combatants sometimes struggle to integrate activity across environmental boundaries As in the case of the war in Ukraine, the value of being able to do so is very evident.

Thinking and Writing about Joint Warfare

It would be fair to say that much more has been written about strategy and warfare in its separate environments than has been written on joint operations. That was true in the past and remains the case today despite an upsurge of interest in joint warfare in recent years. However, it is not the case that nothing was written. Many who focused on land warfare took time to consider the value of cooperation with the navy and this is reflected, for example, in classic works by Antoine Jomini and Colmar von der Goltz.[8] Similarly, classic works on maritime strategy often addressed the same issue from a seaward perspective, and this was particularly true of British writers, including Philip Colomb and Julian Corbett, who showed a better appreciation of the joint nature of maritime operations than was sometimes evident in the work of their great American counterpart, Alfred Mahan.[9] Indeed, for Corbett, joint operations (**combined operations**, in the parlance of his day) represented the very essence of the successful British approach to the conduct of war, a point that was strongly emphasised through all his major works. The same point was taken up after the First World War by the sailor-scholar Herbert Richmond and, with rather less nuance, by Basil Liddell Hart.[10]

For obvious reasons, prior to the twentieth century much of this attention focused on amphibious operations and joint expeditions where the land/sea interface was most evident. It is not surprising that interest should have been sharpest in Britain, given its geographic position and traditional focus on maritime power. Thus, for example, in 1759 James More Molyneux, a British army officer, wrote a treatise on 'Conjunct operations: or expeditions that have been conducted jointly by the fleet and the army', attempting to capture lessons from the past and to make recommendations for more effective joint cooperation in future.[11] Over a century later, in 1897, another British army officer, Colonel George Armand Furse, wrote a two-volume study, *Military Expeditions Beyond the Seas*.[12] Similarly, a Royal Marine, George Aston, wrote a number of books that included a prescient study of 'sea, land and air strategy' published in 1914.[13] The most insightful writer on such matters was yet another army officer, Charles Callwell, who wrote first on the effect of maritime command on land campaigns (1897) and then on the impact of military operations on maritime preponderance (1905), illustrating his work with an array of examples from recent wars, demonstrating the value of joint cooperation.[14] It is unfortunate that these works were not more widely read or better understood. Sadly, and despite the arguments put forth by authors like Aston, Callwell and Corbett, armies and navies of this period tended not to view joint operations as core business. That was not something that changed quickly.

Early writers of air power theory had a tendency to stress the potentially independent uses of systems whose real value in the First World War had been almost entirely within a joint context.[15] To do so was helpful to emerging services desperate for a unique role that might serve them in institutional battles with sceptical generals and admirals, but even this did not stop some from contemplating and publishing on the challenges of joint warfare. Thus for example, John Slessor, a future British Chief of the Air Staff, published *Air Power and Armies* in 1936, although careful readers may detect a slightly apologetic tone as he wrote on a subject that many in his service did not consider to be an important one.[16] Post-war discussion about air power in the Second World War, and in the many conflicts that followed, was often coloured by the desire of different authors to support or undermine air force claims to have an inherent capacity for independent strategic effect and thus to influence debates about policy in a manner that was at least as partisan as the pre-war debate. Here the obvious utility of air power in support of joint forces was sometimes overshadowed by the desire of those in light blue to carve out a unique role for themselves.

Today there remain far fewer scholarly studies of joint warfare and joint operations than there are service specific works. However, the topic does receive more attention than it once did. Moreover, works that study warfare within environmental boundaries now commonly also address joint matters; no serious study of war on land, sea, air, space or cyberspace could afford not to. In addition, armed forces now pay far more attention to joint matters than was ever previously the case, and this is reflected in their published policy and plans, their strategy statements and their doctrine. It is also reflected in their professional journals and associated literature.

Institutional Challenges

A key challenge, historically and through to the present, has been the difficulty of getting different services to understand the needs of the others, and also to accept the compromises inherent in meeting those needs. The dynamic can be very evident at a strategic level where armies, navies and air forces have very often chosen to prioritise their own single service needs ahead of joint assets or capabilities. Indeed, they would be very unusual institutions if they did not do so. This is particularly problematic when resources are scarce, as they often are, and when the services cannot agree on relative priorities, which happens frequently. There is an unfortunate tendency for senior officers to narrowly prioritise the interests of their own service, seemingly with little regard for wider national needs; a forgiving interpretation here might be that, having devoted their lives and careers to the army, navy or air force, they too easily conflate their own interests and priorities with those of the nation. The prominence give to strategic bombing by the British RAF before and during the Second World War may provide an example of this. The heavy emphasis on an independent (i.e., deliberately non-joint) role bolstered the institutional standing of the RAF but encouraged a neglect of joint needs and capabilities that cost Britain dearly in the first half of the war. Ships were sunk, armies defeated and campaigns lost under skies dominated by the enemy at a time when the British bombing campaign brought negligible reward.[17] Similarly, inter-service cooperation between the Japanese Army (focused on the war in China) and Navy (focused on the Pacific) was remarkably poor during the Second World War despite national needs and a recent history of successful joint cooperation in wars against China and Russia.[18]

Even when services are able to agree on strategy and recognise the need to work together as a team, the challenges associated with doing so are formidable. With the best will in the world (and this is not always present) it can be difficult for armies, navies and air forces to recognise the needs of the others, or to understand the best ways to employ limited resources. Assets and techniques optimised to work in one environment may not be well suited to another and it may take much work, and considerable time, to align the tactics, techniques and procedures required to make joint forces truly effective. It might even be difficult for the different services to communicate effectively with each other unless they have invested time and resources into ensuring that this is possible. Ultimately, effective operations require a level of mutual understanding that can be hard to achieve unless it is worked at.

Institutional Structures

There are a number of different approaches regarding the type of institutional structure that might best promote proficiency in joint operations. In the past the tendency was to leave things to the services to sort out for themselves, coordinated to a greater or lesser degree at ministerial level and supported by committees made up of members who were, first and foremost, representatives of their own service. During the Second World War the British experimented with a different approach, with particular reference to the joint aspects of amphibious operations, with the creation of an independent joint Combined Operations Organisation separate from the three services, whose members represented the interests of the joint organisation rather than their parent service. The organisation did a good job of developing British proficiency in amphibious operations, at a time when there was an obvious and pressing need to do so, but foundered in the post-war period as it was starved of funding and priority. It was replaced in the early 1960s by a more traditional system where the services cooperated, argued or ignored each other through a joint committee structure.[19]

Today, at the strategic level, joint cooperation is usually facilitated through a unified defence ministry, such as the French *Ministère des Armées* or the Vietnamese Ministry of National Defence,[20] although the abilities of such ministries to control the power and independence of individual services varies widely. Below this level, activity is commonly coordinated by a chiefs of staff committee, or similar, where the heads of each service meet to discuss issues of policy. Usually, in the past, no one in uniform stood above the chiefs, which could make the development of coordinated policy difficult if they did not agree. Today it is common for the most senior military position to stand above the chiefs, as does the US Chairman of the Joint Chiefs of Staff, who outranks all other officers, coordinates the efforts of the service chiefs and acts as the principal military adviser to the president.

In the American case, the Chairman of the Joint Chiefs of Staff does not have command authority over operational forces. Since the 1986 Goldwater-Nichols Act, EmptyTargetElement such authority has been vested in unified combatant commands, joint commands organised on a functional or a geographical basis (see Box 18.2). The overt shift of the US armed forces to a more joint approach was prompted by a desire to enhance joint cooperation, key to evolving ideas about 'AirLand battle', and also to address the woeful inability of the different services to work together effectively, as had been demonstrated during the 1975 Mayaguez incident and the debacle of Operation Eagle Claw in 1980, where joint forces botched hostage rescue attempts in Cambodia and Iran, and during the muddled operation to invade Grenada in 1983. Success in subsequent operations suggests that much progress has been made since then, even if inter-service debates and disputes continue to figure prominently here, as elsewhere.[21]

Today many armed forces have joint institutions, joint doctrine and joint training that reflects the general acceptance of the need for different forces to work together as a team. It also reflects the hope, particularly important in the post-Cold War retrenchment of the 1990s, that improved jointery might bring with it money-

BOX 18.2 US UNIFIED COMBATANT COMMANDS

In 2025 the US Department of Defense had eleven unified combatant commands, joint military commands organised on either a geographical or a functional basis and with command responsibility over assigned forces in time of peace and war. The unified combatant commands are commanded by an admiral or a general who may come from any service.

Geographical Combatant Commands: Africa Command; Central Command; European Command; Indo-Pacific Command; Northern Command; Southern Command; Space Command.

Functional Combatant Commands: Cyber Command; Special Operations Command; Strategic Command; Transportation Command.

Figure 18.2 The UK Joint Services Command and Staff College at Shrivenham. This college replaced the three single-service staff colleges, creating a joint institution responsible for the training and education of middle ranking and senior officers. Institutions like this are designed to inculcate a joint ethos within the armed forces. Source: www.defenceimagery.mod.uk/Home/Search?Query = 45148046.jpg&Type = Filename

saving efficiencies that would allow for the maintenance of cherished capabilities at reduced cost. For some this process has gone further than in the US. In Britain, for example, the independent service staff colleges were closed in the 1990s and staff training (for middle-ranking and senior officers) moved to a new joint institution, reflecting a belief in the critical importance of joint understanding and integration, particularly at the operational level of war (see Figure 18.2). The same point was also reflected in the creation of a new Permanent Joint Headquarters and the appointment of a Chief of Joint Operations to exercise operational command of UK forces deployed on joint and combined missions overseas. As one might expect, the NATO command structure is both joint and multinational. This is not just a Western phenomenon. China (Theatre Commands) and Russia (Military Districts) both employ joint military commands with responsibility for specific geographical regions (see Box 18.3).

There has been a tendency for some to see the emphasis on joint structures and institutions as a danger, threatening to undermine single service loyalty and competence. The unfortunate impact on morale and esprit de corps of Canadian attempts to create a single unified armed force in the late 1960s is often cited as a cautionary tale. In reality, as Griffin argued, being joint does not require or imply a loss of service identity. It is about finding ways to promote unity of action, not creating a

BOX 18.3 CHINESE THEATRE COMMANDS

In 2015 sweeping military reforms saw Chinese administrative regional commands replaced by five joint theatre commands (Eastern, Western, Southern, Northern, Central) who have taken from the services the command responsibility for training and potential combat operations. In some respects this reflects the approach adopted in the US after the Goldwater–Nichols Act, and the Theatre Commands appear similar to American Unified Combatant Commands (see Box 2). China has also established the Rocket Force, with control of strategic missiles and many conventional strike assets, and the Strategic Support Force (SSF) responsibility for space, cyber and electronic warfare. The latter now controls key capabilities that had previously been held by the separate services and drawing them together into a joint organisation may represent a sign of progress. However, this structure means that the theatre commands must work with the SSF and the Rocket Forces to achieve full integration within their area of interest, creating the possibility of friction in any crisis.[22]

single unitary actor. In many respects it is a state of mind more than anything else.[23] Experience suggests that this state of mind does not happen by accident; it must be worked at, and hence the value of institutions and structures designed to promote this.

Command and Control (C2)

In ancient times there was often no distinction between generals and admirals, reducing the potential for dispute over who should command a joint operation. At the battle of Actium in 31 BC, for example, the rival commanders were Mark Anthony and Marcus Agrippa. Both were successful generals before they were admirals; they understood both environments. Similarly, in the sixth century AD the great Byzantine commander Belisarius was successful as both general and admiral. A thousand years later the distinction between the naval and military professions in Europe was still far from complete. Thus, Charles Howard of Effingham was a cavalry commander on land before he fought and defeated the Spanish Armada in 1588. Robert Blake,EmptyTargetElement one of Britain's most successful admirals ever, was a soldier before he was a sailor, having been a colonel in Oliver Cromwell's New Model Army before he was appointed a 'General at Sea' in 1649.[24]

By the eighteenth century the growing complexity of operations on land and at sea and the growing professionalism of Western armed forces made it increasingly rare for generals and admirals to 'switch code'. There were, of course, exceptions; note that the so-called 'father of the Chinese Navy', Liu Huaqing, was a successful ground force commander before he was drawn to the navy in the 1950s.[25] More typically, however, to be successful in either environment required knowledge and experience that could not be quickly or easily gained, and this was especially true of operations at sea. Armies and navies became very distinct separate organisations with their own traditions, and often with a very different way of viewing the world. This might not matter much when they operated apart, but it could be problematic when they combined, as they had to do when conducting large-scale amphibious or expeditionary operations. Generals and admirals tended to understand war in their own environment, but it was much harder for them to understand fully the business of the other, creating powerful barriers to the achievement of close cooperation. The advent of airpower in the twentieth century added a third element to this, and air forces were as adamant as navies and armies that only they truly understood war within their own environment.

This all raises the question of who should command a joint operation. One option is to divide command equally between representatives of each service, as the British did until the mid twentieth century. This reflected the belief that no one individual would have sufficient competence to decide on matters beyond their own service and that no service could be expected to hand its forces over to someone who lacked such competence. This worked well on some occasions (i.e., Quebec 1759) and badly on others (i.e., Cartegena 1741). The trouble was that in situations where the services disagreed, as they inevitably would, there was no one with authority to settle disputes. The US adopted a similar approach until the late 1930s when it switched to the idea of appointing a unified (joint) commander standing over subordinate land, sea and air commanders. There was no expectation here that any individual could know everything, but they would be advised by their subordinate commanders and by a joint staff and now at least there was one individual with ultimate responsibility for making hard decisions.

The utility of this approach was demonstrated in a series of successful US and Allied operations in the Second World War, with Britain here accepting the need to adopt the American approach. The success of General Eisenhower as Supreme Commander of the Allied Expeditionary Force in Normandy provides a good illustration of the strength of this idea. His ability to balance different interests and to adjudicate between different priorities, and to manage some very difficult characters, while planning and conducting the largest and most complex joint and combined operation in all history, stands as testament to the strength of the system and to the quality of the man. Today the appointment of a unified joint commander at the operational level is standard practice for many countries and is enshrined within NATO doctrine.[26] No one has yet come up with a better system for C2 joint operations.

Combined Operations

The term 'combined operations' is today most commonly used to refer to multinational operations, involving the forces of more than one nation.[27] In the past the term was often employed to refer to what would today be described as joint operations or (in Britain) as a synonym for amphibious warfare. It is helpful to be aware that some commentators continue to conflate combined operations with amphibious operations, but that is not the way in which the term is now most commonly used.[28]

Combined operations, in the modern sense of that term, today represent a key area of military interest and activity. Even the most powerful states often find the need to cooperate with allies and partners for both military and political purposes. Politically, it can be important in terms of domestic and international opinion for military action to be supported actively by others, hence the political significance of the British military contribution to the US-led invasion of Iraq in 2003 and also of French refusal to do the same. Combined operations can also be important militarily, allowing participants to pool their resources to mutual benefit. This is particularly significant for collective security organisations such as NATO, whose strength is derived from the ability of member states to operate together, but is relevant to any situation where two or more nations find need to work as a team. It is worth noting that even superpowers may sometimes struggle to field the scale and range of forces suited to all circumstance and the ability to call on allied help can be important, particularly as allies may offer expertise in niche capabilities or have local knowledge and experience that can be extremely useful.

There are many barriers to the conduct of effective combined operations where, inevitably, forces from different countries think and act in ways that do not always match those of their allies. This can matter at the strategic and operational levels, where decisions must accommodate different interpretations about objectives, methods and means. Political interference is common and can impact on the availability and employment of particular forces; the existence of 'national caveats' provides unwelcome friction into any planning process. At the tactical level, forces may follow different doctrine, have tactics and techniques that are dissimilar and equipment that is incompatible; they may not even speak the same language. The provision of different types of ammunition, replacements and spares, and even differing norms relating to rations, can cause nightmares for logisticians. Different nationalities may have entirely different approaches to C2 or may not even have compatible equipment to enable effective communications and networking between the different force elements. They may also have different rules of engagement, with some elements of a combined force showing more restraint (or having fewer options) than others. None of these issues can be resolved quickly and easily, which raises the value of forces having worked out the problems before they are tested in combat. This is reflected in the emphasis that NATO has placed on interoperability and standardisation, although even here there can be significant divergence in practice and proficiency between different national elements. Given this, it is easy to understand the challenges inherent in planning and conducting operations that are both joint and combined.

Operational Art and Joint Warfare

The operational level of war and operational art have been introduced elsewhere in this volume and need not be repeated here. It has already been noted in this chapter that joint operations are often associated particularly with the operational level, as it is here where command is most likely to be joint and also here where, in planning and coordinating the activity of diverse force elements, joint cooperation has tended to be most evident in the past. Certainly it is difficult today to think of activity at the operational level that is not joint to some degree. The requirement to account for joint activity adds complexity to command at the operational level, and this may often be multiplied by the need to account for the challenge of combined operations within a multinational context. When one also accounts for the need to integrate military activity into a much wider context that includes PMESII dimensions, then the true complexity even of apparently simple military tasks becomes evident. This increases the importance of operational art, as a conceptual framework to help commanders and their staff to think about the complex interactions between all these different elements. Frameworks such as NATO's Comprehensive Operations Planning Directive (COPD) can also help to ensure that different force elements, and different nationalities, share understanding of the decision-making process. As COPD makes clear, this process, to be successful, must be joint and must integrate military activity into the wider context (see Figure 18.3).[29]

Figure 18.3 Regular exercises are important if armed forces are to maintain proficiency in joint operations. Here an Australian Army M1A1 Abrams tank disembarks from a Mexefloat as part of Exercise Alon, a combined amphibious exercise in the Philippines in 2023. Source: https://tinyurl.com/dcr7785a

Multi-domain Operations (MDO) and Integration

Traditional thinking about joint warfare focused on inter-service operations although, as has been noted, many of the same challenges might apply in a situation where one service operates across different environmental boundaries, as would be the case when army attack helicopters provide support to ground forces or when navies coordinate the actions of ships, marines and naval aircraft. In reality, therefore, joint warfare has always been about more than inter-service cooperation. Today there is a growing tendency for some militaries to focus even less on institutional distinctions and instead to think of integrating activities across five '**operating domains**' that can be defined as 'spheres of activity or influence with common and distinct characteristics in which a force can conduct joint operations' (see Box 18.4).[30]

Interest in 'multi-domain' concepts originated in debates in the US, where there has been growing recognition of the need to achieve greater integration across all domains in order to meet the threat posed by adversaries able to exploit new technology and techniques to pose challenges that are not constrained by traditional service boundaries. This has included thinking about greater integration within a military context and also about the need to integrate multi-domain military activity within a whole-of-government response to challenges that might occur both below and above the threshold for war in a condition of persistent strategic competition.

Multi-domain Battle and Multi-Domain Operations (MDO)

The US Army was an early adopter of the multi-domain concept, focusing first on multi-domain battle and then expanding the idea to encompass MDO, defined as 'The combined arms employment of joint and Army capabilities to create and

BOX 18.4 OPERATING DOMAINS

Current NATO doctrine identifies the existence of five distinct domains, as follows: maritime, land, air, space and cyberspace. It is argued that, while the electromagnetic and acoustic spectrums make up an environment formed by physical laws, they do not represent domains in their own right but it is understood that both spectrums are strongly interconnected with the five operating domains listed here.[31]

There is an obvious similarity between the idea of 'domains' and the more established concept of physical environments, although the latter may not have been a very adequate way to conceptualise the way in which space and especially cyber capabilities permeate all types of military activity in a manner that is not environmentally constrained. Moreover, the emphasis on domains has the advantage of refocusing attention away from service boundaries towards a deeper understanding of the challenges inherent in fostering a fully integrated approach.

exploit relative advantages that achieve objectives, defeat enemy forces, and consolidate gains on behalf of joint force commanders.'[32] For the US Army, MDO represents an advanced form of jointery, designed to create synergy across all domains and to enable greater degrees of joint cooperation. This was seen as particularly relevant in the context of potential future operations against China, where land forces might be needed to contribute to a multidimensional battle for access. Thus, the updated 2022 edition of the US Army's capstone doctrine publication 'FM 3-0 Operations' argued that 'all operations are multi-domain operations' and explained that:

> Army forces employ organic capabilities in multiple domains, and they continuously benefit from air and maritime strategic transportation and space and cyberspace capabilities that they do not control, including global positioning, satellite communications, and intelligence, surveillance, and reconnaissance (ISR). Lower echelons may not always notice the opportunities created by higher echelons or other forces that operate primarily in other domains; however, leaders must understand how the absence of those opportunities affects their concepts of operations, decision making, and risk assessment.[33]

In similar vein, the value of MDO is also recognised in recent NATO doctrine, which defines this as the 'orchestration of military activities across all domains and environment, synchronised with non-military activities, to enable the Alliance to deliver converging effects at the speed of relevance'. The idea has quickly become mainstream in Western military thought, although the British articulate similar ideas using the title of Multi-Domain Integration (MDI) rather than MDO, stressing that this includes enhanced cooperation at the tactical as well as the operational level.[34]

It remains to be seen whether the adoption of these snappy new phrases can enhance levels of MDI any more than the profusion of the word 'joint' achieved the same in years gone by. Adoption of this term does have the advantage of focusing the mind more on integration across domains rather than just on institutional cooperation between the services. Certainly the heavy emphasis placed by many armed forces on the need for integration across multiple domains does suggest that they are at least taking the matter seriously.

Joint All-Domain Operations (JADO)

The logic of MDO has been carried further in the US, driven by concern about the challenges of confronting China at a time when ubiquitous sensors, mass data collection and enhanced analysis, AI-driven weapon systems and the increasing development of space and cyber platforms and capabilities have contributed to a situation that, it is claimed, represents a 'fundamental change in the character of war'.[35] In response to this the US military has advanced the concept of JADO and is working to develop a capability for Joint All-Domain Command and Control (JADC2). JADO is defined as 'Actions by the joint force in multiple domains integrated in planning and synchronized in execution, at speed and scale needed to gain advantage and accomplish the mission.'[36] The focus here is on the need to create a 'convergence of effects' across multiple domains, creating and exploiting windows of opportunity within a complex contested environment. This goes beyond traditional ideas of joint coordination, aiming at deeper and more seamless integration across all relevant domains. Thus, for example, recent experiments have tested the ability of army and navy radars to transmit data to Air Force F-22 Raptor and F-35 Lightening aircraft to be used in defence of space assets and to engage cruise missiles. Similarly, army experiments have tested the ability of in-service systems to pass data between themselves and to use AI to help reduce the sensor-to-shooter time for artillery from an average of fourteen minutes to just a few seconds.[37]

To achieve all of this will require a new approach to C2, hence a major focus on JADC2, which represents an attempt to exploit new technology (including AI and ML) to dramatically enhance and speed up decision making and to connect sensors, shooters and data across all domains to all forces, to integrate planning and ensure a convergence of effects across a dynamic battlefield.[38] JADC2 is driven by an awareness of the centrality of information dominance but also by understanding of the continued relevance of mission command as a means to enhance timely and appropriate decision making. The overall approach is nothing if not ambitious, and the US military has invested billions of dollars in a variety of initiatives and exercises designed to turn the idea into reality.[39]

In August 2023, after four years of development, a new Joint Warfighting Concept (JWC) was completed to provide a unifying vision for future warfare and new joint doctrine was published, to show how the vision could be put into effect. The aim of the JWC is to create a multi-domain capable joint force that amounts to more than the sum of its parts and is able to create multiple simultaneous dilemmas for adversaries (see Figure 18.4). General Mark A. Milley, chairman of the US Joint Chiefs of Staff, argued that the JWC built on twenty-five years of thought and experience in joint warfare and that with its completion American forces 'Now have a truly all-domain concept.'[40] The characteristics of joint warfighting were summarised within US doctrine as follows:

> The basis of joint warfighting is in the [combatant commander's] ability to integrate and, to the degree possible, synchronize mutually supporting and unified forces, campaigns, and operations, with all the joint functions throughout all domains and multiple areas of responsibility (AORs). The resultant synergy creates military advantage and maximizes combat capability. In pursuit of unified action, [combatant commanders] recognize the importance and contributions of allies, partners, and the interagency process.[41]

In summary, through the vision provided by the JWC, the US aims to create a multi-domain capable joint force that supports seamless integration of all relevant forces, without reference to traditional service boundaries, that can create multiple simultaneous dilemmas for adversaries. Highly ambitious, if achieved this would represent a super-charged form of jointery.

Figure 18.4 F/A 18F 'Super Hornets' fly over the aircraft carrier USS *Nimitz* during an all-domain joint exercise in the South China Seas in April 2023. Aircraft carriers are vessels with obvious multi-domain capabilities but in future their survival in a high threat environment will likely depend on ever closer synchronisation of joint assets across all domains. Source: www.navy.mil/Resources/Photo-Gallery/igphoto/2003211942/

The Other Side of the Hill

The US vision reflects concern about the challenge of meeting potential Chinese aggression across the continuum of conflict; it is reasonable to assume that Beijing has similar concerns in reverse. Since the 1990s, the Chinese have focused on the need to develop their own joint capabilities after the need to do so was forcefully reinforced by the rapid victory of US-led joint forces in the 1991 Gulf War. This resulted in a new Joint Doctrine publication in 1999, and by the mid 2000s the PLA was advocating a concept of integrated joint operations (IJO).[42] Military reforms announced by Xi Jinping in 2015 created a new C2 structure, replaced regional commands with a new joint theatre command system and reduced the size and importance of the army, relative to the navy and air force, reflecting realisation that joint reforms were necessary if Xi was to achieve his aim to complete Chinese military modernisation by 2035. It is clear that since then China has devoted considerable time and attention to the challenges associated with joint operations, including the production of new doctrinal 'Guidelines on Joint Operations' in 2020.[43]

China does not make its doctrine publicly available but debate amongst Chinese commentators suggest that, in common with its US counterparts, the Chinese military sees the value in an approach that can integrate capabilities across multiple domains to create windows of opportunity within a complex future operating environment. It also shares a heavy emphasis on information/intelligence. As far as we can tell, the PLA does not share the US emphasis on mission command as a core principle of C2, and an over-centralised approach here may inhibit the potential to create true cross-domain synergy. Moreover, most experts agree that, whatever their intent, the Chinese cannot match American experience in the conduct of joint operations, and it may take many years before they can bridge this gap. In this context, joint exercises, such as those now often undertaken with Russian forces, are particularly important to the PLA.[44]

Integrating All Tools of National Power

Accompanying the above has been growing awareness of the need to integrate the actions of joint forces into a wider network of activities that includes multiple non-military agencies. This reflects awareness that the military tool is only one of those available to governments and to be useful it must be flexible enough to be applied in a wide range of scenarios across the continuum of conflict. This was encompassed in the NATO concept of a Comprehensive Approach, the British Integrated Operating Concept, and US ideas about Unified Action, Global Integration and, at a strategic level, Extended Deterrence.[45] It may not be articulated as clearly and publicly in this way by actors such as China, Russia and Iran, but it seems evident that they too think of national strategy in a very joined up manner.[46] In this respect the idea of joint warfare as being team warfare (with the team here extending beyond the military sphere) is highly relevant. Joint military capabilities are thus best understood as representing just one element in a much broader context designed to meet complex challenges in times of war, peace and within the grey zone that lies between.

Conclusion

It is clear that joint operations have always been important and therefore that there is great value in armed forces being able to overcome the barriers created by institutional as well as environmental boundaries. This was true when there were only two recognisable military domains (land and sea), it became even more the case with the advent of air power and it is abundantly clear today that to be truly effective, armed forces need to integrate activity across multiple domains as seamlessly as possible. Proficiency in one environment or domain may count for little unless activity can be coordinated and integrated with the others. As ever, unfortunately, it is easier to recognise the importance of such integration than it is to achieve it. Inter-service cooperation has always been hampered by a range of tangible and intangible barriers that could create friction between the different force elements and, while new technology may help ease some of the practical challenges, by making it easier for forces to communicate and to operate as one cohesive network, it remains probable that different services (and different branches within the same service) will have different interests and priorities and thus will tend to think and act in ways that may not match those of their colleagues wearing different cap badges. Likely it will be impossible to remove entirely such friction, but armed forces will continue to be interested in ways to reduce this to the minimum possible level. The barriers to integration tend to be easier to break down when there is an obvious pressing need, and when resources are plentiful, and these are circumstances more common in time of war than in peace, but to be effective at joint operations requires time and work, and the foundations must be laid before the need arises. The degree to which armed forces succeed in doing this will have a direct bearing on their success on the battlefield and across the broader continuum of conflict. At least now most recognise the need to do so.

RESEARCH QUESTIONS

1. What is joint warfare and why is it so important in the context of twenty-first century military thought?
2. Why has it often proven so difficult to achieve effective joint cooperation?
3. What institutional structures best promote proficiency in joint warfare while protecting core service values and capabilities?
4. What are the key challenges associated with multinational (combined) operations? How can these be overcome?

FURTHER READING

Beaumont, Roger A., *Joint Military Operations: A Short History*, (Westport, CT: Greenwood Press, 1993). Once the standard text on the topic this book still provides a very useful introduction even if, inevitably, if does not discuss the latest developments. The book is particularly useful in identifying the barriers to effective joint operations, which were very evident at the time of writing.

Black, Jeremy, *Combined Operations: A Global History of Amphibious and Airborne Warfare*, (London: Rowman and Littlefield, 2017) As the title suggests, this book focuses on amphibious and airborne operations, rather than joint warfare per se. It provides a brief overview of relevant history from ancient times to the twentieth century.

Burke, Ryan, Michael Fowler and Jahara Matisek (eds.), *Military Strategy, Joint Operations and Air Power: An Introduction*, 2nd ed. (Washington, DC: Georgetown University Press, 2022) Written primarily as a textbook for US Air Force Academy Cadets, this book provides a useful introduction to the topic as it relates to airpower.

Griffin, Stuart, *Joint Operations: A Short History*, (London: Ministry of Defence, 2005). This short (unclassified) work was produced for the UK Ministry of Defence at a time when the latter was keenly interested in exploring and explaining the value of joint operations. The book examines key dynamics of such operations through a number of case studies from the twentieth century. It is well worth a read, if you can find a copy.

Heck, Timothy and B.A. Friedman, (eds.), *On Contested Shores: The Evolving Role of Amphibious Operations in the History of Warfare*, (Quantico, VA: Marine Corps University Press, 2020) Focused on amphibious operations, this volume includes some very interesting essays that explore challenges and opportunities associated with one important type of joint operation.

Vego, Milan, *Joint Operational Warfare: Theory and Practice*, (Newport, RI: US Navy War College, 2009). Vego focuses on operational art and warfare at the operational level, relating this to ideas about joint warfare. The work reflects the importance of operational art as a means of meeting the challenges posed by joint operations.

ONLINE RESOURCES

NATO Joint Warfare Centre homepage, www.jwc.nato.int/.

AJP1 Allied (NATO) Joint Doctrine (with UK national elements), 2022, https://tinyurl.com/ydnxefhj.

Rand Organisation website on Joint Operations, www.rand.org/topics/joint-operations.html.

US Joint Chiefs of Staff, Joint Doctrine Publications, www.jcs.mil/Doctrine/Joint-Doctine-Pubs/.

US Air Force / US Space Force, *The Department of Air Force Role in Joint All Domain Operations*, (November 2021), https://tinyurl.com/bdhsrbwa.

US Department of Defense, *Summary of Joint All Domain Command and Control (JADC2) Strategy* (March 2022), https://tinyurl.com/3mx63u99.

UK Integrated Operating Concept, updated 2021, https://tinyurl.com/yr7ybm6f.

NOTES

1 NATO, *The NATO Terminology Database*, https://nso.nato.int/natoterm/content/nato/pages/home.html?lg = en.

2 US Joint Chiefs of Staff, *JP 1. Joint Warfare of the Armed Forces of the United States*, (14 Nov 2000).

3 US Joint Chiefs of Staff, *Joint Publication (JP) 1. Volume 1. Joint Warfighting*. Unclassified Edition (27 Aug 2023). Glossary

4 See Jeter A. Isely and Philip A. Crowl, *The US Marines and Amphibious War: Its Theory and Practice in the Pacific*, (Princeton, NJ: Princeton University Press, 1951), chs. 4 and 5. Allan R. Millett, *Semper Fidelis: The History of the US Marine Corps*, (New York, NY: Simon and Schuster, 1991), pp. 362–71.

5 Lincoln Paine, *The Sea and Civilisation: A Maritime History of the World*, (London: Atlantic Books, 2015).

6 For a useful overview see Roger Beaumont, *Joint Military Operations: A Short History*, (Westport, CT: Greenwood Press, 1993).

7 Stuart Griffin, *Joint Operations: A Short History*, (London: Ministry of Defence, 2005), p. 17.

8 Antoine de Jomini, *The Art of War* (1828) 1862 ed., transl. G.H. Mendill and W.P Craighill, esp. Article XXIX, Article XL and Appendix 'Sketch of the Principal Maritime Expeditions', www.gutenberg.org/files/13549/13549-h/13549-h.htm. Colmer Van der Goltz, *The Conduct of War, A Short Treatise on Its Most Important Branches and Guiding Rules*, (London: William Clowes & Sons, 1908), esp. ch. XIV.

9 See Ian Speller, *Understanding Naval Warfare*, 3rd ed. (London: Routledge, 2023). Also see Kevin McCranie, *Mahan, Corbett and the Foundations of Naval Strategic Thought*, (Annapolis, MD: Naval Institute Press, 2021).

10 For example, see Julian Corbett, *England in the Seven Years War: A Study in Combined Strategy*, (London: Longmans, 1907) and *Some Principles of Maritime* Strategy, (London: Longmans, 1911). Admiral Sir Herbert Richmond, *National Policy and Naval Strength*, (London: Longmans, 1934) and *Statesmen and Sea Power*, (Oxford: Oxford University Press, 1946). Basil Liddell-Hart, *The British Way in Warfare*, (London: Faber & Faber 1932).

11 Thomas More Molyneux, *Conjunct Expeditions: or Expeditions That Have Been Carried Out Jointly by the Fleet and the Army*, (London: R & J Dodsley 1759).

12 George Furse, *Military Expeditions Beyond the Seas*, two vols. (London: William Clowes, 1897).

13 Sir George Aston. *Letters on Amphibious Wars*, (London: John Murray, 1911) and *Sea, Land and Air Strategy*, (London: John Murray, 1914).

14 Charles Callwell, *The Effect of Maritime Command on Campaigns since Waterloo*, (London: Blackwood, 1897) and *Military Operations and Maritime Preponderance: Their Relations and Interdependence* (Annapolis, MD: Naval Institute Press, 1996 [1905]).

15 See Beatrice Heuser, *The Evolution of Strategy: Thinking War from Antiquity to the Present*, (Cambridge: Cambridge University Press, 2011), part V.

16 John Slessor, *Air Power and Armies*, (Oxford: Oxford University Press, 1936).

17 For the best examination of this campaign see Richard Overy, *The Bombing War in Europe, 1939–1945* (London: Penguin, 2013).

18 Williamson Murray, 'The Evolution of Joint Warfare', *Joint Forces Quarterly*, (Summer 2002), 30–7.

19 Ian Speller, '"Neither Fish nor Fowl nor Yet Good Red Herring" – Joint Institutions, Single-Service Priorities, and Amphibious Capabilities in Postwar Britain', *US Naval War College Review*, 4(73) (Autumn 2020).

20 In Vietnamese: *B⊠ Qu⊠c phòng nư⊠c C⊠ng hòa xã h⊠i chủ nghĩa Vi⊠t Nam.*

21 Beaumont, *Joint Operations*, ch. 5. Also see Alastair Finlan, Anna Danielsson and Stefan Lundqvist, 'Critically Engaging the Concept of Joint Operations: Origins, Reflexivity and the Case of Sweden', *Defence Studies* 21(3) (2021).

22 David Bickers, 'Understanding the Vulnerabilities in China's New Joint Force', *Joint Forces Quarterly* (4th Quarter, October 2001).

23 See Griffin, *Joint Operations*, ch. 1.

24 Ian Speller, 'Command and Control in Amphibious Operations: The Lessons from History', *Revista da Escola de Guerra Navale* (Journal of the Brazilian Naval War College). 25(3) (2019), 561–86.

25 Daniel Hartnett, 'The Father of the Modern Chinese Navy', *CIMSEC*, 8 October 2014. https://cimsec.org/father-modern-chinese-navy-liu-huaqing/.

26 NATO. *ATP-08, Doctrine for Amphibious Operations*, (2017), ch. 2. Also see US Joint Chiefs of Staff, *JP 3-02, Amphibious Operations*, (2019).

27 NATO, *The NATO Terminology Database*, https://nso.nato.int/natoterm/content/nato/pages/home.html?lg = en.

28 For example, see Jeremy Black, *Combined Operations. A Global History of Amphibious and Airborne Warfare*, (London: Rowman and Littlefield, 2017).

29 *AJP 5. Allied Joint Doctrine for the Planning of Operations* (2019).

30 US Air Force/US Space Force, *Air Force/Space Force Doctrine Publication 3-99. The Department of the Air Force Role in Joint All Domain Operations* (November 2021).

31 NATO, *AJP 3.2. Allied Joint Doctrine for Land Operations*, (2022), p. 3

32 Headquarters, Department of the US Army, *FM 3-0 Operations*, (October 2022), pp. 1–2.

33 *FM 3-0 Operations*, pp. 1–3.

34 UK Ministry of Defence, *AJP 01. Allied Joint Doctrine: with UK National Elements,* (December 2022), p. 5.
35 General Mark A. Milley, 'Strategic Inflection Point: The Most Historically Significant and Fundamental Change in the Character of War is Happening Now – Whilst the Future is Clouded in Mist and Uncertainty', *Joint Force Quarterly,* (3rd Quarter, 2023), 8. JP 1, *Joint Warfighting* (2023), xiii.
36 James Black, Alice Lynch, Kristian Gustafson, David Blagdon, Pauline Paille and Fiona Quimbre, *Multi-Domain Integration in Defence. Conceptual Approaches and Lessons from Russia, China, Iran and North Korea,* (Santa Monica, CA: RAND Corporation, 2022), p. 9.
37 See Justin Bronk and Samuel Cranny-Evans, *Building the Capacity to Conduct Joint All-Domain Operations (JADO): Considerations for the UK,* RUSI Occasional Paper (November 2022).
38 AFDP 3-99, p. 5.
39 Travis Sharp, 'JADC2 Spending is Sprawling. DoD Should Keep Watch, but Let It Go' *Breaking Defense,* 20 October 2022, https://breakingdefense.com/2022/10/jadc2-spending-is-sprawling-dod-should-keep-watch-but-let-it-go/.
40 General Mark A. Milley, 'Strategic Inflection Point. The Most Historically Significant and Fundamental Change in the Character of War is Happening Now – Whilst the Future is Clouded in Mist and Uncertainty', *Joint Force Quarterly* (3rd Quarter, 2023), 6–15.
41 JP 1, *Joint Warfighting* (2023), vi.
42 Sugiura Yasuyuki, The PLA's Pursuit of Enhanced Joint Operations Capabilities' *NIDS China Security Report* (2022).
43 David Finkelstein, 'Deciphering the PLA's New Joint Doctrine', Center for International and Strategic Studies Podcast, 12 October 2021, www.csis.org/podcasts/chinapower/deciphering-plas-new-joint-doctrine-conversation-dr-david-finkelstein.
44 Ben Noon and Chris Bassler, 'Schrodinger's Military? Challenges for China's Military Modernization Ambitions', *War on the Rocks,* 14 October 2021, https://warontherocks.com/2021/10/schrodingers-military-challenges-for-the-chinas-military-modernization-ambitions/.
45 NATO, 'A Comprehensive Approach to Crises' April 2023. www.nato.int/cps/en/natohq/topics_51633.htm. US Department of Defense, *The National Defense Strategy of the United States of America* (2022). JP 1, *Joint Warfighting* (2023). UK Ministry of Defence, DCDC, *Integrated Operating Concept* (2019).
46 Black et al., *Multi-Domain Integration,* passim.

19 Cyber Warfare

CHRISTOPHER TUCK

CHAPTER OUTLINE

KEY THEMES

- Cyber warfare has attained a growing prominence in debates on contemporary and future warfare. Cyber tools are an important element in the conduct of information operations and cyber is commonly viewed now as a separate domain of warfare.
- The cyber domain has a range of attributes that appear to give it some unique advantages over the traditional domains of warfare. This has led some commentators to argue that it is an increasingly decisive element in warfare, perhaps able even to substitute for traditional land, air and maritime forces.
- There are counter-arguments that hold that cyber warfare has significant weaknesses as a tool and that it is an important, but still complementary, element in modern warfare.

Introduction

Previous chapters have addressed what might be called 'kinetic' operations: military activity that is concerned with the application, or threat of the application, of physical force. As the twenty-first century has progressed, however, debates have emerged on the effects of new technologies and concepts and their impact on the significance of 'non-kinetic' instruments, especially cyber operations. For some commentators, cyber activities have begun to challenge the importance of traditional land, sea and air operations. It is certainly the case that cyber has had a growing prominence in the last twenty years. Computing, networks and flows of information have come to permeate societies, making them progressively more 'informationalised', strengthening the reach and impact of cyber and information activities. Digital networks have become a foundation of modern military operations for many armed forces. In response, many countries have created organisations, capabilities and doctrines for the use of cyber as a tool of conflict. Cyber is now viewed as its own distinct domain sitting alongside air, maritime, land and space. Nevertheless, cyber's effectiveness as a tool of warfare remains a matter of debate: is cyber warfare independently decisive; or are cyber operations a significant, but complementary, part of modern multidimensional operations? The debate on the significance of cyber operations has also raised a range of other important questions: can one usefully talk of cyber 'war' or 'warfare'? What is the relationship between cyber and information operations? Does cyber genuinely constitute a distinct domain? What are the opportunities and challenges associated with integrating cyber into the tactical and operational detail of military activity?

This chapter is divided into three parts. The first explores the topic of cyber warfare and looks at some important concepts and issues. The second part examines the theory surrounding cyber operations: the attributes of the cyber domain itself, its definitions and characteristics and the application of cyber to modern warfare, in terms of developing capabilities and roles. The chapter then concludes with a discussion of some of the challenges of utilising cyber operations, and possible future developments.

The Significance of Cyber

Cyber-attack is now a pervasive feature of the international system. More than 46 million potential cyber-attacks are detected every day.[1] The significance of cyber is a direct result of the ongoing ' informationalisation ' of human society. The expansion, intensification and integration of political, financial and media networks, driven by satellite communications, the internet and social media, has multiplied dramatically the connectivity between actors in the international system. In the 1990s, the term 'cyber' emerged as an essential element in the debates on change, a phenomenon that reinforced the argument that an information-centric revolution in human affairs was underway. The internet, wireless networks, Big Data, social media and mobile phones accelerate the speed with which information can flow between and amongst producers and users.[2] Amongst other things, this has led to a 'cyberisation' of politics, with elements of the cyber domain now intertwined with political activities. The 'Internet of Things', the growing network of connected electronic devices, from kitchen appliances to wearables, has also expanded the range of sensors and automated data collection that can be employed by information operations.

Political cyberisation has been accompanied by military cyberisation:

> From mechanisation and motorisation, we have passed into the realm of computerisation and networked societies, where even warfare is characterised by the concept of the absolute speed of the cyber domain. Cyberwarfare is part of the evolution of conventional warfare, which itself is linked to broader social and political change.[3]

The cyberisation of modern militaries is embedded in their reliance on computers and networks for many of their most basic functions: C2; communication; navigation; ISR; fire control; and logistics. Cyber is also a vital cross-domain capability, providing a vital means by which the different domains can be combined for joint operations and MDO. As a result, modern Western doctrine has elevated cyber from a supporting capability to a fully-fledged warfighting domain alongside the four physical domains.

What Is Cyber Warfare?

Cyber warfare is sometimes viewed in very expansive ways that include almost any action in cyber space intended to inflict harm. But this view can be politically dangerous and strategically escalatory because it ascribes a particular intent and significance to what are often now routine activities. Used in this way, the term 'warfare' risks lumping together all cyber activities ranging from isolated digital vandalism to coordinated attacks on essential infrastructure. However, in the form of cyber activities designed for espionage, influence, and subversion, cyber forms part of the general competition between political actors that is now a normal part of international relations. James Lewis argues that 'It is not correct to call every bad thing that happens on the internet "war"'.[4]This more general and pervasive activity is perhaps better termed 'cyber conflict'. The term 'cyber war' is often used instead to describe the independent use of cyber activities, often as a substitute for military operations. In 2007, for example, Russia launched a comprehensive cyber-attack on Estonia as part of a diplomatic dispute caused by the Estonian removal of a Soviet era commemorative statue. The targets included banks, media outlets, the telecommunications infrastructure and government servers.[5] For cyber enthusiasts, such as John Arquilla, cyber war reflects the potentially revolutionary impact of cyber, and its development as an independently decisive tool of policy and strategy.

Cyber conflict and cyber war are activities that are best discussed as part of debates on 'political warfare', 'subthreshold warfare' or 'hybrid warfare' (see Chapter 20). This chapter concerns itself with the narrower topic of cyber war*fare*, defined as the use of cyber activities to advance military objectives.[6] Cyber warfare is a 'sequence of coordinated actions with a defined military purpose in cyber space; requiring cyber capabilities'.[7] Some have challenged the use of the term 'warfare' in relation to cyber because it does not exhibit many of the attributes that we ascribe to war, such as major physical destruction or high levels of violence.[8] But cyber warfare helps enable warfare in the other domains: it concerns the use of cyber strategically, in terms of shaping military capabilities, and operationally and tactically as part of military campaigns. As we shall see later in this chapter, cyber warfare is more difficult to execute than we might imagine, especially at the operational and tactical levels.

Are Cyber Operations Different from Information Operations?

There are continuing uncertainties regarding cyber's relationship with information operations. The information environment, the 'Aggregate of individuals, organizations, and systems that collect, process, disseminate, or act on information,'[9] is a very large space, given that information is something that is central to almost every human activity. On the one hand, this has led some to argue that cyber is best thought of as a sub-element of information operations. Information operations are the employment of information-related capabilities and could include everything from strategic-level disinformation campaigns directed by governments, through to Electronic Warfare, cyber, military deception or psychological operations employed by the military at the operational and tactical levels. This was the view taken in US doctrine before 2010, and it is a view that many continue to adhere to. Daniel Moore, for example, argues that cyber operations could be considered as 'The digital network aspect of the larger spectrum of information operations.'[10] Since 2010, however, cyber has been seen alternatively as an 'information-related capability': while it can support information operations, it can also be thought of as separate from them. This is because, while cyber can be used as part of operations designed to have a cognitive effect (to influence and change human views and perceptions), it can also have a direct military effect in the physical domains on land and sea, and in the air and space.[11] But there is no consensus on the nature of this relationship. In Russian doctrine, for example, 'Distinguishing cyber war from IO [information operations] is virtually impossible.'[12]

Cyber as a Means

Even practitioners continue to struggle with these definitional issues. As a former head of US Cyber Command has commented:

> We haven't decided yet what is or isn't information operations, information warfare, cyberspace operations, operations in cyberspace that enable information operations ... Is it about spectrum, is it about IP [internet protocol] space, OT [operational technology] space, is it about cognitive operations, beliefs and understanding and motivations for operations? ... We just haven't yet decided.[13]

An important consequence of the preceding debate is the utility in viewing cyber operations as a means. Cyber provides methods, sometimes as an alternative, but often in a complementary way, to achieve objectives in the other domains or environments. For example, Cyber Electromagnetic Activities (CEMA) are the cyber means that contribute towards electronic warfare, just as cyber influence operations are designed to help contribute to the manipulation of audiences. Cyber can be used as a means to achieve information operations (for example, hacking personal contact details that would allow individuals to be messaged through social media); as a means of supporting physical activities (for example, to disrupt enemy air defence systems); or as a part of wider efforts at coercion (for example, disrupting critical infrastructure).

Cyber Warfare in Theory

As with the other domains, approaches to cyber warfare are shaped by the implications of the characteristics of the cyber domain itself.

Characteristics of the Cyber Domain

As a domain, cyber is commonly identified as having a range of specific characteristics, which also carry consequences for the operations conducted within it.

One important foundation characteristic is that the cyber domain is multidimensional. While the cyber domain is commonly thought of as an essentially technological phenomenon, defined by data and networks, it actually has several different 'layers' or 'planes'. The detail with which these are defined varies: some define as few as three layers, and others as many as six.[14] But, broadly, these dimensions tend to be organised along three themes. The first is a 'logical layer' associated with information and networks. This is the portion that we commonly associate with cyber; it is the realm where data are stored and moved, systems connect, connections are organised and governed, and software and applications reside. This part of the domain is intangible. But cyber also has an important 'physical layer'. This dimension consists of the physical infrastructure required for all cyber activities. This includes computer hardware, microwave receivers, fibre-optics, submarine cables and network devices. This aspect of the cyber domain is tangible and it also has a geographic position; it is physically located somewhere. Finally, the cyber domain also has an important human dimension. This 'user layer' is a manifestation of the way human beings develop and employ cyber systems. This would include how we interact with cyberspace through 'cyber personas': through the different media accounts that we have. But it also includes human predilections and flaws that influence how the cyber domain operates.

The multidimensional character of the cyber domain brings with it some interesting consequences. On the one hand, some parts of the domain are intangible. Computer code and data flows associated with the logical layer lack mass. This means that cyber weapons cannot directly kill a human, although they may do so indirectly. Intangibility also means that it is possible to resurrect aspects of the cyber domain: data can be restored, for example, if there are back-ups available. As a result, some important cyber effects are reversible and may only be temporary. On the other hand, and contrary to many popular assumptions, cyber does have a physical presence. This has political consequences in that governments may have an opportunity to exert influence on those aspects of the cyber domain that are placed within their borders. It also means that cyber warfare can have an important tangible aspect to it – one way of undermining an adversary's cyber capabilities is to destroy the hardware necessary for the networks to function, such as computer systems, routers and cables. The human dimension of the cyber domain is also very significant. It helps to explain many of the fundamental insecurities that exist in cyber systems. Humans design computer hardware and software, and our limitations in doing so create many of the flaws that provide the means by which those systems can be hacked. Human beings also use computers and networks. There has long been a trade-off between security and usability. Many exploitable weaknesses in cyber systems are an avoidable result of making those systems easier for humans to employ.[15] The weak link in many cyber systems is the human link and our often poor 'cyber hygiene'.

Another characteristic of the cyber domain is that, because cyber is an artificial domain, it is a highly variable one. While some aspects of the domain are governed by physical laws, others are elastic and can change depending upon developments in technology, systems and concepts. The activities of humans and automated systems mean that this terrain is constantly changing, making it difficult to map and understand. Rapid change can quickly create new opportunities and render irrelevant existing cyber tools. Paradoxically however, another feature of the cyber domain is its specificity. While the cyber domain is both physical and human in character, the 'logical layer' imposes a particular specificity on the processes and tools that must be employed in cyber operations. This means that while a tank, for example, once created can be used to attack a very wide variety of targets without much specific preparation, cyber tools are often bespoke: they only work against a particular system and through exploiting a particular vulnerability.

The cyber domain is also pervasive. Cyber space is essentially concerned with flows of information, and these flows of information have application across most features of modern society from communications, social media and digital networks, through to industrial infrastructure, government systems and private companies. As a result, cyber is essential to modern military operations and is omnipresent in the other domains of warfare. Increasingly, military capabilities simultaneously have both a physical and a cyber presence. A consequence is that the cyber domain is also globally interconnected. International networks and cloud computing mean that geographic boundaries do not apply in the way that they do in the physical domains. Systems that have effects in one part of the world can be accessed and manipulated from entirely different parts of the world. For that reason, the cyber domain has many potential access points. Given this, cyber also collapses distances, since data can move globally in milliseconds. This gives cyber tools both speed and reach in application.

Despite this interconnectedness, the cyber domain is also fragmented. Much of the cyber domain is owned by private companies. Governments still have influence through the physical dimension of the cyber domain. The US, for example, is often regarded as having privileged cyber access because most internet root servers are on US soil. Countries such as China and Russia have also sought to carve out their own national cyber spaces through technical changes and censorship. These 'splinternets' have had some success in allowing governments to control information flows. Nevertheless, much of the cyber domain remains poorly regulated. The governance structures consist of multiple multilateral institutions and stand-alone treaties such as the Corporation for Assigned Names and Numbers, and the Internet Engineering Task Force. There are also many actors in the cyber sphere that operate outside of direct government control. These include non-government actors and individuals. 'Hacktivist' (politically active hackers) networks have been a public feature of the war in Ukraine, for example; and insurgent groups invariably have an online presence. This makes the cyber domain inherently complex for national militaries because they do not control it, and achieving goals may require cooperation with other agencies, private enterprises and countries.

Because the cyber domain is intangible, globally connected and fragmented, it is also opaque. The cyber 'terrain' is largely invisible and so it isn't clear who owns it, or who is using it. This contributes to problems of attribution. It is often difficult with certainty and in a timely matter to identify the source of cyber-attacks. This is, indeed, one of the attractions of cyber as a tool. As Chapter 2 has discussed, this has also led to debates on whether traditional concepts of deterrence are relevant in the cyber domain.

Because of many of the preceding factors, the cyber domain is also continuously contested. Ease of access to the domain, anonymity, lack of regulation and the importance of cyber economically, politically, socially and militarily, both nationally and internationally, has encouraged its use as a medium for conflict and competition. From individuals or 'hacktivist' groups motivated by politics or entertainment, through to criminal groups motivated by economic gain, or governments and non-state actors attempting to achieve larger political and military goals, the cyber domain is now a central arena for the clash of interests. It is no surprise to find that, as Chapter 20 has demonstrated, cyber is one of the significant means through which hybrid or subthreshold conflict is executed.

These characteristics explain the escalating importance of cyber in modern warfare. Modern militaries offer a large number of potential 'attack surfaces' as a result of the plethora of information entry points, and the ways in which information networks have a pervasive presence; cyber is difficult to attribute; it has global reach; it can be applied rapidly; it is a 'cleaner' more discriminate weapon because it need not inflict physical damage; and the physical costs of failure can be low.

Is Cyber a Domain?

It is worth noting that there continues to be a debate about the extent to which cyber should indeed be viewed as a separate domain of war in the same way that land, air, maritime and space are regarded as such. Unlike the physical domains, the cyber domain is artificial: the 'terrain' is manufactured by humans or by computers created by humans. The cyber domain, therefore, is not defined by the same clear physical characteristics as the others. Allied to this, there is a significant overlap between cyber and the electromagnetic spectrum (EMS), because the EMS provides a significant means through which cyber operates. The EMS comprises 'radio waves, microwaves, heat radiation, visible light, ultraviolet radiation, X-rays, electromagnetic cosmic rays and gamma rays': all of these are defined by differences in frequency and spectrum.[16] The EMS permeates everything. As a result, the UK views cyber and EMS together as a domain rather than just cyber alone. Critics also argue that cyber is an essential presence in the other domains as well. This generates a complexity of interaction 'between technology, society, people, situational awareness and battlefield effects' that makes confining cyber conceptually to its own domain some think is unhelpful.[17] Putting cyber into its own distinct domain risks creating an unhealthy compartmentalisation of the conceptual and practical development of cyber operations. As the example of nuclear weapons demonstrates, new technology may create strategically and militarily significant tools that demand specific thinking or modes of employment; but that does not mean necessarily that they need to be thought of in terms of a distinct domain of warfare.

What Are Cyber Operations?

The building block of cyber warfare is the cyber operation. Cyber operations (sometimes referred to as computer network operations or CNO), as the name suggests are those activities conducted to achieve objectives in or through cyberspace.[18] However, there is no universally accepted definition of what the latter might be. While the term 'cyberspace' is often popularly viewed as essentially being the internet, military perspectives tend to see it as a larger phenomenon. US doctrine defines cyberspace as:

> The domain within the information environment that consists of the interdependent network of information technology (IT) infrastructures and resident data. It includes the Internet, telecommunications networks, computer systems, and embedded processors and controllers.[19]

Therefore, the internet is an important part of cyberspace, but the domain also encompasses the data and processes associated with wider information systems, and implicitly the human interactions that give these systems meaning.[20] As we shall see later, these wider aspects have implications for the nature of cyber operations.

Types of Cyber Operations

There are different ways of categorising cyber operations. One common approach is to emphasise different kinds of objective: attack, defence, and information gathering, for example. Using this approach, offensive cyber operations (OCO) include 'Missions intended to project power in and through foreign cyberspace.' There might be a wide range of targets including enemy weapons systems, C2 and logistics. Defensive cyber operations (DCO) are 'Missions intended to preserve the ability to utilize blue [friendly] cyberspace capabilities and protect data, networks, cyberspace-enabled devices, and other designated systems by defeating on-going or imminent malicious cyberspace activity.' The aim is to protect friendly systems, or, if a breach does take place, to restore the systems as quickly as possible.[21] A third type is cyber ISR, often called cyber-enabled operations (CEO), designed to acquire intelligence that can be used for other military activities.[22]

An alternative way of conceptualising cyber operations is to categorise them according to the method of delivery. Presence-base attacks, as the name suggests, are those built on establishing a long-term clandestine presence in an opponent's systems. They are more likely to require high-level political approval and are likely to require longer periods of time to conduct. Event-based operations, on the other hand, are those that are likely to have more immediate effects, and which target enemy capabilities. They are more likely to be the responsibility of the military.[23]

How Does Cyber Warfare Work?

The methods by which cyber warfare works are often obscured by the vocabulary that is employed to describe cyber operations. The generic term 'cyber hack' does not communicate much about the variety of ways in which cyber can be used. Likewise, common cyber warfare terminology often borrows analogies from the physical domains, a practice that might give the impression that cyber works in similar ways. For example, Western doctrine talks about cyber manoeuvre: 'The application of force to capture, disrupt, deny, degrade, destroy or manipulate computing and information resources in order to achieve a position of advantage in respect to competitors.'[24] Phrases such as 'cyber fires' or the dropping of 'cyber bombs' can also be found in the literature.[25]

Like military operations in the physical domains, cyber is used to create effects. These effects can include things like the disruption, degrading or manipulation of enemy systems. Common objectives for cyber operations include the disruption of enemy C2 systems; the targeting of critical infrastructure; information warfare; deception; targeting logistics and supply chains; causing weapons malfunctions; intelligence and surveillance operations; and counter-intelligence. There are many ways by which cyber can generate effects against these sorts of targets.

- **Capturing** enemy systems: This can be achieved through crashing adversary anti-virus applications; IP hijacking to divert network traffic to one's own country; or gaining root access to an enemy weapon control system.
- **Disruption**: Rendering systems inoperable by deleting data in firmware or on system guard drives; setting system data to invalid values; installing **malware** to slow down a system; sending out spurious router adverts; DDoS attacks (see Box 19.1).
- **Denial**: Locking adversaries out of their systems by changing passwords or encrypting user systems; filling up storage on an email server; forcing a reboot of an enemy security system.
- **Degradation**: Inserting disconnect requests on a wireless network.
- **Destruction**: Erasing a critical application or data from a disk; physical attacks against digital infrastructure; malware attacks to shut systems down.
- **Manipulation**: Tarpitting or sandboxing enemy intrusions; relaying spoofed instructions to humans, or to physical control systems, for example, sending incorrect targeting information to a weapon.

In theory, then, cyber operations are a flexible and dangerous tool of warfare, especially against adversaries reliant on digital architectures.

Who Conducts Cyber Warfare?

In popular culture, cyber warfare is often presented as the arena of the maverick hacker operating outside of established authority. There is an element of truth to this view. Hacktivist collectives such as Anonymous have engaged in many damaging cyber-attacks. In February 2022, Anonymous declared 'war' against Russia after its invasion of Ukraine, conducting a variety of DDoS, information and espionage activities. Equally, many governments make use of semi-autonomous or affiliated hacking groups. Nevertheless, given the growing significance of cyber as a military domain, it is no surprise to find that major state cyber actors have been attempting to develop specific military capabilities and doctrines for cyber warfare.

The US

In the US, new cyber-specific organisations have been created. In 1998, the US created the Joint Task Force – Computer Network Defense (JTF-CND) for defensive cyber operations. By 2005 it had also established an organisation to coordinate offensive operations – the Joint Functional Component Command – Network

BOX 19.1 SOME KEY CYBER TERMS

Malware (malicious software): Malware may have many purposes including deleting, encrypting, corrupting or stealing data, and crashing or taking control of computer systems. Malware can include programs such as *Worms*, designed to be able automatically to replicate themselves and to spread across digital systems; *Trojans*, that disguise themselves as legitimate software to deceive users into downloading them; *Wipers*, intended to erase data ('data-wipe') the target system; and *Logic-bombs*, a type of malware that lies hidden in a system until triggered.

Bot: Programs designed to perform a range of tasks automatically. For example, *Crawlers* index content and *Scrapers* acquire information. *Botnets* are networks of bots, controlled remotely and usually employed for malicious purposes.

Troll farm: Organised groups or bots that flood social media platforms with content designed to mislead and manipulate audiences.

Phishing: The use of online communications such as emails to attempt to deceive targets into revealing private information.

Astro-turfing: Hiding the external origins of a social media communication to make it look as if it emerged from within an existing social media community.

Deepfake: Fabricated images, video or audio content designed to manipulate the perceptions of audiences.

DoS/DDoS (Denial of Service/Distributed Denial of Service): A form of cyber-attack designed to disrupt a target system by subjecting it to an overwhelming volume of network traffic.

Spoofing: Efforts to deceive an adversary's computer systems or users: for example, 'spoof' websites, Internet Protocol (IP), or email addresses that appear genuine but that have been created to facilitate unauthorised access to adversary systems and information.

Sandpit: A controlled and isolated environment that can be used to trap and manipulate adversary cyber intrusions.

Tarpit: A defensive technique utilising a simulated environment (e.g., email system) that mimics a legitimate system but operates much more slowly, trapping an intrusive adversary

APT (advanced persistent threat): Extended, often multistage, cyber espionage attacks conducted over a prolonged period.

Warfare (JFCC-NW). This was followed in 2009 by the creation of Cyber Command (USCYBERCOM), which was created to 'Conduct full-spectrum military cyberspace operations in order to enable actions in all domains.'[26] In 2018, CYBERCOM became a fully-fledged 'unified combatant command'. US CYBERCOM owns the offensive cyber capabilities within the US Department of Defense, and the services conduct

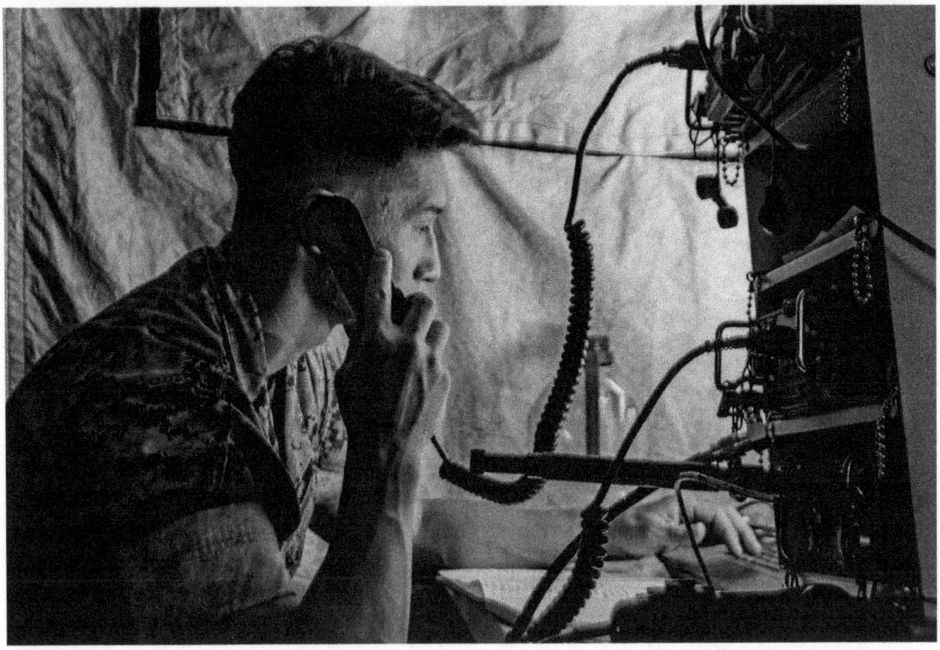

Figure 19.1 A US Marine conducts a communications check during a cyber exercise in 2021. Cyber operations now form an important integrated element in the information warfare capabilities of many modern armies. Source: https://media.defense.gov/2021/Jul/30/2002817453/-1/-1/0/210726-M-TP104-1007C.JPG

offensive cyber operations through CYBERCOM and the cyber mission forces that each service provides to the command. The strength of US cyber forces varies according to different data from 5,000 to 9,000 personnel and has an annual budget of US$7–9 billion.[27]

Each of the services has developed their own cyber organisations. The US Army, for example, has the 11th Cyber Battalion and its own Cyber Center of Excellence; the USN has 'non-kinetic effect teams'; and the USMC has a Marine Corps Information Command and Marine Expeditionary Force Information Groups (MIGs). These generally approach cyber as a capability that is converged with electronic warfare, information operations and intelligence gathering.

Doctrinally, the importance of information operations was reflected in the creation of Joint Publication 3-12 *Cyberspace Operations*, as well as higher direction in the form of the 2015 Cyber Strategy produced by the Department of Defence, Presidential Policy Directive 20 (PPD-20) and 2018's National Security Presidential Memorandum 13 (NSPM-13).[28] The US assumes that cyber will be central to the planning and conduct of future warfare, and that it needs to be fully integrated across commands, partly because cyber is integral to the functioning of assets in the other domains, but also because cyber also relies on an infrastructure that is physically present in those domains (see Figure 19.1).[29] The US is trying to develop a concept of expeditionary cyber operations as a way of enabling higher level-cyber capabilities and expertise to 'reach forward' to the tactical level.

NATO

NATO has its own Cyberspace Operations Centre that serves to support NATO missions by providing cyber situational awareness and coordination. This organisation can also facilitate integration on a voluntary basis by member states through the Sovereign Cyber Effects Provided Voluntary by Allies (SCEPVA) framework. NATO can also provide computer emergency response teams (CERTs) to member states. To develop better cyber expertise, NATO sponsors the Cooperative Cyber Defence Centre of Excellence to encourage cyber cooperation and information sharing. Individual nations also have their own capabilities. In 2017, for example, France established its own Cyber Defence Command.[30] In 2022, the UK created a Cyber Electro Magnetic Activities (CEMA) Effects Group, consisting of the 13 Signal Regiment, reformed in 2020 as a cyber regiment, and the 14 and 21 Signal Regiments, which are electronic warfare effects units.

Russia

Russia sees cyber warfare through the lens of the concept of 'information confrontation' (*Informatsionoye protivoborstvo)*, which embodies a comprehensive view of the need to engage and defeat the foundations of an adversary's information capabilities. In this regard, Russian approaches show strong similarities with their Soviet past in viewing modern strategic competition as something that has information operations at its core. From a Russian perspective, information warfare can be independently decisive in conflict, and, as demonstrated by the Arab Spring in 2011 it might be able to change the views of whole societies.[31]

The importance Russia attaches to information operations has been reflected in progressive increases in funding for these activities, and organisational initiatives including the creation of a cyber command. Russia started forming this structure in 2013. Russian employs between 2000 and 3000 hackers, along with affiliated hacker groups such as FancyBear and Nobilium that are controlled by the GRU (Russian military intelligence).[32] Russia has also created 'information troops' within the armed forces, based on the presumption that information warfare, including cyber, could viewed as something analogous to artillery as a tool for preparing the battlespace. These were announced in 2017, although experimentation had probably been ongoing since 2012. The information troops comprise an array of independent companies with responsibility for activities such as computer security, information security, electronic warfare and cryptography. Russian military districts have also created centres of information combat, and cyber and information operations are included in military exercises.[33]

China

Like Russia, China views information operations as a decisive factor in contemporary international conflict. China has developed its approaches under the concept of 'informationalised warfare.' From this perspective, modern warfare is a struggle to dominate the information space at the strategic, operational and tactical levels to manipulate how adversaries perceive and react. This view emphasises the importance of the cognitive domain and 'cognitive domain operations' as a way of achieving information superiority.[34] China's view of cyberspace is expansive, and encompasses all aspects of the information space. In that sense, cyber warfare for China is also information warfare. The PLA has identified cyber as one of the key 'strategic frontiers' (along with space and the electromagnetic spectrum). However, China's cyber warfare capability had been undermined to an extent by the division in responsibility across several different portions of the General Staff Department. Efforts to improve the functioning and integration of cyber and other capabilities were taken in 2015 with the creation of the SSF, an organisation designed to bring together the capabilities to 'maintain local advantages in the aerospace, space, cyber and electromagnetic fields', and to conduct 'attack and defense in cyber and electromagnetic spaces'.[35] Cyber, electronic warfare and psychological operations were integrated into the SSF's Network Systems Department. In 2024, the SSF was split into three separate organisations: the Aerospace Force; the Cyberspace Force; and the Information Support Force. The PLA has also set about creating network-electronic capabilities with its Joint Staff Department headquarters and within its joint regional commands. The PLA appears to have created information operations groups, a joint wartime formation that would include information support, electronic reconnaissance, electronic countermeasures and UAV troops.[36]

Many other actors have also developed cyber capabilities. For example, North Korea has a variety of units organised under the Reconnaissance General Bureau involved in cyber conflict activities including industrial and military espionage, and ransomware attacks. Iran has an aggressive cyber strategy organised through the Ministry of Intelligence, the Basij Cyber Council, which operates under the Iranian Revolutionary Guard Corps, and various affiliated hacker groups.

How Effective Is Cyber Warfare?

There are fewer examples of cyber warfare than there are for warfare in the other domains, partly because of its relative newness, and partly because cyber operations by their nature are less visible. Nevertheless, there is a growing body of evidence for the conduct of warfare in the cyber domain.

Strategic Cyber Operations

Strategic cyber warfare is a means, according to John Arquilla, 'of striking in very costly, disruptive ways at an adversary without a prior need to defeat opposing military forces in the field, at sea, or in the air.'[37] These sorts of cyber operations may include attempts to attack enemy national military C2 systems, national logistic systems, critical infrastructure and nuclear weapons capabilities, or to conduct high-level espionage and intelligence gathering.

One of the most sophisticated activities of this type was Operation Olympic Games. This operation, probably conducted by the US and Israel, in 2008 injected the Stuxnet malware into Iranian nuclear supervisory control and data acquisition

(SCADA) systems. Reconnaissance and preparation for this operation had probably begun in 2005. This malware damaged the centrifuges used for nuclear enrichment, disrupting Iran's nuclear programme. The Iranians didn't discover the malware until 2010. Another possible example of this sort of operation was Operation Orchard, the Israeli attack on a suspected Syrian nuclear facility at Deir ez-Zor in 2007. The conventional element of this operation was an air attack, but it is also alleged to have included a cyber-attack that was used to deactivate the Syrian air defence systems.

Operational Cyber

At the operational level, cyber-attacks have been used that are designed to prepare the theatre of operations for conventional forces; or, during a campaign, to deliver theatre-wide military effects.

Weeks before Russia's invasion of Georgia in 2008, for example, Russian cyber-attacks were used for information warfare and targeted Georgian media outlets and government websites. When the invasion commenced, DDoS attacks were used to cripple government communications and to block Georgian cyber capabilities. While these attacks did not deliberately target Georgian military capabilities (the Georgians did not have the sorts of advanced systems that would be vulnerable to cyber-attack), Russian cyber operations nevertheless had a military impact in terms of disrupting higher-level Georgian C2 and situational awareness, as well as causing confusion amongst Georgian troops and undermining their morale.[38]

Operational-level cyber was much more in evidence in Russia's invasion of Ukraine in February 2022. Russia had spent more than a year infiltrating Ukrainian networks, engaging in Phishing activities and pre-positioning malware. One hour before the invasion, Russia used malware to interrupt Ukrainian access to Viasat's KA-SAT satellite network: this had an impact on Ukrainian domestic internet services but Viasat was also an important element in Ukrainian's military C2 system. DDoS attacks were then used to disrupt Ukrainian government networks, sowing further confusion. Cyber was also used in major attempts to attack Ukrainian critical infrastructure. 'Industroyer2', a wiper malware, was used to try and turn off the electricity grid. Russian hackers, linked to the GRU, succeeded in causing major disruption to Ukraine's main telecoms provider *Ukrtelecom*. Ukrainian cyber hackers also achieved some successes. One group managed to infiltrate the Belarussian railway signals system and redirect Russian rail traffic. This contributed to the developing Russian logistic problems at the time.[39]

Cyber has played a persistent role in Russian information operations. Within the first month of the war, it was using botfarms to operate more than 100,000 false media accounts spreading Russian disinformation on the war, such as the 'discovery' of US-run biological weapons laboratories on Ukrainian soil.[40] In July 2022, the Russians used a cyber hack to trick Ukrainian radio stations into announcing that President Zelensky was critically ill. Cyber hacking has been used for psychological operations: a Russian hack of Facebook was used to disseminate messages ordering

Ukrainian troops to surrender; others hacks of social media were used to deliver threats and false information to military and civilian recipients.[41]

Russia has also sought to make use of cyber as an information and psychological warfare tool in those areas of Ukraine that it has occupied. In Russian-held areas of Ukraine, the local population is forced to use Russian-controlled telecoms systems, including SIM cards. This routes all communications through a Russian system known as SORM (System for Operative Investigative Activities), which can read emails and texts, censor information and distribute propaganda.[42]

Tactical Cyber Operations

Cyber also has a role on the battlefield, in combination with conventional capabilities. The role of cyber at the tactical level depends to an extent on the capabilities of belligerents and the extent to which they have modern networked weaponry or communications systems. Tactical cyber might include activities such as disrupting enemy UAVs; the conduct of cyber ISR; local social media operations; or gaining access to local enemy networked systems.[43]

One example of tactical cyber operations was a hack by the GRU-affiliated group FancyBear against Ukrainian forces. FancyBear had developed a malware called X-Agent that allowed them to read messages sent using the Popr-D30 application on Android devices. This app was used by Ukrainian artillery to speed up the targeting process for their 122 mm D-30 artillery pieces. X-Agent was able to extract approximate location data for the Ukrainian D-30s, enabling Russia to launch strikes on their positions that inflicted heavy casualties.[44] There have also been examples during the Ukraine War of attempts to coordinate military and cyber effects. For example, in one case, cyber-attack was used to shut down the systems of a nuclear plant immediately before Russian troops arrived to take it over. In another, Russian troops occupied the premises of a Ukrainian internet service provider and forced the company to re-route its services through Russian-controlled networks, allowing Russia to monitor the traffic.[45]

There are also examples of US tactical cyber activities from the war in Iraq (2003–2011). In one case, the US national intelligence service, the National Security Agency (NSA) was able to use Iraqi phone data and correlate this information to geographic positions in order to detonate enemy IEDs, killing some of the insurgents involved in laying them. In another, a combination of Phishing emails and the distribution of infected USB sticks by tactical units on the ground allowed US malware access to Obilisk, which was a form of AQ intranet. In a third example, the US accessed the Iraqi telephone system and used this to send fake messages setting up false meetings with insurgents so that they could be captured by troops on the ground.[46]

However, despite the growing number of examples of cyber warfare operations, it is not clear that cyber warfare is as effective as many enthusiasts believe. Strategically, the Stuxnet malware damaged between 10% and 20% of Iranian centrifuges before it was discovered. This slowed, but it did not halt, Iranian nuclear research. Neither is it clear if Operation Orchard involved a cyber-attack or whether the disabling of Syrian air defence was the result of jamming using electronic warfare capabilities. Operationally, Russian cyber warfare in Ukraine have been far from decisive. Results have often been temporary. For example, Ukraine was quickly able to replace Viasat with access to SpaceX's Starlink system. Cyber warfare has not coerced Ukraine into surrender and cyber generally has played an auxiliary role in operations.[47] Tactically, US operations in Iraq were dismissed by one former head of the US National Security Agency as 'Virtual graffiti on digital subway cars.'[48]

Why Is Cyber Warfare Challenging?

Despite continuing investment in the capabilities and expertise for cyber warfare, the accumulating experience seems to suggest that cyber warfare is not easy to prosecute effectively. Cyber, for example, does not appear to have a high coercive utility against adversaries. Moreover, cyber warfare often appears to be conducted without close integration with parallel military or political initiatives: cyber warfare is often conducted as its own campaign separate from other activity. Why might this be the case?

The challenge is that as a tool, cyber carries with it a range of intrinsic weaknesses. One difficulty is that cyber effects can be difficult to predict: once initiated, a cyber-attack may not work or may not have the expected effect; indeed, it may cause 'blowback', spreading and infecting unintended targets, including friendly systems. Moreover, since cyber-attacks do not physically destroy enemy systems, their effects can be temporary. Cyber operations can also cause fratricide: an adversary may respond to a cyber-attack with security upgrades that don't just negate that cyber event; they may also invalidate a range of other attacks that were being prepared. There are continuing uncertainties regarding the ethical and legal aspects of the use of cyber, especially in terms of proportionality, collateral damage and self-defence. Some attempts have been made to address these issues through NATO's 'Tallinn Manual' on the legal aspects of the use of cyber.[49] Nevertheless, cyber remains an often ambiguous tool in legal and ethical terms.

There seem to be particular challenges involved in tactical cyber warfare, and in integrating cyber with conventional military operations (see Box 19.2). Cyber weapons are not standard weapons that can be mass produced, carried around, and then applied to a wide range of targets. Cyber operations often require long preparation and heavy investment in resources because cyber warfare requires first that exploitable flaws can be identified in enemy systems (see Figure 19.2). Then, bespoke cyber tools must be created to exploit those flaws. The time taken for this process is often too slow for the needs of tactical warfare, which is often conducted at a high tempo, making it difficult to synchronise cyber activities with those in the other domains. The mismatch in the tempo between cyber and tactical conventional operations is magnified by the level at which authorities to use cyber operations are held. The skills and investment needed to create effective cyber tools, combined with the problem of fratricide, means that the authority to employ them is often retained at the strategic level to ensure deconfliction and proper apportionment of assets, further reducing the speed at which cyber can be applied tactically. In any case,

BOX 19.2 CYBER AND OPERATION ODYSSEY DAWN

In 2011, with rebel Libyan forces under pressure from those of President Gaddafi, NATO decided to implement a no-fly zone (Operation Odyssey Dawn). The use of cyber was discussed as a means of disabling Libyan air defence systems, but in the end this option was rejected. The reasons for rejecting a cyber warfare solution illustrate some of the weaknesses of cyber. In rejecting the cyber option, the US concluded that the use of its cyber capabilities might reveal aspects of the US' wider cyber potential; it might establish a precedent for Russia and China to do the same thing in other conflicts; there wasn't enough preparation time to develop the requisite malware tools; the Libyan systems were old, making it more difficult to find useful flaws that cyber could exploit; it wasn't clear how long the Libyan systems could be rendered inoperative for; and it wasn't clear how long a cyber operation could be maintained. In the end, it was simply quicker, more certain and a more permanent solution to destroy the air defence sites with cruise missiles.[51]

Figure 19.2 An aerial view of the UK's Government Communications Headquarters (GCHQ). GCHQ is one of the three UK Intelligence Agencies. Information from this sort of strategic-level organisation forms an important part of cyber warfare efforts. However, synchronising activities at this level with the tempo of operations at the tactical level of cyber warfare can be very challenging. Source: www.defenceimagery.mod.uk/Home/Search?Query = 45154332.jpg&Type = Filename

cyber can also struggle to cope with the physical realities of tactical warfare, including connectivity and bandwidth problems, as well as adversaries that have a limited reliance on digital networks.[50]

On current evidence, cyber warfare is generally a complement to the other domains rather than a substitute. As one commentary has noted on the impact of cyber in the Russo-Ukrainian war: 'Although cyber has been immensely important to both sides since February 2022, it has been as an enabler, not as a weapon of destruction in its own right. Traditional forms of combat have had as high a salience as activity in cyberspace.'[52]

While an increasingly important dimension in modern warfare, cyber evidently can often be challenging to employ, especially at the lower levels of war.

A Future Revolution?

Going forwards, however, there are many who argue that, whatever the limitations now, cyber warfare will inevitably be transformed by further advancements in technology. This is certainly the view of Russian and Chinese commentators who see AI as a transformative dynamic. For Russian theorists, AI constitutes 'the third revolution in military affairs after the invention of gunpowder and nuclear weapons'. AI will make cyber warfare much more dangerous because it will be easier to identify vulnerabilities in enemy systems, and much quicker to provide the means to exploit them. Influence campaigns will attain new levels of effectiveness because AI tools will make disinformation increasingly difficult to separate from the truth, given the fidelity and quantity of misinformation that it will be able to create through techniques such as 'deepfakes'.[53] China's concept of 'intelligentised warfare' (see Chapter 6) also sees a future marked by super-empowered information warfare. As part of this the PLA is exploring information technologies including subliminal messaging, cognitive modelling and brain imaging.[54] In this vision of an AI-driven military revolution, many of the current limits on the effectiveness of cyber warfare may be overcome.

Other technologies might also deliver transformative changes in cyber warfare.[55] **Quantum computing** uses the principles of quantum mechanics to enable computers to solve many types of problems much faster than existing computer systems. This could revolutionise fields such as cryptography and make existing forms of encryption redundant. This could make cyber warfare much more effective. On the other hand, there are developments in security systems that might make it more difficult to hack into enemy networks. Blockchain, for example, is a decentralised and distributed digital ledger technology that records transactions across multiple computers. Because it is distributed across multiple computers, data are more resistant to manipulation and fraud. Data added to a Blockchain are also much more difficult to alter. New storage mediums such as synthetic DNA could also change cyber warfare by altering the character of data vulnerabilities. Synthetic DNA is a form of artificially engineered DNA molecules that can be used to store data. It can store potentially vast amounts of information.

Cyber warfare is therefore a dynamic aspect of modern warfare, and the accelerating processes of technological change might yet yield radically different trajectories in the future.

Conclusion

In recent years, cyber has been elevated from a supporting capability to a fully-fledged warfighting domain. The attributes of this domain give cyber many potential strengths as an instrument of warfare including speed, reach, wide applicability and anonymity. Cyber warfare's significance has been illustrated in many examples of its use in recent years and by the extent to which political actors have been investing in developing cyber capabilities.

Yet it is not clear that cyber warfare has supplanted the relevance of the more traditional domains of warfare. The current evidence suggests that, while cyber operations are an important facet of contemporary military operations, they complement, rather than supplant, land, air, maritime and space operations. Cyber warfare has its own limitations and weaknesses including long preparation times, the narrow specificity of cyber tools and uncertainty in effect. The use, or threat of the use, of physical force still remains the decisive element in modern warfare.

RESEARCH QUESTIONS

1. What is cyber warfare? What are the challenges associated with defining the term?
2. In what ways can cyber contribute to warfare in the other domains?
3. To what extent can cyber be independently decisive?
4. What are the advantages and disadvantages of cyber as a tool of policy?
5. What factors might shape the success or failure of cyber operations?
6. To what extent do modern militaries need to adapt and innovate in order to use cyber most effectively?

FURTHER READING

Conti, Gregory and David Raymond, *On Cyber: Towards an Operational Art for Cyber Conflict* (New York, NY: Kopidion Press, 2017). This volume is worth investigating as a specific discussion of how cyber operations should be conceptualised and executed.

Libicki, Martin, *Cyberspace in Peace and War* (Annapolis, MD: Naval Institute Press, 2016). In addition to discussing some of the general aspects of cyber security, Libicki provides an important analysis and critique of the role of cyber a distinct domain of war.

Moore, Daniel, *Offensive Cyber Operations: Understanding Intangible Warfare* (London: Hurst & Co, 2022). Moore provides a compelling analysis of cyber warfare and its prosecution by key cyber actors.

Rid, Thomas, *Cyber War Will Not Take Place* (London: Hurst & Co, 2017). Read this for a more sceptical view on the impact of cyber. Rid sees cyber as something that reinforces already existing challenges such as espionage and subversion: but cyber's limitations mean that it cannot wage war.

Sanger, David E., *The Perfect Weapon: War, Sabotage, and Fear in the Cyber Age* (London: Scribe UK, 2018). This is an accessible analysis from the viewpoint of an author who sees cyber as something that is likely to be as revolutionary as nuclear weapons.

Whyte, Christopher and Brian M. Mazanec, *Understanding Cyber Warfare: Politics, Policy, and Strategy*, 2nd ed. (Abingdon, Routledge, 2023). This is an excellent and comprehensive introduction to the topic.

ONLINE RESOURCES

Many examples of cyber concepts and doctrines are available online. These include the US joint cyber doctrine, Joint Publication (JP) 3-12, *Joint Cyberspace Operations* (https://tinyurl.com/ydabbrkk), and US Airforce doctrine, Air Force Doctrine Publication 3-12, *Cyberspace Operations* (https://tinyurl.com/27s265p4); and NATO's Allied Joint Publication 3-20, *Allied Joint Doctrine for Cyber Space Operations* (https://tinyurl.com/5n7wnvnh).

NATO's Cooperative Cyber Defence Centre of Excellence (https://ccdcoe.org/) is another important source of cyber-related material.

Given the contemporary significance of cyber operations, there is wealth of material available online that can be found by searching the publications of research institutions including RAND (www.rand.org/), RUSI (www.rusi.org/), Chatham House (www.chathamhouse.org/), the Brookings Institution (www.brookings.edu/) and The Centre for Strategic and International Studies (www.csis.org/).

Military websites and blogs also provide an important source of up-to-date discussions on the applications of cyber. Useful sites include the Modern War Institute (https://mwi.westpoint.edu/) and War on the Rocks (https://warontherocks.com/).

NOTES

1 Les Anderson, 'BTs Cyber Index reveals the scale of today's cyber threat', *BT Press Office*, 9 August 2019, https://newsroom.bt.com/bts-cyber-index-reveals-the-scale-of-todays-cyber-threat/.

2 See David Patrikarakos, *War in 140 Characters: How Social Media Is Reshaping Conflict in the Twenty-First Century* (London: Basic Books, 2017).

3 Jarno Limnell, 'The Cyber Arms Race Is Accelerating – What Are the Consequences?' *Journal of Cyber Policy*, 1(1) (2016), 51

4 James Lewis, *Thresholds for Cyber War, CSIS* (October 2010), www.csis.org/analysis/thresholds-cyberwar.

5 Stephen Blank, 'Cyber War and Information War à la Russe', in George Perkovich, Ariel E. Levite (eds.), *Understanding Cyber Conflict: 14 Analogies* (Washington, DC: Georgetown University Press, 2017), p. 85.

6 Daniel Moore, *Offensive Cyber Operations: Understanding Intangible Warfare* (London: Hurst & Company, 2022), p. 7.

7 Jelle van Haaster, *On Cyber: The Utility of Military Cyber Operations During Armed Conflict* (Thesis, fully internal, Universiteit van Amsterdam, 2019), p. 148, https://pure.uva.nl/ws/files/37093787/Thesis.pdf.

8 Matthias Schulze, 'Cyber in War: Assessing the Strategic, Tactical, and Operational Utility of Military Cyber Operations', in T. Jancarkova, L. Lindstrom. M. Signoretti, I.

Tolga and G. Visky (eds.) *20/20 Vision: The Next Decade: 12th International Conference on Cyber Conflict* (Tallinn: NATO CCDCOE Publications, 2020), p. 184, https://ieeexplore.ieee.org/document/9131733.

9 Joe Kirschbaum, Information Environment: Opportunities and Threats to DOD's National Security Mission (US Government Accountability Office, September 2022), p. 1, www.gao.gov/assets/gao-22-104714.pdf.

10 Moore, *Offensive Cyber Operations*, p. 66.

11 The Joint Chiefs of Staff, Joint Publication 3-12 (R): *Cyberspace Operations*, pp. I-5 and I-6.

12 Blank, *Cyber War and Information War*, p. 81.

13 Gavin Wild, 'Assess Russia's Cyber Performance Without Repeating its Past Mistakes', *War on the Rocks*, 21 July 2022, www.cyberscoop.com/russia-information-war-ukraine-cyber-command-sorm/.

14 *Cyber Primer*, 3rd ed. (UK Ministry of Defence, DCDC, 2022), pp. 6–9, https://tinyurl.com/27d36nzj.

15 Christopher Whyte and Brian M. Mazanec, *Understanding Cyber Warfare: Politics, Policy, and Strategy*, 2nd ed. (Abingdon, Routledge, 2023), p. 15.

16 *Cyber Primer*, 9.

17 David Ormrod and Benjamin Turnbull, 'The Cyber Conceptual Framework for Developing Military Doctrine', *Defence Studies*, 16(3) (2016), 281.

18 DOD Dictionary of Military and Associated Terms (November 2021), p. 55, https://irp.fas.org/doddir/dod/dictionary.pdf.

19 Joint Publication 3-12, *Cyberspace Operations* (Joint Chiefs of Staff, 8 June 2018), p. I-1.

20 Whyte and Mazanec, *Understanding Cyber Warfare*, p. 32.

21 JP 3-12, *Cyberspace Operations*, pp. II-5–9.

22 Department of the Army, Field Manual 3-12: *Cyberspace and Electronic Warfare Operations*, pp. 1–9.

23 Moore, *Offensive Cyber Operations*, p. 5.

24 Scott D. Applegate, 'The Principle of Maneuver in Cyber Operations' (NATO, 2012), p. 185, https://tinyurl.com/yh58ktms.

25 Moore, *Offensive Cyber Operations*, p. 17.

26 Moore, *Offensive Cyber Operations*, p. 64.

27 'Ukraine Experts View Plans to Set Up Cyber Troops', *BBC Monitoring*, 26 October 2021.

28 Moore, *Offensive Cyber Operations*, p. 123.

29 Joshua Rovner, 'Warfighting in Cyber Space', *War on the Rocks*, 17 March 2021, https://warontherocks.com/2021/03/warfighting-in-cyberspace/.

30 See *Cyber Capabilities and National Power: A Net Assessment* (IISS, June 2021), pp. 57–67, www.iiss.org/research-paper//2021/06/cyber-capabilities-national-power.

31 Wild, 'Russia's Cyber Performance'.

32 'Ukraine Experts View Plans to Set Up Cyber Troops'.

33 Volodymir Lysenko and Catherine Brooks, 'Russian Information Troops, Disinformation, and Democracy', *First Monday*, 23(5) (May 2018), https://firstmonday.org/ojs/index.php/fm/article/download/8176/7201?inline = 1#59.

34 See Nathan Beauchamps-Mustafaga, *Chinese Next-Generation Psychological Warfare* (Santa Monica, CA: RAND, 2023), www.rand.org/pubs/research_reports/RRA853-1.html.

35 Moore, *Offensive Cyber Operations*, 177.

36 Elsa B. Kania and John K. Costello, 'The Strategic Support Force and the Future of Chinese information Operations', *The Cyber Defense Review* (Spring 2018), pp. 105–21, https://tinyurl.com/4ff9ts7a.

37 Schulze, 'Cyber in War', p. 185.
38 Stephanie J. Seward, 'Cyber Warfare in the Tactical Battlespace', *Infantry* (April–June 2018), p. 12, https://tinyurl.com/nc3bzm3d.
39 Kenneth Geers, 'Computer Hacks in the Russia-Ukraine War', *TechUkraine*, 22 August 2022, https://tinyurl.com/595rsz2f.
40 Nadiya Kostyuk and Erik Gartzke, 'Why Cyber Dogs Have Yet to Bark Loudly in Russia's Invasion of Ukraine', *Texas National Security Review*, 5(3) (Summer 2022), 122.
41 Greers, 'Computer Hacks'.
42 Suzanne Smalley, 'Mixed Results for Russia's Aggressive Ukraine Information War, Experts Say', *Cyberscoop*, 16 June 2022, https://cyberscoop.com/russia-information-war-ukraine-cyber-command-sorm/.
43 Isaac R. Porche III, Christopher Paul, Chad C.Serena, Colin P. Clarke, Erin-Elizabeth Johnson and Drew Herrick, *Tactical Cyber: Building a Strategy for Cyber Support to Corps and Below* (Santa Monica, CA: RAND, 2017), 7.
44 Seward, 'Cyber Warfare in the Tactical Battlespace'.
45 Smalley, 'Mixed Results'.
46 Schulze, 'Cyber in War', p. 191.
47 Jon Bateman, *Russia's Wartime Cyber Operations in Ukraine: Military Impacts, Influences, and Implications*, Carnegie Endowment for International Peace (December 16, 2022), https://tinyurl.com/373rzfw7.
48 Wild, 'Russia's Cyber Performance'; Michael V. Hayden, 'The Making of America's Cyber Weapons', *The Christian Science Monitor* (24 February 2016), https://tinyurl.com/2sxab58n.
49 See Eric Talbot Jensen, 'The Tallinn Manual 2.0: Highlights and Insights' (March 2017), https://tinyurl.com/4f9886ew.
50 See Jack Watling, *The Arms of the Future: Technology and Close Combat in the Twenty-First Century* (London: Bloomsbury, 2023), pp. 186–9.
51 Schulze, 'Cyber in War', p. 190.
52 Elliot A. Cohen and Phillips O'Brien, *The Russo-Ukraine War: A Study in Analytic Failure*, Centre for Strategic and International Studies (September 2024), p. 10.
53 Rod Thornton and Marina Miron, 'Towards the 'Third Revolution in Military Affairs': The Russian Use of AI-Enabled Cyber', *RUSI Journal*, 165(3) (2020), 14–17.
54 See Beauchamps-Mustafaga, *Chinese Next-Generation Psychological Warfare.*
55 Whyte and Manzanec, *Understanding Cyber Warfare*, pp. 315–20.

20 Hybrid Warfare, Grey Zone Conflict and Strategic Competition

CHRISTOPHER TUCK AND AND JAMES D. KIRAS

CHAPTER OUTLINE

KEY THEMES

- Despite the lack of consensus on definitions, one useful way of conceptualising hybrid warfare, grey zone conflict, and strategic competition is as, respectively, the means employed in conflict, the arena of conflict and the context.
- Hybrid warfare comprises the orchestrated blending of a wide range of military and non-military instruments of power.
- Advocates of the concept assert that hybrid warfare now plays a key role in intensifying competition between the West and its adversaries.
- Critics argue that hybrid warfare is an amorphous and misleading term that hinders our understanding of contemporary conflict more than it helps.

Introduction

The volume in which this chapter appears is titled *Understanding Modern Warfare*. In previous volumes, the term 'warfare' has been defined as something concerned with the use of violence by regular or irregular military forces, and this does indeed remain the focus of much of this third edition. Nevertheless, newer terminology developed, used and debated challenges us to reconsider the framework of warfare and even the validity of our modern understanding of war. Three terms in particular represent this challenge: strategic competition, grey zone conflict and hybrid warfare. While this chapter touches upon the first two, its focus remains on hybrid warfare. To borrow a concept from Russian military thought, this chapter centres on the form (hybrid warfare) rather than its methods, ratios or strategic purpose.

Strategic Competition and Grey Zone Conflict

An important point to identify at the start of any discussion on issues relating to strategic competition, the grey zone and hybrid warfare is that there is a challenging definitional looseness in the literature on these concepts. A wide variety of labels are often applied to the same concepts; and the same labels can often be used to describe different things. For example, what we will define in this chapter as hybrid warfare is also referred to in the literature by a range of terms including grey zone warfare, hybrid war, hybrid threats, asymmetric warfare political warfare, sharp power, malign influence, liminal warfare and more.[1]

Nevertheless, one useful way of thinking about these terms is that, in relation to contemporary conflict, strategic competition provides the context; the grey zone is the arena; and hybrid warfare is the means used.

Strategic Competition

This chapter sees strategic competition as synonymous with terms such as 'great-power competition' and 'political warfare'. Strategic competition 'is fundamentally a long game between revisionist powers and those that want to preserve the status quo of the current international order. Rather than engaging in isolated contests, competitors undertake activities to gain an advantage in pursuit of one of these long-term goals.'[2] Strategic competition is conducted using the full range of instruments available to political actors: political, economic, military and information. It is essentially an exercise in grand strategy (see Chapter 1). While strategic competition is not new and in the past has been a routine feature of international relations, a number of factors have conspired to make it an issue of particular contemporary concern.

One factor has been changing threat assessments. In the decade after the end of the Cold War, optimistic ideas surrounding the possibility of a New World Order or the triumph of liberal democracy sustained the hope that a qualitative change was taking place in the basis of international relations, with cooperation becoming more of a feature than conflict. In the first decade or so of the twenty-first century, this optimism was dashed by the wars in Iraq and Afghanistan. Nevertheless, evaluation of international threats at that time concentrated more on weak states, terrorism, insurgency and civil strife than on more traditional interstate rivalries. In the 2010s, however, Western relations with China and Russia declined dramatically. From a Western perspective it seemed that both of these states sought increasingly to challenge the basis of the rules-based international order. Reflecting this view, the first Trump administration's 2017 *National Security Strategy* and 2018 *National Defense Strategy* refocused the US from counterterrorism towards interstate challenges from peer adversaries. On the other hand, from a Chinese and Russian perspective, the West seemed to be attempting to constrain and undermine the growth in the influence and power of potential challengers.[3] Great-power competition again became the major concern in international relations, a development reflected in the use of terms such as 'the return to competition' or 'an era of constant competition'.

A second factor is the implications of globalisation and technological developments on the character of the international system. The expansion, intensification and integration of political, financial and media networks – driven by satellite communications, the internet and social media – has multiplied dramatically the connectivity between actors in the international system. The rise of mass media, including television, and the processes of globalisation have elevated the relevance of information as a tool of grand strategy. During the Cold War, information was recognised by all sides as an essential dimension of the struggle to expand their power and influence. The Soviet Union, for example, developed highly sophisticated concepts for the prosecution of information warfare under the banner of *aktivnyye meropriatia* or 'active measures'.[4]

However, the salience of information as a tool has grown in step with technological and societal developments that have expanded the volume of information, the methods of delivery and the potential audiences. The cognitive space is now open to a wider range of potential influences. The internet, social media and mobile phones have increased the audiences that can be influenced, both domestic and international, as well as side-stepping the traditional media, such as newspapers and terrestrial television organisations, that had commonly acted as information gatekeepers and mediated the flow of information to audiences. These new technologies have also accelerated the speed with which information can flow between and amongst producers and users.[5] This has promoted a growth in the ubiquity and power of new unconventional tools of conflict, including cyber, space and information operations. In an increasingly interconnected and permeable world, these tools appeared to offer potentially powerful non-military ways of waging conflict.[6] To compound this, Western liberal democracies seemed to some to be especially vulnerable to these new means, given their openness to external interference created by capitalism and democratic processes.

These two factors together conspired to create a third: debates on the meaning of war. Some commentators argued that the West was sleepwalking into defeat because it had not updated its concept of what war was. The West was not taking the challenge from its adversaries seriously enough, because it seemed to assume that war was defined only by major conventional military battle, and thus it was not actually at war with Russia and China. But some disagreed: war could now be fought by other means. The Cold War, even if it had not involved a direct military conflict between the West and the Soviet Union, had nevertheless been an existential struggle that resulted in the elimination of one of the belligerents by processes that had caused it to disintegrate from within. The West's adversaries, so it was argued, were now waging war on it through processes of economic, political and informational attack: but the West had not realised this because it had not updated its view of what war was.

Some commentators resurrected the Cold War concept of political warfare to describe the nature of the strategic competition that applies today. In 1948, the US diplomat George Kennan described political warfare as 'The logical application of Clausewitz's doctrine in time of peace. In broadest definition, political warfare is the employment of all the means at a nation's command, short of war, to achieve its national objectives.'[7] In the contemporary world, authoritarian actors such as Russia, China and North Korea are using old and new means to exploit Western vulnerabilities and wage war:[8] 'If war is politics by other means, then authoritarian political warfare is war by other means.'[9] Strategic competition provides the context that describes intensified strategic competition analogous to a new Cold War.

Grey Zone Conflict

The grey zone describes where much of this form of strategic competition now takes place. The grey zone can be defined as 'the contested arena somewhere between routine statecraft and open warfare' (see Box 20.1 for additional definitions).[10] Strategic competition is associated with the grey zone because this competition operates at a threshold below that of outright conventional warfare. The desire to avoid escalating strategic competition beyond this threshold reflects a rational cost-benefit analysis on the part of those engaged in strategic competition. Aside from the physical and political costs of direct military conflict, armed conflict would involve enormous financial costs, as well as the risks of defeat. A war between the US and China, for example, might result in GDP (gross domestic product) reductions of between 25 and 35% for the former, and 5–10% for the latter.[11]

Grey zone conflict is associated with a number of themes. One is the manipulation of thresholds: activities in the grey zone, even if serious in implication, are designed to be perceived as not significant enough to justify escalation to conventional warfare. Another is the idea of a spectrum of conflict: activities in the grey zone might sit in different places on the continuum from peace to war and are designed deliberately to be difficult to distinguish from the normal processes of competition that form a routine part of the international system. A third theme is ambiguity: one of the factors that helps keep an activity below the threshold of war is an adversary's uncertainty about the source or intentions behind a particular action. Finally, the

BOX 20.1 THE GREY ZONE

The gray zone is defined as *competitive interactions among and within state and non-state actors that fall between the traditional war and peace duality.* They are characterized by ambiguity about the nature of the conflict, opacity of the parties involved, or uncertainty about the relevant policy and legal frameworks' (US Special Operations Command, 2015).[12]

'The grey zone is a murky area, consisting of everything which isn't full-on conflict, but isn't exactly an innocent act either' (UK Strategic Command).[13]

'The image of gray zone conveys the ambiguous and gradual nature of the space in the intermediate conflict spectrum between peaceful competition and armed conflict' (Javier Jordan, 'International Competition Below the Threshold of War', 2020).[14]

'A set of activities that occur between peace (or cooperation) and war (or armed conflict)' (The Atlantic Council)[15].

grey zone is an arena of long-term activity. Grey zone conflict achieves its effects through an accumulation of effects over time and an accomplishment of revanchist or rising power aims without the risk of escalating to conventional conflict.[16]

What Is Hybrid Warfare?

Strategic competition is driving conflictual behaviours between the great powers; the grey zone is where much of this conflict is now being conducted. This zone provides the 'the quintessential terrain' in which the means used to wage this form of war are being conducted: hybrid warfare.[17] Reflecting the definitional fluidity alluded to earlier in this chapter, the term 'hybrid warfare' has had an evolving meaning in the twenty-first century.[18]

Hybrid Warfare as Regular and Irregular Warfare

As a concept, hybrid warfare achieved prominence in the first decade of the twenty-first century largely thanks to the work of the US academic Frank Hoffman. Studying the dynamics of the 2006 war in Lebanon between Israel and Hezbollah, Hoffman argued that the conflict provided an important indicator of the future trajectory of the character of warfare. In 2006, the IDF encountered in Hezbollah a highly adaptive adversary that, despite being a non-state insurgent actor, exhibited in its tactical approaches many features of regular warfare, including conventional capabilities. On the one hand, Hezbollah utilised in its fight against the IDF a cellular structure and fluid methods based on hit-and-run attacks, mobility and evasion. Yet, it had also developed forces capable when required of fighting in manner more associated with regular warfare. In many encounters with the IDF, Hezbollah fighters showed themselves well equipped with sophisticated technologies for C2, night-fighting and anti-tank warfare. Tactically, Hezbollah forces were effectively trained and disciplined and proved able to hold ground and counter-attack when required. Hezbollah represented what Hoffman viewed as being the next major challenge for Western forces: adversaries that would blend regular and irregular warfare into one converged, or hybrid, mode of warfare. While many wars in the past had involved aspects of both regular and irregular warfare, these approaches were applied by different organisations. What made these 'compound wars' different from the new hybrid wars was that in the latter regular and irregular methods would be applied flexibly by the same organisations. As Hoffman argued: 'Instead of separate challengers with fundamentally different approaches (conventional, irregular, or terrorist), we can expect to face competitors who will employ all forms of war and tactics, perhaps simultaneously.'[19]

While some commentators have questioned whether binary distinctions between regular and irregular warfare had ever been useful,[20] this perspective on hybrid warfare was highly influential on debates within Western militaries. The reason is straightforward: it occurred at a point when coalition forces were involved in stability and counterinsurgency operations in Iraq and Afghanistan but highlighted the continuing relevance of competencies to conduct regular warfare.

Nevertheless, this definition of hybrid warfare, which was military-centric and focused on the tactical behaviour of non-state actors, has given way over time to a much broader conception that views hybrid warfare as the means through which strategic competition is conducted.

Hybrid Warfare as a Means of Strategic Competition

The Russian occupation of Crimea in 2014 galvanised Western thinking on the nature of the emerging challenge from state competitors(see Figure 20.1). Russia's actions in 2014 seemed to embody a powerful new approach that sidestepped NATO's conventional military capabilities and exploited through the orchestrated use of multiple policy tools the political difficulties faced by the West in developing a coherent response. While Russia's strategy in 2014 was analysed through the prism of a number of ideas, including 'ambiguous war', 'special war' and 'non-linear war',[21] the label that finally came to dominate debates on Russia's new approach was Hoffman's 'hybrid war'.

This term was defined at the time as the application by Russia of 'a wide range of overt and covert military, paramilitary, and civilian measures ... employed in a highly integrated design.'[22] By 2017, NATO had evolved its definition of the challenge to one of 'hybrid threats':

> Hybrid threats occur where conventional, irregular and asymmetric threats are combined in the same time and space. Conflict could involve a range of transnational, state, group and individual participants operating globally and locally. Some conflicts may involve concurrent inter-communal violence, terrorism, cyberspace attacks, insurgency, pervasive criminality and widespread disorder.[23]

Figure 20.1 The icon of hybrid warfare during Russia's annexation of Crimea was its use of deniable military personnel. Western observers had difficulty attributing these personnel to Russia as their insignia or other identifiable markings had been purposefully removed. Their sudden appearance, in indistinguishable uniforms with common equipment and their faces concealed, meaning they could be pro-Russian Crimeans, a foreign militia or Russian military personnel, only added to the confusion of the situation and complicated Western identification and response. They were dubbed 'little green men' by Western media and 'polite people' in the Russian press. Here 'little green men' patrol outside Simferopol airport. Source: Courtesy of the US Department of Defense; photo by Marine Corps Corporal Armando Elizalde.

While definitions of hybrid warfare (or hybrid war or hybrid threats) vary (see Box 20.2 for examples), the term is generally associated with a number of features. One is that hybrid warfare is 'multimodal': warfare is hybrid because it blends together in an integrated way a wide range of different techniques and forms of conflict including political subversion, the use of proxies, espionage, cyber-attacks, information operations, criminal activity, assassinations, economic coercion and traditional military power.[24] A second feature is that, since hybrid warfare takes place in the grey zone, it is a subthreshold activity. Hybrid warfare uses the tools that it does because these forms of attack might not be easily distinguishable as offensive operations and are much less likely to lead to escalation. Finally, hybrid warfare is not designed to defeat an adversary's military capabilities. Instead, it is designed to attack their political will and cohesion through measures intended to demoralise, polarise, paralyse, distract or otherwise influence negatively domestic political constituencies in the target state.[25]

BOX 20.2 DEFINITIONS OF HYBRID WAR

'Modern adversaries make use of conventional/unconventional, regular/irregular, overt/covert means, and exploit all the dimensions of war to combat the Western superiority in conventional warfare. Hybrid threats exploit the "full spectrum" of modern warfare; they are not restricted to conventional means.'[26]

'The synchronized use of multiple instruments of power tailored to specific vulnerabilities across the full spectrum of societal functions to achieve synergistic effects.' [27]

'Those covert or illegal activities of non-traditional statecraft that are below the threshold of armed organized violence; including disruption of order, political subversion of government or non-governmental organizations, psychological operations, abuse of legal processes, and financial corruption as part of an integrated design to achieve strategic advantage.'[28]

Hybrid Warfare and Information Warfare

While hybrid warfare encompasses a wide range of different activities, information operations have formed a particular point of concern as a hybrid activity. In modern informationalised societies, information networks have a pervasive presence. This has led many to argue that manipulating information in ways designed to influence domestic political constituencies now has a particular power. This form of manipulation has been termed 'information operations'. Information operations are designed for the strategic-level manipulation of audiences. These activities are also often termed 'influence operations', although a variety of different labels are also used, including 'strategic communication', and 'cognitive manoeuvre'. One US definition sees influence operations as:

> The coordinated, integrated, and synchronized application of national diplomatic, informational, military, economic, and other capabilities in peacetime, crisis, conflict, and postconflict to foster attitudes, behaviors, or decisions by foreign target audiences that further U.S. interests and objectives.[29]

Influence operations are typically associated with a variety of overlapping concepts, including disinformation (or misinformation), in which false or partial information is used to try and shape political and societal perspectives; propaganda, the dissemination of biased information in order to manipulate the perceptions of target audiences; social engineering, manipulating individuals or groups to undertake certain actions or reveal desired information; censorship, restricting the access of audiences to information; and social media manipulation, the use of social media platforms to disseminate, shape and distort audience perceptions. Influence operations have three general objectives: to gain international support by influencing relevant audiences; to undermine adversaries by undermining their domestic political stability; and/or to influence domestic audiences.

Information operations have a global reach because they can be conducted without reference to geography or physical boundaries. Another benefit is that information operations are low-cost options relative to many conventional military capabilities and operations. The entry costs for using information tools can be small, and they do not require large a supporting infrastructure. Other costs might also be lower: the physical costs of operational failures should be less than those for conventional military activities, and they are 'cleaner' more discriminate tools that need not inflict mass damage or loss of life. One commonly discussed advantage of information operations is that they can exploit ambiguity in attribution. The origins of information attacks can be heavily disguised, making it more difficult for targets to retaliate and also potentially sidestepping adversary efforts at conventional deterrence. For some, information allows a new form of strategic coercion, between economic sanctions and physical force.[30] In 2007, the Russian Defence Minister Sergei Ivanov argued that: 'The development of information technology has resulted in information itself turning into a certain kind of weapon. It is a weapon that allows us to carry out would-be military actions in practically any theatre of war and most importantly, without using military power'.[31] As a hybrid activity, information can itself be used to wage a form of hybrid warfare, often called information warfare: 'A form of political warfare, where targets include a nation state's government, military, private sector and general population. Ultimately the target of information warfare activities is human cognition.'[32]

The Hybrid Warfare Threat

Hybrid warfare has contributed to a period of profound Western concern over the extent to which the developing security environment has undermined the utility of traditional understandings, concepts and approaches relating to national security.[33] In the context of the intense strategic competition confronting the West, adversaries such as Russia seem to have developed powerful hybrid warfare concepts and practices.

Russian Hybrid Warfare

From a Western perspective, Russia has been one of the principal architects and exponents of hybrid warfare in a process of strategic competition designed to influence political processes, sow discord, exacerbate and exploit political cleavages, and to undermine faith in democracy within targeted countries.

Conceptually, Russian analyses of the changing character of conflict led Russian theorists to conclude that conditions were strengthening the role of non-military instruments of power. Superiority in information and cyber capabilities might be the foundation for success in conflicts as a whole. Strategies involving the coordinated use of levers such as economic coercion, political manipulation, cyber operations, media activities and information warfare might be able to create in that phase termed the 'Initial Period of War', the phase of political contestation before conventional war breaks out, advantages so decisive that war itself might be a formality.[34] In 2015, two Russian military authors asserted that: 'Information warfare in the new conditions will be the starting point of every action now called the new-type warfare (a hybrid war) in which a broad use is made of the mass media and global computer networks.'[35]

Russia sees information warfare through the lens of the concept of 'information confrontation' (*Informatsionoye protivoborstvo)*, which embodies a comprehensive view of the need to engage and defeat the foundations of an adversary's information capabilities.[36] In this regard, Russian approaches show strong similarities with their Soviet past in viewing modern strategic competition as something that has information operations at its core. From a Russian perspective, information warfare can be independently decisive in conflict, and, as demonstrated by the Arab Spring in 2011, it might be able to change the views of whole societies.[37]

One particular expression of Russian thinking that influenced Western perceptions was the contents of a paper published in English in 2014 by the Russian chief of the General Staff, General Valery Gerasimov. Labelled in Western analyses as the 'Gerasimov Doctrine', the paper seemed to contain a definitive statement of Russian thinking on hybrid warfare: the blurring of the relationship between war and peace; the growing salience of non-military levers of power; the utility of the clandestine employment of military power; and the relegation of conventional military combat to the final stages of a conflict.[38]

Russian actions seemed to confirm its commitment to turn hybrid warfare theory into practice. The annexation of Crimea, with the coordinated employment of infiltration, subversion, information operations, proxies and unacknowledged Russian security personnel provided one obvious example. But there have been a wide range of incidences of the Russian use of hybrid warfare as part of its strategic competition with the West. Russian activity has targeted domestic audiences, in order to shore up support for Putin's regime; non-aligned countries, as a way of building international support for Russian policies; and adversaries such as the US, where it has sought to foment conspiracy theories, anti-liberal perspectives and conservative nationalism, in order to polarise society and weaken the legitimacy of democratic processes. Russian narratives portray itself as locked in a battle against a predatory West that sponsors 'degenerate liberal norms', and that does not respect the sovereignty or interest of other states. In conducting these operations, Russia has fully embraced the opportunities produced by new media. While is continues to use state-controlled media outlets, such as RT and Sputnik, especially for domestically focused information purposes, much of its efforts focus on digital platforms and social media, making use of troll-farms, botnets and false accounts. These activities are variously conducted by the Russian Federal Security Service (FSB), Foreign Intelligence Service (SVR) and GRU.[39] High-profile actions have included Russian interference in the 2016 US elections through the use of troll-farms, social media and official news outlets to shape the debate, attacking Clinton and supporting

Trump and Bernie Sanders (the latter being on the left wing of the Democratic party); cyber hacks to undermine the democratic campaign; planting divisive news stories; amplifying and spreading divisive disinformation; and supporting domestic US extremist viewpoints.[40] In 2019, when the COVID-19 pandemic commenced, Russian information operations also helped to fuel conspiracy theories regarding the purpose of lockdown policies, and to inflame anti-vaccination. In the 2020 US elections, Russia used trolls, bots and fake news to bolster Trump and to create distrust in the voting process.[41] Targets have also included the French and German elections in 2017 and Britain's Brexit referendum in 2018.

Chinese Hybrid Warfare

From a Western perspective, China is another major strategic competitor that has employed hybrid warfare to great effect.

China shares similarities and differences with Russia. It has a strong and long-lived theoretical foundation for its thinking on hybrid warfare. Some argue China's strategic culture, dating back some 2,500 years to works such as Sun Tzu's *Bing Fa* (*Art of War*), creates a fertile environment for thinking about more indirect approaches to conflict. Like Russia, however, China views information operations as a decisive factor in contemporary international conflict, suggesting more recent scientific socialist thought. China has developed its approaches under the concept of 'informationised warfare.'[42] Modern warfare is a struggle to dominate the information space at the strategic, operational and tactical levels in order to manipulate how adversaries perceive and react. This view emphasises the importance of the cognitive domain, and the importance of 'cognitive domain operations' as a way of achieving information superiority.[43]

Chinese thinking on the changing character of war sees non-military instruments of power as increasingly influential in shaping the outcomes of international competition. In 1999, two Chinese military officers explored the concept of *Chao Xian Zhan*: 'unrestricted warfare'. Commenting on Western conventional military capabilities demonstrated comprehensively in the Gulf War of 1991 and Kosovo in 1999, 'unrestricted warfare' was a concept that advocated that China needed to avoid a symmetrical conventional conflict with the US. Instead, the concept and prosecution of war needed to be widened to include the widest range of state capabilities and focused on defeating the enemy's political and economic system as a whole.[44] Revising its 'Political Work Guidelines' in 2003, China's PLA also articulated the concept of 'Three Warfares:' media and public opinion warfare; psychological warfare; and legal warfare, a development that seemed to reinforce China's embrace of a wider definition of warfare and the importance of non-military.[45]

This thinking, many argue, is expressed in concrete form today through the actions of the Chinese state. China's use of hybrid warfare in the grey zone as part of its strategic competition with the West has been reflected in a wide variety of activities applied to a range of campaigns. The techniques include political subversion; cyber; espionage; information operations; manipulating economic aid and

Figure 20.2 Many examples of grey zone activities in hybrid warfare are difficult to illustrate as they occur in intangible form. Subversion, cyber activities and other activities are deniable, difficult to attribute or costly to reveal as they may compromise sources and methods of intelligence gathering. Some, however, are concrete and designed to uphold sovereignty claims, as well as harass and send signals. These include the use of 'ghost fleet' ships, commercial vessels flying Chinese flags operating purposefully at the direction and on behalf of the state. Here a crewmember on a Chinese trawler uses a grapple hook in an apparent attempt to snag the towed acoustic array of the USNS *Impeccable*, a military sealift command ocean surveillance ship, in the South China Sea, 8 March 2009. *Impeccable* was conducting routine survey operations in international waters seventy-five miles south of Hainan Island when the Chinese vessels approached it.

debt; targeted investment strategies; intellectual property theft; and low-level military coercion (see Figure 20.2).[46] For one commentator, China is utilising 'A range of mostly indirect, asymmetric strategies that draw on the Chinese Communist Party's (CCP's) deep expertise in unconventional, intelligence-led, subversion-heavy operations.'[47]

For example, China has embraced modern information techniques. It has expanded traditional state media outlets internationally, including *Xinhua*, *China Daily* and the *People's Daily*. It makes extensive use of new media platforms, including social media outlets such as TikTok, We Chat and YouTube. China leverages other resources including the Chinese ethnic diaspora, Chinese cultural organisations, such as the Confucius Institute, as well as expanding Chinese language media and film industries. It makes extensive use of information warfare techniques. For example, in terms of using false media accounts, or 'botnets', to propagate its messages on social media, it has twice as many accounts as Iran, and three times as many as Russia.[48]

These tools are used to further China's goals in a number of different campaigns. These campaigns include, for example, the 'geostrategic manoeuvre' that comprises the Belt and Road Initiative (BRI).[49] Announced in 2013, the BRI is a programme of strategic investment deigned to create a web of economic and financial interconnectivity along land and maritime routes. China has argued that this is a benign development designed to promote trade and development. Critics argue that it is an instrument to expand China's influence through the manipulation of loans, debt and strategic investments in critical infrastructure.[50] Another campaign is the strategic messaging campaign designed to propagate positive images of China abroad.[51] China is presented as a responsible peaceful power, respectful of the sovereignty of other states. In contrast, adversaries such as the US are characterised as aggressive and hypocritical, using issues such as human rights to project their values and influence into other states. The war in Ukraine, for example, is blamed in Chinese narratives on Western aggression towards Russia.[52] China has specific campaigns for other purposes. In relation to Taiwan, it attempts to influence the Taiwanese public and shape international opinion towards a more pro-China view on the dispute. In terms of Hong Kong, Xinjiang and the South China Sea dispute, it attempts to flood social media with positive views of China and to discredit critics.[53]

Other Western adversaries are also employing hybrid methods as part of their conflict with the West. North Korea, for example, has made extensive use of cyber hacking to attack Western interests. Iran is using hybrid warfare, reflected in its support for proxy groups such as Hezbollah in Lebanon and the Houthis in Yemen, as well as its own attempts at cyber conflict and information warfare. Hybrid warfare is dangerous, therefore, because it is a rational and effective response to Western conventional capabilities; and it is one that Western adversaries are using to significant effect.

The Hybrid Warfare Debate

While hybrid warfare, and associated ideas such as grey zone conflict and strategic competition, have formed an important part of contemporary debates on the meaning and conduct of modern warfare, it is nevertheless important to acknowledge that these are ideas that remain controversial. The heart of the controversy focuses on two aspects of war identified by Clausewitz almost two centuries ago: its nature and character.

Arguments for

Those arguing in support of hybrid warfare and grey zone activities suggest that one or both has changed. They draw on three primary observations about modern warfare. These are the blended character of contemporary operations, the blurring of the line between peace and war and the democratisation of violence and therefore war.

Observations about the blended character of contemporary operations had its roots during the Global War on Terrorism (GWOT). These roots related to a Western, but primarily American, realisation that the precision and speed of operations of military operations had increased their tactical but not strategic effectiveness. The 'Afghan model' used to such success in Afghanistan (2001), Libya (2011) and Iraq and Syria (2014) blended together SOF with precision-strike airpower, ISR and local proxy forces to achieve immediate operational or stated policy objectives. They do so rapidly while limiting costs to a minimum, including political ones such as avoiding the need for debate on sending larger regular forces. Such operations, however, rarely translated into strategic success. Some in the West grasped that terrorism could not be defeated by military power, no matter how overwhelming and capable. A more holistic approach that combined military and non-military means was required.

Shortfalls in capabilities drove the need to blend activities. A critical shortfall in Western inventories was the means to conduct influence operations or political warfare to counter terrorist rhetoric. In America, some lamented the dissolution of the US Information Agency in 1999, a victim of post-Cold War peace dividend budget reductions. While vestiges of it were preserved, a lack of coherent policy and messaging in a variety of media and programmes ensured terrorist messaging globally remained relatively uncontested. Operational information sharing, however, increased drastically. This shortfall, identified by the authors of the 9/11 Commission Report, was also identified in the UK, Australia, Spain and elsewhere in the wake of major terrorist attacks. The resulting coordination between military and intelligence activities concerned some, specifically their convergence together and seeming indistinguishability.[54] This indistinguishability was also evident in the capabilities and characterisation of Hezbollah during the 2006 Summer War, as a non-state actor possessed state-like attributes, characteristics and capabilities, including a seeming fusion of political, military and social dimensions. This blended organisation was able to engage in conflict with the most powerful state in the region, Israel, and emerge from it battered but nevertheless claiming victory, thanks to an orchestrated influence campaign.[55]

Two campaigns in 2014 cemented the idea of blended campaigns working. In the first, ISIS emerged from the Syrian Civil War and threatened to overrun Baghdad, with a mixture of civilian and military vehicles including tanks, stymieing efforts of some Western analysts to categorise it.[56] Russia's 2014 campaign to annex Crimea, as mentioned previously, occurred rapidly and caught Western analysts and policymakers by surprise. In subsequent evaluation of Russia's success, analysts noted the blending together of deniable Russian *Spetsnaz* (SOF) personnel working with Russian-sponsored indigenous militias and criminal groups, such as the Night Wolves motorcycle gang, in a coordinated manner. Their very blending made identifying the purpose, direction and coordination difficult to comprehend while the violence was occurring. Russian information operations further contributed to the confusion and success, using Western-backed concepts and vocabulary such as 'democracy' and 'people's choice' to cement their fait accompli, leaving the West little political manoeuvre room for response legally or morally.[57]

Champions of hybrid warfare further claim this obfuscation is not merely operational in nature but rather instrumental. They cite Russian and Chinese writing on the subject, drawing on works such as *Unrestricted Warfare* and Valeri Gerasimov's 2013 article 'The Value of Science Is in the Foresight', and connect these directly to specific actions. To the authors of *Unrestricted Warfare,* modern war relies on 'All means, including armed force and non-armed force, military and non-military, and lethal and non-lethal means to compel the enemy to accept one's interests.'[58] Evidence confirming this approach is China's activities in the South China Sea, which includes island-building in shoals and atolls to achieve political, economic and military objectives, as well as coordinated activities between official Chinese ships and fishing vessels in 'darker grey' tactics designed to test Philippine resolve and commitment but nonetheless involve forms of violence.[59] Gerasimov's article, distributed widely in the West after the annexation of Crimea but published prior to it in Russia, notes the 'Blurring [of] the lines between the states of war and peace' in which the 'Very "rules of war" have changed.'[60] More noteworthy was the graphic representation of conflict contained in the model of conflict development in which non-military methods play a decisive role in setting the conditions for the outcome, which mirrored much of how the campaign in Crimea was conducted.[61]

The third observation has less to do with war than the socio-economic reality surrounding it. The revolution brought on and still underway thanks to information technologies must bring about one in war and warfare. Just as the Industrial Revolution conferred decisive advantage to those who possessed it, so too will the current information one. There are horizontal and vertical dimensions to the information revolution. The former consists of methods to gather intelligence or shape gathering systems. For gathering activities, China's persistent data theft, conducted on an industrial scale and visible in Chinese military platforms, is evidence of hybrid warfare. These efforts, combined with other influence activities such as Confucius Institutes, levying demands on Hollywood to portray China in the most positive light and purchasing land in proximity to US military bases, lead some to one conclusion: 'The acme of skill is to win without fighting', as Sun Tzu proffered.[62] Notions of shaping comport well with Russian writings on reflexive control theory, or getting an opponent to commit to a decision through justification – taking advantage of confirmation bias – or persuasion.[63] Russian attempts to do so in Estonia, Georgia and later in the American elections in 2016 provide tangible proof of the concept in action.

The vertical dimension of information technology can be translated as the erosion of state control due in part to the empowering of individuals and groups. The barriers of entry to advanced capabilities have lowered considerably, resulting in the democratisation of violence. Online, 'digital soldiers' or an electronic '*levee en masse*' is possible with little or no warning, which permits coordinated action of numbers of previously minimally connected individuals. More worrisome is the ability of individuals and small groups to harness technologies once the exclusive preserve of states, as Chapter 15 detailed. When connected to or controlled by other states as proxy forces, however, such groups or militias can become yet another front, potentially capable of launching coordinated attacks. Iranian-backed Houthi drone attacks went from nuisance to a hybrid strategic threat once coordinated with rocket strikes and aimed at critical Saudi and UAE airbases and oil targets.

Arguments against

Arguments critical of hybrid warfare can also be divided along three lines. The first can be summarised as 'the classical strategy' and study line. Arguments along these lines are that classic works of scholarship on war, such as Clausewitz's ideas in *On War*, remain relevant and correct.[64] He concluded that the nature of war is unchanging; it serves an instrumental purpose, one influenced and guided by political considerations. The character of war, however, is constantly changing due to highly specific contextual factors such as the means available and the political and social climates, amongst other factors. Keeping the immutable nature in focus is necessary but comprehending its contemporary character is sufficient. More fully engaging with and understanding dense classics, as opposed to oversimplified summaries comprised of 'key takeaways' for the intellectually lazy, is what is required. For example, comprehension of Thomas Schelling's concept of compellence in *Arm and Influence* is a better guide to decipher the mechanisms of grey zone activities.[65] New concepts often belie a lack of historical knowledge or understanding. Historical conflicts featured hybrid warfare have been 'an integral part of the historical landscape since the ancient world, but only recently have analysts – incorrectly – categorised these conflicts as unique'.[66] Losing sight of these fact is not merely a distraction, it confuses the means and ways they are employed with the ends sought.

A closely related argument to this one against the terms 'grey zone' and 'hybrid warfare', the second line, is conceptual confusion. Modifications of terminology, specifically 'adjectival warfare' (modifying nouns with adjectives in pursuit of a new concept), as is the case with hybrid warfare, or the creation of new terminology such as the grey zone, is more distracting than useful. In common with the first line of reasoning, war is war regardless of its actor[67] or specific form and this reality must be acknowledged.[68] Exercises in lexical semantics have little in the way of consequences academically. For those engaged in national security or defence, however, the pursuit of definitions is not only faddish but has practical consequences. The post-Cold War peace dividend, accompanied by greatly reduced defence budgets and equipment inventories, combined with use of elegant capabilities in the GWOT, has left Western militaries perilously under-resourced.

Attempting to counter the latest definitional focus and fad, particularly one as nebulous as hybrid warfare, diffuses focus unnecessarily at a time when it is needed the most to help guide future force development and employment. Once embraced institutionally, such concepts drive cottage industries devoted to further codifying, refining, distributing and influencing the training and education of, and equipping, forces. The Czech Republic developed a Centre Against Terrorism and Hybrid Threats (2017), NATO and the EU have created a European Centre of Excellence for Countering Hybrid Threats (2017) and a consortium of partner nations have developed a Hybrid Threats and Hybrid Warfare Reference Curriculum complete with frameworks for assessment, scenario and wargames, and recommended practices.[69] The words General James Mattis used to describe effects-based operations, also used to describe the 2006 Hezbollah campaign, are equally applicable to hybrid warfare. He noted that the previous concept was 'Misapplied and overextended to the point that it actually hinders rather than helps joint operations.'[70] Even worse, it elevates a tactical or operational concept to the level of strategy, a phenomenon also observed with counterinsurgency in Afghanistan, suggesting a pathological weakness in Western strategic thinking.[71] As with irregular warfare, rising and revisionist states are driven to hybrid warfare out of necessity, rather than desire or culture, given their weaknesses in organisation, capabilities and experience.

The third line arguing against the value of hybrid warfare relates to the politicising of the term and its implications. Stated simply, this line, argued by Ofer Fridman, suggests hybrid warfare risks becoming a self-fulfilling prophesy both Western and Eastern authors mobilise in support of political goals that each is trying to achieve. Western scholars attempted to make sense of the character of observed contemporary conflicts that did not fit the traditional frame of reference for war. In coining, discussing and debating the term hybrid warfare, some Russian scholars subsequently employed their variation of it, *gibridnaya voina*, as a means to unite individual concepts and theories of subversion developed since the 1990s to explain Western political and military successes against former Soviet client states.[72] Developed in the West and reinterpreted by Russia in the East, hybrid warfare gained momentum and importance after Russia's annexation of Crimea in 2014 as both explanation for its rapid success and cause of NATO's surprise.[73] Politically, hybrid warfare provided a unifying rallying cry, and focus of efforts, for the various member states of NATO after more than two decades of uncertainty of the purpose and future of the Alliance. Particularly for more newly added NATO member states, many of whom were former Soviet Warsaw Pact nations, sharing their 'expertise' as experts in Russian thought and behaviour served to guarantee their defence in the face of future Russian aggression. The result is a dangerous echo chamber: the Russians viewing *gibridnaya voina* as the Western method of further undermining Russian stability and influence, and NATO members seeing it as 'new' form of warfare developed and perfected by Russia.[74]

Conclusion

This chapter discusses hybrid warfare in the context of other prevalent terminology in use to capture the characteristics of modern warfare between states. The term will continue to be used for the foreseeable future for several reasons, including its functional and political value. Functionally, hybrid warfare serves as an umbrella term for a range of state-based activities that occur below the threshold of war. Additionally, it serves to link together military activities with non-military ones, including political and economic mobilisation and influence. Hybrid warfare also provides a label under which actions that defy ready categorisation can be placed and perhaps better understood, for Westerners and Russians alike. Since 1991, military observers have intuited a change in both the conduct and shift in power dynamics within warfare. The strong appear able to accomplish their objectives without resorting to the commitment of large numbers of forces; the outcome seems preconditioned before violence is employed. The weak no longer suffer; they must and are seemingly able to wage effective campaigns that frustrate the ability of modern militaries to translate their formidable capabilities into victory. Far from dispelling this notion, the ongoing conflicts in Ukraine and the West Bank seem to confirm that hybrid warfare as a form of warfare has a future, even if its importance varies based on time or phase. This chapter concluded by presenting the arguments in favour of and against hybrid warfare, leaving its value and utility for you to judge.

RESEARCH QUESTIONS

1. How should hybrid warfare best be defined? What is its relationship to grey zone warfare and strategic competition?
2. What factors have led to the emergence of hybrid forms of warfare?
3. What implications does hybrid warfare have for traditional approaches to warfare?
4. How effective is hybrid warfare as a tool of policy?
5. To what extent is hybrid warfare a valid conceptualisation of the reality of contemporary conflict?
6. How should the West respond to the challenges of hybrid warfare?

FURTHER READING

Fridman, Ofer, *Russian Hybrid Warfare: Resurgence and Politicisation* (London: Hurst and Company, 2018). Fridman explores the origins of hybrid warfare and the differences between Russian and Western conceptions of it.

Galleotti, Mark, *Hybrid War or Gibridnaya Voina? Getting Russia's Non-linear Military Challenge Right* (Morrisville, NC: Lulu Press, 2016). Galleotti is a key interpreter of Russian hybrid warfare. Here, he argues that Russian approaches are distinctive, but not wholly new, and makes recommendations for the ways in which the West should respond.

Hoffman, Frank G., 'Hybrid Warfare and Challenges', *Joint Force Quarterly*, 52 (First Quarter, 2009), 34–9, https://apps.dtic.mil/sti/tr/pdf/ADA516871.pdf. Where the early debates on hybrid warfare began.

Kilcullen, David, *The Dragons and the Snakes: How the Rest Learned to Fight the West* (London: Hurst and Company, 2020). Kilcullen makes a case for the significance of the challenge posed to the West by what he terms 'liminal warfare'.

Murray, Williamson and Peter Mansoor (eds.), *Hybrid Warfare: Fighting Complex Opponents from the Ancient World to the Present* (Cambridge, UK: Cambridge University Press, 2012). Murray and Mansoor take a broader perspective on hybrid warfare, arguing, through a range of historical case studies, that it is nothing new.

Weissman, Mikael, Niklas Nilsson, Bjorn Palmertz and Per Thunholm (eds.), *Hybrid Warfare: Security and Asymmetric Conflict in International Relations* (London: I. B. Tauris, 2021).

This edited volume provides a well-informed assessment of the theory and application of hybrid warfare in the contemporary world. This book is also available through open access at https://tinyurl.com/5ay6xapw.

ONLINE RESOURCES

Given the significance of hybrid warfare to contemporary debates on modern conflict, there is a wide range of quality material available online, including previously cited sources such as RAND (www.rand.org), *Small Wars Journal* (smallwarsjournal.com), and *Strategy Bridge* (thestrategybridge.org).

Other useful sites include the European Centre of Excellence for Countering Hybrid Threats (www.hybridcoe.fi/); NATO's hybrid warfare library guide, which offers access to online reports (https://natolibguides.info/hybridwarfare/reports); the Centre for European Policy Analysis (https://cepa.org/search-results/?term = hybrid+warfare); and the Multinational Capability Development Campaign's 'Countering Hybrid Warfare' project (https://tinyurl.com/3cnec4ra.

NOTES

1 'CSIS Programs: Gray Zone Project', Center for Strategic and International Studies (CSIS), www.csis.org/programs/gray-zone-project.

2 Christopher Paul, Michael Schwille, Michael Vasseur, Elizabeth M. Bartels and Ryan Bauer, *The Role of Information in U.S. Concepts for Strategic Competition* (RAND, 25 October 2022), p. vi, www.rand.org/pubs/research_reports/RRA1256-1.html.

3 Seth G. Jones, *The Return of Political Warfare* (CSIS, 2 February 2018)https://www.csis.org/analysis/return-political-warfare.

4 Ibid., 2.

5 See David Patrikarakos, *War in 140 Characters: How Social Media Is Reshaping Conflict in the Twenty-First Century* (New York, NY: Basic Books, 2017).

6 Kim Wijnja, 'Countering Hybrid Threats: Does Strategic Culture Matter?' *Defence Studies* (June 2021), 5.

7 '269: Policy Planning Memorandum', 4 May 1948 (Foreign Relations of the United States, 1945–1950, Emergence of the Intelligence Establishment), https://history.state.gov/historicaldocuments/frus1945-50Intel/d269.

8 Hal Brands and Toshi Yoshihara, 'Waging Political Warfare', *The National Interest*, No. 159 (January/February 2019,), 16.

9 Ibid., 17.

10 'CSIS Programs: Gray Zone Project'.

11 Jones, 'The Return of Political Warfare', p. 1.

12 'The Gray Zone', United States Special Operations Command, 9 September 2015, https://info.publicintelligence.net/USSOCOM-GrayZones.pdf.

13 Conrad Beckett, 'Getting to Grips with Grey Zone Conflict', Strategic Command Blog, 26 April 2021, https://tinyurl.com/btu2t5vz.

14 Javier Jordan, 'International Competition Below the Threshold of War: Toward a Theory of Gray Zone Conflict', *Journal of Strategic Security*, **14**(1) (2020), 1.

15 'Today's Wars are fought in the 'Gray Zone.' Here's everything you need to know about it' (Atlantic Council Hybrid Warfare Project), 23 February 2022, https://tinyurl.com/2dhwrymz.

16 Jordan, 'International Competition', pp. 3–4.
17 Ibid., 3.
18 Andrew Dowse and Sascha-Dominik Bachmann, 'Explainer: What Is "Hybrid Warfare" and What Is Meant by the "Grey Zone"?', *The Conversation*, 17 June 2019, https://tinyurl.com/4ey53vmv.
19 Frank G. Hoffman, 'Hybrid Warfare and Challenges', *Joint Force Quarterly*, 52 (First Quarter 2009), 35.
20 See, for example, Stephen Biddle, *Nonstate Warfare: The Military Methods of Guerillas, Warlords, and Militias* (Princeton, NJ: Princeton University Press, 2021).
21 Keir Giles, *Russia's 'New' Tools for Confronting the West: Continuity and Innovation in Moscow's Exercise of Power* (London: RUSI, March 2016), p. 5.
22 'Defeating the Hybrid Threat', *NATO News*, (9 January 2015), www.ndc.nato.int/news/news.php?icode = 758.
23 Quoted in Jan Almäng, 'War, Vagueness and Hybrid War,' *Defence Studies*, 19(2) (2019), 192.
24 *Global Strategic Trends: The Future Starts Today,* 6th ed. (Ministry of Defence, 2018), p. 132.
25 'The Operational Environment and the Changing Character of Future Warfare' (TRADOC Pamphlet 525-92, no date), pp. 10, 18, https://adminpubs.tradoc.army.mil/pamphlets/TP525-92.pdf.
26 Damien van Puyvelde, 'Hybrid Warfare: Does it Even Exist?' NATO Review, 7 May 2015, https://tinyurl.com/42ud238n.
27 *MCDC Countering Hybrid Warfare Project: Countering Hybrid Warfare* (March 2019), p. 12, https://tinyurl.com/bpadjwet.
28 Anthony H. Cordesman and Grace Hwang, *Chronology of Possible Chinese Gray Area and Hybrid Warfare Operations* (Washington, DC: Center for Strategic and International Studies, February 2020), p. 2, https://tinyurl.com/4v3bd4se.
29 Erik V. Larson et al., 'Foundations of Effective Influence Operations: A Framework for Enhancing Army Capabilities (Santa Monica, CA: RAND, 2009), p. 12, www.rand.org/pubs/monographs/MG654.html.
30 Brandon Valeriano, Benjamin Jensen and Ryan C. Maness, *Cyber Strategy: The Evolving Character of Power and Coercion* (Oxford: Oxford University Press, 2018), p. 10.
31 Stephen Blank, *Cyber War and Information War à la Russe*, in George Perkovich, Ariel E. Levite (eds.), *Understanding Cyber Conflict: 14 Analogies* (Washington, DC: Georgetown University Press, 2017). p. 85.
32 Gavin Wilson, 'Information Warfare: What Is It, and Why Should We Care?' *The Cove*, 8 January 2022, https://tinyurl.com/bp75xb64.
33 See Maria Mälksoo, 'Countering Hybrid Warfare as Ontological Security Management: The Emerging Practices of the EU and NATO,' *European Security*, 27(3) (2018), 374–92.
34 Lt. Col. Timothy L. Thomas, 'Russian Forecasts of Future War', *Military Review* (May–June 2019), 87.
35 Ibid., p. 89.
36 Daniel Moore, *Offensive Cyber Operations: Understanding Intangible Warfare* (London: Hurst & Company, 2022), p. 148.
37 Gavin Wild, 'Assess Russia's Cyber Performance Without Repeating its Past Mistakes', *War on the Rocks*, 21 July 2022.
38 Giles, *Russia's 'New' Tools for Confronting the West'*, p. 63.
39 Blank, Cyber War and Information War a la Russe, p. 92.
40 Moore, Offensive Cyber Operations, pp. 170–1.

41 Susan Landau, 'Cyberwar in Ukraine: What You See Is Not What's Really There', *Lawfare*, 30 September 2022, www.lawfareblog.com/cyberwar-ukraine-what-you-see-not-whats-really-there.
42 Mike Dahm, 'The Reality of War Should Define Information Warfare', *US Naval Institute Proceedings*, **147**(3) (March 2021), https://tinyurl.com/yenz8mdj.
43 See Nathan Beauchamp-Mustafaga, The Military Applications of Emerging Technologies and Implications for the United States, RAND, 1 June 2023, www.rand.org/pubs/research_reports/RRA853-1.html.
44 David Kilcullen, *The Dragons and the Snakes: How the Rest learned to Fight the West* (London: Hurst and Company, 2020), 202.
45 Peter Mattis, 'China's Three Warfares Perspective,' *War on the Rocks*, 30 January 2018, https://warontherocks.com/2018/01/chinas-three-warfares-perspective/.
46 David E. Sanger, *The Perfect Weapon: War, Sabotage and Fear in the Cyber Age* (London: Scribe, 2018), p. 100.
47 Ross Babbage, *Stealing a March: Chinese Hybrid Warfare in the Indo-Pacific: Issues and Options for Allied Defense Planners*, vol. I (Center for Strategic and Budgetary Assessments, 2019), p. 3, https://csbaonline.org/uploads/documents/Stealing_a_March_Final.pdf.
48 Hannah Bailey, 'Discursive Statecraft: China's Information Operations', Council on Geostrategy, 8 March 2023, https://tinyurl.com/4djr7zbz.
49 Babbage, *Stealing a March*, p. 3.
50 Kilcullen, *The Dragons and the Snakes*, pp. 172–4.
51 'How China and Russia Use Information Operations to Compete With the US', *CNA In-Depth*, 30 June 2023, https://tinyurl.com/2wuuyrar.
52 Bailey, 'Discursive Statecraft'.
53 Albert Zhang and Tilla Hoja, 'China's Information Operations Are Silencing and Influencing Global Audiences on Xinjiang', *Australian Strategic Policy Institute*, 20 July 2022, https://tinyurl.com/yckb2wxx.
54 Robert Chesney, 'Military-Intelligence Convergence and the Law of the Title 10/Title 50 Debate', *Journal of National Security Law & Policy*, **5** (2012): 539–629.
55 William Arkin, *Divining Victory: Airpower in the 2006 Israel–Hezbollah War* (Maxwell Air Force Base, AL: Air University Press, 2007), p. 156.
56 Audrey Kurth Cronin, 'ISIS Is Not a Terrorist Group: Why Counterterrorism Won't Stop the Latest Jihadist Threat', *Foreign Affairs*, **94**(2) (March/April 2015), pp. 87–98.
57 *'Little Green Men': A Primer on Modern Russian Unconventional Warfare, Ukraine: 2013–2014*, U.S. States Army Special Operations Command, 2015, p. 48, www.jhuapl.edu/sites/default/files/2022-12/ARIS_LittleGreenMen.pdf.
58 Liang Qiao and Xiangsui Wang, *Unrestricted Warfare* (Beijing: PLA Literature and Arts Publishing House, 1999), p. 7.
59 Sam Beltran, 'Philippines on Tenterhooks as Beijing Deploys 'Darker Grey' Tactics in South China Sea', *South China Morning Post*, 12 July 2024.
60 Valery Gerasimov, 'The Value of Science is in the Foresight', *Military Review* (January–February 2016), 24.
61 Gerasimov, 'The Value of Science is in the Foresight', p. 28.
62 Sun Tzu, *The Illustrated Art of War*, trans. Samuel B. Griffith (Oxford: Oxford University Press, 2005), p. 115.
63 Timothy Thomas. *Russian Military Thought: Concepts and Elements*, MITRE Report MP190451VI (McLean, VA: MITRE Corporation, August 2019), pp. 4–6.

64 Donald Stoker and Craig Whiteside, 'Blurred Lines: Gray-Zone Conflict and Hybrid War – Two Failures of American Strategic Thinking', *Naval War College Review*, **73**(1) Article 4 (2020): 3–5, https://digital-commons.usnwc.edu/nwc-review/vol73/iss1/4,
65 Adam Elkus,'50 Shades of Gray: Why the Gray Wars Concept Lacks Strategic Sense', *War on the Rocks* blog, 15 December 2015, https://tinyurl.com/y9ewb4vj.
66 Williamson Murray and Peter Mansoor (eds.), *Hybrid Warfare: Fighting Complex Opponents from the Ancient World to the Present* (Cambridge, UK: Cambridge University Press, 2012), p. ii.
67 Biddle, *Nonstate Warfare.*
68 Antulio J. Echevarria II, *Preparing for One War and Getting Another* (Carlisle, PA: U.S. Army War College Press, September 2010), p. 25.
69 See NATO Headquarters, *Hybrid Threats and Hybrid Warfare Reference Curriculum* (Brussels: NATO Headquarters, June 2024), pp. 61–71.
70 Gen J. N. Mattis, commander, US Joint Forces Command, to US Joint Forces Command, memorandum, 14 August 2008, p. 1.
71 Colin Gray, Categorical Confusion? The Strategic Implications of Recognizing Challenges Either as Irregular or Traditional (Carlisle Barracks, PA: U.S. Army War College Press, 2012), pp. 48–9; Emile Simpson, *War from the Ground Up*, rev. ed. (Oxford: Oxford University Press, 2018), pp. 61–71.
72 Ofer Fridman, *Russian Hybrid Warfare: Resurgence and Politicisation* (New York, NY: Oxford University Press, 2018), pp. 92–8.
73 *'Little Green Men'*, p. 17.
74 Fridman, *Russian Hybrid Warfare*, pp. 149–52.

PART VIII
Conclusion

DAVID J. LONSDALE

21 Continuity and Change in Modern Warfare

CHAPTER OUTLINE

Introduction

When seeking to understand a subject as complex as warfare there are various approaches one can take. The following analytical frameworks are not mutually exclusive, but they do reflect particular perspectives on the subject. For example, one can emphasise the technological dimension of warfare, noting developments over time. Alternatively, attention may be focused on the battlespace and/or theatre of operations, giving notice to the tactical and operational levels. Doctrine provides another area of study, whereby developments in warfare are discussed through the prism of ideas or archetypes. Think, for example, of the debates surrounding attrition and manoeuvre or hybrid and grey zone warfare. Warfare can also be understood on the basis of its polymorphous character. This can refer to the regular–irregular spectrum of warfare, or indeed to warfare in the different domains. Equally, the study of warfare can be approached via a cultural model, whereby differences are attributed to strategic, military or service culture. These different paradigms represent just some of the options available to the student of warfare.

When contemplating the Conclusion to the third edition of *Understanding Modern Warfare*, it became immediately apparent that the work has evolved over time. Each edition reflects changes in the environment within which war occurs or developments in the intellectual debates surrounding modern warfare. Indeed, this third edition has arguably seen the greatest changes, adding an entirely new section, *The Future Operational Environment*, which discusses multi-domain operations, hybrid and grey zone conflict and cyber power. At the same time, many ideas, principles, references and so on have remained in each edition. Thus, it became clear that the paradigm of continuity and change would serve as an especially useful approach for the conclusion to this latest version of the book. To that end, eleven constants will be discussed, followed by five changes in modern warfare.

Constants in Modern Warfare

Process and Levels of Strategy

Despite significant shifts in the geostrategic environment and technological basis for modern warfare, the process of strategy continues to function via the five levels of strategy. This statement is not as seemingly obvious as it may at first appear to be. As noted in Chapter 2, the operational level has not always been recognised, nor is its position entirely secure in modern discourse. Nonetheless, it is the contention here that the five levels of strategy remain our best taxonomy for understanding the process of strategy. Specifically, how tactical actions in the battlespace, corralled at the operational level, enable the attainment of military strategic objectives, which in turn work alongside the other instruments of grand strategy to secure the overall policy objectives. Indeed, it can and should be noted that warfare always occurs within a policy context. In this way, warfare is the act of waging war, with the latter being a socio-political activity in broader human affairs. Thus, whatever domain one is operating in, with whatever technology and capabilities, the process of strategy will function through the levels, with policy acting as the driving force.

Combined and Joint Operations

It is true that competence is required in each domain of military activity. That is, each military service must succeed in its own domain before it can contribute effectively to the wider war effort. That being said, across history it is generally true that success in warfare commonly comes from effective combined arms and joint operations. Within context, each form of military power has strengths and weaknesses. Combined arms and joint operations are designed to maximise the former while mitigating the latter. Infantry, for example, are an inherently flexible form of military power and crucial to Wylie's concept of control (see later).[1] They are, however, vulnerable to different forms of firepower and must be protected to the extent that is possible. Typically, one of the roles of artillery is to supress enemy sources of firepower to offer said protection to infantry. The Macedonian art of war under Alexander the Great offers a wonderful example of combined arms. Alexander's infantry phalanx pinned the enemy's forces, while the heavy cavalry acted as the instrument of decision by penetrating the enemy's line. In turn, the heavy Companion Cavalry was supported by light infantry (hypaspists), and the vulnerable flanks of the phalanx were protected by light cavalry. This level of combined arms was replicated in the latter stages of the First World War, when infantry was effectively integrated with artillery, machine gunners and tanks.

In terms of joint operations, surface forces (both land and sea) benefit immeasurably from air cover. As noted in Chapter 3, one of the reasons for the failure of offensives in Ukraine is that neither side has been able to gain control of the air. Perhaps one of the most striking examples of jointery in modern warfare is D-Day. Ground forces, which were essential for the liberation of Europe, had to be transported to the theatre by maritime power, and both were protected and supported by Allied air power. Moreover, the latter also played an important role in preparation for Operation Overlord. This involved an interdiction campaign against the French railway network, as well as dropping paratroopers to help protect the landing forces as they sought to establish a beachhead.

Dominance of the Land Domain

The previous comments regarding the superiority of joint operations do not undermine the principle that land is the decisive domain in warfare. Although the sea, air and cyber domains are important highways for strategic activity and/or contain important resources, it is on land where policy issues are decided. As Admiral J. C. Wylie noted in his 1967 work, *Military Strategy: A General Theory of Power Control*, strategy is fundamentally concerned with the exercise of control. That control is ultimately exercised by the man-on-the-scene-with-a-gun.[2] The reasoning behind this statement is that war is a form of politics, politics is about people, and thus it is people that need to be controlled in some form. And, since humans generally live on the land, the latter is where the real business of politics occurs. Control over human affairs is best exercised by human beings in close proximity. Counterinsurgency is one of the best exemplars of this truism. As noted by James Kiras in his chapters, counterinsurgency tends to be population-centric, with the support or acquiescence of the population central to success. That being the case, the population requires physical security, which is best provided by dismounted infantry, rather than more distant air or sea assets. Moreover, the broader socio-political needs of the population must be met, and these can only really be understood via direct human interaction. In light of these thoughts, technological developments in modern warfare that have introduced or enhanced other domains only end up supporting land power in some form or other. This is clearly evident with reference to the sea, air and cyber domains. All three of these forms of power have undoubtedly become important enablers for strategy. However, none of them have proven decisive.

The Human Dimension

'People matter most', was the stark message in Colin Gray's 1999 book, *Modern Strategy*.[3] The veracity of this statement emanates directly from the previous comments regarding the land domain. War is politics, and politics is about people. And, despite the rise of AI and unmanned systems, ongoing conflicts in the world starkly reveal that people remain central to the waging of war. This leads to some important observations about modern warfare. For example, it means that war is conducted by social organisations, which require social cohesion to function effectively. In turn, that ensures that certain intangible factors are important enablers of military efficacy. Morale, for example, is clearly an important element of combat power. This leads to the realisation that command and leadership are central to tactical, operational and strategic performance. This not only relates to combat power but also to complex interactions that occur between military power and socio-political phenomena. To take just one example, a commander must be conscious of the population amongst whom he is operating, taking into account their culture and systems of governance. Despite the many changes to warfare across the centuries, certain human qualities of command are always evident. Indeed, this may explain why military history is dominated by certain individuals who exhibited these qualities in abundance and in combination. Clausewitz termed such individuals as military geniuses.[4]

Dominance of the Destructive Principle

Because it is a complex socio-political activity, war almost always includes non-violent, even non-military components. And these 'additional' considerations often play a central role in determining the outcome of strategic events. Nonetheless, Clausewitz is convincing when he wrote that war is distinguished from other social activities by the dominance of the destructive principle.[5] For Clausewitz, that meant placing battle at the centre of his theory of war. Despite the socially and technologically driven promises of information operations, cyber power and humane warfare, the destructive principle remains at the heart of modern warfare. This is painfully evident in the ongoing conflicts in Ukraine and Israel/Gaza, where death and human suffering continue unabated at the time of writing.

Why is this the case? Why cannot humanity advance war to be less destructive? There are various reasons for this. Indeed, one can convincingly argue that the opposite has occurred, that war has become ever more destructive. The twentieth century is widely regarded as being the most violent in human history. Additionally, via nuclear weapons humans have developed the means to annihilate both themselves and all other life on the planet. The main answer to the above questions is the nature of war. To cite Clausewitz once again, 'War is a clash between major interests, which is resolved by bloodshed – that is the only way in which it differs from other conflicts.'[6] War is the chosen means when other forms of political interaction have failed. Violence enables us to exert power when persuasion or reasoned argument are insufficient. Moreover, the nature of war is not only violent, but also competitive. This creates an escalatory dynamic in war, whereby each side applies greater or more effective forms of military power to surpass the other. This does not mean that war always escalates to its absolute form, since escalation is limited by friction and socio-political influences. Nonetheless, the nature of war does ensure that each belligerent requires a theory of victory, meaning that the policy objective must be achieved, perhaps with some adjustments to reflect operational realities, via the application, threat or presence of destructive combat power.

Moral Dimension

Despite the dominance of the destructive principle, the nature of war is not merely composed of violence. As noted, the escalatory dynamic of war is restrained by socio-political forces. One of those forces is the moral dimension. Again, this relates to the people dimension. Since humans are moral beings, it is axiomatic that our social activities also exhibit a moral component. That does not mean, however, that the moral component dominates the practice of warfare. Indeed, most wars contain moments when the moral component appears to be sidelined in the name of military necessity or simple brutality. However, even though military ethics sometimes seemingly fade into the background, the moral dimension normally continues to exert some influence over the conduct of war and strategy. This is often due to the significance of legitimacy in strategic matters. Most strategic actors have a constituency to which they must appeal. That being the case, they must be perceived, by said constituency, as a legitimate actor.

Moreover, with important exceptions, warfare is generally waged in a manner that pays some respect to prevalent norms and values, the war convention. This is, at least in part, because complex relationships exist amongst *jus ad bellum*, *jus in bello* and *jus post bellum*. Put simply, the legitimacy of a war with a just cause can be undermined if said war is waged in an unjust manner and in a way that undermines the stability of the post-bellum environment. As a consequence of these moral components, modern warfare cannot be concerned with purely operational issues; it must exhibit a moral dimension, albeit one modified by military or strategic necessity.

Geography

Warfare always occurs within a geographic context. Admittedly, that geographic context can vary considerably, even within the same overall domain. This is especially the case with land power, which must be able to function effectively in many different terrains. The sea is less heterogeneous, but still subject to considerable differences, whether that is due to weather or proximity to land and so on. The air environment is more homogenous, but is still affected by the weather and altitude. Finally, cyberspace initially appears to be chiefly uniform, but due to being largely man-made exhibits considerable variation and is constantly changing in scale and form.

Regardless of the variations in environment one may face, military forces must be masters of their particular domain, while also possessing some knowledge of the other domains to enable more effective joint operations. This all begins with an understanding of the constant features of each particular domain. Occasionally, technological and operational developments will alter how military power interacts with geography. Think, for example, of the impact of air power on the logistical situation in Burma during the Second World War. Air logistics negated some of the terrain-based obstacles initially faced by the British, and thus enabled them to seize the initiative from the Japanese.[7] That being said, geography still represents a reasonably set stage upon which the drama of warfare is played out. Geography was one of the key factors that contributed to the length and costs of the US Civil War. The Eastern theatre was relatively narrow due to the Appalachian Mountains. This restricted operational manoeuvres and ensured that the main armies remained in fairly constant contact, increasing the number of engagements and respective casualties. Operations in the Western theatre were complicated by the Mississippi and its tributaries. Modern forms of warfare will similarly be shaped by geography, and must continue to respect the geographic dimension.

Polymorphous Character of War

As Clausewitz eloquently observed, all wars are things of the same nature.[8] Yet, each individual war is unique in its character. The character of any particular war will be dependent upon a vast range of factors, including, but not limited to, the policy objectives sought; strategic culture of the belligerents; capabilities available to them; geography of the theatre(s); stage of technological development; prevailing moral norms and so on. Thus, considered as a general socio-political activity, this creates the polymorphous character of war. That is, strategic actors must prepare for future warfare without any real certainty on the type of war they will be compelled to wage. This complex reality leads to important debates that have implications for procurement, training and so on. Beyond the challenges of war preparation, the polymorphous character of war also demands, for example, doctrine, forces and command styles that are adaptable. Indeed, Williamson Murray concludes that adaptability is one of the key features of success in war.[9] Interestingly, this may not seem like a constant in warfare, since it is based on the notion of change. However, the polymorphous character of war is itself a constant feature of warfare over time.

War's Competitive Nature

Adaptability is also required as a consequence of war's competitive nature. Again, Clausewitz is correct to highlight that war represents a duel on a larger scale.[10] The existence of an intelligent enemy seriously complicates the conduct of warfare. This is manifest in several different ways. One such manifestation, the paradoxical logic of strategy, is identified by Edward N. Luttwak.[11] The paradoxical logic denotes that over time the enemy adapts and one's successes begin to produce diminishing returns. This phenomenon makes itself present in many different forms. It may be that the enemy develops new technology or techniques to counter your capabilities; they may replicate your tactical approach and operational art; they may forgo battle to deny you tactical success, trading space for time; or they may adopt an asymmetrical form of warfare, adopting the means of small wars, cyber power or even escalating to nuclear weapons, as evident in Russia's 'escalate-to-de-escalate' doctrine.

War's competitive nature complicates the business of warfare in other ways. Alongside the multidimensional nature of strategy, it introduces intangibles and non-linearity into the mix. Clausewitz notes that war is a battle of wills fought through physical means.[12] Consequently, victory requires not only engaging with quantifiable capabilities but also unquantifiable intangibles such as morale, social/political cohesion and pain threshold. These complicate war in general, but are especially troublesome for strategies such as coercion and deterrence that rely on the psychological impact of the use of force. Non-linearity has many causes. In reference to the enemy, non-linearity emanates from the numerous and unpredictable interactions that occur amongst the belligerents of a conflict. One never really knows how these interactions will play out and cross-fertilise until war begins. This range of complications emanating from the presence of the enemy impacts on the significance of the trinity.[13] Another Clausewitzian concept, the trinity, reflects the rational and non-rational forces in war, and identifies the various actors or units that engage with these forces: government, military and people. The complex nature of any particular war can be found within the interplay of the trinities of the various belligerents involved.[14]

Friction

Encompassing a number of the above points is the Clausewitzian concept of friction: 'The only concept that more or less corresponds to the factors that distinguish real war from war on paper.'[15] Military forces must learn to operate within a friction-laden environment. As discussed in Chapter 2, certain actions can be taken to mitigate the impact of friction, but the causes are so widespread that friction itself cannot be eradicated from war. Many implications stem from this truism. One of particular importance is that those waging war must develop strategic and military cultures that are tolerant of friction. For example, societies at war must be prepared for setbacks, unexpected costs and variable timelines for war. This constant of warfare should likewise temper our enthusiasm for the next technological or operational silver bullet.

Change

As will become evident in the next section, and with a twist of irony, one of the constants in warfare is change. This speaks again to the need for adaptability in capabilities, training, doctrine, command, culture and so on. Although war exhibits the above identified constants, and these are of supreme importance, changes, both big and small, constantly alter the challenge of waging modern warfare. In itself, this demands ongoing intellectual engagement with the subject, and one might say the need for new editions of volumes such as *Understanding Modern Warfare*. The real intellectual and conceptual challenge, then, is to effectively incorporate change into the existing body of knowledge on war.

Changes in Modern Warfare

Technology

As alluded to, in the modern period technological change has been rapid. In the realm of warfare, new technology presents both threats and opportunities at all the levels of military strategy. Tactics have regularly had to adapt to new technology, operational art has been further enabled and new strategies have become a reality. In terms of the latter, think, for example, of strategic bombing, which was first enacted less than twelve years after the first heavier-than-air flight. At the tactical level, rifled weapons and precision indirect artillery fire, to name just two innovations, have resulted in more dispersed forces and the so-called empty battlespace. Operational art has arguably benefitted from the internal combustion engine, both in terms of striking power and the logistics to support deep operational manoeuvre.

One of the 'constant' changes that reflects the above is the dynamic relationship between offence and defence. This is evident in all domains of warfare. At different times, technology, depending on how it is utilised in context, may favour either the offence or defence. This is well illustrated by the First World War. Rapid fire machine guns and artillery seemed to favour the defence, but then the same artillery was used to suppress defensive firepower. In response, the defenders adopted defence-in-depth and fortified hardpoints. In turn, the attackers developed infiltration tactics, enabled by new technology that gave attacking forces more organic firepower. Similar dynamics can be witnessed in the sea and air environments. Anti-platform capabilities, which seem to threaten the viability of the aggressive use of ships and aircraft, are themselves countered by technologies such as stealth and standoff munitions.

Technology has also, arguably, increased the scale and scope of warfare. As General Bowder of the British Army notes, 'Battlegroups ... can see further and shoot further ... than we have ever managed before.'[16] This is not to say that, absent of modern technology, warfare was always severely limited. Alexander the

Great managed to campaign from Greece to India, and Napoleon reached Moscow with horses and carts. Nonetheless, it is still evident that technology has increased the range of weapons, the scope of rapid operational manoeuvre and the command structures to support it, and the potential lethality of firepower. Much of this increase in scale and scope is exemplified by nuclear weapons. As was proven time and again in ancient warfare, settlements or cities could be razed to the ground with rocks, swords and torches. Yet, it would take time to do this: days, weeks even months. Moreover, unless endowed with an unusually large army, the attacking force could only assault one city at a time, and would take a considerable time to march to the target, construct the siege engines and so on. In contrast, as evidenced by the Second World War, aircraft made it possible to destroy large parts of a city in one night and at great distances. However, this would still require hundreds of platforms and often be a costly operation in terms of losses of men and equipment. The invention of nuclear weapons, especially when married to intercontinental ballistic missiles, enables the destruction of multiple cities instantaneously, within minutes, and on a global scale.

New Domains and Enhanced Forms of Military Power

As is evident from the structure of *Understanding Modern Warfare*, warfare takes place in distinct domains and with distinct forms of military power. For much of history there were only two domains, land and sea. In the modern period the number of domains and forms of power have increased. The twentieth century bore witness to the arrival of air power, nuclear weapons and the nascent beginnings of the cyber domain. The latter only became officially recognised as a warfighting domain in the twenty-first century. The appearance of a new domain or form of military power is significant because it engenders significant changes in the preparation and conduct of warfare. New organisations or armed services are required, as is new doctrine. Tactics and operations must adapt, and the joint environment is invariably expanded. Think, for example, of the impact of air power on surface forces. Air power is just over one hundred years old, and yet it has become one of the key factors in the outcome of surface operations. As Field Marshall Montgomery noted, 'If we lose the war in the air, we lose the war and we lose it quickly.' With new domains also come new logistical demands and opportunities. Additionally, new strategic options become possible, or older expressions of strategy are enhanced. Cyber power has allegedly democratised strategic attack on a global scale, while nuclear weapons have enhanced the prominence of deterrence in defence and security policies.

All of these changes in domains and forms of warfare are enabled by technological advancements. However, intellectual developments can also bring significant changes in established forms of military power. This is especially evident in small wars. The latter has been an ever-present feature of war, yet the twentieth century arguably witnessed significant development in irregular war via the writings and careers of men such as Mao and Robert Thompson. Small wars have always been a challenge for the powerful, but in response to doctrinal development of irregular warfare the great powers have themselves had to further codify the theory and practice of small wars.

Social, Media, Law

By its very nature, war is a social activity. Nonetheless, historically, especially in relation to larger political communities, the link between society and war was somewhat distant or indirect. With the development of communications technology and the growth in different forms of media, this distance has been reducing. Societies are now deeply enmeshed with the wars waged on their behalf, even when those wars are occurring thousands of miles away. Images and opinions flooding in via mainstream and social media platforms inform socio-political debates on the use of force. At one level democratically empowering, the enhanced social dimension of strategy also causes complications for the conduct of war. This is not lost on the armed services, as evidenced by this recent comment from the British Army, 'With military actions being more closely scrutinised in real time, maintaining surprise, deception and legitimacy will be more of a challenge.'[17] This is especially the case because contested information is rampant in modern media. This is exemplified by the strike on the al-Ahli Arab hospital in Gaza in October 2023. Initially, sections of mainstream and social media subscribed to the narrative that Israel had attacked the hospital, killing over 500 people. As more evidence began to emerge, however, an alternative perspective suggested that the explosion may have been caused by a failed Israel-bound rocket fired from within Gaza. Moreover, it seems that the hospital had not been struck directly, but rather a nearby car park, and that the death toll was lower than originally reported.[18] By the time the situation became clearer, much of the socio-political chaos had already been caused. Those waging modern warfare must navigate this changing and challenging social environment, where every move is carefully scrutinised and contested information is prevalent.

In addition to these social changes, war has become an increasingly litigated activity. As noted above, war has always had a moral dimension. And, at different times and places, norms surrounding the use of force have been codified. To a greater or lesser extent, this has influenced the conduct of war throughout history, acting as a restraining and/or regulatory force. However, the legal dimension of war has expanded considerably since the middle of the nineteenth century. This has important consequences. First, for many strategic actors there now exists a substantial legal aspect to operational planning. Alongside traditional considerations regarding the operational efficacy of an action, it must also be asked whether said action is legal. Secondly, adversaries of legally bound strategic actors may utilise or benefit from the legal dimension of war, creating an asymmetry between belligerents. In this sense, adversaries may engage in 'lawfare', whereby they use legal frameworks to restrict or delegitimise their opponents. This may involve, for example, placing military targets at civilian sites, in the hope that their adversary will either restrain from attacking the military target or do so and suffer the legitimacy consequences.

Complexity

Taken together, technological developments, additional domains and the expansion of the social and legal dimensions, have added considerably to the complexity of modern warfare. In a relatively short period of time, war has evolved from a two-domain activity, with occasional technological developments and limited social and legal intrusion, into the complex beast that we know today. This metaphorical quagmire is further complicated when nation states instruct their military forces to engage in ill-defined activities such as 'nation-building'. This merely complicates the business of war still further. In contrast, Clausewitz is compelling when he extols the virtue of the simple over the complex.[19] While it is true that warfare must be conducted within the confines of strategy, and therefore within a socio-political milieu, the nature of war must also be respected. That is, that the primary focus of military activity must be the defeat of enemy forces.

Firepower and Precision

The final two changes are considered together because their implications are closely interwoven. Tactics, and to some degree operational art, in the modern era have had to adapt to the increasingly lethality and range of firepower. Adaptation has been essential to ensure the continued utility of military forces, especially when prolonged presence is required. Whether it is a ship poised off the coast or the man-on-the-scene-with-a-gun, vulnerable military assets need protection so that they can perform their roles. Additionally, as evidenced most clearly by the US Civil War and the two world wars, the costs of modern warfare have increased considerably. To reference nuclear weapons again, this reached its zenith during the nuclear age, and was starkly noted by Bernard Brodie in his response to the first use of nuclear weapons, 'Thus far the chief purpose of our military establishment has been to win wars. From now on its chief purpose must be to avert them. It can have almost no other useful purpose.'[20] Even theorists such as Colin Gray, a long-time participant in nuclear matters, have concluded that the destruction wrought by nuclear use would likely overwhelm the process of strategy, rendering war as an end in itself.[21]

However, warfare has a habit of adapting, and this includes in response to increases in firepower. Strategic actors have found ways to wage war below the thresholds where massive firepower is unleashed. Limited and small wars have enabled the strategic process to function as ever it did. Moreover, although technology has increased firepower, in recent decades it has also contained it via precision. The latter does not entirely rule out the potential for significant casualties, but it does enable modern military forces to use firepower in more controlled ways that may be more acceptable to modern social and moral mores.

Conclusion

At the risk of belabouring the main point, modern warfare is subject to ever-present features while also being the realm of unremitting change. As a consequence, the art of war is, at least in part, concerned with finding an equilibrium between these two positions. The eternal nature of war must be respected. At the same time, reasonable adaptation is essential to embrace and exploit change for strategic effect. As with much in the theory of war, this position is best expressed by Clausewitz:

> We can thus only say that the aims a belligerent adopts, and the resources he employs, must be governed by the particular characteristics of his own position; but they will also conform to the spirit of the age and to its general character. Finally, they must always be governed by the general conclusions to be drawn from the nature of war itself.[22]

RESEARCH QUESTIONS

1. What is the best approach for the study of modern warfare?
2. What is the most significant constant in warfare?
3. What is the most significant change in modern warfare?
4. How can the practitioner best adapt to changes in modern warfare?

FURTHER READING

Clausewitz, Carl von, *On War*, trans. Michael Howard and Peter Paret (London: David Campbell Publishers Ltd, 1993). Quite simply the best work of strategic theory ever written. Clausewitz gets closer than anyone to defining the true nature of war.

Freedman, Lawrence, *Strategy: A History* (Oxford: Oxford University Press, 2015). A masterly and exhaustive exploration of the theory and practice of strategy.

Gray, Colin S., *Perspectives on Strategy* (Oxford: Oxford University Press, 2016). A deep dive into four of the main influences on strategic behaviour: ethics, culture, geography and technology.

Gruszczak, Artur and Sebastian Kaempf (eds.), *Routledge Handbook of the Future of Warfare* (Abingdon: Routledge, 2024). A varied and comprehensive set of essays on the future of warfare.

Murray, Williamson, *Military Adaptation in War: With Fear of Change* (Cambridge, UK: Cambridge University Press, 2011). Another thought-provoking work from one of the leading analysts and historians of strategic behaviour.

Strachan, Hew, *The Direction of War: Contemporary Strategy in Historical Perspective* (Cambridge, UK: Cambridge University Press, 2013). A superior discussion of modern military strategy from a theoretical and historical perspective.

van Creveld, Martin, *Technology and War: From 2000 BC to the Present* (New York, NY: Free Press, 1991). One of the few classic works on the role of technology in war.

Watts, Barry D., *Clausewitzian Friction and Future War*, McNair Paper 52 (Washington, DC: Institute for National Strategic Studies, National Defense University, October 1996). The best analysis of Clausewitzian friction to date.

ONLINE RESOURCES

https://ssi.armywarcollege.edu/: the website of the Strategic Studies Institute, which contains lots of in-depth analysis of important strategic issues.

www.militarystrategymagazine.com/: an online journal devoted to strategy.

https://thestrategybridge.org/: focused on developing thinking in strategy and military affairs.
https://warontherocks.com/: a site full of articles and podcasts on matters of strategic significance.
www.rand.org/: after many years, RAND continues to keep its finger on the pulse of important strategic matters.
https://nipp.org/: The National Institute for Public Policy offers a wide range of online publications dealing with important issues in contemporary strategy.

NOTES

1 The flexibility of infantry has long been recognised, as evident in Vegetius, *Epitome of Military Science*, trans. N. P. Milner (Liverpool: Liverpool University Press, 1993).
2 J. C. Wylie, *Military Strategy: A General Theory of Power Control* (Annapolis, MD: Naval Institute Press, 1967).
3 Colin S. Gray, *Modern Strategy* (Oxford: Oxford University Press, 1999), p. 26.
4 Clausewitz, Carl von, *On War*, trans. Michael Howard and Peter Paret (London: David Campbell Publishers Ltd, 1993), p. 100.
5 Ibid., p. 228.
6 Ibid., p. 173.
7 Thomas M. Kane, *Military Logistics and Strategic Performance* (London: Frank Cass, 2001).
8 Clausewitz, *On War*, p. 606.
9 Williamson Murray, *Military Adaptation in War: With Fear of Change* (Cambridge, UK: Cambridge University Press, 2011).
10 Clausewitz, *On War*, p. 75.
11 Edward N. Luttwak, *Strategy: The Logic of War and Peace* (Cambridge, MA: Belknap Press, 1987).
12 Clausewitz, *On War*, p. 75.
13 Ibid., p. 89.
14 For a discussion of the nature of war via an analysis of the trinity, see Antulio J. Echevarria II, 'Clausewitz and the Nature of War on Terror', in Hew Strachan and Andreas Herberg-Rothe (eds.), *Clausewitz in the Twenty-First Century* (Oxford: Oxford University Press, 2007), pp. 196–218.
15 Clausewitz, *On War*, p. 119.
16 British Army, 'Army Announces New Way of Winning Future Wars', 16 September 2023, www.army.mod.uk/news-and-events/news/2023/09/army-announces-new-way-of-winning-future-wars/.
17 Ibid.
18 For an early analysis of the attack, see Paul P. Murphy, Katie Polglase, Benjamin Brown, Gianluca Mezzofiore and Eliza Mackintosh, 'CNN Investigates: Forensic Analysis of Images and Videos Suggests Rocket Caused Gaza Hospital Blast, Not Israeli Airstrike', *CNN*, 22 October 2023.
19 Clausewitz, *On War*, p. 229.
20 Bernard Brodie, 'Implications for Military Policy', in Bernard Brodie (ed.), *The Absolute Weapon: Atomic Power and World Order* (New York, NY: Harcourt, Brace and Company, 1946).
21 Colin S. Gray, *Theory of Strategy* (Oxford: Oxford University Press, 2018), p. 123.
22 Clausewitz, *On War*, p. 718.

Glossary

5th Generation Also '5th Gen'. Term used to describe combat aircraft, particularly fighters, with certain characteristics such as low observability ('*stealth*') and sophisticated avionics systems, particularly involving the fusing and processing of data. Exact parameters of the term are not universally agreed upon by commentators. Fighters without low observability and the ability to 'supercruise' (flyi at supersonic speeds without the use of afterburner) but possessing sophisticated avionics are often described as '4.5 Generation' aircraft.

A2/AD Anti-access and area denial: technologies and techniques designed to deny access and freedom of manoeuvre to adversaries within particular areas.

AI Artificial intelligence: simulation of human intelligence by machines, especially computer systems. *'Narrow' or 'weak'* AI systems are designed to perform a specific task or a narrow range of tasks. *'General' or 'strong'* AI (Strong AI) describes a currently theoretical form of AI that can perform any intellectual task a human can do.

Air dominance Having complete control of airspace without any interference from enemy forces. In fact, this is extremely difficult to achieve against an opponent with the ability to fire at aerial systems.

Air interdiction The use of air attack to disrupt or destroy enemy logistical capability and/or enemy equipment beyond the front line. Abbreviated to 'AI', which may create confusion with artificial intelligence.

Air superiority The ability to use air power at a given time and in a given place without prohibitive interference from the enemy.

Air supremacy *Air superiority* in which the enemy is incapable of effective interference.

Aircraft carrier A warship designed to carry and operate numerous fixed-wing aircraft at sea.

Amphibious operation Functioning in land and water. For example, the landing of military forces from the sea against a hostile or potentially hostile shore.

ASAT Air-launched anti-satellite: weapons designed to destroy or disable satellite systems.

Asymmetric warfare Warfare between dissimilar adversaries. A contested concept, asymmetric warfare is often associated with conflict against such unconventional adversaries as terrorists and insurgents.

Attrition Reduction in the effectiveness of a military formation caused by the loss of equipment and/or personnel.

Ballistic missile Missile that follows a ballistic flight path (as opposed to flying, as does a *cruise missile*).

Battalion A military unit normally consisting of 500 to 1,200 troops divided into four to six *companies*. Two or more battalions may be grouped into a *brigade*, or one or more may constitute a *regiment*.

Battle fleet A fleet, usually composed of the most powerful warships designed to contest *control of the sea* in combat with the enemy'.

Battlegroup A flexible *combined-arms* force usually created around the nucleus of a *battalion/regiment*-sized infantry or armoured unit and augmented with other arms.

Battleship A large, heavily armoured warship armed primarily with large calibre guns. Until the mid twentieth century, these were the largest and most powerful warships.

BCT Brigade combat team. The basic large deployable manoeuvre unit of the US Army, consisting of a combat *brigade* with attached supporting units.

Blitzkrieg Second World War German operational level mobile warfare.

Blockade An attempt to deny access to a particular area, often associated with attempts to cut off maritime trade to enemy ports.

Blue water A colloquial term used to refer to the *high seas*.

BMD Ballistic missile defence.

Brigade A military unit consisting of two to five *battalions* or *regiments*. Two or more brigades may be grouped into a *division*.

C2 An acronym to represent the military functions of *command* and *control*. The process by which commanders exercise *command* and *control* of their forces in order to direct, organise and coordinate their activities to maximum effect.

C4I An acronym to represent the following military functions: command, control, communications, computers and intelligence.

C4ISR An acronym to represent the following military functions: command, control, communications, intelligence, surveillance and reconnaissance.

Campaigns A connected series of *tactical* engagements within a *theatre* designed to achieve a *strategic* objective.

Capital ship The most powerful and influential type of warship, often valued for its symbolic as much as its military value.

Centre of gravity Characteristics, capabilities or locations that are key to the ability of an organisation to function effectively.

CIA [US] Central Intelligence Agency.

Close air support Air attacks launched against enemy targets in close proximity to friendly forces.

Close operations Operations on or near the enemy front line, as opposed to *deep operations*, conducted far into the enemy's rear area.

COIN Counterinsurgency operations. Military, paramilitary, political, economic, psychological and civic actions taken by a government to defeat insurgency.

Combined arms The integration of different arms into a single system to achieve a complementary effect.

Combined operations A term traditionally used to describe what is now called *joint operations*. In modern nomenclature, the term is used to describe multinational operations.

Command The authority to *control* the activity and organisation of armed forces.

Command of the sea A concept within maritime strategy that relates to the capacity to use the sea and to deny that use to an adversary'.

Company A military unit consisting of 100–200 troops, divided into two to five platoons.

Compellence The threat or use of force to compel an adversary to behave in a specific manner.

Control The process by which commanders direct, organise and coordinate the activities of the forces under their *command*.

Control of the sea A concept within maritime strategy usually defined as the freedom of action to use an area of the sea for one's own purposes, for a period of time, and if necessary to deny such use to an enemy.'

Corps A military unit consisting of two or more *divisions*. Derived from the French term *corps d'armeé* ('body of the army'), traditionally a corps was a *combined-arms* force capable of fighting independently for a limited period of time.

Corvette A small warship, usually lightly armed.

Cruise missile Guided-weapons designed to fly to their target on a non-ballistic trajectory, often at low altitude.

Counterterrorism As with *COIN*, military, paramilitary, law enforcement, political, economic, psychological and civic actions taken by a government to defeat terrorism. Differs from *COIN* in scale of activities and most often misconceptualised as 'direct action' military raids.

Cyber warfare The use of computers, the internet and other systems to attack an opponent's computers, websites and networks in order to cause harm.

DoS/DDoS: Denial of service/distributed denial of service. A form of cyber-attack designed to disrupt a target system by subjecting it to an overwhelming volume of network traffic.

DCO Defensive cyber operations: 'missions intended to preserve the ability to utilise blue [friendly] cyberspace capabilities and protect data, networks, cyberspace-enabled devices and other designated systems by defeating ongoing or imminent malicious cyberspace activity'.

Deep operations Large-scale, simultaneous attacks against enemy reserve and rear areas as well as the front line. Deep operations can be performed by remote firepower (air, artillery and missile attack) and by the rapid exploitation of breakthroughs by mobile forces.

Destroyer A capable *flotilla* vessel designed to fulfil a range of missions that include anti-submarine operations, air defence and various escort duties, but is capable of operating in support of the battlefleet.

Deterrence The threat of military power to dissuade an adversary from taking a certain action. Deterrence can operate via the threat of punishment or denial. It can be universal or tailored to a specific issue and/or actor.

Dimensions of strategy Factors that impinge upon or play a part in strategy. They can either be external or internal to the process of strategy.

Division A large, usually *combined-arms*, military unit consisting of two or more *brigades*. Two or more divisions may be grouped together in a *corps*.

Doctrine The principles that are codified and taught in order to guide the actions of military forces.

Dreadnought British *battleship* launched in 1906 that, by its exclusive armament of heavy calibre guns and new steam turbine engines, revolutionised battleship construction, lending its name to subsequent vessels of this type.

Echelon As a formation, describes the use of multiple reserve formations to create successive waves of attack. Generally, the term 'second echelon' is sometimes used to describe all of the forces that follow on from the initial attacking forces. The term 'rear echelon' refers generally to non-combat support elements.

EMS Electromagnetic spectrum: the range of all types of electromagnetic radiation, the latter being waves of energy that travel through space at the speed of light. This includes radio waves, microwaves and infra-red radiation.

Envelopment Movement around or over the enemy.

Electronic warfare The use of the electromagnetic spectrum to disrupt, deny, degrade or deceive enemy electronic systems, while protecting one's own systems from such attacks.

Expeditionary operations Operations where military force is projected and sustained at some distance from the home bases, usually across the seas.

Fire control The control and direction of artillery fire, particularly from warships.

Fleet in being The maintenance of one's own fleet intact in the hope that its continued existence will deny options to the enemy.

Fires The coordinated use of indirect and direct fire weapons, including artillery, missiles, mortars and air-delivered munitions, as well as non-kinetic means like electronic warfare or cyber-attacks.

Fire team The building block of modern tactics, the fire team is, in general, a four-person grouping of soldiers. Two or more will comprise a *squad* or *section.*

Flotilla A formation of smaller warships, sometimes included as part of a larger fleet.

Friction: Those factors that make the practice of warfare more difficult than its theory including fear, chance, uncertainty and physical exertion.

Frigate A *flotilla* vessel, usually optimised to focus on either anti-submarine warfare or air defence.

Grand strategy The application of national resources to achieve national/alliance policy objectives.

Grey zone A contested term, one that attempts to capture a level of activities as part of *strategic competition* that deliberately blur the lines between war and statecraft. Often equated with *irregular warfare.*

Guerre de course An attack on enemy merchant shipping at sea.

Gunboat diplomacy The use of naval forces in support of diplomatic activity. It is often associated with the coercive use of naval forces in situations short of armed conflict.

High seas The area of the sea beyond *territorial seas.* Navies are free to navigate through the high seas without restriction.

Hybrid warfare A contested term, hybrid warfare can be characterised by its integration of diverse tactics, designed to create ambiguity, confusion and difficulty in responding. The goal is often to destabilise the target or achieve strategic objectives without triggering a full-scale military conflict.

Hypersonics A class of advanced weapons that can travel at speeds greater than five times the speed of sound, or Mach 5 (approximately 3,836 miles per hour or 6,174 kilometres per hour). These weapons are designed to be highly manoeuvrable, making them extremely difficult to detect, track and intercept with current missile defence systems.

ICBM Intercontinental ballistic missile.

IDF The Israeli Defence Force.

Innocent passage The right provided for under *UNCLOS* for ships to transit through the *territorial seas* of other states providing they do not engage in military activity.

Insurgency An organised movement aimed at the overthrow of a constituted government through the use of subversion and armed conflict, most often guerrilla tactics. Like *terrorism*, however, insurgency is a contested concept. Its essence is the combination of irregular warfare techniques and political mobilisation.

Integration The development of closer, complementary interaction between elements within a military system. Generically, integration is required for effective performance in all aspects of warfare whether *command* and *control*, *logistics*, *combined arms* or *joint* operations. The term has acquired specific importance in relation to contemporary debates regarding the creation of a *system of systems*.

Intelligence In the military context this involves the collection and analysis of information in order to guide actions.

Interdiction Actions to divert, disrupt or destroy the enemy before they reach the area of battle.

Irregular warfare An umbrella term for a range of activities. This differs from others forms of warfare in its forms, approaches and how resources are translated into effective capabilities and effects. Depending on the three, it can be conducted as a coup d'état, revolution, *terrorism*, *insurgency* or civil war. These resources can be physical or psychological, technological or social, or a combination. Groups or states can employ irregular warfare as a means of overthrowing an existing system, imposing costs, through covert or covert means, directly or indirectly. Often confused with *hybrid* or *compound warfare*.

ISR Intelligence, surveillance and reconnaissance.

Joint force In US doctrine, this refers to a force composed of significant elements from more than one service operating under a single commander. More generally, it is often used to refer to any force composed of significant elements from more than one service regardless of the overall command arrangement.

Joint operations Operations involving different military services (usually armies/navies/air forces) working together within an operational context'

Joint warfare Military warfighting activities where elements of at least two services operate together.

Just War A philosophical and theological set of norms that seeks to codify the conditions under which war is necessary and legitimate, and strives to limit the suffering and damage caused when war occurs.

Littoral The coastal region. Sometimes identified as coastal sea areas and the area of land that is susceptible to influence and support from the sea.

Logistics The art of moving armed forces and keeping them supplied.

Malware Malicious software. Malware may have many purposes including deleting, encrypting, corrupting or stealing data, and crashing or taking control of computer systems.

Manoeuvre Movement in relation to the enemy to occupy advantageous positions.

Manoeuvre warfare An approach to warfare developed in the 1980s and 1990s. Rather than focusing on *attrition*, manoeuvre warfare leverages *tempo* to achieve success. Surprise, deception, speed, mobility and the seizing of the initiative are used to confuse and dislocate the enemy, and to invalidate their decision-making.

Manoeuvrist approach A philosophy of war based on the principle of defeating the enemy by attacking such intangibles as cohesion and the will to fight rather than focusing on destroying the enemy's material. Despite its label, manoeuvre is not necessarily a prerequisite for a manoeuvrist approach to war.

Maritime strategy The principles that govern a war (or conflict) in which the sea is a substantial factor.

Mechanised forces Mobile forces where the transport is usually composed of armoured, armed and (often) tracked vehicles. The transport is designed to contribute to combat operations by providing protection and fire support.

Military strategic level The level at which strategic objectives are set and military capabilities are directed to achieve said objectives, in support of grand strategy, in the pursuit of policy objectives.

Mission command A command philosophy based on the principles of decentralisation of responsibility and the use of initiative. Classically, subordinates are informed of what they must achieve (the mission) but are allowed to use their own judgement on how this should best be achieved given local conditions.

ML Machine learning: a subset of artificial intelligence (AI) that involves the development of algorithms and statistical models that allow computers to perform tasks without being explicitly programmed for each step.

MLEA Refers to Maritime Law Enforcement Agencies such as coastguards.

MSO Maritime security operations: designed to enhance maritime security and good order at sea. These can range across a broad spectrum from the benign through to robust action short of warfighting.

MDO Multi-domain operations: generically, operations involving the integration of military activities across multiple *operating domains*. Different nations and services often have different specific definitions. For example, the US Army defines MDO as: 'The combined arms employment of joint and Army capabilities to create and exploit relative advantages that achieve objectives, defeat enemy forces, and consolidate gains on behalf of the joint commander.'

NATO North Atlantic Treaty Organisation.

Nature of war Composed of a combination of ever-present elements that distinguish war from other socio-political activities. War is instrumental, violent, non-linear, uncertain and subject to non-rational forces.

Naval diplomacy The use of naval forces in support of diplomatic activity.

NCO Non-Commissioned Officer such as a Corporal, Sergeant or Warrant Officer. A military officer without a commission (i.e., they are still enlisted soldiers). NCOs provide the crucial interface between commissioned officers and the men and women under their command.

'New wars' A perspective on contemporary and future war that argues that a paradigm shift has occurred in warfare reflected in such characteristics as new participants, new objectives, an increased blurring between war and criminality andobsolescence of much of traditional military thinking.

OCO Offensive Cyber Operations: 'missions intended to project power in and through foreign cyberspace'.

OODA Loop The Observe-Orient-Decide-Act (OODA) process believed by Col John Boyd to underpin effective decision-making.

Operating domains Spheres of activity or influence with common and distinct characteristics in which a force can conduct joint operations. It is usually suggested that there are five distinct operations domains: land, sea, air, space and cyberspace.

Operational analysis The employment of advanced analytical methods, and other problem-solving techniques, to make better decisions.

Operational art The execution of the *operational level* of command.

Operational level The level at which campaigns and major operations are planned, sequenced and directed.

Outflank Movement around the enemy flanks. Although often used synonymously with the term *envelopment*, envelopment often implies a much deeper outflanking movement designed to pin and encircle the enemy.

Paradigm A worldview, conceptual model or framework of thinking.

Paradoxical logic Luttwak's notion that, due to the competitive nature of strategy, success rarely lasts or may produce diminishing returns over time.

Peace operations Crisis response and limited contingency operations to contain conflicts, redress the peace and shape the environment to support reconciliation and re-building and to facilitate the transformation to legitimate governance. Sometimes also termed *peace support operations*.

Peace support operations see *peace operations*.

Peacekeeping A term sometimes used generically to mean *peace operations*, but more properly an operation undertaken with the consent of all major parties to a dispute, and one designed to monitor and facilitate implementation of an agreement to support diplomatic efforts to reach a long-term political settlement.

PGMs Precision-guided munitions such as laser-guided bombs and cruise missiles.

PLA The Chinese People's Liberation Army: the Chinese armed forces. Consists of the Ground Force (the Army), plus a navy air force and Rocket Force.

PLAN The Chinese People's Liberation Army Navy.

Polymorphous character of war War takes many forms, depending upon a range of factors, including the nature of the belligerents, objectives sought, technology, geography, and so on.

Policy In relation to strategic theory, policy represents political objectives. Policy differs from *strategy* in that policy sets the ends to which strategy is directed.

Power projection The ability to project military power overseas.

Quantum computing A type of computing that harnesses the principles of quantum mechanics.

Radar An acronym for radio detection and ranging. The use of electromagnetic waves to detect the range, altitude, bearing and speed of moving objects such as aircraft, ships and vehicles and also the position of fixed installations.

Regiment A tactical or administrative grouping of one of more *battalions*.

RMA Revolution in military affairs. An RMA is a *paradigm* shift in war; 'an observable breaking point between two recognisably different types of warfare'. The RMA refers to a concept that emerged in the 1990s that future war would be revolutionised by combinations of *PGMs*, sensors and networking.

Scouting Activity designed to locate the enemy.

Screening Activity designed to protect forces from enemy observation and enemy action.

Sea control The ability to use an area of the sea for one's own purposes and to deny that use to the enemy for a given period of time.

Sea denial The attempt to prevent an opponent from gaining use of the sea.

Sea lines of communication Commercial shipping routes and sea routes connecting military forces to their sources of supply and reinforcement. Such lanes are notional and are determined by the movement of ships. Unlike roads on land, they do not exist in any physical sense.

SEAD Acronym for suppression of enemy air defences, specifically radar-guided surface-to-air missiles. Pronunciation either 'see-add' or sometimes 'seed'. SEAD involves seeking to prevent enemy air defence systems from operating either by forcing them to shut down for fear of detection and destruction or as a result of jamming radar signals. The method of suppression is irrelevant. Destruction of enemy air defences as a specific task may also be covered by the acronym DEAD (pronounced 'dead' or 'dee-add'), which is less commonly used.

Shock A psychological state marked by fear and disorientation. Shock is a desirable state to induce in an enemy because it may result in slowed, uncoordinated and irrelevant activity. Translated through military organisations, 'systemic shock' undermines the capacity of a military force to operate effectively and may result in heavy defeat without the infliction of large amounts of physical destruction.

SLBM Submarine-launched ballistic missile.

SOF Special operations forces, or in the UK and many Commonwealth countries, special forces. Specialised small units optimised for a high degree of tactical performance based on their unique selection, designation, equipment and joint training. Operators within them assume higher personal and tactical risk than conventional forces. SOF are often used to combat insurgents and terrorists, or conduct irregular warfare against states.

Sonar An acronym for sound, navigation and ranging. The use of sound waves to detect objects under water.

Space Force application The use of space for military purposes, employing weapons systems as opposed to reconnaissance and communications platforms. Defined by US Strategic Command as encompassing 'combat operations in, through and from space to influence the course or outcome of events'.

Squad A small infantry unit comprising two or more *fire teams*. In some armies the squad is known as a section. Two or more squads will be combined to form *platoons*.

Squadron A small formation of aircraft, ships or mobile ground forces such as cavalry or tanks.

Stability operations From a US perspective, tactical activities designed to maintain or re-establish a safe or secure environment, provide essential government services, emergency infrastructure reconstruction and humanitarian relief. But other states have alternate definitions.

Strategic effect In air power doctrine, the use of air power against designated *centres of gravity* to produce higher order political effects. In strategy, any action that has an impact on the relationship between means and ends.

Strategic ethics An approach that respects the instrumental nature of war, whilst at the same time recognising the moral dimension of strategy.

Strategic competition An exercise in grand strategy, the terms reflects the actions of an extended period of time between revisionist powers and those that want to preserve the status quo of the current international order, each seeking mutual advantage. Such competition is conducted using the full range of instruments available to political actors: political, economic, military and information.

Strategic performance The degree to which an action moves measurably towards the achievement of the desired political goals.

Strategic theory: A set of ideas, composed of concepts and principles, concerning the use of military power for policy effect. Strategic theory can be universal or specific to a domain or form of strategic power.

Strategy The process that converts military power into policy effect.

Suppression The neutralisation, rather than destruction, of forces through the psychological effect of firepower. Typically, 'suppressive fire' forces an enemy to remain in cover, pins them and prevents them from firing themselves by rendering them unable (through *shock* or disorientation) or unwilling (through fear) to expose themselves.

System A set of interrelated parts that together constitute a whole. Military organisations are made up of a multitude of systems, such as administrative systems, logistic systems and training systems.

'System of systems' A concept in which very high degrees of *integration* between different military systems, facilitated by improvements in data transfer and *C4ISR*, produce something more resembling a single *system*. In theory, this should dramatically improve the cooperation, coordination, speed and flexibility of a military organisation.

Tactics The conduct of battles and engagements.

Tempo The rhythm or rate of activity of operations, relative to the enemy.

Territorial seas: Under *UNCLOS* these are defined as areas up to twelve miles off the adjacent coast. States enjoy sovereignty within this region and the activities of outside naval forces are circumscribed, notwithstanding a right to *innocent passage*.

Terrorism A basic definition would be 'the use of violence, or the threat of violence, to create fear'. Terrorism, normally considered a tactic, can also form a *strategy* in which violence is important for the psychological effect that it produces. However, terrorism is a contested concept, not least because it has associated moral, political and pejorative connotations; a multitude of different definitions exist.

Theatre Large geographically defined areas of land, water and air that bound the conduct of military operations.

TNW Tactical nuclear weapon.

UAV Unmanned/uncrewed aerial vehicle, more commonly referred to as a 'drone'. Controlled remotely by a crew that is usually based in a ground control facility, using satellite communications to fly the air vehicle. The term 'drone' dates from the early years of using remotely piloted systems that were designed to allow the practice of surface-to-air gunnery by ships and ground forces, with the name stemming from the droning noise of the engine.

UNCLOS: The Third UN Convention on the Law of the Sea that was signed in 1982 and came into effect in 1997.

USAF US Air Force.

USMC US Marine Corps.

USN US Navy.

USV Unmanned surface vehicle (usually referring to a vessel at sea). Also known as autonomous surface vehicles (ASVs).

UUV Unmanned underwater vehicle, including remotely operated underwater vehicles (ROVs) and autonomous underwater vehicles (AUVs).

Vertical envelopment Moving over the enemy in order to threaten their flanks or rear. This may be executed through air-mobile (helicopter-borne) or airborne (parachute or glider) forces.

War Organised violence conducted by political units against each other.

Warfare The military conduct of war; it is concerned centrally with fighting.

WMDs Weapons of mass destruction. A collective term for nuclear, radiological, biological and chemical weapons focusing on their capacity for large-scale indiscriminate damage. Often also referred to as 'weapons of mass effect' because of the potential political, coercive and moral impacts associated with their use or threat of use.

Index

For EU product safety concerns, contact us at Calle de José Abascal, 56–1°,
28003 Madrid, Spain or eugpsr@cambridge.org.

www.ingramcontent.com/pod-product-compliance
Ingram Content Group UK Ltd.
Pitfield, Milton Keynes, MK11 3LW, UK
UKHW052008020426
469625UK00011B/577

* 9 7 8 1 0 0 9 7 2 4 5 0 0 *